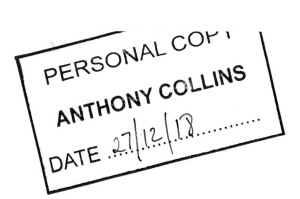

Psychology

FOR THE IB DIPLOMA

SECOND EDITION

Jean-Marc Lawton
Eleanor Willard

The Publishers would like to thank the following for permission to reproduce copyright material.

Photo credits

p.viii, *top* © Jean-Marc Lawton, *bottom* © Eleanor Willard; **p.3** © mrk28 – Fotolia; **p.5** © sola_sola/stock.adobe.com; **p.21** © Sherry LeBlanc-Hayes/stock.adobe.com; **p.28** © pololia/stock.adobe.com; **p.37** © Premium Collection/stock.adobe.com; **p.43** © Chuck Burton/AP/REX/Shutterstock; **p.49** © Lindsey Bowes; **p.59** © Thomas Boggan/East Valley Tribune; **p.74** © ilyabolotov/stock.adobe.com; **p.88** © Texelart/stock.adobe.com; **p.92** © SUNY, Buffalo State Archives & Special Collections, Courier-Express Collection; **p.105**, *left* © NS-Dokumentationszentrum der Stadt Köln, *right* © Juergen Schwarz/Getty Images; **p.116** © jlcst/stock.adobe.com; **p.117** © Ruslan Kudrin/stock.adobe.com; **p.135** © pololia/stock.adobe.com; **p.148** © Eric Isselée/stock.adobe.com; **p.173** © ZoneCreative/stock.adobe.com; **p.188** © Peter Macdiarmid/Getty Images; **p.194** © CORBIS/Getty Images; **p.198** © Bettmann/Getty Images; **p.207** © Melissa Binstock; **p.229**, *left* © Yalcinsonat/stock.adobe.com, *right* © Chones/stock.adobe.com; **p.234** © Trinity Mirror/Mirrorpix/Alamy Stock Photo; **p.236** © Tommaso Lizzul - stock.adobe.com; **p.241** © DR P. Marazzi/Science Photo Library; **p.263** © Glenda Powers/stock.adobe.com; **p.266** © nopgraphic/stock.adobe.com; **p.279** © sheilaf2002/stock.adobe.com; **p.291** © vchalup/stock.adobe.com; **p.302** © highwaystarz/stock.adobe.com; **p.319** © Sergey Nivens/stock.adobe.com; **p.320** © nukul2533/stock.adobe.com; **p.333** © Sam Stephenson/Alamy Stock Photo; **p.334** © Travel21 Impact/Heritage Images/TopFoto; **p.337** © Hubert Boesl/dpa picture alliance archive/Alamy Stock Photo; **p.342** © ajnjuhfabyz/stock.adobe.com; **p.345** © Dr Martin Gruendl, www.beautycheck.de; **p.354** © Caters News; **p.363** © Kellyvandellen/stock.adobe.com; **p.367** © FilmRise/Everett Collection Inc/Alamy Stock Photo; **p.368** © Christian Delbert/stock.adobe.com; **p.378** © Martinedoucet/E+/Getty Image; **p.390** © Carl Mydans/The LIFE Picture Collection/Getty Images; **p.392** © Europan Association of Social Psychology; **p.407** https://commons.wikimedia.org/wiki/File:Hans_Pr%C3%BCfung_1907.jpg# , https://creativecommons.org/licenses/by-sa/3.0/

Acknowledgements

pp. 35–36, *quotation*: Low. "The Cambridge declaration on consciousness" (Low, Panksepp, et al., eds), 2012, p2; **p.276**, *poem*: Excerpt from 'This Be the Verse' from THE COMPLETE POEMS OF PHILIP LARKIN by Philip Larkin, edited by Archie Burnett. Copyright © 2012 by The Estate of Philip Larkin. Introduction copyright © 2012 by Archie Burnett. Reprinted by permission of Farrar, Straus and Giroux.; **p.393**, *Figure 8.10*: Reproduced with permission. Copyright © (1970) Scientific American, a division of Nature America, Inc. All rights reserved.

Every effort has been made to trace all copyright holders, but if any have been inadvertently overlooked, the Publishers will be pleased to make the necessary arrangements at the first opportunity.

Although every effort has been made to ensure that website addresses are correct at time of going to press, Hodder Education cannot be held responsible for the content of any website mentioned in this book. It is sometimes possible to find a relocated web page by typing in the address of the home page for a website in the URL window of your browser.

Hachette UK's policy is to use papers that are natural, renewable and recyclable products and made from wood grown in sustainable forests. The logging and manufacturing processes are expected to conform to the environmental regulations of the country of origin.

Orders: please contact Bookpoint Ltd, 130 Park Drive, Milton Park, Abingdon, Oxon OX14 4SE. Telephone: (44) 01235 827827. Fax: (44) 01235 400401. Email education@bookpoint.co.uk Lines are open from 9 a.m. to 5 p.m., Monday to Saturday, with a 24-hour message answering service. You can also order through our website: www.hoddereducation.com

Contents

Handwritten annotations: TERM 1.   HL + SL   90hrs   35hrs

Handwritten annotations: TERM 2   HL&SL   38hrs

Handwritten annotations: CHRISTMAS.   HL&SL   18hrs

HL   50hp   QUAL

Options

SL   30hrs

HL   3hrs

Internal assessment

HL & SL   40 hrs

Introduction

Psychology emerged from the earlier academic discipline of philosophy in 1879 in two different locations, when Wilhelm Wundt, in Leipzig, Germany, and William James, at Harvard University, USA, both independently set up laboratories for the testing of human mental abilities. This was in an age when science was being applied to many phenomena, including the physical and non-physical aspects of humans and animals. Psychology can thus be defined as 'the study of the mind and behaviour', with both scientific and non-scientific methods being used to achieve this aim, as not all aspects of mental life are seen as having direct physical counterparts.

Psychology consists of several, sometimes conflicting, approaches that reflect its philosophical origins and these are reflected in the IB specification's three core elements of the biological, cognitive and sociocultural approaches. This means that behaviour can often be viewed from different fundamental bases. For example, the formation and maintenance of romantic relationships could be seen from the viewpoint of physiological influences (the biological approach), such as genes, biochemistry and evolution. Then again it could be seen from the standpoint of mental processes (the cognitive approach), such as the consideration of the costs and rewards of a relationship, maybe in comparison to those of possible alternative relationships. Or then again it could be considered by reference to social and cultural influences (the sociocultural approach), such as the tendency for some cultures to favour voluntary relationships, while others prefer arranged marriages, with these tendencies reflecting cultural beliefs.

The first part of this book therefore considers these three approaches in some detail, with the ways in which they overlap and differ from each other being fully explored.

The second part of this book centres upon the optional topics featured in the IB specification and reflects upon how the three core approaches explored in part one can aid psychologists in their study and understanding of a range of topics, namely: human relations, abnormal psychology, health psychology and developmental psychology. There will be differences in how many of these options students need to study depending on which level of the IB qualification is being studied. These optional topics are featured in a way that closely matches the requirements of the IB specification.

A main element of the study of psychology is its focus on research, the methods by which psychologists actually study mental phenomena to acquire knowledge and understanding and then go on to create practical applications of use to society, such as relationship counselling and matchmaking. As mentioned earlier, research methods combine both scientific and non-scientific means, with each having their strengths and weaknesses. There is focus upon relevant research methods and studies throughout the chapters on psychological approaches and the optional topics, but there is also a separate chapter on research methods, which provides both descriptive and evaluative content. Focus upon ethical issues and considerations of conducting research on both humans and animals is also something that is explored in regular fashion throughout the book, while also featured is a chapter giving guidance on how to plan, execute and write up the practical assessment, which is an integral assessed part of the course.

The text of the book is divided into elements that students and teachers will hopefully find engaging and helpful to their learning. Descriptive elements feature heavily – for example, descriptions of theories and models that try to explain behaviour, such as the multi-store model of memory (MSM), which sees memory as consisting of separate stores between which information flows. Research evidence also appears as a regular, separate feature, such as studies that support or conflict with the MSM, with another regular, separate feature being that of evaluative points, such as those detailing the strengths and weaknesses of the MSM. Other regular features, which are often colour-coded for ease of access, are ones that are designed to widen and reinforce students' learning, again in an engaging and motivating manner.

Features of the book

Quotations – *pithy sayings that are designed to provoke thought and give insight into the subject matter being learned.*

Key terms – concise statements that define the meanings of important concepts and operate as retrieval cues for the recall of more detailed knowledge.

IN THE NEWS

Written in the style of an imaginary psychological newspaper, this feature highlights topical news items that illustrate central psychological themes of the topics being discussed, as well as illustrating the central role of psychology in everyday human experience.

FOCUS ON...

An introductory feature for each topic that summarizes in bullet point form the main elements of study that will be featured.

Links to the main approaches

An occasional feature describing how elements of topics being studied relate to the biological, cognitive and sociocultural approaches.

You are the researcher

A feature that focuses upon research methods from the viewpoint of the design of psychological studies. Designed to help foster a greater understanding of why and how psychologists conduct research and assist in the development of the necessary skills for students to plan and undertake their own research.

Research in focus

Using examples in the text, this feature gets students to think about methodological aspects of research studies and asks relevant questions to stimulate learning and understanding.

PSYCHOLOGY IN THE REAL WORLD

Examples of relevant practical applications of psychology that showcase its usefulness within real-world settings and help to form a valuable source of evaluative material for assessed work.

TOK link

A feature centred on exploring how elements of topics being studied relate to a consideration of what knowledge actually is and how we can determine the validity (accuracy) of such knowledge.

Strengthen your learning

Found at the end of each section, this feature focuses upon an appraisal (consideration) of the material covered. Acting as a form of comprehension (understanding) exercise, the questions are used as a means of revision to boost knowledge and understanding before attempting the questions found at the end of each topic.

KEY STUDY

Some studies are particularly important to understand a topic and are covered in greater depth. 'Classic research' focuses upon famous psychological studies, taking students in some detail through the thinking behind such studies, as well as the aims, procedures, findings, conclusions and evaluative considerations, while 'Contemporary research' – similar in focus to the 'classic research' feature, but focused upon more recent cutting-edge research – provides a more up-to-date account of the topic being studied.

■ **Assessment check**

A feature found at the end of each topic that consists of a variety of examination-type questions for students to attempt.

SECTION SUMMARY

A feature that concludes each section of study with a bullet-pointed review of the main points covered.

About the authors

This book has been written by the gruesome twosome of Jean-Marc Lawton and Ellie Willard.

Jean-Marc Lawton is an established writer of psychology books, revision books and study guides. He has many years' experience of lecturing in psychology and was the head of a very academically successful psychology department. He has also been a senior examiner for many years, including for the IB. He currently resides in the Scottish Highlands and has interests, aside from psychology, in conservation, ultra-running and unlistenable music.

Jean-Marc would like to thank his wife, Mara, for all her support (and the flapjacks) and Ellie of Tadcaster for her support and assistance. His part of this book is dedicated to the memory of his father, John, 'the mirror to my future'.

Jean-Marc wrote the following chapters in this book:

■ Cognitive approach to understanding behaviour

■ Approaches to researching behaviour

■ Abnormal psychology

■ Psychology of human relationships

■ Internal assessment

Eleanor Willard is a Senior Lecturer in Psychology at a university in Yorkshire, England. She has written several psychology text books, been a psychology examiner, devised teaching resources and taught psychology to audiences at many stages of education, from introductory level psychology to Masters level courses.

Eleanor would like to thank her support network for their help while she contributed to this book. You know who you are. Much love. Thanks to Jean-Marc too for being a superlative advisor and providing plenty of banter. Eleanor would like to dedicate her part of the book to her parents, Harold and Frances, her nature and her nurture.

Eleanor wrote the following chapters in this book:

■ Biological approach to understanding behaviour

■ Sociocultural approach to understanding behaviour

■ Developmental psychology

■ Health psychology

1 Biological approach to understanding behaviour

Introduction

Psychology is the study of mind and behaviour. Within the discipline, there are several perspectives taken in examining why people do what they do. If you consider the action of an individual it is important to consider all the possible influences on them. This is what the perspectives in psychology do. They vary in terms of level of scrutiny; from the detail of the biology of the body to the effect society and the environment has on an individual.

The case of Elliot Rodger is an example of how a behaviour can be considered at many levels. In May 2014, near Santa Barbara, California, he shot dead seven people and injured seven more. He was 22 years of age. Elliot uploaded a video to YouTube prior to the shootings, in which he stated he was going to exact a revenge attack on people because he felt excluded by his peers. He also explained how he hated women, as they had rejected his approaches. He shot three men who lived in the same apartment block as him and then he got into his car and drove round the neighbourhood, shooting people at random. He shot three more people whom he didn't know, then finally parked the car and shot himself.

This event can be explained due to his feelings of exclusion and anger of rejection. However, it could also be explained as being for biological reasons, such as hormonal levels and atypical thought processes. This illustrates that there are many ways you can explain a behaviour and that it is unlikely there is just one explanation for it.

Three of these 'levels' of explanation (perspectives) – biological, cognitive and socio-cultural – are covered in the first three chapters of this book. This chapter considers biological psychology. Biological psychologists focus on the various ways that the biology of the body can affect behaviour. This happens in many ways and this chapter focuses upon the effect of the brain, hormones and genetics on our behaviour. Also, the role of animal research in the field of biological psychology is examined.

'I am a brain, Watson. The rest of me is a mere appendix.'
Arthur Conan Doyle, 'The Adventure of the Mazarin Stone' (1921)

Assumptions of the biological approach

The core assumption of biopsychologists is that behaviour is affected by the biology of the body and it is the biology that underpins the behaviour. The example of Elliot Rodger above outlines how there are many different levels of explanation for behaviour. At the biological level there are also different ways in which the biology of the body can affect behaviour. These include the following.

1 *The physiology of the brain and the central nervous system.* Biopsychologists use the way the brain is structured and also the way the brain activates to explain many behaviours. The increased technological advancement and use of brain imaging techniques has facilitated much of the recent research in this area.

2 *Biochemistry.* Many chemicals can be found in the brain and the rest of the body. These are called neurotransmitters (found in the brain) and hormones (found in the blood, saliva, etc.). The levels they are found in within the body are part of the explanation for an individual's behaviour.

3 *Genetics.* The unique genetic make-up of an individual is argued, by biological psychologists, to influence their behaviour. Underlying this assumption of genetic influence is a belief in the process of evolution in that behaviour evolves, just like physical characteristics, because it is adaptive, in some way, in the environment.

Another key assumption of the biological approach is that the use of animals in research is appropriate for explaining human behaviour.

Research methods used in the biological approach

The biological approach takes a very scientific stance on researching human behaviour. In many ways, it is able to do this because of the objective nature of what is being measured; there is no opinion involved. For example, if a biopsychologist is examining levels of adrenaline in people who sky dive, they can do this by taking a swab in the mouth for saliva and measure the level of adrenaline within that sample. They will receive a number to signify that level and, assuming the testing is carried out properly, there will be no doubt about its reliability.

This biochemical measurement is a **nomothetic** research method because it can be conducted across large groups of individuals and the respective results compared. This is the case for all biochemical measurements.

In terms of measuring brain activity and brain imaging technology, this, too, is reliable as it measures a physical entity. However, there is an element of interpretation involved and it is currently therefore less objective. The use of brain imaging is discussed in greater depth in the next section. The fact that the brain activity can now be measured relatively accurately has furthered the work of biopsychologists, who have looked to brain physiology to explain behaviour a great deal in recent years, and it is currently one of the key areas in psychology that is progressing rapidly.

Case studies are also traditionally used by biopsychologists. The underlying assumption in using this method is that when behaviour is atypical in some way in an individual and they are found to have atypical biology, then the connection is made between the two in terms of causality. In terms of localization of function in the brain, there are key case studies that have informed the field. Without these case studies, the ability to work out which part of the brain might be implicated in behaviour would have been very difficult.

Ethical considerations of research studies

One of the key issues of research that examines biological explanations of behaviour is that of informed consent. This arises in cases where the person is vulnerable because of brain damage or mental illness. It also occurs when looking at the biology of children.

As much of biological research uses non-human animals, consent is not an issue as it is not sought. However, regulation on the use of non-human animals has to be stringent so that they do not suffer, or suffering is kept to a minimum. The final section of this chapter discusses ethical consideration in research on non-human animals in depth.

At the end of each topic there is a discussion of the ethical considerations that relate to research in that particular topic.

Nomothetic – the idea that people can be regarded as groups and theories/explanations are therefore generalizable.

Case studies – individual (or small group) cases that are unique in some way and therefore studied by researchers for that uniqueness.

FOCUS ON...

- Techniques to study the brain in relation to behaviour, considering the opportunity, available technology and costs.
- Localization within the brain in terms of the idea, the functionality of different parts and limitations of this work.
- Neuroplasticity, namely the ways in which the brain and neural networks will change over time or after injury.
- Neurotransmitters and their effect on behaviour.

Physiology and behaviour

IN THE NEWS

Ψ The Psychological Enquirer

ALIEN HAND SYNDROME SEES WOMAN ATTACKED BY HER OWN HAND

An American woman called Karen Byrne suffered badly from epilepsy and suffered frequent attacks. When Karen reached the age of 27, it was decided that she should have surgery to minimize the effects of the attacks and keep them contained within one hemisphere. This was achieved by severing the corpus callosum, which joins the two sides (hemispheres) of the brain.

After the operation, the frequency of her epileptic attacks was reduced. However, her left hand seemed to function separately from the rest of her body, as if she was not in control of it. She found that the left hand did actions that she did not wish to happen, such as stubbing a cigarette out that she had just lit, unbuttoning her blouse or emptying her handbag and unpacking things she needed in it. It also would hit her on her left cheek, slapping her, and Karen would not be able to control what it did. She was diagnosed with Alien Hand Syndrome.

■ **Figure 1.1** Alien Hand Syndrome means the hand functions separately from the rest of the body

The condition is very rare indeed and does not happen often after the surgical procedure Karen had received. It was thought to occur in Karen's case because the brain could no longer control the body as a cohesive whole because the two hemispheres had been separated. In most cases where the brain has been split this way, there is no such effect, but for Karen this was not the case.

This case study illustrates the direct effect of the structure of the brain on behaviour. This is considered in this chapter, along with other ways an individual's body and biology can affect behaviour.

Neural transmission – the way the signal is transmitted down the neuron to the next synapse.

Neuron – the way the brain can transmit activation. There are billions of neurons in the human brain.

Synapse – the small fluid-filled gap between neurons which is essential for transmission of the nerve signals.

■ The basics of brain physiology

The brain is part of the central nervous system, together with the spinal cord. The central nervous system works alongside the peripheral nervous system and the two are connected by a series of nerves. Information is relayed from the environment to the brain and the brain coordinates movement within the environment. The activation within the brain occurs using electrical signals. This occurs via synaptic and **neural transmission**.

Initially, the electrical nerve impulse travels down the **neuron** and prompts release of neurotransmitters (chemicals in the brain) at the presynaptic terminal. These chemicals are then released into the synaptic fluid in the **synapse**. The adjacent neuron must then quickly take up the neurotransmitters from the fluid and convert them into an electrical impulse to travel down the neuron to the next presynaptic terminal. And so, the impulse continues to be transmitted on.

Synaptic transmission – the process of signal from neuron to neuron.

Synaptic transmission occurs when messages are sent from neuron to neuron at very high speed, in milliseconds through the synaptic fluid. The synapse is the very small and specialized 'gap' between neurons through which the electrical impulse from the neuron is transmitted chemically.

In terms of the structure of the brain there are two hemispheres (left and right) and four lobes in each hemisphere (occipital, parietal, temporal and frontal). See Figure 1.2 below.

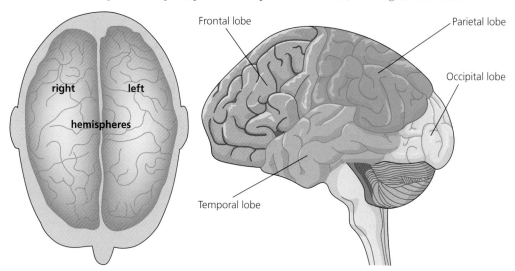

■ **Figure 1.2** Structure of the brain

Initially, this chapter examines the way that the brain can affect behaviour before it looks at the biochemicals within the body and genetics. For those of you studying psychology to the higher level, there is a final section on animal experiments.

Techniques used to study the brain in relation to behaviour

Research into the brain has been helped enormously by the brain imaging techniques developed to look at the structure and activation in the brain. There is a variety of techniques used currently to investigate relationships between the brain and behaviour, all with their own advantages and disadvantages. These brain imaging techniques use varying ways to collect the information on brain structure and activation.

▬ Magnetic resonance imaging and functional magnetic resonance imaging

Magnetic resonance imaging (MRI) – a still picture of the brain which can inform on the structure. The pictures are compiled using the measurement of radio frequency.

Functional magnetic resonance imaging (fMRI) – a brain imaging technique involving detection of differences in magnetization between poor or rich oxygenated blood flow.

Magnetic resonance imaging (MRI) (and the more dynamic **functional magnetic resonance imaging (fMRI)**) uses the measurement of radio frequency waves to gain information. When a radioactive field is generated over the brain, the hydrogen atoms within it move in line with the field. This then gives high-resolution still images of the physiology of the brain. In fMRI, the same measurement of radio waves occurs, but the information is derived from the oxygenation of blood in areas that are activated to a varying degree. When an area of the brain is strongly activated, more oxygenated blood accumulates and hydrogen atoms within the blood are influenced magnetically by the oxygenated blood. This gives a moving picture of the areas of activity.

An example of where the dynamic picture helped with explaining a behaviour is shown in work by **Szycik *et al.* (2017)**. The researchers investigated the idea that playing violent video games makes an individual desensitized to violence. They used fMRI brain imaging to compare the brain activation of users of violent video games to emotionally sensitive pictures. They then compared the pattern of activation with non-violent computer game users. They found that there were no differences between the groups, thus showing that desensitization did not appear to have occurred at the neuronal level. This study would not have been possible without a moving picture of the brain, as it was the pattern of activity that was attended to.

Research

A review of fMRI findings conducted by **Stelzer *et al.* (2014)** highlighted issues with the way the data is analysed, leading the authors of the review to claim that there have been results published that are inaccurate. This is not an issue in the imaging technology, more the subsequent analysis. Given that fMRI is a widely used technique in neuroimaging studies, this means that some work is methodologically weak and should be used with caution. This illustrates that apparently objective measures are still potentially problematic.

Electroencephalography

Electroencephalo-graphy (EEG) – a method of measuring brain activity using electrodes attached to the scalp.

Electroencephalography (EEG) gives an overall picture of activity within the brain. Electrodes are attached to the scalp across all areas and readings taken from the electrodes give a total picture of electrical events in the brain and other areas like the skin, muscles below the electrodes and even the eyes. The EEG technique can be used to measure states of activity such as the stages of sleep and epilepsy. As the signal is a sum of the signals from each electrode generally, it is more difficult to identify a source of atypical activity. This is sometimes, however, possible to do when the differing levels of signal from each electrode are compared.

Technological advances have also made it possible to use EEGs to measure individuals as they move around the environment. The participant wears a dry electrode EEG cap, which can measure brain activity as well as other physiological measures if needed. This means that changes in activity can be detected while individuals negotiate their environment. This is of particular use in the field of sports psychology and for environmental psychologists.

■ **Figure 1.3** EEG gives an overall picture of activity within the brain

Research

Aspinall *et al.* (2015) used mobile EEGs to examine the changes in brain activity when participants walked around three different environments in Edinburgh: an urban shopping street, a path through green space and a street in a busy commercial district. They found that there was an increased level of engagement and arousal in the streets and more meditation together with less frustration in the green space. This study showed that varying activation is dependent on the environment we are in and the mood-enhancing effects of green space. This measurement of brain activity would have been impossible to conduct using other imaging methods within our current technology.

Computerized axial tomography

Computerized axial tomography (CAT) scans provide a still picture of the physiology of the brain using X-rays. To scan the individual's brain using this technique, they must lie still with their head within a large cylinder. One-half of the cylinder projects X-rays across the cylinder to the other side, travelling through the brain. The other side of the cylinder has a detection unit to detect the X-rays. Using this movement across from one side of the cylinder to the other, many still photos can be taken as the cylinder rotates around the head. When all the images are merged they form a 3-D picture of the physiology of the brain.

Research

One issue with using brain imaging in research is ensuring that samples are large enough to give statistical power to conclusions. **Wei *et al.* (2015)** conducted a review of CAT scan studies on post-stroke depression. It was believed that the position that the stroke occurred in the brain would influence the likelihood of depression. Looking at the brains of 5507 patients using CAT scanning in all the studies, they found that there was a significant relationship between right hemisphere strokes and depression. This relationship was not apparent in the left hemisphere stroke patients. CAT scanning does allow for larger numbers than other scanning methods due to the availability of equipment and the cost. In this example, the physiology of the brain was the focus for researchers and patterns of brain activity were not needed. With the numbers of scans conducted over the total studies, there was sufficient statistical power to make claims of an association between the position of the damage and the likelihood of developing depression.

Positron emission tomography

Positron emission tomography (PET) – a brain imaging method that gives a moving picture of brain activity. This is achieved by tracking radiation levels in the brain.

Positron emission tomography (PET) gives us a dynamic picture of brain activity. This is achieved, in one of the most widely used versions of PET, by injecting the individual with radioactive fluorodeoxyglucose (a form of glucose). This is done into the carotid artery in the neck. The radioactivity is therefore introduced into the bloodstream. As the blood circulates around the brain, the areas that are more highly activated need to use a greater amount of the fluorodeoxyglucose. However, the substance, unlike glucose, cannot metabolize so accumulates in the neurons. The PET scanner provides a moving image of the levels of radioactivity in the brain to within a 30-second delay. This helps to establish which areas of the brain were most active at a particular time point.

Research

PET scans, because of the dynamic information they give, can look at experience and processing. Researchers can use the technology to ascertain how activation changes in any given situation. Religious experiences are one such example. **Azari *et al.* (2001)** conducted PET scans on 12 healthy volunteers, six of whom identified as religious. While reciting a religious psalm, the brain activation of the two groups differed in that the religious group activated a circuit which allowed sustained reflexive thought, like a meditative state. This research needed a dynamic picture of activation rather than a still picture of physiology and shows the relative merits of PET imaging as a technique.

Evaluation

To evaluate the various methods of brain imaging it is useful to consider three criteria: level of detail given, risks and cost. Each method is considered below.

MRI/fMRI

Of the two types of scanning technique using this technology, fMRI gives the greatest amount of detail, as it provides a moving picture and therefore gives detail on the pattern of activation as well as the localization. Individuals who have metallic implants are unable to use MRIs or fMRIs as the magnetic fields could dislodge or heat up such items. The tight space involved in an MRI/fMRI can also be psychologically uncomfortable for the individual. Not only can this cause distress, but also, in the case of fMRI, give atypical readings because of the anxiety and, therefore, compromise reliability.

The cost of MRIs and fMRIs, according to figures from 2013, are $592 and $612 respectively.

EEG

There is limited information on localization from this method, as it looks at brain waves over the whole brain. Some information can be ascertained regarding localization from the differences between electrodes, but this is approximate. The EEG has been useful in establishing overall brain activity, though in areas such as sleep and consciousness. The procedure for EEGs is non-invasive and therefore carries a minimal risk.

The cost of an EEG is $200 (in 2013); it is therefore relatively cheap and accessible for researchers. It also means that larger sample sizes can be used within research, increasing the statistical power of the research.

CAT

The CAT scan is a static picture of the physiology of the brain, so in terms of localization it can identify when there is a structural issue or damage but cannot localize activity in typical brains. These scans are widely used, although risk relates to the frequency of use. With frequent use come higher levels of exposure to radiation, and consequently health risks such as cancer and genetic mutations.

The cost (2013) is $271.

PET

The PET scan is a dynamic picture so can give details of localization of brain activity. Whole body PET scans carry some risk of malignancies, as higher doses of radiation are involved. However, for a brain PET scan the radiation, and therefore the risk level, is low

PET scans are the most expensive brain imaging technique at $1266 (2013).

Generally, the neuroimaging techniques can only detect large changes in the blood flow, oxygen uptake, and so on, so small changes are missed. This has implications for findings as there could be potentially 'false negatives' where activity is occurring, but the scanning techniques are not sufficiently sensitive to detect such changes. This means that the sensitivity of the picture taken of activity is reduced. Given that the brain contains approximately 100 billion neurons and 100 trillion synapses (neuronal connections) there is a lot of detail to measure and identify, and, as yet, the imaging techniques cannot provide this.

Many of the brain imaging techniques, particularly the dynamic versions such as PET and fMRI, are slow. The temporal resolution of fMRIs is anything from 2 to 10 seconds, which is actually quicker than the PET scan. This means that the techniques cannot react quickly enough to some stimuli, especially when you consider brain activity is very fast, taking just milliseconds. This means that some research is not suitable for these methods as the resolution is too slow.

YOU ARE THE RESEARCHER

You have been asked to conduct a study comparing the brain activation of violent criminals and non-violent criminals when faced with a stressful situation.

How might you conduct such a study? Justify your methodology.

What are the ethical considerations you should make as a researcher when using these methods?

Strengthen your learning

1 List the ways in which biology can affect behaviour.

2 Explain the basics of brain physiology in terms of synaptic and neural transmission.

3 Outline techniques used to study the brain.

4 Summarize what research studies have suggested about techniques used to study the brain.

5 Assess techniques used to study the brain in terms of their strengths and weaknesses.

Localization

Localization is the ability to identify parts of the brain which serve certain functions. This work is ongoing and there is still much to find out about how the brain works and the function of specific areas. However, we do have some ability to 'map' the brain. The technological advancements in brain imaging techniques have furthered this route of enquiry. Earlier work on localization relied upon post-mortem or surgery techniques. Of particular note was the work of Wilder Penfield (1891–1976), who, as a neurosurgeon, used a technique called neural stimulation on the brain. His work was developed while treating epileptic patients. He destroyed the area of the brain where the seizures originated to reduce the seizures but, prior to this, on the operating table, he would electrically stimulate the brain areas to check the location of the seizures and to try and minimize the effects of the brain damage he was essentially inducing. In that work, it became apparent what areas of the cortex seemed to be responsible for specific functioning. He started to map out certain areas, such as the motor and somatosensory cortices (detailed below). These maps are supported by subsequent enquiry using brain imaging and other techniques. Penfield's brain maps are, as such, robust findings.

The areas of brain which are of particular interest in terms of localization are outlined in the following section. First, hemispheric lateralization is covered, together with the motor, somatosensory, visual, auditory and language centres of the brain.

Hemispheric lateralization

The brain is a fine piece of design. It has two hemispheres that are different to some degree in their function. The two hemispheres are connected by the corpus callosum, which is a bunch of fibres. These fibres help the two hemispheres exchange information and communicate with each other. It should be noted that the brain is contralateral. This means that the right hemisphere relates to the left side of the body and the left hemisphere to the right side of the body. The reason for this design is not clear, but humans are not the only contralateral animals.

There are quite a few myths about the relative functions of the hemispheres, such as, for example, left brain being creative and right brain being practical, but these do tend to generalize too much. It is essential to consider research-based evidence rather than folklore to determine the specific functions of each hemisphere.

The right hemisphere has been found to have three key functions that have been supported experimentally: recognizing emotion and faces, together with spatial functioning. Research (**Dundas et al., 2015**) supports the idea that the right hemisphere is dominant for recognizing faces, as in research it has been shown that participants process faces predominantly in the right hemisphere. It has also been found that this recognition of faces is more strongly associated with the right hemisphere when the recognition is of very familiar faces (**Bombari et al., 2014**). The right hemisphere also appears to specialize in visuospatial processing (**Hugdahl & Westerhausen, 2010**) and there are examples of lesions (damage) in the right hemisphere prompting visuospatial difficulties. This is often called neglect syndrome. A case study that illustrates this was documented by **Clarke et al. (1993)**. A woman who had suffered right hemisphere damage often got lost in both familiar and unfamiliar places (poor visual-spatial processing). However, when she received verbal guidance of which way to go she managed to find her destination. This is thought to be because verbal instructions are processed (in most people) in the left hemisphere and that was not damaged. The functioning deficit was housed in the right hemisphere.

However, it should be noted that the brain becomes less lateralized with age, with the non-dominant hemisphere supporting the superior hemisphere for any given task. This is called the HAROLD model (Hemispheric Asymmetry Reduction in Older Adults). Therefore, in any experimental procedure it is important to consider the age of participants, as a younger group may show more lateralized behaviour than an older group (**Collins & Mohr, 2013**).

KEY STUDY | # CLASSIC RESEARCH

'Hemisphere deconnection and unity in conscious awareness'
Sperry (1968)

The two hemispheres of the brain work closely together. But what happens in cases where the connection is severed?

Aim
Sperry was interested in the effects post-operation for patients who had received split-brain surgery.

Procedure
Sperry (1968) conducted research on epileptic patients who had previously had their corpus callosum severed or removed in an effort to reduce the number of epileptic fits they experienced. The idea was to restrict the attacks to one hemisphere only, reducing the effect to the patient. Sperry was intrigued by how the operation not only reduced the number of attacks, but also did not seem to have any apparent effects cognitively.

Results
When testing in detail for the effects of the operation, Sperry reported that there were actually several effects which indicated the role of each hemisphere. He focused, in particular, on the visual system and used a technique called the divided field technique.

This ascertained the functions that each hemisphere conducted and did that by showing stimuli to one side of the visual field only, which would then be processed in the opposite hemisphere as the brain is contralateral. In non-split brains, this is not possible to do as the two hemispheres can communicate with each other, so the split-brain patients gave Sperry the opportunity to look at the hemispheres in isolation.

When a word was presented to the right visual field the patient could read it out loud. If a word was presented to the right hemisphere using the left visual field, then the right hemisphere could recognize the word and point (with the left hand) at the object corresponding to the word. The patient would not be able to say the word out loud. Sperry also found that they could not explain why they were pointing at the object because the left hemisphere had not processed the word, as it was shown to the right hemisphere.

This disconnection occurred with touch too. When patients held an object in each hand they could name the one in the right hand, but showed little awareness that they were holding anything in their left hand.

Conclusion
These findings clearly indicated that language was localized predominantly in the left hemisphere.

Evaluation
Sperry's findings were examined subsequently by **Pinto *et al.* (2017)** by assessing the effects in two patients who had a 'split-brain'. They examined the reported inability of Sperry's patients to process objects presented to either the left or right visual field in the non-corresponding hemisphere (i.e. left visual field being processed by the left hemisphere as the brain is contralateral). Pinto *et al.*, however, found that contrary to Sperry's findings, the two patients they examined did not show any such problems. They could identify and name objects no matter which side of the brain they were presented to. The found that the visual perception was split but the overall perception was integrated. This was explained by the idea of neuroplasticity or other compensatory mechanisms and that the 'split' in the brain is only temporary.

This means that research suggests hemispheres have a specific function but that this can be compensated for through neuroplasticity.

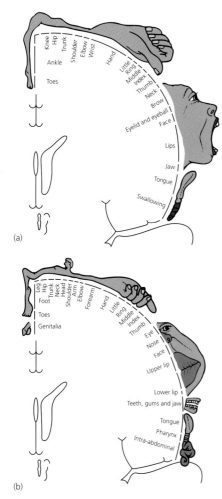

(a)

(b)

■ Figure 1.4
Representation of different parts of the human body on the motor cortex (a) and somatosensory cortex (b). Notice that the face and hands take up more than half of the cortices

Motor centres

The motor centres of the brain are concerned with movement. There are more simple movements like reflexes, coughing, gagging, sneezing, and so on; but the more complex movements we use are coordinated within the motor cortex, which can be found in the parietal lobe of the brain.

The coordination of the neurons and muscles centre on the motor cortex and there are specific areas within it that correspond to the many areas of the body which need to be moved. Figure 1.4 illustrates the approximate placement of the areas of the body. You can see that much of the motor cortex is actually concerned with small areas of the body such as the lips, tongue and hands, as these are areas that require finer motor movements to be performed.

As well as the motor cortex there are other areas of the brain that are involved in movement. For example, the spinal cord and brain coordinate movements; the pre-motor cortex, which is positioned very close in the brain to the motor cortex, plans movements, just before they are actioned. The prefrontal cortex in the frontal lobe also helps to store sensory information from the environment to help the individual work out the movement needed and the possible outcome of that movement.

PSYCHOLOGY IN THE REAL WORLD

Research on localization within the brain is now being used to help individuals who have been paralysed. Ian Burkhart was paralysed in 2012 when he hit a sandbar in the Pacific Ocean while diving into the water. He was paralysed from the neck down. Previously, research into artificial intelligence had developed a way of using signals in the brain to move an artificial limb. However, **Bouton et al. (2016)** devised a way to use artificial intelligence to move Ian's own arm. By inserting a microchip into the motor cortex, in the place that was previously connected to his right arm, they enabled Ian to now think about moving his arm, which then activates the neurons around the microchip. This then transmits a signal to a computer, which decodes them to a specially designed sleeve with 130 electrodes. The electrodes can then activate the muscles needed to conduct the task that Ian is thinking about executing.

The research above illustrates a direct practical application for localization knowledge in the brain. Without knowledge of the motor cortex it would have been difficult to establish where to place the microchip to elicit a response.

Somatosensory centre

The somatosensory area of the brain is focused specifically upon sensory information. It is positioned next to the motor cortex in the parietal lobe and works closely with the motor cortex to allow the individual to move appropriately around their environment. Figure 1.4 shows how the neurons are distributed within the somatosensory cortex. Similarly to the motor cortex, the distribution does not mirror the size of the body part, with the fingers, nose and upper lip (for example) using more of the cortex than large body areas like the trunk. This is due to the complexity of the sensory information gathered in the respective parts.

Visual centre

The area of the brain which processes visual information is positioned in the occipital lobe (see Figure 1.5). It is called the primary visual cortex. There are actually two in the brain, one in both the left and right hemispheres. An area called Area VI within the primary visual cortex seems to be necessary for perceiving visual stimuli (**Daw, 2012**). This is apparent from cases where there has been damage in that specific area.

Auditory centre

There is a primary auditory cortex in both hemispheres (see Figure 1.5). This is required to process complex sounds and is situated in the temporal lobe. If there is a lesion in the area then the individual can still hear some sound, but anything that is complex like speech or music cannot be processed. As the brain is contralateral, sounds heard by the right ear are processed predominantly by the left hemisphere and vice versa. However, unlike the motor cortex, there is not a clearly defined split as some sounds from the right ear are processed on the right side of the brain too.

Language centres

Our production and processing of language occur in many areas across the brain, depending on the function required and modality (i.e. sound, written, oral production) of the language. This section considers two areas: Broca's and Wernicke's areas.

Broca's area

The function of Broca's area is speech production and it is situated in the frontal lobe, very close to the temporal lobe, in the dominant hemisphere (Figure 1.5). Ninety-six per cent of right handers and about 75 per cent of left handers have the left hemisphere as their dominant hemisphere for language. Individuals with a lesion in this area cannot produce speech, but their understanding and processing of other aspects of language remain unimpaired.

Wernicke's area

Wernicke's area is key to understanding language and, more specifically, speech. This area is close to the auditory cortex and can be found where the temporal and parietal lobes meet in the dominant hemisphere for language (which is usually the left hemisphere) (Figure 1.5). It is linked to Broca's area, as the two are closely related, with a bundle of connecting neurons called the arcuate fasciculus. Interestingly, Wernicke's area is also found in deaf people who use sign language, which suggests that its purpose is for more than just speech. Individuals who have a lesion in this area are still able to produce fluent speech as Broca's area is unaffected, although they will sometimes include words they have made up. However, their ability to understand language is severely impaired so someone speaking to them will not be understood, both at sentence and word level.

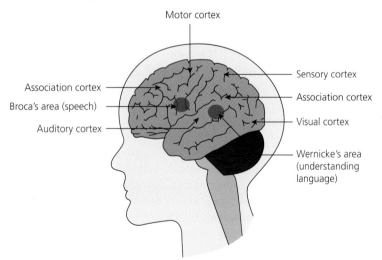

■ **Figure 1.5** Broca's area and other localization of cortical function

Research

Motor centre

Kawai *et al.* (2015) used rats to examine the extent to which the motor cortex is used during learning and executing a skill. When the rats had lesions (damage) in the motor cortex they were still able to execute actions, but not learn new ones. This suggests that the motor cortex is vital for learning new motor skills, but that it is not always necessary for executing the skills once learned.

Somatosensory centre

Research has shown that perception of pain is processed in the somatosensory cortex. This is particularly problematic when a limb is amputated and yet the brain perceives pain from a limb that is no longer there. This is called phantom limb pain. **Hu (2016)** found that the somatosensory cortex was sensitive to pain, despite there being no actual presence of tissue, and this was worse when the pain had continued for a prolonged period. It appeared as if the brain had rewired from the memory of pain and that this was reinforced by phantom limb pain.

Visual centre

There are a few documented case studies of people with damage in Area VI who experience a phenomenon called 'blindsight'. This is when someone feels as though there is something in their visual field but they have no actual vision of it **(Overgaard, 2011)**. This suggests that the visual processing in the brain has two pathways from the eyes and is more complex than studies suggest. Blindsight is extremely rare, however, and as such it is widely accepted that a damaged connection between the eyes and the occipital lobe will result in no vision at all.

Auditory centre

Hyde *et al.* (2009) looked at how the brain developed following 15 months of training on musical instruments in six-year-old children. There was a significant difference in the structure of the participants' auditory centre in the temporal lobe, but also in other key areas such as the motor cortex. These differences were not observed in the control group that had not learned instruments and they were not evident in the participants prior to the musical instruction. This showed that music is processed predominantly in the temporal lobe, but that other areas of the brain are also used. It also suggests that there is no predisposition for musical ability evident in the structure of the brain.

Language centres

Broca's area is named after a neurologist called Paul Broca, who worked with a patient called LeBorgne. LeBorgne was unable to say any words other than 'Tan'. Sadly, in 1861, he died at the age of 51 and Broca conducted a post-mortem examination of his brain. He found a lesion in the area now known as Broca's area which accounted for the inability of LeBorgne to produce speech **(Domanski, 2013)**.

◼ Evaluation

- ◼ Many areas of the brain are activated at any one time, so this makes localization particularly difficult. For example, in a review of studies conducted looking at brain localization for psychopathy, **Santana (2016)** found that there were structural abnormalities highlighted in at least 11 areas of the brain, including the hippocampus and amygdala. The extent to which those individual areas play a part in psychopathy is hard to establish and therefore stating that specific areas are implicated is really all that can be done. Causation is hard to ascertain. It seems unlikely that one area of localization of specific function can ever be established, as it is argued that localization by area is a simplification of the human brain. Associationist theories purport that function is actually a combination of areas being activated. **Thiebaut de Schotten *et al.* (2015)** used brain imaging techniques to revisit some of the famous case studies that have informed localization of function. One of the cases was LeBorgne, whose brain led to the documentation of Broca's area. An MRI was conducted on the brain, which is kept in a medical museum in Paris. The scan showed that it is likely he had damage to other areas connected to the main lesion and that language production is therefore not likely to be confined solely to Broca's area.

- ◼ Some of the localization literature has been derived from case studies, as in the case of Broca's area. This work does support the idea that specific areas do indeed serve specific functions, as the individual with the brain damage can no longer perform specific functions. However, generally this methodology is problematic as a case study is essentially a sample of one person and therefore generalizing to others from someone who may have an atypical brain in terms of localization is problematic.

- ◼ An argument against specific function within the brain can be made when looking at brain injury rehabilitation. The fact that some people recover from brain injury demonstrates that neuroplasticity exists and that therefore the brain is more flexible in terms of function than localization might suggest.

Strengthen your learning

1 Explain what is meant by localization of the brain.

2 Explain localization in terms of hemispheric lateralization.

3 For Sperry's classic 1968 study into hemispheric brain disconnection, in your own words, state the:
   a aims
   b procedure
   c results
   d conclusions
   e evaluative points.

4 Explain localization in terms of how the brain is involved with movement of the body.

5 Explain localization in terms of the functions of the following brain areas:
   a somatosensory centre
   b visual centre
   c auditory centre
   d language centres
   e Broca's area
   f Wernicke's area.

6 Summarize what research studies have suggested about localization of the brain in terms of:
   a hemispheric localization
   b movement of the body
   c the brain areas focused upon in question 5.

Neuroplasticity

Neuroplasticity – the ability of the nervous system, especially the brain, to adapt to the environment and to replace function following damage.

It used to be thought that brain development and change occurred only in childhood and that the brain of an adult was fixed and unchangeable. However, this is now known not to be the case, and neuroscientists call this ability to change and regenerate at all life stages 'neuroplasticity'. As we learn we forge pathways through the brain and as we repeat the action or thought, the pathways become more robust; essentially they become our preferred route. However, it is possible to change our habits and thought patterns, and this is done through neuroplasticity. The more we practise at changing our thought patterns, the stronger they become and they eventually supersede the original pattern as they are stronger.

Neuroplasticity can also occur when there has been damage. This happens in several ways: increased brain stimulation, axon sprouting, and denervation supersensitivity.

Increased brain stimulation is when an area that lies close to the damaged area, or has a similar function on the opposite hemisphere, is stimulated by practising tasks that use that area specifically. The non-affected areas can also function at a lower level initially following damage and it has been found that increasing activation to the close/mirrored areas also helps the one that has been damaged. Axon sprouting is when the link between two neurons is severed by damage but when there are other neurons connected in the same way that sprout extra connections. This compensates for the lost connections and re-establishes a strong link. Denervation supersensitivity is like axon sprouting in that it compensates for lost connections. However, instead of establishing new connections, as in axon sprouting, denervation supersensitivity activates neurons with the same function, meaning the functionality is increased. Basically, this means that the neurons unaffected by damage must work harder.

It would be useful to imagine these methods of neuroplasticity following damage using the metaphor of a factory. Increased brain stimulation would mean that another factory, which produces the same goods, must work harder to help the damaged factory to recover. Axon sprouting is when new workers are employed to compensate for those who can no longer work and denervation supersensitivity is when the undamaged workers must work hard to compensate for the loss of their damaged co-workers.

These three ways that neuroplasticity occurs mean that recovery is possible following trauma to the brain and that a full recovery can be possible, in some cases.

KEY STUDY   **CONTEMPORARY RESEARCH**

'Is a lone right hemisphere enough? Neurolinguistic architecture in a case with a very early left hemispherectomy'
Danelli *et al.* (2013)

The functions of the hemispheres do show some difference, but case studies can illustrate specific effects of hemisphere damage.

Aim
The researchers wished to document the details of a case study of a boy who had one functioning hemisphere.

Procedure
1 When he was two years old EB was operated upon to remove a large tumour that was in his left hemisphere. As the benign tumour was very large, surgeons had no alternative but to remove almost all his left hemisphere. This caused issues with language at the time, as the language centre of the brain is in the left hemisphere of 95 per cent of right-handed people. EB was right-handed and therefore lost his linguistic abilities because of the operation.

2 Following the operation, he underwent an intensive rehabilitation programme. It took three years of intensive therapy to see an improvement, but six years after the operation the recovery was complete.

3 He was tested again when he was 17 years old and comparisons made with 'control' participants who had suffered no such damage. Overall, it appeared that the remaining right hemisphere had compensated for the loss of the left hemisphere and there were only minor issues with grammar processing and speed of oral response to naming objects. When they scanned the brain, they found little difference in processing between EB and the control participants.

4 Now in his early 20s, EB has regained all his previous linguistic ability and there are very few deficits presenting in his linguistic abilities now.

Results
The right hemisphere seems to have compensated almost fully for the loss of the left hemisphere.

Conclusions
This indicates that hemispheric lateralization can be compensated for by the other hemisphere, even though it is not usually used for certain functions. This is a case study though, so the findings cannot be generalized to all individuals. It is important to remember that this is a very young brain and therefore he will have made a more comprehensive recovery than an individual who is older might in the same circumstances.

Evaluation
Caution should be used in terms of the generalizability of this case study. As the sample is effectively one person, the ability to say that all people function similarly is problematic. It may be that this boy's brain was atypical prior to the damage.

Research

■ **Takatsuru *et al.* (2009)** found that function could be regained following strokes if the subjects received brain stimulation. In the research, a stroke was induced in mice in their somatosensory cortex. They then received stimulation on the non-damaged hemisphere and neuroplasticity was observed after two days. Recovery continued, and a full recovery of functioning was reported after four weeks. This demonstrated that the non-affected hemisphere could compensate for function in the damaged hemisphere.

■ Neuroplasticity does not just occur in damaged brains, it occurs in the learning brain, throughout all stages of the lifespan. Evidence from research suggests that the idea that the brain does not change after childhood is wrong. **Fuhrmann *et al.* (2015)** found that adolescence was a particularly sensitive period for brain development and learning, showing that learning and hence neuroplasticity continues later into the lifespan.

Evaluation

■ There are factors that affect neuroplasticity such as perseverance, age and gender. Perseverance has been shown to be important so that the brain exercises the surrounding neurons, which increases the chances of neuroplasticity. In terms of age, the older the individual is the less chance there is that recovery of function will occur. A study by **De la Plata *et al.* (2008)** found that individuals aged 40 or over recovered less function following a brain trauma than younger individuals. The gender, too, can have an effect and, overall, women seem to recover better than men **(Ratcliff *et al.*, 2007)**. Neuroplasticity seems more efficient in women. All these factors are potentially influential in recovery from brain trauma and seem to affect the mechanisms involved in neuroplasticity. The underlying reasons for these are not yet clear, but the sample used in any research into the area should factor these effects in before ascertaining clear progress due to neuroplasticity.

■ Research that gauges the level of recovery following trauma is problematic, as there is often no record of the level of functioning prior to the trauma. It is therefore difficult for researchers to reliably establish the extent of the recovery.

■ The success of rehabilitation programmes from brain injury is strong evidence that the brain can recover from trauma and damage. This would only be possible if neuroplasticity occurred. There are still elements of the process that are unknown, but neuroplasticity is evident from individuals who have benefited from it.

Strengthen your learning

1   Explain the role of neuroplasticity in brain development and change.

2   Summarize what research studies have suggested about the role of neuroplasticity in brain development and change.

3   Assess the role of neuroplasticity in brain development and change in terms of strengths and weaknesses.

4   For Danelli *et al.*'s 2013 contemporary study of the boy who learned to speak again after losing half his brain, in your own words, state the:
    a aims
    b procedure
    c results
    d conclusions
    e evaluative points.

Neurotransmitters and their effect on behaviour

Neurotransmitters – biochemicals found within the brain that play an important part in transmitting messages from neuron to neuron.

An essential part of the transmission of brain signals is the synaptic transmission. This is the point between neurons where the nerve impulse is transferred chemically. Within the brain there are chemicals that are called **neurotransmitters**. They circulate in the synaptic fluid, which lies between the neurons, and they affect the activation of the neurons depending on their levels.

However, the reaction to neurotransmitters is not always the same and depends on the way that the message is responded to by the neuron receiving it.

Cell membrane
– the outer covering
of neurons. The cell
membrane for neurons
is composed of layers
that allow it to transmit
electrical impulses.

It works in a way similar to a lock and key system. The neurotransmitters in the synapse act as the key, and this needs to match with the correct receptor, like a lock, in order for the message to be transmitted across the synapse. This matching process triggers a specific area of the **cell membrane** in the receptor to open up. The 'door' is essentially then opened up for the signal to be received. Ions flow through the membrane, causing an action potential to occur. This can transmit the signal electrically through the neuron (which is called excitatory) or the ionic flow can cause an inhibitory action potential that stops or reduces the transmission level through the neuron.

In summary, excitatory potentials make it more likely for the neuron to fire, so, if a synapse is more likely to cause the post-synaptic neuron to fire, it is called an excitatory synapse. Inhibitory potentials make it less likely to fire and if the message is likely to be stopped at the post-synaptic neuron, it is called an inhibitory synapse.

The pedals of a car may be used as a metaphor to help understand the role of excitation and inhibition. Pressing the accelerator creates an excitatory potential, causing the car to move, while pressing the brake creates an inhibitory potential, which results in slowing down or stopping the car.

Examples of neurotransmitters are serotonin and dopamine, which are both monoamine neurotransmitters; this is because they are synthesized from a single amino acid. The effect that these have on behaviour is considered in the following section.

Serotonin

Serotonin seems to play a regulatory role within the brain and, as such, is implicated in many types of behaviour. There is evidence to suggest that it is involved in emotion, motor, cognitive and basic autonomic behaviour too. The arousal level of the nervous system is mediated by serotonin levels and it also, as a biochemical, seems to coordinate behaviours. Serotonin is perhaps best known for its effect on well-being and happiness. It is found in the gastrointestinal tract as well as the brain and is implicated in mood regulation. Changes in the levels within the brain are evident when an individual is experiencing an elevated mood and lower levels are observed when there is a depressed mood. The recreational drug ecstasy raises levels of serotonin and its ameliorating effect on mood is well-researched. Low levels of serotonin are associated with depression and SSRIs (selective serotonin uptake inhibitors), which are antidepressants, raise the levels of serotonin within the brain and help some patients suffering from depression.

Another potential effect of serotonin levels on behaviour is aggression. This relationship, as with other behaviours, is not clearly defined but some evidence of increased levels of aggression when serotonin levels are low have been found in humans (**Passamonti *et al.*, 2011**). This is thought to occur through the serotonin levels affecting emotion processing in the brain.

Despite this controversy on the extent to which serotonin can be implicated in behaviour, it is clear that it has a general role in terms of regulation. However, this will be alongside other influences that could be found in the environment.

Research

A relationship has been found between reduced levels of serotonin and increased aggression. In research by **Moeller *et al.* (1996)** of ten men who took drugs to reduce their serotonin levels, it was found that aggression levels increased five hours after the drug was administered. The aggression was measured using the Point Subtraction Aggression Paradigm. This is a laboratory-based measure of behaviour in response to provocations via a computer screen. This research shows a relationship between serotonin and aggression, but the laboratory setting does mean that generalizing it to aggression in the world outside the laboratory is problematic. Causation can also not be established.

Dopamine

One of the key areas of behaviour where dopamine has been implicated is schizophrenia. The dopamine hypothesis focuses on the idea that high levels of dopamine in the system of an individual are linked to the onset of schizophrenia. High levels of dopamine appear to increase the activity within the neurons, which means the level of communication is also increased.

This is argued to prompt symptoms experienced in thought-process disorders (e.g. disturbance of thought and communication). However, causation is not proven. There is a body of evidence to suggest that schizophrenia cannot be explained by levels of dopamine alone.

Research

Work by **Davis *et al.* (1991)** found that not all people with schizophrenia had high levels of dopamine and therefore it could not be exclusively responsible for explaining the disorder. However, it was felt by Davis and his fellow researchers that abnormal levels, not low levels, were implicated. This is supported by the fact that Clozapine, which has no effect on decreasing dopamine levels, is successful in the treatment of individuals with schizophrenia.

Evaluation

- There are issues with establishing causality of behaviour from neurotransmitters. Clearly, the objective measurement of the monoamines produced by the neurotransmitters being processed can indicate a link, but the order in which this link occurs is not clear. It could be that the atypical levels prompt behaviour, or equally it could be that the behaviour triggers the levels to deviate from what is typical. Therefore, causation cannot be established. There is also an argument that the role of serotonin in depression specifically is exaggerated, and that the administration of medication to combat low serotonin levels is unhelpful. **Healy (2015)** acknowledges that serotonin plays a part in mood regulation, but he asserts that to imply that it causes depression is mistaken.

- The fact that the measurement of neurotransmitters is objective is a strength of research in this field. As there is no opinion or biases involved in the judgement, the results given are very reliable. Reliability adds academic weight to the research and also makes the findings more persuasive. However, there is an issue with the explanation being reductionist, in that it looks to biochemistry to explain really quite complex behaviour. It is unlikely that any single behaviour can be explained by the levels of one neurotransmitter and, therefore, it can be argued that the neurotransmitter explanations are incomplete. An example of this point is that serotonin has been implicated in eating behaviours and, as such, some researchers have focused on this in an attempt to explain the causes of eating disorders. It is thought to play a part in satiety (feeling full). However, the exact role it plays is not clear and it seems likely that it is only one small element of a bigger picture into how the body regulates appetite (**Voigt & Fink, 2015**).

TOK link

Reductionism is when a single explanation or cause is given for a behaviour. Biological explanations are sometimes described as reductionist and this is argued to be too simplistic, as human behaviour is said to be more complex than a singular cause.

Ethical considerations

The key methods used within this section are measurement of neurotransmitters, case studies and brain imaging technology. These all require consent (in the case of human participants) and this can be problematic if there is some brain damage or mental illness. When using case studies the very nature of their use is that they relate to individuals who have atypical functioning and therefore great care must be taken to ensure that their individual well-being is not compromised by scientific inquisitiveness.

Brain imaging techniques also come with issues to do with consent. Even being part of a typical control group can cause issues if the brain imaging inadvertently discovers an abnormality in the brain that the participant was not aware of. Ethical procedures are put in place to ensure that any discovery that is relevant to an individual in terms of their health and well-being is communicated sensitively and appropriately.

Some brain imaging techniques come with potential risk (such as the substances used in PET scans and the radiation levels in CAT scans) and this means that any participant should be fully informed about the risk involved prior to taking part in the research.

Strengthen your learning

1   Explain how neurotransmitters affect behaviour, including the role of serotonin and dopamine.

2   Summarize what research studies have suggested about how neurotransmitters affect behaviour.

3   What other evaluative points can be made about how neurotransmitters affect behaviour?

SECTION SUMMARY

- There are two hemispheres in the brain, which differ in function. The function of the left hemisphere is language, for most of the population, whereas the right hemisphere specializes in visuospatial processing and emotion/face recognition.
- There is research indicating localization of function of movement (motor cortex), sensory information (somatosensory cortex), vision (occipital lobe), hearing (temporal lobe) and language (Broca's and Wernicke's areas).
- Although there are areas identified for specific functions, a combination of activation in several areas is most likely with processing.
- Neurotransmitters have been implicated in behaviour; for example, serotonin and well-being/aggression and dopamine in schizophrenia.

■ Assessment check

1 Explain how the function of one or more parts of the brain is determined.	(9 marks)
2 Outline one study investigating neuroplasticity.	(9 marks)
3 With reference to a study investigating neurotransmitters and their effects on behaviour, outline one strength and one limitation of a research method used in the study.	(9 marks)
4 Outline one or more techniques used to study the brain in relation to behaviour.	(9 marks)
5 Evaluate techniques used to study the brain in relation to behaviour.	(22 marks)
6 Discuss neuroplasticity of the brain.	(22 marks)
7 Discuss the limitations of localization as a model of the brain and behaviour.	(22 marks)
8 Discuss two or more studies related to neurotransmitters and their effect on behaviour.	(22 marks)

Hormones and behaviour

> 'Hormones are very powerful things. We are helpless in their wake.'
> Meg Cabot (2015)

> 'Hormones are nature's three bottles of beer.'
> Mary Roach, 'Bonk: The Curious Coupling of Science and Sex' (2008)

FOCUS ON...

- Hormones and behaviour; one or more examples of hormones are necessary here.
- Pheromones and behaviour; one or more examples of pheromones are necessary here.

Hormones – chemical messengers released from glands throughout the body.

Neurotransmitters are not the only biochemicals implicated in behaviour. **Hormones**, which are found in the bodily fluids of an individual, are also seemingly involved in certain behaviours. They are secreted via the endocrine system, which includes glands such as the pituitary gland, the adrenal glands and the thyroid gland. These glands can be found in various locations throughout the body. The pituitary gland is sometimes called the 'master gland', as it monitors hormone levels and facilitates secretion and is found within the brain. The adrenal glands are situated on top of the kidneys and the thyroid gland is in the throat. There are many hormones in the body, but this section outlines the effect of oxytocin, testosterone and adrenaline (which is also a neurotransmitter in its noradrenaline form) on behaviour.

Oxytocin

Oxytocin levels are maintained by the pituitary gland. Oxytocin's key effects relate to reproductive behaviour and maternal behaviour, too, such as nurturing, caring and feeding. **Campbell (2008)** found that oxytocin could increase maternal behaviours in female rats, even when they were not pregnant. It also intensifies contractions, aiding the speed of delivery during labour, and increases milk production in new mothers. There is research to suggest that oxytocin helps attachment formation (**Tops *et al.*, 2013**). These findings should be taken with caution, however, as most of the research upon which the effects are found was conducted on animals. **Extrapolation** to humans is therefore problematic. This is discussed in greater depth in 'The role of animal research in understanding human behaviour' in the final section of this chapter.

KEY STUDY

CONTEMPORARY RESEARCH

'Effects of MDMA and intranasal oxytocin on social and emotional processing'
Kirkpatrick *et al.* (2014)

MDMA is a recreational drug which increases feelings of empathy, sociability, and interpersonal closeness. These effects are thought to occur by releasing oxytocin.

Aim
Kirkpatrick *et al.* were interested in investigating the immediate effects of MDMA and oxytocin.

Procedure
Sixty-five human participants were administered MDMA, some oxytocin (nasally), and the control group received a placebo (a substance with no effect). They were then given measures of emotion recognition and sociability (i.e. measuring how much they wanted to be with others). Physiological measures were also taken.

Results
In the groups that received the MDMA or oxytocin there was an effect. They found that MDMA raised feelings of euphoria and the oxytocin raised feelings of sociability and enhanced recognition of sad facial expressions.

Conclusions
This suggests that, in both forms (i.e. either MDMA or oxytocin only), oxytocin increased sociability and favourable perception of others.

Evaluation
The use of a control group in this study is essential to show potential causality. However, there are many other potential factors that will affect a participant's reaction in this study, so unless all variables were controlled for causality is still difficult to discern.

Testosterone

Testosterone is an androgen: a male hormone. It is not found exclusively in males but generally the amount found in females is much lower than that found in the male population. Testosterone is often linked to aggression and research has shown a link between the hormone and aggressive behaviour. However, this appears to be predominantly in non-human animals. In humans, the relationship is more complex, with testosterone not being implicated in all aggression, but mainly aggressive reactions to social provocation (**Mehta & Beer, 2010**).

It is also implicated in behaviour classified as masculine, as it is an androgen. The contemporary research study below by **Beltz *et al.* (2011)** illustrates that researchers are looking to testosterone to explain 'masculine' behaviour and choice.

KEY STUDY   ## CONTEMPORARY RESEARCH

'Gendered occupational interests: Prenatal androgen effects on psychological orientation to Things versus People'
Beltz *et al.* (2011)

It is difficult to establish the extent to which hormones are responsible for our behaviour and the stereotypes that abound in society.

Aim

Beltz *et al.* were interested to find out the effect of testosterone levels on subsequent career choice.

Procedure

A genetic condition called congenital adrenal hyperplasia (CAH) causes higher-than-normal levels of testosterone in those affected. Beltz *et al.* looked at the jobs of 46 women who have CAH and compared them with 31 of their brothers, 27 males with CAH and 21 of their sisters who were unaffected. Their choice of career was classified into person-centred or non-person-centred.

Results

They found that the females with CAH, and consequently higher levels of testosterone, chose non-person-centred career choices, which were similar findings to the career choice of males with and without CAH, whereas the non-CAH affected females erred towards the person-centred career choices.

Conclusion

These findings, the researchers asserted, indicate that exposure to higher levels of androgens in the womb affects the psychological orientation sufficiently to influence career choice.

Evaluation

There are many factors affecting career choice, such as academic level and personality. The results do indicate a connection, but the sample size is not sufficient to identify testosterone levels as the key consideration.

▨ Adrenaline

The heightened state brought about by an adrenaline increase is well-known. The term 'adrenaline rush' is widely used for the feeling that an arousing situation can bring about, and the description 'adrenaline junkie' is used to describe someone who actively seeks an adrenaline rush. Adrenaline is secreted by the adrenal glands located on top of each kidney. When an individual perceives a threat or potentially stressful situation, adrenaline rushes through the system triggering a racing heart and tense muscles, along with other effects. All these are part of the fight-or-flight response. The term 'fight or flight' is used to describe the circumstances under which adrenaline is released into the body; this response will probably save everybody's life at some point. It is designed to allow the body to deal with threat and danger. When experiencing the fight-or-flight response, an individual can move faster (due to the tensed muscles) and take in more oxygen (due to the respiratory changes). This enables a rapid exit from the stressful situation, or indeed the ability to fight. The raised heartbeat helps to send the adrenaline around the system and gets blood to the muscles and organs. This means that a relationship between the physiological and behavioural reaction to situations and adrenaline is likely.

LINK TO SOCIOCULTURAL LEVELS OF ANALYSIS

Work such as the Beltz study (see 'Contemporary research' above) conducted on the effects of genetics or hormones on gender makes assumptions about the social role of the genders. In the Beltz study the link between testosterone and types of career was examined. A core assumption was made about person-centred professions being more feminine. This is a stereotype which could have emerged from gender differences in general behaviour, potentially triggered by hormonal differences and, as such, is a biosocial explanation of career choice.

High levels of both adrenaline and testosterone have been found in a personality type called 'sensation seeking'. People who are sensation seekers are able to cope with, and like, high levels of stimulation in the environment because they like their body to be in a heightened state of arousal. They like to participate in situations that involve sensations of flying, speed and being out of your comfort zone, such as riding roller-coasters, parachuting and car racing (**Zuckerman, 1983**).

There is also some suggestion that it is implicated in aggression, but research on the relationship indicates it is not always clear.

■ **Figure 1.6** Roller-coaster rides take individuals out of their comfort zone

Research

- **Gerra *et al.* (1999)** looked at the levels of norepinephrine and epinephrine (the American terms for noradrenaline and adrenaline) in 74 healthy males. They found a positive relationship between adrenaline and noradrenaline (the neurotransmitter equivalent of adrenaline) and their level of sensation-seeking temperament. This suggests that an individual with high residual levels of adrenaline is more likely to be a sensation seeker. Causation cannot be proven, but the researchers suggested that the higher adrenaline levels could be responsible for the development of this personality type.

- **Klinteberg & Magnusson (1989)** looked at the relationship between behaviour and adrenaline levels in 13-year-old boys. Levels of adrenaline found in the urine of the sample of 86 boys were measured in both a resting situation (while they were watching a non-violent film) and a stressful situation (performing a mental maths test). The researchers gathered teacher ratings in terms of fidgeting, concentration difficulties and aggression. They found that the boys who were hyperactive (high fidgeting and low concentration) had lower levels of adrenaline secretion in both the stressful and 'normal' conditions. They did not find a relationship to aggression. This suggests that adrenaline is implicated in restless behaviour but that it is not related to aggressive behaviour in this kind of situation.

Evaluation

■ As with the evaluation of neurotransmitter explanations for behaviour, the hormone levels are measured objectively, which means that the reliability of the data is very good. And this means the research is well regarded by many psychologists. However, again similarly to the neurotransmitter explanations, using hormones to explain complex human behaviours is seen as reductionist and shows little consideration of environmental, social or cognitive influences.

■ There are circumstances where levels of hormones can be explained by very similar emotions. For example, adrenaline can be raised with differing emotional states: stressed or happy. This means that the validity of explanations is compromised in some research into hormones. In the case of adrenaline, it can be argued that the level of hormone is related to the level of emotion rather than a specific emotion or feeling.

Strengthen your learning

1   Explain how neurotransmitters affect behaviour, including the role of serotonin and dopamine.

2   Summarize what research studies have suggested about how neurotransmitters affect behaviour.

3   What other evaluative points can be made about how neurotransmitters affect behaviour?

4   Explain the role of hormones on behaviour, including oxytocin, testosterone and adrenaline.

5   For Kirkpatrick *et al.*'s 2014 contemporary study of oxytocin and friendliness, in your words, state the:
    a aims
    b procedure
    c results
    d conclusions
    e evaluative points.

6   For Beltz *et al.*'s 2011 contemporary study of testosterone and career choice, in your own words, state the:
    a aims
    b procedure
    c results
    d conclusions
    e evaluative points.

7   Summarize what research studies have suggested about the role of hormones on behaviour.

8   What other evaluative points can be made about the role of hormones on behaviour?

Pheromones and behaviour

Pheromones are chemical substances that are emitted by humans and non-human animals into their environment. This can occur in several ways, but the most frequent release of pheromones is in the sweat of the individual. These chemical substances are thought to elicit an effect on the environment itself and other animals in the environment. The effect on other animals in terms of behaviour is the focus of psychologists in this field.

In non-human animals, pheromones are a method of communication. Transmission occurs via sweat and other bodily fluids such as urine. Humans are also thought to be affected by pheromones. Those argued to elicit a specific behavioural effect are called releaser pheromones and, in certain contexts or situations, they trigger specific behaviour. In other situations, the same pheromone may act as more of a primer. An example of the distinction between these two effects is found in the pheromones in male mouse urine. The releaser effect is to make behaviour more aggressive when an intruder is perceived, but the pheromone also promotes menstrual synchrony in the female mice; this is the primer effect.

KEY STUDY | ## CLASSIC RESEARCH

'Olfactory influences on the human menstrual cycle'
Russell *et al.* (1980)

Pheromones are believed to transfer their effect to humans in several ways, one of which is via smell. The pheromones can act as an olfactory cue.

Aim
Russell *et al.* aimed to examine the effect of pheromones administered nasally.

Procedure
1   The researchers compared two groups of women regarding the timing of their menstrual cycle. One group was administered the pheromones of a single female by rubbing their top lips with a mixture of underarm perspiration from the female and alcohol. Plain alcohol only was rubbed under the noses of the other group.
2   The substance (whether pheromones plus alcohol or alcohol only) was administered to both groups daily for five months.
3   Researchers then compared the timing of the onset of the menstrual cycles in both groups with that of the woman who had donated the sweat.

Results
1   The group which received the pheromones plus alcohol showed a significant shift in the timing of their menstrual cycles, and this shift corresponded with the timing of the donor female.
2   The shift did not occur in the control (alcohol-only) group.

Conclusion
This suggested that transference of pheromones can affect those in the environment, if they receive olfactory cues.

Evaluation of research
●   This research is intriguing and important, because experimentally it shows how menstrual synchrony can appear through transferral of pheromones.
●   Menstrual synchrony is something which is unaffected by methodological procedures, as it is out of the conscious influence of the individual. This means there can be no effect from bias or experimenter effects, meaning the findings are potentially solid.

▮ Research into attraction
Pheromones are implicated in attraction in both humans and non-human animals. There are specific pheromones secreted that arouse and encourage sexual activity in males and females. In the animal kingdom, the boar pheromone is secreted via the male boar's saliva when he is sexually aroused and this transfers to the air. The sow will detect the pheromone nasally and assume a standing position that makes it possible for the boar to mount her.

In humans, there is thought to be an effect from secretion of a steroidal compound found in male sweat called androstenedione. It is found in women too, in lower levels, but women are able to detect it to a varying degree. **Verhaeghe *et al.* (2013)** conducted a review of the research looking at the effect of the pheromone on mood (increasing positivity), heightened focus and mate attractiveness. They found that the literature indicates that exposure to androstenedione does indeed increase attractiveness in mates, improves mood and focus and also increases sexual arousal and desire.

Research into menstrual effects

Stern and McClintock (1998) found that when women received 'odourless compounds' from the armpits of women in the latter half of their menstrual cycle, their menstrual cycle was shortened, presumably by the effect of the other women's pheromones as they approached the end of their cycle. The compounds were transferred by the women wiping a pad, which had previously been wiped across the donor's armpit, above their upper lip. However, if the compounds (which included pheromones) were collected from women at the beginning of their cycle, this had the opposite effect, lengthening the cycle of those who had received the compound. This shows that the menstrual cycle of a woman can be altered by communication via pheromones. This is a priming effect.

Research into learning

Recent research has indicated that pheromones are part of a learning process that some animals acquire. Female mice are attracted to the urine of males they have previously encountered. It is as if the pheromones have rewarding properties that encourage a female to stay with a mate. In ants, there is a contribution from pheromones to helping forager ants to remember their routes (**Czaczkes et al. 2013**).

In humans, the role of androstadienone in attention to various stimuli was examined by researchers. They found that following administration of the substance to the upper lip of 50 men and women there was increased attention paid to emotional information in the environment, although this effect was not reported in non-emotional stimuli (**Hummer & McClintock, 2009**).

Evaluation

- The pheromonal explanation for behaviour can be evaluated in the same way as neurotransmitter and hormone explanations; the measurement is objective, so reliable but the explanation is reductionist. Measurement of pheromones is objective in the same way as other biochemicals; there is no subjectivity involved. Pheromones are released via bodily fluids so the measurement is also relatively easy and non-invasive. This means it is not only objective, it is also easy to use methodologically. However, it is correlational; in other words, there can only be a link established between the pheromones and the behaviour, and causation cannot be stated.

- It is also important not to overemphasize the role pheromones play in human attraction and sexuality. A review of the literature by **Mostafa et al. (2012)** suggests that they play a major role in non-human animal behaviour but a minor role in human reproductive behaviour. This warning of the overemphasis of pheromones was supported further by **Hare et al. (2017)**, who looked specifically at the level of effect that the two sex pheromones, androstadienone and estratetraenol, had on gender perception, attractiveness ratings, or judgements of unfaithfulness. They found no effect and argued that the two pheromones are not human pheromones at all. This undermines much of the previous work on the effect these substances have on human behaviour.

YOU ARE THE RESEARCHER

As a researcher, you have been given the job of researching the interaction between pheromones and attraction. You have decided to use a questionnaire to determine the level of attraction.

What items could you include on the questionnaire? What kind of response option would you give the participants (i.e. Likert scale, true/false)? Justify your item wording and response choices in terms of reliability and validity.

Finally, draw up a plan of the research procedure.

■ Ethical considerations in research into hormones and behaviour

Research into hormones requires non-invasive techniques to be used, such as mouth swabs and sweat collection. This means that there is little risk and harm involved and therefore the research is ethically sound. Sometimes blood samples may also be involved and, as this is a more invasive technique, ethical procedures are more stringent.

Consent is sought from human participants and therefore if the participant group is vulnerable in some way, this is an ethical consideration. Parents, carers and families will be approached in this instance, but they must be fully informed regarding the proposed procedure.

Much of the research in this area is also conducted on non-human animals so if hormonal levels are being measured or manipulated, the level of suffering must be kept to a minimum. For a fuller discussion around non-human animals and ethical considerations, please see 'Ethical considerations in animal research' in the final section of this chapter (page 39).

Strengthen your learning

1 Explain how pheromones affect behaviour.

2 Summarize what research studies have suggested about how pheromones affect behaviour.

3 What other evaluative points can be made about how pheromones affect behaviour?

4 For Russell *et al.*'s classic 1980 study of olfactory influences on the human menstrual cycle, in your own words, state the:
   a aims
   b procedure
   c results
   d conclusions
   e evaluative points.

SECTION SUMMARY

- Hormones are chemical messengers that are part of the endocrine system. They are released from glands throughout the body. They move around the body in the bloodstream and can be measured in bodily fluids.
- Examples of hormones that seem to affect behaviour are: oxytocin, which fosters sociability and encourages formation of attachments; testosterone, which is implicated in behaviours such as aggression; and adrenaline, which helps the body to respond to threat.
- Pheromones are a chemical substance produced and released into the environment. They affect the behaviour or physiology of others in the environment.
- Pheromones can affect behaviour in terms of attraction and reproductive behaviour. There is also research to suggest they affect learning and menstrual synchrony.
- Caution should be taken to not overemphasize the role of hormones and transmitters in human behaviour, as causation is not proven.

■ Assessment check

1	Explain how pheromones may influence one human behaviour.	(9 marks)
2	Outline one study of how hormones affect human behaviour.	(9 marks)
3	With reference to a study, outline the ethical considerations of investigating the effects of pheromones and behaviour.	(9 marks)
4	Discuss the effects of hormones on human behaviour.	(22 marks)
5	Evaluate evidence that pheromones play a role in human behaviour.	(22 marks)

Genetics and behaviour

'We are survival machines – robot vehicles blindly programmed to preserve the selfish molecules known as genes. This is a truth which still fills me with astonishment.'
Richard Dawkins, 'The Selfish Gene' (1976)

FOCUS ON...

- Genetic similarity and how this relates to twin and family research and genetic heritability.
- Gene regulation and expression, and factors that affect gene expression.
- Evolutionary explanations for behaviour, including survival of the fittest and natural selection.

There are several ways that biology can affect behaviour; along with brain physiology and biochemicals, there is also the role of genetics. Each human has a genotype, which is a genetic code unique to them. This is the case for all individuals except identical twins, who share a genotype. That genetic code determines physical characteristics such as eye colour, but there is a lot of work being conducted examining the extent to which it plays a part in behaviour. The field is known as human behaviour genetics. Genes are coded into an individual's genetic make-up, but the way that they affect development throughout the life span is called genetic expression. They are not always active and only affect the individual when they are 'switched on'. Sometimes there will be an environmental switch that will trigger activation of the gene to affect the individual physiologically. This can result in a psychological effect. It is important to remember that a genetic predisposition for a behaviour in the genetic code of the individual (called the genotype) is not the same as the genetic code plus the environment (called the phenotype.) The phenotype is the result of the individual's interaction with their environment and is what we observe in behaviour research.

TOK link

Iceland is a country with two key elements that make it particularly helpful for genetics research: a small population and a low level of immigration. This has meant that the potential for genetic research is great as the genetic picture is clearer.

In 1998 a company called deCODE collected the DNA of one-third of the population of the country. Over 11 years, it conducted research that made links between many genes and specific diseases. Indeed, by 2007 there had been 15 variants identified as increasing the risk of developing a range of disorders from asthma to diabetes, including schizophrenia.

This illustrates the potential help that research in one country can confer to the global population. It also shows how data on genetic relatedness (i.e. similarity) can be gathered successfully without using twin samples.

There is research conducted into nearly all aspects of human behaviour, but the following section will consider aggressive behaviour specifically.

Aggression

The link between testosterone and aggression was discussed briefly in the previous section, 'Hormones and behaviour'. It is also entirely possible that the high levels of testosterone implicated in aggression are a consequence of the individual's genetic code. If this is indeed the case then it would be expected that the higher levels of testosterone would also be evident in the individual's relatives. Other biochemicals such as serotonin, dopamine and adrenaline are implicated too.

Genes can affect testosterone levels, as they have an effect on the way that the hormone is metabolized (this is the word used when a biochemical is processed by the body). Genes can also affect the brain physiology of an individual in the extent to which receptors are available to process the testosterone in the neurons. In terms of brain physiology, the frontal lobe is known to have properties that exert control and therefore some individuals' brain physiology will mean that the control element is not as strong, leading to aggression. This frontal lobe physiology could be genetically determined. However, merely demonstrating how the genes could prompt changes to the physiology and biochemical make-up of an individual is not sufficient; there needs to be an identifiable gene, or series of genes, if the genetic link to behaviour can be made.

Research

■ In the case of aggression this link has been suggested by the MAOA gene (in full the name is monoamine oxidase A). The genetic link was found through observations that the men in a Dutch family seemed to be particularly aggressive (see 'Classic research' below)

■ This observation was supported by evidence from animal research (**Cases *et al.*, 1995**) which showed that mice presenting with the MAOA gene had increased secretions of monoamines too, and that behaviourally they were much more aggressive than other mice who did not present with the gene. The mechanism that underpinned these differences was thought to be that the MAOA gene controlled not the levels of the biochemicals directly, but the enzyme that helps to process them. Some people have the low-activity form of the gene, which is called MAOA-L, and this leads to higher levels of the monoamines in the urine. This is the type linked to aggression. In the high-activity version (MAOA-H), there is a higher level of the enzyme and therefore less trace of the monoamines in the urine. It should be noted that all individuals with the shortened form of the gene (MAOA-L) are male.

Evaluation

■ Not all occurrences of specific behaviours can be explained using genetics. For example, only one-third of men have the shortened form of the gene so, in theory, the MAOA explanation can only explain aggression within that population. It also cannot explain aggression in women. This means that the explanation is incomplete if seen to be a general explanation for aggression.

■ Another argument against genetic explanations is that even when a gene is identified as implicated in behaviour, individuals who possess the gene do not always demonstrate the behaviour. The MAOA gene is an example of this argument too, as one-third of men have the MAOA shortened version of the gene but they are not all aggressive. This is explained by the diathesis–stress model, a theory which states that genetics can explain predispositions to acting a certain way (diathesis) but that will not develop unless the environment triggers the development. This is often due to environmental stressors (stress). The environment can affect the individual's psychological equilibrium, which triggers development of that predisposition. This idea underlines the reductionist nature of genetic explanations, in that it is rarely the case that possessing a gene implicated in behaviour means that that specific behaviour will definitely develop.

KEY STUDY   ## CLASSIC RESEARCH

'Abnormal behaviour associated with a point mutation in the structural gene for monoamine oxidase A'
Brunner et al. (1993)

The potential effect of a gene on behaviour is fascinating research. This work uses a family case study to examine how the genetics in the family affects behaviour.

Aim
In 1993 H.G. Brunner published a paper on Brunner syndrome, which was identified within a Dutch family. His aim was to establish the genetic influence on behaviour of the individuals.

Procedure
Brunner measured the levels of monoamine in the urine of all family members.

Results

1   Five of the men in that family showed high levels of monoamines in their urine, produced when noradrenaline, serotonin and dopamine are processed. The reason behind this excess of monoamine levels was found to be genetic; they possessed a shortened version of the MAOA gene, which was unable to absorb the monoamines and remove them from the system.

2   Brunner found that not only did the biochemistry of the male members of the family exhibit atypical biochemical measurements, they also displayed higher-than-normal levels of aggression when in a position where they felt threatened, angry or frustrated. This behaviour would escalate and manifest in such behaviours as attempted rape, arson and extreme violence.

Conclusion

Brunner syndrome demonstrates a possible relationship between biochemicals and aggression. The fact that the abnormal levels of monoamines are genetic implicates genetics too.

Evaluation

● While this study is essentially a case study, as it looks at a small sample and just one family, it supports genetic explanations of aggression.

● However, overall, it does not explain why some men with the genetic indication of Brunner syndrome do not exhibit high levels of aggression. The area is clearly more complex than this study suggests.

▨ Genetic similarities

One of the key ways that genetic research can be conducted is by using twin studies. By using twin pairings, the level of heritability for any given behaviour can, in theory, be calculated due to the genetic relatedness of the individuals. There is a core assumption that underpins this type of methodology. As identical (monozygotic or MZ) twins come from the same fertilized egg, they are 100 per cent genetically similar and non-identical (dizygotic or DZ) twins share half their genes, as they come from different fertilized eggs, so any differences in behaviour should be attributable to how similar the twins' genetics are.

This works on the assumption that the environment is the same for both twins (i.e. shared womb and home environment). For example, if all the identical twins demonstrate a behaviour and only half of the non-identical twins do so, then there is the suggestion that genetics can explain the behaviour. In the real world, this rarely happens and concordance rates are used to ascertain the level of heritability.

■ **Figure 1.7** Twin studies are used in genetic research as the level of heritability for any given behaviour can, in theory, be calculated due to the genetic relatedness of the individuals

Concordance rates are expressed as a percentage. The percentage is calculated from the number of twin pairs, where both twins exhibit the behaviour. If identical twins have a concordance rate of 80 per cent for a behaviour and non-identical twins have a 32 per cent concordance rate for the same behaviour, the difference between the two concordance rates can be attributed to the differences between the two types of twins (MZ or DZ) in terms of genetic similarity. However, it can also be said from the concordance rates that there are environmental influences because otherwise the concordance rate for identical twins would be 100 per cent.

Family studies are also conducted to examine behaviour and its heritability level. By looking through a family tree and looking at members who may be diagnosed with a condition, geneticists have estimated heritability of that condition.

Research

- Researchers (**Crisp *et al.*, 1985**) conducted a study into anorexia nervosa, an eating disorder, to ascertain how genetic similarity affected development of the eating disorder. They looked at 34 sets of twins, one set of triplets and an adoptive family. They found that the disorder was presented by 55 per cent of identical twin pairs (both twins) and 7 per cent in non-identical twins (both twins); the concordance rates were 55 per cent and 7 per cent respectively. This is argued to show a genetic component in the development of the disorder as the concordance rates between the two types of twins were different and there was a significantly higher concordance rate for identical twins. However, there was no indication of a genetic influence in the triplets or family data (although that was just one triplet set and one family involved in the research, so this is weak evidence against the genetic component).

- In a family study conducted by **Gottesman *et al.* (1987)** rates of schizophrenia were examined, looking at the genetic similarity of family members. The study showed that relatives of people with schizophrenia were more likely to develop the condition than the public. The risk of this occurring increases as the genetic similarity increases. So, the study found that the percentage of grandchildren of people with schizophrenia to develop schizophrenia themselves was 2.84, whereas children of those with schizophrenia presented a percentage of 9.35. As grandchildren are 25 per cent genetically similar to their grandparents and children are 50 per cent genetically similar to their parents, the figures demonstrate that genetic similarity plays a part in development of schizophrenia.

Evaluation

- Twin studies rely upon large sample sizes to ascertain reliable concordance figures. The fact that twin pregnancies are rarer than single pregnancies means that finding a sample is difficult. There are twin registries now in some countries, including the UK where there is a registry that has 12,000 identical and non-identical twins. However, this information is not always available in other countries and, even with registries, the sheer volume of twin research needed means that not all projects can access the database. There is also the problem of finding twins in large numbers if looking at specific populations where the prevalence is low in the general population and numbers therefore are very low in the twin population. This means that unusual conditions may be unsuitable for twin research.

- The idea that twins share an environment is a key assumption of twin research. However, stating that both identical and non-identical twins have the same level of environmental similarity is argued to be problematic. Due to physical similarity, it is argued that parents treat identical twins more similarly than parents of non-identical twins do (**Ohlson, 2002**). When comparing the concordance rates of the two twin types, any differences cannot therefore necessarily be attributed to genetic similarity, rather environment.

- Assumption of genetic similarity, based on the relationship of the individual, can sometimes be inaccurate. In the case of paternity, there is sometimes an inaccurate picture given in that the father is not always the biological father and both the child and the man concerned might be unaware of this fact. In 2007–2008 the UK Government found that about 20 per cent of claims by mothers of paternity for child support were disproven with a DNA test. This means that the level of genetic similarity within families cannot be assumed.

■ Evolutionary explanations for behaviour

Evolutionary psychologists are interested at looking at why some behaviours may have been helpful to us through the generations. The core idea is that as humans, like our ancestors, we live in an environment of evolutionary adaptation (EEA). The primary purpose for evolutionary adaptation is firstly to survive, with the ability to survive described in the phrase 'survival of the fittest'. The second purpose for any behaviour is to increase the chance of reproduction. Therefore, a behaviour should increase an individual's attractiveness to the opposite sex. This reproductive focus is different for men and women. Evolutionary theory states that men increase their chances of reproducing offspring by having sex with as many partners as possible, as in that way, in theory, they will increase the chance of making lots of women pregnant. For women, the emphasis is on not only getting pregnant, but doing so with a mate who will stay around to help to provide for the children. They also need to try and pick a mate that is well-resourced so that both they (as the mother of the child) and the child itself will be well provided for. It is argued by evolutionary psychologists that most behaviours serve some function in terms of one or both aims.

KEY STUDY   ## CONTEMPORARY RESEARCH

'Averageness or symmetry: which is more important for facial attractiveness?'
Komori et al. (2009)

There is some suggestion that facial symmetry is linked to attractiveness, as it is an indicator of health and therefore reproductive fitness.

Aim

Komori *et al.* investigated the facial symmetry and averageness of men and women's faces using a mathematical method of comparison called 'geometrics morphometrics' to test the idea that the two were related.

Procedure

Geometrics morphometrics compares the extent to which 72 facial feature points deviate from the gender average and from the opposite side of the face.

Results

They found that averageness increased the attractiveness for both men and women, but that facial symmetry was equally as influential in terms of attractiveness in men.

Conclusion

The evolutionary argument given for this finding by the researchers was that symmetry in men's faces increases the perception of masculinity, which would suggest that the person has good prospects as a reproductive partner... making them more attractive.

Evaluation

● With women, a raised level of perceived masculinity may not be evolutionarily adaptive in the same way, as evolutionary theory would argue that women are more attractive if they are more feminine.

● There are other variables such as personality and interests that make someone more attractive, so this really only can relate to initial attraction. Therefore, perhaps evolutionary theory can only really explain superficial attraction and not the formation of a relationship.

The following section will consider how anxiety may be environmentally adaptive.

Anxiety

Anxiety is a feeling of apprehension and worry. For many sufferers of anxiety disorders, anxiety is not enabling in any way, indeed it means that life can be difficult as the individual is held back by their anxiety. Evolutionary psychologists argue, however, that anxiety is evolutionarily adaptive. It prevents the person who is experiencing the anxiety from potentially putting themselves in danger, which increases their chances of survival.

The problem comes when the anxiety levels become too high and are not adaptive. **Nesse & Williams (1995)** called the anxiety regulation mechanism the 'smoke detector principle'. They argue that it is an evolutionary adaptation to have a heightened awareness of potential threat and that manifests itself as anxiety. However, like a smoke detector it is set to be triggered at the smallest sign of threat and, like the smoke detector, it is necessary for us to be aware of problems.

Some individuals can tell when the anxiety triggered is unnecessary. However, others cannot detect a false alarm and the anxiety is acted upon, and the situation avoided. Evolutionary psychologists attribute anxiety disorders to some disorders that are due to design rather than genetic flaws. This is where the 'smoke detector principle' works for some individuals but not others.

There is further discussion and research on the evolutionary influence on anxiety in Chapter 5 'Abnormal psychology', where evolutionary explanations for obsessive-compulsive disorder (OCD) are considered. OCD is classified as an anxiety disorder and the evolutionary explanation examines how such a debilitating disorder can be seen as evolutionarily adaptive.

Research

■ A research review of family studies was conducted by **Hettema et al. (2001)**. It found that, looking at the results of all the studies reviewed, panic disorder, generalized anxiety disorder, phobias, and OCD all have significant clustering within families and that there were also environmental factors involved in individuals to anxiety. The family predisposition could be due to a shared environment, but Hettema et al. looked at the level of non-shared environment and found the contribution to be significant, suggesting a genetic influence.

■ A twin study conducted by **Torgersen (1983)** looked at 85 twin pairs (32 identical [MZ], 53 non-identical [DZ]). The results showed that anxiety disorders were more than twice as likely in MZ twins and the genetic influence is particularly strong for some anxiety disorders such as agoraphobia with panic attacks. Torgersen found no indication of genetic influence for generalized anxiety disorders, which cannot easily be explained in evolutionary terms.

Evaluation

■ The idea that sex occurs merely to have children is outdated. Couples are given control now as to whether having sex will result in a pregnancy. This ability to choose has arisen, following more reliable contraception methods. Indeed, most intercourse is for fun and pleasure rather than pregnancy. This means that explaining behaviour using the likelihood of passing on genes can be argued to be a misnomer.

■ The general principles of survival and reproduction as underpinning behaviour are global. This then should mean that there would be very similar behaviour across the world, as, arguably, all the behaviour is driven by the same principles. Instead, we find that there is variation from culture to culture. Relationships are an example of such variation. Divorce is not unusual in many cultures, whereas monogamy with the same partner is expected within other cultures and divorce is rare. Both these cultures therefore vary significantly and they illustrate that explaining behaviour the same way in evolutionary terms can be inappropriate.

■ Evolutionary psychologists have found some cross-cultural consistencies in their research, suggesting that evolutionary explanations may be appropriate for some behaviours. One example is mate preference work by **Buss (1989)**. The research is detailed in 'Classic research' (below).

KEY STUDY   ## CLASSIC RESEARCH

*'Sex differences in human mate preferences: Evolutionary
hypotheses tested in 37 cultures'*
Buss (1989)

A key part of evolutionary theory is that behaviour is observed cross-culturally.

Aim
This was the focus of the work by Buss (1989). He wished to test evolutionary theory,
cross-culturally.

Procedure
1   Buss conducted his study in 37 different cultures (within 33 countries) globally. The work
    involved a sample of 10,047 participants. Buss looked specifically at mate preferences.
2   He focused upon how males and females rated reproductive capacity, ambition–
    industriousness (resource acquisition), youth, physical attractiveness, and chastity. He
    also collected data on age of marriage, where appropriate, in most of the countries.

Results
1   He found that there was indeed consistency shown across nearly all the cultures.
2   Women rated the resources of potential partners higher than men did. Ambition and
    good financial prospects were important to them. This suggests that the need for a
    mate to provide for any offspring is important to women in mate selection.
3   Similarly, across most cultures, men rated appearance in potential mates as more
    important than women did. They also indicated that a younger mate by about two
    and a half years was ideal. It could be argued that men prioritize the reproductive
    fitness of a mate. Attractiveness is purported to indicate good health and a younger
    mate will also potentially have a higher chance of being fertile.

Conclusions
These findings demonstrate the reproductive strategy of both males and females, but
also support the evolutionary psychology idea that behaviour is influenced by the need to
reproduce successfully.

Evaluation
- Subsequent research has highlighted that there are other influences on findings such
  as these.
- **Conroy-Beam *et al.* (2015)** found that mate preference of males and females was
  negatively correlated to the gender equality level of the culture. In other words, if
  the culture was generally of high gender equality, the difference in mate preference
  between the sexes was reduced. This suggests that evolutionary theory may not be
  applicable in all cultures equally, which reduces the persuasive power of the theory.
- Research conducted by **Schwarz & Hassebrauck (2012)** looked at age and mate
  preference in a single adult population. There was little to no effect of education
  level and age on the observed findings of Buss in gender differences. This supports
  evolutionary theory in terms of mate preference.

YOU ARE THE RESEARCHER

You have decided to research the potential genetic underpinning of the personality trait 'neuroticism'. Neuroticism can be described as 'the extent to which an individual worries and becomes anxious'. You have decided to conduct a twin study on identical and non-identical twins to do this.

What methodological issues could you encounter in this experimental field?

Ethical considerations in research into genetics

The key ethical issue with genetics research is the implications of the findings. If, for example, a gene is identified as underpinning aggressive behaviour, that then casts doubt over the culpability of an individual who commits a violent crime, if they possess that gene. This was the issue with regard to the court case of Davis Bradley Waldroup Jr, who lived in the USA. In 2006, he was arrested and charged with the attempted murder of his estranged wife and the murder of her friend. However, his defence argued that he was not culpable for the crimes, as he had the shortened version of a gene nicknamed the 'warrior gene' (or MAOA gene), which is implicated in aggressive behaviour.

An expert defence witness, Dr William Bernet, gave testimony that presence of the gene in Mr Waldroup's genotype, combined with the abuse he had experienced, increased his chance of a violent offence by 400 per cent. As a consequence of this testimony, the charge was reduced from murder to manslaughter and Mr Waldroup was given a 32-year sentence. This is argued by some to be an ethical dilemma with respect to genetics research. Are those in possession of potentially 'dangerous' genes culpable for their actions?

Another issue of gene identification is the potential to use the information for modification of the population prior to birth. So-called 'designer babies' are chosen to be taken to full term, following genetic testing. This allows foetuses to be tested for both positive and negative characteristics. A most healthy foetus can then be selected. As things stand at the moment, a gene for intelligence has not been identified, but it could be feasible in the future for selection of the most intelligent foetuses to be made following scrutiny of their genetic profile. This will be a key ethical issue that will need legislation.

The work of Cyril Burt in the 1940s and 1950s on intelligence levels in different ethnic groups was controversial and later disproved, but he argued that some ethnicities were more intelligent than others. Not only does this kind of research have far reaching political and racist implications, it also suggests that educational resources are not best spent on some ethnicities. This is clearly problematic.

Strengthen your learning

1 Outline the role of genetics in behaviour, with especial focus upon aggression.

2 For Brunner's classic 1993 study of the MAOA gene and aggression in a Dutch family, in your own words, state the:
   a aims
   b procedure
   c results
   d conclusions
   e evaluative points.

3 Explain how studies of genetic similarity are used to investigate the role of genetics in behaviour.

4 Summarize what research studies of genetic similarity have suggested about the role of genetics in behaviour.

5 What other evaluative points can be made about what studies of genetic similarity have suggested about the role of genetics in behaviour?

6 Outline evolutionary explanations of behaviour, including explanations of anxiety and attractiveness.

7 For Komori *et al.*'s 2009 contemporary study of facial symmetry and attractiveness, in your own words, state the:
   a aims
   b procedure
   c results
   d conclusions
   e evaluative points.

8 For Buss's classic 1989 study of sex differences in human mate preferences, in your own words, state the:
   a aims
   b procedure
   c results
   d conclusions
   e evaluative points.

9 Summarize what research studies have suggested about evolutionary explanations of behaviour.

10 What other evaluative points can be made about evolutionary explanations of behaviour?

11 Outline ethical considerations of research into the role of genetics on behaviour.

SECTION SUMMARY

- Each individual is born, typically, with a genotype and this forms the basis for our development. The work of geneticists and psychologists has suggested that there may be a genetic underpinning for certain behaviours.
- The genotype of the individual is affected by the environment in which they live. The product of that interaction is called the phenotype.
- Twin and family studies can be useful in ascertaining the extent to which genetics influences behaviour. Comparison of the concordance rates of identical and non-identical twins and genetic similarity can give us an indication of how much genetics has had an influence on behaviour.
- The evolution of human behaviour is thought, by biological psychologists, to develop in the same way as the physical characteristics of humans. The idea is based around adaptiveness.

The role of animal research in understanding human behaviour

'The question is not, can they reason? nor can they talk? but can they suffer?'
Jeremy Bentham (1748-1832)

'Animal tests… less predictive than tossing a coin.'
Kathy Archibald

'Without animal testing, there will be no new drugs for new or hard-to-treat diseases…'
The Lancet (2004)

FOCUS ON...

- The role of animal research in understanding behaviour.
- The value of animal models in psychology research.
- Whether animal research can provide insight into human behaviour.
- Ethical considerations in animal research.

There are areas in psychology which require human-only research. However, the discipline has used animal research in the past to inform our understanding of human behaviour and continues to do so. This is sometimes done in addition to work with humans, or it is sometimes also done instead of working with human participants.

The key reasons for using animals as participants are to refine and improve on existing theories and when there are practical or ethical reasons for not being able to use human participants. The case for using animal research in psychology was made by Allyson Bennett in an opinion piece to the American Psychological Association (2012), in which she argued that animal research had been historically essential in informing the area and, furthermore, the need was still there.

A key example she gave was that of Harlow's research into attachment theory (**Harlow, 1959, 1969**), whereby in some of the experimental conditions a baby rhesus monkey was raised without the presence of a real mother. The infant monkey, instead, had a mother made of wire that would provide milk from a feeding bottle and a wire mother covered in soft cloth. When the infant monkey was scared, it ran to the cloth mother, thereby demonstrating that attachments are not formed for food. The research from Harlow provided a starting point for subsequent research and contradicted the operant conditioning explanation of attachment (as the milk did not provide reinforcement for attachment behaviour). Indeed, the principles of operant conditioning were derived from work on rats.

Harlow's work could clearly not be conducted on humans ethically and practically (as human babies are unable to seek comfort as they are not mobile at a young age).

Harlow's work, at the time and subsequently, was targeted for its negative treatment of animals and is used as an example of unethical practice with animals. However, it is argued that the cost to the rhesus monkeys is less than the benefit to society that the research has brought.

Bennett (2012) in her article highlights the benefits that research on animals has given, and continues to give, and urges the psychological community to be careful of placing too many restrictions on the use of animals, which she believes would stem advances in the field of psychology. She uses gene therapy and drug research as areas where animal research, in particular, benefits humans too. The animal research into the field of genetics has been very helpful in terms of subsequent research for humans. It should also be borne in mind that the developmental cycle of rodents (who comprise 95 per cent of animal research participants) takes substantially less time than the gestation and developmental cycle of humans and therefore allows for observations to be made in a shorter time span.

■ The value of animal models in psychology research

An animal model, in the psychological sense, is when a non-human animal is used in research to test physiology, behaviour and pathology to extrapolate the findings to humans.

Work using animals has been successful in several ways in terms of insight into human pathological behaviour; for example, obsessive-compulsive disorder. A review conducted by **Pitman (1989)** demonstrated how work on animals showed how the compulsive behaviour was reinforced. However, attempts to find research support for explaining hoarding behaviour by using animal models in a review by **Andrews-McClymont et al. (2013)** were not successful, and the link between human and non-human animal behaviour was not supported. This shows that the value of using animal research is not always apparent.

In the 1980s there was a move to reading animal mental states from their behaviour (**Dawkins, 1990**). This had obvious implications for the animal model in psychology. Many scientists and psychologists resisted this move. They did not trust the idea that mental states could be projected on to animals (**Kennedy, 1992**). It was argued that it was erroneous to use adjectives to describe animal behaviour. Words such as 'anxious' were not applicable to animal behaviour and inferences like this could not be made, as animals do not have a conscious motive for actions. This debate remains for some psychologists.

In 2012 The Francis Crick Memorial Conference, held at the University of Cambridge, debated the extent to which animals could be seen as conscious and acting intentionally. Following the debate there was a declaration, named the Cambridge Declaration on Consciousness, which stated: 'The absence of a neocortex does not appear to preclude an organism from experiencing affective states. Convergent evidence indicates that non-human animals have the neuroanatomical, neurochemical, and neurophysiological substrates of conscious states along with the capacity to exhibit intentional behaviours. Consequently, the weight of evidence indicates that humans are not unique in possessing the neurological substrates that generate consciousness. Non-human animals, including all mammals and birds, and many other creatures, including octopuses, also possess these neurological substrates' (Low *et al.*, 2012, p.2). This gives a clear indication that the extrapolation of animal research, and the animal model, to human behaviour is supported by many in the scientific community.

Research: brain and behaviour

Action potentials – electrical activity which travels down the neuron. At the synapse, they may be transmitted to the next neuron, or they may be stopped.

Hodgkin & Huxley (1952) conducted work on the mechanism of neural **action potentials** on the squid giant axon. The squid's physiology means that the researchers could insert voltage clamp electrodes on to the giant axon as its diameter is big enough. This would not be possible with the human brain. This research methodology was useful in establishing the accuracy to which action potential characteristics could be measured (**Kandel & Squire, 2000**).

Research: hormones and behaviour

Direct manipulation in the levels of testosterone levels in animals allows for the effect in aggressive behaviour, which is difficult to do ethically with humans. **Conner & Levine (1969)** studied young rats who had been castrated (and so had lower levels of testosterone) and compared them with rats who had been castrated when fully grown. Even if the young rats were injected to raise their levels of testosterone, they still displayed lower levels of aggression.

Not only does this study demonstrate that sensitivity to testosterone is part of the developmental process, it also gives an example of when research could not be conducted ethically with humans. The fact that it is also studying the developmental process is important because the maturation process of a rat to sexual maturity is only five weeks, as opposed to the years involved in the same process in humans. This illustrates two instances where research on humans would have been more difficult to conduct than on animals.

Research: genetics and behaviour

Genetic alteration and reproductive cloning are both areas where experimentation on humans is problematic. An example of where this kind of methodology has informed psychology is in work conducted by **Clapcote *et al.* (2007)**, where researchers genetically modified mice to present with the mutation of the DISC1 gene. The DISC1 gene is potentially a risk factor in schizophrenia. When induced in mice they demonstrated depressive-like symptoms and reduced activity, suggesting that some of the behavioural indicators observed in individuals with schizophrenia could be induced in animals by gene manipulation. Clearly this could not have taken place with humans due to ethical issues and the maturation process of humans taking much longer than that of mice.

Can animal research provide insight into human behaviour?

Many argue there is an issue with extrapolating animal research into human behaviour. A key argument is that humans are more complex than animals and therefore experimentation on animals can provide few insights into human behaviour.

Indeed, the work by Harlow was heavily criticized by **Mason (1991)** as being irrelevant to humans. The monkeys were observed (due to their inability to communicate) and the behaviour of clinging to a cloth-covered wire mother was seen to be indicative of the fact that they had a closer bond with the 'comforting mother' than the 'food-providing mother'. Mason argues that clinging behaviour is not used by babies and therefore demonstrates the lack of applicability of the research to humans. Equally, however, it could be argued that the underpinning sentiment behind the clinging behaviour can be expressed in other ways by human babies, such as crying for comfort and relaxing once they are picked up.

There is a field of psychology named comparative psychology. This is used for research that has investigated non-human animals from insects to primates, to look at behaviour and mental processes, and then compared it with human behaviour. These comparisons are thought to be useful in four ways, outlined by Tinbergen but stated originally by **Lorenz (1935)**: causation, survival value, evolution and ontogeny.

Causation is the idea that behaviour is not a reflex reaction in non-human animals; it is a planned and motivated action which can be compared with humans.

Survival value in the animal kingdom is argued to underlie the motivations for behaviour and the simplicity of some animal actions illustrates that motivation. In humans, although some behaviours are seemingly complex, the basic survival value behind a behaviour is supported when comparing with non-human animals.

Evolution is the idea that it is not just survival value that is an important motivation. Reproduction is also important for the evolution of behaviour, after all it is not going to help the ancestral line if you survive but do not reproduce. The mating strategies of non-human animals and their mate choice can offer insight into the human behaviour surrounding reproduction. This is illustrated in research by **Lycett & Dunbar (2000)** (see 'Psychology in the real world' below).

Ontogeny is the development of a behaviour from the earliest stage through to maturation. Comparison of behaviour in animals allows for a practical way to study the ontogeny of a behaviour. When comparing a rat's development and lifespan with a human, there are clear practical reasons why using rats in research helps. The lifespan of the black rat is 12 months and the gestation period is three weeks. Given that the rats also only take 12 to 16 weeks to reach sexual maturity, this means the time from infant to adult is only months rather than the years in human terms. Therefore, research can be conducted much quicker and, depending on the behaviour, within a realistic time scale. For behaviours that are appropriate for comparison, it can be argued that using comparison with animal behaviour to human behaviours is invaluable regarding practicalities of research.

PSYCHOLOGY IN THE REAL WORLD

Research on mobile phone behaviour has been compared to the animal kingdom to offer insight for motivation. What people do with their mobile phones when engaged in social activity was argued to be an indicator of peacocking, a behaviour used by a man to attract a woman. **Lycett & Dunbar (2000)** observed the behaviour of men in drinking establishments in Liverpool over a period of four months. They focused upon what men did with their mobile phones when they weren't using them, that is, where they put them, how much they fiddled with them and the rate of checking. The observations highlighted several aspects of this behaviour.

There was an increased display of telephones in groups with more males and this was not related to usage (i.e. the making and receiving of calls):

1 Single males tended to use and touch their phones more.

2 There was a positive relationship between the number of visible telephones (i.e. on the table) and the ratio of males to females.

■ **Figure 1.8**
Peacock expanding its feathers using a lekking strategy to attract a peahen

These results were analysed using comparative psychology, and comparing specifically with peacocks. Peacocks use a lekking strategy to attract a mate, which means when gathered they will try to maximize the display of their tail feathers in order to attract a peahen. The more males there are, the wider they spread their tail feathers. Lycett & Dunbar used this comparison with the human male behaviour and the phones (which they called cultural ornaments). They explained that the motivation behind the mobile phone behaviour was to attract a mate, supported by the frequency of attention single men paid to their devices and the fact there was more focus on the devices when the male-to-female ratio was greater.

This demonstrates comparison between non-human animal and human real-world behaviour and the value of using animal models for ascertaining motivations underpinning behaviour.

KEY STUDY   ## CLASSICAL RESEARCH

'The ape and the child: a study of environmental influence upon early behaviour'
Kellogg & Kellogg (1933)

Aims
Kellogg and Kellogg wished to see if a chimpanzee baby could be socialized if brought up alongside a human infant in their home.

Procedure
1 In 1931 two married scientists, Luella and Winthrop Kellogg, were interested in how language is acquired and decided to bring their research into their home. When their son Donald was ten months old they brought a baby chimpanzee called Gua into the home to raise alongside their son. Gua was slightly younger at almost eight months old. Donald and Gua lived alongside each other and interacted daily.
2 Donald's parents recorded what they saw and tested Gua and Donald too.

Results
1 Several differences in their abilities became apparent, such as recognizing people. Donald recognized visitors to the home by their faces, whereas Gua used their clothes and smell. It also appeared that Gua outperformed Donald in comprehension tests at one year, responding to 20 command words appropriately, whereas Donald could only respond to three.
2 Significant differences became apparent in language acquisition too. Donald was able to form words and did so spontaneously, whereas Gua was unable to do this and could make only the chattering and clicking sounds of a chimpanzee. From that point onwards Gua outperformed Donald in physical tasks, but linguistically was unable to keep up.
3 Nine months into the experiment the Kelloggs stopped the co-rearing as their son was starting to make chimpanzee sounds to communicate with Gua.
4 Gua was returned to a primate centre in Florida.

Conclusion
This case study shows the direct comparison of a chimpanzee and human as problematic. It does, however, show that there is transference between species, but that the two species are qualitatively different.

Evaluation
This research took a case study approach and used an immersion technique for Gua to establish the extent to which she could be socialized into being human. However, the ethical considerations for both the child and the chimpanzee at an early and impressionable stage of development are questionable.

Andics *et al.* (2014) conducted a comparative study using fMRI technology, measuring the brain activity of humans and dogs when they heard words and sounds. The words were presented alongside non-words to see if the activity of the dogs' brains showed differentiation between words and sound. The researchers found that vocalizations of words are familiar in both humans and dogs and a similar pattern of activity was found, which suggests dogs can recognize that words are different from sound and from each other. The dog brain appears to have an area which is able to process human language in a more sophisticated way than originally thought.

This suggests that the animal model will be able to offer insight even with such complex processing as human language.

When examining potentially toxic substances in the environment, scientists use animal species to test for the potential effects in human brains. In their review of how effective this is, **Clancy et al. (2007)** considered some of the animal research conducted. They concluded that some of the ways that the data were analysed did not allow for them to be related to humans. They said, however, that using a technique called neuroinformatics, which incorporates elements of neuroscience, genetics and computer science, extrapolation from animal brain data to human brains is possible.

Research: hormones and behaviour

Mazur (1983) makes the point that sometimes inferring the sentiment or emotion behind a behaviour from animals is problematic. In the case of aggression, animal research has inferred aggression from dominance behaviour. This behaviour is not always aggressive. There is also the issue that some aggressive behaviour is expressed verbally in humans and this cannot be observed in animals.

Research: genetics and behaviour

Work in the field of drug addiction has used animal research extensively in the development of drugs to aid rehabilitation. **Peck & Ranaldi (2014)** looked at the level of similarity between humans and animals in terms of the mechanisms that underpin abstinence. They found that some abstinence behaviours in humans are similar in animals, specifically those that give negative consequences if the individual takes drugs again. Peck & Ranaldi argue that animal research is therefore valid in the development of rehabilitation drugs that give unpleasant consequences when relapses occur.

Ethical considerations in animal research

One of the key arguments given for animal research is that it can facilitate research that would not otherwise be possible, for ethical reasons, on humans. However, there is an increasing amount of legislation to protect the rights of animals, too. Cultures vary to the extent by which they consider animal research to need ethical guidelines. In some cultures, all life is sacred, and therefore research which causes any type of suffering to humans or non-human animals alike is not conducted. However, other cultures may see animals as a resource and, as such, are less prohibitive.

In UK law, special protection for animals in research is not equal across all species and seems to be centred on the relationship we have with them as a society and the level of genetic similarity. Historically, animals with which we have a companionship or use as pets are protected (examples being dogs, cats and horses). So, too, animals that look like us (i.e. are genetically similar) are also protected, so research on primates is restricted. European law focuses on the usefulness of the research for the greater good.

This is a difficult decision to make and one model used for this is Bateson's cube. This model asserts that three domains should be considered: the quality of the research, the certainty of medical benefit and the degree of animal suffering. Research that is of high quality, high benefit medically and low suffering in animals is seen to be worthwhile and has a good purpose. Likewise, poor quality research, with little benefit and high levels of suffering would be seen, by this model, to be unreasonable. Bateson's model is constructed in such a way that high levels of suffering in animals are unacceptable. Looking at Figure 1.9 on the next page, the 'gaps' in the cube denote research that is acceptable (according to this model). High suffering is never acceptable, but medium suffering in animals, high research quality and high levels of benefit would make the research permissible by these standards.

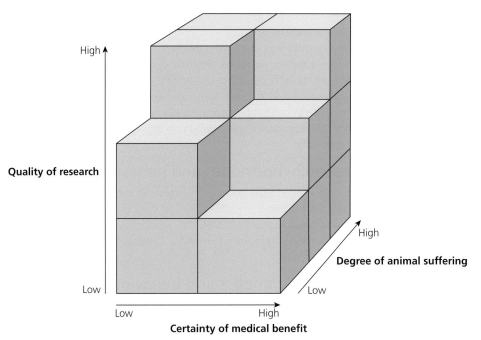

High

Quality of research

Low

Low   High

Certainty of medical benefit

High

Degree of animal suffering

Low

■ **Figure 1.9** Bateson's cube: a model used to determine the usefulness of research. Three domains should be considered: the quality of the research, the certainty of medical benefit and the degree of animal suffering

Further guiding principles designed to determine the acceptability of animal research are the 3Rs: replacement, refinement and reduction. Replacement as a principle means that other research methods that replace animal research should be used wherever possible. These include the use of cell cultures, human volunteers and computer modelling. Refinement means that research techniques that reduce pain and suffering in animals should be used wherever possible, and finally, reduction refers to using research strategies that are efficient and reduce the number of animal experiments used wherever possible.

Research

■ **McMahon *et al.* (2012)** advocated the use of Bateson's cube for wildlife research. Conservation groups see some research as helping species to thrive, but animal welfare groups have different priorities. McMahon *et al.* argued that the use of the cube would ensure research continued in a way agreeable to both groups. This shows how applicable the method is and how difficult the decision can be without such a reference point.

■ One of the key aims of the 3Rs is to reduce the number of animal studies conducted. **Hooijmans *et al.* (2010)** suggested this would be possible if systematic reviews were conducted with animal research. Systematic reviews are an overview of all the research published in a field of study. These are rarely used in animal research due to the issues of control (i.e. comparing 'like with like'). Hooijmans *et al.* suggested that this was a missed opportunity to reduce the amount of animal research and, following their review of animal research, designed and developed a gold standard publication checklist to help systematic reviews be conducted. This included consideration of the housing environment for the animals and their health. The researchers argued that not only would this reduce the number of studies conducted (as more conclusions could be drawn from the large samples gathered within systematic reviews), but also it would encourage the appropriate treatment of animals in both planning and conducting research.

■ **Dawkins (1990)** argued that more care needs to be made when deciding the level of suffering an animal could potentially experience. In her research, she makes the point that some animals suffer when they are prevented from doing something they naturally want to do. This has, she argues, the effect of exerting psychological stress on them. As one of the elements of Bateson's cube is the level of animal suffering, the way animals are housed and the environment they are kept in are important to minimize suffering. However, this is not the only issue. As soon as an animal is put in a non-natural situation, as often occurs in captivity, the behaviour observed will lack validity and as such will not extrapolate well to humans.

Evaluation

■ Even using methods of acceptability such as Bateson's cube there is a problem with deciding the levels of suffering. How do we know what is low/high suffering for an animal? The assumption of level of suffering will always need to be inferred.

■ The push for statistical power in experiments, however, has meant that it is widely seen that the larger the sample size and numbers of experiments the better. This makes reduction difficult.

■ There is also a potential issue with validity in animal research, not just because of the fact that there is extrapolation to humans, but also because reducing the number of experiments means greater control over the conditions used. This means that the controlled environment becomes even less generalizable to real-world functioning. This applies to humans and non-human animals alike.

YOU ARE THE RESEARCHER

A key argument for the use of animal research is that there is some research which cannot be conducted ethically on humans. You are a researcher being asked to conduct research into aggression following the influence of illegal drugs. Can you think of two experiment designs that could be conducted to investigate this area:

• using animal research?
• using human participants?

Strengthen your learning

1 Outline the role of animal research in understanding human behaviour.

2 Explain the value of animal models in psychological research.

3 To what degree can animal research provide insight into human behaviour?

4 Summarize what studies have suggested about animal research and animal models, as a means of understanding human behaviour.

5 For Kellogg & Kellogg's classic 1933 study of teaching a chimp language, in your own words, state the:
   a aims
   b procedure
   c results
   d conclusions
   e evaluative points.

6 What ethical considerations are there when conducting psychological research on animals?

7 Summarize what research studies have suggested about ethical considerations of psychological research on animals.

8 What other evaluative points can be made about ethical considerations of psychological research on animals?

SECTION SUMMARY

■ For many, the value of animal research is not clear, even though there have been clear advancements made using the results of animal studies.

■ The use of the animal model is widespread, but there is a debate on the extent to which it is useful. The extent to which animal research can be extrapolated to human behaviour is not clear.

■ The 3Rs (replacement, refinement and reduction) have been put in place to help regulate the ethics of animal research.

■ There are also methods used to help make the decision about whether research should be conducted, taking animal suffering into account. One such method is Bateson's cube.

■ Assessment check

1	Explain how genes affect human behaviour.	(9 marks)
2	Outline one twin study of genes and behaviour.	(9 marks)
3	Outline evolutionary explanations for one human behaviour.	(9 marks)
4	Explain ethical considerations in animal research.	(9 marks)
5	Evaluate the evidence for links between genes and behaviour.	(22 marks)
6	Discuss studies of genetic relatedness.	(22 marks)
7	Discuss evolutionary explanations for behaviour.	(22 marks)
8	With reference to research studies, evaluate the role of animal research in understanding human behaviour.	(22 marks)

IN THE NEWS

Ψ The Psychological Enquirer

PICKING COTTON

■ **Figure 2.1** 'I was certain, but I was wrong' – Jennifer Thompson and Ronald Cotton

Back in 1984, college student Jennifer Thompson was confronted by an intruder in her flat. He overpowered her, held a knife across her throat and raped her. During the ordeal Jennifer carefully memorized every detail of his face, determined that if she survived she would ensure he was captured and imprisoned. She went straight to the police and constructed a sketch of the rapist, looking carefully through hundreds of images of facial features to get it absolutely right. A few days later she identified Ronald Cotton as the attacker. She was certain it was him and picked him out again at a police identity parade. On the strength of Jennifer's eyewitness testimony (EWT) Ronald was convicted and sent to jail – she said it was the happiest day of her life and she was so convinced of his guilt that she wanted him electrocuted, desiring to flip the switch herself.

But Ronald Cotton was innocent. Eleven years later in 1995, DNA samples proved it was another man who had committed the crime. Ronald was released from prison and Jennifer begged his forgiveness, which Ronald gave. The two have become close friends and have written a book, 'Picking Cotton', about their experience, which illustrates how schema, a readiness to interpret sensory information in a preset manner, can lead to inaccurate memories of events we actually witnessed. Schema can affect many cognitive (mental) processes, such as memory, perception, thinking and decision-making. Emotional factors can also affect how schema influences cognitive processes. In this chapter we will examine some cognitive processes and especially how schema affects them. A better understanding of how cognitive processes work might lead to fewer miscarriages of justice, such as that which occurred to Ronald Cotton.

Introduction and history

Although mental processes had always interested psychologists, it was not until the 1950s that the 'cognitive revolution' occurred, where the dominant behaviourist approach was replaced by a new model of 'Mind' based on computer science. It was Alan Turing, who famously helped defeat the Nazis in the Second World War, by decoding messages sent by German enigma coding machines, and who in 1950 suggested human intelligence operated similarly to the workings of a computer. However, the term cognitive psychology was first used by Ulric Neisser (1967) to refer to the mental processes by which sensory information is dealt with in the mind. Cognitive psychology therefore involves the study of mental structures and processes existing in the mind; although, as 'mind' is a vague, difficult to define term, cognitive psychologists refer instead to mental processes in terms of information processing.

An easy way to understand this is to compare the workings of the mind to a computer. Data enters a computer via an input, like a keyboard, while data enters a human in the form of sensory inputs through specialized sensory organs, such as the eyes and ears, and so on. In both computers and humans, data is converted to electrical impulses and conveyed along either circuitry or nerve fibres. In a computer, data travels to a central processing unit (CPU) for analysis, a function performed in humans by the brain. After information is processed, a response is initiated, for example a print-out in a computer or a behaviour in a human. Information processing in a computer is dependent on which analytical programmes the computer is running, while in humans information processing depends on which cognitive processes occur; perception, language, memory, decision-making, problem-solving, attention, and so on – in a sense the programmes that our minds are running.

Until the 1950s, the dominant approach in psychology was behaviourism, where only observable behaviour was studied, with no place for the scientific study of invisible mental processes. Behaviourism had replaced the earlier approach of introspection, with its emphasis on observing and analysing mental processes. The problem with this was that it was not possible to directly observe other people's mental processes and one's own mental processes could not be generalized to others; what is true of how one person's mind works isn't necessarily true of how other people's minds work.

Behaviourism, especially when applied to humans, also had problems, as it could not reveal motivating forces behind behaviour, or how behaviour was directed at future goals. Only by exploring the hidden workings of the mind, the ways in which humans process sensory information, could these problems be solved, with cognitive psychology presenting an opportunity to do just that, especially as interest in mental processes had been stimulated by Jean Piaget with his research into cognitive development in children.

The earlier comparison of a computer with a human mind is fitting, as the development of computer technology went hand-in-hand with cognitive psychology. Although computers can be traced back to Charles Babbage's difference engine of 1822, it was not until after the Second World War that computer science really took off, and it was not long before psychologists were borrowing from computer science to better understand the mind by perceiving it as an information-processing device. In doing so, psychology was returning to the earlier approach of introspection, but in a more objective and scientific way. More recent developments within cognitive neuroscience, where the biological basis to cognitive processes is studied, have made it possible to do this in an even more scientifically rigorous manner, especially through scanning, such as MRI, which permits the physical workings of mental processes in the brain to be directly observed and analysed.

Although cognitive psychology is a separate psychological approach, with many psychologists seeing themselves purely as cognitive psychologists, it also overlaps with other approaches, including computer science, linguistics and artificial intelligence. Indeed, the idea that mental processes are only understood by including reference to biological and sociocultural influences is a core part of cognitive psychology. Cognitive psychology has made, and continues to make, huge contributions to a better understanding of the mind.

▨ Assumptions of the cognitive approach

Schema – a readiness to interpret sensory information in a preset manner.

While behaviourists see behaviour as resulting from unthinking stimuli and responses, cognitive psychologists focus on the mental processes, such as attention and thinking, which occur between these stimuli and responses. Such processing is influenced by the mental representations that individuals have of their world, with **schemas** being important examples of such mental representations.

Schemas are mental representations that help us to organize and interpret information. They are ever-changing and dependent on our experiences and knowledge, whether correct or not, that we have of the world. Schemas therefore are structured sets of beliefs about the world that allow information to be perceived in preset ways, that is, in ways that fit your world view. Thus you never really experience objective reality, but instead experience your own subjective interpretation of information dependent on the mental representations (schemas) of the world that you hold at a particular time. For example, **Turnbull (1961)** reported on Kenge, a BaMbuti pygmy who lived in dense rainforest with no experience of wide open spaces. When he was first taken to the shores of a huge lake, Kenge perceived a boat that was far away as a stick on a puddle just a short distance away. This occurred because Kenge's life experiences had given him little sense of distance perception. His schema limited his ability to see what was actually right in front of him.

The other main principle behind cognitive psychology, which separates it from introspection, is that mental processes can be scientifically investigated, with support from biological means of investigation, like cognitive neuroscience, giving assistance to this process. This means that mental processes – which behaviourism saw as invisible and unavailable to scientific scrutiny – could be tested scientifically, through laboratory experiments, where hypotheses are formulated and subjected to rigorous testing.

Overall cognitive psychology is based on the assumptions that:

■ Behaviour is underpinned by mental representations, like schemas, which allow humans to perceive and understand the world differently from each other, due to their differing experiences and knowledge of the world.

■ The 'hidden' world of mental processing that behaviourism saw as incapable of study can actually be investigated by scientific methods, allowing a more sophisticated view of behaviour than that gained through behaviourism.

■ A deeper understanding of human behaviour is gained by combining the cognitive with biological and sociocultural approaches.

■ The contribution of research methods used in the cognitive approach to understanding human behaviour

FOCUS ON...

■ The use of research methods to investigate the cognitive approach.
■ Examples of research studies used to investigate the cognitive approach.

Cognitive psychologists use several research methods that reflect the principles on which the cognitive approach is based, such as:

Independent variable (IV) – the factor manipulated by researchers in an investigation.

Dependent variable (DV) – the factor measured by researchers in an investigation.

1 *The experimental method*, where an **independent variable** is manipulated under controlled conditions to assess its effect on a **dependent variable**. For example, **Bruner & Mintern (1955)** presented participants with an ambiguous figure that could be either a letter 'B' or a number '13'. Those who saw the figure in-between a letter 'A' and a letter 'C', perceived it as a letter 'B', while those who saw the figure in-between a number '12' and a number '14' saw it as a number '13'. This suggests that the perceptual schema influences perception by people seeing what they expect to see, based on previous experience.

2 *The case study method*, where one person or a small group of people are studied in detail. For example, **Scoville & Milner (1957)** studied HM, who, as a result of brain surgery to treat his epilepsy, could not create new long-term memories, though his short-term memory was fine, which suggests we have separate short and long-term memory stores.

3 *Self-reports*, such as interviews where participants answer questions in a face-to-face situation. For example, **Kohlberg (1969)** studied the development of moral thinking by giving participants from different cultures moral dilemmas (hypothetical stories where a choice between two alternatives has to be made based on morality). He found the same sequence of moral development in all cultures, which suggests it is an innate biological process. (Questionnaires [such as used in **Loftus & Pickrell's 2003** study – see page 83] and surveys [for example, the **Kaspersky laboratory international survey 2015** – see page 98] are other types of self-reports also used.)

4 *The correlational method*, where a relationship between co-variables is measured. For example, **Schmidt et al. (2000)** found a negative correlation between the number of times Dutch participants had moved house since they were at elementary school and the number of

street names they could remember in the school area. This supports the idea that forgetting can occur due to newly learned information (e.g. the street names of where you live now) interfering with the recall of previously learned information (e.g. the street names around where you used to live).

5 *The observational method*, where naturally occurring behaviour is observed and recorded. For example, **Slatcher & Trentacosta (2011)** observed that parental depression negatively affected children's behaviour and cognitive socialization, which suggests parental-mood states affect childhood cognitive development.

6 *Non-invasive brain-scanning techniques* are used to identify brain areas associated with specific cognitive processes (see page 89). For example, **D'Esposito *et al.* (1995)** used fMRI scans to find that the prefrontal cortex is associated with the workings of the central executive, the controlling system of the working memory model.

TOK link

Laboratory experiments allow the methods employed by the natural sciences, such as physics, to be directed at human behaviour. This produces quantitative data that can be statistically analysed to show causality (cause-and-effect relationships), the accepted basis behind scientific truth.

Experiments form a nomothetic approach, showing generalizations of what humans have in common, in other words the information-processing abilities of the average person. Idiographic methods are used too, however, reflecting specific types of processing that different individuals possess, which make them unique; for example, the case study method, where one individual, or a small group of individuals, is studied in detail. **Trojani & Grossi (1995)** reported a case study of SC, who had brain damage affecting the functioning of just one part of his memory, which suggested there are separate memory stores. The problem is that due to participants' uniqueness it is difficult to generalize case study findings to everybody.

◾ Ethical considerations in the investigation of the cognitive approach to understanding human behaviour

FOCUS ON...

- ◾ The effect of ethical considerations upon the investigation of cognitive processes.

Cognitive psychologists, like all researchers, must consider the ethical aspects of research in advance and design and conduct research in ways that meet the ethical guidelines laid down by psychological governing bodies such as, for example, the British Psychological Society (BPS). All research methods are subject to similar ethical considerations, but some of these are more important in different research settings.

The main consideration with laboratory experiments is informed consent, where participants are not deceived and are given full details of research in advance, in order to make a considered decision as to whether they wish to take part. Participants should not be harmed in any way, for example, being subjected to stress greater than in everyday life. Informed consent can be difficult to gain with field and natural experiments if participants are unaware of being studied. Such participants should be fully debriefed and offered a chance to withdraw their data.

A major ethical concern with case studies is that researchers may investigate individuals with unusual abilities or brain damage; therefore, aside from ensuring harm does not occur in the form of psychological stress, care should also be taken to protect the confidentiality and anonymity of participants.

With neuroimaging techniques, like brain scans, the main consideration is ensuring that participants are not harmed, as scanning can make many nervous. Therefore, participants need to be fully informed of procedures in advance, put at ease at all times and be aware of their right to withdraw at any time.

Finally, with self-report methods, ethical issues arise over the sensitivity of material being discussed. Protection from harm is paramount, with interviewers asking questions in a way that does not offend the dignity of those being interviewed and emphasizing confidentiality and anonymity. This applies to the questions posed in questionnaires, too.

With all research methods there should be no inducements offered to take part and participants should always be fully debriefed after research is concluded.

TOK link

Ethical considerations are important, as there is a need to protect the health and dignity of participants. Doing so also protects the reputation of psychology. A lack of ethical practices could lead to people being reluctant to participate in research, meaning psychology would not advance its understanding of human behaviour.

LINK TO THE BIOLOGICAL APPROACH

The use of biological means of investigation, such as cognitive neuroscience techniques – for example, brain scanning – has allowed cognitive processes to be studied in a more objective, scientific manner.

Strengthen your learning

1 Explain, using examples, how the following research study methods are used in the study of cognitive processes:
   a the experimental method
   b case studies
   c self-reports
   d correlational studies
   e observations
   f brain scans.

2 Explain how the following ethical issues relate to the study of cognitive processes. Include in your answers details of how these issues should be dealt with (see 'Research methods' on page 148).
   a informed consent
   b harm
   c deceit
   d confidentiality
   e anonymity
   f inducements to take part.

SECTION SUMMARY

- Cognitive psychology studies the mental processes by which sensory inputs are dealt with within the mind.
- Cognitive psychology views the mind and behaviour as similar to the workings of a computer, where information is inputted, processed and responded to.
- The dominating principle behind cognitive psychology is that humans have mental representations of their world and these differ between individuals.
- Cognitive psychologists use a combination of methods, both experimental and non-experimental, to further our understanding of mental life.

■ Assessment check

1 Discuss ethical considerations linked to research into the cognitive approach to understanding human behaviour. (22 marks)
2 Evaluate the contribution of research methods used in the cognitive approach to understanding human behaviour. (22 marks)
3 With reference to a study investigating biases in thinking and decision-making, outline one strength and one limitation of the research method used in the study. (9 marks)
4 With reference to a study investigating cognitive processing in the digital world, outline ethical considerations associated with the study. (9 marks)

These questions should only be attempted after studying sufficient relevant topics on the specification for the cognitive approach to understanding behaviour.

The multi-store model of memory

'Memory is the diary we all carry about with us.'
Oscar Wilde

FOCUS ON ...

- How information passes between separate storage systems.
- The differences between sensory, short-term and long-term memory systems.
- The features of encoding, capacity and duration in the multi-store model (MSM).
- What research studies inform about the MSM.
- An assessment of the MSM in terms of its strengths and weaknesses.

....

Sensory memory (SM) – a short-duration store holding impressions of information received by the senses.

Short-term memory (STM) – a temporary store holding small amounts of information for brief periods.

Long-term memory (LTM) – a permanent store holding limitless amounts of information for long periods.

Multi-store model (MSM) – an explanation of memory that sees information flowing through a series of storage systems.

Capacity – the amount of information that can be stored at a given time.

Encoding – the means by which information is represented in memory.

Duration – the length of time information remains within storage.

....

Information gathered by the sense organs enters **sensory memory (SM)**. Only the small amount paid attention to passes to **short-term memory (STM)** for further processing; the rest is lost very quickly. Information in STM that is actively processed enough (thought about), mainly through rehearsal, transfers to **long-term memory (LTM)** for more permanent storage.

Sensory memory

SM is not under cognitive control, but is an automatic response to the reception of sensory information by the sense organs and is the first storage system within the **multi-store model (MSM)**. All information contained within LTM will have originally passed through SM, though in an unprocessed form.

Encoding, capacity and duration of sensory memory

Information is stored in a raw, unprocessed form, with separate sensory stores for different sensory inputs: the echoic store for auditory information, the iconic store for visual information, the haptic store for tactile information, the gustatory store for taste information and the olfactory store for smell. Information that is paid attention to passes on to the STM; the remainder fades quickly through trace decay, leaving no lasting impression.

The **capacity** of each sensory memory store is very large, with the information contained in an unprocessed, highly detailed and ever-changing format.

All sensory memory stores have limited duration, though the actual duration of each store is not constant. Different types of information within each store decay at different rates. Different sensory stores have different capacities and capacity seems to decrease with age.

Research

- **Crowder (1993)** found that SM only retains information in the iconic store for a few milliseconds, but for 2 to 3 seconds within the echoic store, which supports the idea of sensory information being **encoded** into different sensory stores (it also suggests they have different **durations**).

- **Sperling (1960)** flashed a 3 × 4 grid of letters on to a screen for 1/20th of a second, and asked participants to recall the letters of one row. As the information would fade very quickly, he sounded different tones (high, medium or low) to indicate which row had to be recalled (1st, 2nd or 3rd). Recall of letters in the indicated row was high, which suggests all the information was originally there, indicating that the capacity of SM (especially for the iconic store) is quite large.

- **Walsh & Thompson (1978)** found that the iconic sensory store has an average duration of 500 milliseconds, which decreases as individuals get older. This suggests duration of sensory memories is limited and dependent on age.

- **Treisman (1964)** presented identical auditory messages to both ears of participants, with a slight delay between presentations. Participants noticed the messages were identical if the delay was two seconds or less, suggesting the echoic store has a limited duration of two seconds, while also illustrating the difference in duration from the iconic store.

■ Evaluation

■ After-images of visual events provide good evidence of sensory memories. The light trail produced by a moving lighted stick was noted as early as 1740. Such phenomena led to early experiments into SM in the 1960s.

■ Although evidence exists that the iconic store can hold about 15 to 20 images, the capacity of other sensory memory stores is not well studied, as they last so briefly and generally only at a pre-conscious level.

■ The brief duration of sensory memories is seen as due to their physical traces (engrams) fading quickly. This suggests a biological explanation to the duration of information within SM.

■ The brief duration of SM can be understood from an evolutionary perspective, as people only need to focus on perceptual information with an immediate survival value. Retaining non-useful information diminishes the ability to do this.

■ Short-term memory

Short-term memory (STM) temporarily stores information received from SM. It is an active (changing) memory system, as it contains information currently being thought about. STM differs from LTM especially in terms of coding, capacity and duration and how information is forgotten.

Encoding, capacity and duration of STM

Information arrives from SM in its original raw form, such as in sound or vision, and is then encoded (entered into STM) in a form that STM can more easily deal with. For example, if the input into SM was the word 'platypus', this could be coded into STM in several ways:

■ visually – by thinking of the image of a platypus

■ acoustically – by repeatedly saying 'platypus'

■ semantically – (through meaning) by using a knowledge of platypuses, such as their being venomous egg-laying aquatic marsupials that hunt prey through electrolocation.

Chunking – method of increasing STM capacity by grouping information into larger units.

STM has a limited capacity, as only a small amount of information is held in the store. Research indicates that between 5 and 9 items can be held, though capacity is increased by **chunking**, where the size of the units of information in storage is increased by giving them a collective meaning. For example, the 12 letters of SOSABCLOLFBI may be grouped into four chunks of SOS/ABC/LOL/FBI.

The amount of time that information remains within STM without being lost is limited to a maximum of about 30 seconds. This can be extended by rehearsal (repetition) of the information, which if done long enough will result in transfer of the information into LTM, where it will become a more long-lasting feature.

KEY STUDY

CLASSIC RESEARCH

'Influence of acoustic and semantic similarities on long-term memory for word sequences'
Baddeley (1966)

Professor Alan Baddeley of York University started his research into memory when he received a grant from the British Post Office to test how well different sorts of postcodes could be remembered. His preferred option wasn't adopted, but he did become famous for helping develop the working memory model (1974). He also carried out lots of other memory research, including the following experiment into coding in STM and LTM.

■ **Figure 2.2**
Professor Alan
Baddeley

Aim
To assess whether coding in STM and LTM is mainly acoustic (by sound) or semantic (by meaning).

Procedure

1 75 participants were presented with one of four word lists repeated four times.

   List A – acoustically similar words (sounded the same as each other) ('cat', 'mat', 'sat')

   List B – acoustically dissimilar words (sounded different to each other) ('pit', 'day', 'cow')

   List C – semantically similar words (meant the same as each other) ('big', 'huge', 'tall')

   List D – semantically dissimilar words (had different meanings to each other) ('hot', 'safe', 'foul')

2 To test coding in STM, participants were given a list containing the original words in the wrong order. Their task was to rearrange the words in the correct order.

3 The procedure for LTM was the same, but with a 20-minute interval before recall, during which participants performed another task to prevent rehearsal.

Findings

1 For STM, participants given List A (acoustically similar) performed the worst, with a recall of only 10 per cent. They confused similar-sounding words, for example recalling 'cap' instead of 'cat'. Recall for the other lists was comparatively good at between 60 to 80 per cent.

2 For LTM, participants with List C (semantically similar) performed the worst, with a recall of only 55 per cent. They confused similar-meaning words, for example recalling 'big' instead of 'huge'. Recall for the other lists was comparatively good at between 70 to 85 per cent.

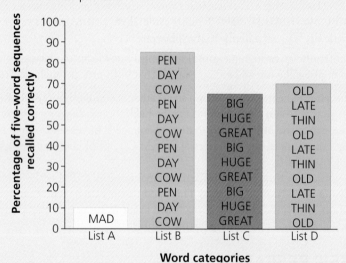

■ **Figure 2.3** Baddeley's 1966 acoustic/semantic study findings

Conclusions

- For STM, since List A was recalled the least efficiently, it seems there is acoustic confusion in STM, suggesting STM is coded on an acoustic basis.

- For LTM, since List C was recalled the least efficiently, it seems there is semantic confusion in LTM, suggesting LTM is coded on a semantic basis.

Evaluation

- Baddeley's findings make 'cognitive sense'. For example, if you had to remember a shopping list, you would probably repeat it aloud (acoustic rehearsal) while walking to the shops, but if you recall a book you have read, you remember the plot, rather than every single word.
- The small difference in recall between semantically similar (64 per cent) and semantically dissimilar (71 per cent) lists, suggests there is also semantic coding in STM.
- This was a laboratory study and therefore shows causality (cause-and-effect relationships), but may lack ecological validity (not representative of real-life activities).
- As a laboratory study it can be replicated to check the results.

RESEARCH IN FOCUS

1 **Baddeley's 1966** studies into encoding of STM and LTM were experiments, but what type of experiment were they?

2 What experimental design was used in both studies?

3 Give one strength and one weakness of this design.

4 What were the IV and DV in each study?

5 What is a DV always a type of?

Research

- **Jacobs (1887)** tested STM capacity with the serial digit span method, where participants are presented with increasingly long lists of numbers or letters and have to recall them in the right order. For example, '3, 9, 1' are presented (followed by recall); then '8, 5, 3, 9' (followed by recall); then '2, 4, 7, 1, 3' (followed by recall), and so on. When participants fail on 50 per cent of tasks, they are judged to have reached their capacity. Jacobs found that the capacity for numbers was nine items and for letters seven items, which illustrates how the capacity of STM is limited. Numbers may be easier to recall as there are only nine single-digit numbers (0–9), compared to 26 letters in the English language (A–Z). One criticism is that experimental tasks such as recalling lists of letters have little relevance to everyday activities and so lack **mundane realism**.

- **Miller (1956)** reviewed research to find the capacity of STM to be between 5 and 9, but that the 'chunk' (pieces of information grouped together into meaningful sections) was the basic unit of STM. This means 5 to 9 chunks can be held at any one time, increasing the store's capacity. Simon (1974) found that although STM capacity should be measured in terms of chunks, this varies with the type of material being recalled and the amount of information contained within the chunks.

- **Peterson & Peterson (1959)** read nonsense trigrams (words of three letters that do not form recognizable words, like ZFB) to participants, and then got them to count backwards in threes from a large three-digit number (to prevent repetition of the letters) for varying periods of time. They found that around 90 per cent of trigrams were recalled correctly after three seconds, but only 5 per cent after 18 seconds, which suggests STM duration has a capacity of between 20 and 30 seconds. However, the results may be due to flawed methodology. Because different trigrams were used on each trial, this may have led to interference between items, leading to decreased recall. Also, recalling nonsense trigrams has little relevance to STM tasks in everyday life and therefore lacks mundane realism.

- **Marsh et al. (1997)** found that if participants weren't expecting to have to recall information, STM duration was only between 2 and 4 seconds, which suggests duration of STM is affected by the amount of time taken to process information.

Mundane realism – the extent to which findings of studies can be generalized to real-life settings.

YOU ARE THE RESEARCHER

Design and carry out an experiment into STM duration. You will need some nonsense trigrams for your participants. You will also need a stop-watch to time the intervals between presentation and recall. One condition will involve a short time interval, say three seconds, and the other condition a longer time interval, say 18 seconds.

What experimental design will you use? What will be the IV and DV? How many participants are needed? Use Peterson & Peterson's study (see page 51) to work out whether you need a directional or non-directional hypothesis and then construct suitable experimental and null hypotheses.

Draw up a table to record your data. Calculate totals and relevant measures of central tendency and dispersion. What conclusions can you draw from your data?

For more on research methods, see Chapter 4.

Evaluation

- Other factors, like age and practice, also influence STM capacity and nowadays STM limitations are mostly seen as due to processing limitations associated with attention.

- There may be individual differences in STM capacity. **Daneman & Carpenter (1980)** found capacity varied between five and twenty items, between those with advanced and poor reading comprehension.

- **Reitman (1974)** suggested that the brief duration of STM is due to displacement; as new information comes into STM it pushes out existing information due to its limited capacity.

- There is little in the way of research evidence considering the STM duration of other forms of stimuli, like visual images.

- Although research shows that coding in STM is mainly acoustic, other sensory codes, such as visual, are used too. Indeed, some stimuli such as faces or the smell of food would be difficult to code acoustically. What would the sound of treacle be?

Long-term memory

Long-term memory (LTM) involves storing information over lengthy periods of time, indeed for a whole lifetime, with information stored for longer than 30 seconds counting as LTM. All information within LTM will have originally passed through the sensory register (SR) and STM, though may have undergone different forms of processing during the process. Research indicates that there are several different types of LTM, such as semantic (what something means), episodic (when something was learned) and procedural (how to do something), and LTMs are not of equal strength. Strong LTMs can be retrieved easily, such as when your birthday is, but weaker LTMs may need more prompting. LTMs are not passive (unchanging) – over time they may change or merge with other LTMs. This is why memories are not necessarily constant or accurate. Research also indicates that the process of shaping and storing LTMs is spread through multiple brain regions.

Encoding, capacity and duration of LTM

Coding involves the form by which LTMs are stored – the means by which information is shaped into representation of memories. Coding of information will be stronger (and thus the memory more retrievable) the deeper the level of processing of a stimulus that occurs while it is being experienced.

With verbal material, coding in LTM is mainly semantic (based on meaning), though coding occurs in other forms too, with research indicating a visual and an acoustic code.

The potential capacity of LTM is unlimited. Information may be lost due to decay and interference, but such losses do not occur due to limitation of capacity.

Duration of LTM depends on an individual's lifespan, as memories can last for a lifetime; many elderly people have detailed childhood memories. Items in LTM have a longer duration if originally well coded and certain LTMs have a longer duration, such as those based on skills rather than facts. Material in STM that is not rehearsed is quickly forgotten, but information in LTM does not have to be continually rehearsed to be retained.

Research

- **Frost (1972)** gave participants sixteen drawings in four categories (e.g. animals), differing in visual orientation, such as angle of viewing perspective. The order of recall of items suggested that participants used visual and semantic coding, implying evidence for a visual as well as semantic code in LTM.

- **Nelson & Rothbart (1972)** showed that acoustic coding also occurs in LTM, as participants made recall errors involving homophones, words that are pronounced the same, but have different meanings, like 'night' and 'knight', again suggesting that coding in LTM has several varieties.

- **Anokhin (1973)** estimated the number of possible neuronal connections in the human brain is 1 followed by 10.5 million kilometres of noughts. He concluded 'no human yet exists who can use all the potential of their brain', suggesting the capacity of LTM is limitless.

- **Wagenaar (1986)** created a diary of 2400 events over six years and tested himself on recall of events rather than dates, finding he too had excellent recall, again suggesting the capacity of LTM is extremely large. Diary studies, however, are a type of case study and therefore not representative of the general population and there could also be an element of bias as people are testing themselves.

- **Bahrick *et al.* (1975)** showed 400 participants aged between 17 and 74 years a set of photos and a list of names, some of which were ex-school friends, and asked them to identify ex-school friends. Those who had left high school in the last 15 years identified 90 per cent of faces and names, while those who had left 48 years previously identified 80 per cent of names and 70 per cent of faces, suggesting memory for faces is long-lasting.

- **Goldman & Seamon (1992)** asked participants to identify odours of everyday products experienced in the last two years and odours not experienced since childhood. Although identification (by name) was better for more recent odours, there was significant identification of less-recent odours, suggesting duration of olfactory (smell-based) information in LTM is very long-lasting.

Evaluation

- It is difficult to see how smells and tastes could be coded semantically and reason suggests songs are encoded acoustically, supporting the idea of several forms of encoding in LTM.

- Different types of LTM involve different brain areas, with research suggesting that they are encoded in different ways, which implies that there are varying forms of coding within LTM.

- The capacity of LTM is assumed to be limitless, as research has not been able to determine a finite capacity.

- There may be an evolutionary basis to LTM; animal studies, such as that by **Fagot & Cook (1996)**, showed that pigeons can memorize 1200 picture response associations. Baboons still had not reached their capacity after three years of training, memorizing 5000 associations. This suggests that an enlarged memory capacity has a survival value, which has been acted upon by natural selection.

- Sometimes information in LTM appears to be lost, but may be a problem of access to the information rather than it not being in LTM.

- The type of testing techniques used may affect findings from studies of duration of LTM. Recall is often better when asking participants to recognize stimuli, rather than getting them to recall stimuli. See Table 2.1 for details of the differences in encoding, duration and capacity between the SR, STM and LTM.

	Sensory register		**Short-term memory**		**Long-term memory**	
Encoding	Separate sensory stores for different sensory inputs	Crowder (1993)	Mainly acoustic (by sound), other codes used too	Baddeley (1966): immediate recall study	Mainly semantic (by meaning), other codes used too	Baddeley (1966): delayed recall study
Capacity	Huge	Sperling (1960)	Small: 5 to 9 chunks of information	Jacobs (1887)	Huge	Anokhin (1973)
Duration	Brief: varies between different sensory stores	Walsh & Thompson (1978)	Short: maximum of 30 seconds	Peterson & Peterson (1959)	Potentially for a lifetime	Bahrick *et al.* (1975)

■ **Table 2.1** Differences in encoding, duration and capacity between the SR, STM and LTM

■ Overall evaluation of the MSM

- The MSM was the first cognitive explanation of memory and thus was influential, inspiring interest and research, and formed the basis for the working memory model leading to a greater understanding of how memory works.
- There is considerable research evidence for the existence of the separate memory stores of the SR, STM and LTM (see studies of encoding, capacity and duration).
- The model is supported by amnesia cases (loss of memory). Patients either lose their LTM or their STM abilities, but not both, supporting the idea that STM and LTM are separate memory stores (see below).
- The serial position effect (**Murdock, 1962**) supports the MSM's idea of there being separate STM and LTM stores. Words at the beginning and end of a list are recalled better than those in the middle. Words at the beginning of the list, the primacy effect, are recalled because they have been rehearsed and transferred to LTM, while words from the end of the list, the recency effect, are recalled as they are still in STM.
- The main criticism of the MSM is that it is oversimplified, as it assumes there are single STM and LTM stores. Research indicates several types of STM, like one for verbal and one for non-verbal sounds, and different types of LTM, like procedural, episodic and semantic memories (see 'Long-term memory' on page 60 for more information about types of LTM).
- **Cohen & Levinthal (1990)** believe memory capacity cannot be measured purely in terms of the amount of information, but rather by the nature of the information to be recalled. Some things are easier to recall, regardless of the amount to be learned, and the MSM does not consider this.
- MSM describes memory in terms of structure, namely the three memory stores and the processes of attention and verbal rehearsal. However, MSM focuses too much on structure and not enough on processes.
- Case studies of amnesia support the MSM, as retrograde amnesia affects retrieval from LTM abilities, while anterograde amnesia affects the ability to transfer information from STM to LTM. They also support the idea of there being separate types of LTM, as generally not all forms of LTM will be affected. **Lawton (2015)** reported on Scott Bolzan (see page 59), an example of retrograde amnesia, who lost access to his LTMs (though not his procedural LTM) due to a head injury, but could still create new memories by transferring STMs to LTM. **Scoville & Milner (1957)** reported the case study of HM, who had brain tissue removed in an attempt to treat his epilepsy, and who incurred anterograde amnesia, where he was unable to encode new long-term memories, although his STM seemed unaffected, supporting the idea of separate memory stores. HM donated his brain to science on his death in 2008, aged 82. **Sacks (2007)** reported on musician Clive Wearing who in 1985 caught a virus that caused brain damage and amnesia, robbing him of the ability to transfer STMs into LTMs, as well as some LTM abilities. However, his procedural LTM was intact; he could still play the piano, though he had no knowledge that he was able to do so.

LINK TO THE BIOLOGICAL APPROACH

Case studies of brain damage, such as those by **Scoville & Milner (1957)** and **Sacks (2007)** have allowed cognitive psychologists to understand more about how memory works.

1 Explain why it is only really possible to investigate examples of amnesia, such as **Sack's (2007)** study of Clive Wearing, by using the case study method?

2 What are the strengths and weaknesses of the case study method?

3 What other study methods do case studies often use?

Strengthen your learning

1 Draw a diagram to show how the MSM sees information as flowing between separate storage systems.

2 Explain what is meant by:
a encoding
b capacity
c duration.

3 What is chunking?

4 Outline the encoding, capacity and duration of SM, STM and LTM.

5 For Baddeley's (1966) study, in your own words state the:
a aims
b procedure (remember to state the difference in procedure between the studies of encoding in STM and LTM)
c findings
d conclusions
e evaluative points.

6 Explain what research has suggested about the encoding, capacity and duration of SM, STM and LTM.

7 Provide an overall assessment of the MSM based on its strengths and weaknesses.

Working memory model (WMM) – an explanation that sees short-term memory as an active store holding several pieces of information simultaneously.

Central executive (CE) – oversees and coordinates the components of working memory.

Visuospatial sketchpad (VSS) – component of the WMM that deals with visual information and the physical relationship of items to each other.

Phonological loop (PL) – component of the WMM that deals with auditory information.

Episodic buffer (EB) – temporary store of integrated information from the central executive, phonological loop, visuospatial sketchpad and LTM.

The working memory model

'*Kiss me goodbye and make it impressive; I have issues with my short-term memory….*'
Jennifer Delucy (2010)

FOCUS ON …

■ Working memory as an explanation of short-term memory through consciously holding several pieces of information simultaneously.
■ The roles of the central executive, phonological loop, visuospatial sketchpad and episodic buffer in working memory.
■ What research studies inform about the working memory model (WMM).
■ An assessment of the WMM in terms of its strengths and weaknesses.

Baddeley & Hitch (1974) questioned the existence of a single STM store (their model does not concern LTM), arguing that STM was more complex than simply a temporary store for transferring information to LTM. They saw STM as an 'active' store, holding several pieces of information while they were being worked on (hence 'working' memory). **Cohen & Levinthal (1990)** described working memory as: 'the focus of consciousness – it holds information consciously thought about now'. The **working memory model (WMM)** should not be seen as a replacement for the MSM, but more as an explanation based upon the MSM.

To replace the single STM store of the MSM, Baddeley and Hitch proposed a multi-component working memory (WM) of initially three components. At the head of the model is the **central executive (CE)**, which oversees the two 'slave' systems, the **visuospatial sketchpad (VSS)** and the **phonological loop (PL)**, temporary stores that process specific types of information. A fourth component, the **episodic buffer (EB)**, was added in 2000 to address shortcomings of the model.

The central executive

The central executive (CE) is a supervisory system that acts as a filter to determine which information received by the sense organs is and is not attended to. It processes information in all sensory forms, directs information to the model's slave systems and collects responses. It is limited in capacity and can only effectively cope with one strand of information at a time. It therefore selectively attends to particular types of information, attaining a balance between tasks when attention needs to be divided between them, for example talking while driving. It also permits us to switch attention between different inputs of information.

Research

- **Baddeley (1996)** discovered that participants found it difficult to generate lists of random numbers while simultaneously switching between pressing numbers and letters on a keyboard, suggesting the two tasks were competing for CE resources. This supports the idea of the CE being limited in capacity and only being able to cope with one type of information at a time.
- **D'Esposito *et al.* (1995)** found using fMRI scans that the prefrontal cortex was activated when verbal and spatial tasks were performed simultaneously, but not when performed separately, suggesting the brain area to be associated with the workings of the CE.

Evaluation

- Little is known about the CE. It is not clear how it works or what it does. This vagueness means it can be used to explain almost any experimental results. If two tasks cannot be performed together, then the two processing components are seen as conflicting, or that the tasks exceed the CE's capacity. If two tasks can be done simultaneously, it is argued they do not exceed the available resources, in essence a circular argument (an argument that continually proves itself).
- The CE is probably better understood as a component controlling the focus of attention rather than being a memory store, unlike the PL and the VSS, which are specialized memory stores.

Phonological loop

The phonological loop (PL) is a slave system that deals with auditory information (sensory information in the form of sound) and the order of the information, such as whether words occurred before or after each other. The PL is similar to the rehearsal system of the MSM, with a limited capacity determined by the amount of information that can be spoken out loud in about two seconds. As it is mainly an acoustic store, confusions occur with similar sounding words.

Baddeley (1996) divided the PL into two sub-parts; the **primary acoustic store (PAS)** and the **articulatory process (AP)**. The PAS, or inner ear, stores words that have recently been heard, while the AP, or inner voice, keeps information in the PL through sub-vocal repetition of information, and is linked to speech production.

Primary acoustic store (PAS) – part of the phonological loop, stores words heard.

Articulatory process (AP) – part of the phonological acoustic store, allows sub-vocal repetition of information within the store.

Research

- **Trojani & Grossi (1995)** reported a case study of SC, who had brain damage affecting the functioning of his PL, but not his VSS, suggesting the PL to be a separate system.
- **Baddeley *et al.* (1975)** reported on the word length effect, where participants recalled more short words in serial order than longer words, supporting the idea that capacity of the PL is set by how long it takes to say words, rather than the actual number of words.

RESEARCH IN FOCUS

Studies of the WMM and the MSM generally use laboratory-based experiments.

1 Laboratory experiments establish causality; explain what causality means.

2 Causality can be established, as experiments have independent (IV) and dependent (DV) variables. Explain what an IV and DV are and why they allow causality to be established in an experiment.

3 Select one experimental study of the WMM and identify the IV and DV within the study.

Evaluation

PET scans show that different brain areas are activated when doing verbal and visual tasks, which suggests that the PL and the VSS are separate systems, reflected in the biology of the brain.

The PL is strongly associated with the evolution of human vocal language, with the development of the slave system seen as producing a significant increase in the short-term ability to remember vocalizations. This then helped the learning of more complex language abilities, such as grammar and expressing meaning.

Visuospatial sketchpad

The visuo-spatial sketchpad (VSS), or inner eye, is a slave system that handles non-phonological information and is a temporary store for visual and spatial items and the relationships between them (what items are and where they are located). The VSS helps individuals to navigate around and interact with their physical environment, with information being coded and rehearsed through the use of mental pictures.

Logie (1995) suggests sub-dividing the store into a **visual cache (VC)**, which stores visual material about form and colour, and an **inner scribe (IS)**, which handles spatial relationships and rehearses and transfers information in the VC to the CE.

Visual cache (VC) – part of the VSS, stores information about form and colour.

Inner scribe (IS) – part of the VSS, stores information about the physical relationships of items.

Research

■ **Gathercole & Baddeley (1993)** found participants had difficulty simultaneously tracking a moving point of light and describing the angles on a hollow letter F, because both tasks involved using the VSS. Other participants had little difficulty in tracking the light and performing a simultaneous verbal task, as they involve using the VSS and the PL, indicating the VSS to be a separate slave system.

■ **Klauer & Zhao (2004)** reported more interference between two visual tasks than between a visual and a spatial task, implying the existence of a separate VC and IS.

YOU ARE THE RESEARCHER

Design an experiment to test whether participants can do two acoustic tasks at the same time. First get someone to speak some numbers into a participant's ear; the participant has to add them up. Then get two people to simultaneously speak different numbers into both of the participant's ears and see if the participant can add them both up separately.

What would be your IV and your DV?

How could you do something similar for: a) two visual tasks; b) one visual and one acoustic task?

Evaluation

■ As well as showing the PL and the VSS to be located in different brain areas, PET scans also show brain activation in the left hemisphere of the brain with visual tasks, and activation in the right hemisphere with spatial information, which further supports the idea of dividing the VSS into a separate VC and IS.

■ Studies of the VSS (and the PL) often feature a dual-task technique, where participants have to perform two simultaneous activities. However, the actual tasks performed are often not ones encountered much in everyday life, so such studies can be accused of being artificial and lacking in mundane realism.

The episodic buffer

Baddeley (2000) added the episodic buffer (EB), a third slave system, as the model needed a general store to operate properly. The PL and the VSS deal with the processing and temporary storage of specific types of information, but have limited capacity and the CE has no storage capacity, so cannot contain items relating to visual and acoustic properties. Therefore, the EB was introduced to explain how it is possible to temporarily store information combined together from the CE, the PL, the VSS and LTM.

Research

- **Prabhakaran *et al.* (2000)** used fMRI scans to find greater right frontal brain activation for combined verbal and spatial information, but greater posterior activation for non-combined information, providing biological evidence of an EB that allows temporary storage of integrated information.

- **Alkhalifa (2009)** reported on a patient with severely impaired LTM who demonstrated STM capacity of up to 25 prose items, far exceeding the capacity of both the PL and the VSS. This suggests the existence of an EB, which holds items in working memory until they are recalled.

Overall evaluation of the WMM

- The WMM explains much more about memory than the MSM does, because not only does it acknowledge that there is more than one type of STM, it also includes a wide range of mental processes, such as attention, reasoning, reading, comprehension, problem-solving and spatial and visual processing.

- The model is supported by a wide range of research evidence for its slave systems of the PL, VSS and EB. However, relatively little is known about the workings of the CE, nor what its capacity is, and as this is seen as the controlling component of the model, this weakens overall support for the model.

- The model explains the execution of everyday tasks; for example, reading, through use of the PL, and navigation around one's environment, through use of the VSS.

- The WMM is not a full explanation of memory (not that it was ever intended to be), as it does not include explanation of the workings of SM and LTM. Indeed the MSM can be seen as a better overall explanation of memory.

- The WMM should not really be seen as a separate alternative model of memory, but rather as an extension of the MSM.

- A negative criticism of the WMM is its inability to explain accelerations in processing ability that occur with practice or over time.

- The term 'slave system' has been criticized, as being racist. However, the term is derived from engineering to simply mean a subsidiary or secondary system to the supervisory system of the CE and has no connections to race.

- Although the existence of the episodic buffer is supported by research evidence, it is not clear how the EB combines information together from other parts of the model and from LTM.

PSYCHOLOGY IN THE REAL WORLD

The WMM suggests practical applications; especially for children with Attention Deficit Hyperactivity Disorder (ADHD) relating to impairments of working memory (WM). **Alloway (2006)** recommends several methods to help children focus on the task at hand:

1 Use brief and simple instructions so they do not forget what they are doing.

2 Break instructions down into individual steps.

3 Frequently repeat instructions.

4 Ask the child to periodically repeat instructions.

Klingberg *et al.* (2002) additionally report that computerized working memory training, using systematic exercises to produce cognitive gains, is beneficial to those with poor working memory (WM).

Strengthen your learning

1 Name the four main components of the WMM and briefly describe their functions.

2 Explain the difference between:
   a the primary acoustic store (PAS) and the articulatory loop (AL)
   b the visual cache (VC) and the inner scribe (IS).

3 Give details of a study that suggests a visual and an auditory task can be performed at the same time.

4 Summarize what other research studies have suggested about the WMM.

5 Provide an assessment of the WMM in terms of its strengths and weaknesses.

6 Explain how the WMM can be seen as an extension of the MSM, rather than being a separate theory.

7 What practical applications are there of the WMM?

IN THE NEWS

Ψ The Psychological Enquirer

THE MAN WHO FORGOT EVERYTHING, BUT NOT HOW TO LOVE...

■ **Figure 2.4** Scott Bolzan and wife Joan

Forty-six-year-old Scott Bolzan had played American football for the New England Patriots and the Cleveland Browns, before going on to run his own successful charter aeroplane business. Then, in December 2008, he slipped and banged his head. When he woke up he didn't know his name or recognize his friends or family, or remember any past events.

Scott had suffered severe retrograde amnesia, probably as he had had no blood flow to his right temporal lobe, a brain area associated with long-term memory. His memory loss was so severe that he had no understanding of concepts most people would take for granted, like the meaning of birthdays or what the relationship between a husband and a wife is. Fortunately, Scott was able to relearn things, as his short-term memory ability was still intact, as was his ability to create new long-term memories.

Scott found it was not easy rekindling his love for his wife, a woman he no longer recognized. He had to be wooed and fall in love with her again. Eventually, they spent a night on a boat and restarted their sex life; he had retained a lot of procedural memory and 'thank goodness for that', said his wife.

Scott's loss of long-term memories shows how STM and LTM involve different storage systems, as theorized by the MSM. But Scott still had some LTMs; he could understand written and spoken speech and perform old skills such as riding a bicycle, which are examples of procedural LTM. It was his episodic and semantic LTMs he had lost. So Scott's case also suggests that there are different types of LTM – Scott's accident hadn't affected them all.

Long-term memory

'Love, like long-term memories, lasts forever.'
Leslie Drawill (2017)

FOCUS ON...

- LTM existing as several separate types.
- LTM dividing into explicit (declarative) and implicit (non-declarative) forms.
- The differences between and characteristics of semantic, episodic and procedural LTMs.
- What research studies inform about different types of LTM.
- An assessment of different types of LTM.

The WMM shows that the MSM is oversimplified as an explanation of memory, as there is more than one type of short-term memory store and the situation is the same with LTM. Research indicates the existence of several types, each having a separate function and associated with different brain areas. The main subdivision of LTM is into explicit (also known as declarative, as it is easy to put into words) and implicit (also known as non-declarative, as it is not easy to express in words) types. Explicit LTMs are ones recalled only if consciously thought about, while implicit LTMs do not require conscious thought to be recalled. Explicit memories are also often formed from several combined memories.

Two types of explicit LTM are featured here: semantic and **episodic memories (EM)**, and one type of implicit LTM, procedural memory.

> **Episodic memory (EM)** – a form of LTM for events occurring in an individual's life.

Episodic LTM

Episodic LTM, first suggested by **Endel Tulving (1972)**, is the memory that gives individuals an autobiographical record of personal experiences: when their birthday is, the circumstances of their children being born, and so on. The strength of episodic memories is influenced by emotions present at the time a memory is coded, for example traumatic events are often well-recalled due to their high emotional content. Strength of episodic memories is also affected by the degree of processing of information at coding, with highly processed episodic events recalled more easily. It is thought that episodic memory helps individuals to distinguish the difference between real events and imagination/delusions.

The prefrontal cortex brain area is associated with initial coding of episodic memories, with consolidation (strengthening) and storage of the memories associated with the neocortex. Memories of the different parts of an event are located in the different visual, auditory, olfactory, and so on, areas of the brain, but are connected together in the hippocampus to create a memory of an episode, rather than remaining a collection of separate memories.

Research

Herlitz et al. (1997) assessed explicit LTM abilities in 1000 Swedish participants, finding that females consistently performed better than males on tasks requiring episodic LTM, although there were no differences in semantic LTM ability. This suggests that there are gender differences in episodic memory ability, which may be explained in part by females generally having higher verbal ability.

Evaluation

> **Semantic memory** – type of LTM for meanings, understandings, and other concept-based knowledge.

- The extent to which episodic and **semantic memory** systems are different is unclear, as although different brain areas are involved, there is also a lot of overlap between the two systems, with semantic memories often clearly originating in episodic memory. Whether therefore the gradual transformation of an episodic into a semantic LTM means a change in memory systems cannot be certain.

- It may be that episodic memory differs from that of semantic memory in terms of different types of thinking and emotion; episodic memories are associated with conscious awareness of events and emotional feelings related to them, while semantic memories are associated with objective analysis of phenomena.

PSYCHOLOGY IN THE REAL WORLD

Scientists at Vanderbilt University, USA are programming episodic memory into their robot ISAC, the aim being to more closely mimic the brain functions of humans.

Already ISAC can recall specific past experiences to solve a current problem, just like humans do, and can indirectly carry out tasks by influencing information placed in working memory. When given a new task, ISAC creates associations between the new task and stored experiences and then uses these associations to decide which information is entered into working memory. ISAC also uses episodic memory to relate past experiences of success and failure in different situations to decide preferences in new situations, which allows ISAC to influence goal and task setting.

Attempts are now being made to give ISAC an EB, so that it can combine information from separate memory channels involving different types of sensory input (just like the VSS and PL do in a human) into single memory chunks.

Semantic LTM

Semantic LTM is another type of explicit memory and contains all knowledge (facts, concepts, meanings, etc.) an individual has learned (though, of course, not when the knowledge was learned). The strength of semantic memories, like episodic memories, is positively associated with the degree of processing occurring during coding, though in general semantic memories seem to be better sustained over time than episodic ones. Semantic LTMs are linked to episodic LTMs, as new knowledge tends to be learned from experiences, with episodic memory therefore underpinning semantic memory. Over time there will be a gradual move from episodic to semantic memory with knowledge becoming increasingly divorced from the event/experience that it was learned from.

There is disagreement over which brain areas are involved in semantic LTM; some evidence suggests involvement of the hippocampus and related areas, while others believe several brain areas are used. Coding is mainly associated with the frontal and temporal lobes.

Research

- **Azar (2007)** created 64 imaginary but believable drawings of animals, one of which was the prototype for 'crutters' (animals that shared three particular features). Alzheimer's sufferers and non-sufferers then had to decide which of the 64 drawings were of crutters. Participants had to use either direct comparison to make their assessments – judging which animals were crutters based on their similarity to the picture of the prototype – or they based their comparison on a stated rule that crutters matched the prototype on three of the four target features. Alzheimer's sufferers were as good as non-sufferers when using direct comparison, but inferior when using the stated rule. As using a stated rule involves higher-level processing, it suggests semantic memory involves different processes and brain areas.
- **Vicari et al. (2007)** reported on the case study of CL, an eight-year-old girl who suffered brain damage due to the removal of a tumour. She demonstrated deficiencies in her episodic LTM functions, especially in creating new episodic memories, but was still able to create and recall semantic memories. This suggests that episodic and semantic memories are separate systems using different brain areas, with the hippocampus associated with episodic memory and the perirhinal cortex with semantic LTM.

Evaluation

- Semantic memory may involve more of a network of associated links performed in different brain areas, rather than being a single form of memory ability. Some links may be stronger than others or quicker to access, explaining why some semantic memories appear to be easier to recall than others.
- The fact that damage to different areas of the brain can affect semantic memory abilities differently supports the idea that semantic memory abilities are spread throughout brain structures, while also supporting the idea that semantic memory may consist of several interrelated memory abilities and therefore not be a single type of memory.

▨ Procedural LTM

Procedural memory (PM) – type of LTM for the performance of particular types of action.

Procedural LTM is a type of implicit memory permitting individuals to perform learned tasks with little conscious thought, for instance riding a bicycle. Although seemingly easy to do, procedural LTMs are difficult to explain in words (so are classed as being non-declarative). Many procedural LTMs occur early in life, involving the learning of important motor skills, like walking, dressing, and so on. Procedural LTM is also involved in language, helping individuals to speak automatically, using grammar and syntax without thinking how to. This shows how procedural and semantic memories work together. As **procedural memory** does not require conscious thought, it permits people to simultaneously perform other cognitive tasks that require attention.

Procedural LTM is associated mainly with the neocortex brain areas of primary motor cortex, cerebellum and prefrontal cortex, and unlike explicit forms of LTM, does not need the hippocampus to function.

▨ Research

- **Finke *et al.* (2012)** reported the case study of PM, a 68-year-old professional cellist who suffered damage to various brain areas after contracting encephalitis, resulting in severe amnesia. His episodic and semantic LTM were very affected, but although he could not remember musical facts, such as the names of famous composers, his ability to read and play music was unaffected, including learning new complex pieces.

- **Van Gorp *et al.* (1999)** compared 37 heavy cocaine users with 27 non-abusing controls on memory ability for a 45-day period after abstaining from the drug. The interesting finding was that the former cocaine users showed a faster increase in procedural memory ability than non-users. As abstinence from cocaine causes dopamine production to be much increased, it suggests dopamine plays a part in procedural LTM.

▨ Evaluation

- One problem in deciding which brain areas are involved in procedural memory is the relative lack of research. What is needed are case studies of people with brain damage that affects procedural memory, but not explicit memory (semantic and episodic memory). However, such cases are rare.

- Procedural memories generally take longer to learn than explicit memory abilities. This may be because procedural memory involves motor functions and spatial abilities, while explicit memory tends not to (though the learning of procedural memories can also involve higher-level processing too).

Strengthen your learning

1   Explain what is meant by explicit and implicit LTMs and how this relates to episodic, semantic and procedural LTM.

2   Outline the following:
    a episodic LTM
    b semantic LTM
    c procedural LTM.

3   Summarize what research has suggested about episodic, semantic and procedural LTMs.

4   What other evaluative points can be made about episodic, semantic and procedural LTM?

5   Explain how Scott Balzan (see 'In the News' on page 59) lost his episodic and semantic LTMs, but not his procedural LTMs.

Schema theory

'Humans see what they want to see.'
Rick Riordan

'The eye sees only what the mind is prepared to comprehend.'
Robertson Davies

FOCUS ON...

- Schema as a means of perceiving and remembering events in a preset manner.
- Describing and evaluating Gregory's theory as an explanation of top-down (indirect) processing of sensory information.
- Describing and evaluating Gibson's theory as an explanation of bottom-up (direct) processing of sensory information.

Perception – the interpretation of sensory data.

■ **Figure 2.5** Paris in the spring

A schema is a cognitive framework for structuring information about the physical world and the events and behaviour occurring within it. Knowledge therefore becomes stored within memory in an organized way so that future experiences become perceived in preset ways. Schema processing generally does not require conscious thought and thus is a largely automatic process. Although this is beneficial to individuals in reducing the amount of cognitive 'energy' used up, it has a large negative effect in creating biases in cognitive processes, such as thinking, **perception** and memory, which then limit an individual's ability to think about, perceive or remember events in an accurate way.

A simple way to see how situations are perceived wrongly, as they do not fit what is expected, is to present the written statement *'Paris in the the spring'* to participants and ask them to state what they can see. Many participants continually read 'Paris in the spring', even though this is wrong, because that is what they think they should see, based on previous experiences of language.

Allport & Postman (1947) illustrated this type of recall error. Participants saw a picture of a black man and a white man arguing, with the white man brandishing a knife (Figure 2.6 overleaf). On recall many participants remembered the black man holding the knife, because the idea of black men as oriented to violence and carrying weapons was a cultural stereotype of the time that was reflected in people's schemas.

It seems, therefore, that memories are reconstructed to fit personal beliefs about the world.

Snyder & Uranowitz (1978) also demonstrated the influence of schemas on recall. Participants heard the story of Betty, which contained information that Betty was a popular girl who had lots of dates, but no steady boyfriend. Participants asked to recall the story after being told that Betty got married remembered that she was popular and had lots of dates; those told that Betty became a lesbian recalled her never having a steady boyfriend, a fact not recalled by those told she got married. This illustrates how memories become selective on the basis of whichever schemas are being used.

■ **Figure 2.6** The knife held by the black man illustrates a type of recall error based on cultural stereotypes: Allport & Postman (1947)

Schemas even occur as 'scripts', a phenomenon demonstrated by **Schank & Abelson (1977)** with their restaurant study. The researchers went beyond describing what schemas contain, to showing how schemas were organized and used to allow understanding of recurring social situations involving stereotyped behaviour, like visiting a restaurant. Knowledge of such events was stored as scripts describing sequences of events in a particular order; for example, arriving at the restaurant, hanging up your coat, being seated, ordering your food, and so on. Recall and understanding of such social situations is therefore influenced by reference to stored cognitive scripts, as when participants compared written scripts about visiting a restaurant there was general agreement about events that had occurred.

(For a fuller picture of how schema influences memory, see 'Reconstructive memory' on page 79.)

LINK TO THE BIOLOGICAL APPROACH

Schemas can be seen in evolutionary terms as having an adaptive survival value, as they allow situations/events to be quickly understood and responded to appropriately

■ Schema theory and perception: top-down and bottom-up processing

'There is no truth, there is only perception.'
Gustave Flaubert

Top-down (indirect) processing – perception that involves cognitive processing that goes beyond mere sensory input.

Bottom-up (direct) processing – perception that arises directly from sensory input without further cognitive processing.

Top-down processing concerns cognitive analysis involving more than just the sensory information received by the brain. **Bottom-up processing**, however, concerns cognitive analysis involving only the sensory information received by the brain, without any further cognitive analysis. Top-down and bottom-up processing are probably best understood through reference to the cognitive process of perception, the interpretation of sensory data.

Eyes do not directly 'see' and ears do not directly 'hear'. They are just sensory organs that respond to specific types of physical energy, converting this energy into electrical impulses that are relayed by the nervous system to the brain for processing into what is experienced as perception. Yet the brain cannot directly perceive. Shine a torch onto the brain and it will not be dazzled; plug an iPod into the brain and it will not hear music – it is a silent, unseeing bodily organ. This is because sensing and perceiving are two separate yet interdependent processes, where sensations have no meaning on their own and perception cannot occur without sensations to comprehend. Therefore, when a tree falls down in a wood with no one there to hear it, it does not make a noise; indeed the noise only occurs when there is someone there to perceive the sound of the falling tree.

Perception is a cognitive process concerning how sensory information is understood. This is about how sensations are received, processed and experienced (as touches, tastes, smells, sights and sounds) as meaningful experiences and create a predictable world of objects, which can be moved about in and interacted with.

Top-down processing (as described by Richard Gregory's theory) best explains perception when sensory information is incomplete, through the use of schema to make inferences (educated guesses) about our physical world. Bottom-up processing (as described by Jerome Gibson's theory) best explains perception when sensory information is sufficient for perception to occur directly, without any need for the use of schema to facilitate higher-level cognitive processing.

Gregory's top-down theory

Gregory (1970) argued that perception is an unconscious, ongoing process of testing hypotheses; an active search for the best interpretation of sensory data based on previous experience. The search is indirect, going beyond data provided by sensory receptors to involve processing information at a higher, 'top-down' cognitive level.

Gregory sees sensory information as weak, incomplete or ambiguous. For example, the retinal image of a banana cannot display its taste. Perception therefore isn't directly experienced from sensations, but involves a dynamic search for the best interpretation of stimuli, with what is perceived being richer than the information contained within sensory data. The eye for Gregory is not a camera to view the world directly.

Sensory data is often incomplete or ambiguous, and hypotheses are constructed about its meaning. For example, the experience of reversible figures, like being able to see a vase or two faces in Figure 2.7. Both are perceived, as Gregory believes separate hypotheses are generated and tested out, though usually there would be enough sensory data to decide which interpretation of information is correct. Visual illusions are therefore experienced when confusions occur.

■ **Figure 2.7** A vase or two faces?

▨ Perceptual schema

Perceptual set sees individuals as biased in how they perceive, due to previous experiences, cultural factors and emotional and motivational influences. Thus, people see what they want or expect to see, cutting down the number of possible interpretations that data may suggest, making perception quicker, though increasing opportunities for errors to occur. Perceptual schema occurs in several ways.

Expectation

Expectation involves individuals perceiving what they expect to perceive based on previous experience.

▨ Research

Brochet *et al.* (2002) (see also confirmation bias, on page 85) gave 54 expert wine tasters a selection of white wines, which they described as 'fresh', 'honeyed', and so on. They were then given red wines, some of which were white wine altered to look red by adding a tasteless, odourless substance. No one spotted the frauds, describing them with words relating to red wines, like 'intense' or 'spicy'. As experts have better knowledge of wine they were more influenced by colour, which created an expectation that determined actual perception.

> ### YOU ARE THE RESEARCHER
>
> A simple way of demonstrating perceptual schema experimentally through context and expectation can be achieved as follows. (It works best if participants are blindfolded.) In one condition get participants to hold identical objects of equal weight, one in each hand. Ask them whether they are the same weight or different (they should say the same). Then get them to hold a reasonably heavy object in one hand, while simultaneously holding a much lighter object in their other hand. Do this for about 30 seconds and then replace the objects (at the same time) with those used in the first condition. Participants should now report the object in the hand that held the heavy object as being heavier.
>
> What advantage is there in using the same participants in both conditions?
>
> What are order effects and how would you control for them?

PSYCHOLOGY IN THE REAL WORLD

The idea of schema through expectation is used in food frauds, the passing off of inferior foods as superior ones. In the USA in 2007 DNA testing showed that 77 per cent of fish labelled as expensive red snapper was actually much cheaper types of fish. If fish is labelled as red snapper and coloured to look like it, people's expectations shape their perception and they taste it as being red snapper.

Emotional influences

Emotional factors affect perception by forming a bias to perceive, or not, certain features of sensory data, such as perceptual defence, where emotionally harmful stimuli take longer to perceive.

Research

Lazarus & McCleary (1951) found that nonsense syllables presented so quickly that they were not consciously perceived increased anxiety levels if previously paired with electric shocks. This suggests that emotional factors influence perception unconsciously.

Motivational influences

Perception is influenced by motivational factors like hunger, with pictures of food seen as more appetizing as people become hungrier. This may have an evolutionary origin, with perception focused on the elements necessary for survival, like finding food.

Research

Solley & Haigh (1948) found that children drew a bigger Santa and sack of toys as Christmas approached, but afterwards Santa and his sack shrunk, which implies that motivational factors do influence perception.

Cultural factors

Cultural factors influence individuals to perceive environmental features in set ways. People from different cultural groups may perceive identical sensory data differently, because of different environmental experiences. For example, the Müller-Lyer illusion consists of two equally long lines, but line A appears longer than line B; however, the illusion is only perceived in cultures where individuals live in a 'carpentered' world of manufactured straight lines, angles, and so on. Those from cultures where buildings are made from natural materials do not experience the illusion, as they subconsciously read the third dimension of depth into it from experience.

Research

Stewart (1973) found that Tongan rural children were less likely to experience the Müller-Lyer illusion, but the more experienced they became with an environment of straight lines and rectangles, the more prone to the illusion they became, illustrating how environmental experience shapes perception through the use of schema.

LINK TO THE SOCIOCULTURAL APPROACH

Cross-cultural studies, like that of Stewart (1973) into the Müller-Lyer illusion, allow psychologists to see if behaviours are innate (shared by members of all cultural groups) or are learned (occur differently in different cultural groups).

Visual illusions

Gregory believes visual illusions occur because expectations based on previous experience are used to create and test hypotheses from incoming sensory information, but that sometimes this is prone to error, with false perceptions occurring. With the Kanizsa illusion, an upright white triangle is perceived over an upside-down white triangle with black edges and three black circles. The upright triangle appears ultra-white, with sharp edges, but is a perceptual invention, as previous experience of what objects look like when superimposed on each other is used to experience the illusion. The

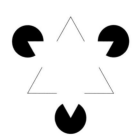

■ **Figure 2.8**
The Kanizsa illusion

third dimension of depth is read into a flat, two-dimensional image, with individuals going beyond the sensory data to perceive something that is not there.

■ Evaluation of Gregory's top-down processing theory

- Gregory's theory increased the understanding of perception, generating interest and research and creating much evidence to support the theory.

- It seems logical that interpretations based on previous experience would occur when viewing conditions are incomplete or ambiguous. For example, if incomplete features indicated an animal could be a duck or a rabbit, the fact it was on water would determine that it was a duck.

- **Eysenck & Keane (1990)** argue that Gregory's theory is better at explaining the perception of illusions than real objects, because illusions are unreal and easy to misperceive, while real objects provide enough data to be perceived directly. However, Gregory's explanation of visual illusions is not without criticism; according to him, once it is understood why illusions occur, perception should alter so the illusion is not experienced anymore. However, they still are, so weakening Gregory's explanation.

- Most research supporting Gregory involves laboratory experiments, where fragmented and briefly presented stimuli are used, which are difficult to perceive directly. Gregory thus underestimates how rich and informative sensory data can be in the real world, where it may be possible to perceive directly.

- People's perceptions in general, even those from different cultures, are similar. This would not be true if individual perceptions arose from individual experiences, weakening support for Gregory.

- Gregory's theory suggests that memory is constantly searched to find the best interpretation of incoming sensory data. This would be time-consuming and inefficient, casting doubt on Gregory's explanation.

Gibson's bottom-up theory

Optical array – the structure of patterned light received by the eyes.

Texture gradient – surface patterns that provide sensory information about objects.

Optic flow patterns – unambiguous sources of information that directly inform perception.

Affordances – the quality of objects that permits actions to be carried out on them.

Gibson (1966) argued that there was enough information within the **optical array** (the pattern of light reaching the eyes) for perception to occur directly, without higher-level cognitive processing. Individuals' movements and those of surrounding objects within an environment aid this process. This involves innate mechanisms that require no learning from experience.

Gibson saw perception as due to the direct detection of environmental invariances, unchanging aspects of the visual world. These possess enough sensory data to allow individuals to perceive features of their environment, like depth, distance and the spatial relationships of where objects are in relation to each other.

Gibson believed that **texture gradients** found in the environment are similar to gradients in the eye, and these corresponding gradients allow the experience of depth perception. This grew into a theory of perception that includes the optical array, textured gradients, **optic flow patterns**, horizon ratio and **affordances**.

Gibson believed perception was a 'bottom-up' process, one constructed directly from sensory data. He saw the perceiver not as the brain but as an individual within their environment. The purpose of perception therefore is to allow people to function in their environment safely and he argued that illusions were two-dimensional, static creations of artificial laboratory experiments.

■ The optical array

The optical array is the structure of patterned light that enters the eyes. It is an ever-changing source of sensory information, occurring due to the movements of individuals and objects within their world. It contains different intensities of light shining in different directions, transmitting sensory data about the physical environment. Light itself does not allow direct perception, but the structure of the sensory information contained within it does. Movement of the body, the eyes and the angle of gaze, and so on, continually update the sensory information being received from the optical array.

The optical array also has invariant elements, providing constant sources of information, which contribute to direct perception from sensory information and are not changed by the movements of observers.

Optic flow patterns

Optic flow patterns are unambiguous sources of information concerning height, distance and speed that directly inform perception and provide a rich, ever-changing source of information.

'Optic flow' refers to the visual phenomena continually experienced concerning the apparent visual motion that occurs as individuals move around their environment. Someone sitting on a train looking out of the window sees buildings and trees seemingly moving backwards; it is this apparent motion that forms the optic flow. Information about distance is also conveyed; distant objects such as hills appear to move slowly, while close-up objects seem to move quicker. This depth cue is known as motion parallax.

 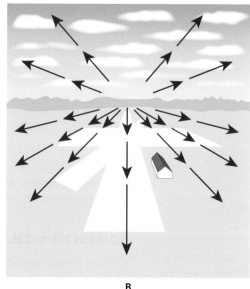

A   B

■ **Figure 2.9** Optic flow patterns as seen by a train driver (A) and a pilot (B)

As speed increases, the optic flow also increases. The optic flow also varies in relation to the angle between an observer's direction of movement and the direction of an object being viewed. When travelling forwards, the optic flow is quickest when the object being regarded is 90 degrees to the observer's side, or when directly above or below. Objects immediately in front have no optic flow and seem motionless. However, the edges of such objects appear to move, as they are not directly in front and thus seem to grow larger.

Research

Maher & West (1993, cited in Lawton et al., 2011) filmed the movements of black-clad animals with lights on their joints, finding that the species of animal was recognizable to observers. This demonstrates the strength of information gained from movement in optic flow patterns, and shows that these can provide enough sensory information for perception to occur directly.

Texture gradient

Texture gradients are surface patterns providing sensory information about depth, shape, and so on. Physical objects have surfaces with different textures that allow direct perception of distance, depth and spatial awareness. Due to constant movement, the 'flow' of texture gradients conveys a rich source of ever-changing sensory information to an observer – for instance, as objects come nearer they appear to expand.

Two depth cues central to the third dimension of depth being directly available to the senses are motion parallax (see above) and linear perspective. The latter is a cue provided by lines apparently converging as they get further away. These both permit the third dimension of depth to be directly accessible to the senses.

There are several classic texture gradients – for example, frontal surfaces provide a uniform gradient, while longitudinal surfaces, like roads, project gradients that lessen with greater distance from the observer.

▇ Research

Frichtel & Lecuyer (2007) presented participants with a film of a car driving through scenery and found that infants as young as four months old could perceive using texture gradient, implying that the ability is innate, supporting Gibson's idea that perception depends on innate mechanisms.

▇ Horizon ratios

Horizon ratios
– invariant sensory information concerning the position of objects in relation to the horizon.

Horizon ratios are another type of invariant sensory information permitting direct perception. These concern the position of objects in relation to the horizon. Objects of different sizes at equal distances from an observer present different horizon ratios, which can be calculated by dividing the amount of an object above the horizon by the amount below.

Different-sized objects at equal distances from the observer present different horizon ratios, while objects of equal size standing on level surfaces have the same horizon ratio. When nearing objects, they seem to grow, though the proportion of the object above or below the horizon remains constant and is a perceptual invariant.

▇ Research

Creem-Regehr et al. (2003) found that restricting participants' viewing conditions did not affect their ability to judge distances using horizon ratio information, suggesting that this form of invariant sensory information is an important means of establishing direct perception.

▇ Affordances

Affordances involve attaching meaning to sensory information and concern the quality of objects to allow actions to be carried out on them (action possibilities). For instance, a cup 'affords' drinking liquids. Affordances are therefore what objects mean to observers and are related to psychological state and physical abilities. For an infant who cannot walk properly a mountain is not something to be climbed.

Gibson saw affordances as relaying directly perceivable meaning to objects, because evolutionary forces shaped perceptual skills so that learning experiences were not necessary. This rejects Gregory's belief that the meaning of objects is stored in LTM from experience and requires cognitive processing to access.

▇ Research

Warren (1984) studied whether participants could judge if staircases portrayed with differently proportioned steps could 'afford' to be climbed; whether they actually could be climbed depended on the length of a participant's legs. It was found that participants were sensitive to the affordance of 'climbability', and according to Gibson this was achieved by the invariant properties of the light reflected from the staircases. This therefore supports the concept that affordances do not rely on experience.

LINK TO THE BIOLOGICAL APPROACH

There may be a biological basis to Gibson's theory. **Logothetis & Pauls (1995)** identified neurons in the brains of monkeys that seemed to perceive specific objects regardless of their orientation, implying that a biological mechanism allows direct perception. This was supported by **Rizzolati & Sinigaglia (2008)**, who found that the anterior intraparietal brain area is involved in direct perception of object affordances.

▇ Evaluation of Gibson's bottom-up processing theory

■ Gibson's theory explains how perception occurs quickly, which Gregory's theory cannot, though Gibson cannot explain why illusions are perceived. He dismissed them as artificial laboratory constructions viewed under restrictive conditions. But some occur naturally under normal viewing conditions.

■ The idea that the optical array provides direct information about what objects permit individuals to do (affordances) seems unlikely. Knowledge about objects is affected by cultural influences, experience and emotions. For example, how could an individual directly perceive that a training shoe is for running?

■ Gibson's and Gregory's theories are similar in seeing perception as hypothesis-based. Gregory explains this as a process of hypothesis formation and testing, with the flow of information processed from the top down, while Gibson sees it as an unconscious process originating from evolutionary forces, with the flow of information processed from the bottom up. Another similarity is that they both agree that visual perception occurs from light reflected off surfaces and objects and that a specific biological system is required to perceive.

■ Gregory's and Gibson's theories involve the nature versus nurture debate. Gregory's indirect theory emphasizes learning experiences and thus the influence of nurture, while Gibson's direct theory sees more of a role for nature.

TOK link

Sometimes, rather than one explanation being superior to others, a unification of different theories may work better. For instance, uniting Gregory and Gibson's very different theories actually provides the most valid explanation; Gibson's theory works best for ideal viewing conditions and Gregory's works best for less-than-ideal conditions.

PSYCHOLOGY IN THE REAL WORLD

One practical application of Gibson's theory is putting parallel lines increasingly close together as road junctions approach, giving a false impression of speed to slow drivers down. In this way, Gibson's theory can be seen to save countless lives each year.

■ **Figure 2.10** Road markings giving a false impression of speed to slow drivers down

Strengthen your learning

1 Explain what is meant by top-down (indirect) and bottom-up (direct) processing.

2 Why does Gregory see perception as a top-down process?

3 Explain how schema affects perception in terms of:
a expectations
b motivational influences
c emotional influences
d cultural factors.

4 How does Gregory explain visual illusions? Does research support his view?

5 Summarize the extent to which research supports Gregory's idea of schema determining perception?

6 Why does Gibson see perception as a bottom-up process?

7 What is the optical array?

8 Outline Gibson's theory in terms of:
a optic flow patterns
b texture gradients
c horizon ratios
d affordances.

9 Summarize the extent to which research supports Gibson's theory.

10 In terms of evaluation, is Gregory or Gibson's theory more supported? Construct a balanced argument in bullet-point form.

■ Evaluation of schema theory

FOCUS ON...

■ An assessment of schema theory in terms of its strengths and weaknesses.

■ One question that interested researchers is where within the information processing procedure do schemas exert their influence? Most interest centred on encoding, which occurs early on in information processing, and retrieval, which occurs later on. **Bartlett (1932)** believed schemas were influential during retrieval, but **Anderson & Pichert (1978)** presented a story about two boys spending the day at one of their homes while absent without permission from school. At encoding, participants were given the schema of concentrating on the perspective of a burglar, or a prospective house buyer. At recall, participants remembered details that fitted their schema; for example, those with the burglar's perspective recalled that the house contained valuable items and what these items were, but didn't recall that the house was musty with a leaky roof. Those with the house buyer's perspective did recall this, but not the list of valuable items. Participants then recalled the story from the other perspective, that is, those presented with the schema of the burglar's perspective had to switch to the prospective house buyer's perspective and vice versa. Participants then recalled details that fitted their new schema, which they hadn't recalled originally. Participants had developed a richer representation of the details in the story than could be explained in terms of the schema used during encoding; else they wouldn't have retained information relevant from another schematic perspective. 'Irrelevant' information must have been originally encoded for it to be recalled using a later different schema, even though participants claimed that they had originally recalled everything they could. This suggests that schemas exert an influence at both encoding and retrieval.

■ Schema theory has allowed psychologists to develop a unified theory of cognition that shows how all cognitive processes, for example thinking, memory, learning, attention, and so on, work in conjunction with each other through the influence that schemas collectively exert on these processes. This therefore suggests that cognition is a holistic process consisting of cognitive sub-skills operating together.

■ Schemas allow psychologists to comprehend how memory errors occur, but also how prejudices arise through the formation of schemas containing negative stereotypes of people. Such a comprehension is important in devising effective practical applications to reducing such socially harmful prejudices.

■ Schemas are activated automatically and effortlessly and so are energy-efficient. They are also resistant to change, ensuring continuity in how information is processed and responded to, though sometimes errors and distortions can occur if events are completely new and unknown, or if inappropriate schemas are referred to.

■ A flaw in schema theory is the lack of explanation on how schemas are acquired and the process by which they work. Schemas are hypothetical ideas of how the mind works, with no physical presence, and so cannot be directly observed.

■ Schema theory aids understanding of how the mind works and has withstood rigorous testing to provide an effective explanation of how human learning occurs. Schema theory demonstrates how knowledge is organized within a cognitive framework that influences expectations and interpretations of new events and also how new learning is influenced by previous knowledge.

Strengthen your learning

1 Explain what is meant by schema.

2 Explain how schema can affect:
   a memory   b perception.

3 Compile an evaluation of how schema affects cognitive processes in terms of strengths and weaknesses.

SECTION SUMMARY

■ Schema theory sees humans as perceiving and remembering events in a preset way, based on experience, emotion and available information.
■ Gregory's top-down theory sees perception as involving cognitive processing that goes beyond sensory input.
■ Gibson's bottom-up theory sees perception as occurring directly from sensory input.

Thinking and decision-making

'It is easy to make good decisions when there are no bad options.'
Robert Half

'I think therefore I am.'
Descartes –

'I'm pink therefore I'm Spam.'
Monty Python

FOCUS ON...

■ The relationship between thinking and decision-making.
■ Understanding thinking and decision-making by reference to the information processing approach.
■ The role of heuristics as mental short-cuts in selecting and processing information.
■ Understanding and assessing the adaptive decision maker framework and its role in choice in decision-making.
■ The effect of decision task variables upon decision-making strategies.
■ The role of emotions and goals in decision-making.
■ The use of coping theory to explain decision-making in response to negative emotions.
■ What research has suggested about the adaptive decision maker framework.

Thinking and **decision-making** are related cognitive processes that involve pondering on knowledge and information in order to select from options available. However, humans do not necessarily think in the most rational (sensible) way and thus do not necessarily make logical choices when making decisions.

Hastie & Dawes (2001) argued that different sorts of people in very different types of situations actually think about making decisions in the same way, which seems to suggest that people have a common set of cognitive processes. It is the limitations of these processes that restrict choice and can lead to illogical decisions being made.

There are two basic types of theory concerning thinking and decision-making: *normative theories*, which focus on how we should make decisions from a logical point of view, and *descriptive theories*, which focus on how people actually do make decisions. It is descriptive theories that are supported by research evidence and will be focused on here.

The information processing approach

The information processing approach (IPA) of thinking and decision-making sees:

- humans as very selective about which available information they attend to and how they use it
- the acquisition and processing of information as having cognitive and emotional costs
- humans as using heuristics (mental short-cuts) to select and process information
- heuristics as chosen according to the nature of a decision to be made
- beliefs and preferences as constructed through the decision-making process.

The adaptive decision maker framework

The adaptive decision maker framework (ADMF) is part of the IPA and focuses upon choice in decision-making, especially with preferential choice problems (when no single option is best in all aspects of choice). Preferential choice problems are solved by acquiring and evaluating information about possible choices. Available options vary according to:

- their perceived desirability
- the degree of certainty of their value
- the willingness of a decision-maker to accept loss on one aspect of a choice in return for gain on another aspect.

■ **Figure 2.11** There are a number of heuristics Siusaidh could use to decide which house to buy

For example, Siusaidh is fed up of living in the city and wants to move house. She must first decide on the desirability of the attributes to the decision-maker (which aspects of choice are important to her). For example, the house is in a rural location, within one hour of travelling to work, has an easy to maintain garden, is in a low-crime area and has a good school nearby. Other aspects are not as important, such as the need for shopping facilities, pubs and restaurants and having a garage. Also, some possible choices have unique aspects, such as one house that has a conservatory and another that has a pretty view.

Then there is the degree of certainty of receiving an attribute value. This concerns the fact that some aspects are more certain than others, such as a house being in a rural location, but others are less certain, such as a garden being easy to maintain or how accurate the ratings of low-crime and good local school are.

There is also the willingness to accept loss on one attribute for gain on another, for example having to travel more than one hour to work in return for having a good school nearby.

There are a number of strategies (heuristics) that Siusaidh could use to make a decision between choices involving several aspects. Which strategy is chosen depends on the demands of the task (such as the number of alternative choices of houses), how accurate a decision must be in terms of important aspects and individual differences (such as how important the decision-making is to Siusaidh). Some strategies might use all information, others only selected information. Some might focus on possible house choices, processing each house in turn, while other strategies may consider all possible houses on one aspect, before considering them on another aspect.

Heuristics

Heuristics involve using simpler decision-making processes. Such processes involve less cognitive effort by only focusing on some relevant information. This leads to less logical decisions being made, especially when there are a greater number of important aspects to consider. Several types of heuristics have been identified:

- Lexographic strategy (LEX) – involves selecting the option with the best value on what is perceived as the most important aspect.
- Satisficing strategy for decisions (SSD) – involves each option being considered in terms of whether all perceived important aspects meet a certain minimum level. If any aspect fails to reach that level, that option is rejected and the next option is then considered.
- Majority of confirming decisions (MCD) – involves options being considered in pairs on all important aspects, with the 'winning' option being retained and then compared against the 'winning' option of another pair, and so on, until only one option is left.
- Elimination by aspects (EBA) – involves rejecting options that do not meet a minimum level on the most important aspect. This process is then repeated for the second most important aspect, and so on, until only one option is left.

The use of heuristics can make big savings in cognitive effort, but more effective decisions are made when a mix of heuristics is used. To some extent EBA can be seen as combining aspects of LEX and SSD heuristics.

■ **Figure 2.12** Which heuristic is Mara using to decide her record of the year?

Strengthen your learning

Mara buys a lot of vinyl records. At the end of each year she plays them in pairs to determine which she likes best, with the winning record going through to the 'next round' (like sports teams in a cup competition) where it is paired against the winner of another pair of records. Mara continues in this way until she has her 'record of the year'.

1 Which heuristic is Mara using to determine her record of the year?

Decision task variables

Choice of decision-making strategy can be affected by decision task variables; for instance, time pressure, where decisions have to be made within a certain time period. Errors in judgement-making can occur through rush-to-judgement (making decisions too quickly) and delay-to-judgement (making decisions too slowly). Choice of decision-making strategy is also affected by the number of choice alternatives, for example whether a choice has to be made from two options or from ten options.

Role of emotions and goals in decision-making

'You can't make decisions based on fear and the possibility of what might happen.'
Michelle Obama

Originally the ADMF focused on the accuracy of decision-making and the amount of cognitive effort in decision-making, but the ADMF was later extended to include the role of emotion and goals (desired outcomes of a decision), as these can greatly affect decision-making.

Choice goals framework for decision-making

There are several important factors when deciding between available choices:

- maximizing accuracy of decision-making
- minimizing cognitive effort
- minimizing negative emotions while making decisions and afterwards
- maximizing the ease of justifying a choice to yourself and others.

The importance of these factors varies with different choice-making situations. For example, if it is important to be able to justify a decision, then this may lead to using a decision-making strategy that clearly shows the similarities and differences between available options.

When decision-making involves negative emotions, simpler decision-making strategies are often selected that lead to cognitive performance being worsened through decisions taking longer to arrive at and by an increased risk of error in choice occurring.

Negative emotions can especially be aroused when a trade-off has to be made between two highly valued options; for example, painful surgery that may improve health versus poor health, but without enduring painful surgery. In such situations, individuals will often avoid decision-making strategies involving trade-offs, for example, making no decision at all. This is an example of emotion focused coping (see below).

Coping theory

Folkman & Lazarus (1988) argue that individuals respond to negative emotions in one of two ways:

1 *Problem focused coping* – negative emotions are seen as indicating how important a decision is to an individual, so they concentrate on making the best choice and avoid being influenced by the experience of negative emotions.

2 *Emotion focused coping* – an individual focuses more on minimizing negative emotions, rather than the quality of decision-making; for example, refusing to make a choice, getting someone else to make the choice, avoiding the distressing aspects of a choice, making a choice that is easier to justify, and so on. Negative emotions can be generated when trade-offs between two desirable options have to be made; for example, whether to allow fracking, which may have the desirable outcome of generating money for a community, but may have the negative outcome of damaging the environment.

In this case an individual might try to get someone else to make the choice, or put off making the choice.

▨ Research

- **Payne *et al.* (1988)** got 16 participants to choose between sets of gambling options, with each set containing four options and each option having four possible outcomes that ranged from winning 1 cent to $9.99. In condition one, participants could take as long as they liked to reach a decision, while in condition two they only had 15 seconds. It was found that, as expected, when under time pressure participants selected less available information to consider and spent less time considering this information than when they had limitless time. Participants also used processing strategies (heuristics) that focused on what they perceived as the most important aspects of available information. This supports the idea that people vary their decision-making strategies in response to environmental conditions, for example time constraints.

- **Payne (1976)** found, when getting participants to make choices between flats to rent on a number of important aspects, such as price, size and location, when a choice had to be made between two options, participants considered information relating to more aspects than when a decision had to be made between several flats. When choosing between several flats, decision strategies were used that eliminated possible choices as quickly as possible. This illustrates that thought processes concerned with decision-making vary with task complexity.

- **Hancock & Warm (1989)** reported that negative emotions associated with choice decisions damaged cognitive performance, with decisions taking longer to make and more chance of errors in choice occurring. This illustrates the harmful influence that negative emotions can have on decision-making, as stated by the ADMF.

- **Bettman *et al.* (1998)** found that when the most important aspect of a decision was being able to justify that decision, it led to the use of decision-making strategies based upon easily viewable and explicable options, a strategy known as relational heuristics. This supports the central idea behind the choice goals framework for decision-making that decision-making strategies vary according to which factor is seen as most important when making a decision.

- **Schwartz *et al.* (2002)** reported that satisficers were people who will select the first option they find that meets their threshold for acceptability (one that is 'good enough'), not necessarily the best option. Satisficers were also unlikely to experience regret if they later encountered a better option. Maximizers, however, were individuals who were motivated to consider all options in order to select the best one and so were often reluctant to commit to choices and worried if they had made the right choice. This suggests that decision-making style is related to individual differences in personality.

Strengthen your learning

1 Outline the information-processing approach to thinking and decision-making.

2 Briefly describe, in terms of its main features, the adaptive decision maker framework.

3 What are heuristics?

4 Explain the following heuristics:
 a lexographic strategy
 b satisficing strategy for decisions
 c majority of confirming decisions
 d elimination by aspects.

5 What is meant by decision task variables?

6 Outline the choice goals framework for decision-making.

7 Explain the difference between problem-focused and emotion-focused coping strategies.

8 Summarize what research has suggested about the ADMF.

■ Dual process model

'Those who play badminton well make decisions quickly.'
Dmitry Medvedev

FOCUS ON...

- System 1 thought as an intuitive, unconscious means of thinking.
- System 2 thought as an analytical, conscious means of thinking.
- The interaction between System 1 and System 2 thought in decision-making.
- What research has suggested about the dual process model (DPM).

Part of the IPA, the dual process model (DPM) sees thinking as occurring on a continuum, from System 1 (intuitive mainly unconscious) through to System 2 (analytic, controllable, conscious) thought. The IPA was initially focused more on System 2 thinking, but now also focuses on the affect System 1 thinking has upon System 2 thinking when making decisions.

System 1 thinking occurs without the use of language and gives a feeling of certainty. It permits quick, automatic decision-making that involves little cognitive effort. System 1 thinking generally occurs when an individual has to make a decision quickly or cannot expend much cognitive effort on a decision, as cognitive energy is simultaneously being used elsewhere (like when paying attention to driving a car and being asked to make a decision about food choices). System 2 thinking, however, is limited by working memory, is rule based, develops with age, uses language in its operation and does not necessarily give feelings of certainty. System 2 thinking involves higher-level information processing activities that require attention and which characterize most decision-making, but System 1 thinking, which occurs below the level of consciousness, is seen as having an effect on System 2 thinking.

The correction model argues that initial decisions occur quickly through System 1 thinking, with this decision either being expressed immediately, or confirmed/corrected by System 2 thinking. In this way, System 2 thinking is seen as a check upon System 1 thinking.

Research has surprisingly suggested that unconscious thought (System 1) produces better decisions compared to conscious thought (System 2). This may be because unconscious thought is an active (ever-changing) process that organizes information in memory in 'clusters' that relate to a specific choice option and which clearly separate out different choice options from each other.

Research

- **Dijksterhuis (2004)** got 63 participants to individually consider 12 pieces of information (such as location, size, cost, etc.) about four possible flats to rent (48 pieces of information in total). Flat B was the most attractive, having eight positive aspects and four negative aspects, while Flat D was the least attractive with four positive and eight negative aspects. Flats A and C, were of middling attractiveness. In the immediate-decision condition participants had to give an instant decision, while in the conscious-thought condition participants had three minutes to consider the information before making a decision. In the unconscious-thought condition, participants had three minutes before making a choice, but had to perform a distractor activity to stop them thinking about the information. Participants in the immediate-decision and considered-thought conditions made poorer selections than those in the unconscious-thought condition. This supports the idea that unconscious thinking leads to the best decisions, as unconscious thought is an active process that leads to information in memory about choice options being arranged in a more clearly separate and organized fashion.

- **Ares *et al.* (2013)** got 71 participants to choose yoghurt pots from information printed on labels concerning nutrition, fat, sugar, etc. levels. There were eight choices to make, with labels appearing in pairs on a computer screen. Eye movements were tracked during this process. It was found that participants who used System 2 thinking searched through more information in a more analytical way than those using System 1 thinking. This highlights how there are individual differences in the way in which thinking and decision-making occurs.

YOU ARE THE RESEARCHER

Test out System 1 and 2 thinking by getting participants to consider eight pieces of information (such as price, comfort, durability, etc.) about four pairs of trainers. One pair should be superior in having six positive pieces of information and two negative pieces of information. One pair should be inferior in having only two positive pieces of information, but six negative pieces. The other two pairs should have four positive and four negative pieces of information (not the same ones).

One group of participants has to make an immediate decision as to which pair they most favour, one group is given three minutes to make a decision, while a third group makes a decision after three minutes, but in that time has to perform simple maths questions (to distract them from thinking about the trainers).

See if your findings match those of **Dijksterhuis (2004)**. If so, then the third group should be better at selecting the superior trainers. Can you explain why?

Strengthen your learning

1 Explain what is meant by:
   a System 1 thinking
   b System 2 thinking.

2 Outline the correctional model.

3 Explain why System 1 thinking is seen as producing better decisions than System 2 thinking.

4 Summarize what research has suggested about the DPM.

Evaluation of the information processing approach upon thinking and decision-making

FOCUS ON...

- An assessment of thinking and decision-making in terms of the information processing approach.

TOK link

A common problem when studying psychological phenomena is that of defining such phenomena, like the decision choices people have, in an objectively measureable way. Often such definitions do not exist, or may be so artificial as to have little relevance to real life.

■ Much of the research into thinking and decision-making has involved laboratory experiments and while this method, due to its highly controlled nature, allows causality (cause and effect) relationships to be established, the method can be said to lack ecological validity, with the artificial nature of laboratory experiments meaning that results cannot necessarily be generalized to real-life situations. For instance, in experiments participants are often told what the important aspects of a decision-making choice are, while in real life, people would generate their own important aspects, with different ones for different individuals.

■ The experimental method also allows for single variables to be isolated and rigorously tested. However, such variables may not actually occur in isolation in real-life situations, with several variables, like the different important aspects of a decision-making choice, working together to affect the decision-making process.

■ Satisficers (individuals who accept the first acceptable option they encounter) tend not to experience regret if they later encounter a better option. Maximizers, however, are motivated to consider all options in order to select the best one and so are often reluctant to commit to choices and worry if they have made the right choice. This suggests that decision-making style is related to individual differences in personality.

■ There are, however, potential negative practical applications of research into the information processing approach. Knowledge gained could be used to exploit the thinking and decision-making processes of consumers by the advertising industry so that people form positive impressions of and buy certain products. Chartered psychologists, such as those belonging to the BPS and the American Psychological Association, are not supposed to use psychology for unethical purposes, such as the exploitation of others.

■ Models of thinking and decision-making allow psychologists to identify the reasons why humans do not necessarily make the most logical choices when making decisions, which leads to a greater understanding of the decision-making process.

■ Research into thinking and decision-making has also allowed psychologists to better understand how cognitive processes work in unison with each other, for example the role that memory and attention play in thinking and decision-making.

■ A criticism of the information processing approach is that it somewhat neglects the role of social influence in thinking and decision-making. For example, the important influence of conformity on decision-making. Research into minority influence has shown that, over time, the views of a persistent, committed minority group can greatly affect the thinking and decision-making of individuals, indeed to the point that such minority influence can become the majority viewpoint.

PSYCHOLOGY IN THE REAL WORLD

Research into the information processing approach, like that on the ADMF and the DPM, has practical applications in helping organizations, such as business and institutional groups, in reaching effective decisions. Individuals can be trained to use their thought processes to make logical choices, thus avoiding decisions that have a negative impact.

Another practical application of research into the IPA is in counselling and therapy. Many people with anxiety problems tend to be maximizers. Encouraging such individuals to use satisficing strategies when making decisions, where they accept the first acceptable option they encounter, can lead to them being less anxious about their decision-making and therefore more content in general.

TOK link

One way to evaluate a theory is to assess its contribution to real-world applications. Good theories should lead to effective practical applications. Therefore, theories of information processing, such as the ADMF and the DPM, can be considered valid, as they have produced useful practical applications (see 'Psychology in the real world' above).

Strengthen your learning

1 Provide an assessment of the information processing approach upon thinking and decision-making. Make sure you provide a balanced assessment by considering the approach in terms of its strengths and weaknesses.

■ Assessment check

1	Discuss models of memory.	(22 marks)
2	Evaluate one model of memory.	(22 marks)
3	To what extent do findings from one or more psychological studies related to schema theory support the understanding of thinking and decision-making.	(22 marks)
4	Discuss schema theory in relation to two cognitive processes.	(22 marks)
5	Consider what schema theory has informed about thinking and decision-making.	(22 marks)
6	Discuss schema processing in relation to top-down and bottom-up processing.	(22 marks)
7	Outline one study investigating schema theory.	(9 marks)
8	Evaluate one research study of one model of memory.	(9 marks)
9	Explain how schema theory affects perception.	(9 marks)

SECTION SUMMARY

■ The information processing approach sees humans as not generally making decisions in the most logical way.
■ Humans use heuristics as mental short-cuts to select and process information when making decisions.
■ The adaptive decision maker framework sees humans as making decisions by acquiring and evaluating information about possible choices.
■ Decisions are also affected by emotions, especially negative ones.
■ The dual process model sees thinking as a continuum ranging from System 1 to System 2 types of thought.

Reliability of cognitive processes

■ Reconstructive memory

'Memory is a complicated thing, related to truth, but not its twin.'
Barbara Kingsolver (2002)

FOCUS ON...

■ The reconstructive nature of memory due to the actions of schemas active at the time of recall.
■ The effects of misleading information and questions upon the accuracy of recall.
■ The effects of post-event information on the accuracy of recall.
■ The idea that recovered memories are confabulations, false memories believed to be true, that are actually products of the suggestive techniques of psychotherapists.
■ What research has suggested about the reconstructive nature of memory.
■ An assessment of the reliability of memory due to its reconstructive nature.

Reliability of memory – the extent to which memory produces consistent results.

Eyewitness testimony (EWT) – the recall of observers of events previously experienced.

(Material on the reliability of memory could also be used to answer exam questions on schema theory and memory.)

The **reliability of memory** especially interests psychologists due to its effects within the legal system.

The accuracy of judgements in court cases depends heavily on the reliability of **eyewitness testimony (EWT)**, which concerns what witnesses to events recall as having occurred, with decisions as to the guilt or innocence of those accused often reliant on such evidence. In 75 per cent of cases where people are found on the basis of DNA to have been wrongly convicted of crimes, the original guilty verdict was formed based on unreliable EWT.

Bartlett (1932) argued that memories are not accurate versions of events, but instead are reconstructed over time, influenced by active schemas, ready-made expectations based on previous experiences, moods, existing knowledge, contexts, attitudes and stereotypes. Schemas are used to interpret the world and fill in the gaps in knowledge. With EWT, events are not recalled as they happened, but are reconstructed from schemas active at the time of recall. For example, **Allport & Postman (1947)** (see page 63) found that participants who saw a picture of a black man and a white man arguing, where the white man had a knife and the black man was unarmed, often recalled the black man as brandishing the knife, as participants often held schemas about black people being aggressive and carrying weapons.

Inaccurate EWT can have severe repercussions. In 1984, American college student Jennifer Thompson (see page 43) was raped at knifepoint by a man who burst into her flat. During her ordeal Jennifer concentrated on every detail of her attacker so she could later accurately recall him. She was determined that if she lived, he would be caught and punished. Later that day she worked with police officers to compose an accurate sketch of the assailant. A few days later she identified Ronald Cotton as the rapist and picked him out of an identity parade. On the strength of her EWT Ronald Cotton was imprisoned; Jennifer was so sure of his guilt that she wanted him electrocuted, declaring that she would throw the switch herself. In 1995, after serving 11 years in prison, DNA evidence proved that Ronald Cotton was innocent and that it was another man, Bobby Poole (who was already in prison for another rape), who was guilty. Remarkably Jennifer and Ronald became close friends and now campaign against the unreliability of EWT.

There is the serious prospect that innocent people have been executed in the USA on the basis of unreliable EWT. More encouragingly, the 'Innocence Project' in America has helped to overturn the wrongful convictions through faulty EWT of 351 people. This is an important area for psychology to investigate, as there are such serious implications from unreliable EWT.

Reconstructions of memory can be influenced by several factors. Giving **misleading information** or asking **misleading questions** can 'suggest' to people that events occurred in a certain way, which is how that event is then recalled (see 'Classic study, Loftus & Palmer', below). Providing **post-event information** (misleading information added to an event after it has occurred) can lead to people remembering completely false elements of that event (see 'Contemporary study, Loftus & Pickrell', page 83). There is even the concept of false memory syndrome (FMS) (see also 'cognition and emotion', page 87). This concerns the Freudian concept of repressed memories, where traumatic events are seen as being 'hidden' in the unconscious mind. Recovered memory therapy is a controversial technique used by psychotherapists to retrieve such memories. However, research suggests that such memories are merely false reconstructions based on 'suggestions' given by a therapist. This is an example of confabulation, the spontaneous production of false memories that are believed to be true. Recovered memory syndrome is now banned as a therapeutic technique.

Misleading information/ questions – information or questions that suggest a desired answer.

Post-event information – misleading information added to an event after it has occurred.

KEY STUDY ## CLASSIC RESEARCH

'Reconstruction of automobile destruction: an example of the interaction between language and memory'
Loftus & Palmer (1974)

Elizabeth Loftus would go on to find fame based around research into EWT and the formation of false memories. In this early study she found that participants' memories of important details of an event witnessed on video could be influenced by the use of misleading questions.

Aim

To assess the extent to which participants' estimates of the speed of cars involved in accidents witnessed on video could be influenced by misleading questions.

Procedure

1 Experiment one: 45 university students were each shown seven video clips of car crashes. After each accident, participants wrote an account of what they could recall and answered specific questions, the 'key' question being to estimate the speed of the vehicles. There were five conditions (with nine participants in each condition), and the conditions varying through which verb was used in asking the key question.

Key question: About how fast were the cars going when they … each other?

The blank space was filled with 'contacted', 'hit', 'bumped', 'collided' or 'smashed'.

Participants' estimations of speed were then recorded.

2 Experiment two: 150 student participants viewed a video of a car crash. Of these, 50 were asked the key question with the word 'smashed' in it, 50 with the word 'hit' and a control group of 50 were not asked at all. One week later they were questioned about their memory of the event, with the key question being, did you see any broken glass? (There was none.)

The number of participants who recalled broken glass was then recorded.

Findings

The findings of experiment one and experiment two are shown in Tables 2.2 and Table 2.3.

Experiment one – estimated speed of cars in accident

Verb	Mean estimate of speed in miles per hour
Contacted	31.8
Hit	34.0
Bumped	38.1
Collided	39.3
Smashed	40.8

■ **Table 2.2** Findings of experiment one

As the intensity of the verb used in the key question increased, so did the estimation of the speed of the cars.

Experiment two – number of participants recalling broken glass

Answer	Smashed	Hit	Control
Yes	16	7	6
No	34	43	44

■ **Table 2.3** Findings of experiment two

Participants were twice as likely in the 'smashed' condition to recall the false memory of broken glass.

Conclusions

● Experiment one showed that misleading information in the form of leading questions can affect memory recall of eyewitnesses.

● Experiment two showed that misleading information in the form of post-event information can also affect memory recall of eyewitnesses.

● Both studies suggest that at recall misleading information is reconstructed with material from the original memory.

Evaluation

● The study is a laboratory experiment centred on an artificial task (watching videos) and, as such, lacks ecological validity (lacks relevance to real-life scenarios). Witnessing real car crashes would have much more of an emotional impact and thus would affect recall differently.

- The results may be due to demand characteristics, rather than genuine changes in memory; participants may have just given the answer they thought the researchers wanted, as suggested by which verb they heard in the key question.
- The researchers also found that more participants mistakenly remembered a week later seeing non-existent broken glass if they were originally given the verb 'smashed' (32 per cent) rather than 'hit' (14 per cent), which suggests that at recall, misleading information is reconstructed along with material from the original memory.

Research in focus

1 A limitation of **Loftus & Palmer's 1974** study is that demand characteristics may have caused the results. What are demand characteristics and how may they have occurred in this study?

2 How might including 'filler' questions as well as the 'key' question help reduce demand characteristics?

▨ Research

- **Bartlett (1932)** got participants to read 'The War of the Ghosts', a Navajo Indian story, which makes little sense to people of other cultures. Participants then had to either write down their memory of the story, which is then read by another participant and written down from memory, and so on, for a total of six or seven participants (serial reproduction), or the same participant read and wrote the story from memory about six or seven times (repeated reproduction). It was found that the story got increasingly shorter and changed to fit the viewpoints of the reader's cultural background. This supports the idea that memories are reconstructions based on schema; we remember what we think should have happened based on experience and knowledge rather than what actually happened.

- **Loftus (1975)** found that 17 per cent of participants who watched a film of a car ride and were asked, 'How fast was the car going when it passed the white barn?', when there was no barn, recalled seeing a barn one week later. This supports the idea that post-event information, where information is added after an event, affects recall.

- **Loftus & Pickrell (1995)** gave 24 participants aged 18 to 53 four stories about their childhoods provided by relatives: three of the stories were true, but one was false, involving being lost in a department store aged five then rescued by an elderly lady before being returned to their family. Participants were then asked what they could remember of these incidents and to report 'I do not remember this' if they had no recollection of an event. Sixty-eight per cent of true incidents were recalled and 29 per cent of the false ones, with details and clarity of false memories being lower than for true ones. The findings imply that false memories can be created from suggestion.

- **Kaplan & Manicavasagar (2001)** reviewed three case studies of FMS, finding that 'retrieved' memories were actually false and induced by therapy, giving support to the notion that false memories can be created by suggestion. The researchers also commented on the shattering consequences for families when such cases involve allegations of sexual abuse, and so on, highlighting the important role research can play in showing such claims to be false.

YOU ARE THE RESEARCHER

Design a study based on Bartlett's 'The War of the Ghosts' to investigate how schema can affect recall. You'll need to write a story that has no clear plot. Create some opportunities for participants to change the story using schema. For example, including a librarian who likes to go out clubbing and a racing car driver who is shy and retiring, as the librarian may then get recalled as shy and retiring, as that fits the typical view of librarians.

You will need about eight participants. Only tell the story to the first participant, who then tells it to the second participant and so on. The last participant writes down what they recall. How will you record and analyse your data?

▧ Evaluation

■ Much research into EWT is laboratory based, where inaccuracies in recall have only minimal consequences, plus witnessing real-life events also has more of an emotional impact. **Foster *et al.* (1994)** demonstrated that EWT was more accurate for real-life crimes than for simulations, supporting the notion that laboratory situations may not reflect real-life incidents.

■ It is unclear whether recall inaccuracies due to misleading information are due to genuine changes in memory or to demand characteristics. Also participants do not expect researchers to deliberately mislead them, so inaccurate recall is to be expected, as they believe researchers are telling the truth.

■ Misleading information only affects unimportant aspects of memory. Memory of important events is not easily distorted. Also information that is obviously misleading does not tend to lead to inaccurate recall.

KEY STUDY | # CONTEMPORARY RESEARCH

'Make my memory: How advertising can change our memories of the past'
Loftus & Pickrell (2003)

Motivated by their earlier success in creating false memories in individuals of being lost as a child in a shopping mall, Elizabeth Loftus and Jacqueline Pickrell were motivated to perform several studies centring on childhood memories of visits to Disneyland, an emotional experience that would presumably be remembered clearly. In this particular study, the researchers showed how both verbal and pictorial suggestions created false memories of meeting Bugs Bunny at Disneyland. An impossibility, as he is a Warner Brothers character.

Aims

1 To see whether false memories could be created through the use of suggestion.

2 To investigate whether autobiographical advertising can make memories become more consistent with images evoked in advertising.

Procedure

1 120 students who had visited Disneyland in childhood were divided into four groups and instructed to evaluate advertising copy, fill out questionnaires and answer questions about a trip to Disneyland.

2 Group 1 read a fake Disneyland advertisement featuring no cartoon characters.

3 Group 2 read the fake advertisement featuring no cartoon characters and was exposed to a cardboard figure of Bugs Bunny placed in the interview room.

4 Group 3 read the fake Disneyland advertisement featuring Bugs Bunny.

5 Group 4 read the fake advertisement featuring Bugs Bunny and saw the cardboard figure of Bugs Bunny.

Findings

1 30 per cent of participants in group 3 and 40 per cent of participants in group 4 remembered or knew they had met Bugs Bunny when visiting Disneyland.

2 A ripple effect occurred whereby those exposed to misleading information concerning Bugs Bunny were more likely to relate Bugs Bunny to other things at Disneyland not suggested in the advertisement, such as seeing Bugs and Mickey Mouse together.

Conclusions

● Through the use of post-event information false memories can be created.

● Both verbal and pictorial suggestions can contribute to false memories.

● Memory is malleable and vulnerable to inaccuracy.

Evaluation

- The study can be considered superior to Loftus's famous study of car crashes, as it uses memory of a real-life event rather than something watched on video.
- The study shows the power of subtle association changes on memory.

PSYCHOLOGY IN THE REAL WORLD

Research into the impact of false eyewitness testimony has real-world implications. In Britain the **Devlin report (1976)** into the misidentification of suspects in criminal cases led to a change in the law, whereby a person cannot now be convicted of a crime by uncorroborated EWT (where only one person identifies someone as a criminal).

A practical application of post-event information is that of advertisers using nostalgic images to manufacture false positive memories of their products to get people to buy them.

RESEARCH IN FOCUS

1 **Loftus & Palmer's 1974** study lacks ecological validity. Explain what is meant by ecological validity and why this study is lacking in it.

2 However, **Loftus & Pickrell's 2003** study can be said to have ecological validity. Explain why this is so.

Strengthen your learning

1 Explain why Bartlett thought memories were reconstructions, rather than accurate versions of events.

2 What kind of serious consequences can occur because of unreliable EWT?

3 Explain how i) misleading information/questions, ii) post-event information, and iii) false memory syndrome can affect the accuracy of memory.

4 For both Loftus & Palmer's (1974) and Loftus and Pickrell's (2003) studies of memory, state in your own words the:
   a aim(s)
   b procedure
   c findings
   d conclusions
   e two evaluative points.

5 Summarize what other research has suggested about the accuracy of memory.

6 What other evaluative points can be made about **reconstructive memory**?

Reconstructive memory – the phenomenon by which memories are not accurate versions of events experienced, but instead are built from schemas active at the time of recall.

■ Cognitive biases in thinking and decision-making

'Go in the direction your head is pointed in.'
Jung Chang

FOCUS ON...

- How heuristics contain cognitive biases that negatively affect decision-making.
- Different types of cognitive bias and the ways in which they exert an influence upon thinking and decision-making.
- What research suggests about the role of cognitive bias on decision-making.
- Assessment of the influence of cognitive bias.
- An assessment of the reliability of decision-making due to the influence of cognitive bias.

Cognitive biases – illogical, systematic errors in thinking that negatively affect decision-making.

Evolution has equipped humans with a range of cognitive skills to deal effectively with the environments they find themselves in. These include heuristics (mental short-cuts) that allow individuals to make quick decisions when deeper analysis is not possible. However, such thinking strategies are irrational as they contain **cognitive biases** (illogical, systematic errors in thinking that negatively affect decision-making). There are several ways in which cognitive biases can exert an influence on thinking and decision-making:

■ *Framing effects* – how a situation is perceived can affect the way in which a decision will be made; for example, in positions of loss or gain, like when gambling. If an individual perceives themselves as in a position of gain (having previously won a bet) they may have a reduced chance of taking risks (such as then making a large bet or betting on an unlikely outcome for a big gain). If they perceive themselves in a position of loss (having previously lost a bet) they may take risks to recover losses.

■ *Use of information* – how information is used can be biased in several ways. Information that is easily available may be paid more attention to, while information which is easily memorable (usually because it has an emotional or personal connection) is seen as more important. Also, information that displays an individual in a positive way will be favoured (**self-serving bias**), as will information that supports an established belief (**confirmation bias**); for example, an individual with certain political views may seek out the opinions of others with similar views, which only has the effect of them backing up that person's views.

■ *Judgement* – due to the sheer amount of sensory information around us, humans have to be selective in what they pay attention to. However, this occurs in a biased way for two reasons. First, we like to be confident in our judgements and this leads to us not paying attention to any potential sources of uncertainty. Any potentially problematic or worrying information tends to get ignored. Secondly, there is **insufficient anchoring judgement**, which involves not updating our decisions as new information becomes available. Once an initial judgement has been made, it acts as a 'mental anchor', a source of resistance to our changing a decision. This leads to our ignoring any information that is inconsistent with the original judgement.

■ *Post-decision evaluation* – as maintenance of self-esteem (self-value) is important to us, we do not pay attention to information that may show us in a negative way. This involves **fundamental attribution bias**, a tendency to see favourable outcomes as being a result of actions under our control and unfavourable outcomes as being due to factors not under our control. This form of bias therefore helps protect us against loss of self-esteem. Additionally, humans like to feel they have influence over external events, so we distort our understanding of such events so that we believe we have more control over them than we really do. This **illusion of control** can lead to superstitions, like believing that if you wear your 'lucky' yellow pants then your football team will win. This leads to our underestimating how poor our decisions might be and prevents us from learning from experience, due to our ignoring information that suggests we are not in control of events. **Hindsight bias**, sometimes known as the *I-knew-it-all-along effect*, is the phenomenon to see an event as having been predictable, even though there was no information for predicting this occurrence at all.

■ Research

■ **Marsh & Hanlon (2007)** gave two groups of behavioural biologists differing sets of expectations about salamander (lizard-like creatures) behaviour and then got them to observe and record salamander behaviour from real-life and videotaped examples. It was found that expectations did bias observations, demonstrating the effect of confirmation bias, even among experts in a field. Additional support came from **Brochet *et al.* (2001)** who gave 54 expert wine tasters an array of white wines, which they described correctly as 'fresh', 'honeyed', and so on. They then gave them an array of red wines to taste, some of which were actually white wines, doctored to look red by the addition of an odourless, tasteless additive. No experts spotted the fraud and described the white wines in terms that applied to red wines, such as 'intense', 'spicy', and so on. The colour had created an expectation that led to confirmation bias.

■ **Rahman & Crouch (2015)** divided participants into two conditions. In each condition participants had to choose between two options of booking a flight. In the first (*gain-framed*) condition participants had the option of either paying two months in advance and saving $300 off the price, or paying one week in advance with a 50 per cent chance of saving

---

Self-serving bias – favouring information that displays oneself in a favourable way.

Confirmation bias – favouring information that supports an established belief.

Insufficient anchoring judgement – the tendency to not update decisions as new information becomes available.

Fundamental attribution bias – the tendency to see favourable outcomes as being a result of actions under our control and unfavourable outcomes as being due to factors not under our control.

Illusion of control – the idea that people's understanding of a situation is illogical in order for them to believe they can influence external events.

Hindsight bias – the tendency to see an event as having been predictable, even though there was no information for predicting this occurrence at all.

nothing off the normal price or a 50 per cent chance (if demand is low) of saving $600. In the second (loss-framed) condition participants had the option of booking two months in advance and losing $300 of the maximum possible discount (which was $600) or paying one week in advance and having a 50 per cent chance of losing all the maximum possible discount or a 50 per cent chance (if demand was low) of losing none of the maximum possible discount. Results showed that in the gain-framed condition, 73 per cent chose the riskless (pay two months in advance) option and 22 per cent the risky (pay a week in advance) option, while in the risk-framed condition 44 per cent chose the riskless option and 46 per cent the risky option. The findings thus support the idea of framing effects, where individuals in a position of gain will have a reduced chance of taking risks, while those in a position of loss will have an increased chance of taking risks.

■ **Brandt *et al.* (1975)** got teachers to believe they were giving lessons to a non-existent student (apparently hidden behind a screen). When teachers were told the student did well on a test of the material taught, the teachers generally attributed this success to their personal teaching skills, while when the student scored badly, the teachers attributed this to the poor quality of the student. This supports the idea of a self-serving bias that information which displays an individual in a positive way will be favoured.

■ **Fluke *et al.* (2010)** investigated post-decision evaluation, finding from questionnaires done by 200 students that the main reason for a belief in superstitions was to gain control over uncertain situations. This supports the idea of an illusion of control, where people's understanding of a situation is illogical in order for them to believe they can influence external events.

▧ Evaluation

■ Studies of bias often use artificial laboratory situations and thus may suffer from a lack of ecological validity, producing results that do not apply to real life. For example, **Lawson & McKinnon (1999)** report that in studies of self-serving bias, attributional bias is much less evident when real classroom situations are used, rather than when false laboratory situations using deception are used. This suggests that researchers should use real-life scenarios more in order to produce realistic results.

■ People who hold paranormal beliefs – for instance, that psychic forces exist, such as telekinesis (the ability to move objects with your mind) – often have an illusion of control; for example, that they have skill in picking winning lottery numbers. They also often indulge in confirmatory bias, where they over-focus on information that confirms their beliefs, such as focusing on parts of their horoscope that come true and ignoring elements that do not.

■ Studies that involve the use of deception, like those used to investigate self-serving bias, can be seen as unethical. When studies involve deception it is not possible to gain informed consent. The use of debriefing and the right to withdraw can go some way to reducing the effects of deception, but do not take away from the stress such deception may initially cause to participants.

PSYCHOLOGY IN THE REAL WORLD

Cognitive bias in decision-making can have serious consequences. It has been argued that the financial crash of 2008 was at least partly due to illogical decisions taken through cognitive biases of financiers.

Cognitive biases negatively affect jury decisions so that wrongful convictions occur (or guilty people are found innocent). This is why some argue that legal decisions should be made by judges who are trained to avoid cognitive biases and not juries whose decisions may be illogical and thus wrong.

Bookies (people who take bets from people) get rich as they exploit the cognitive biases individuals make when placing bets. The odds they offer on horse racing do not necessarily reflect the actual chances individual horses have of winning. For example, by the last race of a meet, most punters (people who bet) will have lost money, so the bookies set odds that centre on the fact that most punters will want to try and win their losses back, for instance by shortening the odds on favourites to win and lengthening the odds on less-fancied horses to win.

Research in focus

Brochet's *et al.* 2002 experiment assessed whether wine experts would be fooled by white wine dyed red. What was the purpose, therefore, of getting them to rate genuine white wines first?

YOU ARE THE RESEARCHER

Test out **Brochet *et al.*'s 2001** study findings by carrying out an experiment to see whether participants would perceive lemonade as cola if they expected it to be so.

Get participants to sip genuine lemonade and select from a list of adjectives (you will need to draw some up) describing the taste. Repeat the procedure, but with lemonade disguised as cola (you will need a tasteless additive that makes the lemonade cola-coloured). If perception is altered by confirmation bias, the adjectives selected for the disguised lemonade should be different from ones selected for the real lemonade.

Why do you need to ask participants to rate real lemonade as well as the fake lemonade?

In what order would you present the drinks to participants to avoid bias?

What ethical considerations are there in this study, and how would you deal with them?

Strengthen your learning

1 Explain what is meant by cognitive bias.

2 Explain how cognitive biases can influence thinking and decision-making through:
   a framing effects
   b use of information, including: i) self-serving bias, and ii) confirmation bias
   c judgement, including: i) potential sources of uncertainty, and ii) insufficient anchoring
   d post-decision evaluation, including: i) fundamental attribution bias, ii) illusion of control, and iii) hindsight bias.

3 Summarize what research has suggested about cognitive biases in thinking and decision-making.

4 What other evaluative points can be made about cognitive biases in thinking and decision-making?

SECTION SUMMARY

- Memory is reconstructive due to the action of schemas active at the time of recall.
- Memory can be affected by misleading information/questions as well as post-event information.
- Cognitive biases are illogical errors in thinking that negatively affect decision-making.
- Humans tend to portray illogical understanding of events in order to believe they can influence external events.

■ Assessment check

1	Discuss the reliability of one cognitive process.	(22 marks)
2	Outline reconstructive memory. Evaluate reconstructive memory with reference to studies.	(22 marks)
3	Outline and evaluate the reliability of cognitive processes in relation to biases in thinking and decision-making.	(22 marks)
4	Evaluate the reliability of two cognitive processes.	(22 marks)
5	Outline the reliability of reconstructive memory.	(9 marks)
6	Describe one study relevant to the reliability of cognitive processes.	(9 marks)
7	Evaluate biases in thinking and decision-making by reference to one or more studies.	(9 marks)

Emotion and cognition

FOCUS ON...

- The evolutionary nature of emotion.
- Methods used to study the influence of emotion on cognitive processes.
- Lazarus's cognitive appraisal theory as an explanation of emotion.
- What research suggests about Lazarus's cognitive appraisal theory.
- Strengths and weaknesses of Lazarus's cognitive appraisal theory.
- What research suggests about the effect of schema upon perception through emotional factors.
- An assessment of the effect of schema upon perception through emotional factors.

IN THE NEWS

Ψ The Psychological Enquirer

DISCOVERING 'REPRESSED' MEMORIES

■ **Figure 2.13**
Are 'repressed memories' real or false?

In 1989, Laura B's sister, Amy, claimed to have discovered 'repressed' memories of sexual abuse by her own father, Joel Hungerford, when she was young. Laura B then attended 100 sessions of psychotherapy over nine months, often with her sister, building up a close relationship with her therapist.

Five 'memories' of abuse were recovered that Laura B had no previous recollection of. These 'memories' would often start as unpleasant feelings (such as a dream of people walking in on her when on the toilet and feeling uncomfortable with it), which the therapist would then enlarge on through questioning; for example, 'do you want to find out where that bathroom is?' Attempts to visualize the incident would occur and eventually actual sexual abuse by her father would be 'remembered', including being raped with a gun when a little girl. Laura B recalled the abuse continuing until two days before her wedding. These revelations were then reported to the police and charges brought against her father. Her sisters also broke off all contact with their father.

But Joel Hungerford was a lot luckier than many who had been in his position; in 1995 the Supreme Court of New Hampshire ruled that the recovered memories were not admissible as evidence, due to their being 'not scientifically reliable'. Joel then sued the psychotherapist. From this case came the term 'Hungerford's law', whereby accusations involving recovered memories can only be heard in court if they pass strict criteria to ensure their validity. The problem with such memories is the often highly suggestive questioning and methods used by therapists (e.g. 'guided visualization'), leading to one accusation of them being a 'lobotomy for the modern age'. Before Joel Hungerford, many individuals, often loving fathers, had been publicly ruined and wrongly jailed for long periods over allegations of sexual abuse. Hundreds of accusers have subsequently withdrawn allegations of sexual abuse, many successfully suing their therapists. Emotion can often influence cognitive processes, like perception and memory, to be inaccurate due to the influence of schema, while cases like the Hungerford one suggest that repression, the 'burying' of emotionally distressing memories into the unconscious mind, may also be false.

'There can be no knowledge without emotion. To the cognition of the brain must be added the experience of the soul.'
Arnold Bennet

■ The influence of emotion on cognitive processes

Emotion – a state of mind determined by one's mood.

Emotion is a state of mind that is determined by one's mood. Emotions are seen as having evolved, as they have an adaptive survival value in helping shape human reactions to environmental stimuli. In prehistoric times individuals who showed the 'correct' emotional and behavioural responses (ones that helped them survive in life-and-death situations) would have survived to sexual maturity and passed on the genes for demonstrating such responses to their children. Over time, through the process of natural selection, the genes for these emotional and behavioural responses would have become more widespread throughout the population, leading to the possession by humans of the 'flight-or-fight' response (an innate reaction to flee or stand and fight in response to potentially harmful stimuli).

Theories of emotion have changed greatly over the years, with cognitive factors increasingly being seen as important in the experience of emotion. The experience of emotion can also be seen to have effects upon specific cognitive processes, such as perception, memory and decision-making.

■ Methods of study

Traditionally, the relationship between emotion and cognition has been investigated by the use of laboratory-based experiments, the scientific nature of cognitive psychology lending itself to such a study method. However, the rise of cognitive neuroscience (which seeks to identify the areas of the brain within which specific cognitive processes function) has seen the use of non-invasive scanning techniques, such as functional magnetic resonance imaging (fMRI) and positron emission topography (PET). For example, accidental damage to the human brain, such as through illness and physical injury, allows the cognitive and emotional effects of brain damage to be studied and localized to specific brain structures.

Amygdala – brain area associated with the influence of emotion on cognitive processes.

Scanning techniques have shown that the brain area most associated with emotional memory is the **amygdala**, which seems to be involved in assessing the emotional impact of events and, because of its involvement in processing sensory information, also seems involved in assessing the impact of emotion on perception and decision-making. Brain scanning also suggests that the cerebellum, a brain area associated with coordinating motor skills, is involved in the memory of emotional events.

LINK TO THE BIOLOGICAL APPROACH

As cognitive processes are located within the physical structures of the brain, neuroimaging techniques, such as fMRI, PET and CAT scans, which show specific areas of brain activity during different types of information processing, are also used. For example, **D'Esposito et al. (1995)** used fMRI scans to find the prefrontal cortex is associated with the workings of the central executive, the controlling system of the working memory model. This informs us about the biological basis to memory. The use of research activities like these demonstrates the flexibility of cognitive psychology to combine with other levels of analysis, like the biological and sociocultural levels.

Self-report methods of questionnaires and interviews are also used, as they allow participants to directly report on subjective experiences of mental representations. For example, **Christianson & Hubinette (1993)** interviewed witnesses to a bank robbery to find that increased emotional arousal led to greater accuracy of memory recall. Although such data is useful, especially when complementing data drawn from more scientific methods, its validity is often dependent on how such self-reports are conducted, for example the degree of bias in data analysis.

Overall, cognitive psychology uses several research methods, often in combination with each other, reflecting the ability of the discipline to draw on different sources of investigation and different levels of analysis, like the biological and sociocultural ones, to further the understanding of mental processes.

■ Theories of emotion

Lazarus's cognitive appraisal theory (1982)

Early theories, such as the James-Lange, Cannon-Baird and Schachter & Singer theories of emotion, saw emotion as tied very much to physiological experience. However, Lazarus's theory was the first to see emotion as arising from an individual's interpretation and explanation of a particular event, even in the absence of physiological arousal. Lazarus identified two crucial factors in the cognitive aspects of emotion: first, the nature of cognitive appraisals that underlie separate emotional responses, for example fear, happiness, and so on; and secondly, the determining preceding conditions (those that come before) of those cognitive appraisals. Two types of appraisal methods are perceived as underpinning appraisal: primary appraisal, concerning the meaning and significance of an event to an individual; and secondary appraisal, concerning an individual's assessment of their ability to cope with the consequences of that event. Primary appraisal assesses the importance of an event, while secondary appraisal assesses coping mechanisms, which Lazarus divided into direct actions and cognitive reappraisal processes. Overall, Lazarus stresses the importance of cognition (thinking), as when we experience an event thoughts precede physiological arousal and the sensation of emotion (which occur simultaneously). Therefore, some cognitive processing must occur before an individual can experience an emotional response to an event.

Research

Speisman *et al.* (1964) found that when shown a film about Aboriginal circumcision, participants experienced the most physiological arousal when the traumatic element of the film was heightened through manipulation of the soundtrack, so that emphasis was focused on the jaggedness of the knife, pain of the boys, and so on. This suggests that the cognitive appraisal of what people think about a situation affects the level of arousal experienced, giving support to Lazarus's theory.

Evaluation

- **Zajonc (1984)** argued that although emotion and cognition are independent of each other and that cognition usually precedes emotion and physiological arousal, it is quite possible for emotion to be experienced without cognition occurring. For example, if suddenly confronted by a hissing snake, physiological reactions of increased heartrate, rapid breathing, and so on, would occur before the sensory data concerning the snake was cognitively processed. Zajonc showed that participants had a preference for pictures they had previously been shown subliminally (too quickly for conscious recognition to occur), even though they did not recall being shown them, than for pictures never seen before. This supports Zajonc's idea that emotion can occur without cognition.

- Lazarus counter-argues that human liking for stimuli experienced subliminally does not mean that such stimuli were not processed cognitively, as awareness does not necessarily equate with conscious thinking.

- Lazarus's theory has been superseded by more recent cognitive neuroscience explanations, which see emotion and cognition as controlled by separate, but interacting, brain systems. Emotional systems are seen as assessing the biological significance of external and internal stimuli, like thoughts and memories, with these assessments occurring before conscious awareness and with only the results of such assessments becoming conscious. Therefore, while all emotional processes have a cognitive component, not all cognition has an emotional component.

- **Le Doux & Brown (2017)** argue that research into cognitive neuroscience suggests that emotions are part of higher-order cognitive processes. They believe that the brain mechanisms which lead to the experience of conscious emotional feelings are fundamentally the same as those that lead to conscious perceptual experiences. Basically, emotions are not innately programmed into our brains, but are instead cognitive states generated from sensory information. This suggests emotion is a cognitive process in itself.

TOK link

Although psychologists conduct experimental research into the experience of emotion and attempt to identify the associated physiological features and cognitive processes underlying the phenomenon, there are many who would argue that emotional experience is beyond the scrutiny of scientific investigation.

Perceptual defence
– the process by which stimuli are not perceived or are distorted due to their threatening or offensive nature.

Emotion and perception

We have seen how perception can be biased by schema (see page 63), so that individuals perceive what they wish and expect to perceive based on previous experiences, expectations, cultural factors, and so on. Another way in which schemas affect perception is through emotional factors creating a bias to perceive (or not) certain features of incoming sensory data. An important factor here is **perceptual defence**, where emotionally threatening stimuli take longer to perceive.

Research

- **McGinnies (1949)** presented participants with eleven emotionally neutral words (e.g. 'apple') and seven emotionally threatening words (e.g. 'rape'), with each word presented for increasingly long durations until it was recognized, finding that emotionally threatening words took longer to recognize, which suggests that perceptual defence influences perception through emotional factors.

YOU ARE THE RESEARCHER

Test out the idea of perceptual defence in the following way.

For both conditions set out below, write out a list of words vertically (one above the other) on a sheet of paper (or you could use a computer screen). One of these words is the target word. Ask the participant to say out loud (or point to) the target word. Time how long this takes.

For one condition, use a neutral word, for example 'carrot'. Ask the participant to point to the word with six letters.

For the other condition, use an emotionally threatening word, for example 'cancer'. (Note that the words have the same number of letters and start with the same letter.)

Repeat the procedure for about ten pairs of neutral and emotionally threatening words (you will need to randomize the order of presentation), add up the total times for each condition and then calculate the mean times for each condition.

Consider what other measures you will need to take to avoid confounding variables.

If it takes longer to identify the emotionally threatening words, then you have evidence of perceptual defence.

- **Lazarus & McCleary (1951)** found that nonsense syllables presented so rapidly they could not consciously be perceived raised anxiety levels if previously paired with electric shocks, which suggests that emotional factors influence perception unconsciously.

- **Hardy & Legge (1968)** presented participants with an acoustic stimulus that increased in intensity, while emotive or neutral words were flashed subliminally on a screen, to find that the stimulus was detected at a higher intensity with the emotive than with the neutral words. This further supports the idea that perceptual defence affects perception.

- **Phelps et al. (2006)** manipulated emotion by briefly showing participants either fearful or neutral faces in various locations on a screen. An image then appeared briefly and participants selected in which direction it tilted. Participants performed best when the figure was paired with fearful faces, especially those in the same orientation as the tilted figure, which implies that emotion facilitates perception early in the processing system. **Zeelenberg & Bocanegra (2010)** further found that acoustic presentation of negative emotional words enhanced the perception of subsequent visually presented emotionally neutral target words, but impaired performance when they were presented visually. This suggests that emotional stimuli affect perception differently in different sensory modalities, perhaps due to the focusing of attention.

- **Brasel et al. (2006)** presented a picture, the central image of which was a woman leaping to her death, to assess the perception of 56 participants. An eye-tracker device showed that 88 per cent of participants fixated at least once on the falling woman, with the average fixation time being 25 per cent of exposure time. Only 35 per cent recalled the woman, however, with 30 per cent recalling no central image, though remembering other elements of the image in accurate

■ **Figure 2.14** The Genesee Hotel suicide picture

detail; 35 per cent used schematic processing to transform the image of the falling woman into something safe, like 'the image of an angel'. This again suggests that perceptual defence is used to restrict the perception of emotionally threatening events.

■ Evaluation

■ Findings from early studies of perceptual defence, like McGinnies (1949), may have occurred, as participants were too embarrassed to speak the words aloud. However, when **Bitterman & Kniffin (1953)** repeated the study, but with participants writing the words down instead of speaking them, no differences in recognition time were found, which suggests that perceptual defence is a valid concept.

■ When using emotionally threatening stimuli, such as the Genesee Hotel suicide picture (Figure 2.14), to assess perceptual defence, care should be taken not to psychologically harm participants, with fully informed consent being gained prior to participation and full debriefing afterwards.

■ The use of subliminal stimuli, which are presented too quickly for conscious recognition to occur, suggests that perceptual defence is a real phenomenon rather than a response bias, where participants are embarrassed to recognize such stimuli or are genuinely unfamiliar with them. However, the paradox here is how participants can selectively defend themselves against emotionally threatening stimuli, unless they have already consciously recognized them as threatening?

Strengthen your learning

1 Explain how evolution has shaped emotions.

2 How do brain scans contribute to the study of emotions?

3 Which brain areas are associated with the experience of emotions?

4 Outline Lazarus's cognitive appraisal theory.

5 Explain how Speisman *et al.*'s (1964) study supports Lazarus's theory.

6 Summarize evaluative points concerning Lazarus's theory.

7 What does Le Doux & Brown (2017) believe that research into emotions suggests?

8 How might schemas affect perception through emotional factors?

9 Explain what is meant by perceptual defence.

10 Summarize what research suggests about the effects on emotion of perception.

11 What other evaluative points can be made about the relationship between emotion and perception?

....
Confabulation – the spontaneous production of false memories, which are believed to be true.

Repression – a form of motivated forgetting where emotionally threatening memories are hidden in the unconscious mind to prevent feelings of anxiety.
....

'There are lots of people who mistake their imagination for their memory.'
Josh Billings (1860)

■ Emotion and memory

We have also seen previously how memory can be affected by schema, where individuals reconstruct memories according to which particular schemas they are using at the time of recall; for example, through misleading information/questions, post-event information, **confabulation**, and so on. Memory can also, though, be affected by emotional factors in a number of ways, such as through flashbulb memory, **repression** and contextual emotional effects. Emotion seems to affect memory at all stages of the process: encoding, storage and retrieval.

Emotionally arousing stimuli have also been seen to lead to amnesia, even though no physical damage to brain structures associated with memory have occurred. This can occur as retrograde amnesia, where memories occurring before a traumatic event are lost, or anterograde amnesia, where new memories cannot be created after experiencing an emotional event.

The effects of emotion upon memory as a process

Encoding

Encoding concerns the means by which information is represented in memory. The **cue-utilization theory** argues that high levels of emotion focus attention mainly on the emotionally arousing elements of an environment and so it is these elements that become encoded in memory and not the non-emotionally arousing elements. Emotional arousal may also increase the length of time attention is focused on emotionally arousing elements of an environment, which aids the encoding of such elements.

Storage

Storage relates to the amount of information that can be retained in memory. Emotional arousal can increase the consolidation of information in storage, making such memories longer lasting. This is not an immediate effect, as emotional arousal seems mainly to enhance memory after a delay in time, possibly because the hormonal processes involved in memory consolidation take a little time and because emotional experiences incur more elaboration (creating links between the new information and previously stored information).

Retrieval

Retrieval concerns the reconstruction of memories with this process influenced by contextual emotional effects, which relates to the degree of emotional similarity between the circumstances of encoding and the circumstances of retrieval, through either the **mood-congruence effect** or **mood-state dependent retrieval**. These effects occur because when information is encoded, an individual not only stores the sensory aspects of the information (what it looks like, sounds like, etc.), they also store their emotional state at that time.

The mood-congruence effect concerns the ability of individuals to retrieve information more easily when it has the same emotional content as their current emotional state.

Mood-state dependent retrieval concerns the ability of individuals to retrieve information more easily when their emotional state at the time of recall is similar to their emotional state at the time of encoding.

◼ Research

- ◼ **Loftus *et al.* (1987)** found that if a person is carrying a weapon, a witness to this focuses on the weapon rather than the person's face, negatively affecting their ability to recall facial details of the person. This 'weapons effect' supports the idea that emotion affects the encoding of memories by focusing attention on the emotionally arousing elements of a stimulus.

- ◼ **Ochsner (2000)** reviewed studies into the effects of emotion on encoding, to find that emotion does indeed focus attention onto the emotionally arousing elements of a stimulus, in line with Loftus's (1975) study, but also that emotion increases the length of time attention is focused on emotionally arousing elements, illustrating how this further strengthens the encoding of such elements.

- ◼ **LaBar & Phelps (1998)** got participants to rate emotionally arousing and neutral words, while their arousal levels were recorded by an arousal scale questionnaire and skin-conductance responses. Participants had heightened arousal when the words were presented, with recall of the words at that time poor. But they had a higher recall of the words one hour later, thus demonstrating how emotional arousal enhances memory over time.

- ◼ **Drace (2013)** subjected 38 female participants to positive, negative and neutral mood conditions (through the presentation of music and pictures) and then asked them to recall three personal memories. Mood was measured physiologically (through electromyography ratings) and by questionnaire, with memories rated from positive to negative by independent judges (who were unaware of which mood conditions participants had been subjected to). The results showed that more positive memories were recalled when in a positive mood and more negative memories when in a negative mood. This supports the idea of the mood-congruence effect, where individuals retrieve information more easily when it has the same emotional content as their current emotional state.

■ **Bower (1981)** reviewed studies of mood-state dependent retrieval, finding that participants' recall of word lists, personal experiences recorded in diaries and childhood experiences were related to the mood they were in at the time of recall. This supports the idea that people retrieve information more easily when their emotional state at the time of recall is similar to their emotional state at the time of encoding.

Evaluation

■ There has been some criticism of mood-state dependent memory being a product of confounding variables in artificial laboratory-based experiments. **Ucross (1987)** did a meta-analysis of studies, finding some support for this argument, for example that the phenomenon occurred more when participants were paid for taking part in a study, which suggests demand characteristics at work.

■ Focusing on emotionally threatening aspects of an experience makes evolutionary sense. There is an immediate survival value in doing so and remembering such aspects helps an individual be prepared for similar future situations.

■ Care should be taken with studies that manipulate participants' mood not to cause harm, a key ethical consideration when conducting research. The procedure of such studies should be fully stated when gaining informed consent, the right to withdraw emphasized and participants given a full debriefing afterwards to reduce the impact of any emotional stress.

PSYCHOLOGY IN THE REAL WORLD

Research into the effect of emotion on memory suggests several practical applications. For instance, emotional memories seem to be encoded best during sleep, so students could pair up material they need to learn for an exam with information that has an emotional impact just before going to sleep, in order to heighten recall of the exam-based information.

Emotional stimuli can also be used to facilitate better recall in people with amnesia, as emotional stimuli can often serve as effective retrieval cues to prompt the recall of apparently forgotten information.

Sundstrom (2011) found that giving objects to Alzheimer's patients as birthday presents improved their recall of such objects compared to just giving them the objects. This shows how the emotional arousal associated with a birthday can facilitate memory, suggesting the technique as a means of improving recall in people with the condition.

Flashbulb memory

Flashbulb memory – a strong, vivid memory of an event with a high emotional impact.

Brown & Kulik (1977) stated that important emotional events are stored in a complete and detailed manner that contains the circumstances and the emotional reaction, as well as the details of an event. They argued that when an emotional event occurs, there isn't time to analyse it properly, so a vivid memory of it is stored, so you can analyse and learn from it later. Such events may be shared by many, like a traumatic news event, or be personal, like the birth of your child. People tend to be confident their **flashbulb memories** are accurate, as they are so important to them, but research suggests that such memories may not be completely accurate.

Repression

Repression, also known as motivated forgetting, is a Freudian concept (see also 'Reconstructive memory' on page 79). Freud believed that traumatic events are so distressing that we store the memory of them in our unconscious mind, a part of the mind that we are unaware of, but which motivates conscious behaviour. There are some claims of research evidence for repression, though others disagree. The most controversial aspect of the concept is that of recovered memory therapy, a psychotherapeutic technique used to retrieve such memories. Research suggests that such memories are merely false reconstructions based on 'suggestions' given by a therapist.

Research

- **Hirst *et al.* (2011)** reported on memory surveys completed after ten days, and one, three and ten years, by about 200 participants, concerning their recall of the terrorist attacks in the USA on 11 September 2001. Participants recalled flashbulb memories (details of the event, emotional reactions, etc.) and were confident of their accuracy. However, compared to their memories taken after ten days, accuracy was reduced to 65 per cent after one year and 60 per cent after ten years. Memory was best for central facts (e.g. how many planes were involved) than minor facts. This gives support to flashbulb memory as a phenomenon, but suggests such memories are not completely accurate.

- **Karon & Widener (1997)** found that many Second World War veterans who suffered battlefield trauma repressed the memories and the resulting mental disturbance was only relieved by those memories being recovered in therapy, giving support to repression as an explanation of forgetting.

- **Holmes (1990)** reviewed 60 years of research into repression and did not find any solid evidence of the phenomenon, weakening support for repression being a valid explanation.

RESEARCH IN FOCUS

1 **Hirst *et al.*'s 2011** study used surveys. Explain why surveys are a self-report study method.

2 What other types of self-reports are there?

3 Although self-reports are relatively easy to conduct, they have their faults. Explain each of the following weaknesses:

    a leading questions   **b** socially desirability bias   **c** idealized answers.

4 What other strengths and weaknesses are there of the different types of self-report?

Evaluation

- Flashbulb memories are vulnerable to post-event information, incorrect information that is added to an event after it has occurred. This again suggests that flashbulb memories are not always completely accurate recollections, though individuals will believe they are due to their intense, vivid nature.

- **Deffenbacher (1983)** argued that moderate levels of emotional arousal improved the detail and accuracy of memory, but after an optimal (highest) point of arousal is reached, further increases in emotional arousal lead to a decline in recall. This suggests that it is the amount of emotional arousal that affects the quality of recall, not emotional arousal itself.

Emotion and decision-making

Emotion also has a strong role to play in the cognitive process of decision-making. Emotions, especially negative ones, can lead to changes in decision-making strategies that impact on the effectiveness of decisions made (see 'Role of emotions and goals in decision-making' on page 74).

Strengthen your learning

1 Explain how emotion can affect the:
    a encoding of memories; include comments on the cue-utilization theory in your answer
    b storage of memories
    c retrieval of memories; include comments in your answer on: i) mood-congruence effects and ii) mood-state dependent retrieval.

2 Summarize what research has suggested about the effect of emotion on the encoding, storage and retrieval of memories?

3 What other evaluative points can be made about the effect of emotion on the encoding, storage and retrieval of memories?

4 Explain what a) flashbulb memory and b) recovered memory therapy are.

5 Why could memories recovered from repression actually be false?

6 Summarize what research has suggested about flashbulb memory and repressed memories.

7 What other evaluative points can be made about flashbulb memory and repressed memories?

SECTION SUMMARY

■ Emotion is increasingly being seen as less of a physiological and more of a cognitive process.

■ The amygdala is the brain area most associated with the influence of emotion on cognitive processing.

■ Schemas affect perception through emotional factors creating a bias to perceive certain features of sensory information.

■ Memory can be affected by emotional factors at all stages of the process.

■ Flashbulb memories are representations of emotional events recalled in detail.

■ Repression is the Freudian concept that traumatic memories are hidden in the unconscious mind and can be recovered by psychotherapy, an idea that has little support.

■ Assessment check

1	Discuss the influence of emotion on two cognitive processes.	(22 marks)
2	Evaluate the effect of emotion on memory.	(22 marks)
3	Outline and evaluate the influence of emotion upon one cognitive process other than memory with reference to studies.	(22 marks)
4	Discuss what studies have suggested about the influence of emotion on cognitive processes.	(22 marks)
5	Outline one research study of the influence of emotion upon one cognitive process.	(9 marks)
6	Outline the influence of emotion on memory.	(9 marks)
7	Evaluate one or more studies of the influence of emotion upon one cognitive process, other than memory.	(9 marks)

Cognitive processing in the digital world

'It's been my policy to regard the internet not as an information highway, but as an electronic asylum full of babbling loonies.'
Mike Royko

FOCUS ON...

■ The nature of digital technologies (DTs) and their influence on cognitive processes.

■ The positive and negative effects of DTs on cognitive processes.

■ What research suggests about the positive and negative effects of DTs on cognitive processes.

■ An assessment of the positive and negative effects of DTs on cognitive processes.

....

Digital technology (DT) – electronic devices and systems that generate, process and store data.

Myth of multitasking – the false belief that humans can simultaneously perform cognitive tasks.

....

■ The influence of digital technology on cognitive processes

Digital technologies (DTs) consist of electronic devices and systems that generate, process and store data. DTs include social media, such as Facebook, online gaming, such as 'Minecraft', applications (apps) and mobile devices (such as smartphones). Such technologies are ever-changing, as the digital world tends to develop very quickly.

In recent years digital technology has come to greatly affect many individuals' lives, leading to the formation of what has been called the 'Information Society'. Psychologists are thus interested in how such technologies affect cognitive processes.

DTs affect a wide range of cognitive processes. Psychologists are interested in the effects they have on attention, especially the effects of multitasking (for example, using DTs in lectures). Indeed the **myth of multitasking,** which is the false belief that humans can simultaneously perform cognitive tasks, suggests that humans do not perform several tasks simultaneously, they just switch from one task to another very quickly, which expends cognitive energy and leads to errors being made. Cognitive psychologists are also interested in the effects of DTs on learning processes and memory.

| KEY STUDY | ## CONTEMPORARY RESEARCH |

'Google effects on memory: cognitive consequences of having information at our fingertips'.
Sparrow *et al.* (2011)

If you were asked how many countries have a flag of only one colour, would you start to think about flags or would you immediately go online to find the answer? People nowadays are so used to looking information up online that the researchers decided to investigate whether this has become a memory source in itself.

Aim
To assess:

1 Whether the internet has become an external memory system, motivated by a desire to acquire information.

2 Whether internal encoding of memory is focused more on where information can be found, rather than the information itself.

Procedure
Four laboratory experiments were conducted.

1 *Experiment one* – would participants be 'primed' to use a computer when they did not know the answer to a question? Participants answered either easy, or hard 'yes/no' questions. Then, on a separate task they were timed on how long it took them to say whether computer- or non-computer-related words were printed in blue or red ink.

2 *Experiment two* – would participants recall information they believed they could access online later on? Participants read 40 easy-to-remember statements of the type often found online; for example, 'an ostrich's eye is bigger than its brain'. They then had to type the statements into the computer to ensure they had been paid attention to. In one condition, participants believed the computer would erase the statements, while in a second condition participants believed the computer would retain them. Half the participants in each condition were explicitly asked to try and remember the information. All participants then had to write down as many statements as they could recall.

3 *Experiment three* – would participants recall where specifically to find information they believed would be available online? Participants read and typed out 30 easy-to-remember statements. For one-third of the questions participants received the message 'your entry has been saved', for another third of the questions they received the message 'your entry has been saved in folder X' (there were six different folders that were individually named), and for the final third of the statements participants received the message 'your entry has been erased'. Participants then did a recognition task of all 30 statements, but half had been altered slightly. Participants had to say whether or not the statements were the original ones, whether statements had been saved or erased and whether statements had been saved to a folder or not and, if so, which folder.

4 *Experiment four* – would participants recall where to find information more than the information itself? Participants again read and typed out easy-to-remember statements, which they believed were saved to one of six specific folders (as in experiment three). Participants then had ten minutes to write down as many statements as they could recall. They were then given an identifying feature of a statement and asked which folder it was saved in (e.g. 'which folder is the statement about the ostrich in?').

Results

1   *Experiment one* – computer-related words were read more quickly on hard questions than easy ones.

2   *Experiment two* – participants who thought the computer would erase the statements had the best recall. Being asked, or not, in advance to try and remember the information had no effect on recall.

3   *Experiment three* – participants recalled best those statements they believed had been erased. Participants also accurately recalled which statements had been saved and which had been saved to a folder, though they did not generally have good recall of which specific folder the information was in.

4   *Experiment four* – participants generally recalled the folders where statements were stored more than the statements themselves.

Conclusions

- When we do not know the answer to a question (i.e. when a question is hard) people seem to be primed to use a computer to find the answer (because in the study, when a question was hard, it took participants longer to identify the colour of non-computer-related words than computer-related words).

- When we believe we will be able to look something up online, we do not make the effort to remember it; we do not feel we need to internally encode the information.

- Believing we will not have access to information in the future improves memory of that information, whereas believing information has been saved externally (within a computer) increases memory of the fact that the information can be accessed.

- We do not generally recall specifically where external memories can be located (e.g. in which specific file, web page, etc.).

Evaluation

- Participants have recalled the folders where information was kept better in experiment four than experiment three, as in experiment four they received a memory cue (an identifying feature of the statement).

- Overall, it seems that when people expect the source of information, for example the internet, to remain available, they recall the source of the information, but not the information itself. In other words, the computer has become an external source of memory in itself – maybe human memory is adapting to digital technologies and, in doing so, is gaining the advantage of quick access to a vast range of information.

RESEARCH IN FOCUS

1   The aim of **Sparrow *et al.*'s (2011)** study was to see whether the internet has become an external memory system. Explain how an aim differs from a hypothesis.

2   For each of **Sparrow *et al.*'s** four experiments, construct a suitable:

   a   non-directional hypothesis   b   directional hypothesis   c   null hypothesis.

■ Research

Digital amnesia – the tendency for individuals to forget information that has been stored on digital devices.

Kaspersky laboratory international survey (2015) surveyed 6000 European participants aged 16 to 55, to find a phenomenon called **digital amnesia**: the tendency for all age groups and genders to forget information that has been stored on a digital device. Thirty-six per cent said they would use the internet rather than trying to remember something and 24 per cent immediately forget facts found online (on the basis they could find them again if necessary). Around 50 per cent of people admit they store digitally almost all important information they need to recall, which suggests digital devices are replacing autobiographical memory (memory for personal information).

The positive and negative effects of modern technology on cognitive processes

'The Internet has been a boon and a curse for teenagers.'
J.K. Rowling

Positive effects

There are some positive effects of DTs on cognitive processes, though only if DTs are used in specific ways. For example, DTs seem to work best when used by small groups rather than by individuals, as group usage stimulates deeper-level analysis of material than individual use does. DTs also seem to aid learning more when used in a short and focused way and can be especially beneficial to lower-attaining students and those with learning disorders or from disadvantaged backgrounds, as they can provide intensive support to aid learning. DTs seem to be most beneficial when used as a support for learning, rather than the sole means of learning, and in certain subjects, like mathematics, where deeper levels of cognitive processing may not be necessary. Overall, DTs improve learning if they are focused on assisting what is to be learned rather than being seen as a means of learning in themselves.

Research

- **Liao (2007)** conducted a meta-analysis of 29 studies that compared computer teaching versus traditional teaching in Taiwan. The results showed that computer teaching produced better test scores, but only when used in small-group rather than individual learning situations, which suggests DTs are effective learning tools when they encourage deeper-level cognitive processing through discussion.

- **Moran *et al.* (2008)** conducted a meta-analysis of 27 studies investigating the use of digital video in teaching, finding that the method led to students generally gaining better test scores than traditional methods of teaching, when used in a focused way over short periods of time. This suggests that DTs can be effective when used as a means of supporting learning, rather than a means of learning in themselves.

- **Lou (2001)** conducted a meta-analysis of 122 studies, involving 11,317 participants, into the use of DTs and the social context of learning, finding that (in line with Liao's 2007 study) DTs were an effective method of learning in small groups, rather than when used by individuals. It was also found that results were best when DTs were used with lower-attaining students, which supports the idea of DTs providing intensive support learning to those requiring it.

RESEARCH IN FOCUS

1 Liao's 2007, Moran *et al.*'s 2008 and Lou's 2001 studies are examples of meta-analyses. How is a meta-analysis conducted?

2 What is the main advantage of carrying out a meta-analysis?

3 What are the weaknesses of the method?

'Multi-tasking is the opportunity to screw up more than one thing at a time.'
Neaj Cram Notwal (2017)

Negative effects

Although DTs present new opportunities for enhanced learning, through use of the internet, and so on, concern has arisen that such technologies also have negative effects, for example increases in Attention Deficit Hyperactivity Disorder (ADHD) and Internet Addiction Disorder, as well as decreasing cognitive performance, by overloading visual working memory. Concern has also grown that younger individuals, who have grown up only knowing DTs, are increasingly unable to use other forms of perceptual media effectively, such as reading books and magazines.

The relatively recent growth of computer usage has led to changes in cognitive functioning. Use of computers can quickly lead to an overload of visual working memory and thus a decrease in an individual's cognitive performance.

DTs may also lead to individuals who are easily distracted from learning tasks and who possess short attention spans, with inferior writing skills, due to the predominant use in digital media of short snippets of information. This has a negative effect on the development of critical skills with students conditioned to give easy, quick answers rather than considered viewpoints. Students who engage in digital multitasking, such as accessing their phones or emails while in lectures, tend to get lower test scores.

The constant recording of information on digital devices makes individuals less likely to commit such information to LTM and can distract individuals from properly encoding information as it is experienced.

Interesting evidence has emerged that taking notes by pen and paper leads to higher-quality learning, as writing seems to facilitate more effective means of storing and organizing information in memory. Writing seems to enhance learning (compared to typing) as it allows the brain to receive feedback from motor actions that leave a more meaningful motor memory. This appears to help individuals to establish connections between reading and writing. It may also be that the longer time it takes to write by hand has a temporal (time related) effect that affects the learning process.

Overall, digital technology could be turning people into 'shallow thinkers'. When we actively recall information (think about the information) it helps to create a strong, detailed memory of that information. But passively recalling information (by constantly looking it up on the internet and thus not thinking deeply about it) does not lead to such strong, detailed memories and instead helps to create individuals who process information in a shallow, moment-to-moment fashion.

Research

- **Mayer & Moreno (1998)** got participants to watch a cartoon with the text presented visually or auditorily (by sound) and then tested them on their memory of the event. Performance was best when the cartoon was presented with text in an auditory form. This suggests that visual working memory is overloaded when materials are presented in the same sensory modality (e.g. visual), but multi-modal presentations do not incur such information processing overload (e.g. visual and auditory).

- **Roediger & Karpicke (2006)** assessed the degree to which taking a memory test improves memory of the knowledge being tested. Participants read some material and were then either repeatedly tested on their recall of the material, or allowed to reread the material for an equal number of times. All participants then took a final recall test five minutes, two days or one week later on. For those tested after five minutes, participants who had reread the material had better recall than those who had been repeatedly tested. However, for those tested two days or a week later these results were reversed; with those repeatedly tested having better recall than those who had reread the material. This shows how testing is an effective way of improving long-term memory of information and thus suggests that unless DTs similarly allow opportunities for rehearsal and revision, they can have a negative effect on learning.

- **Wood et al. (2012)** used student participants to compare the effects on learning of four digitally based multitasking activities (using a mobile phone, emailing, MSN messaging and Facebook) with three control activities (paper and pen note-taking, word-processed note-taking and using digital technology however they wished), while being given three lectures on research methods. At the end of each lecture, participants sat a test on the content of the lecture. Participants who did not use DTs during the lectures outscored those who did. This suggests that multitasking through the use of DTs has a negative effect on learning by diverting attention. This was supported by **Carr (2010)**, who found that students who used a laptop during a lecture to access internet information related to the lecture did worse in a test on the content of the lecture than those who used no form of DT during the lecture.

■ **Mueller & Oppenheimer (2014)** got participants to listen to a lecture and make notes while doing so, either on a laptop, or by pen and paper. The results of a test given half an hour later showed that both groups remembered the same number of facts, but the pen-and-paper group scored better for understanding of ideas, concepts, inferences and applications of the material presented, which suggests they had a deeper understanding of the topic. A second study copied the first study exactly, except that recall occurred a week later, allowing students to review their notes. The pen-and-paper group outscored the laptop group on all aspects. This supports the idea of typing as leading to 'mindless processing' and suggests that pen-and-paper writing is superior, as it prompts individuals to go beyond passively hearing and recording information.

TOK link

Psychological studies into the influence of DTs on cognitive processes provide a good example of how science works. Such research means explanations get regularly updated, leading to ever better understanding of phenomena – a process known as the search for verisimilitude: closeness to the truth.

YOU ARE THE RESEARCHER

Is multitasking a myth? Find out by getting participants to conduct this test.

For each participant :

Draw two horizontal lines on a piece of paper.

Time the participants as they write on one line 'I am a great multitasker' and on the other line write the numbers: '1, 2, 3, 4, 5, 6, 7, 8, 9, 10 ,11, 12 ,13, 14, 15, 16, 17, 18, 19, 20'.

It should take them about 20 seconds.

Now get the participants to multitask by drawing two more horizontal lines and time each participant, as they write the first letter 'I' on one line and then the number '1' on the next line, then the next letter in the sentence 'a' on the upper line, then the number '2' on the lower line, and so on, until both lines are complete.

If multitasking is a myth it will take participants a lot longer to complete this task. Can you explain why?

Evaluation

■ Studies of DTs in assisting learning are often focused on those subjects where DTs are used more, such as in mathematics and science. This means that the results from such studies may not be generalizable to other subjects, where DTs are less effective in the learning of required skills, such as critical thinking in history and psychology classes.

■ DTs are not effective or ineffective means of learning in themselves. It is whether they are used in a targeted, engaging and motivating way that is key to their providing a positive effect on cognitive processes.

■ Many schools and colleges are rushing headlong into trying to create digital learning environments in the belief that doing so will in itself provide positive effects on students' cognitive performance. However, research suggests that DTs are only effective when used in certain ways and possibly in certain subjects. Traditional learning methods, such as note-taking using pen and paper, are seen as more effective in some situations in stimulating deeper levels of processing. The best learning environment, therefore, is one that combines DTs with traditional learning methods in a targeted way.

■ As the respective positive and negative effects of DTs have now been identified, future research should be directed at identifying the ways in which DTs can enhance cognitive performance, especially as an aid to learning, and formulating strategies to lessen the negative impact of DTs, such as by reducing the use of multitasking involving DTs in learning environments.

◼ Methods used to study the interaction between DTs and cognitive processes

Meta-analyses involve looking at similar studies and pooling the data to look for recurrent themes that may not be so apparent when conducting individual studies. Meta-analyses are a useful tool in researching the impact of DTs, as many similar studies have often been done into research areas. For example, **Liao's (2007)** study comparing computer versus traditional learning methods in Taiwan was composed of results drawn from 29 similar studies performed on Taiwanese students.

The experimental method is also used to research the effect of DTs, as cognitive psychology adheres to the scientific method of rigorously testing selected variables under controlled conditions in order to establish causality (cause-and-effect relationships). For example, **Carr (2010)** used the experimental method to assess the effect on test scores (dependent variable) of either using or not using a laptop during lectures to access internet information on the content of the lecture (independent variable).

The self-report method of conducting surveys is also used to investigate the effect of DTs. Surveys gather factual information and opinions about specific research areas. This is especially useful as DTs and their usage develop at such a fast pace in the modern world that surveys are a very effective method of detecting changes and tracking the impact of such changes. For example, the **Kaspersky laboratory international survey (2015)** highlighted the new phenomenon of 'digital amnesia' where people can often forget information they have stored on digital devices and how digital devices may be replacing autobiographical memory.

Strengthen your learning

1 What are digital technologies? Give examples.

2 For Sparrow *et al.*'s (2011) study, in your own words state the:
   a aims
   b procedure
   c findings
   d conclusions
   e evaluative points.

3 What is meant by 'digital amnesia'?

4 Why does the Kaspersky laboratory international survey (2015) suggest that digital devices are replacing autobiographical memory?

5 Use research to summarize the positive and negative effects of digital technologies.

6 What other evaluative points can be made about the positive and negative effects of digital technologies?

7 Explain how a) meta-analyses, b) experiments, and c) self-reports can be used to investigate the interaction between digital technologies and cognitive processes.

SECTION SUMMARY

- Digital technologies are having an increasing influence on cognitive processing.
- Digital technologies can have positive effects if they are targeted in the right way.
- Digital technologies can negatively affect cognitive processing, which has implications for education.

◼ Assessment check

1	Discuss the influence of digital technology on cognitive processes.	(22 marks)
2	Outline and evaluate the positive and negative effects of digital technology on one or more cognitive processes.	(22 marks)
3	Discuss what studies have suggested about cognitive processing in the digital world.	(22 marks)
4	Evaluate the negative effects of digital technology on cognitive processes.	(22 marks)
5	Outline the positive influences of digital technology on one or more cognitive processes.	(9 marks)
6	Discuss one research study of the effect of digital technology on one cognitive process.	(9 marks)

3 Sociocultural approach to understanding behaviour

Introduction

The sociocultural approach to understanding behaviour originates from the belief that it is essential to look at context. Looking at the behaviour of an individual in isolation is an incomplete viewpoint. They are members of social groups such as their family, neighbourhood and society, membership of which makes their situation and context unique. The culture individuals live in and consequently the cultural influences upon them also mean that their behaviour is a reflection of that influence.

This sociocultural chapter will consider the ways in which the context and others in it can affect an individual. The two elements of effect from people and effect from culture are covered in this chapter, with the first section, 'The individual and the group', covering the social element. The culture aspect of the approach is covered in the sections entitled 'Cultural origins of behaviour and cognition', 'Cultural influences on individual attitudes, identity and behaviours' and finally (for HL students only) 'The influence of globalization on individual behaviour'.

■ Assumptions of the sociocultural approach to understanding behaviour

First, it is important to consider that there are three key assumptions of the sociocultural approach: individual behaviour is influenced by the environment we live in; we have a need to be connected to others; and each individual constructs their own self-concept and social self.

Environmental influence on an individual

The sociocultural approach focuses upon the context in which an individual lives and the potential influences on their behaviour. The emphasis is at the macro level, so the approach looks at the attitudes and ideologies of the culture. However, it also considers the environment such as the mass media, schools, type of environment (urban or country) and family circumstances. There are many other considerations which the approach considers, but a key one is the influence of others on what we do.

Sense of belonging and connectedness

The sociocultural approach believes that humans have a desire and need to be connected to others. This connectedness brings about a feeling of belonging. It is believed we are essentially social animals that like to function in groups. Being, and wishing to be, independent of others is rare for humans. Therefore, this is seen as a need or drive of an individual, and this affects behaviour and decision-making. Social relationships are important to well-being and we are driven to conform to others so that we fit in.

Construction of the self and social self

The development of the self is seen by the sociocultural approach to be constructed through our engagement with others. However, the 'others' are also influenced by the environment and therefore the culture we live within affects how we see ourselves. Our selves can differ from context to context (consider how different you are with friends compared to how you behave at home). This approach also believes that were we to live in another culture our self could be very different; the culture has a big influence on the self.

■ The contribution of research methods used in the sociocultural approach to understanding human behaviour

Observation (ethnography)

The sociocultural approach, due to its emphasis on context, often prefers naturalistic settings. If research is conducted in a real-world setting it is believed to have higher validity, especially if the focus is on the context in which the behaviour occurs. One of the key methodologies used is observation. It is believed that by observing an individual and how they interact with others in a natural setting, you can gain insight into their behaviour. Ethnography is also used. This is where the researcher becomes part of the context as this allows for them to understand and observe behaviours fully.

Interviews and focus groups

Interviews and focus groups are used in the sociocultural approach because they allow researchers to question the individual about what may be influencing them. Focus groups are also useful because essentially they provide an opportunity to observe and record the effect of others on an individual. This is a key aspect of the approach.

Case studies

The sociocultural approach focuses upon how an individual is influenced by their immediate environment and the culture too. This means that each individual has a very individual set of influences, as it is rare for all environments to be shared. Case studies are therefore useful to the approach because the detail they provide allows for a thorough analysis of all the various influences on an individual, or small groups of people.

■ Ethical considerations in the investigation of the sociocultural approach to understanding behaviour

Deception

As naturalistic settings are favoured by this approach, any manipulation of that environment can mean deception, as the individuals may not even be aware of the fact they are part of an experiment. Traditionally, this approach has provoked ethical debate as the experimentation of the 1950s and 1960s, in many cases, used deception. Examples include the experimentation of Asch (see page 114), which would not have been possible if the participants had not been deceived.

Lack of informed consent

Part of the issue with deception is the inability to give informed consent. In much early experimentation from this approach, deception was deemed necessary for the research to work. If participants were given informed consent, the aims of the research would have to be made apparent to them. This was not possible and so there were issues with consent. This can lead to psychological harm of an individual if they are not fully aware of what their research involvement requires them to do. The British Psychological Society deems it reasonable not to get full informed consent if the setting is not going to put the participant under any risk of harm. Therefore, researchers in using this approach must ensure that the level of risk is considered when planning research.

IN THE NEWS

Ψ The Psychological Enquirer

BECOMING A PIRATE GROUP

■ **Figure 3.1** The Edelweiss Pirates (Jean Jülich, first left)

In November 2011 the press reported on Jean Jülich, who had died aged 82. He was one of the last surviving Edelweiss Pirates – working-class German teenagers who resisted the Nazis during the Second World War. Distinctive by their long hair, checked shirts, Edelweiss badges and their love of jazz music, by 1944 5,000 'Pirates' were living as outlaws in bombed-out cities throughout Germany.

Throughout the war, Jean and his friends (both male and female) provided food and shelter to concentration-camp escapees, fugitive Jews and German army deserters. They attacked Hitler Youth patrols, derailed ammunition trains, vandalised weapons factories and sabotaged machinery.

■ **Figure 3.2** Jean Jülich as an older man

Jean was arrested at age 15, held in solitary confinement and tortured for four months. His 16-year-old friend, Barthel Schink, was hanged along with 11 other Pirates, in public, without trial, on orders from Heinrich Himmler. Jean survived beatings, starvation and typhus in a concentration camp until he was freed by American troops in 1945.

One popular explanation for the atrocities committed by the Nazis in the Second World War, such as the extermination of Jewish people and Gypsies, was that Germans had a personality defect that led them to unquestioningly obey and commit such horrific acts. However, the bravery of Jean and the Edelweiss Pirates in opposing the Nazis shows that not all Germans responded with blind obedience; indeed, there were groups of Pirates in most German cities.

A strong element of social influence can be seen in the hairstyle, clothing and music that the Pirates conformed to. They had their own social norms and a group identity. The actions of the teenagers also highlight how social influence can be resisted in some cases, but it is unquestionably the strength of being in a minority group, rather than alone, that helped them to fight their cause. It was not until 2005 that their actions against the Nazis were no longer officially seen as criminal acts.

The individual and the group

*'No man is an island, Entire of itself, Every man is a
piece of the continent, A part of the main…'*
'No man is an island', John Donne (1572–1631)

FOCUS ON…

- Social identity theory, including the role of in-groups and out-groups.
- Social cognitive theory, including modelling and observational learning.
- Self-efficacy and its effect on social cognition.
- Reciprocal determinism and its role in affecting the environment.
- Stereotypes.
- Socialization, including social and cultural learning.

Social identity theory

This theory considers group membership, and how it can become an essential part of our individual identity. A strong group identity promotes cohesiveness.

The theory works on the idea that an **in-group** will seek out negative aspects of an **out-group** in an effort to make their group appear superior. The membership of an in-group is part of an individual's identity and that sense of membership is implicated in their behaviour.

The theory is centred on the work of Tajfel and his team in the 1970s. Not only did they emphasize the idea that in-groups try to make themselves superior to others, but also that they will work together to raise their status if they feel undermined.

The strength of feeling in terms of the cohesiveness of the in-group is clearly important for social identity to have an effect on the behaviour of an individual. There are a multitude of groups to which an individual can belong.

> **In-group** – the group
> an individual belongs to.
>
> **Out-group** – the
> groups that an individual
> is not a member of.

In-group and out-group

Examples of in-groups and out-groups range from genders to football teams. Our ability to form in- and out-groups happens from childhood. Bullying is an example of an in-group undermining an out-group. Jane Elliott illustrated this in her 1968 research conducted as a primary school teacher. The day after Martin Luther King, an American black civil rights activist, was assassinated she found herself teaching an all-white class to whom the effects of the assassination were not personally salient. She decided to raise awareness of the assassination and to understand the effects on the 'out-group' of black children with her students. The following day she told her class, who were about eight years old, that the blue-eyed students were now better and cleverer than their brown-eyed peers and that they should not play together. She also said that the brown-eyed children had privileges withdrawn (such as only being able to drink water out of paper cups – not the water fountains). Within hours she was appalled to see that the blue-eyed children became arrogant and superior and treated the out-group (brown-eyed children) with disdain, even those with whom they had been close friends prior to the experiment. The activity was then reversed with similar effects. It seemed that the children were able to form in-groups and out-groups without issue, implying it is a natural human behaviour.

KEY STUDY **CLASSIC RESEARCH**

'Social categorization and intergroup behaviour'
Tajfel *et al.* (1971)

The membership of an in-group is known to affect identity, but to what extent? And how important do the groups need to be to affect behaviour?

Aim

Tajfel and colleagues were interested to see how, and to what extent, group membership is influential in behaviour and attitude change.

Procedure

1 Tajfel and the research team conducted experiments using the minimum group paradigm, a methodology designed to test for intergroup discrimination and in-group favouritism. Participants in the experiments were 14 to 15-year-old boys, all living in Bristol, UK. The boys were placed into one of two groups, with no real justification of why they were placed in those groups other than it being due to their preferring a particular painter (Klee or Kandinsky). The group placement was, in fact, random.

2 The researchers asked the boys to participate in some tasks. This required them to allocate points in different combinations to boys who were members of their own group (the in-group) or to boys in the other group (the out-group). The points were then converted to cash and the group was able to spend the money.

Results

1 The boys favoured their own group in most instances and usually allocated them more points than they did to members of the out-group.

2 However, interestingly, when the out-group stood to gain if they put more points on the table, the boys chose to sacrifice the points to their own group so that the other group could not benefit. This seemed to be so that the out-group was disadvantaged and the difference between the two groups maximized.

Conclusion

Their behaviour showed favouritism for their own group members and deliberately discriminated against the out-group. This showed the strength of group membership in influencing behaviour. A key point to remember when we consider these findings is that the original group membership was decided (or so the participants thought) on a trivial reason. The findings therefore show our tendency to align with members of social groups we belong to, and the findings also clearly demonstrate how willing we are to discriminate against other social groups, even when there has previously been no reason for hostility.

Evaluation

It should be borne in mind that while this experiment does show, very clearly, the perils of in-group membership, it cannot be merely group membership that can be seen as the cause of these findings. The prospect of financial gain is a big incentive and would have been a motivating factor for the favouritism/discrimination shown.

◼ Research

◼ **Rabellino *et al.* (2016)** examined how decision-making is affected when mediated by someone in the same group as you (in-group) or a different group (out-group). The researchers asked participants to play a game asking for decisions on whether to administer economic third-party punishment to other players. Groups were defined on their nationality: Chinese or Italian. They found that participants were more likely to administer third-party punishment if they felt there was unfair play towards one of their own nationality. This demonstrates that membership of a group can foster strong allegiance, even in a hypothetical game context.

■ Favouring in-group members over out-group members is also apparent in children. **Neto (2002)** asked 366 Portuguese children ranging from 10 to 11 years old to rate other Portuguese in terms of personality characteristics. These ratings were then compared to ratings of Brazilians and people from Cape Verde. Neto found that the children rated the Portuguese with a greater number of positive features and fewer negative features than the other two nationalities. There was a bias to their own in-group and no effect from gender, so the boys and girls reacted similarly. This demonstrates that in-groups are formed in childhood and favouritism to one's own in-group is evident in childhood.

■ **Hildebrand et al. (2013)** looked at the level of influence that in-group membership has on behaviour in adults and compared minority groups with majority groups. They gave homosexual men and heterosexual men questionnaires that asked about making purchasing decisions (i.e. shopping habits) and to whom they would listen to the most in terms of making those decisions. Participants were given a vignette about buying a pair of trainers and choosing between two pairs: one that they liked and one that the other person liked. The 'other person' could be a parent, a close friend or a boss/teacher. The researchers found that the homosexual men were more likely to be swayed in terms of choice by the close friend than heterosexual men and they also indicated that they would be less likely to be swayed by out-group members such as a boss or teacher. This supports the idea that when in a minority in-group the cohesiveness and influence is strong for members within that group.

Evaluation

■ History and the current day shows evidence of in- and out-groups and the effects on behaviour. The idea of social identity theory occurring in everyday life is therefore well supported. Examples are sports fans and nationality.

■ Sometimes in-groups have sub-groups which can cause different behaviours and attitudes between settings. For example, as an England fan at an international game, an individual will be standing with and in an 'in-group' with other English fans. In a league game the following week, however, they could support a local club and be separate from the opposing team's fans, even if they are all England fans. This suggests that the membership of groups is not straightforward.

■ Social identity theory has been very influential in terms of helping us understand the damage stereotypes can do and how prejudice can occur. Stereotypes are discussed in greater depth later in this chapter (see page 117). By understanding the cognition behind the behaviour, we gain greater insight into why conflict occurs.

■ The theory has a good practical application. Knowing that people make judgements made on group membership means that steps can be taken to reduce the prejudice, emphasizing similarities between individuals from different groups.

Strengthen your learning

1 Outline the three key features of the sociocultural approach to understanding behaviour.

2 Outline social identity theory, including reference to in-groups and out-groups.

3 Summarize what research studies have suggested about social identity theory.

4 Assess social identity theory in terms of its strengths and weaknesses

5 For Tajfel *et al.*'s classic 1971 social categorization and intergroup behaviour study, in your own words, state the:
   a aims
   b procedure
   c results
   d conclusions
   e evaluative points.

Social cognitive theory

Social cognition

Social cognition is defined as how individuals process information about the world including other humans, based on elements such as schemas and stereotypes.

Social cognitive theory suggests that behaviour is modelled by other members of a group and acquired through observation or imitation based on consequences of a behaviour. A key theoretical influence on this theory is the social learning theory of Bandura.

Social learning

The basic assumptions of this theory are that:

1 Behaviour is learned from the environment, so therefore it does not regard genetics as an influence on behaviour.

2 Behaviour is learned from observing others and the reinforcement or punishment they receive.

Social learning theory considers cognitive processes and, as such, is social cognition. The theory was conceived by Albert Bandura in the 1970s. Albert Bandura (born 1925) is a learning theorist. He argues that reinforcers and punishments experienced by other individuals and observed inform the individual of likely consequences and it is for the individual to decide whether their behaviour is affected by the potential consequences. Bandura's basic idea is that we learn behaviour by observing the positive and negative consequences of someone else's behaviour. This means we learn the behaviour vicariously, so we do not receive the reward or punishment, the person who is modelling the behaviour does.

The key processes in social learning are outlined below.

Imitation

This is the term used to describe when an individual observes a behaviour from a role model and copies it. The term imitation is more appropriate than copying as it is often not possible to copy the behaviour exactly, it is merely an imitation.

Identification

Identification is when an individual is influenced by another because they are in some way similar or wish to be like them. The 'model' is the person with whom they identify. There are many factors influencing the choice of model by someone. These include same gender and ethnicity, higher status and greater expertise. These need not all be present, but identification does not occur unless there is a reason.

Modelling

When someone is influential on an individual in some way, they are referred to in social learning theory as a model. If they then imitate that behaviour later it is called modelling the behaviour. This term is only used when referring to behaviour that is imitated.

Vicarious reinforcement is the term used to describe the reinforcement the observer sees the model receiving. They do not receive the reward themselves; they see someone else get it. This makes it vicarious reinforcement.

The role of mediating processes

We do not automatically observe the behaviour of a model and imitate it. There is some thought prior to imitation and this consideration is called 'mediational processes'. This occurs between observing the behaviour (stimulus) and imitating it, or not (response).

There are four mediational cognitive processes documented by **Bandura (1977)**: attention, retention, reproduction and motivation.

1 *Attention.* For a behaviour to be imitated it has to grab our attention. We observe many behaviours on a daily basis and many of these are not noteworthy. Attention is therefore pivotal in whether a behaviour has an influence on others copying it.

2   *Retention.* The behaviour may be noticed, but it is not always remembered, which obviously prevents imitation. It is important therefore that a memory of the behaviour is formed for it to be performed later by the observer. Much of social learning is not immediate so this process is especially vital in those cases. Even if the behaviour is reproduced shortly after seeing it, there needs to be a memory to refer to.

3   *Reproduction.* We see much behaviour on a daily basis that we would like to be able to imitate but that is not always possible. We are limited by our physical ability and, for that reason, even if we wish to reproduce the behaviour we cannot. This influences our decision of whether to try and imitate it, or not. Imagine the scenario of a 90-year-old lady (who struggles to walk) watching 'Dancing on Ice'. She may appreciate that the skill is a desirable one, but she will not attempt to imitate it because she physically cannot do it.

4   *Motivation.* The rewards and punishments that follow a behaviour will be considered by the observer. If the perceived rewards outweigh the perceived costs (if there are any) then the behaviour will be more likely to be imitated by the observer. If the vicarious reinforcement is not seen to be important enough to the observer then they will not imitate the behaviour.

For example, Aman notices his father spending a little time, every evening, when he gets home, completing press-ups (attention). He then hears his Mum complimenting his Dad on how he looks. He remembers these compliments (retention). He thinks he knows how to do press-ups and is confident about how to do them (reproduction). He wants to get compliments from his Mum and Dad too and wants to look grown up like his Dad (motivation). In all likelihood, Aman will imitate the behaviour.

KEY STUDY   CLASSIC RESEARCH

'The Bobo Doll experiment'
Bandura *et al.* (1961)

The theory of social learning was generated from work conducted by Bandura that looked at how individuals influence each other's behaviours. The key study was conducted by Bandura and colleagues in 1961 and is detailed here.

Aim

1   Bandura's study was designed to examine the role of a model on influencing an observer's behaviour. This had already been documented (**Bandura & Huston, 1961**) but Bandura was interested to find out if the influence continued once the role model was no longer present.

2   Together with the aim of examining the effect of continued influence of the model, another aim was to see if the sex of the model influenced same-sex and opposite-sex participants to a differing degree.

Procedure

1   There were 36 male and 36 female participants in the study. Their ages ranged from 37 to 69 months, and the mean age was 52 months (just over four years).

2   Two adults, a male and a female, served in the role of model for the experiment. There were eight experimental groups (each with six participants). Half the groups observed an aggressive role model and the other half saw non-aggressive behaviour from their role model. The groups were further subdivided by gender and whether the model was the same sex or opposite sex of the participants.

3 Participants were put into a room one at a time and observed the adult role model's behaviour (either aggressive or non-aggressive). In the room there was a Bobo doll (an inflatable doll that is weighted at the bottom), a hammer and other toys. The aggressive model had to hit the Bobo doll with the hammer and shout abuse at it at the same time. Examples of the abuse were 'Punch him in the nose', 'He sure is a tough fella' and 'Pow'.

4 After witnessing the behaviour for about ten minutes, participants were taken down the corridor to another room. Initially, there was aggression arousal where the participants were taken straight to a room where they were told they could not play with the toys as they were being saved for other children, but that they could play with the toys in a neighbouring room. They were then allowed to go into that room with the experimenter (about two minutes later) and play with any toys that they wanted.

5 The room contained a range of toys: a three-foot Bobo doll, a mallet, dart guns, etc. and 'non-aggressive toys' such as dolls, crayons and a plastic farm. The participants were observed in that room for 20 minutes and rated for the extent they imitated the behaviour they had just seen.

Results

The researchers found that the children who had observed aggressive behaviour acted more aggressively when observed and that boys acted more aggressively than girls. There was also a greater level of imitation of behaviour if the role model was the same gender as the child.

Conclusion

It seems there is a behavioural effect from observing aggressive behaviour and that this behaviour continues after a delay.

Evaluation

- The effects of social learning are still only short term in this experiment and it is difficult to see whether there are any long-term effects on the children.
- There are issues with interpreting the behaviour as all being influenced by social learning. Most people would hit a Bobo doll as it is designed for this purpose. This affects the validity of the experiment.

Research

- **Mesoudi (2016)** looked at variation of social learning within the global human population. They found that there was considerable variety globally. For example, some cultures teach social learning by using social learning, whereas others leave it to the individual to develop the skill. This has implications for cultural socialization and the way it occurs (see section on 'Enculturation' on page 129).

- Social learning does not only appear to happen in humans, but also in non-human animals too. **Schuetz et al. (2017)** looked at the extent to which horses can learn from humans by observation. They tested 24 horses for their ability to watch humans open up a feeding apparatus and learn how to execute the action themselves. Half the horses were shown how to open the apparatus and the other half were not. Researchers found that more (8/12) horses that had seen the demonstration were able to open the apparatus as opposed to the non-demonstration group (2/12). This seems to suggest that some non-human animals learn across species by observation.

- **Fitneva et al. (2013)** found through experimentation with children aged 4–6 years old that they preferred, in some cases, to observe and look rather than ask someone else a question. This was dependent on context, so even children who have no issues with communication may have a preference for social learning in some contexts. This shows how instinctive and comfortable children find social learning to be.

Evaluation of social learning theory

■ The social learning approach takes thought processes into account and acknowledges the role that they play in deciding if a behaviour is to be imitated or not. This combination of levels of sociocultural and cognitive explanations makes the theory stronger, as behaviours are rarely focused on one level of explanation.

■ The approach can successfully explain the initiation of certain behaviours, such as, for example, why someone would start smoking. Many other theories can explain why a behaviour continues, but not why it occurs initially. More information detailing the initiation of smoking and the addiction is given in Chapter 7, 'Health psychology', on page 305. You will see that the behaviourist and biological explanation cannot explain why smoking started initially.

■ There is not a full explanation for all behaviour. This is particularly the case when there is no apparent role model in the person's life to imitate for a given behaviour. This occurs, for example, in the case of psychopathic behaviour in just one individual in a family. Social learning cannot successfully explain who the behaviour is imitated from.

■ Social learning theorists use a variety of research methods in their work; this means that they can sometimes be criticized for being unscientific. Much of the behavioural aspect is observational research, the cognitive aspects are also difficult to test, and both of these methods are potentially less scientific. Usually, research only focuses on one aspect too, which is incomplete evidence.

YOU ARE THE RESEARCHER

As a researcher you are asked to examine whether role models affect the decision to start smoking. How might you do this? What cognitive processes in social learning theory would you need to test?

Reciprocal determinism

Reciprocal determinism – a term defined by Bandura as the way an individual affects their environment and vice versa.

Another important element of Bandura's work was his theory of **reciprocal determinism**. This theory explains how both the environment and an individual affect each other. Often, we see that someone is affected by the context they are in; indeed, this is a key consideration for the sociocultural approach. However, Bandura also argued that the individual can have an effect on their immediate environment. The effect works both ways.

He argued that the effect works on three levels: behavioural, cognitive and environmental. He called this triadic reciprocity, as the three all interlink to maintain a cycle of behaviour, thought and environment.

An example of this might be Malcolm, who does not like visiting his Auntie June because he thinks she is strict. Malcolm, upon arrival, may behave badly because he does not like being there, but, as a consequence of both his and Auntie June's dispositions and the behaviour, Auntie June is strict with him. The behaviour then becomes worse and so the cycle continues. Identifying the start of the problem is difficult; it seems that they are just closely linked.

Much of the work in this theory looks at self-efficacy, a cognitive construct, and the effect it has on behaviour and the environment. If someone has low self-efficacy in, for example, mathematics, then they will believe they cannot do mathematics well. This, in turn, raises their anxiety levels when faced with mathematical work and this means they will not be able to process the information as needed to complete the work satisfactorily. This then perpetuates the idea that they cannot do the work, their teacher (the environment) may also react to them as lacking ability and the behaviour continues. As described here, the behaviour stems from the thought process; however, it could equally start from a bad experience in the environment that makes them think they cannot do mathematics.

LINK TO THE COGNITIVE EXPLANATION

The mediational cognitive processes and self-efficacy discussed in Bandura's work are cognitive constructs. This theory then combines elements of both cognitive and sociocultural levels of explanation.

Research

■ The relationship between self-efficacy and reciprocal determinism was examined in 33 countries by **Williams & Williams (2010)**. The researchers used the PISA 2003 data, which is international data collected worldwide on achievement and attitudes to education. The data includes measures of self-efficacy. Using a statistical analysis on the data of all the countries the researchers found that there was a feedback loop between self-efficacy and mathematics achievement in 24 of the 33 countries. This illustrates that they are closely related, and that reciprocal determinism occurs in the learning of school children.

■ **Wardell et al. (2012)** examined the role of reciprocal determinism in alcohol consumption in adolescents. They conducted an online survey asking participants to detail their drinking habits. They found, unsurprisingly, that if someone had positive alcohol expectancies they were more likely to drink more and often. However, when considering what was normal, and 'what others did' they were more likely to moderate their intake in terms of the amount they drank in line with the norms they observed. Sometimes they believed others drank more than they actually did, which had a negative effect, but this illustrates that referencing to others in the environment is important in decision-making. Researchers also found that their drinking behaviour influenced how they viewed their peers' drinking habits, which in turn affected the 'norms', so the decision to drink was influenced both ways.

■ **Pourrazavi et al. (2014)** examined the excessive use of mobile phones by university students in Iran. They found that the use became excessive if an individual had a boyfriend or girlfriend. This illustrates the influence of others in terms of mobile use. However, they also found that this was moderated by self-control and attitude, which in turn affected the use by the girlfriend/partner. The researchers argued that this was a good example of reciprocal determinism.

Evaluation

■ Empirical work on reciprocal determinism is not widespread. This may be in part because it is difficult to test methodologically, as it requires examination of three elements: the environment, the behaviour and the cognitive processes. However, the idea is upheld by many and the link between reciprocal determinism and self-efficacy is well documented, perhaps because of its potential for application to education and other areas of learning.

■ Reciprocal determinism, as a theory, has practical applications. For example, in the field of education it is (or should be accounted for) in feedback given by teachers on work. Giving feedback showing that good results come from hard work can mean a child will feel that they have the potential to achieve. By feeling that potential, they then have a positive mindset when they approach a task in future, which then increases the chance of doing well in subsequent work.

■ The theory of reciprocal determinism explains how a pattern of behaviour is perpetuated. The interaction between the environment and the individual is acknowledged by the theory and the way that the two interact shows how behaviour can escalate. This consideration of a two-way effect is quite rare in theories and they mainly document the direction of effect as one way only.

Conformity and/or compliance

Conformity and compliance are important features of social cognitive theory as they explain how the presence of others can often lead to changes in beliefs and behaviours. This then results, in the case of conformity, in changing how the individual's beliefs and norms thinking influence their behaviour. First, it is important to highlight the difference between compliance and conformity.

Conformity is defined as yielding to group pressure. Conformity occurs when an individual's behaviour and/or beliefs are influenced by a larger group of people, which is why conformity is also known as majority influence. When conformity reduces a person's independence and leads to harmful outcomes, it can be a negative force. Generally, though, conformity has positive outcomes, helping society to function smoothly and predictably. Much human activity is socially based, occurring in groups, so there is a need for individuals to agree in order for groups to form and operate efficiently. Conformity helps this process; by conforming we can make it easier to get along with each other.

There are several situational variables that affect rates of conformity, such as the size of the majority influence, the unanimity (amount of agreement within a group) of the majority influence, task difficulty, group identity, whether responses are made publicly or privately, and social norms. There are also individual factors such as gender, mood, personality and culture.

On the other hand, compliance occurs when individuals adjust their behaviour and opinions to those of a group to be accepted or avoid disapproval. Compliance therefore occurs due to a desire to fit in and involves public, but not private, acceptance of a group's behaviour and attitudes. It is a fairly weak and temporary form of conformity, only shown in the presence of the group. For example, you may claim to support a certain football team, because many others of your age group do, and you want to be accepted and not ridiculed by them. However, privately you may have little interest in this team, or indeed football at all.

Explanations for conformity

Deutsch and Gerard (1955) distinguished between informational social influence (ISI) and normative social influence. This distinction, they believed, was crucial to understanding majority group influence on behaviour.

ISI occurs when someone is unsure that the answer they give or the way they behave will be seen as correct. They therefore look to the group they are with for the answer or direction on the way they act. **Abrams & Hogg (1990)** think that we are only influenced by others' opinions in ambiguous situations when we see ourselves as sharing characteristics with them. Thus, we are much more likely to internalize the opinions of friends than strangers. The membership of the individual to the in-group has an influence.

LINK TO THE BIOLOGICAL LEVEL OF ANALYSIS

Informational social influence can be seen to have an evolutionary basis to it, as looking to others for guidance in new situations that are potentially dangerous could have a survival value.

Normative social influence occurs when individuals want others to like and respect them and not reject or ridicule them. The best way of gaining the acceptance of others is to agree with them. However, this does not necessarily mean that we truly agree with them.

The classic research by **Asch (1955)** illustrates this well (see 'Classic research' below). Asch got participants to conform to answers given by others that were obviously incorrect. If the participants gave the correct answers, they risked being ridiculed by the majority. A conflict had been created between an individual's opinion and that of the group. In the post-experimental debriefing, many said 'I didn't want to look stupid' or 'I didn't want to be the odd one out'. So, they compromised, with what they said (publicly) and what they believed (privately) being completely different, demonstrating an example of compliance.

KEY STUDY   CLASSIC RESEARCH

'Opinions and social pressure'
Asch (1955)

Solomon Asch, a Polish immigrant to the USA, transformed the study of social influence with his ground-breaking research at Harvard University. He also taught Stanley Milgram, who achieved later fame with his studies of obedience.

Asch was interested in testing conformity to obviously incorrect answers. He criticized research that only involved ambiguous tasks and uncertain situations. Beginning in 1951, Asch conducted a series of experiments, adding and publishing new data as he progressed.

Aim

The aim was to investigate the degree to which individuals would conform to a majority who gave obviously wrong answers.

Procedure

1 123 American male student volunteers took part in what they were told was a study of visual perception. Individual participants were placed in groups with between seven and nine others, sat either in a line or around a table, who in reality were pseudo-participants (confederates). The task was to say which comparison line, A, B or C, was the same as a stimulus line on 18 different trials. Twelve of these were 'critical' trials, where pseudo-participants gave identical wrong answers, and the naïve (real) participant always answered last or last but one.

2 There was also a control group of 36 participants who were tested individually on 20 trials, to test how accurate individual judgements were.

Results

Asch found:

1 The control group had an error rate of only 0.04 per cent (3 mistakes out of 720 trials), which shows how obvious the correct answers were.

2 On the 12 critical trials, there was a 32 per cent conformity rate to wrong answers.

3 75 per cent of participants conformed to at least one wrong answer (meaning also that 25 per cent never conformed).

4 5 per cent of participants conformed to all 12 wrong answers.

5 Post-experiment interviews with participants found three reasons for conformity:

   a Distortion of action – where the majority of participants who conformed did so publicly, but not privately, as they wished to avoid ridicule.

   b Distortion of perception – where some participants believed their perception must actually be wrong and so conformed.

   c Distortion of judgement – where some participants had doubts concerning the accuracy of their judgements and so conformed to the majority view.

Conclusions

- The judgements of individuals are affected by majority opinions, even when the majority is obviously wrong.

- There are big individual differences in the extent to which people are affected by majority influence. As most participants conformed publicly, but not privately, it suggests that they were motivated by normative social influence, where individuals conform to gain acceptance or avoid rejection by a group.

Evaluation

- Asch's method for studying conformity became a paradigm, the accepted way of conducting conformity research.

- As only one real participant is tested at a time, the procedure is uneconomical and time-consuming. **Crutchfield (1955)** performed similar research, but improved on the procedure by testing several participants at once.

- The situation was unrealistic and so lacked mundane realism. It would be unusual to be in a situation where you would disagree so much with others about what was the 'correct' answer in a situation.

- Asch's study was unethical, as it involved deceit; participants believed it was a study of visual perception. It also involved psychological harm, with participants put under stress through disagreeing with others (see **Bogdonoff *et al.* 1961**).

Research

- **Jenness (1932)** aimed to investigate whether individual judgements of jelly beans in a jar were influenced by discussion in groups. The task Jenness gave his participants, estimating the number of jellybeans in a jar, had no obvious answer; it was difficult to assess the amount so participants then made individual, private estimates of the number of jelly beans in a jar. They then discussed their estimates either in a large group or in several smaller groups, discovering in the process that individuals differed widely in their estimates. After discussion, group estimates were created and participants then made a second individual, private estimate. Jenness found that typicality of opinion was increased – individuals' second private estimates tended to converge (move towards) their group estimate. He also found that the average change of opinion was greater among females – women conformed more. This shows that individuals' judgements are affected by majority opinions, especially in ambiguous or unfamiliar situations. Discussion is not effective in changing opinion, unless the individuals who enter into the discussion become aware that the opinions of others are different to theirs.

- **Mori & Arai (2010)** designed a study to improve on the previous methodology used to study conformity. Participants wore filter glasses, allowing them to look at the same stimuli, but see different things. One participant in each group wore different glasses, thus perceiving a different comparison line to match to the stimulus line. No confederates were needed. They found that the 78 'majority' participants who saw the correct-sized comparison lines answered incorrectly 8 per cent of the time. Also the 26 'minority' participants who saw the different-sized comparison lines answered incorrectly nearly 20 per cent of the time. This showed that the frequency of conformity of minority participants was similar regardless of whether the majority answered unanimously or not. This suggests the number of people in a majority group has little effect on conformity levels. Additionally, as no majority participants laughed at the performance of minority participants, conformity cannot have occurred due to fear of ridicule.

■ **Figure 3.3** How many jelly beans are in the jar?

Evaluation

- A key issue with conformity research is the method used to test it. Asch's study became a paradigm study, but a major criticism was that of demand characteristics. The confederates were not trained actors and therefore participants may have realized that the confederates' answers were not real so just pretended to conform, as that is what they thought the researcher wanted them to do. The **Mori & Arai (2010)** study dealt with this issue and found that conformity effects were lessened considerably, suggesting much of the early work was methodologically flawed.

- Conformity is hard to test ethically. The new procedure used by **Mori & Arai (2010)** is still unethical, as participants were deceived into thinking the sunglasses were worn to prevent glare. It seems that it is difficult to avoid a level of deceit.

- Conformity as a construct is worthy of study to consider how our behaviour is affected by the influence of others. History is littered with examples of where conformity can become dangerous, but also positive. It has the potential to affect individuals at a one-to-one level but also, in groups, it has the potential to change society for both the good and bad.

Strengthen your learning

1 Explain what is meant by:
   a social cognition
   b social cognitive theory.

2 Outline social learning theory, including reference to a) imitation, b) identification, c) modelling, d) vicarious reinforcement, e) the role of mediating processes, f) attention, g) retention, h) reproduction and i) motivation.

3 Summarize what research studies have suggested about social learning theory as an explanation of behaviour.

4 Assess social learning theory in terms of its strengths and weaknesses.

5 For Bandura *et al.*'s classic 1961 Bobo doll study, in your own words, state the:
  a aims   b procedure   c results   d conclusions   e evaluative points.

6 Explain the concept of reciprocal determinism.

7 Summarize what research studies have suggested about reciprocal determinism.

8 What other evaluative points can be made about reciprocal determinism?

9 Define conformity.

10 What is compliance and why does it occur? Give an example of your own to show your understanding.

11 Explain what is meant by a) normative social influence and b) informational social influence. For both explanations, give an example of your own to show your understanding.

12 Summarize what research studies have suggested about conformity.

13 What other evaluative points can be made about conformity?

14 For Asch's classic 1955 study of normative social influence, in your own words, state the:
  a aims   b procedure   c results   d conclusions   e evaluative points.

■ Stereotypes

IN THE NEWS

Ψ The Psychological Enquirer

SHOE NAMES AND SEXISM

■ **Figure 3.4** Campaigners have argued against what they consider to be gender-stereotyped clothing

A footwear firm in the UK was lobbied by campaigners for gender neutral children's clothing when they released a shoe aimed at the female market called 'Dolly Babe'. The campaign group called 'Let Clothes be Clothes'

argued that the shoe was gender stereotyped and that the boys' equivalent was similarly stereotyped. The 'Dolly Babe' was a flat black shoe with a heart print insole, designed for wear at school. The 'boy' equivalent had an insole with a football print on the inside and was called 'Leader'. Campaigners also argued that the styling was more robust for boys, with a thicker sole, whereas the 'Dolly Babe' was thinner and not designed for outdoor activity.

This was the most recent campaign by the group. There have also been instances of their highlighting that there was too much sparkle and glitter on the girls' collection in a children's clothing brand and the group also argued against the description of girls' shoes having sensitive soles and the boys having airtred soles.

This is an example of stereotypes in everyday life and how they can lead and be reinforced by advertising campaigns.

Stereotypes – a collection of beliefs or attitudes held towards someone due to their membership of a group.

A **stereotype** is a collection of beliefs or attitudes we have towards someone due to their membership of a group. We make judgements on initially meeting someone from their name, to their appearance, indeed even the first conversational exchange. These judgements are made at an individual level and influenced by our previous experiences of in- and out-groups. Our judgements are influenced by the expectations we have, because of the perceived groups the individuals are part of: nationality, gender, age and so on. The expectations we hold about them are dependent on stereotypes that we hold. A stereotype occurs when we have the same expectancies for all members of that group. If you tell someone you are a psychology student, various stereotypes may emerge such as that you must be reading their mind or working out who they are from their body language. Labels such as feminist, soldier and politician also evoke stereotypes in the general population, but many people do not acknowledge that they use stereotypes. Stereotypes are formed through schema. These are discussed in greater detail in Chapter 2 (see page 43) and in Chapter 8 (see page 342).

As humans, we like to be able to predict and stereotypes seem to be a way of making generalizations so that behaviour can be predicted. However, this can of course be very damaging as it means creating prejudice and discrimination against groups, which can impact on their ability to get jobs or access other social groups. Two examples are sex stereotyping and racial stereotyping.

Sex stereotyping is when generalizations are made by people based on the biological sex of an individual. There is an underlying assumption by some people that a male will act in a certain way and have preferences in terms of colours, hobbies and clothes. The same occurs with females.

The 'In the News' feature (above) illustrates the ways in which society perpetuates gender stereotyping.

These stereotypes are perpetuated by the environment with clothes marketed for boys and girls separately, advertising in the media 'aimed' at gender-specific markets. They basically centre on the old saying of 'blue for boys and pink for girls'.

Cultural stereotyping is also widespread. This is where the nationality of an individual places them in a group which some people have an opinion about. Generalizations are made, and a judgement passed on the individual based upon the beliefs held about their nationality. This occurs in all areas of society.

PSYCHOLOGY IN THE REAL WORLD

In 2016 Raymond Lynn and Daniel Clayton set up the charity 'Fair Football' in the UK. Its key purpose is to tackle discrimination in football through educational sessions, and it has run sessions to over 500 pupils in its first year. The idea is that by challenging discriminatory attitudes in children they will be able to reduce racism and prejudice not only in football, but also society in general. Specifically, they explore the influence and impact that culture has on society; that is, attitudes, thinking and behaviour. This involves exploring hidden assumptions, stereotypes and bias that people are not really aware that they have, which then starts the process of building awareness and understanding of 'cultural difference' and respecting it rather than fearing it.

Cleland & Cashmore (2016) examined the extent to which racism was embedded into the beliefs of football fans and found that some fans expressed negative stereotypes of players and managers depending on their nationality or skin colour. Indeed, 83 per cent of respondents said that they believed that racism was still an issue in the sport. This highlights that there is still work that needs to be done in terms of negative racial and cultural stereotyping, and Fair Football, along with other interventions, is tackling these effects.

KEY STUDY   # CONTEMPORARY RESEARCH

'Accuracy of national stereotypes in central Europe: Out-groups are not better than in-group in considering personality traits of real people'
HŘebíČková & Graf (2014)

National stereotypes are undoubtedly formed and perpetuated, but the question is whether they are indicative of the population. Exactly how accurate are they?

Aim

To examine the accuracy of racial stereotypes within Europe.

Procedure

1   HŘeblČková & Graf (2014) examined the accuracy of stereotypes across nations in central Europe. The countries involved in the research were Austria, the Czech Republic, Germany, Poland and Slovakia. The researchers looked specifically at the relationship between personality traits of individuals within a country and how closely that related to the national stereotype. In terms of the rating scales, the country stereotypes were rated on 30 items that related to the 5-factor theory of personality (extraversion, neuroticism, agreeableness, conscientiousness and openness). This allowed for direct comparison with individual personality data that was gathered using the same 5 factors.

2   They examined this by asking 2241 participants to complete the National Character survey for both their own (autostereotype), and the other countries participating in the study (heterostereotype). They then used personality data from 17,377 participants from other studies to compare how the data sets related to each other.

Results

The findings showed that:

1   There was evidence of national stereotypes both within cultures as well as across countries.

2   Heterostereotypes had a higher level of agreement when compared with raters from cultures that were less similar (i.e. linguistic differences).

3   With national autostereotypes, there was a difference between typical representatives of central European countries. However, when compared with the personality data, the nationalities actually showed a lot of similarity, suggesting that the perceived similarity of a nationality is widespread across the region, encompassing other nationalities. People are more similar than they realize.

Conclusions

● This study illustrates not only that people hold stereotypes for other nationalities, but also hold stereotypes about themselves.

● There is also evidence of an in-group effect with nationalities that are similar in terms of language and geography. The personality data actually highlighted that there was similarity across nationalities and that the stereotypes held suggested that they should be more different. This demonstrates the inaccuracies of generalizing across a group of people.

Evaluation

● The response method of using a questionnaire is sound for this type of research, as it fosters a higher level of honesty than one-to-one interviewing would elicit. Admitting to stereotyping of others can be seen to be socially inappropriate, therefore the chances of social desirability bias affecting results is greater if face to face with participants.

● Another potential negative effect of stereotyping is stereotype threat. Whether you believe in stereotypes or not, you may be aware of the stereotypes that people hold about you, whether it is because of your gender, profession, nationality or any other group you are a member of. Sometimes, you become aware that you may do something which reinforces that stereotype, such as choosing a bright pink dress because you are female. This is called stereotype threat and is not related to believing the stereotype, more about trying to counteract it.

Research

- **Shih *et al.* (1999)** conducted research looking at how stereotyping can enhance performance. This is the case when a stereotype suggests that someone may be better at something. The researchers compared the skills performance of Asian students and to those of non-Asian students. They also considered gender. Stereotypes of Asian students are that they are better at mathematical tasks and these were the tasks used in the research. There are similar stereotypes saying that men are better at mathematical tasks than women. The researchers subtly 'primed' ethnicity and gender in some of the participants so they took the test with their group membership in their mind. They found that Asian–American women performed better on a mathematics test when their ethnic identity was activated, but the opposite was true when their gender identity was activated. The performance was compared with groups who did not have their group membership primed. This suggests that stereotypes affect performance, both negatively and positively.

- **Steele & Aronson (1995)** focused their research on stereotype threat in black students. Stereotypes about the performance of black students can be negative and the researchers wanted to examine whether knowledge of this stereotype affected the behaviour of students who were classified this way by the stereotype. To do this, they examined two groups of black students; one group took the test after being told that it was to diagnose their academic ability and the second group were told it was merely a problem-solving exercise. Students in the former group did not perform as well as students in the latter group, suggesting that those students who felt their performance was under scrutiny, and therefore could possibly fulfil the stereotype, could have been more nervous and underperformed. This suggests that stereotype threat affects performance.

Evaluation

- Stereotype threat is an important idea because it can show how stereotypes affect behaviour, even if the person does not believe the stereotype; the fact it exists has a potentially negative effect.

- Research shows that stereotype threat can have a beneficial outcome as well as a negative one, depending on whether the stereotype is positive or not. This idea is supported by the research of **Shih *et al.* (1999)** detailed above.

- The research on stereotype threat is argued to be affected by other variables, so the extent to which performance change can be attributed to stereotype threat could be less than reported. This was highlighted in a review by **Pennington *et al.* (2016)**, who found that other factors such as anxiety, negative thinking and mind-wandering were also implicated in behaviour change and could therefore be confounding variables in testing for stereotype threat.

Strengthen your learning

1 What is a stereotype? Give an example of your own to show your understanding.

2 Give one reason for humans having stereotypes.

3 Explain:
   a sex stereotyping
   b cultural stereotyping.

4 Summarize what research studies have suggested about stereotyping.

5 What other evaluative points can be made about stereotyping?

6 For HŘebíČková & Graf's contemporary 2014 study of the accuracy of national stereotypes, in your own words, state the:
   a aims
   b procedure
   c results
   d conclusions
   e evaluative points.

SECTION SUMMARY

- Social identity theory looks at how our identities as individuals are affected by membership to an in-group. This includes how we view members of out-groups.
- Social cognitive theory looks at the way our behaviour is affected by other people in our environment and how we learn from them.
- Social learning is a theory outlined by Bandura that documents learning from observing others.
- Stereotypes are ideas formed about others based on the social groups they belong to; this includes gender and racial stereotypes.

■ **Assessment check**

1	Outline one study investigating social identity theory.	(9 marks)
2	With reference to a study investigating social cognitive theory, outline one strength and one limitation of a research method used in the study.	(9 marks)
3	Explain how stereotypes influence behaviour.	(9 marks)
4	Evaluate research studies related to stereotypes.	(22 marks)
5	Discuss social identity theory.	(22 marks)
6	Evaluate social cognitive theory.	(22 marks)

Cultural origins of behaviour and cognition

The sociocultural explanation for behaviour has two elements: social and cultural effects and learning. The previous section explained how both the social identity theory and the social cognitive theory look at how 'others' affect the individual, with both focusing on the social element. The end of the last section moved onto cultural learning and this will be continued in this section, which looks at culture and the influence it has on behaviour and thought (cognition).

'[O]ne person's "barbarian" is another person's "just doing what everybody else is doing."'
Susan Sontag, 'Regarding the Pain of Others'

FOCUS ON...

- How culture can influence behaviour and cognition, referencing cultural norms.
- What are cultural dimensions?
- How cultural dimensions affect behaviour.

■ Culture and its influence on behaviour and cognition

Culture can be described as the learned and shared behaviour of members of a particular society, including shared beliefs, attitudes and values. This definition talks about learning but emphasizes the word 'shared', using it twice. This part of the definition is important because, for ideas to be cultural, they should be shared. This shows the influence of the majority of people within that culture and that the ideas, beliefs and values often derive from the dominant religion or from the geographical context.

The idea that behaviour and cognition are separate from cultural influences is widely regarded as erroneous. The extent to which culture influences both behaviour and cognition varies enormously. Teasing apart cultural influence from other types of influence such as cognitive is difficult, partly because one can argue that culture influences thoughts.

There are differing levels to cultures: surface culture and deep culture. They both affect behaviour in different ways and at different levels. Deep culture refers to the beliefs, values, thought processes and assumptions of a culture; in other words it is culture at the cognitive level.

This is difficult for people moving into the culture to understand, as their thought processes will have been formed in a different culture. However, if you are brought up and socialized into that culture the processes seem reasonable and comprehensible. Surface culture is, much like its name suggests, at a shallower level than deep culture. It is usually what people think of when we refer to culture and its differences and focuses upon the behaviours, customs, words and traditions of a culture. These are easier for someone from a different culture to understand and adopt as they can easily be observed and require no thought processes to be considered.

This section considers areas of psychology where work has been documented on the cultural effects on behaviour and cognition at both surface and deep levels.

The areas discussed below are culture and day care, mental health and obedience.

Culture and day care

Day care – care provided for children while their parents are occupied, usually at work. Day care can include nurseries, nannies and childminders.

Parenting practices vary across the world and leaving a child to be looked after by someone other than a parent is widespread practice in some cultures, especially if both parents work outside of the home. **Day care** is seen by many to reflect the parenting practices used within the culture, and there are differences in the way that day care is organized globally. In comparative studies there have been differences recorded in terms of accepted class sizes, response to bad behaviour and the emphasis placed on values. These are predominantly cultural influences at the surface level; however, the emphasis placed on certain values is a form of oblique cultural transmission and is designed to socialize the child into taking on such values at the deep cognitive level.

▨ Research

■ **Tobin (1987)** looked at the cultural differences between American and Japanese preschool nurseries. He found that one of the most noticeable differences was the class sizes. When asked, Japanese educators said they found the small class sizes of the American system surprising and felt that it would have a detrimental effect on the child's social development as they would not interact with as many children, whereas the American educators thought that the large class sizes in Japan would have a negative effect on the children because it would limit the amount of attention they could receive from the adults in the room. This illustrates that the cultural expectations differ and that the emphasis on social skills in Japanese culture was an extension of the collectivist society. Equally the American idea that children need attention to develop is an individualist influence.

■ **Fuller *et al.* (1996)** examined the sub-cultural effects of day care choice. The researchers looked at why parents chose specific day care and found that they always looked for one that aligned with their parenting practices. Ethnic minorities' (African–American) choices were different from Latino and white choices in that there was a focus on putting their child into childcare based in centres. This was thought to be due to the focus on structured play in centres and also the community feel that mimicked the neighbourhood feel for African–American families. This shows how culture affects choices in bringing up a child and that decision-making is heavily influenced by cultural ideas.

Culture and mental health

Cultures have their own set of social norms. These are the shared behaviours that all living in that culture understand are the expected way to behave, and are called cultural norms. If good mental health is gauged by the extent to which an individual fits within their cultural norms, then poor mental health is a deviation from it. This means that across the world behaviour can be seen as typical or atypical, depending on context. This has led to culture-bound syndromes arising globally. Examples are Koro (Southeast Asia) and Pibloktoq (Greenland, Alaska, Canadian Artic). Koro is described as an intense fear that the penis will retract into the body and this will lead to death. This is only witnessed and diagnosed in Southeast Asia, as it is conceivably a cognitive effect of the culture. The same can be said of Pibloktoq, which is characterized by the urge to take all clothes off and run around in freezing temperatures crying and screaming. This is only found among the Eskimo (Inuit) people and, rather like Koro, a factor of the culture.

Both these syndromes suggest that they are culturally learned and are examples of how good mental health and poor mental health differ from culture to culture. The behaviour and thought processes behind the syndrome are culture-specific and Koro, in particular, shows cognitive effects of the culture, that is, the belief that a penis will retract is not reported globally, suggesting that it is a feature of the thinking within that specific culture.

Research

- **Ventriglio *et al.* (2016)** argue that culture-bound syndromes are less likely to occur as globalization increases. They acknowledged that perceptions of mental health are culturally influenced, however, and that the number of syndromes outlined in DSM-V in 2013 has reduced and changed. They assert that clinicians should be aware of the cultural effects of symptoms, but that the extent to which culture is influential in mental health is declining and the norms are becoming homogenized.

- **Roldán-Chicano *et al.* (2017)** looked at Bolivian culture-bound syndromes and what happens with a migratory population. They examined the culture-bound syndrome of Susto and whether it disappeared if Bolivian migrants settled in Spain. Susto is characterized by extreme fear and death by fright. When Bolivians moved to Spain they continued, in many cases, to believe that Susto could appear and that the elements that 'caused' it were still present in Spanish society. This suggests that the cognitive constructs detailed in the syndrome were still present and influential.

Culture and obedience

Much of the research looking at obedience is focused in North America and Europe. The research suggests that obedience occurs cross-culturally and that we are likely to obey an authority figure, in both a natural setting and in a laboratory context. One of the most famous psychology experiments to consider obedience was designed and conducted by **Milgram (1963)** to test the obedience level of individuals. It involved participants being told to administer electric shocks to someone who had given incorrect answers on a memory task. The shocks were fake ones and the person receiving them was an actor, but the participant was unaware of this detail. In about 65 per cent of cases the participants administered (or believed they administered) shocks that were potentially fatal. This experimental design has been conducted across the world and the levels vary according to culture. When conducted on male populations the replications suggest high obedience levels of 90 per cent (Spain) and lower levels of 40 per cent in other cultures (Australia). The variation is striking, and researchers have suggested various reasons why this may occur. One is that cultures regard status differently and that the status of scientist may be perceived differently across cultures. The parenting styles and expectation of obedience also vary cross-culturally as do the historical context and effect on obedience levels. Cultures at war may expect higher levels of obedience than in peace time.

Research

- **Lavine (2009)** in his research suggests that the level of obedience cross-culturally is determined to some extent by personality characteristics in that culture. Looking at the interaction between personality traits and obedience levels, Lavine found a relationship between high neuroticism and low conscientiousness being linked to uncertainty avoidance. This means that people with this personality profile do not like uncertainty and are more likely to obey rules and authority figures as a consequence. The data suggested that this type of personality was more prevalent in cultures that had high obedience levels. This relationship suggests not only cultural influences on obedience levels, but also personality.

- **Bond & Smith (1996)** argued that the cross-cultural differences found in research studies cannot be attributed to cultural influence in all cases. They argued that the differences reported could be affected by problems with the suitability of the methodology and that the validity of the results could be low. They did acknowledge that there were cultural differences, but they argued that this could potentially be a byproduct of the experimental design.

Evaluation of the cultural origins of behaviour and cognition

- Establishing the extent to which culture affects behaviour and thought is very difficult. It seems that it plays a part but the possibility of influence from other factors such as genetics, gender and other variables means it is difficult to quantify.

- A key argument around the cultural differences of behaviour is that there are more similarities than differences between cultures (**Church *et al.*, 2010**) and this means that difference is focused upon when it should not be. Therefore, it could be said that the cultural influence is actually not a major factor compared with other influences, as the differences are smaller than the similarities between cultures. If this was not the case, the cultural influence could be seen as greater.

- One way in which the influence is thought to occur is through cultural dimensions, which are measures of the differences between cultures. An understanding of cultural influence on behaviour and cognition has become more important than ever now, with the rise of globalization. Trade and knowledge exchange occurs on a day-to-day basis and the understanding of the way in which other cultures think and act differently is needed for successful globalization. This has led to glocalization, where there is a combination of cultures. There is more detail on this in the final section of this chapter.

Strengthen your learning

1 What is meant by culture?

2 Explain, with examples of your own, the difference between surface and deep culture.

3 Explain the relationship between culture and:
   a day care
   b mental health
   c obedience.

4 Summarize what research studies have suggested about culture and:
   a day care
   b mental health
   c obedience.

5 What evaluative points can be made about the cultural origins of behaviour and cognition?

Cultural dimensions

Cultures vary in many ways. In an effort to gain insight into the cultural differences of countries across the world, **Hofstede (1983)** conducted research with 50 countries, across three regions and at two separate time points. Questionnaires were administered across organizations in all countries and a factor analysis conducted. A factor analysis is a statistical analysis technique that looks at patterns within data gathered. Once the analysis is run it identifies themes (called factors) to arise from the data.

In the case of Hofstede's results there were four overarching dimensions identified; individualism/collectivism, uncertainty avoidance, power/distance, and masculinity/femininity.

Individualism/collectivism

Individualism – a perspective that emphasizes the well-being and needs of the individual.

Collectivism – a perspective that emphasizes the well-being and needs of the group or nationality.

Hofstede described the **individualism/collectivism** dimension as the extent to which a culture focuses upon the needs of the individual or the greater good. A country that scores highly on individualism would emphasize the needs of each person and their need to be able to live their life in a way that suits them. Collectivist societies expect actions that show consideration of the bigger picture for everyone else. In a collectivist society it would be expected for social roles to be very important, as they affect others, and there will be a high level of interconnectedness. People are seen as a group not as a group of individuals, as one might expect in an individualist society. Figure 3.5 indicates that Australia and Sweden are highly individualist societies.

Uncertainty avoidance

Uncertainty avoidance is a factor that denotes the extent to which a country, and the working climate within it, is one that maintains the status quo. There is no risky behaviour and security is valued. The higher the score, the more anxious the country is about change. Japan and Panama (see Figure 3.5) both score highly in this aspect and, as such, are countries where jobs are more likely to be 'jobs for life'.

Power/distance

This dimension in Hofstede's research indicates the extent to which the countries are hierarchical. If there is an autocratic leadership within the organizations within that culture the country would score highly on that particular dimension. With reference to Figure 3.5, Panama scores particularly highly on the power/distance dimension, meaning that respondents to the questionnaire indicated a structured set up within their society, where people are at a stage of the hierarchy. This hierarchy means that key decisions are made towards the top of the hierarchy and those lower down accept that this is the way, on the whole.

Masculinity/femininity

This factor considers the way in which ambition, money and recognition are emphasized. A country that focuses on these aspects is deemed to be 'masculine'. Conversely, feminine countries are more focused upon negotiation, cooperation and maintaining a pleasant working environment. Hofstede asserted that this dimension reflected the gender roles within societies globally. This dimension came from the gender differences indicated by men and women in the same job and their key motivators and ways of working.

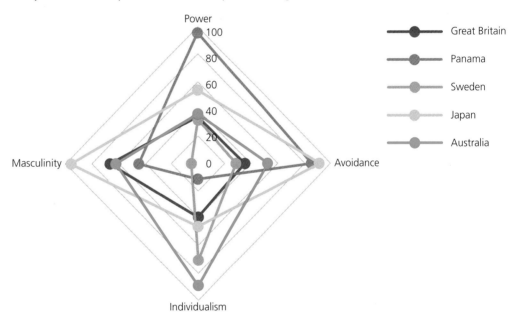

■ **Figure 3.5** Hofstede (1983) ranking for select countries

Hofstede has reviewed and reworked his ideas, and this has culminated in the addition of further determinants from the original four from his 1983 work.

Long term/short term

This determinant was added in response to criticism that the original four cultural dimensions did not adequately reflect Asian cultures. In 2001, he then added the short-term/long-term dimension to indicate cultures that encourage looking at the long-term reward. Traits such as persistence and resilience are fostered in some cultures more than others. This determinant looks at the maintenance of personal status (keeping face) and a respect for tradition. This dimension is also sometimes called Time orientation. It is essentially the extent to which long-term gain is encouraged rather than short-term gain in some cultures.

Indulgence/restraint

This dimension was added, as the sixth dimension, in 2010. It is based on the work of a Bulgarian sociologist, Minkov, using data from the 'World Values survey'. Some societies, he and then Hofstede subsequently argued, expect immediate gratification of their needs. This often corresponds closely with the individualism/collectivism dimension in that the focus is on the wishes and needs of the individual. There is an implicit expectation in 'indulgent' countries that the needs will be met quickly. Happiness of the population is seen to be important at an individual level. Individuals in indulgent societies have a greater level of personal control and freedom in their actions.

■ Evaluation

■ **McSweeney *et al.* (2016)** criticized Hofstede's work in that they argued that the determinants were not the exclusive cause of behaviour at both individual and national level and that the factors had no predictive power. They did not disagree with Hofstede's determinants, as such, more the explanatory power he asserted they had.

■ Behaviour within a country is very diverse and different among individuals. The argument that cultural dimensions filter into behaviour is potentially flawed in that the variety of behaviour in a nation would suggest cultural dimensions have little influence. If they did influence the behaviour it would be more similar. It is likely that the differences within nations are greater than the difference between nations, reducing the likelihood of a strong influence. There is evidence that behaviour is affected at the individual level (see the following section); however, this effect may be over-exaggerated.

■ The validity of the cultural dimensions has also been criticized. This is, in part, because the number has not remained at four, and more are being added following research by other researchers. This seems to suggest that the picture is much more complex in terms of explaining and predicting the behaviour of countries and the individuals within it.

■ In addition to the number of determinants, work testing validity of the original four dimensions has cast doubt on their validity. For example, **Schmitz & Weber (2014)** found that the uncertainty avoidance dimension had no supporting evidence and did not appear to be a valid construct.

■ How the dimensions affect behaviour

Hofstede's work looked at a more macro level at the profiles of countries, almost as if they have personalities. How do these translate to behaviour in the population? What is the effect on individual behaviour of these dimensions? This section will consider one of these dimensions and how the individuals within the countries are influenced: individualism/collectivism.

Individualism/collectivism

The individualism/collectivism dimension is outlined above and described as the extent to which a culture focuses upon the needs of the individual for the greater good. Clearly, this has the potential to permeate through to behaviour in the whole population, including childhood, as the dimension is likely to affect parenting style.

Relationships are one area in which there is an effect from the dimension. In China, a collectivist culture, the term 'guanxi', translates as 'relationships', but in the Chinese business meaning of the term there is an implicit addition of cooperation and support for one another in relationships in the workplace. Guanxi is very important in China and a lot of effort is put into establishing guanxi between people who work together. In conducting deals, this is seen as vital so a lot of hosting and dining out takes place to establish the connection. Guanxi also is about maintaining face, so interactions are respectful and polite. The way it is written in Mandarin is a combination of the characters for 'connection' and 'system'. This means that within the language the collectivist ideals are evident and affect day-to-day interactions.

The dimension of individualism/collectivism has also been implicated in conflict resolution at a one-to-one level. Much research has found that the conflict resolution styles differ between the East and West, with East Asians using non-confrontational styles and the West using a more assertive style. This is sometimes attributed to individualism and collectivism in the culture.

◼ Research

- **Rhee *et al.* (2017)** looked at guanxi and its relationship to collectivism. They considered emails and online survey data and found that there was indeed a link between collectivism and guanxi, especially where the relationship was hierarchical or competitive (i.e. a boss/ worker relationship).

- **Kim & Coleman (2015)** found that the individualism/collectivism dimension was more influenced by how embedded into the dimension an individual is. If they have a strong individualist/collectivist perspective they were actually more likely to be assertive or very conflict-averse respectively, whereas those along the middle of the continuum were more likely to have an integrative style, showing concern for both themselves and others. This illustrates that within cultures there is a variability of conflict styles and that it is influenced by the identification level with the cultural dimension of the culture they are part of.

KEY STUDY ## CONTEMPORARY RESEARCH

'Waiting for the second treat'
Lamm *et al.* (2017)

In the 1960s a test to study delayed gratification in children aged about four years was developed by Walter Mischel. It involved a child being in a room, at a table with a marshmallow or cookie or pretzel on a plate. Prior to being left alone, the child was told that they could eat the marshmallow (or other food), but that if they waited they would be given more of the reward. Essentially, they were rewarded if they could wait (delay gratification). This test was developed from an earlier piece of work that had tested stereotypes of ethnic minorities living in Trinidad, so was originally designed to test cross-cultural differences in behaviour (Mischel, 1958).

Aim
The study aimed to look at the cultural effect on a standard child development test of delaying gratification and see how that may have been affected by culture.

Procedure
Lamm and colleagues used the marshmallow methodology on 76 children who lived in Cameroon and compared it with 125 German children of the same age. Lamm *et al.* then conducted a second experiment looking at the parenting style across cultures to see if that could account for the differences in performance. The Cameroonian parenting style is a responsive control style, characterized by bodily closeness, training, and control, which differs from the German child-centred style that explores the mental world of the infant, reacts to infant moods, and provides opportunities for children to exert influence over their environments. The regulation of mood is therefore not of paramount concern in Germany.

Results
The researchers found that the children from Cameroon actually were able to delay gratification for the treat in more instances than the children from Germany. The percentage of children who managed to wait was 69.7 per cent and 28 per cent respectively.

For the second experiment, the researchers found, following more observation of the children with their mothers, that this difference in cultural parenting could account for the differences in gratification delay.

Conclusion

- This research relates to cultural determinants in that the cultural determinants are potentially influential in cultural socialization, such as parenting. The extent of the cultural influence on what is seen to be the correct way to bring up a child is difficult. However, when considering Hofstede's determinants, it can be seen how the long-term/short-term determinant in particular might have influenced how able children are to delay gratification. The German parenting style could be argued to be more rapidly reactive to a child's individual needs and as such they are not used to waiting.

- The researchers did not directly test the six proposed cultural determinants, but the results show clear differences that could be accounted for this way.

Evaluation

- This research provides a useful cross-cultural perspective on the development of delaying gratification in children which could be in part due to cultural determinants. The use of a standardized methodology also means that the cross-cultural comparison is valid.

- Research supports the idea that cultural determinants affect individual behaviour. This illustrates that the way a culture operates filters through to the individual level and this is perpetuated by the process of socialization.

- Evidence suggests that assuming that an individual is affected in the same way by some cultural dimensions is erroneous. It seems that within cultures the level to which an individual aligns with the cultural determinants varies on an individual level. So, the strength of the determinant does not transfer to the corresponding behaviour of every individual. This means individual behaviour may not be affected by cultural determinants at all.

The cultural determinants could be argued to underpin stereotypes of different cultures. However, there is always the possibility that the stereotypes affect how the working practices are perceived, and generalizations may be made from that. The relationship cannot be said to be causal.

Strengthen your learning

1 What four cultural dimensions were identified by Hofstede (1983)?

2 Explain, in your own words, providing relevant examples where appropriate, the following cultural dimensions. You should include in your explanations details of how these cultural dimensions affect behaviour:
   a individualism/collectivism
   b uncertainty avoidance
   c power/distance
   d masculinity/femininity
   e long term/short term and time orientation
   f indulgence/restraint.

3 Summarize what research studies have suggested about cultural dimensions.

4 What other evaluative points can be made about cultural dimensions (including criticism of Hofstede's work)?

5 For Lamm *et al.*'s contemporary 2017 study of 'waiting for the second treat', in your own words, state the:
   a aims
   b procedure
   c results
   d conclusions
   e evaluative points.

■ Assessment check

1	Outline one or more studies investigating cultural dimensions.	(9 marks)
2	Outline how culture can affect behaviour.	(9 marks)
3	Explain ethical considerations relating to one study of cultural dimensions.	(9 marks)
4	With reference to a study investigating the influence of culture on behaviour and cognition, outline two strengths of a research method used in the study.	(9 marks)
5	Discuss culture and its influence on behaviour and cognition.	(22 marks)
6	Evaluate research studies of cultural dimensions.	(22 marks)
7	Discuss one or more aspects of the cultural origins of behaviour and cognition.	(22 marks)

Cultural influences on individual attitudes, identity and behaviours

This section considers the processes of how culture affects an individual, either in their own culture, or in a new culture. Enculturation explains the process of socialization into one's own culture and explanations are given for acculturation, and its various levels. It is also important to consider how the researcher can influence the way in which culture affects the individual and whether they look at it with an 'outsider' perspective or as an 'insider'. The extent to which behaviour can be generalized cross-culturally is also examined in the section headed 'Universalism/relativism' on page 134.

'I'm a little like Marco Polo, going around and mixing cultures.'
Gianni Versace

FOCUS UPON...

- Enculturation, i.e. what it is and how it occurs.
- Acculturation, i.e. what it is and how it occurs.
- Universalism/relativism and how this affects research.
- Factors underlying cultural change.

■ Enculturation

Enculturation – the process by which an individual learns culturally appropriate behaviour and cultural norms of their own culture.

Enculturation is the process of learning about the culture we live in. As a child this is learning about our home culture. The learning involves understanding the social norms (i.e. what is acceptable and expected), such as behaviours, language, values and morals of the specific culture.

Socialization, including cultural learning and cultural transmission

Socialization is the process by which we learn to become part of a group. It ensures that the person understands how to behave in the society that they live. It is how enculturation occurs.

Social identity theory has previously considered how our identity is affected by group membership, which in turn affects our behaviour. Social cognitive theory also highlights how we learn from others in our environment; however, its focus is very much on the interpersonal one-to-one process of learning. This is social learning.

Cultural learning stems from this social learning. Both the model and the learner are immersed in a culture and its effect is also important in the process of socialization. Cultural transmission is the means by which we learn to behave appropriately in our culture specifically.

A good example of cultural transmission is learning language. Linguists state that this transmission is evident globally, as all cultures have their own language and dialects. It is also apparent in non-humans; bird song, for example, is locally determined. This cultural transmission occurs in three different directions: horizontal, vertical and oblique (**Gong, 2010**).

Horizontal transmission occurs between individuals in the same generation, so relates to language learning among peers. This occurs within their culture and sub-culture until it becomes language accepted and understood by their generation. Often language transmitted this way remains within the generations, an example being the varied ways that people express that something is good. Consulting any online slang dictionary will bring up a multitude of words expressing the sentiment that something is good; however, these are reflected at different points in the generations. People who are over 70 do not generally say something is 'awesome' and, likewise, under 25-year-olds would not usually refer to something as 'super'.

Vertical transmission relates to cross-generational communication between individuals who are genetically related. This refers, for example, to cultural learning from parents or grandparents, which is a key point of language learning for a child and ensures continuity over time. There are slight variations across geographic areas in terms of what words are used for specific objects, but parents will usually teach a child to use the appropriate vocabulary for that area. This sometimes does not happen if parents have moved into the area and were socialized themselves elsewhere.

Finally, oblique transmission is between two individuals of different generations who are not related. A good example of oblique transmission of language would be a child listening to a teacher's language within a school.

An important part of socialization is cultural transmission. It ensures that individuals learn appropriate information for the context they find themselves within. It is a vital part of the process of enculturation. Using the example of cultural transmission of language, it can be seen how important appropriate communication is for the successful socialization of a child. If the child learns to use language in an appropriate way, then their enculturation will be easier.

Research

- **Wang & Vallotton (2016)** looked at variations in the use of infant signing across cultures. Infant signing is an approach used by parents with pre-language children to symbolize objects (such as milk, nappy) or actions (drink, listen). This is a method that can help to socialize children and helps them to express their needs. The researchers observed the frequency that American parents and Taiwanese parents use object and action signs and found that there was a significant cultural difference. American children were taught to use more object signs than the Taiwanese children, who learned more action words. Researchers argued that this difference reflected the parenting practices within the cultures, illustrating that vertical cultural transmission is used by parents in socializing their children.

- **Kaya & Oran (2015)** looked at oblique cultural transmission. They examined how Turkish is taught to people learning it as a second language. There was a disparity of cultural reference dependent on whether the classes were in Turkey or abroad. There was considerably less sociocultural input in lessons taught abroad. Kaya and Oran argue that this means the learner is not aware of the nuances and subtle interaction differences that are culture-dependent. They also argued that there should be an emphasis on key elements of the Turkish culture, such as respect for teachers and scholars and helping others, for successful language learning to take place.

- Horizontal cultural transmission was examined by **Maes *et al.* (2006)** when they studied the cultural transmission of smoking behaviours between twins. They looked at smoking initiation specifically and found that both horizontal and vertical cultural transmission had an effect. This was not the only reason, however, for there to be shared smoking behaviours between twins; biology and environmental effects also played a part. This shows that cultural learning is one element of learning a behaviour, but that there are many other reasons why people do what they do.

Evaluation

■ Cultural transmission, as a process within enculturation, has much supporting evidence and cross-cultural studies distinguish it from social learning as the content of the learning is culture dependent. The idea is therefore well supported.

■ It is likely that much cultural transmission occurs with mass media. The focus in the research, however, is on interactions between individuals and, while this is clearly important, the role of mass media is probably increasing as access is much more widespread.

■ Globalization is the interconnectedness of cultures globally due to media, trade and culture agreements between countries. This means that there is far more communication between countries and it can be argued that this means cultural transmission is less important as cultures are becoming more similar. This is discussed in more detail in the final section of the chapter, 'The influence of globalization on behaviour'.

Link to the biological level of analysis

Cultural transmission is argued to be one of the elements that makes humans 'human'. However, evidence from animal studies shows that there are non-human animals that also use cultural transmission. Research has found evidence in dolphins of passing on knowledge of tool use, wolves who learn hunting strategies from their pack and birdsong that is essential for survival in some cases. This illustrates that it is not a uniquely human phenomenon, and could therefore have a biological, genetic basis.

Strengthen your learning

1 What is meant by:
   a enculturation
   b socialization?

2 Explain, giving an example of your own, what is meant by cultural transmission.

3 Outline the following types of cultural transmission:
   a horizontal transmission
   b vertical transmission
   c oblique transmission.

4 Summarize what research studies have suggested about cultural transmission.

5 What other evaluative points can be made about cultural transmission?

Acculturation

Acculturation – the process by which an individual learns culturally appropriate behaviour and cultural norms for a new culture.

Acculturation is the process of enculturation, but in a new culture (i.e. a non-home culture). The understanding of how to act clearly means that a change of culture may mean a change of behaviour for a successful transition. However, our culture is part of our identity so the shift to another culture is not always easy. There are varying stages of acculturation: assimilation, separation, integration and marginalization. These refer to acculturation when a move to another culture occurs from a home culture, not the enculturation of a child learning about their home culture. The level of acculturation depends on two factors: the level of acceptance of the new culture and the level of rejection of the old culture.

Assimilation

Assimilation is used as a term to describe when an individual takes on the values, morals and behaviours of a new culture they have moved to and lose or reject all the aspects of their home culture. This is acculturation in its fullest form as the new culture essentially becomes all-encompassing.

Separation

Separation occurs when an individual rejects all the cultural change involved in becoming part of the new culture they have moved to and they retain the behaviour and beliefs of their home culture. There is little acculturation at all in this instance.

Integration

Integration is where an individual retains some of their own cultural values and behaviours, but also adopts some of the new culture. This is also sometimes called bicultural. For example, Catherine, whose home culture is the UK, moves to China and adopts some of the social norms, such as not queuing when taking the Shanghai metro and using chopsticks to eat. However, she does not adopt the social norm of spitting, which is common on Chinese streets but not in Yorkshire where her family live.

Marginalization

Marginalization is less usual and occurs when an individual rejects both their home culture and the culture they move to. This is unusual because there is then a change to their identity in relation to others.

KEY STUDY **CONTEMPORARY RESEARCH**

'*Getting the most out of living abroad*'
Tadmor et al. (2012)

Does acculturation benefit all? Acculturation is often portrayed as advantageous. But is this the case for all people?

Aim

Tadmor *et al.* (2012) were interested at looking at why living in another culture has benefits, but only for some people.

Procedure

1   The researchers gathered a sample of 78 MBA students in Europe. All the participants had spent a period of living abroad for at least a year. They were placed into three groups
    a   Bicultural – participants who had embraced elements of the new culture but also retained aspects of their own culture.
    b   Separated – participants who had retained their own cultural practices while living abroad.
    c   Assimilated – these were participants who had adopted the new culture of the host country as their own.
2   Tadmor *et al.* ran a series of tests to see whether the effects of living abroad affected all the groups equally. The tests included a measurement of integrative complexity. This is a construct which is described as the ability to take on multiple perspectives. It also allows them to combine ideas in a unique way. In essence, it is a type of creativity.

Results

The researchers found that the bicultural participants outperformed the other groups in their measures of integrative complexity. Subsequently, they also created more products and more innovative businesses in their years following the MBA course.

Conclusions

Tadmor and colleagues suggested that this was because they had a greater level of flexible thinking, fine-tuned by integrating two cultures. The process of acculturation can encourage some people to become more flexible in their thinking and problem-solving. However, this does not work for all.

Evaluation

The direction of causality is not clear here – perhaps it is the flexible thinkers that choose to adopt both cultures and integrate them rather than becoming more flexible. Integration is not the choice of all people moving abroad and this could be due to their psychological make-up.

Research

- **Asendorpf & Motti-Stefanidi (2017)** looked at the relationship between the level of acculturation of an individual and their acceptance by non-immigrant peers. They looked specifically at 1057 13-year-old students in Greece. This was a longitudinal design over three years. For measurement of acculturation the researchers adapted a questionnaire to be age-appropriate, which was designed to measure the level of acculturation. In terms of acceptance, a peer nominations measure was used where students were asked to put down the names of three classmates they liked the most and three classmates they liked the least. They were also asked about their immigrant status at that particular time point and the proportion of immigrants within the class was noted. Researchers found that gradually, over the three years, the immigrants and Greeks did not differ in being rejected at all, implying that they had integrated fully. They also found that immigrants in classrooms with few immigrants became increasingly more accepted. Those students that embraced more of the Greek culture were rejected less. This research illustrates that acculturation as a process helps with social integration into a new culture.

- Research by **Serafini *et al.* (2017)** highlighted the negative effects of acculturation. The team looked at drug use among Spanish speaking Latinos in the United States of America. The team then looked at the relationship between level of acculturation and drug abuse, together with treatment success. The two types of acculturation which took on board a higher level of the American culture – that is, integrated and assimilated – showed higher levels of substance abuse than the separated and marginalized levels. However, they found no difference in the success of treatment in any of the groups. This suggests that acculturation can be negative and also that recovery from substance abuse transcends culture.

- **De Mamani *et al.* (2017)** examined how level of acculturation can affect mental health and quality of life in mental health patients in a sample of black and Hispanic patients with schizophrenia. The researchers found that symptom severity was not affected by level of acculturation, but quality of life was affected. Integrated individuals showed the best quality of life scores, followed by assimilated, then separated, then marginalized patients. This demonstrates that acculturation level can help with individuals who have poor mental health but also that retaining some of one's own culture helps too.

Evaluation

- The role of the mass media is an important part of the acculturation process. It allows for an individual not only to be immersed in the language of a culture, but also for some understanding of the cultural norms. It also means that there is little pressure on the individual other than absorption. Face-to-face interaction can be stressful. This means that mass media as a strategy of acculturation is very helpful initially.

- Strategies adopted in the acculturation process can be both helpful and unhelpful. If an individual spends a lot of their time with other immigrants from the same culture, they will initially settle quicker but eventually it will hinder them. This has implications for culture-specific communities and other communities around them.

- Language and communication are argued by researchers such as **Lakey (2003)** to be the most important aspect of acculturation. It facilitates social cognitive learning and cultural transmission, both of which play a part in acculturation.

- Acculturation is often seen as the best course of action for an individual moving to another culture, but it should be borne in mind that learning the negative aspects of a culture also occurs in the process.

Strengthen your learning

1 Explain what is meant by acculturation.

2 Outline the following stages of acculturation:
   a assimilation
   b separation
   c integration
   d marginalization.

3 In what ways does acculturation benefit an individual?

4 Summarize what research studies have suggested about acculturation

5 What other evaluative points can be made about acculturation.

6 For Tadmor *et al.*'s contemporary 2012 study of 'getting the most out of living abroad', in your own words, state the:
   a aims
   b procedure
   c results
   d conclusions
   e evaluative points.

Universalism/relativism

Universalism – the viewpoint that all humans are the same and behaviour is generalizable globally.

Relativism – the viewpoint that behaviour is culture-dependent and therefore not generalizable across cultures.

Universalism and **relativism** are concepts derived from anthropology but adopted and used by psychology to explain the differing ways that behaviour can be considered.

Universalism in psychology is the viewpoint that all humans are the same and any variation between them is superficial, whereas relativism argues that differences are at the psychological level as thought is affected by the culture we live in; it is socially constructed. There is an assumption in some research that the findings of their study will generalize globally. The scientific tradition of clustering people into groups and formulating laws which apply to them all has meant that cultural bias has occurred in psychology. Much of the research has been conducted in western universities and, as a consequence, the results are really applicable to that population only. The assumption of universality from these research studies has meant that findings have been generalized globally and this is a mistake. Cultural differences should have been tested and although it has occurred in some areas, it has not in all. Some biased researchers have assumed that their culture is the norm – this is ethnocentrism.

As much of the psychological research is carried out in western cultures, the ethnocentric bias in psychology is therefore based on western culture. However, it should be noted that this is not always the case. Psychological research often considers the perspectives of many cultures and as such the claim for universality can be supported by good research.

Cultural relativism

Cultural relativism is the opinion that there is no global 'right' and 'wrong' and that it is important to consider the behaviour of the individual within their culture before making a judgement. Context is vital. Social norms are culturally relative as what is considered acceptable in one culture may be unacceptable elsewhere.

Mental health disorders are affected by culture greatly. For anxiety disorders, the culture seems to determine what situations/objects are likely to cause the anxiety or fear. For example, in Japan there is a syndrome called 'taijin kyofusho'. Sufferers have a fear of upsetting or displeasing others. They also fear blushing and refuse to make eye contact. In the UK this would be diagnosed (along with other diagnostic criteria) as a social phobia. However, in the UK this is usually a fear of embarrassment rather than the fear of upsetting others. This emphasis is culturally determined. Culture-bound syndromes from across the world are culturally driven, such as kayak angst suffered by the Inuit people of western Greenland. The sufferer has acute anxiety about drowning or getting lost at sea. This is observed in seal hunters who often sail alone and the fear they experience is clearly linked to their environmental threats.

For more details on cultural relativism please see page 205 in Chapter 5.

IN THE NEWS

Ψ The Psychological Enquirer

RESIGNATION SYNDROME IN SWEDEN: 'THE APATHETIC'

■ **Figure 3.6** Resignation syndrome causes those affected to fall into a coma-like state

Georgi is a Swedish immigrant with Russian parents. He had embraced the Swedish culture and language but was, however, at risk of deportation. On finding out that the family were being deported to Russia he fell into a coma-like state, where he could not be reached. He didn't eat or drink and was admitted to hospital, having lost almost a stone in weight in a week.

Swedish doctors have named the syndrome 'uppgivenhetssyndrom' or resignation syndrome. It only exists in Sweden, and only within the refugee community. There is no evidence of underlying physical or neurological disease, but the doctors describe sufferers as having no will to live. Between 2000 and 2005 more than 400 children (aged between 8 and 15) had been diagnosed with the condition. If children suffering from uppgivenhetssyndrom are deported, they remain in the same coma-like state in the new culture. Swedish researchers have visited the home cultures of the immigrants, who usually come from Eastern Europe, and have found no evidence of the state being a reaction to trauma within the culture. It seems specific to immigrants who are at risk of deportation. Swedish doctors argue that the withdrawal and loss of will to live is due to a lack of 'trygget', a Swedish word that has no equivalent term in English. It is best described as a feeling of security, trust, a sense of belonging and a release from danger and anxiety.

The Swedish National Board of Health and Welfare produced a report in 2013 on how to treat 'uppgivenhetssyndrom' but makes it clear that the only real chance of recovery from the illness is permission to stay in Sweden. This underlines the very specific and context-dependent nature of the illness. When recovery does occur it takes months, as the body has been unresponsive and immobile, in many cases, for years. No one has yet died of the condition, but it can last for as long as four years.

Georgi was given permission to stay in Sweden and he started to make a recovery, which took several months, and is not yet complete. As he was in a non-communicative state the family was not able to reassure him that they now had permanent residence in Sweden, but they did 'awaken' him eventually by telling him constantly and reassuring him of his safety. He woke up several weeks after the permission to stay was granted, although it was a gradual process from there on. There are still cognitive effects, but he has returned to school.

Whatever the reasoning behind the syndrome, it is clear that it is culture specific. This supports the idea of cultural relativism and demonstrates that universalism is not appropriate for all behaviour. It seems there are circumstances where behaviour is influenced by the context and environment.

Emic and etic perspectives

Emic – when the researcher conducts research within their own culture and has a relativist viewpoint (an insider's viewpoint). They therefore do not generalize the findings to other cultures.

Etic – when a researcher conducts research outside of their culture and holds a universalist perspective. This then becomes an imposed etic (an outsider's viewpoint).

Emic and **etic** perspectives refer to the kind of analysis used by a researcher. As with universalism and relativism, this is a stance or bias that a researcher has. A researcher can conduct research within a new culture and see that as generalizable globally. This is an etic viewpoint. An imposed etic is the idea that what they have found is globally relevant. This is a strongly universalist viewpoint. Conversely, researchers can conduct research in their own culture, and see it only as relevant to the culture they are researching within. So, a researcher taking an emic perspective will think that their findings only relate to the culture where the research was conducted and therefore it cannot be generalized to a global population (a relativist viewpoint).

Conducting cross-cultural research is prone to the problem of an imposed etic, where researchers use research methods and tools relevant and applicable in their own culture but alien and non-applicable to other cultures, which can result in flawed conclusions being drawn. Many replications of western cultural studies in other cultures have involved an imposed etic.

Research

- **Henrich *et al.* (2010)** conducted a review of cognition experimentation and its applicability globally. The idea behind this was the argument that much of research is conducted on participants that are WEIRD (Western, Educated, Industrialized, Rich, Democratic), so Henrich *et al.* wanted to test the extent to which this is an issue in cognitive psychology and, as such, compared research cross-culturally. They found that there was considerable difference cross-culturally in findings in the fields of visual perception, fairness, cooperation, spatial reasoning, categorization and inferential induction, moral reasoning, reasoning styles, self-concepts and related motivations, and the heritability of IQ. They found that WEIRD participants are one of the least representative populations globally, meaning that cognitive research findings are over-generalized if conducted on a WEIRD population. It seems that the assumption we think in the same way across the world is problematic.

- Margaret Mead was an anthropologist who conducted research into gender differences between tribes in Papua New Guinea. In the Arapesh both males and females exhibited feminine, caring behaviours. In the Tchambuli, the men exhibited what would be seen in western culture as female behaviours, while women exhibited traditional (western) male behaviours. In the Mundugumor, both men and women exhibited masculine aggressive personalities. This work was used by Margaret Mead to argue that gender roles are culturally constructed. This was influential, but she later came to believe that gender roles were predominantly biological in nature. This dramatic conversion is argued by **Booth (1975)** to have occurred due to Mead marrying a man with very 'traditional' views on the roles of men and women, and to her having her own child. This suggests that the personal viewpoints investigators bring to their research have strong effects on the conclusions they ultimately draw. This is supported by **Errington & Gewertz's (1989)** study of the Tchambuli, which did not find the gender role reversals that Mead did. This illustrates that the researcher's viewpoint is influential in the analysis and conclusions drawn from research.

- Globalization may be contributing to the lessening of cultural differences; this may in turn mean that there is less difference between cultures. In terms of the emic/etic perspective this could mean that the imposed etic occurs more frequently as researchers may believe behaviour is more similar than it actually is.

Evaluation

- It is difficult to look at research through completely objective eyes, as we all have a gender and a culture. However, it should be noted that the vast majority of researchers give due consideration to these matters. A recognition that bias can occur is important in ensuring the effect it can have is minimized. An acknowledgement of how the bias could have affected analysis when research is published is also important.

- There is an issue of reactivity in human research as the gender of the researcher can alter the outcomes of the research. This is also the case depending on whether the researcher is from the ethnic majority or ethnic minority of the culture in which the research is conducted.

This makes biases hard to avoid, although, again, an acknowledgement of this reactivity is important to ensure interpretation of the findings is as fair as possible.

■ Qualitative research traditionally requires the researchers to acknowledge their biases and argues that universalism is not appropriate. When using and writing up qualitative methods, there is a requirement to write about the perspective of the researcher and many papers do not attempt to generalize out to global populations. Much qualitative research is ethnographic, which means it relates to the culture in which it is conducted. Therefore, it could be argued that some research rejects universalism completely.

■ Factors underlying cultural change

Cultures do not remain constant. The cultural norms change, and with those the values and behaviour vary. It is argued that the change can be swift over a matter of years, such as when political systems change leaders, an example of this being the collapse of communism in East Europe in the late 1980s. Change can also take decades or hundreds of years, as a much more gradual process. There are underlying factors which prompt change. These include the education system, the affluence of the nation and modernization. This section will focus upon geographical mobility and the way it can act as a transmission mechanism for cultural change.

According to a report on World Migration (2005), at the turn of the century in 2000, there were 175 million international migrants living in a country that was different to where they were born. A historical example of how the migration can lead to cultural change is in Karelia, Russia in the 1930s. The region of Karelia shares a border with Finland, and in the 1930s 7000 North American Finns moved to that area of Russia. With the migration the Finns brought more efficient and productive ways of working together with a strong work ethic. The working practices of the region changed as a consequence. There was also an introduction to North American ideas and culture. The social identity of the immigrants became part of the Soviet state, but their influence on the culture was significant. This illustrates the way in which migration and the process of acculturation have an effect on the culture the immigrants have made home.

The geographical mobility of a population within a culture can also have cultural effects. Many cultures have high levels of movement within the country. Many people in the UK and other countries live in a city or area of their country which is different from where they were born and where their family is. This has a cultural effect on friendship styles and the influence of the family.

There was a distinction between communities made by **Tönnies & Loomis (1957)** in terms of gemeinschaft (little movement into and out of the area, a traditional community) and gesellschaft (a mobile population, a more modern society). Gemeinschaft was the way communities worked before the geographical mobility of the modern world, with an emphasis on familiarity and families that settled and remained for generations. As more and more of the population move within their country, the influence of the family has diminished. They are no longer nearby to see and interact with on a daily basis and, as a consequence, people have to rely upon friends for social support. However, within some areas currently, the level of geographical mobility is so high that the friendship and social style varies, because of the transient nature of the friendships formed.

The size of friendship groups in different areas varies due to social mobility. If it is high, then residents will make a larger number of friends but fewer close friends so that as a friend moves in and out, they will still have a social support to call upon. This is not, apparently, a conscious decision but is behaviour that is observed in such areas. It results in a cultural change of friendship networks if an area, because of the job market, has large numbers of people moving in and out of the area.

The types, not just number, of friendships also are different. In areas of high geographical mobility, the friendships are not as 'involved' and long term and there are lower levels of obligations because the friendships are not as deep. These are called duty-free friendships. What becomes important in a friendship varies with high levels of mobility. For example, in the USA, in areas where there is residential mobility the attributed value in friendships include being active and energetic. This is argued to be because participation and action are needed in an area that relies upon friends for support.

▨ Research

- **Efremkin (2016)** reviewed the role that migrants have played historically in cultural change. He noted the positive influence that migrants can have in terms of modernization and intellectual exchange. He therefore argued that immigrants acted as agents of social and cultural change.

- **Oishi (2010)** studied the effect mobility has on social relationships. He found, within the USA, that geographical mobility was linked to different friendship styles within areas of high social mobility. This illustrates that geographical mobility can have a sociocultural effect on sub-groups in terms of the kind of interactions and relationships formed.

- **Adams & Plaut (2003)** looked at cross-cultural friendships and the relationship style. They found that in Ghana, where there are low levels of geographical mobility, a smaller number of friendships are formed, as opposed to the number with the American population. When asked, 29 per cent of Ghanaians agreed that having a large number of friends was foolish, compared to only 4 per cent of Americans. The Ghanaians also showed that they were cautious in forming friendships because they felt that there was a large amount of obligation involved in being a friend. This was not expressed by Americans to the same extent.

▨ Evaluation

- Friendship formation is a complicated area and there are many reasons why we form friendships, and not just for social support. It is evident that there is an influence from geographical mobility in terms of friendship numbers and type. However, how large this influence is, as compared with other influences such as personality type, is difficult to establish.

- Causation cannot be established easily in this research area. Research is necessarily naturalistic and therefore correlational. It is not possible to manipulate geographical mobility experimentally. It is possible that the type of people who move from their home area have a preference for 'duty-free friendships' anyway, and it is not their movement that affects the friendship style.

- Income can have a confounding effect on what individuals need out of friendships. The idea that friends are needed for practical support in areas of high mobility is not as strong when the areas are affluent. In wealthy areas, it is possible to pay for support services such as childcare and this means that friendships are entirely duty free. Therefore, when analysing the effect on the culture of friendship formation in an area, it is necessary to consider both geographical mobility of the population and affluence. The research area is a complex one.

LINK TO THE BIOLOGICAL EXPLANATION

Cultural change is argued, by some theorists, to be related to evolutionary theory. They say it arises as an adaptation to a changing environment. For example, when referring to relationships, when there is geographical mobility it becomes more important to have many friendships as support because the likelihood of a friend moving away from the area again increases. However, there is an issue with this argument in that cultural change can be rapid and this would not occur in evolutionary theory.

Strengthen your learning

1 Explain what is meant by universalism/relativism.

2 Explain what is meant by cultural relativism. Give an example of your own to show your understanding.

3 Explain what is meant by emic and etic perspectives.

4 Summarize what research has suggested about emic and etic perspectives.

5 What other evaluative points can be made about universalism/relativism?

6 Outline factors underlying cultural change.

7 Summarize what research has suggested about factors underlying cultural change.

8 What other evaluative points can be made about factors underlying cultural change?

SECTION SUMMARY

- Enculturation is the process of learning to act in a culturally appropriate way within the culture we are born into; and it is the way cultural norms are transmitted.
- Acculturation is similar to enculturation, but it is the socialization process within a new culture. There are different levels of acculturation: assimilation, separation, integration and marginalization.
- Universalism is a perspective that believes all humans are the same globally, so behaviour can be generalized across the global population. Relativism is the opposite viewpoint where all behaviour is seen as culture-specific.
- An etic perspective is when a researcher conducts research outside of their culture and holds a universalist perspective. This then becomes an imposed etic (an outsider's viewpoint).
- An emic perspective is when the researcher conducts research within their own culture and has a relativist viewpoint (an insider's viewpoint). They therefore do not generalize the findings to other cultures.

The influence of globalization on behaviour

Globalization – global trade, cooperation and geographical mobility across cultures.

Globalization is the cooperation and involvement of countries, both culturally and economically. There are exchanges of goods and capital between cultures but also people, knowledge, culture and fashion are exchanged across borders. This section will consider the effects of this exchange on attitudes, identities and behaviour, but also then look at what can happen when local and global influence mix. Finally, the research methods used to investigate globalization will be considered.

'One day there will be no borders, no boundaries, no flags and no countries and the only passport will be the heart.'
Carlos Santana

'Globalization has made national boundaries more porous but not irrelevant. Nor does globalization mean the creation of a universal community.'
Joseph S. Nye Jr.

FOCUS ON....

(With reference to research studies)
- How globalization may influence behaviour.
- The effect of the interaction of local and global influences on behaviour.
- Methods used to study the influence of globalization on behaviour.

Please note: This section is for HL students only.

How globalization may influence behaviour

This section will consider the influence of globalization on behaviour. For this it is necessary to consider how attitudes and identity are affected, as this leads to behavioural effects. This section will consider the effect on nationalism attitudes and biculturalism identity as globalization effects. It will also look at body image and eating disorders behaviour change.

Nationalism

Nationalism is an attitude towards your own and other countries. A nationalist attitude can be patriotic and has much national pride, but also sometimes, with a highly nationalist attitude, there is a feeling of superiority of one's own country over others.

It has been argued that globalization both increases and reduces nationalism. The increase can occur due to multiple reasons. The strength of national identity is perceived by some to be under threat from globalization. There can be a feeling of being overwhelmed by 'foreign ideas and goods'. This can make people feel threatened in terms of their identity and they sometimes

Xenophobic – a dislike of people from other countries.

wish to accentuate their membership to the nation (i.e. the in-group). As globalization has increased levels of migration, the presence of ethnic minorities within some countries is perceived by some to be a threat to their way of life. Global recessions also prompt resentment and when the economy is weak there can often be a call for immigration to be curbed. This can lead to **xenophobic** behaviour.

However, globalization is also argued to reduce nationalism. The global economy has meant that there is interdependence on other countries for imports. This means that the 'foreign' becomes familiar. There is the potential to learn about the cultures of other countries and this reduces xenophobic attitudes, weakening of national boundaries and increased interdependence on other countries. The exchange of ideas, goods and cultures across borders occurs at such a rapid rate now that it is hard to avoid globalization.

Identity effects

Globalization has been seen as a threat to national identity. As the world becomes, culturally, a smaller place and there is more cultural exchange it can be understood how cultural identity is reduced. Terms such as 'citizen of the world' and 'transnational' are now used to describe people who are no longer living or working in their place of birth and who are used to living in many different cultures.

George Ritzer (1993) wrote about McDonaldization – the idea that we can buy an identical burger in identical surroundings in cities around the world. The term 'McDonaldization' is used as a derogatory expression against globalization and the negative effect, some argue, it has on local culture and identity. A French sheep farmer, José Bové, was arrested for bulldozing a McDonald's franchise which was under construction in his local area in Roquefort, France. Bové was protesting against the introduction of McDonald's into his home area because he did not agree with the introduction of cheap and tasteless food. He argued it was a 'profound revolt against the American nutritional model, which produces a nation where 30 per cent of people are obese'. He also objected to the American heavy taxation of high-quality European food, such as Roquefort cheese. Bové was responsible for introducing a new phrase into the French language, 'la sale bouffe', which roughly translates as 'dirty food'. Bové was sent to prison for his vandalism of the building site and served his sentence of three months but then went on to continue as an anti-globalization activist.

Some people are happy to be described as bicultural and the increase in bicultural marriages has meant that this is, indeed, a more common occurrence in children. Immigration and globalization have resulted in more cross-border workforce movement and, as a consequence, more exposure to people from foreign cultures. This, in turn, increases the number of relationships that arise. For bicultural individuals, this means that one culture is not influential, on its own, in terms of identity. This is particularly the case if both parents live in a third culture, which is not where they grew up.

The effects of identity on behaviour are discussed in the first section of this chapter (page 106).

The effect on body image and eating disorders

Exposure to how people think and act globally (usually by the mass media) has had behavioural effects on populations across the world. One example of where this occurs is in body image behaviour. The introduction of global media to countries can mean that there is a shift in the 'ideal' body image or an exaggeration of effects that are already there.

An example of this is the increase of 'bleaching syndrome' globally, which is the behaviour of applying products to skin to make it appear whiter. This occurs across cultures in women of colour and also can be found within cultures too. Some women with dark skin feel that a paler skin is more attractive. Japanese women see pale skin as more refined, while Nicaraguan women of Costenos descent try to appear more like their 'Mestizos' peers, who form the light-skinned majority. There is an association within some cultures that pale skin is a sign of affluence and attractiveness.

Eating disorders are discussed in more detail in Chapter 5, 'Abnormal psychology', on page 188.

KEY STUDY | **CLASSIC RESEARCH**

'Eating behaviours and attitudes following prolonged exposure to television among ethnic Fijian adolescent girls'
Becker et al. (2002)

One element of the effect of eating disorders and body image behaviour is the globalization of the media, where American and European programmes are exported to many areas of the world. The effect this can have on the population is outlined here.

Aim

Becker and her research team aimed to look at the effect of introducing media to a previously media-naïve population.

Procedure

1 The study was conducted in Fiji, which did not have television until the mid-1990s. The body image ideal was heavier in Fiji than some western cultures and cultural traditions were protective against body image dissatisfaction.

2 The researchers took a measure of eating attitudes and interviewed 63 participants, initially aged about 17 years old, before television was introduced, and then interviewed another group after television had been in place for three years. The second group were older by an average of five years. The measures and interviews were conducted in English, but also in the local dialect in cases where a respondent struggled with English.

Results

Becker *et al.* found that:

1 There was a significant increase in indicators of eating disorders.

2 The interview responses after the introduction of television showed that the interviewees had an increased level of anxiety about their weight and there were changes in attitudes to diet, weight loss and ideal body image.

Conclusion

The researchers concluded that owing to the introduction of television there had been a cultural shift in perception of body image and that the introduction of television and the western programmes broadcast had been responsible for this attitude and behaviour change.

Evaluation

- There was no clinical diagnosis of eating disorders made in the study so the argument that eating disorder prevalence had increased cannot be upheld.

- The different groups used in the study may have meant that the results were due to individual differences rather than television.

Research

- **Sobol et al. (2018)** examined the effect of globalization on consumer behaviour in the Netherlands. They found that there was an effect of national identity, depending on which type of goods the Dutch consumers bought. National identity affected purchasing of food, so there remained a preference for Dutch snacks and meals. However, with fashion and luxury items, there was a preference for global brands. This shows that globalization occurs to a greater degree in some areas more than others and therefore the effect on attitudes, identity and behaviour varies.

- **Hall (2013)** found that there were worldwide effects on body image perception from globalization in terms of ideal skin colour. He argued that globalization was to blame for the bleaching of skin in many cultures.
- **Roca & Urmeneta (2013)** found there was an increasing number of binational marriages in Spain, with 8000 in 1996 and almost 30,000 by 2009.

Evaluation

- The extent to which globalization can be held responsible for changes in attitudes, identity and behaviour is difficult to ascertain. It is one part of a complex socio-political landscape and, as such, is combined with other forces of change. This is difficult to test methodologically.
- Globalization can be seen in both positive and negative terms and the effects it has on the psychology of an individual are varying. However, it can be argued that globalization is now inevitable, due to technological advancements such as the internet. An awareness of the potential threat to identity and the effect that could have on behaviour is important; hence, the use of glocalization (see following section).
- Much of the research on globalization focuses upon consumer behaviour and therefore the focus is on effects within businesses. This means that there is a bias towards the effect of consumerism and global brands. This focus can often mean that it appears as if western countries are dominating. However, it should be remembered that globalization has also meant that medical advancements can be accessed across the world and goods are sold from poorer countries to richer countries. The function of globalization is not all in a one-way direction.

The effect of the interaction of local and global influences on behaviour

Glocalization and localization (the opposite of globalization; keeping a behaviour specific to the area of the world it comes from) are at the opposite ends of a continuum. Somewhere in the middle of the two ends of the spectrum is behaviour that is adaptive but yet retains its cultural uniqueness. **Glocalization** is a portmanteau word, as it combines globalization and localization, and is used to describe the product of combining both behaviour that is global but identified as originating in a specific culture. The saying 'Think locally, act globally' is associated with glocalization, and reiterates the need to take both the local and global perspectives into account.

> **Glocalization –**
> the adaptation of
> globalization to the local
> environment.

An early example of glocalization is the incorporation of foreign words into a local language. This occurred in the English language when French was used by the British elite in the Norman years. Examples are menu, chic, and fiancé, words all incorporated from another culture and now widely used by English speakers.

Consumer behaviour

Glocalization occurs mostly in terms of consumer behaviour. Global companies acknowledge the need for cultural identity to be preserved. This was not always the case and the need to adapt seems to have coincided with the rise of Asian economies in particular. A global brand cannot be too arrogant and expect consumers to buy its goods, merely because it comes from the West. There is strong national identity to cater for.

In terms of global brands taking local behaviour into account, food companies such as McDonald's and Kentucky Fried Chicken have altered their menu to accommodate local food preferences. So, for example, McDonald's has introduced the Maharaja Mac in India and the Ebi Filit-O in Japan. In Nigeria, Guinness not only changed the formulation of its beer to suit cultural tastes by increasing the alcohol content to 7.5 per cent and making it sweeter, the company also changed the marketing to focus upon the drink as good for virility. This is, apparently, a focus for men living in Africa. Indeed, it is known locally as Viagra, which is a drug that helps sexual functioning.

Communications companies such as Nokia have responded to local needs too by introducing dust-resistant keypads, anti-slip grip and phone flashlights, specifically for rural Indian customers (particularly lorry drivers). This was following observation that the dusty roads in India caused problems for their customers.

All these adaptations are designed to increase sales, and marketing is targeted closely to the potential consumers to encourage purchasing behaviour and brand loyalty.

Hybrid cultures emerge from glocalization, and imported global influence is often incorporated into the local culture. Globalization has meant that people are introduced to new choices and these are often integrated to the way of life of the culture. An example is the introduction of Indian food into Britain, to the point now where curries are eaten widely by many, with curry houses employing about 100,000 people in the UK. It was the Asian immigrants who introduced the food locally, and its popularity grew. In the 1960s there were just 300 curry restaurants in Britain, but the industry has since flourished.

Sport

Glocalization also occurs in sporting behaviour and choice. The National Basketball Association (NBA) looked at how it could change to encourage basketball as a sport in China. One key strategy that helped was the focus on fan engagement; that is, understanding the game and using games as an opportunity for socialization in groups of friends and families. NBA teams were taken to China to play exhibition matches. The competitive element was underplayed, acknowledging the collectivist cultural roots. The NBA also found that they needed to emphasize the American aspects of the game such as bringing in cheerleaders, mascots and even the authentic wooden floor, to recreate the events watched by Chinese people on television. However, entertainment during the breaks was Chinese in origin; for example, there would be dancing dragons, especially in games that coincided with local festivals.

▧ Research

- **Gineikiene & Diamantopoulos (2017)** looked at psychological ownership of a product and how it affected the likelihood of buying the goods. The researchers defined psychological ownership by whether a brand is perceived as domestic or foreign. This can be affected by whether those around you use a brand or not. Gineikiene and Diamantopoulos found that if someone perceived goods as domestic they were more likely to buy them. This shows that it is important, for global brands at least, to adapt the presentation of their goods to make them appear as 'local' as possible.

- **Lim & Park (2013)** conducted a cross-cultural study of consumer behaviour on participants in the USA and South Korea. They wanted to look at the effect of cultural context and cosmopolitan (global) attitude on consumer behaviour in new electronic goods. They found that variation occurred across the two countries and that the receptiveness to new innovations in the field was related to the levels of individualism and masculinity. American consumers were more likely to try new innovations than South Korean consumers and this related, the researchers argued, to how the countries measure in terms of Hofstede's cultural dimensions, with the USA being more individualistic and masculine than South Korea.

- **Zhou *et al.* (2017)** conducted one-to-one interviews and focus groups on Chinese men who attended exhibition matches of basketball in China. They were asked about their thoughts on the game, and the likelihood of playing themselves. They indicated in their answers that they had been enthused by the matches and liked the social atmosphere. They also said that it had encouraged them to get better at playing the sport. They appreciated the combination of American and Chinese culture, indicating that it did not threaten the cultural identity, despite being a western sport. This shows the importance of acknowledging cultural identity when introducing non-local activities/brands.

▧ Evaluation

- Social identity theory appears to play a part in consumer behaviour. The perception of a brand being domestic is a strong force in determining its success and therefore combining a global brand with local considerations is important. Global brands should acknowledge the cultural identity of those who are potential consumers so that they fit with the in-group.

- Sometimes for a brand to be perceived as foreign is seen as attractive. This happens in the luxury goods market, where designer goods are bought as non-local and are phenomenally successful.

■ There are many considerations as to why someone might buy goods or participate in an activity and this is not always related to whether it is global or local. Therefore, it is important not to overemphasize the role of globalization and glocalization in behaviour.

PSYCHOLOGY IN THE REAL WORLD

It is evident that cultural stereotypes and 'in-group, out-group' behaviour could be reduced if awareness and understanding of other cultures were increased. In the world of business, internationally cultural competence is a necessary skill. One such way of achieving this is by cultural training. This aims to increase awareness of behavioural differences in other cultures and understanding how cultures operate in the working environment. This is designed to increase an individual's CQ (cultural intelligence).

The effectiveness of this training was tested by **Eisenberg *et al.* (2013)**. They looked at levels of CQ prior to training, and after. Initially, the researchers measured students' international experience by the number of countries in which students lived, worked, or were educated for at least six months. This was to gauge the probable prior level of CQ. This measure was added to by a questionnaire, before and after the training. Results indicated that there was a significant increase in CQ following the training.

This supports the idea that cultural IQ can be taught and therefore an individual does not need to be well travelled to have a cross-cultural perspective. It also shows how working or living in a cultural situation that is unfamiliar to your own requires acknowledging local behaviour and customs.

Methods used to study the influence of globalization on behaviour

When looking at the influences of globalization on behaviour, research is conducted across boundaries; these are not simply border lines but include functional barriers. The suitability of measures is therefore an issue.

In some ways, it is necessary to study the effects of globalization on behaviour by adoption of a sort of glocalization of research methodology. The western methods readily adopted by many researchers may be wholly inappropriate and a hybrid version between the requirements of the western measurement and locally appropriate methodology is needed. This is done through the adaptation of measures.

Adaptations of measures

In the 1920s there was a series of tests used on immigrants to the United States. They included knowledge of the American culture, such as past presidents, and many of the immigrants struggled to answer the questions correctly, partly due to their knowledge being based on the culture they had come from and also, in a large part, due to the fact that many could not speak English. Their poor performance on the tests was taken to indicate they were 'feeble minded'.

It is evident from this historical example that tests need to be adapted appropriately for use with different cultures. This adaptation includes consideration of linguistic, construct validity, cultural response and sample factors. These are outlined below, and the methods used to combat the issues are discussed.

Linguistic considerations

It is clear from the historical example above that linguistic considerations must be made on tests if they are to be used globally. Mere translation of a measure is not sufficient, as the wording may affect the validity of the questionnaire. When measuring constructs cross-culturally the researcher has to be sure they are measuring the same construct. If poorly translated, the validity of the questionnaire is threatened. Researchers developing research globally therefore have to ensure adaptation of a questionnaire is conducted systematically and that the properties of the final product correspond with the questionnaire as it is presented in the language of origin.

There are often five stages to the process: forward translation, synthesis, back translation, expert committee review, and pilot testing.

1   *Forward translation*: As the initial stage, forward translation is the translation of the scale into the second language. This is often conducted by a bilingual group of individuals (ideally), as fluency in both languages is needed. It is also helpful if one of the translators is

aware of the topic and the other is naïve because then there can be a translation conducted that is appropriate to the topic, together with one which is similar to the perspective of the participants.

2 *Synthesis*: At this point the translations are brought together and differences in terminology and phrasing used are discussed. Researchers are always present in this process because there is a need to ensure the research construct is considered appropriately.

3 *Back translation*: The third stage of back translation is when the resultant questionnaire from the translation is translated back into the language it was originally translated from. Though seemingly strange, this actually ensures that the translation and the original are similar. The translation is conducted by new translators who were not involved in the process. Again, the process is supervised and discussed.

4 *Expert committee review*: The fourth stage is an expert committee review, which discusses any discrepancies between the two versions and how to deal with them. There is then a pre-final questionnaire produced.

5 *Pilot testing*: The final stage is pilot testing the questionnaire with the target sample. The sample size varies, but at least 40 participants are necessary to check the reliability and validity of the questionnaire. Essentially, it is a check to ensure the questionnaire 'behaves' in the same way as the original on a home population.

Construct validity considerations

Construct validity is also an issue with tests generated from western universities. This can occur owing to imposed etic by western researchers who believe their perspective is universal. An emic perspective is seen by some to be more appropriate in looking at the effects of globalization on behaviour because it is context-dependent. Examples of this kind of issue include research centring on education, for example in studies of collaborative learning. In the West, this may be seen as students sharing an activity, with everyone in the group being responsible. In collectivist societies such as the Middle East or Far East, this might mean that the strongest group members do most of the work and the weaker ones then feel less likely to fail. From this example, it is evident that the cultural understanding of the construct of collaborative learning is qualitatively different between cultures.

A way of dealing with this issue is to combine emic and etic perspectives when designing research. Researchers should always familiarize themselves with the culture they are studying, much like companies should do when moving their goods or services into a culture. This means any cultural biases they have can be challenged by what they observe. To see the effect of globalization it is clearly important to consider what the social norm is.

Sampling considerations

There can be differences in cultures that need to be acknowledged, for example with demographic levels of age, gender, job position, status, job tenure and education. If they are not taken into account, there can be criticisms levelled at the research in terms of stereotyping and bias. A good knowledge of the sub-cultures that occur within a culture is necessary. For example, taking a sample of residents in a London borough such as Chelsea compared with a group from a town in the Highlands will vary considerably. The best way to ensure a representative sample, therefore, is to match samples across as many variables as possible.

Sampling frames are a method used to try and ensure a representative sample of participants. Sampling frames are essentially a list of all the various 'types' of people within a population. These vary from culture to culture. The key step is to give due consideration to all possible elements of the population along demographic and sub-cultural variables. If careful consideration is given at this point, then the researcher has a chance of finding a suitably representative sample. Once those elements are included in the sampling frame it is then important for the researcher to ensure they are included in appropriate proportions. Then if that process is conducted, the level of representativeness will be equivalent in all cultures involved, giving sampling equivalence.

Cultural response considerations

Cultures and sub-cultures demonstrate varying response biases to each other. A measure administered in a cultural context may elicit quite different results, not because of the differences in behaviour but actually due to response differences. The response patterns vary on scales such as Likert scales and semantic differential scales (e.g. 'always', 'sometimes', 'rarely', 'never'). Even the position on the scale can elicit different cultural responses. In the UK a response on the middle point is deemed to be that the individual cannot decide beyond the mid-point and does not have a strong opinion. This is not the case, for example, in South Korea where a mid-point response would be interpreted as mild agreement. Asian cultures will also avoid the far ends of scales because this is seen as being too different from the norm or collective. South European cultures have been shown to avoid the mid-point due to wishing to be seen as decisive. If the scales are not calibrated appropriately, perhaps by avoiding mid-points, then the data collected can be unreliable. It is also important that researchers consider response biases within cultures during analysis of results to ensure the appropriate interpretation of the findings.

Research

■ **Koopmans *et al.* (2016)** adapted a work performance questionnaire for use in English-speaking countries. The original questionnaire was written in Dutch. The researchers undertook the five-stage translation process (see above) to adapt the questionnaire. The adaptation was successful, and when run with target populations the questionnaire's measurement properties seemed promising. This illustrates how adaptation to other cultures is possible if a rigorous process is used.

■ **Schaffer & Riordan (2003)** reviewed cross-cultural research and highlighted issues with conducting research globally. They found problems with transferring constructs and finding representative samples between cultures, which has obvious implications for the measures used in research into the effects of globalization.

■ **Kim & Kim (2016)** looked at response bias to questionnaires in the Korean population. They found that these were different from the western patterns and this was attributed to cultural differences. This highlights how the measurements used should be adapted, and the responses given should be analysed, with culture in mind.

Evaluation

■ It is known that most academics who publish in the top European and American journals are trained and based in US and European universities. This creates a bias towards their culture. In cross-cultural research on globalization, this could affect the analysis and interpretation of findings (see emic/etic and universalist/relativist perspectives in the previous section). Researchers with a universalist and etic mind-set are less likely to think that their research tools need adapting for the culture they are studying. This means that this adaptation does not always occur.

■ Research tool adaptation is a lengthy and detailed process. This means that it is not always carried out as thoroughly as is needed and there are still issues with the measurement tool. Unfortunately, this is difficult to distinguish from actual behavioural effects, so findings can be reported with poor validity.

■ Ideally, globalization research should always include the involvement of a combination of researchers from all cultures in the research. This means that an imposed etic is avoided and it also ensures that both measurement and sampling are carried out in a culturally appropriate way.

Strengthen your learning

1   Explain what is meant by globalization.

2   Explain how the following factors relate to globalization:
    a nationalism
    b identity effects
    c body image and eating disorders.

3   Summarize what research studies have suggested about globalization.

4   What other evaluative points can be made about globalization?

5   For Becker *et al.*'s classic 2002 study of eating behaviours of Fijian girls, in your own words, state the:
    a aims
    b procedure
    c results
    d conclusions
    e evaluative points.

6   Outline the effects of globalization on:
    a consumer behaviour
    b sport.

7   Summarize what research studies have suggested about:
    a consumer behaviour
    b sport.

8   What other evaluative points can be made about:
    a consumer behaviour
    b sport?

9   Why are adaptations of measures necessary when studying the influence of globalization on behaviour?

10 Explain the following adaptations of measures:
    a linguistic considerations
    b construct validity considerations
    c sampling considerations
    d cultural response considerations.

11 Summarize what research studies have suggested about adaptations of measures.

12 What other evaluative points can be made about adaptations of measures?

SECTION SUMMARY

■ Globalization affects behaviour by changes in attitude (e.g. nationalism) and identity (e.g. the number of bicultural individuals and cultural transference). Behavioural effects include behaviour relating to body image and eating disorders.

■ The blending of cultures following globalization is called glocalization. This has occurred all over the world in many domains, for example consumer and sport behaviour.

■ When researching globalization, it is important to consider how culturally appropriate the measures used are. Adaptation may be necessary. The researcher must consider linguistic, validity, sampling and response factors.

■ Assessment check

1	Explain how enculturation affects cognition and/or behaviour.	(9 marks)
2	Outline one research study relating to acculturation.	(9 marks)
3	Outline one or more methods used to study the influence of globalization on behaviour.	(9 marks)
4	Discuss enculturation.	(22 marks)
5	Evaluate research studies related to acculturation.	(22 marks)
6	Contrast enculturation and acculturation.	(22 marks)
7	Discuss how globalization may influence attitudes, identities and behaviour.	(22 marks)
8	Evaluate the effect of the interaction of local and global influences on behaviour.	(22 marks)

4 Approaches to researching behaviour

'Equipped with his five senses, man explores the universe around him and calls the adventure science.'
Edwin Powell Hubble (1929)

IN THE NEWS

Ψ The Psychological Enquirer

THE WAR AGAINST THE BIRDS

■ **Figure 4.1** The War against the Birds: the consequences of acting upon unproven 'facts'

In 1958, Chinese leader Mao Zedong made the observation that sparrows always seemed to be feasting on the rice fields. He estimated that each sparrow ate 4.5 kilos a year of rice, so for every 1 million sparrows killed there would be food for 60,000 people. He therefore announced that all citizens were to participate in a campaign to kill the sparrows, so that food production could be increased and famine avoided. On 13 December *The Shanghai Newspaper* reported on the start of the 'total war' against the birds, of the waving flags and scarecrows, the whistles and gongs to keep the birds airborne, the poisoning and shooting of sparrows, the destruction of their nests and eggs. Hundreds of millions of sparrows were killed and the bird became nearly extinct. Yet, as early as April 1960 it was realized with horror that what the birds had mainly been snacking on were the locust grubs that attacked the rice crop. Without the sparrows the grubs literally had a field day, swarms of locusts rampaged unchecked, and between 1958 and 1961, during a period known in China as 'the great famine', it is estimated that up to 60 million people starved to death.

This is an example of the negative consequences that can occur when practical applications are based on flawed evidence. Mao Zedong's intentions were good, but if he had subjected his beliefs to proper scientific research, this disaster would never have happened. Practical applications that truly benefit society should be based upon objective, unbiased research that is capable of being replicated in order to check its credentials. In this chapter we look at the many ways in which psychologists can conduct research, their individual strengths and weaknesses, and the techniques that can be employed, so that research is carried out in a responsible manner.

Research methods

- The experimental method.
- The different types of experiment used in psychological investigations.
- Non-experimental research methods used in psychology: observations, self-reports (questionnaires and interviews), correlational studies and case studies.

Research methods – the means by which explanations are tested.

Experimental method – a research method using random allocation of participants and the manipulation of variables to determine cause and effect.

Independent variable (IV) – the factor manipulated by researchers in an investigation.

Dependent variable (DV) – the factor measured by researchers in an investigation.

Operationalization of variables – the process of defining variables into measureable factors.

Extraneous variables – variables other than the IV that might affect the DV.

Confounding variables – uncontrolled extraneous variables that negatively affect results.

There are several **research methods** in psychology. Like a golfer selecting the most appropriate club, psychologists choose the most appropriate method for research. No single method is perfect; each has strengths and weaknesses.

The experimental method

The **experimental method** is a scientific method involving the manipulation of variables to determine cause and effect. A variable is any object, characteristic or event that varies in some way. Participants are randomly allocated (without bias) to the different testing groups, so that the groups should be fairly similar. All procedures in an experiment should be standardized (kept the same for all participants).

In an experiment a researcher manipulates an **independent variable (IV)** to see its effect on a **dependent variable (DV)**. For example, caffeine consumption (IV) could be manipulated to see its effect on reaction time (DV).

Operationalization

Variables must be operationalized, which means clearly defining them so they can be manipulated (IV) and measured (DV). Some variables are more difficult to operationalize; for instance, anger levels. Another problem is that **operationalization of variables** leads to only one aspect of a variable being measured. However, without accurate operationalization, results will be unreliable and could not be replicated to check their validity.

Extraneous and confounding variables

Extraneous variables (other variables that could affect the DV) are controlled so that they do not vary across any of the experimental conditions or between participants. Uncontrolled extraneous variables can become **confounding variables** and 'confuse' the results by affecting the DV. For example, if researchers wished to investigate the effect of background music (Condition 1) or silence (Condition 2) on homework performance using two classes, they would have to control a number of extraneous variables, including age, homework difficulty, and so on. If these were all controlled, the results would be trustworthy. However, if the participants in Condition 1 were brighter than those in Condition 2, intelligence would be a confounding variable. The researchers could not then be sure whether differences in homework performance were due to the presence of the music or intelligence. Results would be confounded and worthless.

There are three main types of extraneous variables:

1 *Participant variables* – concern factors such as participants' age and intelligence.

2 *Situational variables* – concern the experimental setting and surrounding environment, for example temperature and noise levels.

3 *Experimenter variables* – concern changes in personality, appearance and conduct of the researcher. For example, female researchers may gain different results from male ones.

Replicability

Replicability – being able to repeat a study to check the validity of the results.

Replicability involves repeating research to check the validity of the results. Therefore, research has to be fully and clearly written up so that it can be repeated under identical conditions. **Fleischmann & Pons (1989)** claimed to have created cold fusion, raising hopes of producing abundant and cheap energy. However, replications of their experimental technique failed to get the same results. They had made an error in their procedure and only by replication were scientists able to realize this.

Demand characteristics

Conducting research involves interaction between researchers and participants and such interactions can affect research findings.

There are several features of research studies that enable participants to guess what a study is about and what is expected of them. Such **demand characteristics** can involve participants:

- guessing the purpose of research and trying to please the researcher by giving the 'right' results
- guessing the purpose of the research and trying to annoy the researcher by giving the wrong results; this is called the 'screw you effect'
- acting unnaturally out of nervousness or fear of evaluation
- acting unnaturally due to social desirability bias (see page 156).

The single-blind procedure is a technique that reduces demand characteristics. It involves participants having no idea which condition of a study they are in. In drug trials, for example, they would not know whether they were being given a real drug or a placebo drug (sugar pill).

Investigator effects

Investigator effects are the ways in which researchers unconsciously influence the results of research and can occur in several ways:

- Physical characteristics of investigators may influence results, such as age or ethnicity. For example, male participants may be unwilling to admit sexist views to female researchers.
- Less obvious personal characteristics of investigators, like accent or tone of voice, can influence results; for example, participants may respond differently to someone with a stern voice.
- Investigators may be unconsciously biased in their interpretation of data and find what they expect to find.

The double-blind procedure is a technique to reduce investigator effects, which involves neither participants nor investigators knowing which condition participants are in. They are both 'blind' to this knowledge. This prevents investigators from unconsciously giving participants clues as to which condition they are in and therefore reduces demand characteristics. For example, in drug trials, the drug and placebo would be allocated in such a way that neither the participant, nor researcher would know who was receiving which.

Reflexivity is a means of controlling the personal biases of researchers when conducting research; for example, bias in their selection of research area, the research method to be used and which participants are selected. Reflexivity helps researchers become aware of any biases they have, in order for them to be addressed. Reflexivity can be established in several ways:

- Multiple investigators – using several researchers can help individual investigators to become aware of any biases they have.
- Reflexive journal – during the research process an investigator records methodological decisions and the reasons for them, as well as reflecting upon the progress of the study.
- Reporting research perspectives – a researcher's preconceptions, expectations, values, and so on, concerning a study, are presented in the final research report.

> **Demand characteristics** – a research effect where participants form impressions of the research purpose and unconsciously alter their behaviour accordingly.

> **Investigator effects** – a research effect where researcher features influence participants' responses.

Strengthen your learning

1 Describe the experimental method in terms of:
   a manipulation of variables
   b random allocation
   c operationalization
   d extraneous and confounding variables.

2 What are:
   a demand characteristics
   b investigator effects?

3 How can the risk of demand characteristics and investigator effects be reduced?

4 What is replication and what is its purpose in research?

5 What is reflexivity and how can it be established?

Types of experiment

'No amount of experimentation can ever prove me right;
a single experiment can prove me wrong.'
Albert Einstein (1920)

Laboratory experiments

**Laboratory
experiment** –
experiment conducted
in a controlled
environment, allowing
the establishment of
causality.

Laboratory experiments are performed in a controlled environment, using standardized procedures, with participants randomly allocated to experimental groups.

Advantages of laboratory experiments

■ *High degree of control* – experimenters control all variables and the IV and DV are precisely operationalized (defined) and measured, leading to greater accuracy and objectivity.

■ *Replication* – other researchers can repeat the experiment to check results.

■ *Cause and effect* – as all other variables are controlled, the effect (change in the value of the DV) must be caused solely by the manipulation of the IV.

■ *Isolation of variables* – in the laboratory, individual pieces of behaviour can be isolated and rigorously tested.

LINK TO THE BIOLOGICAL APPROACH

The research method that the biological approach mainly relates to is the experimental method. For example, the role of genetics can be assessed through twin and adoption studies, as well as gene-mapping studies.

Correlational studies can be of use too, such as assessing evolutionary theory of human reproductive behaviour by correlating the degree of symmetry in faces with their perceived level of attractiveness.

Occasionally self-reports may be of use, such as **Simmons *et al.* (2003)** assessing the evolutionary explanation of relationships by using questionnaires to measure levels of unfaithfulness in males and females (see page 348).

Weaknesses of laboratory experiments

■ *Experimenter bias* – experimenters' expectations can affect results and participants may be influenced by these expectations.

■ *Problems operationalizing the IV and DV* – to gain precision, measurements can become too specific and not relate to wider behaviour; for example, defining 'getting fatter' as putting on two pounds per week.

■ *Low external (ecological) validity* – high degrees of control make experimental situations artificial and unlike real life. Therefore, it can be difficult to generalize results to other settings. Laboratory settings can be intimidating places so people may not act normally.

■ *Demand characteristics* – participants are aware they are being tested and so may unconsciously alter their behaviour.

Research in focus

Have a look at **Darley & Latane's (1968)** laboratory experiment into bystander behaviour (page 370).

1 Can you identify the IV and the DV?

2 What aspects of this study make it a laboratory experiment?

3 What are the advantages and weaknesses of conducting this study as a laboratory experiment?

Field experiment –
experiment conducted
in a naturalistic
environment where the
researchers manipulate
the independent variable.

Field experiments

Field experiments, for example **Piliavin *et al.*'s (1969)** study of bystander behaviour (see page 371), occur in 'real world' settings rather than the laboratory. The IV is manipulated by the experimenter and as many other variables as possible are controlled.

YOU ARE THE RESEARCHER

Construct a field experiment that looks at whether people are more willing to help females or males when asked to change a bank note for some coins (even looking to see if they have change could be counted as 'willing' behaviour).

Why would this be a field experiment rather than a laboratory or natural experiment? What would be your IV and DV? What type of sample would you be using? Compose a suitable null hypothesis for your study.

Natural and quasi-experiments

Natural experiment – experiment where the independent variable varies naturally.

Quasi-experiment – experiment where the independent variable occurs naturally without manipulation from the researcher.

In **natural experiments** the IV varies naturally; the experimenter does not manipulate it, but records the effect on the DV. For example, **Costello *et al.* (2003)** studied the mental health of Native Americans on a reservation. During the study a casino opened, giving an opportunity to study the effect of decreasing poverty on mental health. In **quasi-experiments** the IV occurs naturally, such as in a study of gender where males and females are compared. Natural and quasi-experiments are often used when it is unethical to manipulate an IV. In such studies random allocation of participants is not possible.

Advantages of field and natural experiments

- *High ecological validity* – due to the 'real world' environment, results relate to everyday behaviour and can be generalized to other settings.
- *No demand characteristics* – often participants are unaware of the experiment, so there are no demand characteristics.

Weaknesses of field and natural experiments

- *Less control* – it is more difficult to control extraneous variables, so causality is harder to establish.
- *Replication* – since the conditions are never exactly the same again, it is difficult to repeat field and natural experiments exactly to check the results.
- *Ethics* – when participants are not aware that they are in an experiment it incurs a lack of informed consent. This applies more to field experiments, since in natural experiments the IV occurs naturally and is not manipulated by the experimenter.
- *Sample bias* – since participants are not randomly allocated to groups, samples may be not comparable to each other.

YOU ARE THE RESEARCHER

Design a quasi-experiment that assesses whether children who regularly attend day care are more aggressive than children who are raised at home.

Why would this be a natural rather than a field or laboratory experiment? What would the IV and DV be? Refer to the section on inferential testing (page 182) to work out what type of statistical test you would need. What advantages and limitations would there be compared to a laboratory study?

■ Non-experimental research methods

Observational techniques

Observations involve watching and recording behaviour, for example children in a playground. Most observations are naturalistic (occur in real-world settings), but can occur under controlled conditions, for example **Ainsworth's (1971)** 'Strange Situation' study (see page 280).

There are two main types of observation:

1 *Participant observation* involves observers becoming actively involved in the situation being studied to gain a more 'hands-on' perspective, for example, Zimbardo's (1973) prison simulation study that examined the behaviour of prisoner and guards, where Zimbardo took on the role of 'prison superintendent' (**Haney** *et al.***, 1973**).

2 *Non-participant observation* involves researchers not becoming actively involved in the behaviour being studied, for example, **Ainsworth's (1971)** 'Strange Situation' study (see page 280).

Observations can also be:

1 Overt – where participants are aware they are being observed, for example Zimbardo's prison simulation study (**Haney** *et al.***, 1973**).

2 Covert – where participants remain unaware of being observed, for example **Festinger's (1957)** study where he infiltrated a cult that was prophesizing the end of the world.

Advantages of observational techniques

- *High external validity* – since observations usually occur in natural settings, participants behave naturally and so results can be generalized to other settings.

- *Practical method* – can be used in situations where deliberate manipulation of variables would be unethical or impractical, for example studying football hooliganism. It is useful where cooperation from those being observed is unlikely and where the full social context for behaviour is needed. It is particularly useful when studying animals or children.

- *Few demand characteristics* – with covert observations participants are unaware of being observed and so there are no demand characteristics.

Weaknesses of observational techniques

- *Cause and effect* – causality cannot be inferred, since the variables are only observed, not manipulated, and there is little control of extraneous variables.

- *Observer bias* – observers may see what they want to see, though this can be reduced by establishing inter-observer reliability (see next page).

- *Replication* – the lack of control over variables means conditions can never be repeated exactly to check the results.

- *Ethics* – if participants are unaware of being observed, issues of invasion of privacy and informed consent arise (though if participants are informed of the study, then there is a possibility of demand characteristics).

- *Practical problems* – it can be difficult to remain unobserved and there can be problems recording behaviour, for example seeing all behaviour exhibited. It can also be difficult to categorize observed behaviours accurately.

Observational design

Naturalistic observations – surveillance and recording of naturally occurring events.

Behavioural categories – dividing target behaviours into subsets of behaviours through use of coding systems.

There are several ways in which data can be gathered in **naturalistic observations**, including visual recordings such as videos and photographs, audio recordings, or 'on-the-spot' note-taking using agreed rating scales or coding categories. The development of effective behavioural coding categories is integral to the success of observational studies.

Behavioural categories

Observers agree on a grid or coding sheet on which to record the behaviour being studied. The **behavioural categories** chosen should reflect what is being studied. For example, if observers are interested in the effect of age and sex on the speed of car driving, they might want to develop behavioural categories like those given in Table 4.1.

Driver	Sex (M/F)	Age (estimate)	Number of passengers	Observed behaviour	Type of car	Speed (estimate in km per hour)	Safe driving rating 1 = very unsafe 5 = very safe
A	M	55	0	M-P	Ford	40	2
B	F	21	2	T	VW	30	5
C	F	39	3	D	BMW	50	3
D etc.	M	70	0	C	Jensen	60	5

■ **Table 4.1** Behavioural categories of driving behaviour. Observed behaviour code: D = Distracted; T = Talking; M-P = Using mobile phone; C = Concentrating

Rather than writing descriptions of behaviour observed, it is easier to code or rate behaviour using previously agreed scales. Coding can involve numbers (such as age of driver) or letters to describe characteristics (e.g. M = male) or observed behaviours (e.g. T = talking). Observed behaviour can also be rated on structured scales, for example 1–5 on a scale of 'safe driving'.

Field notes

Field notes are qualitative descriptions recorded by observers during or soon after a study is conducted. The purpose of such notes is to permit a deeper meaning and understanding of the phenomena being observed.

Sampling procedures

In observational studies it is difficult to observe all behaviour, especially as it is usually continuous. Breaking behaviour down into categories helps, but decisions must also be made about what type of sampling procedure (methods of recording data) to use. Types of sampling procedures include:

■ *Event sampling* – counting the number of times a behaviour occurs in a target individual or individuals.

■ *Time sampling* – counting behaviour in a set time frame, for example recording what behaviour is being exhibited every 30 seconds.

LINK TO THE SOCIOCULTURAL APPROACH

The sociocultural approach uses the full range of research methods. Scientific experiments are used, especially quasi-experiments, for example **Lin & Rusbult's (1995)** investigation of the investment theory of relationships by comparing males' and females' levels of relationship satisfaction (see page 357). Correlational studies are also used, such as **Dainton's (2003)** study, which assessed perceived levels of inequity in relationships with levels of relationship satisfaction (see page 355). Other research methods used in the sociocultural approach include self-reports, for example **Canary & Stafford's (1992)** use of the Relationship Maintenance Strategies Measure (RMSM) to assess the degree of equity in romantic relationships (see page 355). In addition case studies are used, such as **Chlebowski & Gregory's (2009)** assessment of five cases of psychodynamic therapy in treating OCD (see page 248). Finally, observations are used too, such as **Slatcher & Trentacosta's (2011)** observational study of parental depression upon children's behaviour (see page 46).

Inter-observer reliability

Inter-observer reliability – where observers consistently code behaviour in the same way.

Inter-observer reliability occurs when independent observers code behaviour in the same way (for example, two observers both agree on a score of '3' for safe driving) and lessens the chances of observer bias, where an observer sees and records behaviour in a subjective way (i.e. sees what they want to see). Inter-observer reliability needs to be established before an observation begins and it is easier to achieve if behavioural categories are clearly defined and do not overlap with each other.

YOU ARE THE RESEARCHER

Design and carry out an observation in your school/college cafeteria to assess gender differences in healthy eating. Behavioural categories will need to be established, e.g. healthy/unhealthy food items, as well as ratings of food items. How would you:

- determine inter-observer reliability
- analyse and present the data?

How could you incorporate time and/or event sampling into your study? How long would you conduct the observation for?

Self-report techniques

Self-report techniques –
participants giving
information about
themselves without
researcher interference.

Questionnaires –
self-report method where
participants record their
own answers to a preset
list of questions.

Self-report techniques are research methods in which participants give information about themselves without researcher interference.

Questionnaires

When completing **questionnaires**, respondents record answers to a preset list of questions, usually concerning behaviour, opinions and attitudes – for example, **Adorno *et al.*'s (1950)** F-scale questionnaire (see page 399). Two main types of question are asked:

1 Closed (fixed) questions – these involve yes/no answers, for example 'Do you believe in UFOs?' ('yes' or 'no'); or a range of fixed responses to questions, for example 'Do you eat meat?' ('always', 'usually', 'sometimes', or 'never'). Such answers are easy to quantify, but restrict participants' answers.

2 Open questions – these allow participants to answer in their own words. They are more difficult to analyse, but allow freedom of expression and greater depth of answers. For example, what kinds of music do you like and why?

RESEARCH IN FOCUS

Becker *et al.* (2002) used a questionnaire to investigate eating habits in Fijian girls (see page 141).

Explain why the data from this study may lack validity due to a) idealized answers and b) socially desirable answers.

Advantages of questionnaires

- *Quick* – compared to other methods, large amounts of information can be gathered in a short period. Postal questionnaires can gain relatively large samples for the cost of a stamp.
- *Lack of investigator effects* – questionnaires can be completed without researchers present.
- *Quantitative and qualitative analysis* – closed questions are easy to analyse statistically, while open questions provide richer, fuller detail.
- *Replication* – as questionnaires use standardized questions (the same for everyone), they are easy to replicate. This is particularly true of questionnaires using closed questions.

Weaknesses of questionnaires

- *Misunderstanding* – participants may misinterpret questions. (For example, what is meant by 'do you "usually" do your homework?') There can also be problems with technical terms, emotive language and leading questions.
- *Biased samples* – questionnaires are suitable for people who are willing and able to spend time completing them. Certain types of people may be more willing to fill in questionnaires and not be representative of the whole population.
- *Low response rates* – questionnaires are an uneconomical research method as they can get very low return rates.

- *Superficial issues* – questionnaires, particularly those using closed questions, are not suitable for sensitive issues requiring detailed understanding.
- *Social desirability/idealized answers* – participants may lie in order to give answers expected of them (for example, not revealing racist beliefs) or may give answers that reflect how they would like to be, rather than how they actually are.

Questionnaire construction

There are several important considerations in designing questionnaires that people will actually complete and provide useful data to.

- Aims – having an exact aim helps, as it is then easier to write questions that address the aim.
- Length – questionnaires should be short and to the point, as the longer the questionnaire, the more likely it is that people will not complete it.
- Previous questionnaires – use examples of questionnaires that were previously successful as a basis for the questionnaire design.
- Question formation – questions should be concise, unambiguous and easily understood.
- Pilot study – questionnaires should be tested on people who can provide detailed and honest feedback on all aspects of the design of the questionnaire.
- Measurement scales – some questionnaires use measurement scales to assess psychological characteristics or attitudes. These involve statements on which participants rate levels of agreement or disagreement. See an example below in Table 4.2.

Rate your level of agreement with the following statement: 'Vigorous regular exercise is good for your health.'

1	2	3	4	5
Strongly agree	Agree	Undecided	Disagree	Strongly disagree

■ **Table 4.2** Example of a Likert measurement scale

There are usually a number of statements on a particular topic and the answers to these statements are combined to create a single score of attitude strength. However, it is not easy for participants to judge answers, so many choose the middle score. When this happens it is impossible to know whether they have no opinion or cannot decide between their attitudes in both directions. The best known of these attitude scales is the Likert scale (as shown in the example above).

YOU ARE THE RESEARCHER

Compose three open and three closed questions for a questionnaire examining people's smoking habits and attitudes to smoking. What type of data would:

- open questions generate
- closed questions generate?

Explain how:

- social desirability bias could affect the answers given
- idealized answers could affect the answers given.

Interviews

Interviews – self-report method where participants answer questions in face-to-face situations.

Interviews involve researchers asking face-to-face questions – for example, **Stice *et al.*'s (2004)** study of eating disorders (page 204). There are four main types: structured, unstructured, semi-structured and focused group interviews.

1 *Structured* – involves identical closed questions being read to participants, with the interviewer writing down answers. Interviewers do not need much training, as such interviews are easy to conduct.

2 *Unstructured* – involves an informal discussion on a particular topic. Interviewers can explore interesting answers by asking follow-up questions. Interviewers need considerable training and skill to conduct such interviews.

3 *Semi-structured* – involves combining structured and unstructured techniques, producing quantitative and qualitative data.

4 *Focused group interviews* – involve asking questions to a specific group of people, such as a cultural group, about a particular issue, with group members able to interact with each other when producing answers.

Advantages of interviews

■ *Complex issues* – complicated or sensitive issues can be dealt with in face-to-face interviews by making participants feel relaxed and able to talk. This is particularly true of unstructured interviews.

■ *Ease misunderstandings* – any misunderstood questions can be explained and individual questions can be adapted so they are understood by all participants.

■ *Data analysis* – semi-structured interviews produce both quantitative and qualitative data, which can be used to complement each other. Structured interviews produce quantitative data that can be easily analysed.

■ *Replication* – the more standardized or structured an interview, the easier it is to replicate. Unstructured interviews are less easy to replicate, but it should be possible for other researchers to review data produced.

■ *Ecological validity* – focus group interviews are often conducted in more naturalistic settings, so findings relate more to real-life settings.

■ *Reduced cost* – focus group interviews process several people at once, so are relatively cheaper to conduct.

Weaknesses of interviews

■ *Interviewer effects* – interviewers may unconsciously bias answers, such as by their appearance; for example, women may be less willing to talk about sex with male interviewers. Interviews are also subject to demand characteristics and social desirability bias.

■ *Interview training* – a lot of skill is required to carry out unstructured interviews, particularly concerning sensitive issues, and such interviewers are not easy to find.

■ *Ethical issues* – participants may not know the true purpose of an interview and there is also the danger that participants may reveal more than they wish.

■ *Participant answers* – interviews are not suited to participants who have difficulty putting their feelings, opinions, etc. into words.

■ *Loss of control* – with focus group interviews there is less control than in one-to-one interviews and so time can be lost through irrelevant discussion.

RESEARCH IN FOCUS

In 1984 Linda Williams interviewed 129 women who had been sexually abused in childhood, finding that 38 per cent had no memory of the abuse.

1 Explain why the results may have been different if a male had interviewed the women.

2 Was this a focused group interview? Explain your answer.

Design of interviews

Aside from deciding whether to use a structured, unstructured or semi-structured interview and open or closed questions, decisions need to be made about who would make the most appropriate interviewer. Several interpersonal variables affect this decision:

■ Gender and age – the sex and age of interviewers affect participants' answers when topics are of a sensitive sexual nature.

■ Ethnicity – interviewers may have difficulty interviewing people from a different ethnic group to themselves. **Word et al. (1974)** found that white participants spent 25 per cent less time interviewing black job applicants than white applicants.

■ Personal characteristics and adopted role – interviewers can adopt different roles within an interview setting and use of formal language, accent and appearance can also affect how someone comes across to the interviewee.

Interviewer training is essential to successful interviewing. Interviewers need to listen appropriately and learn when to speak and when not to speak. Non-verbal communication is important in helping to relax interviewees so that they will give natural answers. Difficult and probing questions about emotions are best left to the end of the interview when the interviewee is more likely to be relaxed, whereas initial questions are better for gaining factual information.

Interviews are generally seen as a qualitative research method (though quantitative data can be produced through yes/no type questions). Interviews can be followed by a more targeted survey, which asks questions targeted at a specific area and which are framed in such a way so as to produce quantitative data.

YOU ARE THE RESEARCHER

Design and conduct a semi-structured interview examining student attitudes to relationships. You will need some questions that are asked of all participants, but you will also need to ask follow-up questions to explore answers further. Try and create open and closed questions in order to generate quantitative and qualitative answers.

How could you analyse and present your quantitative data? How could you use content or inductive content (thematic) analysis (see page 175 and page 176) to analyse and present your qualitative data? What ethical issues must you consider when writing your questions?

'Men love to wonder and that is the seed of science.'
Ralph Waldo Emerson (1860)

Correlational studies

Correlational studies
– a research method that measures the strength of relationship between co-variables.

Co-variables – the variables measured in a correlation.

Experiments look for a difference between two conditions of an IV, while **correlational studies** involve measuring the strength and direction of relationships between **co-variables**, for example **Murstein's (1972)** study of the matching hypothesis (page 351):

■ A positive correlation occurs where one co-variable increases as another co-variable increases, for example ice cream sales increase as the temperature increases.

■ A negative correlation is where one co-variable increases while another co-variable decreases, for example raincoat sales decrease as sunny weather increases.

Scattergrams (also known as scattergraphs) are a type of graph used to display the extent to which two variables are correlated. The measurement of one co-variable goes on one axis and the measurement of the other co-variable on the other axis. See Figure 4.2.

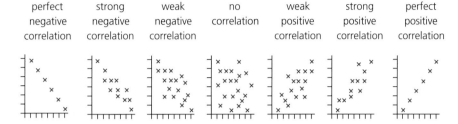

−1 −0.9 −0.8 −0.7 −0.6 −0.5 −0.4 −0.3 −0.2 −0.1 0 +0.1 +0.2 +0.3 +0.4 +0.5 +0.6 +0.7 +0.8 +0.9 **+1**

| perfect negative correlation | strong negative correlation | weak negative correlation | no correlation | weak positive correlation | strong positive correlation | perfect positive correlation |

■ **Figure 4.2**
Scattergrams and correlation strength

RESEARCH IN FOCUS

1   For **Einstein & Menzies's (2003)** study of OCD patients (see page 217) identify the co-variables.

2   This study found a positive correlation, but explain why a cause and effect relationship could not be established.

Advantages of correlational analysis

■ *Allows predictions to be made* – predictions can be made from correlations, like predicting the number of ice creams that will be sold on hot days.

■ *Allows quantification of relationships* – correlations show the strength of relationship between two co-variables. A correlation of +0.9 means a high positive correlation, while a correlation of −0.1 indicates a weak negative correlation (see Figure 4.2).

■ *No manipulation* – correlations do not require manipulation of variables and so can be used when carrying out an experiment may be unethical.

Weaknesses of correlational analysis

■ *Quantification problem* – correlations that appear low (e.g. + 0.28) can sometimes be significant (meaningful) if the number of scores is high, while correlations that seem high, (e.g. +0.76) are not always statistically significant if the number of scores is low.

■ *Cause and effect* – as they are not done under controlled conditions, correlations do not show causality. Therefore, we cannot say that one co-variable has caused the other.

■ *Extraneous relationships* – other variables may influence the co-variables. For example, many holidays are taken in the summertime and people eat ice creams on holiday; therefore, the variable 'holiday' is related to both temperature and ice cream sales.

■ *Only works for linear relationships* – correlations only measure linear (straight-line) relationships. For example, correlations cannot show the relationship between temperature and aggression, as it is curvilinear (not a straight line), as temperature increases, aggression levels increase up to an optimum point. Then any further increase in temperature leads to a decline in aggression levels.

YOU ARE THE RESEARCHER

Design a correlational study that studies the relationship between age and memory ability. What would be your co-variables and how would you measure them?

Previous research into whether memory declines with age is contradictory; with this in mind, compose a suitable correlational hypothesis. What type of graph would be used to plot the data?

TOK link

Experiments look for differences between variables, while correlations look for relationships, so they appear to be two totally opposite research methods with nothing in common. However, correlations can often be used to research areas that would be unethical through experimentation, such as researching into the effects of smoking upon lung cancer. But correlations can also be used to identify relationships that are interesting enough to warrant further more-scientific research through the use of experiments. In this way, correlational and experimental methods are combined in the pursuit of knowledge and understanding.

Case studies

Case studies are in-depth, detailed investigations of one individual or a small group. They usually include biographical details, behavioural information and experiences of interest. Case studies allow researchers to examine individuals in great depth. Explanations of behaviour are outlined in subjective ways, describing what an individual feels or believes about particular issues. For example, **Chlebowski & Gregory's (2009)** study of OCD (see page 248).

A case study can also occur as a detailed analysis conducted over a period of time (longitudinal study) into a topic of interest (a case), which produces findings relevant to that particular context.

> **Case studies** – individual (or small group) cases that are unique in some way and therefore studied by researchers for that uniqueness.

PSYCHOLOGY IN THE REAL WORLD

Case studies often have a high real-world significance, as they allow important areas to be researched that would not be possible by any other means and which can have great benefits to society.

For example, developmental psychologists have been very interested to see if children can recover from traumatic early life experiences and, if they can, what conditions are necessary for such recovery to occur. Cases of severe privation are rare, meaning samples of sufficient size would not be possible to amass, and anyway this phenomenon could not be studied by experiments or observations, as this would be unethical.

Therefore, case studies are conducted of actual examples. For instance, **Koluchova (1972, 1991)** and **Freud & Dann (1951)** both found from case studies of children who had endured awful early life experiences that recovery was possible if long-term, sensitive care was provided. These findings have helped to form strategies to help children who have undergone similar experiences to develop into normally functioning adults of benefit to society.

Advantages of case studies

- *Rich detail* – case studies provide great depth and understanding about individuals and acknowledge human diversity. Because case studies are about 'real people', they have a feeling of truth about them. Information relates to a real person, not an average gathered from many.

- *The only possible method to use* – case studies allow psychologists to study unique behaviours or experiences that could not have been studied any other way. The method also allows 'sensitive' areas to be explored, where other methods would be unethical, like the effects of sexual abuse.

- *Useful for theory contradiction* – the findings from just one case study can refute (disprove) a theory.

Weaknesses of case studies

- *Not representative* – as no two case studies are alike, results cannot be generalized to others. But do we always have to find universal truths of behaviour?

- *Researcher bias* – researchers conducting case studies may be biased in their interpretations or method of reporting, making findings suspect.

- *Reliance on memory* – case studies often depend upon participants having full and accurate memories.

RESEARCH IN FOCUS

Chlebowski & Gregory (2009) conducted a case study into psychodynamic treatment of OCD (see page 248).

1 Why was the case study method the only viable way of studying this form of therapy?

2 What advantages and weaknesses of the case study method may apply in this particular study?

Strengthen your learning

1 What similarities and differences are there between laboratory, field and natural experiments?

2 What strengths and weaknesses are there of:
   a laboratory experiments
   b field experiments
   c natural experiments?

3 For the following research methods:

   Observations

   Questionnaires

   Interviews

   Correlations

   Case studies

   a Explain how they work.
   b Detail their strengths and weaknesses.

SECTION SUMMARY

- There are several research methods in psychology; which one is used depends on specific research circumstances.
- Experiments assess the effect of an IV or a DV to establish causality.
- Observations record behaviour, generally in naturalistic, but also sometimes controlled, environments.
- Self-reports, like questionnaires and interviews, generate data produced by participants about themselves.
- Correlational studies assess the level and direction of relationship between co-variables.
- Case studies are in-depth assessments of individuals or small groups and also occur as detailed investigations of a specific topic area over time.

Scientific processes

'The great tragedy of science – the slaying of a beautiful hypothesis by an ugly fact.'
Thomas Huxley (1870)

FOCUS ON...

- The role of aims and hypotheses in psychological research.
- The role of sampling in the testing of target populations.
- Types of sampling used in psychological investigations: random, opportunity self-selected (volunteer), purposive and snowball samples.

▨ Aims

Aim – a precise statement of why a study is taking place.

An **aim** is a precise statement of why a study is taking place/what is being studied; for example, to investigate the effect of caffeine on reaction times. An aim should include what is being studied and what the study is trying to achieve.

Hypotheses

A **hypothesis** is a precise, testable prediction of what is expected to happen. For example, 'caffeine consumption will affect reaction times'.

The *experimental/alternative hypothesis* predicts that differences in the DV will be beyond the boundaries of chance (they will occur as a result of manipulation of the IV). Differences beyond the boundaries of chance are significant differences and this can be incorporated into a hypothesis. For example, 'caffeine consumption will significantly affect reaction times'. Statistical tests are used to see if results are significant (see page 182). The term 'experimental hypothesis' is only used with the experimental method. Other research methods use the term 'alternative hypothesis', but the definition is the same.

The *null hypothesis* is 'the hypothesis of no differences'. It predicts that the IV will not affect the DV. Any differences in results will be due to chance factors, not the manipulation of the IV and will therefore not be significant, and this can be incorporated into a null hypothesis. For example, 'there will be no significant difference in reaction times as a result of caffeine consumption'.

One of the two hypotheses, null or experimental, will be supported by the findings and thus be accepted, while the other one will be rejected.

There are two types of experimental/alternative hypotheses:

1   Directional ('one-tailed') hypothesis – predicts the direction of the results. For example, 'there will be a significant reduction in the speed of reaction times as a result of caffeine consumption'. It gets its name from predicting the direction the results will go.

    Directional hypotheses are used when previous research suggests that results will go in one direction, or when replicating a previous study that also used a directional hypothesis.

2   Non-directional ('two-tailed') hypothesis– predicts that there will be a difference, but does not predict the direction of the results. For example, 'there will be a significant difference in the speed of reaction times as a result of caffeine consumption'. Reaction times will either be quicker or slower.

RESEARCH IN FOCUS

1   Have a look at **Klauer & Zhao's (2004)** study of the working memory model (page 57). For this study compose a suitable:

    a   directional (one-tailed) hypothesis

    b   non-directional (two-tailed) hypothesis

    c   null hypothesis.

Sampling

A population is all of something, for example all the grains of sand on a beach. Researchers generally do not have the means to test whole populations, so they test a sample (part of the population). Ideally a sample is representative (contains the same characteristics as the population from which it was taken) and the term target population is used to indicate the group of people the results are targeted at. Psychologists use several **sampling** techniques, each with strengths and weaknesses.

Random sampling

Random sampling is where each member of a population has an equal chance of being selected. One way to achieve this is to place all names from the target population in a container and draw out the required sample number, while computer programs are also used to generate random lists. This results in a sample selected in an unbiased fashion.

Strengths of random sampling

- *Unbiased selection* – there is no bias in selection, increasing the chances of getting an unbiased and thus representative sample.
- *Generalization* – as the sample should be fairly representative, results will be generalizable to the target population.

Weaknesses of random sampling

- *Impractical* – random sampling is difficult to achieve, as it is sometimes difficult to get full details of a target population and not all members may be available or wish to take part.
- *Not representative* – unbiased selection does not guarantee an unbiased sample; for example, all females could be randomly selected, making the sample unrepresentative and thus the results not generalizable.

Opportunity sampling

Opportunity sampling involves selecting participants who are available and willing to take part; for example, asking people in the street who are passing. **Sears (1986)** found that 75 per cent of university research studies use undergraduates as participants, simply for the sake of convenience.

Strengths of opportunity sampling

- *Ease of formation* – opportunity samples are relatively easy to create, as they use people who are readily available.
- *Natural experiments* – opportunity sampling usually has to be used with natural experiments, as the researcher has no control over who is studied.

Weaknesses of opportunity sampling

- *Unrepresentative* – the sample is likely to be biased by excluding certain types of participants and thus be unrepresentative so that findings cannot be generalized to the target population. An opportunity sample collected in town during the day on a week day would not include those at work or college.
- *Self-selection* – participants have the option to decline to take part and the sampling technique thus turns into a self-selected sample.

Volunteer (self-selected) sampling

Volunteer or self-selected sampling involves people volunteering to participate. They select themselves as participants, often by replying to adverts.

Strengths of self-selected sampling

- *Ease of formation* – creating the sample requires little effort from the researchers (other than producing an advert), as participants volunteer themselves.
- *Less chance of 'screw you' phenomenon* – as participants are eager to take part there will be less chance of their deliberately trying to sabotage the study.

Weaknesses of self-selected sampling

- *Unrepresentative* – the sample will be biased, as volunteers tend to be a certain 'type' of person and thus unrepresentative, making results not generalizable to a target population.
- *Demand characteristics* – volunteers may be eager to please, which increases the chances of demand characteristics, for example participants giving the answer they think is required.

Purposive sampling

With purposive sampling (also known as selected sampling) participants are selected as they have qualities that are relevant to a research study. There are several sub-types:

1 Maximum variation type – as many different types of people as possible in a population are selected in order to get a wide range of views/behaviours.

2 Homogenous type – selecting people who are of a certain 'type'; for example, as many red-haired people as possible in a population, in order to get a representative view of that type of person.

3 Typical case sampling – selecting people who seem the most 'average' in a population in order to get the 'mean' view.

4 Extreme case sampling – selecting non-typical people in a population; for example, the most and least intelligent, in order to understand the range of views/behaviour.

5 Critical case sampling – selecting just one 'typical' case to study, such as the most average high school, in order to get a representative view.

6 Total population sampling – selecting all of the population that has one or more shared characteristics, in order to obtain summaries of views/behaviours.

7 Expert sampling – selecting people who have a certain type of skill, in order to become better informed about an area of study.

Strengths of purposive sampling

- *Focused* – allows selection of participants for a particular research purpose. Different types of purposive sampling can be used, depending on what the research purpose is.
- *Time-saving* – does not waste time on selecting and testing participants whose data will not be useful to the research.

Weaknesses of purposive sampling

- *Non-representative* – selection is not unbiased, so findings cannot be generalized to whole populations.
- *Small samples* – some forms of purposive sampling generate very small samples, which can make them unrepresentative and difficult to generalize from.

Snowball sampling

With snowball sampling, initial participants generate additional participants from their friends and acquaintances, that is, like a snowball getting bigger as it rolls down a hill.

Strengths of snowball sampling

- *Locates hidden participants* – participants can be obtained that the researchers would never have been able to find.
- *Ease of formation* – aside from obtaining the initial participants the sample generates itself.
- *Locates hidden populations* – can be useful in obtaining difficult-to-find types of people; for example, those with radical views, homeless people, etc.

Weaknesses of snowball sampling

- *Unrepresentative* – selection is biased in terms of participants selecting who they want. Therefore, results cannot be said to be representative.
- *Anchoring* – as only a few participants are initially selected, who then select similar people, there is a risk the sample becomes 'anchored' on the type of people initially selected.

Strengthen your learning

1 What is the difference between:
   a an aim and a hypothesis
   b a directional (one-tailed) and a non-directional (two-tailed) hypothesis
   c an experimental and a null hypothesis?

2 For the following sampling methods:

   Random sampling

   Opportunity sampling

   Self-selected sampling

   Purposive sampling

   Snowball sampling

   a Explain how they are conducted.
   b Detail their strengths and weaknesses.

■ Assessment check

A researcher wanted to assess the effect of revision on students studying for the IB psychology examination. Twenty-four participants responded to a poster asking for people to take part. The participants were then assigned, without bias in selection, to two conditions. In the first condition participants revised for two hours a day for the month before the exam, while in the second condition participants did no revision before sitting the exam. Participants were informed before the study started that they were under no obligation to take part and that they could leave at any time. No names were recorded; participants instead were referred to by number.

The researchers planned to publish their findings in a peer-reviewed journal.

Table 4.3 below shows the number of marks out of 100 that each participant gained in the exam.

Participant	Revision condition	Participant	No-revision condition
1	75	7	52
2	52	8	67
3	92	9	32
4	78	10	52
5	66	11	32
6	78	12	52

■ **Table 4.3** Number of marks each participant gained in the exam out of 100

The results were subjected to statistical testing and a significant difference was found.

1a Identify the research method used and outline two characteristics of the method. (3 marks)
1b Describe the sampling method used in the study. (3 marks)
1c Suggest an alternative or additional research method, giving one reason for your choice. (3 marks)
2 Describe the ethical considerations in reporting the results and explain additional ethical considerations that could be taken into account when applying the findings of the study. (6 marks)
3 Discuss the possibility of generalizing the results. (9 marks)

FOCUS ON...

- The role of pilot studies in psychological investigations.
- Type of experimental design: independent groups, repeated measures and matched pairs designs.
- Ethical considerations in psychological research.
- The importance and formation of reliability and validity in psychological investigations.
- The conventions concerned with writing up research studies.

◼ Pilot studies

Pilot studies are small-scale practice investigations, carried out prior to research to identify potential problems with the design, method or analysis, so they can be fixed. Participants may also suggest appropriate changes; for example, if participants admit that they guessed the purpose of the study and acted accordingly (demand characteristics), changes could be made to avoid this. Pilot studies also identify whether there is a chance of significant results being found.

◼ Experimental designs

There are three main types of experimental design: the repeated measures design, the independent groups design and the matched pairs design.

Independent groups design

An **independent groups design (IGD)** uses different participants in each of the experimental conditions, so that each participant only does one condition (either the experimental or control condition). Different participants are therefore being tested against each other.

> ### LINK TO THE COGNITIVE APPROACH
> The cognitive approach focuses on mental processes and this is generally investigated through the use of experiments, such as **Baddeley's (1966)** experiment into encoding in short- and long-term memory (see page 49). Cognitive neuroscience combines, through experimentation, the cognitive and biological approaches, by investigating in which brain areas specific mental processes appear to operate, such as **D'Esposito et al.'s (1995)** study using fMRI scans to assess brain areas associated with components of the WMM (see page 56). The cognitive approach does use correlations too, such as **Schmidt et al.'s (2000)** study into forgetting (see page 45) and self-reports can be used to get participants to reflect on their mental processes, such as **Loftus & Pickrell (2003)** using questionnaires to assess the validity of participants' memories of childhood visits to Disneyland (see page 83). Occasionally, the observational method is used, such as **Marsh & Hanlon's (2007)** study of confirmation bias in behavioural biologists (see page 85).

Strengths of the IGD

- *No order effects* – as different participants do each condition there are no order effects, whereby the order in which the conditions are done may have an effect on the outcome (see next page).

- *Demand characteristics* – participants do one condition each, so there is less chance that they can guess the purpose of the study and act accordingly.

- *Time saved* – both sets of participants can be tested at the same time, saving time and effort.

Weaknesses of the IGD

- *More participants needed* – with participants each doing only one condition, twice as many participants are needed as for a repeated measures design (RMD).

- *Group differences* – differences in results between the two conditions may be due to participant variables (individual differences) rather than manipulations of the IV. For example, participants in one condition may be more intelligent than another condition. This is minimized by random allocation of participants to each condition.

Repeated measures design

In a **repeated measures design (RMD)** each participant is tested in all conditions of an experiment. Participants are therefore being tested against themselves.

Strengths of the RMD

- *Group differences* – as the same people are measured in both conditions, there are no participant variables (individual differences) between the conditions.

- *More data/fewer participants* – as each participant produces two scores, twice as much data is produced compared with an independent groups design (IGD). Therefore, half as many participants are needed to get the same amount of data.

Weaknesses of the RMD

- *Order effects* – with a RMD, participants do all conditions and the order in which they do these conditions can affect the results. Participants may perform worse in the second condition, due to fatigue or boredom (negative order effect), or perform better due to practice or learning (positive order effect). Counterbalancing can control this, where half the participants do Condition A, followed by Condition B, and the other half do Condition B and then Condition A.

- *Demand characteristics* – by participating in all conditions, it is more likely that participants may guess the purpose of the study and act accordingly.

- *Takes more time* – a gap may be needed between conditions to counter the effects of fatigue or boredom. Each condition may also need different materials; for example, in a memory test the same list of words could not be used for both conditions.

RESEARCH IN FOCUS

Herlitz *et al.* (1997) assessed long-term memory abilities in 1000 Swedish participants (see page 60).

1   Explain why an IGD was used for this study.

2   What would the advantages and weaknesses of using this design be compared to a RMD?

Matched pairs design

Matched pairs design (MPD) – experimental design where participants are in similar pairs, with one of each pair performing each condition.

A **matched pairs design (MPD)** is a special kind of RMD. Different, but similar, participants are used in each condition. Participants are matched on characteristics that are important for a particular study, such as age. Identical (monozygotic) twins are often used as they form perfect matched pairs, sharing identical genetic characteristics.

Strengths of the MPD

- *Order effects* – as different participants do both conditions there are no order effects.

- *Demand characteristics* – participants do one condition each, therefore there is less chance of their guessing the purpose of the study.

- *Group differences* – as participants are matched, there should be less chance of participant variables (individual differences) affecting the results.

Weaknesses of the MPD

- *More participants* – with participants each doing only one condition, twice as many participants are needed as for a RMD.

- *Matching is difficult* – it is impossible to match all variables between participants and an unmatched variable might be vitally important. Also, even two closely-matched individuals will have different levels of motivation or fatigue at any given moment in time.

- *Time-consuming* – it is a lengthy process to match participants.

YOU ARE THE RESEARCHER

Design a laboratory experiment that assesses whether memory recall is affected by the amount of sleep a person has had. How would you do this using an IGD, a RMD and a MPD? Compose a suitable aim and non-directional (two-tailed) hypothesis. Explain how you would attempt to control extraneous variables. How could you reduce the risk of demand characteristics? Explain how you would get a snowball sample for the study.

Ethical issues

'A man without ethics is a wild beast loosed upon this world.'
Albert Camus

Ethical issues – the rules governing the conduct of researchers in investigations.

Ethical issues involve researchers assessing and acting upon all ethical considerations involved in a research study before it is conducted. The main consideration is that the health and dignity of participants should be protected. The BPS has published a Code of Ethics that all psychologists should follow and most research institutions, such as universities, have ethical committees which have to okay research projects before they commence. Researchers should also, before conducting research, seek peer advice (colleagues), consult likely participants for their views, consider alternative research methodologies, establish a cost–benefit analysis of short-term and long-term consequences and assume responsibility for the research. Also if, during the research process, it becomes clear there are negative consequences resulting from the research (for instance, harm to participants), it should be stopped and every effort made to correct the negative consequences. Any researcher having ethical concerns about a colleague's work should contact them in the first instance, and if their concerns are not met, contact the BPS.

TOK link

Often when research on humans is considered unethical, investigators use animals instead; for example, when creating lesions (damage) to specific areas of the brain to assess its effect on behaviour. In the 1950s many such experiments were done on rats' brains to assess the impact of the hypothalamus brain area on eating behaviour (something that might give insight into the causes of obesity and anorexia nervosa), which would not have been ethical to do on human brains. However, aside from the important issue of whether animals should be considered to have the same ethical rights as humans in regard to participating in studies is the issue of generalization. Are the findings taken from animal studies applicable to humans? When the drug thalidomide was tested on animals in the late 1950s, it produced no harmful effects and so was then given to pregnant women to reduce morning sickness (nausea). However, hundreds of children were born with severe deformities, due to its effect on developing foetuses.

The Code of Ethics includes:

1 *Informed consent* – investigators should give participants sufficient details of an investigation that enable them to make a considered choice as to whether they wish to participate. Parental consent should be obtained in the case of children under 16 years of age. Informed consent cannot be gained from those under the influence of alcohol or drugs or those mentally unfit to do so.

2 *Avoidance of deception* – withholding of information or misleading participants is unacceptable if participants are likely to object or show unease once debriefed. Intentional deception over the purpose and general nature of investigations should be avoided. Participants should not deliberately be misled without scientific or medical justification. If deception occurs, informed consent cannot be gained from participants. It is often necessary that participants do not know the purpose of a study in order to get realistic results. In such cases, deception must be dealt with in an ethical way. There are a number of ways to achieve this:

   a Presumptive consent – this is gained from people of a similar background to participants in a study. If they state that they would have been willing to participate, then it is deemed that the actual participants would too.

   b Prior general consent – this involves participants agreeing to be deceived without knowing how they will be deceived. As participants know they will be deceived, this can affect their behaviour.

   c Retrospective consent – this involves asking participants for consent after they have participated in a study. However, they may not consent and yet have already taken part.

   If deception is used, participants must be told immediately afterwards and given the chance to withhold their data from the study.

3 *Adequate briefing/debriefing* – all relevant details of a study should be explained to participants before and afterwards. A debrief is important if deception has been used.

Participants should leave the study in no worse state than when they started it. Debriefing does not provide justification for unethical aspects of a study.

4 *Protection of participants* – investigators have a responsibility to protect participants from physical and mental harm during the investigation. Risk of harm must be no greater than in ordinary life.

5 *Right to withdraw* – participants should be aware that they can leave a study at any time, and can even withdraw their data after the study has finished.

6 *Confidentiality/anonymity* – participants' data should not be disclosed to anyone unless agreed in advance. Numbers should be used instead of names in published research papers. Confidentiality means that data can be traced back to names, whereas anonymous data cannot, as the researchers collect no names. Confidential data collection is preferable in cases where participants might be followed up later.

7 *Observational research* – observations are only made in public places where people might expect to be observed by strangers.

8 *Incentives to take part* – participants should not be offered bribes or promised rewards for their participation, as this puts pressure on them to do so.

TOK link

It is important that psychological research is conducted in a way that protects the dignity and health of participants, as well as the reputation of the subject. Therefore, over time, ethical considerations have become increasingly more important when planning and conducting research. Studies like that of **Piliavin et al. (1969)** where a person pretended to collapse on a train to see what bystanders' reactions would be (see page 371) would not now be permitted, as deceit was used (the person was not really ill and pseudo-participants were used to manipulate people's behaviour), no informed consent was gained, there was no right to withdraw from the study and participants were subjected to stress. There is no indication either that they were debriefed at the end of the study. The pursuit of knowledge is important, but treating participants properly is more important.

▧ Reliability

Reliability – the extent to which a test or measurement produces consistent results.

Reliability refers to consistency. If a study is repeated using the same method, design and measurements and the same results are obtained, the results are said to be reliable. Reliability can be improved by developing more consistent forms of measurement, using clearly defined operational definitions and by improving inter-observer reliability (see below).

- Internal reliability concerns the extent to which something is consistent within itself; for example, a set of scales should measure the same weight between 50 and 100 grams as between 150 and 200 grams.

- External reliability concerns the extent to which a test measures consistently over time.

Ways of assessing reliability

Ways of assessing reliability are:

- The split-half method measures internal reliability by splitting a test into two and having the same participant doing both halves of the test. If the two halves of the test provide similar results this indicates that the test has internal reliability.

- The test–retest method measures external reliability, by giving the same test to the same participants on two occasions. If the same result is obtained, then reliability is established.

- Inter-observer reliability is a means of assessing whether different observers are viewing and rating behaviour in the same way. This can be achieved by conducting a correlation of all the observers' scores, with a high correlation indicating that they are observing and categorizing behaviour consistently. Inter-observer reliability is improved by developing clearly defined and separate categories of observational criteria.

- If results are unreliable, they cannot be trusted. However, results can be reliable, but not be valid (accurate). For example, if you add up 1 + 1 several times and each time calculate the answer as 3, then your result is reliable (consistent), but not valid (accurate).

Validity

Validity – the extent to which results accurately measure what they are supposed to measure.

Validity concerns accuracy, the degree to which something measures what it claims to. Therefore, validity refers to how accurately a study investigates what it claims to and the extent to which findings can be generalized beyond research settings, as a consequence of a study's internal and external validity. Validity can be improved by improving reliability (see above) and by improving internal and external validity (see below).

- Internal validity concerns whether results are due to the manipulation of the IV and have not been affected by confounding variables. Internal validity can be improved by reducing investigator effects, minimizing demand characteristics and the use of standardized instructions and a random sample. These factors ensure a study is highly controlled, leaving less doubt that observed effects are due to poor methodology.

- External validity refers to the extent to which an experimental effect (the results) can be generalized to other settings (ecological validity), other people (population validity) and over time (temporal validity). External validity can be improved by setting experiments in more naturalistic settings.

Ways of assessing validity

Ways of assessing validity include:

- Face validity is a simple way of assessing validity and involves the extent to which items look like what a test claims to measure.

- Concurrent validity assesses validity by correlating scores on a test with another test known to be valid.

- Predictive validity assesses validity by predicting how well a test predicts future behaviour; for example, do school entrance tests accurately predict later examination results?

- Temporal validity assesses to what degree research findings remain true over time.

RESEARCH IN FOCUS

Researchers often use questionnaires to assess mental disorders, such as the Yale–Brown Obsessive Compulsive Scale used in the assessment of OCD.

Explain why such a questionnaire could be reliable, but not valid.

Strengthen your learning

1 Why is it important that research be carried out in an ethical way?

2 Explain what is meant by the following ethical considerations:
   a informed consent
   b avoidance of deception
   c briefing/debriefing
   d protection from harm
   e the right to withdraw
   f confidentiality/anonymity
   g incentives to take part.

3 How can deception be avoided?

4 To what do the following terms refer:
   a reliability
   b validity?

5 Explain what is meant by:
   a internal reliability
   b external reliability
   c internal validity
   d external validity.

6 How can each of items a–d in question 5 be assessed?

7 Explain what is meant by inter-observer reliability and how it can be achieved?

8a What is a pilot study?

8b Why would a pilot study be conducted?

9 For the following experimental designs:

Independent groups design

Repeated measures design

Matched aairs design

a Explain how they would be conducted.

b Detail their strengths and weaknesses.

Reporting psychological investigations

Progress in science depends on communication between researchers. It is therefore essential to describe the results of research as accurately and as effectively as possible. To get research published in eminent peer-reviewed journals, psychologists have to write reports in a conventional manner. This means that reports are written in such a way that replication would be possible, allowing others to repeat the research to check results.

The basic requirements of a report are to communicate:

- what was done
- why it was done
- what was found
- what it means.

There is no single best way to set out a report, but the general format is as follows:

1 Title	5 Aims	9 Discussion
2 Table of contents	6 Hypotheses	10 Conclusion
3 Abstract	7 Procedure/method	11 References
4 Introduction	8 Findings/results	12 Appendices

PSYCHOLOGY IN THE REAL WORLD

Over one million scientific papers are published each year. But before research can be published it has to be written up in a conventional way (so that it can be replicated by other researchers to check the validity of the results) and subjected to peer review, inspection by experts in the field. The aim of this is to stop flawed or unscientific research being published, which could have harmful implications or practical applications in the real world.

Peer review is supposed to be unbiased and independent, but the process is not without its critics. There are accusations of reviewers rejecting papers purely because they go against mainstream ideas or challenge work done by the reviewers themselves. It has even been alleged that reviewers often have links (for example, sponsorship by organizations such as drug companies) that do not want certain research published. The consequences of flawed research being published as having scientific validity and being safe could be disastrous, but it is equally disturbing that valid research, backed up by scientific evidence, may be prevented from publication, and thus not permitted to have real-world benefits.

TOK link

Psychological investigations are written up in an accepted 'conventional' manner so they can be replicated to check the validity of the findings and are subjected to peer review before they can be published in a scientific journal. But another reason for them being written in such a conventional manner is the idea of verisimilitude (closeness to the truth). This is a scientific concept where, through research that builds on previous research findings, science gradually gains a greater understanding of the phenomena being studied. Indeed, in the discussion part of a research report, it is customary to suggest some ideas for future research that emerge from the study's findings.

- Scientific processes involve forming aims and hypotheses, which are tested on samples drawn from target populations.
- Experiments can be conducted using independent groups, repeated measures and matched pairs designs.
- Research can only occur after ethical considerations have been addressed.
- Measures should be taken to ensure research findings are reliable and valid.
- Psychological investigations are written up in a conventional manner, so they can be replicated in order to check their validity.

■ Assessment check

A team of researchers decided to assess the effect of anxiety on memory recall.

An opportunity sample of an equal number of male and female participants aged between 18 and 53 was recruited from a university common room and were shown a tray containing 30 unrelated items for 30 seconds, after which time the tray was removed from sight.

Participants were placed in different states of anxiety, by being made to wear fake electrodes that they were told would give them electric shocks, ranging from 15 volts and going up in 15 volt increases to 150 volts for every item they failed to recall. One participant was told they would receive 15 volts, another 30 volts, another 45 volts, and so on, up to one participant being told they would receive 150 volts. A total of 10 participants were used.

Before the study began participants were given full details of the study and signed an informed consent form. They were also given a debriefing afterwards to reduce the effect of their incurring any harm from taking part in the study.

It was found that as the level of electric shock that participants believed they would receive for failing to recall items went up, the number of items forgotten went down.

It was recommended that future research should take place to assess whether high levels of anxiety would produce a different effect on memory recall than very low anxiety.

1a Identify the research method used and outline two characteristics of the method. (3 marks)
1b Describe the sampling method used in the study. (3 marks)
1c Suggest an alternative or additional research method, giving one reason for your choice. (3 marks)
2 Describe the ethical considerations in reporting the results and explain additional ethical considerations that could be taken into account when applying the findings of the study. (6 marks)
3 Discuss the possibility of generalizing the results. (9 marks)

Data analysis

'Data! Data! Data! I can't make bricks without clay.'
Sherlock Holmes (1892)

IN THE NEWS

Ψ The Psychological Enquirer

A GLASS OF WINE A DAY DOUBLES THE RISK OF CANCER

The newspaper headline above seems to suggest a strong link between drinking alcohol and developing life-threatening illness. The story, reported in the British press, was taken from US research, which indicated that middle-aged women drinking just a single glass of wine a day, half the recommended safe level, doubled their risk of developing lobular cancer, a common type of breast cancer, when compared with people who didn't drink at all. It was reported that scientists had concluded that excessive consumption of alcohol was causing a worldwide rise in breast cancer, pointing to the fact that in Britain the number of cases has risen by 80 per cent in the past 30 years. Over the same period, alcohol consumption had nearly doubled.

■ **Figure 4.3** Does drinking wine cause cancer?

This type of article is not uncommon in the popular press. Although highlighting issues that have a serious side to them, like the undesirability of excessive drinking, such articles show a basic misunderstanding of what scientific data actually display. The data talked about in this article, that cancer cases have increased at the same time that alcohol consumption has increased, are correlational evidence, which shows a relationship between two co-variables. But what the data do not show is that excessive drinking causes a rise in the incidence of cancer.

Correlational data do not display cause-and-effect relationships, only experiments are capable of doing that. It is important that scientific data are properly understood, in order that people comprehend fully the impact of scientific knowledge upon their daily lives.

FOCUS ON...

- Quantitative and qualitative data.
- The establishment of credibility in qualitative data; triangulation and member-checking.
- The establishment of transferability in qualitative data.
- Forms of data analysis: meta-analysis, content analysis and inductive (thematic) content analysis.
- Measures of central tendency: the mean, the median and the mode.
- Measures of dispersion: the range and standard deviation.
- Percentages.
- Correlational data.

■ Quantitative and qualitative data

Quantitative data is numerical (occurs as numbers), for example counting the number of stressful incidents in a study, while **qualitative data** is non-numerical (occurs in forms other than numbers), such as describing the emotional experience of each stressful incident. Research involves the collection of both quantitative and qualitative data. Qualitative studies tend to produce subjective, detailed, less reliable data of a descriptive nature, whereas quantitative studies produce objective, less detailed, more reliable data of a numerical nature. Although they are different forms of data, they can often be used collectively to give stronger emphasis to research findings and a deeper insight.

Qualitative data provides insight into feelings and thoughts that quantitative data cannot, though analysis of such data can be very subjective, based on the researcher's own interpretation. Qualitative data can be converted into quantitative data though through content analysis (see page 175) and then be presented in quantitative forms, such as tables and graphs, and be analysed by numerical means such as by statistical tests.

Experiments are seen as producing mainly quantitative data, though qualitative data in the form of opinions/comments from participants can also be gathered. Observations, through the use of behavioural categories and ratings of behaviour, produce quantitative data, while questionnaires produce quantitative data from closed questions and qualitative data from open questions. Similarly interviews produce quantitative data from structured interviews and qualitative data from unstructured interviews. Correlational data tends to be quantitative, while case studies produce mainly qualitative data. (See Table 4.4.)

Qualitative data	Quantitative data
Subjective	Objective
Imprecise non-numerical measures used	Precise numerical measures used
Rich and detailed	Lacks detail
Low in reliability	High in reliability
Used for attitudes, opinions, beliefs	Used for behaviour
Collected in 'real-life' setting	Collected in 'artificial' setting

■ **Table 4.4** Qualitative and quantitative data

Credibility

Credibility is a concept relating to the validity of qualitative findings, in other words can the findings be trusted, as truly matching the participants' feelings, beliefs, experiences, and so on. The techniques of triangulation and member-checking are used to assess credibility.

Triangulation

Triangulation involves multiple-methods, sources of data, observers and theories to gain a fuller comprehension of the research area being studied. There are four types of triangulation.

1 *Methods triangulation* – involves using different data collection methods to assess the reliability (consistency) of the findings; for example, seeing if data from surveys, interviews, case studies, experiments, and so on, match those found in the original study.

2 *Triangulation of sources* – involves using different sources of data within the same research method. For example, if two groups were being tested, then participants could be tested at different times, or in public and private settings, and so on.

3 *Analyst triangulation* – involves using another researcher or researchers to analyse the findings to assess the inter-rater reliability of findings.

4 *Theoretical triangulation* – involves using several different theories to assess the validity of the findings, that is, which theories do the findings 'fit'?

Member-checking

Member-checking involves giving participants access to a study's data and conclusions drawn from it, in order to assess their degree of agreement. This allows an opportunity for errors to be amended and for greater insight to be obtained.

Transferability

Transferability relates to the degree that findings from a qualitative research study are applicable to settings and populations other than those used in a study. For transferability to be established, findings need to be corroborated with findings from similar studies. For example, if the findings from a case study match those from other similar case studies.

TOK link

The most scientific form of research studies used in psychology are experiments that produce quantitative (numerical) data, which can be subjected to statistical analysis to establish causality, a prime aim of science. However, quantitative data does not display the full picture of the human condition; for example, it does not inform much, if at all, about feelings and beliefs. This type of information is gained through qualitative (non-numerical) data. However, quantitative and qualitative forms of data should not be seen as separate or superior/inferior to each other – instead the best insight into the human condition is probably gained from a combination of the two.

■ Forms of data analysis

Meta-analysis

Meta-analysis – a statistical technique of combining the findings of several similar studies to give a more typical overview.

Meta-analysis is a statistical technique for combining the findings of several studies of a certain research area, for example **Bulik *et al.*'s (2007)** meta-analysis of therapies for anorexia nervosa, taken from several studies (see page 254). As a meta-analysis involves combining data from lots of smaller studies into one larger study, it allows the identification of trends and relationships that would not be possible from individual smaller studies. The technique is especially helpful when a number of smaller studies have found contradictory or weak results, in order to get a clearer view of the overall picture.

RESEARCH IN FOCUS

Grootheest *et al.* (2005) performed a meta-analysis into twin studies and the incidence of OCD (see page 211).

1 How was this achieved?

2 What are the main strengths of conducting a meta-analysis?

3 Can you think of any problems with this type of research?

Content analysis

Content analysis – a method of quantifying qualitative data through the use of coding units.

Content analysis is a method of quantifying qualitative data through the use of coding units and is commonly performed with media research. It involves the quantification of qualitative material, in other words, the numerical analysis of written, verbal and visual communications. For example, **Davis (1990)** analysed 'lonely hearts' columns to find out whether men and women look for different things in relationships.

Content analysis requires coding units to categorize analysed material, such as the number of times women commentators appear in sports programmes. Analysis can involve words, themes, characters or time and space. The number of times these things do not occur can also be important. (See Table 4.5.)

Unit	Examples
Word	Count the number of slang words used
Theme	The amount of violence on TV
Character	The number of female commentators there are in TV sports programmes
Time and space	The amount of time (on TV) and space (in newspapers) dedicated to eating disorders

■ **Table 4.5** Coding units for content analysis

Strengths of content analysis

- *Ease of application* – content analysis is an easy-to-perform, inexpensive research method, which is non-invasive, as it does not require contact with participants.

- *Complements other methods* – content analysis can be used to verify results from other research methods and is especially useful as a longitudinal tool (detecting trends; changes over time).

- *Reliability* – establishing reliability is simple as a content analysis is easy to replicate, through others using the same materials.

Weaknesses of content analysis

- *Descriptive* – content analysis is purely descriptive and so does not reveal underlying reasons for behaviour, attitudes, and so on ('what' but not 'why').

- *Flawed results* – limited by availability of material, so observed trends may not reflect reality; for example, negative events receive more coverage than positive ones.

- *Lack of causality* – content analysis is not performed under controlled conditions and therefore does not show causality.

Inductive content analysis

Inductive content (thematic) analysis is a qualitative analytic method for identifying, analysing and reporting themes (patterns) within data, with patterns identified through data coding. Ultimately inductive content analysis organizes, describes and interprets data. The identified themes become the categories for analysis, with inductive content analysis performed through the process of coding involving six stages:

1 *Familiarization with the data* – involves intensely reading the data, to become immersed in its content.

2 *Coding* – involves generating codes (labels) that identify features of the data that are important to answering the research question.

3 *Searching for themes* – involves examining the codes and data to identify patterns of meaning (potential themes).

4 *Reviewing themes* – involves checking the potential themes against the data, to see if they explain the data and answer the research question. Themes are refined, which can involve splitting, combining, or discarding them.

5 *Defining and naming themes* – involves a detailed analysis of each theme and creating an informative name for each theme.

6 *Writing up* – involves combining together the information gained from the analysis.

Inductive content analysis goes beyond just counting words or phrases, but instead involves identifying ideas within data. Analysis can involve the comparison of themes, identification of co-occurrences of themes and using graphs to display differences between themes.

▓ Descriptive statistics

'Beware of averages, by definition the average person has one breast and one testicle.'
Dixie Lee Ray

Descriptive statistics provide a summary of a set of data drawn from a sample, which apply to a whole target population. They include measures of central tendency and measures of dispersion.

Measures of central tendency

Measures of central tendency are used to summarize large amounts of data into averages ('typical' mid-point scores). There are three types: the median, the mean and the mode.

Inductive content (thematic) analysis – a method of qualitative research linked to content analysis, which involves analysing text in a variety of media to identify the patterns within it. A coding system may be needed to sort the data and to help to identify patterns.

Measures of central tendency – methods of estimating mid-point scores in sets of data.

The median

The median is the central score in a list of rank-ordered scores. With an odd number of scores, the median is the middle number. With an even number of scores, the median is the mid-point between the two middle scores and therefore may not be one of the original scores.

Advantages of the median

■ It is not affected by extreme 'freak' scores.

■ It is usually easier to calculate than the mean.

■ The median can be used with ordinal data (ranks), unlike the mean.

Weaknesses of the median

■ It is not as sensitive as the mean, because not all the scores are used in the calculation.

■ It can be unrepresentative in a small set of data. For example:

1, 1, 2, 3, 4, 5, 6, 7, 8 – the median is 4.

The mean

The mean is the mid-point of the combined values of a set of data and is calculated by adding all the scores up and dividing by the total number of scores.

Advantages of the mean

■ It is the most accurate measure of central tendency as it uses the interval level of measurement, where the units of measurement are of equal size (for example, seconds in time).

■ It uses all the data in its calculation.

Weaknesses of the mean

■ It is less useful if some scores are skewed, such as if there are some large or small scores.

■ The mean score may not be one of the actual scores in the set of data. For example:

1, 1, 2, 3, 4, 5, 6, 7, 8 – the mean is 4.1 (1+1+2+3+4+5+6+7+8 = 37. 37/9 = 4.1).

The mode

The mode is the most common, or 'popular', number in a set of scores.

Advantages of the mode

■ It is less prone to distortion by extreme values.

■ It sometimes makes more sense than the other measures of central tendency. For example, the average number of children in a British family is better described as 2 children (mode) rather than 1.75 children (mean).

Weaknesses of the mode

■ There can be more than one mode in a set of data. For example, for the set of data 2, 3, 6, 7, 7, 7, 9, 15, 16, 16, 16, 20, the modes are 7 and 16.

■ It does not use all the scores.

TOK link

Measures of central tendency (the mean, mode and median) give 'typical' or 'average' scores and many statistical tests are based around usage of such measures, though supplemented by measures of dispersion (the range and standard deviation), which show the spread of scores in a set of data. However, the problem with this is that it is very nomothetic, an approach favoured by science, as it produces a very 'general' view that is supposed to apply to everyone. This is fine in, say, chemistry where all atoms of an element are identical and behave in exactly the same way. However, humans have many individual differences that make each of us unique, something that is accommodated more by the idiographic approach. It should be remembered that mean scores often do not apply to anyone. For instance, the average number of children in a British family is 1.75, an occurrence that is impossible for any individual family.

Measures of dispersion

Measures of dispersion provide measures of the variability (spread) of scores. They include the range and standard deviation.

The range

The range is calculated by subtracting the lowest value from the highest value in a set of data.

Advantages of the range

- It is fairly easy and quick to work out.
- It takes full account of extreme values.

Weaknesses of the range

- It can be distorted by extreme 'freak' values.
- It does not show whether data are clustered or spread evenly around the mean.

  For example, the range of the two sets of data below is the same (21 − 2 = 19), despite the data being very different.

  Data set one: 2, 3, 4, 5, 5, 6, 7, 8, 9, 21

  Data set two: 2, 5, 8, 9, 10, 12, 13, 15, 16, 18, 21

Standard deviation

Standard deviation is a measure of the variability (spread) of a set of scores from the mean. The larger the standard deviation, the larger the spread of scores will be.

Standard deviation is calculated using the following steps:

1 Add all the scores together and divide by the number of scores to calculate the mean.

2 Subtract the mean from each individual score.

3 Square each of these scores.

4 Add all the squared scores together.

5 Divide the sum of the squares by the number of scores minus 1. This is the variance.

6 Use a calculator to work out the square root of the variance. This is standard deviation.

Advantages of standard deviation

- It is a more sensitive dispersion measure than the range since all scores are used in its calculation.
- It allows for the interpretation of individual scores. Thus, in Figure 4.4, anybody with an IQ of 131 is in the top 5 per cent of the population, between +2 and +3 standard deviations of the mean.

Weaknesses of standard deviation

- It is more complicated to calculate.
- It is less meaningful if data are not normally distributed (see Figure 4.4).

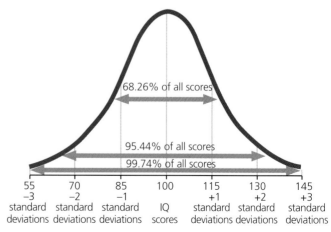

■ **Figure 4.4** Standard deviation: IQ scores

Percentages

Percentages are a type of descriptive statistic that shows the rate, number or amount of something within every 100. Data shown as percentages can be plotted on a pie chart.

Data can be converted into percentages by multiplying them as a factor of 100; for example, a test score of 67 out of a total possible score of 80 would be: $67/80 \times 100/1 = 83.75\%$.

Correlational data

Correlational studies provide data that can be expressed as a correlation coefficient (see page 181), which shows either a positive correlation, negative correlation or no correlation at all. The stronger a correlation, the nearer it is to $+1$ or -1. Correlational data is plotted on a scattergram, which indicates strength and direction of correlation (see Figure 4.2, page 159).

■ Presentation of quantitative data

FOCUS ON...

- Presenting data in graphs, charts and tables.
- The idea of normal distribution.
- The analysis and interpretation of correlational data.

....

Graphs – easily understandable, pictorial representations of data.

Correlational data – data produced from correlational studies.

....

Quantitative data can be presented in various ways. Although emphasis is primarily on statistical analysis, data can also be presented through tables that summarize data to reveal findings of interest, as well as visually through **graphs** and charts, pictorial representations of data that allow viewers to more easily see patterns in data. **Correlational data** are presented via scattergrams, while other types of graphs exist for different types of research data.

'The most beautiful curve is the one that rises on a graph.'
Ralph Loewy

Graphs and charts

Bar charts

Bar charts show data in the form of categories to be compared, like male and female scores concerning chocolate consumption. Categories are placed on the x-axis (horizontal) and the columns of bar charts should be the same width and separated by spaces. The use of spaces illustrates that the variable on the x-axis is not continuous (for example, males do not at some point become females and vice versa). Bar charts can show totals, means, percentages or ratios and can also display two values together. For example male and female consumption of chocolate as shown by gender and age (see Figure 4.5).

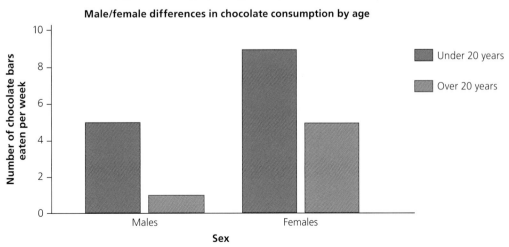

■ **Figure 4.5** An example of a bar chart displaying two values together

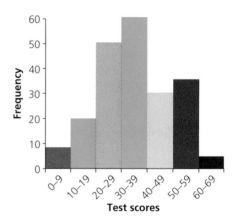

■ **Figure 4.6** Example of a histogram

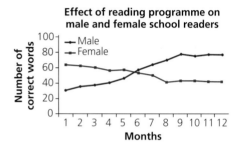

■ **Figure 4.7** Example of a frequency polygon

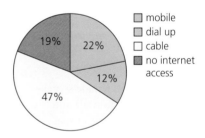

■ **Figure 4.8** Pie chart showing the different ways British people accessed the internet in 2010

Histograms

Histograms and bar charts are somewhat similar, but the main difference is that histograms are used for continuous data, such as test scores, like the example shown in Figure 4.6. The continuous scores are placed along the x-axis, while the frequency of these scores is shown on the y-axis (vertical). There are no spaces between the bars since the data are continuous and the column width for each value on the x-axis should be the same width per equal category interval.

Frequency polygon (line graph)

A frequency polygon is similar to a histogram in that the data on the x-axis are continuous. The graph is produced by drawing a line from the mid-point top of each bar in a histogram. The advantage of a frequency polygon is that two or more frequency distributions can be compared on the same graph (see Figure 4.7).

Pie charts

Pie charts are used to show the frequency of categories as percentages. The pie is split into sections, each one of which represents the frequency of a category. The sections are colour-coded; with an indication given of what each section represents and its percentage score (see Figure 4.8).

Tables

Results tables summarize the main findings of data and so differ from data tables which just present raw, unprocessed scores (ones that have not been subjected to statistical analysis) from research studies. It is customary with results tables to present data totals (though percentages can also be shown) and relevant measures of dispersion and central tendency (see Table 4.6 below).

	Males	**Females**
Total scores	160	132
Mean	8	6.6
Range	9	13
Number of participants	20	20

■ **Table 4.6** Table showing male and female scores on a test of concentration

YOU ARE THE RESEARCHER

For Table 4.6, construct a suitable graph to display the data. Ensure you title and label it appropriately.

What statistical test would be suitable to analyse the data? Give three reasons for your choice of test. What significance level would you use? Justify your choice.

Explain how you would decide if the result of your test was significant or not.

Normal distribution

The idea of **normal distribution** is that for a given attribute, for example IQ scores, most scores will be on or around the mean, with decreasing amounts away from the mean. Data that is normally distributed is symmetrical, so that when plotted on a graph the data forms a bell-shaped curve with as many scores below the mean as above it (see Figure 4.9).

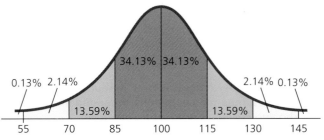

■ **Figure 4.9** Normal distribution of IQ scores

There are several ways that data can be checked to see if it is normally distributed:

1 Examine visually – look at the data to see if most scores are clustered around the mean.

2 Calculate measures of central tendency – calculate the mean, mode and median to see if they are the similar.

3 Plot the frequency distribution – plot the data on a histogram (see above) to see if it forms a bell-shaped curve.

Analysis and interpretation of correlation

A correlational study produces a correlation coefficient: a numerical value showing the degree to which two co-variables are related. Measurements range from +1 (perfect positive correlation) to –1 (perfect negative correlation). The closer the correlation to a perfect correlation, the stronger the relationship between the two variables. If there is little correlation, the result will be near to zero (0.0).

Data from correlational studies can be analysed with both the Spearman's rho and Pearson's product moment statistical tests (see page 183).

Strengthen your learning

1 What is the difference between quantitative and qualitative data?

2 What is meant by a meta-analysis?

3 Explain how the following work:
   a content analysis
   b inductive content (thematic) analysis.

4 Describe the different types of measures of central tendency and measures of dispersion and give the strengths and weaknesses of each.

5 What is the:
   a difference between a bar chart and a histogram
   b similarity between a histogram and a frequency polygon
   c difference between a results table and a data table?

6 When would a pie chart be used to display data?

7 What is meant by credibility with qualitative data?

8 Explain how triangulation and member-checking can be used to establish credibility.

9 What is meant by transferability?

10 Explain what is meant by normal distribution.

11 Explain what correlational data are and how they are analysed.

Introduction to statistical testing

'A single death is a tragedy; a million deaths is a statistic.'
Joseph Stalin

FOCUS ON...

- Levels of measurement: nominal, ordinal and interval/ratio.
- Reasons for the selection of different inferential tests.
- Probability and significance.
- Type I and Type II errors.
- Statistical tests used in psychological investigation: sign test, chi-squared, Mann-Whitney, Wilcoxon signed-matched ranks, independent t-test, repeated t-test, Spearman's rho and Pearson's product moment.
- The interpretation of significance.
- A worked example of the sign test.

Inferential testing

Inferential testing – statistical procedures that make predictions about populations from mathematical analysis of data taken from samples.

Research studies produce data that, in order to be made sense of, have to be analysed. This can be achieved using descriptive statistics (measures of central tendency and dispersion, graphs, tables, etc.) to illustrate the data. But a more sophisticated means of analysis is the use of **inferential testing**, which allows researchers to make inferences (informed decisions) about whether differences in data are significant ones (beyond the boundaries of chance) that can be applied to the whole target population which a sample represents.

In order to decide which statistical test to use it needs to be decided:

1 Whether a difference or a relationship between two sets of data is being tested for.

2 What level of measurement the data is. There are three basic levels of measurement: nominal, ordinal, and interval/ratio.

3 What design has been used: either IGD or RMD (including MPD, as it is regarded as a type of RMD).

Levels of measurement

Nominal, ordinal and interval/ratio data are ranked in relation to one another, getting gradually more informative each time. The mnemonic 'NOIR' (Nominal, Ordinal, Interval/Ratio) can be used to remember this order. The level of data produced by a research study affects which statistical test will be chosen.

Nominal data – Involves counting frequency data, for example how many days of the week were rainy or sunny? Tally charts are used to record this type of data. Nominal data is the crudest, most uninformative type of data. For example, although we might know how many days were sunny/rainy overall, nominal data does not show how rainy or sunny each day was hour-by-hour.

Ordinal data – involves ranking data into place order, with rating scales often being used to achieve this. Ordinal data is more informative than nominal data, but still lacks being fully informative. For example, the finishing places in an athletics race, 1st, 2nd, 3rd, 4th, and so on, show which athletes are better than others, but does not inform us about the distances between individual athletes. The distance between 1st and 2nd may be shorter than between 2nd and 3rd. Similarly, one person's subjective rating of 7 may be very different to another's rating of 7.

Interval/ratio data – standardized measurement units such as time, weight, temperature and distance are interval/ratio measures and are the most informative and accurate form of measurement, as they use equal measurement intervals; for example, one second in time is the same length as any other second in time. Interval and ratio data are classed together, as they apply to the same statistical tests, but the difference between them is that interval data has an arbitrary zero point, whereas ratio data has an absolute zero point. For example, zero degrees temperature does not mean there is no temperature (interval data), whereas someone with zero pounds in their bank account would have no money (ratio data).

Selecting an inferential test

Once it has been determined (i) whether a difference or relationship is being sought between two sets of data, (ii) what level of measurement has been used, and (iii) whether an IGD or a RMD has been used, the appropriate statistical test can be selected. (See Table 4.7.)

Nature of hypothesis	Level of measurement	Type of research design	
		Independent (unrelated)	Repeated (related)
Difference	Nominal data	Chi-squared	Sign test
	Ordinal data	Mann-Whitney U test	Wilcoxon (matched pairs)
	Interval data	Independent t-test	Related t-test
Correlation	Ordinal data		Spearman's rho
	Interval data		Pearson product moment

■ **Table 4.7** Choosing an appropriate statistical test

> ### RESEARCH IN FOCUS
>
> 1   What statistical test would you use to analyse the data from **Akert's (1992)** study of relationship break-ups (see page 364)?
>
> 2   You will need to decide if a difference or relationship was being sought, what design was used and what level of measurement was used. Do the same thing for **Carlo *et al.* (2007)** (see page 381), who found a positive correlation between parental styles and prosocial behaviour in American teenagers.

■ Probability and significance

When differences and relationships are found between sets of data it is important to determine whether such differences and relationships are significant ones, beyond the boundaries of chance.

If a coin is tossed 100 times, then by the law of averages there should be 50 heads and 50 tails. However, it might be 52 heads and 48 tails, meaning there is a difference between the two sets of data, but is it beyond the boundaries of chance? Probably not, but how is the cut-off point determined between the two sets of data being significant or insignificant? 55 heads to 45 tails? 60 to 40? This is where the idea of **probability** comes in.

Probability is denoted by the symbol p and concerns the degree of certainty that an observed difference or relationship between two sets of data is a real difference/relationship, or whether it has occurred by chance. It is never a 100 per cent certainty that such differences and relationships are real ones, that is, beyond the boundaries of chance. This is why it is impossible to prove something beyond all doubt, so an accepted cut-off point is needed and in psychology, and in science generally, a significance (probability) level of $p \leq 0.05$ is used. This means there is a 5 per cent possibility that an observed difference or relationship between two sets of data is not a real difference, but occurred by chance factors. This is seen as an acceptable level of error.

On certain occasions a stricter level of significance may be needed, for example if testing out untried drugs or in new research areas. Then a significance level of $p \leq 0.01$ might be used, meaning there is a 99 per cent certainty that an observed difference/relationship is a real one, but there is still a 1 per cent chance it occurred due to chance factors. An even stricter level of $p \leq 0.001$ would mean there is a 99.9 per cent certainty of a real difference/relationship, but there is still a 0.1 per cent possibility it occurred by chance.

Probability – the likelihood of events being determined by chance.

PSYCHOLOGY IN THE REAL WORLD

Probability has real-world applications in determining if treatments, such as drug therapies, are effective and safe for general use by clinicians. It could potentially threaten lives if drugs were allowed to be prescribed that had not been shown to be harmless by scientifically conducted research. This is why experiments are conducted where large samples of participants are given drugs and are compared against participants given placebos, to assess their effectiveness and safety.

Significance levels in such experiments are set at a very high level, such as $p \leq 0.001$, so that there is only a very small chance of making a **Type I error** and accepting a treatment as safe when it is not. Such research has also to be written up in a conventional manner, so it can be replicated by others to check the validity of the findings, and subjected to independent peer review to assess its scientific acceptability.

Significance levels – statistical criteria determining if observed differences/relationships are beyond the boundaries of chance.

Type I errors – when a difference/relationship in a data set is accepted as a real one and is not.

Type II errors – when a difference/relationship in a data set is rejected, but actually does exist.

Type I and Type II errors

A Type I error occurs when a difference/relationship is wrongly accepted as a real one; that is, beyond the boundaries of chance, because the significance level has been set too high. This means the null hypothesis is wrongly rejected. For example, if a pregnancy test revealed a woman to be pregnant when she was not. With a 5 per cent significance level this means, on average, for every 100 significant differences/relationships found, 5 of them will have been wrongly accepted.

A **Type II error** occurs when a difference/relationship is wrongly accepted as being insignificant; that is, not a real difference/relationship, because the significance level has been set too low (for example, 1 per cent). This means that the null hypothesis would be wrongly rejected. For example, a pregnancy test reveals a woman not to be pregnant when she is.

The stricter the significance level is, the less chance there is of making a Type I error, but more chance of making a Type II error and vice versa. One way to reduce the chance of making these errors is to increase the sample size.

A 5 per cent significance level is the accepted level, as it strikes a balance between making Type I and Type II errors.

Statistical tests

- **Sign test** – used when a difference is predicted between two sets of data, the data is of at least nominal level and a RMD has been used.
- **Chi-squared** – used when a difference is predicted between two sets of data, the data is of at least nominal level and an IGD has been used. It is also possible to use chi-squared as a test of association (relationship).
- **Mann-Whitney** – used when a difference is predicted between two sets of data, the data is of at least ordinal level and an IGD has been used.
- **Wilcoxon signed-matched ranks** – used when a difference is predicted to occur between two sets of data, the data is of at least ordinal level and a RMD or MPD has been used.
- **Independent (unrelated) t-test** – used when a difference is predicted between two sets of data, the data is normally distributed, the data is of interval/ratio level and an IGD has been used.
- **Repeated (related) t-test** – used when a difference is predicted between two sets of data, the data is normally distributed, the data is of interval/ratio level and a RMD or MPD has been used.
- **Spearman's rho** – used when a relationship (correlation) is predicted between two sets of data, the data is of at least ordinal level and the data are pairs of scores from the same person or event.
- **Pearson's product moment** – used when a relationship (correlation) is predicted between two sets of data, the data is normally distributed, the data is of at least interval/ratio level and the data are pairs of scores from the same person or event.

Interpretation of significance

Statistical analysis produces an observed value, which is compared to a critical value in order to determine if the observed value is significant (beyond the boundaries of chance). Critical value tables need to be referenced, taking into consideration such information as whether a hypothesis is directional or non-directional (one-tailed or two-tailed), the number of participants or participant pairs (N) used and what level of significance, for example 5 per cent, is being used.

The Mann-Whitney, Wilcoxon and sign tests require observed values to be equal to, or less than, the critical value to be accepted as significant, allowing the null hypothesis to be rejected. The chi-squared, independent (unrelated) t-test, repeated (related) t-test, Spearman's rho and Pearson's product moment tests require an observed value to be equal to, or greater than, the critical value to be accepted as significant, allowing the null hypothesis to be rejected.

In order to have a better understanding of how statistical testing works, let's have a look at an example of a statistical test being used to analyse data. One such statistical test is the sign test, which is used when a difference is predicted between two sets of data (such as in an experiment), the data is of at least nominal level (see levels of measurement on page 182) and a RMD has been used. The test assesses the direction of any difference between pairs of scores.

Statistical analysis produces an observed value, which is compared to a critical value in order to determine if the observed value is significant (beyond the boundaries of chance) (see probability and significance on page 183). The sign test requires observed values to be equal to, or less than, the critical value to be accepted as significant, allowing the null hypothesis to be rejected (see interpretation of significance, above).

A worked example of the sign test

A food manufacturer wishes to know if its new breakfast cereal 'Fizz-Buzz' will be as popular as its existing product 'Kiddy-Slop'. Ten participants try both and choose which they prefer. One participant prefers the existing product, seven the new product and two like both equally. See Table 4.8.

Participant number	Preference	Direction of difference
1	Fizz-Buzz	+
2	Fizz-Buzz	+
3	No difference	Omitted
4	Kiddy-Slop	−
5	Fizz-Buzz	+
6	Fizz-Buzz	+
7	Fizz-Buzz	+
8	No difference	Omitted
9	Fizz-Buzz	+
10	Fizz-Buzz	+

■ **Table 4.8** Participants' preferences for breakfast cereals

To calculate the sign test:

■ Insert the data into a table as above.

■ Use a plus or minus sign to indicate the direction of difference for each participant.

■ To calculate the observed value, add up the number of times the less frequent sign occurs (this is s). This equals 1 in this case.

■ Get the critical value of s from a critical value table. This shows the maximum value of s that is significant at a given level of probability. To do this you need the value of N, the number of pairs of scores, omitting scores with no + or − sign. In this case N = 8.

■ Work out whether you have used a one-tailed (directional hypothesis) or a two-tailed (non-directional hypothesis)? This affects what the cv (critical value) will be – we will assume here it is two-tailed.

■ A significance level of $p \leq 0.05$ is normally used.

- The cv is found from a critical values table.

Level of significance for a two-tailed test				
	0.05	0.025	0.01	0.005
Level of significance for a one-tailed test				
N	0.10	0.05	0.02	0.01
5	0	-	-	-
6	0	0	-	-
7	0	0	0	-
8	1	0	0	0
9	1	1	0	0
10	1	1	0	0
11	2	1	1	0
12	2	2	1	1
13	3	2	1	1
14	3	2	2	1
15	3	3	2	2
16	4	3	2	2
17	4	4	3	2
18	5	4	3	3
19	5	4	4	3
20	5	5	4	3

■ **Table 4.9** The critical values of *s* in the sign test. Note: N = 8, two-tailed hypothesis, significance level $p \leq 0.05$, cv = 0, observed value *s* = 1

- The observed value *s* is 1 and the cv is 0. Therefore not significant, accept the null hypothesis.
- It might surprise you that 7 preferences for one product against 1 preference for another product is not a difference beyond the boundaries of chance, but this is probably because the sample was too small, that is, there were not enough participants to show such a difference.

SECTION SUMMARY

- Data generated from research studies can either be quantitative (numerical) or qualitative (non-numerical).
- There are various forms of data analysis, including meta-analysis, content analysis and inductive (thematic) content analysis.
- Measures of central tendency summarize data into average scores, while measures of dispersion show the spread of scores within a set of data.
- Data can be displayed visually in graphs, or numerically in tables.
- Data can be subjected to inferential tests to detect significant trends and relationships that are beyond the boundaries of chance.
- Different statistical tests are used to suit different research situations.

Strengthen your learning

1 Explain what is meant by inferential testing.

2 What is meant by the following levels of measurement:
   a nominal
   b ordinal
   c interval/ratio?

3 What three criteria should be considered when choosing a statistical test?

4 With reference to probability, what is meant by a significant difference/relationship?

5 What are Type I and II errors and when do they occur?

6 What is meant by a critical value?

7 Give three reasons for the selection of each of the following statistical tests:
   a sign test
   b chi-squared test
   c Mann-Whitney test
   d Wilcoxon signed-matched ranks test
   e independent t-test
   f repeated t-test
   g Spearman's rho test
   h Pearson's product moment test.

■ Assessment check

Researchers decided to conduct a study of a young girl, aged about seven years, who was found living with a troop of monkeys in an Ecuadorean forest. When discovered, she made noises like a monkey, but had no human language abilities. She preferred to walk on all fours and spent a lot of time climbing trees. She had an intense fear of humans and behaved very aggressively in their presence. She was fostered by a child-centred couple and gradually with sensitive care came to trust people and develop human abilities. By the age of 21 she was normal in all respects, had an IQ of 110 and was studying to be a teacher at university.

Data was collected through interviews with her foster parents and interviews with the girl herself (after she developed language abilities) about her recall of her early life living with the monkeys.

Before the study began, informed consent was gained from her foster parents and care was taken to not identify the girl by name, referring to her instead in the findings by a fake name.

It was hoped that the results would be useful in devising strategies to help children overcome the negative effects of early life trauma so that they could develop normally.

1a Identify the research method used and outline two characteristics of the method.   (3 marks)
1b Describe the sampling method used in the study.   (3 marks)
1c Suggest an alternative or additional research method, giving one reason for your choice.   (3 marks)
2 Describe the ethical considerations in reporting the results and explain additional ethical considerations that could be taken into account when applying the findings of the study.   (6 marks)
3 Discuss the possibility of generalizing the results.   (9 marks)

'Yesterday on the stair I met a man who wasn't there, he wasn't there again today, I wish to God he'd go away.'
William Hughes Mearns

'And then I decided I was a lemon for a couple of weeks.'
Ford Prefect in 'The Hitchhiker's Guide to the Galaxy' by Douglas Adams

IN THE NEWS

Ψ The Psychological Enquirer

THE LONG WALK HOME – NAKED

■ **Figure 5.1** Stephen Gough's second naked ramble

It is ex-Royal Marine Stephen Gough's heartfelt belief that being naked in public is a fundamental freedom and he wishes by doing so to separate nudity from sexual behaviour. So in 2003–04 and again in 2005–06 he walked the length of Great Britain, from Land's End to John O'Groats, in just his boots and occasionally (on sunny days) a hat. He was arrested 18 times and has spent six years in prison (naked) in isolation. His spells of freedom are often for a few seconds, with arrest following his refusal to wear clothes on leaving prison. The cost for his imprisonment now runs into several hundred thousand pounds. In 2012, he was allowed to walk home from Scotland to Hampshire, as long as he did so with 'consideration for others'. Three days later, he was arrested for walking naked past a children's playground in Fife and put back in prison, with Gough refusing to allow social workers to assess his mental health. The authorities have generally seen him as confrontational, intolerant and inconsiderate and, in January 2014, he was again jailed for 16 months for breaking an ASBO to not be naked in public.

Stephen Gough's behaviour by many definitions of abnormality would be seen as abnormal; he is deviating from the social norm of being dressed in public, displaying elements of failure to function adequately (such as displaying behaviour that causes offence to others), showing statistically infrequent behaviour (being naked in public) and deviating from ideal mental health (such as not having environmental mastery by not being competent in all aspects of life). But then again, many of us would say he's quite sane and is just behaving according to his principles, and that it is the objectors to his behaviour who have a problem.

Introduction

Psychopathology is a branch of psychology focusing on abnormal psychological conditions, with the aim of gaining an understanding into these conditions in order that effective treatments can be developed. This is important, as one in ten people will spend time in a mental institution at some point in their life and one in three will receive treatment for an abnormal condition. If not you, then someone close to you will be affected.

◼ Factors affecting abnormality

FOCUS ON...

- Understanding abnormality through reference to definitions of deviation from social norms, failure to function adequately, deviation from ideal mental health and statistical infrequency.
- The strengths and weaknesses of definitions of abnormality.

Abnormality – a psychological or behavioural state leading to impairment of interpersonal functioning and/or distress to others.

Abnormality is difficult to define; psychologists disagree about the causes of mental disorders and how they reveal themselves. One point of view sees abnormality resulting from flawed biology, another that abnormality is due to 'incorrect' learning or defective thought processes. Others argue that mental disorders originate from problems of the mind and personality. Different viewpoints have been favoured at different times and across different cultures. **Rosenhan & Seligman (1989)** believe that normality is merely an absence of abnormality. This means that by defining abnormality, decisions are being made about what is normal.

Four criteria for defining abnormality are examined here, each with its strengths and weaknesses.

◼ Deviation from social norms definition

Deviation from social norms – behaviour that violates a society's accepted rules.

Each society has norms, unwritten rules for acceptable behaviour, for example not being naked in public. Any behaviour that varies from these norms is abnormal, so abnormal behaviour is, therefore, behaviour that goes against social norms (**deviation from social norms**). The definition draws a line between desirable and undesirable behaviours and labels individuals behaving undesirably as social deviants and allows interference into their lives in order to help them, for instance putting them into a mental hospital. These norms will vary across cultures, situations, ages and even gender, so that what is seen as acceptable/normal in one culture, situation, age group and gender type will not be so in others. One important consideration is the degree to which a social norm is deviated from and how important society sees that norm as being.

Strengths of the definition

- *Helps people* – the fact that society gives itself the right to intervene in abnormal people's lives can be beneficial, as such individuals that need it may not be able to get help themselves.
- *Social dimension* – the definition gives a social dimension to the idea of abnormality, which offers an alternative to the isolated 'sick-in-the-head' individual.
- *Situational norms* – the definition considers the social dimensions of behaviour; a behaviour seen as abnormal in one setting is regarded as normal in another, for instance while being naked in town is seen as abnormal, it is regarded as normal on a nudist beach.
- *Developmental norms* – the definition establishes what behaviours are normal for different ages; for example, filling a nappy aged two is considered normal, perhaps not so if you are 40.
- *Distinguishes between normal/abnormal* – the definition gives a clear indication of what is and is not seen as normal behaviour.
- *Protects society* – the definition seeks to protect society from the effects an individual's abnormal behaviour can have on others.

Weaknesses of the definition

- *Subjective* – social norms are not real, but are based on the opinions of ruling elites within society rather than majority opinion. Social norms are then used to 'control' those seen as a threat to social order. A true definition of abnormality should be objective and free from subjective factors. **Szasz (1960)** sees the term 'mental illness' as a form of social control. Those labelled as abnormal are discriminated against. Some countries, for example China, have been known to label political opponents as abnormal and confine them to mental institutions.

- *Change over time* – the norms defined by society often relate to moral standards that vary over time as social attitudes change. As an example, homosexuality was not removed from the International Classification of Diseases classification of mental disorders until 1990.

- *Individualism* – those who do not conform to social norms may not be abnormal, but merely individualistic or eccentric and not problematic in any sense.

- *Ethnocentric bias in diagnosis* – western social norms reflect the behaviour of the majority 'white' population. Deviation from these norms by ethnic groups means that ethnic minorities are over-represented in the mental illness statistics. **Cochrane (1977)** found that black people were more often diagnosed as schizophrenic than white people or Asians. However, while this high rate of diagnosis for black people is found in Britain, it is not found in such countries as Jamaica where black people are the majority, suggesting a cultural bias in diagnosis among British psychiatrists.

- *Cultural differences* – social norms vary within and across cultures and so it is difficult to know when they are being broken. If a male wears a skirt, does it indicate abnormality? Would the same be true of a Scottish male? Therefore, this definition of abnormality is culturally relative.

LINK TO THE SOCIOCULTURAL APPROACH

The deviation from social norms definition gives a sociocultural dimension to abnormality, with **Szasz (1960)** arguing that a prime function of psychiatry is to exclude from society individuals seen as being from cultural and sub-cultural groups that exhibit socially unacceptable behaviour or beliefs.

■ Failure to function adequately definition

Failure to function adequately – an inability to cope with day-to-day living.

The **failure to function adequately** definition sees individuals as abnormal when their behaviour suggests that they cannot cope with everyday life. Behaviour is considered abnormal when it causes distress leading to an inability to function properly, like disrupting the ability to work and/or conduct satisfying interpersonal relationships. Such people are often characterized by not being able to experience the usual range of emotions or behaviours. The definition focuses on individual suffering, thus drawing attention to the personal experiences associated with mental disorders.

Rosenhan & Seligman (1989) suggest that personal dysfunction has seven features. The more an individual has, the more they are classed as abnormal (see Table 5.1).

Features of personal dysfunction	Description of a feature
Personal distress	A key feature of abnormality. Includes depression and anxiety disorders.
Maladaptive behaviour	Behaviour stopping individuals from attaining life goals, both socially and occupationally.
Unpredictability	Displaying unexpected behaviours characterized by loss of control, like attempting suicide after failing a test.
Irrationality	Displaying behaviour that cannot be explained in a rational way.
Observer discomfort	Displaying behaviour causing discomfort to others.
Violation of moral standards	Displaying behaviour violating society's moral standards.
Unconventionality	Displaying unconventional behaviours.

■ **Table 5.1** Rosenhan & Seligman's features of personal dysfunction

To assess how well individuals cope with everyday life, clinicians use the Global Assessment of Functioning Scale (GAF), which rates their level of social, occupational, and psychological functioning.

Strengths of the definition

- *Matches sufferers' perceptions* – as most people seeking clinical help believe that they are suffering from psychological problems that interfere with the ability to function properly, it supports the definition.

- *Assesses degree of abnormality* – as the GAF is scored on a continuous scale, it allows clinicians to see the degree to which individuals are abnormal and thus decide who needs psychiatric help.

- *Observable behaviour* – it allows judgement by others of whether individuals are functioning properly, as it focuses on observable behaviours.

- *Checklist* – the definition provides a practical checklist that individuals can use to assess their level of abnormality.

- *Personal perspective* – it recognizes the personal experience of sufferers and thus allows mental disorders to be regarded from the perception of the individuals suffering from them.

Weaknesses of the definition

- *Abnormality is not always accompanied by dysfunction* – psychopaths, people with dangerous personality disorders, can cause great harm yet still appear normal. Harold Shipman, the English doctor who murdered at least 215 of his patients over a 23-year period, seemed to be a respectable doctor. He was abnormal, but didn't display features of dysfunction.

- *Subjective nature of the features of dysfunction* – although GAF measures levels of functioning, it does not consider behaviour from an individual's perspective. What is normal behaviour for an eccentric, like wearing flamboyant clothes, is abnormal for an introvert.

- *Normal abnormality* – there are times in people's lives when it is normal to suffer distress, like when loved ones die. Grieving is psychologically healthy to overcome loss. The definition does not consider this.

- *Distress to others* – behaviour may cause distress to other people and be regarded as dysfunctional, while the person themselves feels no distress, like Stephen Gough, the naked rambler (see page 188).

- *Personally rewarding abnormality* – an individual's apparently dysfunctional behaviour may actually be rewarding. For example, a person's eating disorder can bring affection and attention from others.

- *Cultural differences* – what is considered 'normal functioning' varies from culture to culture and so abnormal functioning of one culture should not be used to judge people's behaviour from other cultures and sub-cultures.

▊ The ideal mental health definition

'Perfect sanity is a myth put forward by straitjacket salesmen.'
Rebecca McKinsey

This definition perceives abnormality in a similar way to how physical health is assessed, by looking for signs of an absence of well-being, but in terms of mental rather than physical health. Therefore, any deviation away from what is seen as normal is classed as abnormal.

Deviation from ideal mental health – failure to meet the criteria for perfect psychological well-being.

The definition needs a set of characteristics of what is required to be normal and these were provided by **Marie Jahoda (1958)**, who devised the concept of ideal mental health. She described six characteristics that individuals should exhibit in order to be normal (see Table 5.2). An absence of any of these characteristics indicates individuals as being abnormal, in other words displaying **deviation from ideal mental health**.

Characteristics of ideal mental health	Description of characteristics
Positive attitude towards oneself	Having self-respect and a positive self-concept.
Self-actualization	Experiencing personal growth and development. 'Becoming everything one is capable of becoming.'
Autonomy	Being independent, self-reliant and able to make personal decisions.
Resisting stress	Having effective coping strategies and being able to cope with everyday anxiety-provoking situations.
Accurate perception of reality	Perceiving the world in a non-distorted fashion. Having an objective and realistic view of the world.
Environmental mastery	Being competent in all aspects of life and able to meet the demands of any situation. Having the flexibility to adapt to changing life circumstances.

■ **Table 5.2** Jahoda's characteristics of ideal mental health

The more characteristics individuals fail to meet and the further they are away from realizing individual characteristics, the more abnormal they are.

Like the deviation from social norms and the failure to function adequately definitions, this definition focuses on behaviours and characteristics seen as desirable, rather than what is undesirable.

YOU ARE THE RESEARCHER

Design a questionnaire to measure Jahoda's characteristics of ideal health. Include questions that produce both qualitative and quantitative data. How easy/difficult was this to do? How would you use content analysis to make sense of your qualitative data?

Strengths of the definition

- *Positivity* – the definition emphasizes positive achievements rather than failures and distress and stresses a positive approach to mental problems by focusing on what is desirable, not undesirable.

- *Targets areas of dysfunction* – the definition allows targeting of which areas to work on when treating abnormality. This could be important when treating different types of disorders, such as focusing upon specific problem areas a person with depression has.

- *Holistic* – the definition considers an individual as a whole person rather than focusing on individual areas of their behaviour.

- *Goal setting* – the definition permits identification of exactly what is needed to achieve normality, allowing creation of personal goals to work towards and achieve, thus facilitating self-growth.

PSYCHOLOGY IN THE REAL WORLD

Both the deviation from ideal mental health and failure to function adequately definitions have real world applications.

They both identify areas of a person's psychosocial functioning that need improvement and can be worked upon, either through therapy or through humanistic self-growth methods, such as encounter groups like alcoholics anonymous or eating disorder support groups.

Weaknesses of the definition

- *Over-demanding criteria* – most people do not meet all the ideals. For example, few people experience personal growth all the time. Therefore, according to this definition, most people are abnormal. Thus the criteria may actually be ideals (how you would like to be) rather than actualities (how you actually are).

- *Subjective criteria* – many of the criteria are vague and difficult to measure. Measuring physical health is more objective, using methods like X-rays and blood tests. Diagnosing mental health is more subjective, relying largely on self-reports of patients who may be mentally ill and not reliable.

- *Contextual effects* – mental health criteria are affected by context. Spitting while out jogging is quite normal, but is not considered normal in the college cafeteria.
- *Changes over time* – perceptions of reality change over time. Once seeing visions was a positive sign of religious commitment, now it would be perceived as a sign of schizophrenia.
- *Cultural variation* – the criteria used to judge mental health are culturally relative and should not be used to judge others of different cultures. Some types of abnormality exist only in certain cultures, like Koro, which is a syndrome found in South-east Asia, China and Africa, where a man believes that his penis is fatally retracting into his body.
- *Non-desirability of autonomy* – collectivist cultures stress communal goals and behaviours and see autonomy as undesirable. Western cultures are more concerned with individual attainment and goals, so the definition is culturally biased.

Statistical infrequency definition

Statistical infrequency –
exhibiting behaviours that numerically are rare.

The idea of **statistical infrequency** is that behaviours that are statistically rare should be seen as abnormal. Statistics are gathered that claim to measure certain characteristics and behaviours, with a view to showing how they are distributed throughout the general population.

What is regarded as statistically rare depends on normal distribution. A normal distribution curve can be drawn to show what proportions of people share the characteristics or behaviour in question (see Figure 5.2). Most people will be on or near the mean for these characteristics or behaviour, with declining amounts of people away from the mean (either above or below it). Any individuals who fall outside 'the normal distribution', usually about 5 per cent of a population (two standard deviation points away from the mean) are perceived as being abnormal. So, for example, individuals whose moods were elevated above or below that of the normal distribution would be classed as abnormal.

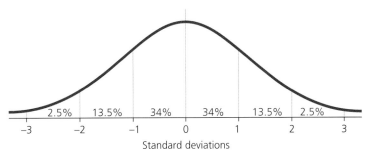

■ **Figure 5.2** Standard deviation

The definition goes no further than declaring which behaviours are abnormal and makes no judgements about quality of life or the nature of mental disorders.

Strengths of the definition

- *Can be appropriate* – in many situations statistical criterion can define abnormality, for example mental retardation.
- *Objective* – once a way of collecting data about a behaviour/characteristic and a 'cut-off point' has been agreed, it becomes an objective way of deciding who is abnormal.
- *No value judgements* – no judgements are made, so, for example, homosexuality, which was defined as a mental disorder under early versions of diagnostic criteria used by psychiatrists, would not be seen under this definition as 'wrong' or 'unacceptable', but merely as less frequent than heterosexuality.
- *Evidence for assistance* – statistical evidence that a person has a mental disorder can be used to justify requests for psychiatric assistance.
- *Based on real data* – the definition relies on real, unbiased data and so again is an objective means of defining abnormality.
- *Overall view* – the definition gives an overview of what behaviours and characteristics are infrequent within a given population.

Weaknesses of the definition

- *Where to draw the line* – it is not clear how far behaviour should deviate from the norm to be seen as abnormal. Many disorders, like depression, vary greatly between individuals in terms of their severity.

- *Not all infrequent behaviours are abnormal* – some rare behaviours and characteristics are desirable rather than being undesirable. For example, being highly intelligent is statistically rare, but desirable.

- *Not all abnormal behaviours are infrequent* – some statistically frequent 'normal' behaviours are actually abnormal. About 10 per cent of people will be chronically depressed at some point in their lives, which suggests depression is so common as to not be seen as abnormal under this definition.

- *Cultural factors* – the definition does not consider cultural factors. What is statistically normal in one culture may not be in another (cultural relativism). This can lead to the problem of judging people of one culture by the statistical norms of another culture.

TOK link

There are various criteria of abnormality, as well as different psychological approaches that try to explain abnormal conditions. All have their criticisms, however, which give rise to the possibility that the whole concept of abnormality is one that is beyond the understanding of science.

Approaches to abnormality

'*To study the abnormal is the best way to understand the normal.*'
William James

Biological approach
– model of abnormality that perceives mental disorders as illnesses with physical causes.

FOCUS ON...

- The biological approach to abnormality, including bacterial infections and viruses, brain damage, biochemistry and genetic factors.
- The cognitive approach to abnormality.
- The sociocultural approach to abnormality.

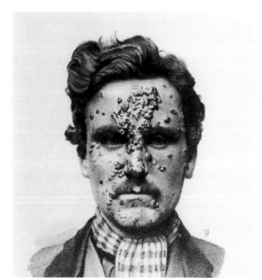

■ **Figure 5.3** Bacterial infections and viruses can cause abnormal conditions, such as the neuropsychiatric disorder general paralysis of the insane, caused by the syphilis bacterium

■ The biological approach

The **biological approach** (medical model) perceives abnormality in a similar way to physical ill health, as being due to malfunctioning biological processes, especially in the structure and working of the brain. As with physical medicine, mental health practitioners diagnose abnormal conditions from their symptoms, using criteria set out in diagnostic manuals. The two most popular are the International Classification of Diseases (ICD) and the Diagnostic and Statistical Manual of Mental Disorders (DSM). Each disorder is seen as separate, with its own particular pattern of symptoms, and brain scans are also used to determine diagnosis.

Four types of biological factors cause abnormal conditions, with some overlap between factors.

Bacterial infections and viruses

Bacterial infections and viruses can damage the brain, causing abnormalities of function. For example, general paralysis of the insane is a neuropsychiatric disorder caused by syphilis. The bacterium treponema palladium enters the body through sexual activity, initially causing ulcers in the genital area. Later on tumours develop in the brain, impairing memory and intellect, with personality and mood also affected, and delusions and bizarre behaviour commonplace. Eventually patients are bedridden, with death occurring after 3–5 years.

Brain damage

Brain damage leads to abnormality through physical damage or illness within the brain. For example, Alzheimer's disease, caused by destruction of cells within the nervous system, leads to chronic memory impairment.

Biochemistry

Biochemical factors can lead to abnormality by affecting levels of neurotransmitters, chemicals that facilitate communication between brain nerve cells, and hormones, chemical messengers that regulate the activity of cells and organs. For example, heightened levels of the neurotransmitter acetylcholine are associated with depression.

Genetic factors

A genetic component is associated with increased risk of developing abnormal conditions. For example, research indicates that obsessive-compulsive disorder is heritable, suggesting a genetic involvement. Several genes combine to give a heightened susceptibility to abnormality, rather than single genes determining mental disorders on their own.

■ The cognitive approach

Cognitive approach
– model of abnormality that perceives mental disorders as due to negative thoughts and illogical beliefs.

The **cognitive approach** perceives abnormality as due to dysfunctional thought processes. The model acknowledges the role of maladaptive learning, but sees the mental processes that occur between stimuli and responses – cognitions, appraisals, thoughts, and so on – as more important, because they inform individuals as to how they feel about stimuli. Abnormal conditions are therefore seen as due to distorted and irrational thought processes, such as negative thoughts and illogical beliefs, referred to by **Beck (1963)** as cognitive errors. These exert influence over emotions and behaviour, leading to abnormalities.

The approach sees individuals as making sense of the world through cognitive processes. Automatic thoughts are ones that occur unconsciously and are more negative in abnormal conditions. Attributions refer to how individuals attempt to make sense of and explain their own and others' behaviour, with those individuals who exhibit abnormal conditions making more inaccurate attributions, like attributing their failed relationships to a lack of social skills. Such attributions can lead to inaccurate expectations, for example expecting relationships to fail, which turn into reality as self-fulfilling prophecies. Illogical thoughts do not therefore have to reflect reality, but do affect behaviour.

Overall the cognitive approach sees abnormal conditions as occurring when dysfunctional thought processes lead to maladaptive behaviour. For example, **Beck (1963)** saw depression as occurring through the cognitive triad, three illogical thought processes that result in irrational, negative feelings and lead to actual depression:

1 *The self* – where individuals regard themselves as being helpless, worthless and inadequate.

2 *The world* – where obstacles are perceived within one's environment that cannot be dealt with.

3 *The future* – where personal worthlessness is seen as hindering any improvements.

Examples of these types of thoughts:

1 Negative feelings about themselves – 'Nobody loves me.'

2 Negative feelings about the world – 'I cannot influence events.'

3 Negative feelings about the future – 'I will always be unlovable.'

The sociocultural approach

The **sociocultural approach** sees one's social and cultural environment as important factors in determining abnormality. The social and cultural context in which individuals live affects the kind of stressors they are exposed to and thus the types of disorders they are vulnerable to. This is backed up by the fact that different disorders occur in different cultures. For example, pibloktoq is a culture-bound syndrome found among arctic and sub-arctic Eskimo communities. It is characterized by a brief period of intense excitement, during which the sufferer tears off their clothes, breaks furniture, shouts obscenities and eats faeces, followed by seizures and a coma lasting up to 12 hours, after which sufferers have no recollection of the incident.

The fact that certain disorders have different rates of occurrence is explicable by sociocultural factors. For instance, anorexia nervosa, where sufferers fail to eat enough to maintain a healthy body weight, is predominately a western cultural phenomenon, with females the main sufferers. In western societies there is a cultural obsession, reinforced by the media, of attaining and maintaining a low body weight in order to be attractive. When non-western cultural groupings are exposed to western cultural norms, the rates of anorexia increase. The sociocultural approach also considers socio-economic background, which may explain why anorexia nervosa is predominately found among middle-class, white females.

The fact that incidence rates of abnormal disorders change in cultural groups who emigrate to become ethnic minorities within other cultural groupings is also explicable through sociocultural means. For example, the incidence of schizophrenia worldwide is 1 per cent, a fact true of people of Caribbean cultures. However, the rate of schizophrenia among people of Caribbean origin living in Great Britain is much higher, which can be explained by the high rate of social stressors, like poor housing, low socio-economic status, racism, and so on, to which they are exposed.

Overall, the sociocultural approach sees abnormality as arising from the influence society and culture has on individuals. It considers society's norms, roles within social environments, cultural background, family and the views of others, with its focus centring on cultural rules and ideals, social networks, family structures and religious beliefs. Abnormality is therefore not a disease, but instead is seen as arising from dysfunctional sociocultural systems.

Strengthen your learning

1 Describe the following definitions of abnormality:
   a the deviation from social norms definition
   b the failure to function adequately definition, including Rosenhan & Seligman's features of personal dysfunction
   c the deviation from ideal mental health definition, including Jahoda's characteristics of ideal mental health
   d the statistical infrequency definition

2 Evaluate each of the definitions given in question 1 in terms of their strengths and weaknesses.

3 Explain how the following approaches view abnormality:
   a the biological approach
   b the cognitive approach
   c the sociocultural approach.

Classification systems

'Science is the systematic classification of experience.'
George Henry Lewes

FOCUS ON...

- Diagnosis of mental disorders through DSM-V and ICD-10 classification systems.
- Rosenhan's classic 'On being sane in insane places' study.
- The role of clinical biases in diagnosis, including influences of the placebo effect, the medical model, psychoanalytic theory, drug companies and cultural bias.

The diagnosis of mental disorders

As with physical illness, mental disorders must first be diagnosed, whereby the nature and cause of a disorder are identified and determined. For this, clinicians use classification systems, which are based on the idea that certain groups of symptoms can be grouped together as a syndrome (an illness or disease), with an identifiable underlying cause that is separate from all other syndromes.

However, many mental disorders have no physical symptoms and clinicians are reliant on the non-physical subjective experiences that sufferers report, along with any observed signs of dysfunctional behaviour. This, coupled with the fact that many dispute whether mental disorders exist as separate, diagnosable conditions, makes **diagnosis** more unreliable and invalid compared to diagnoses of physical conditions.

Diagnosis – identification of the nature and cause of a mental disorder.

LINK TO THE BIOLOGICAL APPROACH

The concept of diagnosis comes from the medical (biological) model, based on the idea that, similarly to physical illnesses, causes and types of mental disorders can be diagnosed (identified), treated and cured, with a cure being seen as an absence of physical symptoms.

DSM-V

DSM-V – diagnostic classification system produced and used in the USA.

The Diagnostic and Statistical Manual of Mental Disorders, 5th edition (**DSM-V**) (published 2013) is the classification system of the American Psychiatric Association, but is used in many countries worldwide.

Section I – describes the revision of DSM since DSM-IV from the previous multi-axial system.

Section II – lists diagnostic criteria and codes:

- *Neurodevelopmental disorders*, such as autism spectrum disorder and intellectual development disorder
- *Schizophrenia spectrum and other psychotic disorders*, such as schizophrenia and catatonia
- *Bipolar and related disorders*, such as bipolar disorder (manic-depression)
- *Depressive disorders*, such as major depressive disorder and persistent depressive disorder
- *Anxiety disorders*, such as specific phobia and separation anxiety disorder
- *Obsessive-compulsive and related disorders*, such as OCD and body dysmorphic disorder
- *Trauma and stressor related disorders*, such as post-traumatic stress disorder and unspecified trauma
- *Dissociative disorders*, such as dissociative amnesia and dissociative identity disorder
- *Somatic symptom and related disorders*, such as conversion disorder and somatic symptom disorder
- *Feeding and eating disorders*, such as pica (eating non-nutritious foodstuffs), anorexia nervosa
- *Elimination disorders*, such as enuresis (repeatedly defecating in places other than a toilet) and encopresis (repeatedly urinating in places other than a toilet)
- *Sleep-wake disorders*, such as insomnia disorder and narcolepsy
- *Sexual dysfunctions*, such as delayed ejaculation, female orgasmic disorder
- *Gender dysphoria*, such as gender dysphoria and unspecified gender disorder
- *Disruptive, impulse control and conduct disorders*, such as intermittent explosive disorder and kleptomania (recurrent urges to steal without any need)
- *Substance related and addictive disorders*, such as alcohol related disorders and cannabis withdrawal
- *Neurocognitive disorders*, such as delirium and Alzheimer's disease
- *Personality disorders*, such as general personality disorder and dependent personality disorder
- *Paraphilic disorders*, such as voyeuristic disorder and sexual sadism disorder
- *Other mental disorders*, such as unspecified mental disorder due to a medical condition

- *Medication induced movement disorders and other adverse effects of medication*, such as neuroleptic induced Parkinsonism and tardive dyskinesia

- *Other conditions that might be the focus of clinical attention*, such as abuse and neglect and relational problems

Section III – emerging measures – contains techniques and skills that enhance clinical decision-making and help understand the cultural context of mental disorders, as well as emerging diagnoses for further study.

LINK TO THE COGNITIVE APPROACH

With DSM-V, cognitive tests are used to determine cognitive dysfunctions and IQ tests are used to differentiate between mental disorder and mental retardation, thus providing a link to the cognitive approach.

ICD-10

ICD-10 – diagnostic classification system produced by the World Health Organization and used in Great Britain.

The International Classification of Diseases, 10th revision (**ICD-10**) is a classification system of illnesses and health complaints, including mental disorders, created by the World Health Organization. Similarly to DSM-V, signs and symptoms are used to categorize diagnoses and regular revisions occur to reflect changes in clinical knowledge. ICD-10 recognizes 11 general categories of mental disorders, like schizophrenia, mood disorders, stress-related disorders, and so on.

Attempts are being made to unify the categories of DSM-V and ICD-10 to create better reliability, with the USA moving towards 'officially' using ICD-10.

■ Evaluation

There have been criticisms that DSM-V revisions (from DSM-IV) lack research support, inter-rater reliability for many disorders is low, some descriptions are contradictory and that the drugs industry had influence over its creation, with a majority of panel members (who wrote the revision) having ties to the drugs industry.

KEY STUDY   CLASSIC RESEARCH

■ **Figure 5.4** David Rosenhan

'On being sane in insane places'
Rosenhan (1973)

David Rosenhan was one of the most famous of psychologists. His work in abnormal psychology was truly ground-breaking and led to many positive changes in the treatment of the mentally disordered. He died in 2012, aged 82.

In this classic study of the reliability and validity of psychiatric diagnosis, nine healthy people (including Rosenhan himself) presented themselves at psychiatric hospitals in five American states claiming to hear voices. Eight were admitted (three females and five males), one being refused entry due to falsifying personal details. After admission all eight behaved normally and participated in ward activities, each making notes about their experiences, though such note-taking was often perceived to be part of their abnormal condition. The pseudopatients noted how clinicians ignored them, even when they were speaking directly to them (asking questions like, 'Pardon me, doctor, but could you tell me when I will be presented at the staff meeting?'); it was as if they were 'invisible' (see Table 5.3). It was left to each pseudopatient to secure their release, with the length of hospitalization before release ranging from 7 to 52 days (average stay 19 days). All were released with the diagnosis of 'schizophrenia in remission' after treatment involving being given 2100 tablets (of which only two were swallowed). Although no pseudopatients were detected by clinicians, many fellow patients had suspicions concerning their authenticity (35 out of 118 patients in the first three hospitalizations). Comments from fellow patients included, 'You're not crazy. You're a journalist or a professor' and 'You're checking up on the hospital'.

On the basis of these results it seems that psychiatric diagnoses had low validity (though reliability was high, as 7 out of 8 were diagnosed as schizophrenic, demonstrating how reliability can be high while validity is low). However, this criticism was somewhat unfair, as clinicians do not expect people to fake abnormal symptoms to attempt admittance to hospital and it is better to admit those who may be ill than to deny admittance, on the basis that the prime function of hospitals is to help people.

To counter this criticism Rosenhan falsely informed staff at a teaching and research hospital, who were aware of his initial study, that an unspecified number of pseudopatients would attempt to gain admittance during the next three months. Staff rated on a 10-point scale the likelihood of new patients being fake. Out of 193 new patients, 83 aroused suspicions of faking (43 per cent). Rosenhan sent no pseudopatients, however; all were genuine. These results strongly suggested that clinicians could not reliably diagnose who was mentally disordered.

	Percentage making contact with patient	
Response	Psychiatrists	Nurses
Moves on with head averted	71	88
Makes eye contact	23	10
Pauses and chats	2	4
Stops and talks	4	0.5

■ **Table 5.3** Responses of clinicians towards pseudopatients

■ Role of clinical biases in diagnosis

'Bias and impartiality is in the eye of the beholder.'
Lord Barnett

Clinicians' beliefs and desires about diagnosis and treatment, coupled with patients' high levels of susceptibility (believing what they're told by 'experts'), often have an effect on the diagnosis and treatment of mental disorders. There can be a powerful self-deception effect from a combination of misinformed clinicians and gullible patients. The ultimate effect of this is reduced reliability and validity of diagnosis.

Placebo effect

Placebo effect –
where improvement in a patient's condition is due to expectation of improvement rather than any actual therapeutic effect.

How could highly trained clinicians be misinformed? Well, this can easily occur, if theories of abnormality and diagnostic criteria are incorrect. Clinicians may over-estimate the validity of the diagnoses they make, and the treatments given, on the basis of such diagnoses. This can produce a **placebo effect**, where diagnosis and treatment lead to an improvement in a patient's mental health, not because the diagnosis and treatment are correct, but because of the expectation of recovery they create in the patient. The patient gets better, because they expect to get better and the clinicians then assume this was because their diagnosis and prescribed treatment was correct (and the theories upon which they were based). Such incorrect diagnoses are easier to make with mental disorders, as most mental disorders do not have physical symptoms that clinicians can base their judgements on, but instead diagnoses are made based on the symptoms that patients report.

Clinical bias –
systematic deviation from validity of diagnosis.

Clinical bias can occur as *over-diagnosis*, where patients are diagnosed as having a condition when they do not (usually because of system errors due to incorrect theories and diagnostic criteria), and as *under-diagnosis*, where patients are not diagnosed as having a condition when they do (usually because of errors by individual clinicians). It is believed that over-diagnosis is more common.

Medical model

In the world of mental health treatment, the medical model is the most preferred, which sees the causes of mental health as having a physiological basis, such as through abnormally functioning genetics, biochemistry and brain structures. Mental disorders are seen as similar to physical illnesses, with diagnosis based on physical symptoms, which are then treated by biological means, such as with drugs, ECT or psychosurgery, and a cure being seen as attainable by removal of the physical symptoms. In other words, mentally disordered people are just objects that need their biology readjusting. However, this approach neglects the fact that many mental disorders are characterized by non-physical psychological factors that the medical model cannot explain or treat. Clinicians making diagnoses (and prescribing treatments) on this basis can easily therefore make biased, incorrect diagnoses.

Psychoanalytic theory

Similar bias in diagnosis can occur by clinicians who subscribe to Freudian psychoanalytic ideas about the origins and treatments of mental disorders. Mental disorders here are seen as being due to unresolved, unconscious traumas that occur during psychosexual stages of development during childhood. For example, anxiety disorders are seen as occurring from an over-developed super-ego, the moralistic part of personality that blocks unacceptable urges of the id, the irrational, pleasure-seeking part of personality. To reduce such anxiety, threatening thoughts and impulses are repressed (hidden) in the unconscious mind, which then has an effect on adult, conscious behaviour, such as by exhibiting phobias. These are then treated by psychoanalysis, which seeks to reduce anxiety by giving a sufferer insight into the origins of their problem. However, there is very little evidence than any of this is actually true. Therefore, clinicians acting on psychoanalytic principles can easily give incorrect, biased diagnoses and treatments.

Drug companies

There are many who argue that companies who produce drug treatments for mental disorders (and who make vast profits when such drugs are given as treatments) have an undue influence over the diagnoses of clinicians. Promoting biological explanations for mental disorders, such as through sponsoring research that suggests such disorders have biological components, can lead to clinicians making biased diagnoses that favour the medical model. It has also been alleged that drug companies had an unjustifiable influence on the construction of the DSM-V classification system; 56 per cent of panel members (who wrote the revision of the system) had ties to the drugs industry. The accusation is that DSM-V may therefore be inclined towards getting clinicians to make biased, incorrect diagnoses that favour the medical model and thus the drug companies.

Cultural bias

Cultural bias – the tendency to over-diagnose members of other cultures as suffering from mental disorders.

Cultural bias concerns the tendency to over-diagnose members of other cultures as suffering from mental disorders. In Britain, for example, people of Afro-Caribbean descent are much more likely than white people to be diagnosed as schizophrenic. Also Afro-Caribbean schizophrenics in Britain are more likely to be compulsorily confined in 'closed' (secure) hospitals than white schizophrenics, with the accusation being that most British psychiatrists are white and thus more likely to perceive black schizophrenics as more 'dangerous' than white schizophrenics. There is also the possibility though that the heightened stress levels people from ethnic minorities experience, from poverty and racism for instance, may actually contribute to higher levels of schizophrenia in such cultural groups.

▧ Research

- **Goldberg & Huxley (1992)** assessed the validity of diagnosis of depression and anxiety disorders by British clinicians, finding that up to 50 per cent of cases went undiagnosed. Although some patients were diagnosed at later medical inspection and some recovered without treatment, 14 per cent of patients with persistent depression went undiagnosed, which suggests that under-diagnosis of mental disorders is quite a common occurrence.
- **Cochrane (1977)** reported the incidence of schizophrenia in the West Indies and Britain to be similar, at around 1 per cent, but that people of Afro-Caribbean origin are seven times more likely to be diagnosed with schizophrenia when living in Britain. This suggests either that Afro-Caribbean people living in Britain have more stressors leading to schizophrenia, or that invalid diagnoses are being made due to cultural bias.
- **Kirsch *et al.* (2002)** used the Freedom of Information Act to gain unpublished data on the effectiveness of the six most prescribed antidepressants in the USA between 1987 and 1999.

It was found that more than half of drug trials sponsored by drug companies failed to find a significant positive effect for these drugs. This suggests that incorrect viewpoints about mental disorders that favour the medical model are being encouraged, which could lead to clinicians making biased diagnoses in favour of such viewpoints.

■ **Holmes (1990)** reviewed 60 years of research into repression and did not find any solid evidence of the phenomenon, weakening support for the explanation. This suggests that diagnoses of disorders based on the psychoanalytic model are biased and incorrect.

Evaluation

■ **Stewart** *et al.* **(2003)** argues that clinicians need to move away from the clinical 'disease-centred' method, where mental disorders are diagnosed in a biased way based on the medical model, towards a 'patient-centred' method, where doctors become more aware of their biases in diagnosis. This would reduce the effect of their deceiving their patients and causing expectations that lead towards a placebo effect, which in turn perpetuates the myth that such diagnoses are valid. Doctors should also have a more human relationship with their patients that gives more consideration to the psychological factors at play in the causation of patients' disorders. It is believed that such measures would have the effect of reducing clinical bias.

■ The majority of clinicians in mental health are white, middle-to-upper class males, so the suggestion is that until clinicians become more representative of the populations they treat, clinical diagnoses will continue to be biased.

■ One way to reduce the possibility of clinical bias occurring is to reduce the influence of the drug companies. To achieve this, further reviews of diagnostic categories should be conducted by people with no connections to the drug industry and the influence of drug companies over research into psychotherapeutic drugs should be heavily curtailed. One suggestion by some in the field is that results of all studies into the effectiveness of drug treatments should be published and not just ones that favour the validity of the medical model.

■ **Szasz (1960)** argues that the mind does not exist in a physical sense and so cannot be 'diseased' in a biological sense. He believes that the diagnosis of mental 'illness' is actually a means of 'socially controlling' undesirable elements of society. This suggests that diagnoses based on the medical model are not only biased, but are being used in an unjustifiable way to negatively stigmatize certain types of people.

TOK link

The psychological study of abnormality has led to ethical changes in the ways in which mental patients are perceived and treated. Only through research that highlights unethical practices is it possible for radical changes to occur, permitting a more humane treatment of the mentally afflicted.

Strengthen your learning

1 Explain how DSM-V and ICD-10 are used to diagnose mental disorders.

2 For Rosenhan's classic 1973 study, in your own words, state the:
   a aims
   b procedure
   c results
   d conclusions
   e evaluative points.

3 Explain how the following affect the role of clinical biases in diagnosis:
   a the placebo effect
   b the medical model
   c psychoanalytic theory
   d drug companies
   e cultural bias.

4 Summarize what research studies have suggested about the role of clinical bias in diagnoses.

5 What other evaluative points can be made about clinical bias in diagnoses?

Reliability and validity of diagnosis

'Not all truths are truthful.'
Raheel Farooq

FOCUS ON...

- The reliability and validity of diagnosis.
- The reliability and validity of diagnosis of OCD and anorexia nervosa.
- Cultural relativism and diagnosis.
- Ethical considerations in diagnosis.

Reliability

....
Reliability of diagnosis – the consistency of diagnosis.
....

Reliability of diagnosis refers to the consistency of symptom measurement and affects classification and diagnosis in two ways:

1   Test–retest-reliability – occurs when a clinician makes the same consistent diagnosis on separate occasions using the same information.

2   Inter-rater reliability – occurs when several clinicians make identical diagnoses of the same patient, independently of each other.

Evaluation

- Making reliable diagnoses is difficult, as clinicians cannot base decisions on physical signs, but only on what symptoms patients report.

- Due to the wording of DSM-V, for example comparing patients to 'average people', clinicians have to make subjective decisions regarding diagnosis.

- Classification systems are not objective, as they have an arbitrary number of symptoms that must be evident for diagnosis to occur; for example, under DSM-V, depression requires a depressed mood plus four other symptoms.

- Another factor in clinicians making reliable diagnoses is comorbidity, where patients simultaneously have two or more mental disorders; for example, simultaneously having schizophrenia and depression, which creates confusion for clinicians as to which actual disorder they are diagnosing. (This also raises issues of descriptive validity, as it suggests some mental disorders may not actually be separate disorders.) Similarly, the reliability (and thus validity) of diagnoses may also be affected by symptoms of a disorder also being an identifying symptom of other mental disorders. For example, hallucinations can be a symptom of bipolar disorder, but also of schizophrenia.

Validity

....
Validity of diagnosis – the accuracy of diagnosis.
....

Validity of diagnosis refers to how accurate, meaningful and useful a diagnosis is. Validity is assessed in several ways:

- *Reliability* – a valid diagnosis must first be reliable, though reliability itself does not ensure validity.

- *Predictive validity* – if diagnosis leads to successful treatment, the diagnosis is seen as valid.

- *Descriptive validity* – for a diagnosis to be valid, patients diagnosed with different disorders should be different from each other in terms of classification.

- *Etiological validity* – to be valid, patients with the same disorder should have the same cause.

- *Convergent validity* – for a diagnostic measuring tool to be valid, it must correlate with another diagnostic tool already known to be valid.

▨ Evaluation

- No matter how much reliability of diagnosis improves, it does not ensure validity.

- Descriptive validity is reduced by comorbidity, where patients have two or more simultaneous disorders, which suggests such disorders may not be separate at all.

- Predictive validity is difficult to attain, as therapies are often assigned from clinicians' biased viewpoints as to what constitutes effective treatments.

- **Winter (1999)** believes that 'diagnostic systems are only aids to understanding, not descriptions of real disease entities'.

- Research has assessed the reliability and validity of diagnoses, with initial findings suggesting low levels of reliability and validity for the diagnoses of many disorders. The positive outcome of this is that classification systems were amended and methods used in classification, such as clinical interviews, have greatly changed. For example, specialist inventories are used in the diagnosis of specific disorders, like the Geriatric Depression Scale (GDS), used in the diagnosis of depression among the elderly. Recent research suggests that diagnosis of many disorders is now much more reliable and valid.

▨ Reliability and validity of the diagnosis of OCD

The development of standardized rating scales, like the Yale–Brown Obsessive Compulsive Scale (Y-BOCS), has improved the reliability and validity of diagnosis, though such scales still have their criticisms. There is also a lack of agreement among clinicians as to whether OCD is a separate disorder.

▨ Research

- **Di Nardo & Barlow (1988)** found an excellent 80 per cent reliability of diagnosis, second only to simple phobias in diagnosis of anxiety and mood disorders. This was supported by **Foa *et al.* (1987)**, who used Likert scales to find high correlations among patients', therapists' and independent observers' ratings of OCD features, suggesting good inter-rater reliability.

- **Geller *et al.* (2006)** assessed the reliability of the Child Behaviour Checklist, finding it reliable and possessing psychometric properties that identified children with OCD, which supports the idea that the development of specialist inventories has improved the reliability of diagnosis.

- **Leckman & Chittenden (1990)**, while assessing the validity of diagnosis of OCD, found that 50 per cent of Tourette's syndrome patients also had OCD, which suggests that OCD is not a separate disorder.

- **Deacon & Abramowitz (2004)** applied the Yale–Brown Obsessive Compulsive Scale (Y-BOCS), the 'gold standard' measure for OCD, to 100 patients, finding problems with the Y-BOCS sub-scales' ability to accurately measure OCD components, which implies the scales lack validity and need revision.

> **YOU ARE THE RESEARCHER**
>
> Design a correlational study to assess inter-rater reliability of diagnosis of OCD. What would your co-variables be and how would you measure them?
>
> Construct suitable correlational and null hypotheses for your study, as well as a suitable graph to plot your correlational data on. What kind of graph would this be? Plot the data as if you had found a positive relationship between the co-variables.

▨ Evaluation

- The high incidence of OCD in young people, coupled with the secretive nature of the disorder, which leads to its under-recognition, and the lack of specialized child psychiatry services, implies a need for a quick, reliable diagnostic tool to identify cases.

- OCD has easily observable symptoms that assist in clear diagnosis, thus contributing towards high levels of reliability. The American Psychiatric Association (1987) reported that, compared to other anxiety disorders, the diagnostic reliability of OCD is highly favourable.

- Diagnoses of OCD incur long-term negative effects on sufferers, yet such diagnoses are made with little evidence of the disorder actually existing as a separate condition.

Reliability and validity of diagnosis of anorexia nervosa

As with many other disorders, reliability and validity of diagnosis has improved over time, as diagnostic categories and methods of assessment have been amended. Reliability of diagnosis among young patients has been problematic, which is worrying, with many anorexia nervosa (AN) sufferers being of young age. Diagnosis of AN and bulimia nervosa (BN) as separate disorders seems possible, but the idea of AN having separate sub-types is not yet proven.

Research

- **Nicholls *et al.* (2000)** assessed the inter-rater reliability of diagnostic tools for eating disorders for children and young adolescents. Eighty-one participants aged 7–16 years were rated by two clinicians (ignorant of each other's ratings). A concordance rate of 35 per cent was found when using ICD-10, 63 per cent when using DSM-IV and 88 per cent using Great Ormond Street (GOS) criteria. When using DSM criteria, 50 per cent of the children could not be classified. This suggests that DSM and ICD criteria are of little use in classifying the eating disorders of children, but the GOS criteria, specially developed for this age group are more reliable.

- **Sysko & Walsh (2011)** assessed the test-retest reliability of the new DSM-V classification criteria for eating disorders. Participants conducted two telephone interviews with trained assessors. Agreement rates of between 81 and 97 per cent were found for AN, which suggests that test-retest reliability of AN diagnosis is highly reliable if conducted by experienced interviewers.

- **Stice *et al.* (2004)** conducted four studies into the reliability and validity of the widely used Eating Disorder Diagnostic Scale (EDDS), a self-report interview method of diagnosing AN (as well as BN and binge-eating disorder). The scale was found to have internal consistency (reliability), convergent validity, and predictive validity in anticipating responses to a prevention programme and future onset of eating disorders and depression. This suggests the scale to be both reliable and valid for clinical and research use.

- **Eddy *et al.* (2008)** investigated the validity of the DSM classification system to distinguish between AN, BN and AN sub-types. The researchers assessed 216 AN and BN patients every week for seven years using the Eating Disorder Longitudinal Interval Follow-Up Examination (EDLIFUE). Most AN patients were diagnosed as having diagnostic 'crossover', with one-third switching from AN to BN (though were likely to relapse back to AN) and more than half switching from one sub-type of AN to another. BN patients were unlikely to cross over to AN. This suggests that there is a general distinction between AN and BN, but that the idea of sub-types of AN is not supported.

Evaluation

- Early indications are that the usefulness of the new DSM-V classification system in the reliability and validity of AN diagnosis is reasonably effective, but further research needs to be done before a more certain view can be reached.

- One criterion for diagnosing AN is a refusal to maintain 'normal' body weight, with falling below 85 per cent of expected body weight used as a 'cut-off' point for whether someone has AN or not, but **Wilfley *et al.* (2007)** found 28 per cent of sufferers had body weight greater than expected. Also, this criterion does not take into account age, gender, ethnicity or frame size and has low predictive validity in forecasting treatment outcomes.

- The diagnostic criterion of fear of gaining weight is criticized for being culture-bound, as this criterion comes from studies of western cultural participants and again has poor predictive validity in forecasting treatment outcomes. The criteria do not take into account factors like not eating due to religious fasting.

■ Criteria for diagnosis are also criticized for being influenced by western sociocultural factors, for example the way in which body weight and shape is perceived. **Khandelwal et al. (1995)** assessed five cases of AN from India to find little body image distortion, as is common with western sufferers, possibly because thinness is not associated with feminine beauty in India. This criticism is backed up by **Mumford et al. (1991)** finding Asian girls with higher scores for 'westernization' reported greater dissatisfaction with their body shape.

PSYCHOLOGY IN THE REAL WORLD

Diagnostic classification systems like DSM-V and ICD-10 have real-world applications, as they are used to diagnose patients, which then affects the treatment they are prescribed. It is therefore important that classification systems are reliable and valid, which is why they are periodically revised, such as the revision of the DSM system in 2013.

Cultural relativism

Cultural relativism – the idea that definitions of what is normal functioning vary from culture to culture and have equal validity.

Definitions of abnormality suffer from **cultural relativism**, meaning that no one definition applies to everyone, as normal functioning varies between cultures. This creates problems when clinicians of one culture evaluate and diagnose those from other cultures. Unless clinicians are aware of an individual's cultural background, norms and reference points, they may diagnose the individual's culturally normal behaviour as abnormal from their own cultural viewpoint. In some cultures it is normal to hear the voices of departed loved ones during the grieving process, but in western cultures this could be an indication of schizophrenia.

LINK TO THE SOCIOCULTURAL APPROACH

Cultural considerations in diagnosis are more widespread in multicultural societies, where several distinctive sub-cultures, each with their own perceptions of what constitutes normality, exist side by side, especially in those sub-cultures forming ethnic minorities within a larger society.

Ethical considerations in diagnosis

The aim of diagnosis is to correctly identify disorders so that appropriate treatment can be given. However, there are several ethical consequences of diagnosis. First, diagnosis can be used to discriminate against and even punish certain people. For example, diagnostic criteria have been used to classify homosexuality as a mental disorder, thus justifying the forcible 'treatment' of homosexuals to 'cure' their abnormality. Such treatments as aversion therapy, where electric shocks are given if patients become aroused by homosexual images, do not 'cure' homosexuals and turn them into heterosexuals, instead patients often become stressed, depressed and suicidal. Certain regimes have also used diagnostic criteria to classify political and religious dissidents as abnormal and punish them for their beliefs, by incarcerating them in psychiatric institutions to undergo forcibly applied treatments. **Xia (2012)** reported that China has imprisoned political dissidents in psychiatric institutions and subjected them to forced treatments, such as electroconvulsive therapy (ECT).

To be diagnosed as abnormal involves being given a stigmatizing label that is difficult to remove. Rather than being classed as 'people with schizophrenia', sufferers are labelled as 'schizophrenics', as if that is their whole being, and even when symptoms are absent they are still referred to as 'schizophrenic in remission', a lifelong identity that negatively affects employment chances and how others view them. **Abelson & Langer (1974)** showed a video of a young man telling an older man about his work experience. Psychoanalytic clinicians who were told the young man was a job applicant perceived him positively, while those told he was a mental patient viewed him negatively, illustrating the stigmatizing impact of labelling (though there was no difference in judgement among behavioural therapists).

Labelling therefore can sentence those diagnosed as abnormal to a lifetime 'career' as mental patients, with frequent periods of hospitalization, treatment and unemployment. Those placed within psychiatric hospital environments may succumb to institutionalization, where they cannot function meaningfully outside the hospital environment. Another aspect of hospitalization is the powerlessness and depersonalization experienced by patients, as reported by Rosenhan's pseudopatients commenting on how they were ignored by clinicians (see page 198). An additional danger with labelling people as mentally disordered is that of self-fulfilling prophecy, where people behave in the way that the label suggests they should.

There is also the ethical issue of the use of psychoactive drugs as a 'chemical cosh' to control patients rather than treat them. There is even the viewpoint that drug companies exert an unhealthy influence over doctors and public health figures to promote their wares even though there is evidence that such drugs are often ineffective or even dangerous, with the accusation that the drug companies are suppressing such evidence. It is a lucrative market; sales of antipsychotic drugs topped £10 billion globally in 2008.

TOK link

The psychological study of abnormality has led to ethical changes in the ways in which mental patients are perceived and treated. Only through research that highlights unethical practices is it possible for radical changes to occur, permitting a more humane treatment of the mentally afflicted.

Strengthen your learning

1 Explain the difference between reliability and validity of diagnosis.

2 What is meant by:
   a test-retest reliability
   b inter-rater reliability?

3 What evaluative points can be made about reliability of diagnosis?

4 What is meant by:
   a predictive validity
   b descriptive validity
   c etiological validity
   d convergent validity?

5 What evaluative points can be made about validity of diagnosis?

6 Summarize what research studies have suggested about the reliability and validity of diagnosis of OCD.

7 What other evaluative points can be made about the reliability and validity of diagnosis of OCD?

8 Summarize what research studies have suggested about the reliability and validity of diagnosis of anorexia nervosa.

9 What other evaluative points can be made about the reliability and validity of diagnosis of anorexia nervosa?

10 Explain how definitions of abnormality suffer from cultural relativism.

11 Outline ethical considerations in diagnosis.

SECTION SUMMARY

- There are several definitions of abnormality, each with its own strengths and weaknesses.
- Different psychological approaches are used to explain abnormality.
- Classification systems, based on the medical model, are used to diagnose mental disorders.
- The reliability and validity of diagnosis are not always accurate.
- Clinical biases often serve to reduce the reliability and validity of diagnosis.
- Reliability refers to consistency of diagnosis, while validity refers to accuracy of diagnosis.

■ Assessment check

1	Discuss classification systems used in the diagnosis of abnormality.	(22 marks)
2	Discuss the role of clinical biases in diagnosis of abnormality.	(22 marks)
3	Discuss psychologists' attempts to define abnormality.	(22 marks)
4	Evaluate the reliability and validity of diagnosis in abnormality.	(22 marks)
5	Discuss one or more studies relating to the reliability and validity of diagnosis in abnormality.	(22 marks)
6	Discuss ethical considerations in the diagnosis of abnormality.	(22 marks)

Etiology of abnormal psychology

IN THE NEWS

Ψ The Psychological Enquirer

'OBSESSED WITH CONTROL' – A BATTLE WITH OCD

■ **Figure 5.5** Melissa Binstock

Melissa Binstock's troubles began aged eight when the unpredictable movements of her Tourette's syndrome left Melissa feeling not in control of her life. So control became her obsession; first it was her belongings at school, books and pencils, perfectly sharpened of course, had to be arranged in order. Before starting work she had to close her eyes and touch the tip of each pencil five times. Her desire was for a safe, predictable world, which she felt her rituals could provide, without them she was consumed with overwhelming anxiety. However, control over the external world then progressed to controlling herself. So her rituals now included wearing the same T-shirt every day; it gave her a sense of power and stability. Then she moved on to what she ate; 12 grams of fat per day, 12 grams of sugar per item, and only eating at one restaurant. By the time she went to high school, rituals controlled every moment of her life: the way she dressed, undressed, only eating white foods. At university Melissa spiralled out of control, as the constant battle between the comfort of her rituals and a great desire to be 'normal' became too much and she collapsed from lack of food; she had been surrounded by people all day and her rule was that she could only eat in private. Her saving moment came when, during a lecture about cognitive behavioural therapy (CBT), Melissa realized it might be possible for her to change her thoughts and feelings. Through practice exposure and response prevention (ERP), she forced herself repetitively into anxiety-provoking activities until they no longer produced feelings of fear. Eventually, Melissa aged 22 was free of her obsessions, compulsions and the anxiety that came with them.

Melissa was suffering from OCD, an anxiety disorder characterized by persistent unpleasant thoughts and repetitive behaviours. Sufferers generally realize their thoughts and behaviour are inappropriate, but cannot control them. Like Melissa, sufferers often have symptoms of Tourette's syndrome too. Research has brought a greater understanding of the condition, allowing effective therapies, like that received by Melissa, to be developed.

Obsessive-compulsive disorder

'I put gloves on before I put gloves on, so I don't get my gloves dirty.'
Jarod Kintz

- Description of OCD.
- Gender and cultural variations in prevalence of OCD.

Description

Obsessive-compulsive disorder (OCD) is an anxiety related mental disorder. As with all anxiety disorders, OCD is characterized by fear reactions that are so high they become maladaptive, negatively affecting sufferers' ability to function effectively in everyday life, with 2 per cent of the population suffering from OCD.

Obsessions consist of forbidden or inappropriate ideas and visual images, leading to feelings of extreme anxiety. Common obsessions include:

- *Contamination*, e.g. by germs
- *Losing control*, e.g. through impulses to hurt others
- *Perfectionism*, e.g. fear of losing important things
- *Unwanted sexual thoughts*, e.g. fear of being homosexual
- *Religion*, e.g. fear of being immoral.

Compulsions consist of intense, uncontrollable urges to repetitively perform tasks and behaviours, such as constantly cleaning door handles. Compulsive behaviours serve to counteract, neutralize or make obsessions go away, and although OCD sufferers realize that compulsions are only a temporary solution, they have no other way to cope so rely on their compulsive behaviours as a short-term escape. Compulsions can also include avoiding situations that trigger obsessive ideas or images. Compulsive behaviours are time-consuming and get in the way of meaningful events, such as work and conducting personal relationships. Behaviours are only compulsive in certain contexts, for example arranging and ordering books is not compulsive if the person is a librarian. Common compulsions involve:

- *Excessive washing and cleaning*, e.g. teeth-brushing
- *Excessive checking*, e.g. doors are locked
- *Repetition*, e.g. of body movements
- *Mental compulsions*, e.g. praying in order to prevent harm
- *Hoarding*, e.g. of magazines.

Most OCD sufferers understand their compulsions are inappropriate, but cannot exert conscious control over them, resulting in even greater levels of anxiety.

OCD is an exaggerated version of normal behaviour and is perceived as a mental disorder when an individual's behaviour becomes detrimental to everyday functioning. For instance, when a sufferer's obsession with contamination means they cannot perform any meaningful work. Not all repetitive behaviours are compulsions; learning a new skill often involves endless, ritualistic repetition, but this is normal and beneficial.

Symptoms of OCD often overlap with those of other disorders, such as Tourette's syndrome and autism, which suggests that OCD may not actually exist as a truly separate disorder.

Symptoms

Obsessions

Recurrent and persistent – recurrently experiencing unwanted thoughts, impulses and images that are inappropriate and intrusive, leading to high levels of anxiety and distress.

Obsessive-compulsive disorder (OCD) – anxiety disorder characterized by persistent, recurring, unpleasant thoughts and repetitive, ritualistic behaviours.

Obsessions – forbidden or inappropriate ideas and visual images leading to feelings of extreme anxiety.

Compulsions – uncontrollable urges to repetitively perform tasks and behaviours.

Irrelevant to real life – experiencing thoughts, impulses and images that are not relevant to real-life situations and are time-consuming so that they hinder an individual's ability to pursue valued activities.

Suppressed – sufferers attempt to suppress thoughts, impulses and images with alternative thoughts or actions.

Recognized as self-generated– sufferers understand that their obsessional thoughts, impulses and images are self-invented and not inserted externally.

Compulsions

Repetitive – sufferers feel compelled to repeat behaviours and mental acts in response to obsessional thoughts, impulses and images.

Aimed at reducing distress – behaviours and mental acts are an attempt to reduce distress or prevent feared events, even though there is little chance of doing so.

Other symptoms

Recognized as excessive – sufferer realizes obsessions/compulsions are excessive.

Time-consuming – obsessions/compulsions are time-consuming, cause distress and interfere with the ability to conduct everyday working and social functioning.

Not related to substance abuse – disorder is not related to substance abuse or other medical condition.

LINK TO THE COGNITIVE APPROACH

OCD has a cognitive component, as it is characterized by persistent, recurrent unpleasant thoughts (as well as repetitive, ritualistic behaviours). Sufferers endure persistent and intrusive thoughts occurring as obsessions or compulsions, or a combination of both.

Gender variations in the prevalence of OCD

There is little gender difference in the prevalence of OCD, though there are gender differences in types of OCD. Preoccupations with contamination and cleaning are more apparent in females, while male sufferers focus more on religious and sexual obsessions. OCD is more common among male children than female, as males have an earlier, gradual onset with more severe symptoms, while OCD in females generally has a later, sudden onset with fewer severe symptoms.

■ Research

Mathis *et al.* (2011) found male OCD sufferers were more likely to have early onset of the disorder, to be single, to have greater social impairment and more sexual or religious symptoms, while females generally had later onset and more contamination or cleaning symptoms. This illustrates that there are gender differences in the onset and expression of OCD.

LINK TO THE BIOLOGICAL APPROACH

Lomax *et al.* (2009) found that the brains of people with early onset OCD, who tend to be male, have a reduction in size of some brain areas, which isn't apparent in those with later-onset OCD, who tend to be female. This suggests that male OCD may be more biological in nature.

■ Evaluation

■ OCD in females may be more influenced by sociocultural factors, as it tends to have a sudden onset often in response to stressful life events, like the death of a loved one. OCD in males seems more biological in origin, as it tends to have a gradual, earlier onset with more severe symptoms.

■ Not all patients with early onset OCD are male, nor are those with later-onset OCD all female. This therefore weakens the argument that male OCD is more biological in nature.

> ### YOU ARE THE RESEARCHER
>
> Design a questionnaire that determines whether there is a gender difference in the experience of OCD. Ensure your questions measure the age of onset, as well as the types of obsessions and compulsions that male and female sufferers develop. How will you record and analyse your data? Create a suitable table and graph to display your findings.

Cultural variations in prevalence of OCD

Sociocultural factors are not prime causes of OCD, but increase the chances of its onset in vulnerable individuals by raising anxiety levels, through influences like major life events and family disharmony. Sociocultural factors, such as family tensions, additionally assist in the maintenance of the disorder. There has also been speculation that some childhood experiences, like contracting streptococcal infections, in association with social factors, such as parental over-protectiveness, predispose individuals to OCD. Sociocultural influences also help shape the expression of the disorder; for example, in highly religious environments obsessions often reflect the particular religious views of that cultural setting. It is also important, if clinicians are to understand the origins of a sufferer's OCD, to consider the specific sociocultural context of an individual, in terms of what is considered shameful or dirty, and so on.

▧ Research

- **Gothelf *et al.* (2004)** reported that anxiety-raising major life events appear to precede the onset of OCD. This suggests such events do not cause OCD, but act as triggers in those biologically or psychologically predisposed to OCD, as not everyone subjected to such life events develops the disorder.

- **Fontenelle *et al.* (2004)** found that while the exact symptoms of OCD may reflect sociocultural factors, there was no consistent evidence that any particular sociocultural factor has a causal role, which implies that sociocultural factors merely shape the expression of OCD.

- **Greenberg & Witztum (1994)** found that 13 out of 19 ultra-religious Jews from Jerusalem with OCD exhibited symptoms that reflected religious beliefs relating to prayer, dietary habits, cleanliness and menstrual practices, which suggests that religious rituals do not cause OCD, but help to shape its expression.

▧ Evaluation

- **Horwath & Weissman (2000)** argue that as studies from different cultures reveal similar prevalence rates and a consistency in the forms of obsessions and compulsions, OCD is likely to be more biological than sociocultural in origin.

- Although OCD appears to be primarily biological in origin, for treatments to work it is important that clinicians understand the origins of each individual sufferer's OCD in terms of their sociocultural background, as only by sensitively targeting the underlying triggers that precipitate the condition can it effectively be addressed.

Strengthen your learning

1 Explain OCD in terms of obsessional thinking and compulsive behaviours.

2 Outline the symptoms of OCD.

3 Think of an example of OCD and explain it in terms of obsessional thoughts and compulsive behaviour.

4 What gender and cultural variations are there in the prevalence of OCD?

5 Summarize what research studies have suggested about gender and cultural variations in the prevalence of OCD.

6 What other evaluative points can be made about gender and cultural variations in the prevalence of OCD?

Explanations for OCD

'I have CDO, it's like OCD, but all the letters are in alphabetical order as they should be.'
Anonymous

FOCUS ON...

- Biological explanations for OCD, including the genetic explanation, neural explanations and the evolutionary explanation.
- Grootheest *et al.*'s. contemporary twin study of OCD.

Biological explanations

....

Biological explanation of OCD – the perception of the disorder as determined by physiological means with treatments based upon chemical means.

....

Biological explanations see OCD as arising from physiological factors. Three possible biological explanations are first hereditary influences through genetic transmission, second the occurrence of OCD through damage to neural (brain) mechanisms and third that OCD has an evolutionary adaptive survival value that has been acted upon by natural selection.

LINK TO THE BIOLOGICAL APPROACH

The genetic, neural and evolutionary theories of OCD all link to the biological approach, as they see OCD as physiologically determined.

Genetic explanation

....

Genetic explanation of OCD – the perception of the disorder as transmitted through inherited factors.

....

The **genetic explanation** here centres on OCD being inherited through genetic transmission, with research originally centring on twin and family studies to assess whether this viewpoint is valid and, if so, to what extent genes do play a part. However, as in other areas of psychology, the problem with twin studies is separating out the relative influences of genes and environment.

With the introduction of DNA profiling, more recent attention has been upon gene-mapping studies, which involve comparing genetic material from OCD sufferers and non-sufferers. Such studies also permit researchers to see whether OCD truly is a separate disorder, as OCD sufferers often also have Tourette's syndrome. Results from both forms of study indicate a genetic link to OCD, with particular genes being involved that make some individuals more vulnerable to developing the disorder than others. It is unlikely that single genes cause OCD; more likely is that it is a combination of genes that determine an individual's level of vulnerability to the condition. Although there seems to be some genetic similarity between OCD and Tourette's syndrome, current thinking is that they are two separate disorders. One interesting finding is the possibility that the genetic contribution to the disorder varies among different age groups. Future research in this area needs to be done to identify whether there are varying rates of genetic influence upon different sub-types of OCD.

KEY STUDY — CONTEMPORARY RESEARCH

'Twin studies on obsessive-compulsive disorder: A review'
Grootheest *et al.* (2005)

Twin studies of OCD began in 1929 and varying degrees of genetic influence have been suggested. In this meta-analysis the researchers assessed 70 years of twin studies into OCD. In a twin study MZ (identical) twins are compared against DZ (non-identical) twins. If the chances of both twins in an MZ pair having OCD is greater than that of both twins in a DZ pair having the disorder, it suggests a genetic component, as MZ twins are 100 per cent genetically similar, while DZ twins are only 50 per cent genetically similar. Case studies of single pairs of twins were also included in the review.

Aims

1 To see if there is any indication of the extent to which OCD is inherited.
2 To see if there is any difference in the extent to which OCD is inherited between children and adults.

Procedure

1 Twin studies of two broad types were reviewed:
   a 'Old literature' – comprising studies performed between 1929 and 1965, where it is not known if patients would be diagnosed with the disorder under modern diagnostic criteria.
   b 'Studies meeting modern criteria' – comprising studies where patients were diagnosed under DSM criteria.
2 In all, 10,034 twin pairs included in 28 twin studies formed the review. There were 9 studies from 1929 to 1965 comprising 37 twin pairs, and 19 modern era studies comprising 9,997 twin pairs.

Findings

1 From studies where methodology and statistical analysis was deemed sufficiently objective to gain useful data, it was estimated that in children, obsessive-compulsive symptoms are heritable, with genetic influences ranging from 45 per cent to 65 per cent.
2 From studies where methodology and statistical analysis was deemed sufficiently objective, it was estimated that in adults, obsessive-compulsive symptoms are heritable, with genetic influences ranging from 27 per cent to 47 per cent.

Conclusions

● Twin studies indicate a genetic component to the transmission of OCD.
● Heritability of OCD appears to be greater in adults than among children.

Evaluation

● The majority of twin studies of OCD were not performed in large enough numbers or under methodological conditions sufficient to gather objective data; therefore, there is a need for further properly controlled twin studies to investigate the heritability of OCD.
● There is a need to assess whether the different sub-types of OCD have different levels of genetic transmission.
● There is a need to include, along with MZ–DZ twin comparisons, data from more gene-mapping studies, which look for similarities in genetic material in the DNA of sufferers and non-sufferers.

▓ Research

■ **Lenane *et al.* (1990)** performed a study into the prevalence of OCD among related family members, finding evidence for the existence of heritable contributions to the onset of the disorder, lending support to the genetic viewpoint.

■ **Samuels *et al.* (2007)** used gene-mapping to compare OCD sufferers who exhibited compulsive hoarding behaviour with those who did not, finding a link to chromosome 14 marker D14S588, implying a genetic influence to compulsive hoarding behaviour, which may also indicate the existence of a separate OCD sub-type.

■ **Stewart *et al.* (2007)** performed gene-mapping on OCD patients and family members, finding a variant of the OLIG-2 gene commonly occurred, which suggests a genetic link to the condition.

- **Davis *et al.* (2013)** used a study method called genome-wide complex trait analysis, which allows simultaneous comparison of genetic variation across the entire genome, rather than the usual method of testing genes one at a time. The genetic datasets of 1500 participants with OCD were compared against 5500 non-OCD-controls (the study also compared the datasets of 1500 Tourette's syndrome sufferers with 5200 non-Tourette's controls). The results showed that both OCD and Tourette's syndrome had a genetic basis, though more so in Tourette's syndrome, and that although there were some shared genetic characteristics, the two disorders had distinct genetic architectures. This suggests the two are separate disorders, though with some overlap.

- **Tang *et al.* (2014)** decided, as complex genetics hinders attempts to understand their role in OCD in humans, to perform research using dogs. Dogs suffer from naturally occurring compulsive disorders that closely model human OCD, but the limited diversity within dog breeds makes identifying genetic influences easier. Gene analysis showed that OCD-affected dogs had significantly higher levels of particular gene variants than dogs without the condition, which suggests a genetic link to OCD. The extent to which findings can be generalized to humans is debatable.

Evaluation

- Although research suggests a genetic component to OCD, there must be some environmental influences upon the disorder, else the concordance rate between MZ twins would be 100 per cent.

- There does not appear to be a single gene involved in the transmission of OCD, instead what research suggests is that many genes scattered throughout the genome each contribute a small amount to an individual's overall risk of developing the disorder. Whether an individual does go on to develop the disorder is then dependent on the degree of environmental triggers that an individual encounters.

- **Pato *et al.* (2001)** report that a substantial amount of evidence suggests OCD is a heritable condition, but that few details are understood about actual genetic mechanisms underpinning the disorder, indicating the need for more focused research.

- As evidence indicates genetic factors are at work in the expression of some forms of OCD, especially obsessions about contamination, aggression and religion and compulsions involving washing, ordering and arranging, it may well be that some types of OCD are more genetic in nature than others.

- As studies like **Grootheest *et al.* (2005)** find, OCD originating in childhood is more genetic in nature than that originating in adulthood, which suggests there may be different types of OCD with different causes.

- The fact that family members often display dissimilar OCD symptoms, for example a child arranging dolls and an adult constantly washing dishes, weakens support for the genetic viewpoint, as if the disorder was inherited then surely exhibited behaviours would be the same?

Neural explanation

Some forms of OCD have been linked to breakdowns in immune system functioning, such as through contracting streptococcal (throat) infections, Lyme's disease and influenza, which would indicate a biological explanation through damage to neural mechanisms. Such onset of the disorder is more often seen in children than adults.

PET (positron emission tomography) scans also show relatively low levels of serotonin activity in the brains of OCD patients and as drugs that increase serotonin activity have been found to reduce the symptoms of OCD, it suggests the neurotransmitter may be involved with the disorder.

PET scans also show that OCD sufferers can have relatively high levels of activity in the orbital-frontal cortex, a brain area associated with higher-level thought processes and the conversion of sensory information into thoughts. The brain area is thought to help initiate activity upon receiving impulses to do so and then to stop the activity when the impulse lessens.

A non-sufferer may have an impulse to wash dirt from their hands; once this is done the impulse to perform the activity stops and thus so does the behaviour. It may be that those with OCD have difficulty in switching off or ignoring impulses, so that they turn into obsessions, resulting in compulsive behaviour.

Research

- **Pichichero (2009)** reported that case studies from the US National Institute of Health showed that children with streptococcal (throat) infections often displayed sudden indications of OCD symptoms shortly after becoming infected. Such children also often exhibited symptoms of Tourette's syndrome. This supports the idea that such infections may be having an effect on neural mechanisms underpinning OCD.

- **Fallon & Nields (1994)** reported that 40 per cent of people contracting Lyme's disease (a bacterial infection spread by ticks) incur neural damage resulting in psychiatric conditions, including OCD. This suggests that the **neural explanation** can account for the onset of some cases of OCD.

- **Zohar et al. (1987)** gave mCPP, a drug that reduces serotonin levels, to 12 OCD patients and 20 non-OCD control participants, finding that symptoms of OCD were significantly enhanced in the OCD patients. This suggests that the sufferers' condition was related to abnormal levels of serotonin.

- **Hu et al. (2006)** compared serotonin activity in 169 OCD sufferers and 253 non-sufferers, finding serotonin levels to be lower in the OCD patients, which supports the idea of low levels of serotonin being associated with the onset of the disorder.

- **Saxena & Rauch (2000)** reviewed studies of OCD that used PET, fMRI and MRI neuroimaging techniques to find consistent evidence of an association between the orbital-frontal cortex brain area and OCD symptoms. This suggests that specific neural mechanisms are involved with the disorder.

Neural explanation of OCD – the perception of the disorder as resulting from abnormally functioning brain mechanisms.

TOK link

Although experiments permit cause-and-effect relationships to be established, psychological findings are never completely beyond chance factors. This is why findings can only ever 'suggest' a conclusion and not establish an absolute truth.

Evaluation

- It is thought that infections which reduce immune system functioning do not actually cause OCD, but may instead trigger symptoms in those more genetically vulnerable to the disorder. The onset of the disorder generally occurs very quickly after infection, usually within 1–2 weeks.

- To what extent abnormal levels of serotonin and activity within the frontal orbital cortex are actual causes of OCD or merely effects of the disorder has not been established.

- There may well be a genetic connection to neural mechanisms, through such mechanisms, for example levels of serotonin activity, being regulated by genetic factors. An **NIMH (National Institute for Mental Health)** study examined DNA samples from sufferers and found OCD to be associated with two mutations of the human serotonin transporter gene (hSERT), which lead to diminished levels of serotonin.

- Despite the fact that research indicates there are neural differences between OCD sufferers and non-sufferers, it is still not known how these differences relate to the precise mechanisms of OCD.

- Not all sufferers of OCD respond positively to serotonin enhancing drugs, which lessens support for abnormal levels of the neurotransmitter being the sole cause of the disorder.

Evolutionary explanation

Historical evidence indicates that OCD has been around for a long time. The fact that it continues to be apparent in the population suggests that OCD has an adaptive value and therefore an evolutionary basis. If OCD had no useful purpose, natural selection would not have favoured it and OCD would have died out. So, rather than perceiving OCD in maladaptive terms, evolution views the disorder as fulfilling a useful purpose. OCD involves repetitive behaviours like washing and grooming and these would have had an adaptive value in protecting against infection. Other similar behaviours may have increased vigilance and alertness, again incurring a survival value. Therefore, behaviours like continually cleaning door handles may merely be exaggerations of prehistoric adaptations.

The **evolutionary explanation** also includes the idea of biological preparedness, a concept suggested by **Seligman (1971)** that sees animals as possessing an innate ability to display certain anxieties as they possess an adaptive value linked to survival and reproduction abilities. Thus we may develop some conditioned anxieties easier than others. For example, a fear of infection, as this would have constituted a serious threat in the Pleistocene era (when most evolution occurred). Such anxieties have genetic and environmental components, as anxieties have to be learned from environmental experience, with the predisposition to learn the anxiety being the inherited component. It would be much harder to develop an anxiety about being shot, as a risk of being shot did not exist in the Pleistocene era.

Evolutionary explanation of OCD – the perception of the disorder as being acted upon by natural selection through having an adaptive survival value.

▨ Research

- **Marks & Nesse (1984, cited in Lawton, 2012)** reported that lacking concern for others incurs a risk of ostracism (being cut off) from social groups, and so because many OCD sufferers have concern for the welfare of others, this risk is reduced, which suggests the condition has an adaptive value.
- **Chepko-Sade *et al.* (1989)** found rhesus monkeys who performed the most grooming of others were retained within a group following group in-fighting, suggesting OCD tendencies have an adaptive value, as continued group membership is crucial to survival.
- **Abed & Pauw (1998)** believe OCD is an exaggerated form of an evolved ability to foresee situations and predict the outcome of one's own thoughts and behaviour, so that dangerous scenarios can be coped with before they happen, suggesting OCD helps in the avoidance of harm.
- **Polimeni (2005)** reported that OCD tendencies like counting and checking possess the potential to benefit society, which suggests an ancient form of behavioural specialization with evolutionary origins.
- **Garcia & Koelling (1966)** found that rats quickly learned not to drink a sweet-tasting liquid paired with an injection that made them sick, as this is a natural adaptive response, but did not develop such a taste aversion when the sweet-tasting liquid was paired with an electric shock, as this would not be an adaptive response – electric shocks not being apparent in the Pleistocene era – thus supporting the idea of biological preparedness.

▨ Evaluation

- The explanation is a biological one that can be seen as an extension to the genetic explanation rather than an opposing explanation, as genes are the medium by which evolution occurs. There is a common-sense value to OCD having occurred through the process of evolution and thus having a genetic basis, leading to neuroanatomical and biochemical influences.
- Behavioural features of OCD, like precision and hoarding, would be beneficial in hunting and foraging and therefore useful in the EEA and remain now, due to genome lag, where genes take time to evolve and fit current environments.
- Evolutionary explanations of OCD may help clinicians and patients gain a better understanding of causes and symptoms that could lead to more effective therapies.

■ It may be that OCD results from an over-activation of warning signals of evolutionary importance. Therefore, gender differences in OCD reflect the evolutionary differences in male/female priorities like mating and parenting.

Strengthen your learning

1 Explain the following biological explanations of OCD:
   a the genetic explanation
   b neural explanations
   c the evolutionary explanation.

2 Summarize what research studies have suggested about biological explanations of OCD.

3 Assess biological explanations of OCD in terms of their strengths and weaknesses.

4 For Grootheest *et al.*'s (2005) twin study of OCD, in your own words, state the:
   a aims
   b procedure
   c results
   d conclusions
   e evaluative points.

▧ Psychological explanations for OCD

FOCUS ON...

■ Psychological explanations of OCD, including behaviourist explanations, the cognitive explanation and the psychodynamic explanation.
■ The diathesis-stress explanation.

....

Behaviourist explanation of OCD
– the perception of the disorder as being learned from environmental interactions.

Cognitive explanation of OCD
– the perception of the disorder as resulting from maladaptive thought processes.

Psychodynamic explanation of OCD
– the perception of the disorder as resulting from unresolved traumatic experiences occurring during psychosexual stages of development in childhood.
....

Psychological explanations see OCD as arising from non-physiological factors. Three possible psychological explanations for OCD are: first the **behaviourist explanation**, which sees OCD as a learned condition through reference to classical and operant conditioning and social learning; second the **cognitive explanation**, which sees OCD as being caused through irrational thought processes; and third the **psychodynamic explanation**, which sees OCD as linked to the anal stage of psychosexual development.

The behaviourist explanation

The behaviourist explanation sees OCD as being a learned condition, through the application of classical conditioning (CC), operant conditioning (OC) and social learning theory (SLT).

Via the *two-process model*, CC and SLT are used to explain the acquisition (onset) of OCD, with OC used to explain how OCD is maintained.

The acquisition of OCD is seen as occurring through CC, where a neutral stimulus becomes associated with threatening thoughts or experiences and this leads to the development of anxiety. For example, the neutral stimulus of shaking hands with people becomes associated with thoughts of becoming contaminated with germs by doing so (or through the experience of actually being contaminated in this way). This can also occur through SLT, where an individual sees or hears about this event occurring to someone else and then imitates it.

The maintenance of OCD is then seen as occurring through OC, where an individual gains reinforcement (reward) from exhibiting a behaviour that reduces anxiety. For example, an individual washes their hands and this reduces the anxiety of being contaminated. This reinforces the behaviour as it increases the chances of it being done again, when the anxiety returns.

Classical conditioning

Classical conditioning (CC) is based upon the work of **Ivan Pavlov (1903)**, who explained how dogs learned to salivate in anticipation of being fed rather than to actually being fed. The process by which Pavlov explained this as occurring can be also used to explain the acquisition of OCD, where a natural response that causes anxiety becomes associated with a neutral stimulus, so that the neutral stimulus by itself causes an anxiety response.

Operant conditioning

Operant conditioning (OC) involves learning through the consequences (outcomes) of behaviour. A behaviour that is rewarding reinforces the chances of the behaviour being repeated in future similar circumstances. An outcome of a behaviour that is pleasant is known as a positive reinforcement, while an outcome of a behaviour that results in escaping something unpleasant is known as a negative reinforcement. As detailed by the two-process model OC explains how OCD is maintained, as when an avoidance response (a behaviour that lessens the chances of contact with the feared object or situation) is made the anxiety response is reduced, reinforcing the avoidance response, making it more likely to occur again. Washing one's hands is negatively reinforcing, as it reduces the anxiety associated with shaking hands. This reinforces the behaviour, that is, it increases the chances of them washing their hands again when the anxiety returns. OCD therefore becomes very resistant to extinction (dying out) because of the sufferer constantly making the reinforcing avoidance response.

LINK TO THE SOCIOCULTURAL AND COGNITIVE APPROACHES

The behaviourist explanation for OCD relates to the sociocultural approach, as it focuses on social and environmental learning experiences, while social learning theory also relates to the sociocultural approach, as it too focuses on social and environmental learning experiences, but also to some extent the cognitive approach, as it additionally focuses on mental processes, such as memory.

Social learning theory

Along with CC, SLT can also explain the acquisition of OCD. SLT sees behaviour as learned by modelling through observation and imitation. Watching (or hearing about) someone else experience an anxiety-causing event can cause the observer to subsequently experience the anxiety response in the presence of the same stimulus. For example, reading about someone who becomes seriously ill through shaking hands with an infected person. SLT focuses on thought processes as well as learned behaviour and so has a cognitive element to it.

▨ Research

- **Rachman & Hodgson (1980)** found that when OCD patients were exposed to situations that triggered their obsessional thoughts, this resulted in their experiencing high levels of anxiety, but when they were then permitted to enact their compulsive behaviours, levels of anxiety declined considerably. This supports the two-process theory that CC explains the acquisition of OCD, while OC explains its maintenance.

- **Meyer & Cheeser (1970)** demonstrated how compulsions are learned responses, reducing the heightened anxiety levels brought on by obsessions, thus providing a behaviourist explanation for this aspect of the disorder.

- **Einstein & Menzies (2003)** gave 60 OCD patients the Magical Ideation Scale, which measures beliefs in magical thinking, and found a significant correlation between magical thinking (the belief that the mind can have a direct effect on the physical world) and OCD symptoms, suggesting a link between superstition and OCD, in line with Skinner's behaviourist superstition hypothesis (that repetitive behaviours, such as washing your hands, can affect outcomes, like not becoming contaminated).

- **Carr (1974)** found that ritualized behaviours are demonstrated when activity in a sufferer's autonomic nervous system (ANS) was heightened, such behaviour then leading to a reduction of arousal in the ANS, which implies that such compulsive behaviours are reinforcing, as they reduce anxiety levels associated with OCD.

- **De Rosnay et al. (2006)** found that previously non-anxious toddlers began to demonstrate high levels of anxious behaviour after observing their mothers' fearful reactions, providing support for the idea that OCD can be learned through observation and imitation of role models.

Evaluation

- **Baxter (1992)** reported behavioural therapies to be effective in reducing OCD symptoms and also that behavioural therapies incur changes in biochemical activity, giving support to the behaviourist explanation. This was backed up by **Schwartz *et al.* (1996)** finding similar results.

- The avoidance behaviours often characterizing OCD, performed to reduce anxiety, like persistent washing, actually create more anxiety. Therefore, it is difficult to view such behaviours as reinforced responses, weakening the behaviourist viewpoint.

- Although certain OCD features are explicable by behaviourism, intrusive thoughts, often a key feature, cannot be explained, again weakening the explanation.

- The explanation is oversimplified, as it only focuses on learning, thus ignoring other important aspects, such as biological and cognitive factors. The explanation can also be seen as supporting nurture, as it sees OCD as purely learned. However, this ignores the important aspect of nature, as the evolutionary explanation explains why certain stimuli are easier to condition.

- The explanation is good at explaining compulsions, but not obsessive thinking, which is better explained by the cognitive approach. Although research supports the idea of anxious behaviours being learned through social learning (observation and imitation of role models) there is little specific evidence of this being true for OCD.

The cognitive explanation

The cognitive viewpoint sees some people as being more vulnerable to developing OCD because of an attentional bias, where perception is focused more upon anxiety-generating stimuli. Those with OCD also tend to have maladaptive thoughts and beliefs about stimuli, with OCD sufferers having faulty, persistent thought processes that focus upon anxiety-generating stimuli, such as assessing the risk of infection from shaking hands being much higher than it is in reality. Behaviours that lessen impaired obsessive thoughts become compulsions because of their anxiety-reducing qualities.

The cognitive explanation also sees compulsive behaviours as being due to cognitive errors, based on sufferers having a heightened sense of personal responsibility, which motivates them to carry out compulsive behaviours to avoid negative outcomes. This has a behaviourist element, where compulsive behaviours are seen to be reinforcing by reducing anxiety. However, the demonstration of compulsive behaviours means sufferers do not get to test out their faulty thinking and realize that actually there will not be a negative consequence if they do not demonstrate compulsive behaviours.

LINK TO THE COGNITIVE APPROACH

OCD links to the cognitive approach through the presence of typical cognitive errors, such as:

- being intolerant of uncertainty due to a need for certainty and control
- having a need to be in control of all thoughts and emotions at all times
- believing thoughts must be important, as they are being thought about
- having unwanted, involuntary thoughts means that an individual is abnormal
- having intrusive thoughts and doing what they suggest are the same, morally
- thinking about doing harm and not preventing it is just as bad as committing harm
- having unwanted, involuntary thoughts means an individual will act on them.

Even when OCD sufferers feel less anxious as a result of compulsive behaviours, the cognitive doubts quickly return.

Research

- **Rachman & Hodges (1987, cited in Lawton, 2012)** report that some individuals are more susceptible to obsessional thinking because of their increased vulnerability due to genetic factors, which links cognitive factors to the genetic explanation.

- **Gehring *et al.* (2000)** found that the irrational thought processes of nine OCD patients were associated with activity within the orbital-frontal cortex that was not seen in non-OCD control patients. This illustrates how the neural and cognitive models can be combined to explain the occurrence of OCD.

- **Barrett & Healey (2002)** compared children with OCD against anxious children and non-anxious children, finding that OCD children had higher ratings of cognitive appraisals, such as probability, and severity of events and the fusing of thoughts with actions. This suggests that the cognitive conceptualization of OCD occurs in childhood.

- **Clark (1992)** reported that intrusive thinking is significantly more common in OCD sufferers than in non-sufferers, again supporting the cognitive explanation.

- **Buttolph & Holland (1990)** found that 69 per cent of female OCD sufferers had an onset or worsening of symptoms during pregnancy, which supports the idea of sufferers having an inflated sense of personal responsibility, as the imminent birth of a child is a big responsibility for the unborn child's welfare.

Evaluation

- OCD sufferers have impaired thought processes that could be due to them having impaired neural functions, which allows the cognitive explanation to be put into a biological framework by being seen as linked to the neural explanation, rather than being a separate explanation.

- The fact that there are different sub-types of OCD, each focusing upon different forms of anxiety arousal and impaired thought processes, for example emotional contamination, where people fear that by associating with people with negative emotions they will become like them, and sexual identity, where sufferers fear being of an opposite sexual orientation, supports the idea of OCD being largely determined by cognitive rather than biological factors.

- **Abramowitz (2006)** argues that the irrational thought processes shown by OCD sufferers gives support to the idea of them having an inflated sense of personal responsibility, as such cognitive errors include the belief that their thoughts can help cause events with negative consequences, such as by believing that wishing someone dead actually increases the chances of their dying. He also argues that OCD sufferers believe mistakes and imperfection are intolerable and that they therefore should strive to be perfect at all times. However, **Tallis (1995)** argues that if an inflated sense of personal responsibility was the prime factor in causing OCD, then many more people would have the disorder.

- Support for the explanation is also reduced by the fact it does not explain why those with OCD would accept responsibility for events with negative but not positive consequences.

- Most research focuses on describing the types of thinking found in sufferers, rather than what causes such irrational types of thinking. Also, it could be that irrational thinking results from having OCD, rather than being a cause of the disorder.

- The cognitive viewpoint is further weakened by the fact that compulsive behaviours tend to centre on checking and cleansing behaviours, which the theory does not explain.

- Cognitive treatments of OCD have proven effective in correcting cognitive bias and in helping sufferers become less vigilant, giving support to the cognitive theory upon which the treatments are based. However, the treatment aetiology fallacy argues that just because a disorder responds to a treatment does not necessarily mean the treatment addresses the cause of that disorder.

The psychodynamic explanation

The psychodynamic explanation of OCD (which was called 'obsessional neurosis' by Freud) sees the ego (the conscious, rational part of personality) as being disturbed by obsessions and compulsions, which leads to sufferers using ego defence mechanisms (unconscious strategies that reduce anxiety), such as:

1 *Isolation*, where the ego of a sufferer separates itself from the anxiety produced by unacceptable urges of the id (the irrational, pleasure seeking part of personality) by perceiving such urges as not belonging to them. However, such urges intrude as obsessive thoughts.

2 *Undoing*, where the anxiety produced by undesirable urges can be addressed by performing certain compulsive behaviours (such as reducing fears of contamination by hand-washing).

3 *Reaction formation*, where the anxiety produced by undesirable urges is addressed by adopting behaviours that are the opposite of the undesirable urges (like becoming celibate to cope with obsessive sexual impulses).

The explanation also sees the anal stage of psychosexual development, which occurs around two years of age, as linked to the formation of OCD. During this stage, where pleasure is gained from defecation, children are potty trained. If parents criticize children for 'making a mess', it can lead to children having a conflict between being 'anally retentive' (resisting the urge to defecate for fear of being 'dirty') and wanting to rebel and deliberately soil themselves. It is this conflict which is seen as leading to OCD, where anxieties arise over individuals becoming anxious about being controlled and clean and tidy. Conflict over sexual restriction is also seen as providing a similar route to developing OCD.

LINK TO THE BIOLOGICAL AND SOCIOCULTURAL APPROACHES

The psychodynamic explanation relates to the biological approach, as it has innate features, such as the concept of the id (the selfish, pleasure-seeking part of personality), but it also relates to the sociocultural approach, as it additionally focuses on social and environmental learning experiences.

Adler (1930) argued for a slightly different psychoanalytic explanation, as he saw OCD as developing from children being prevented, by over-strict parents, from developing a secure sense of competence, which leads to an anally fixated personality. Individuals therefore develop OCD through feelings of inferiority and exhibit a need for control, which is expressed through being obsessively clean and tidy.

▨ Research

■ **Gross (1996)** reports that studies which have examined how people were potty trained as children have found no difference in the potty training of those with anal personality types and those with other types of personality. This therefore lowers support for the explanation.

■ **Leichsenring & Steinert (2016)** reviewed research to find that short-term psychodynamic therapy (STPP) is effective in treating OCD, which suggests that the psychodynamic explanation upon which the therapy is based is valid (see psychodynamic treatment of OCD on page 247).

■ **Rachman & Hodgson (1980)** found no relationship between 'anal' personality traits and those of OCD. Clinical studies showed that some people with OCD had anal personality traits, but many do not show these traits, and many who have them do not go on to develop OCD in later life.

■ **Fisher & Greenberg (1996)** reviewed studies of anal and oral personalities, but found no evidence that these types are associated with early childhood experiences of anal and oral fixations, which suggests the psychodynamic explanation of OCD is incorrect. Support for the explanation is further weakened by **Peterson *et al.* (1992)** finding no research support for the idea that people with obsessive personality types are likelier to develop OCD than those with non-obsessive personality types.

■ **Noonan (1971)** reported that treatment for OCD with psychoanalysis actually increases, rather than decreases, the symptoms of OCD. This viewpoint was supported by **Salzman (1980)**, who found psychodynamic therapies of little, if any, help in treating anxiety disorders such as OCD. The fact that psychodynamic therapies actually have a negative rather than a positive effect on OCD sufferers implies the theory to be invalid.

▓ Evaluation

■ There is a lack of scientific research evidence for the explanation. This is mainly because psychoanalytic concepts are difficult to operationalize so that they can be objectively tested in a scientifically credible way. For example, it would be very difficult to measure the level of anxiety produced by conflicts over potty training, sexual restriction, and so on.

■ The explanation is also weakened as it only seems to relate to certain obsessions and compulsions. For example, it is difficult to apply the theory to checking and orderliness compulsions (such as compulsions to check that doors are locked or a need to be excessively tidy), as it is difficult to see how these could relate to potty training or sexual restriction.

■ Even if links could be argued to exist between potty training, this would not establish a causal relationship (of cause and effect) because it would not show that a certain type of potty training causes people to develop OCD. It could be instead that there are other non-considered factors, such as personality factors, which have an influence on both potty training and the development of OCD.

■ Psychodynamic explanations are reliant on case studies of single individuals, which are analysed through non-empirical, subjective means. This suggests a lack of scientific rigour in such explanations, as well as producing problems of generalizing findings to all sufferers of OCD

Diathesis-stress explanation

Rather than viewing OCD as resulting from any single explanation, it may be more sensible to regard the disorder as due to a combination of explanations that include both nature and nurture elements. For instance, it could be that certain personality types that result from genetic influences (through effects upon neural functioning) are more vulnerable to developing the disorder through environmental learning influences (as explained by behaviourism). The irrational thinking associated with the disorder that is the central feature of the cognitive explanation could also be seen as under genetic influence, which is itself transmitted through evolutionary means. A **diathesis-stress explanation** could account for individual differences, such as where one identical (MZ) twin develops the disorder and the other does not. Both twins would have an equal genetic vulnerability to developing OCD, but only one does due to having different environmental learning experiences.

Diathesis-stress explanation of OCD – the perception that the disorder results from a combination of factors that include both nature and nurture elements.

Strengthen your learning

1 Explain the following psychological explanations of OCD:
   a behaviourist explanations, including the two-process model
   b the cognitive explanation
   c the psychodynamic explanation.

2 Summarize what research studies have suggested about psychological explanations of OCD.

3 Assess psychological explanations of OCD in terms of their strengths and weaknesses.

4 Outline the diathesis-stress explanation of OCD.

Anorexia nervosa

'To lose confidence in one's body is to lose confidence in oneself.'
Simone de Beauvoir

FOCUS ON...

- Description of AN, including signs, symptoms and effects, behaviour and sub-types.
- Gender and cultural variations in the prevalence of AN.

Description

**Anorexia nervosa
(AN)** – an eating
disorder characterized
by an obsessive desire to
lose weight by refusing
to eat.

Anorexia nervosa (AN) is a mental disorder characterized by three main criteria: a) self-starvation, b) strong motivation to lose weight through fear of being fat and c) medical signs and symptoms that result from starvation. AN has existed for a long time, but has become more widespread in recent years. There are several theories, biological and psychological, for AN and different explanations may apply in different circumstances. AN can occur at different times of life and to differing degrees: 20 per cent of sufferers recover after one episode, 60 per cent continue to have periodic episodes, while 20 per cent will be hospitalized for lengthy periods. About 15 per cent of sufferers will die from starvation, suicide, electrolyte imbalances and organ failure. It is believed that AN has the highest mortality rate of any mental disorder. Brain damage and infertility can also occur.

Signs, symptoms and effects

Aside from chronic thinness there are many other signs, symptoms and effects of AN, such as elevated liver enzymes, irregular heart rate, low blood pressure, poor circulation, constipation, osteoporosis (brittle bones), dehydration, dizziness, feeling cold, fatigue, brittle nails, thin hair, absence of menstruation, lanugo (soft, down-like body hair), dry skin, blotches, bruising, bloated stomach, halitosis (bad breath) and aching joints.

Behaviour

Many sufferers have trouble maintaining sleep, are extremely self-obsessed, have little interest in sexual relationships and are facile (believable) liars, going to great lengths to convince people that they are fine/improving, and so on. They will often wear baggy clothing to hide their thin appearance and pretend to eat meals (and if they do, then vomit the food up later). They can also use vast quantities of diuretics (to make them lose fluid) and laxatives. If being weighed they will hide weights inside their clothes/body and drink large quantities of water to appear heavier than they are. They can be very interested in food, know the calorific content of most foodstuffs and enjoy cooking food for others. Many will hoard food that they will never eat. Vigorous exercise will often be pursued, as will frequent self-weighing.

Sub-types of AN

Some clinicians believe there are separate sub-types of AN, though not all clinicians agree.

- *Restricting type* – a sub-type where weight loss is achieved through dieting, fasting and/or excessive exercise. There are no regular episodes of binging or purging.
- *Binge-eating/purging type* – a sub-type where there are regular episodes of binging and/or purging. Self-induced vomiting and use of laxatives, diuretics and enemas to elicit purging.

Gender variations in the prevalence of AN

One per cent of adolescent females, compared to 0.3 per cent of adolescent males are hospitalized with AN. Overall, about 85 per cent of sufferers are female and 15 per cent male, though male prevalence is on the increase. A disproportionate number of male sufferers are homosexual, though it is difficult to get accurate figures for this. Male and female anorexia seems to have different environmental triggers, which probably explains different prevalence rates, especially at different ages. For example, there seems to be a higher proportion of older females than older males who develop the disorder and most male sufferers develop the disorder in adolescence and early adulthood. More research, especially with male sufferers, is needed to get a clearer picture.

▣ Research

- **Darcy & Lin (2012)** reported that most assessment tests for AN are designed primarily for use with females, which may have led to an underestimation of male sufferers, who are not seen as anorexic by such tests, or that such tests stigmatize male sufferers leading to them not coming forward for assessment.

- **Raevuori *et al.* (2014)** reviewed available studies to find that risk of mortality from being anorexic (and from other eating disorders) is higher for males than it is for females, most probably due to a higher risk of suicide among male sufferers.

- **Weltzin *et al.* (2012)** reported that men are likelier than women to have comorbid conditions (other simultaneous conditions) alongside AN, such as depression, substance abuse and anxiety. This could have the effect of making valid diagnoses of AN for males more difficult than with females.

- **Allen (2013)** found that 1.2 per cent of males had an eating disorder at age 14, rising to 2.6 per cent at age 17 and 2.9 per cent at age 20. The increase in prevalence matches increases in female prevalence rates at similar ages, with the ratio of female to male sufferers in childhood and adolescence being about five females to every one male sufferer. In adulthood, however, this rises to ten female sufferers to every one male sufferer, which suggests AN is more prevalent over a wider age range in females then males.

- **Feldman (2007)** found that 15 per cent of American homosexual males had an eating disorder, compared to only 5 per cent of heterosexual males, which supports the idea that AN is more prevalent among homosexual than heterosexual males.

▣ Evaluation

- It is difficult to calculate prevalence rates for males, due to problems with the suitability of assessment criteria for men. It is believed that the overall percentage of sufferers who are male is on the increase, with some current estimations as high as 25 per cent of all sufferers.

- It may be that some signs and effects of AN in males are different to those in females, which may lead to errors in diagnosis. For example, male anorexics will often have a preoccupation with weights and body building that is not generally found in female sufferers.

- Research suggests that separate diagnostic assessment categories may need to be constructed for males and females (and possibly even for heterosexual and homosexual males) in order for more valid diagnoses of males to occur. This is especially important as effective treatments can only occur after diagnosis, a fact made doubly important with the mortality rate for male sufferers being so high.

- Increasing numbers of females, but not males, seem to be developing AN in middle age. This may be because divorce makes women feel pressurized to lose weight in order to be 'attractive' to potential new partners, or due to the stress of an aging body reducing female perceptions of 'attractiveness', or the loneliness associated with children leaving home or the trauma of parents dying. It suggests overall that there are different triggers for AN between males and females that diagnosis needs to consider.

Cultural variations in prevalence of AN

A dominant feature of AN is the difference in prevalence rates in different cultures, which suggests that sociocultural factors are at play, such as cultural perceptions of attractiveness and media pressure to conform to cultural body type stereotypes. For example, prevalence rates are much higher in western cultures than non-western cultures, which are seen as being a reflection of western cultures emphasizing slim body types, especially for females, as being desirable. Media sources in western cultures heavily promote examples of ultra-slim females as being something that females need to conform to in order to be attractive and have high self-esteem. Dieting is something that is also heavily promoted in western cultures, with a highly profitable industry marketing products and methods of weight loss as being desirable.

Research

- **Gunewardene *et al.* (2001)** reported that prevalence rates for AN in non-western cultures, such as China and Middle Eastern countries, are on the increase and this increase correlates with exposure to western cultural ideals of body image brought by globalization. This supports the idea that sociocultural factors are linked to the development of AN.

- **Makino *et al.* (2004)** reviewed studies to compare prevalence rates of AN in western and non-western cultures. Prevalence rates in western countries were found to be 2.6 per cent in Norwegian students and 1.3 per cent in Italian students, but in non-western countries were only found to be 0.05 per cent in Malaysia, 0.025 per cent in Japan and 0.01 per cent in China. This supports the idea that prevalence rates are higher in western cultures where cultural ideals of slimness are held in higher regard.

- **Becker *et al.* (2002)** compared the incidence of disordered eating in 65 Fijian girls before and after the introduction of TV that exposed the population to western ideals of desirable body images. 12.7 per cent of the girls had evidence of disordered eating patterns, as indicated by answers to the EAT-24 eating habits questionnaire, before the introduction of TV, but this had risen to 29.2 per cent three years after the introduction of TV. Also, the incidence of self-induced vomiting to control weight was non-existent before the introduction of TV, but was at 11.3 per cent after its introduction. This supports the idea that cross-cultural levels of AN vary due to exposure to western cultural ideals of body image.

- **Nasser (1986)** administered the Eating Attitudes Test (EAT-40) to two matched groups of Arabian female students: one attending university in Cairo, Egypt and the other attending university in London, England. Only 12 per cent of the Cairo sample showed disordered eating patterns, while 22 per cent did so in London, which again suggests cultural factors influence AN prevalence rates.

Evaluation

- For an explanation of AN to be considered valid would require that explanation to be able to explain why there are cross-cultural prevalence rates for AN, as well as explaining prevalence differences between males and females and why relatively high levels of male homosexuals develop the disorder.

- If the prevalence rates for AN were similar across cultures (as they generally tend to be for OCD), then this would suggest that the disorder is primarily biological in origin. However, as prevalence rates differ across cultures, this suggests the disorder is more environmental and a result of nurture, not nature.

- The idea that the onset of AN is heavily influenced by sociocultural factors is backed up by the fact that when a culture becomes more westernized, or when people from non-western cultures move to a western culture and are exposed to western cultural ideals of body image, there are increases in levels of the disorder.

- Many cross-cultural studies of AN, such as **Makino *et al.* (2004)**, only look at female prevalence rates and often only in student populations. More representative samples are needed and ones including cross-cultural male prevalence rates, in order for more valid conclusions to be drawn.

Strengthen your learning

1 Describe anorexia nervosa in terms of signs, symptoms, effects and behaviour.

2 What sub-types of AN might there be?

3 Outline gender and cultural differences in prevalence rates of AN.

4 Summarize what research studies have suggested about gender and cultural differences in prevalence rates of AN.

5 What other evaluative points can be made about gender and cultural differences in prevalence rates of AN?

Explanations for anorexia nervosa

'Nothing tastes as good as skinny feels.'
Kate Moss

FOCUS ON...

- Biological explanations for anorexia nervosa, including the genetic explanation, neural and biochemical explanations, and evolutionary explanations.
- Oberndorfer *et al.*'s contemporary study of anorexia and disturbance in the brain region.

Biological explanations

Biological explanations see AN as resulting from physiological factors. Three possible biological explanations are first the genetic explanation, which sees AN as an inherited condition, second neural explanations, which sees AN as linked to defective brain structures, and third evolutionary explanations, which sees AN as having an evolutionary adaptive survival value that has been acted upon by natural selection.

Genetic explanation

Genetic explanation of anorexia nervosa – the perception of the disorder as resulting from an inherited predisposition.

The **genetic explanation** sees AN as transmitted through hereditary means from the genetic material passed from parents to children. Evidence indicates an increased risk for individuals with close relatives with the disorder, which suggests that the disorder is in part genetically transmitted. However, the genetic explanation is seen as only a contributory factor in the causation of the disorder. What genes may do is give individuals a level of inherited vulnerability to developing the disorder, with different individuals having differing levels of vulnerability. Whether a given individual goes on to develop AN would depend upon the presence of other factors, for example levels of environmental stress, types of family structure, and so on. Study methods involve examining the incidence of AN among related individuals, such as twin studies, as well as gene profiling studies that search for common genes among sufferers.

Research

- **Bulik *et al.* (2006)** used a sample of 31,406 Swedish twin pairs to find that the overall incidence of AN was 1.2 per cent for females and 0.29 per cent for males, with the heritability of the disorder calculated as 56 per cent, suggesting a significant genetic influence in the development of the disorder.
- **Kortegaard *et al.* (2001)** assessed the level of AN among 34,000 pairs of Danish twins, finding the concordance rates for MZ (identical twins who share 100 per cent of genetic material) was 0.18 while for DZ (non-identical twins who share 50 per cent of genetic material) was 0.07. In other words, if one MZ twin had anorexia then there was an 18 per cent chance the other twin would too, but if one DZ twin had the condition there was only a 7 per cent chance the other twin would too. This supports the genetic explanation, while also suggesting a large role for environmental factors.
- **Hakonarson *et al.* (2010)** compared DNA material from 1003 mainly female AN participants and 3733 non-sufferers, finding variants of the OPRD1 gene and HTR1D gene were commonly associated with the disorder. These findings confirmed those of earlier studies, supporting the idea of several genes contributing to an advance risk of developing AN.
- **Scott-Van Zeeland *et al.* (2014)** compared 152 genes in 1205 women with anorexia and 1948 without the condition and found that variants of the EPHX2 gene, which is involved with cholesterol function in the body, were more common in those with anorexia. The findings suggest a contributory role for this gene, though the results only apply to female sufferers.

YOU ARE THE RESEARCHER

Design a twin study to assess the heritability of AN. What kind of experimental design would you be using? What would be the independent variable (IV)? What would be the dependent variable (DV)? Identify one important confounding variable.

Your study should produce a heritability estimate. What does this mean?

What other research methods could be used to check your results?

Evaluation

■ Although research indicates that genes are a factor in the causation of anorexia, the fact that multiple genes are involved, as well as environmental factors, makes it difficult to identify and quantify the role of individual genes: many genes are involved, each having different levels of influence. These genes may also exert different levels of influence in different people.

■ If genes were solely responsible for AN, concordance rates between MZ twins would be 100 per cent, and as they are not it confirms that other non-genetic factors are also involved, though an interaction between genetic and environmental factors seems most probable.

■ The genetic explanation cannot account for why the disorder primarily affects females (a large amount of homosexual males also have AN), nor can it explain the heightened incidence of the disorder nowadays. The inheritance of genes from generation to generation has not greatly changed, yet the disorder has increased its prevalence.

■ Genes may exert a non-direct influence upon the development of AN. Many sufferers display perfectionist personality characteristics and genes may be influencing such personality traits. For instance, **Bachner-Melman et al. (2007)** found three genes associated with AN that are also associated with perfectionist personality.

LINK TO THE BIOLOGICAL APPROACH

The biological measure of body mass index (BMI), a ratio of body weight to height, is used as an accurate and reliable way of measuring AN. Normal BMI is between 18.5 and 24.9. A person is seen as anorexic if their BMI falls below 17.5, though BMI is not designed for those under 18 years of age.

Neural and biochemical explanations

Neural explanation of anorexia nervosa – the perception of the disorder as arising from abnormally functioning brain mechanisms.

Leptin – a hormone produced by fat cells associated with the regulation of energy intake and expenditure.

Neural explanations involve the idea that AN is linked to defective brain structures. Early research focused on possible damage to the hypothalamus, especially damage to the lateral hypothalamus, but more recent research has concentrated on identifying specific brain mechanisms. One area of interest is the insula dysfunction hypothesis as the biological root of anorexia. This sees the insula brain area, part of the cerebral cortex, as developing differently in anorexics. Various symptoms of AN are associated with dysfunction in several brain areas, with the common factor being the insula, which is responsible for more neural connections than any other part of the brain, including brain areas associated with AN. Contemporary research appears to back up the hypothesis.

Neural explanations also involve the idea that faulty biochemistry is related to the development of AN. The neurotransmitter serotonin is especially linked with the onset and maintenance of anorexia, though noradrenaline is also of interest, with its role in maintaining restriction of eating by influencing anxiety levels.

Leptin also attracts interest, as anorexics can have low levels of leptin, probably due to their low levels of fat. It is thought that leptin influences the regulation of the neuroendocrine system during starvation. Low leptin levels are also known to affect the hypothalamic-pituitary-gonadal axis, which leads to the amenorrhea (cessation of periods) often seen in anorexics.

CONTEMPORARY RESEARCH

'Anorexia linked to disturbance in brain region'
Oberndorfer *et al.* (2013)

Researchers are undecided as to whether anorexia is due to psychological factors, such as an obsession with body image, or biological factors, like a disturbance in the brain system that regulates eating behaviour. Tyson Oberndorfer set out to investigate the degree to which brain structures play a role in the development of anorexia.

Aim
To confirm the findings of earlier studies indicating that altered function of neural circuitry associated with appetite contributes to the reduced eating of anorexics.

Procedure

1 Fourteen female recovered anorexics and fourteen non-anorexic females were the participants (recovered anorexics were used to avoid the confounding variable of altered nutritional state). (Fourteen recovered sufferers of BN were also studied for another aspect of the study, not reported here.)

2 Participants fasted overnight and received a standardized breakfast of 604 calories, before having an fMRI scan as a control for satiety state.

3 fMRI scans were then used to test neurocircuitry by measuring brain responses to sweet tastes, where participants were given 120 doses of either sucrose or sucratose (to distinguish between neural processing of calorific and non-calorific sweet tastes).

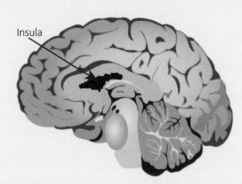

Insula

■ **Figure 5.6**
Obendorfer *et al.*'s research associated the insula brain area with anorexia nervosa

Results
Anorexic participants had greatly reduced responses to sweet tastes, especially the taste of sucrose, in the right anterior insula brain area.

Conclusions

● The findings confirm earlier studies suggesting a relationship between AN and neural processes in the insula brain region, an area where taste is sensed and integrated with reward signals, which determines whether an individual feels hungry or not.

● Altered functioning of neural circuitry appears to contribute to the restricted eating feature of anorexia.

● The restricted eating and weight loss seen in anorexics may occur because the brain fails to accurately recognize hunger signals.

● Anorexics appear to have altered balance or sensitivity in brain mechanisms that signal the calorific content of food.

Evaluation

● The findings may offer a practical application in the development of effective treatments for AN, like enhancing insula activity in anorexics by using biofeedback or mindfulness training to adjust the brain's response to food stimuli. Alternatively, medications could be manufactured that enhance the reward response of food or decrease inhibition to food consumption in the brain's reward circuitry.

● The research does not determine whether faulty brain mechanisms cause anorexic behaviour or whether anorexic behaviour leads to changes in brain mechanisms. One way of addressing this would be to scan the brains of at-risk children to see if their brains exhibit such faulty mechanisms.

Research

- **Anand & Brobeck (1952)** found that lesions to the lateral hypothalamus led to aphagia (undereating) and weight loss, which suggests that damage to this brain area can cause AN, a view further supported by **Stellar (1954)** finding that when the lateral hypothalamus was stimulated it increased eating, but when lesioned decreased eating.

- **Brooks *et al.* (2011)** used fMRI scans of anorexic and non-anorexic participants' brains and found heightened activity in the dorsolateral prefrontal cortex brain area of anorexics (a brain area associated with self-control that helps to decrease impulsive behaviours) when they imagined eating plates of high calorific food, like chocolate cake, but activity was not heightened when they imagined plates of inedible objects like clothes pegs. This suggests that the brains of anorexics are regulating control over their desire to eat when confronted with food.

- **Bailer *et al.* (2005)** used fMRI scans to compare serotonin activity in recovered female anorexics and female non-sufferers, finding heightened serotonin levels in several brain areas of the anorexics, especially those with the highest levels of anxiety. This suggests that prolonged disruption of serotonin levels produces heightened anxiety levels, which then triggers AN.

- **Nunn *et al.* (2012)** reported that abnormal noradrenaline functioning is seen as being genetically determined, leading to high anxiety and insula brain area dysfunction that results in negative body image distortion. This gives rise to intense dieting, which helps reduce anxiety in the short-term. Anxiety then increases again, illustrating how noradrenaline leads to a cycle of anorexia being maintained.

- **Grinspoon *et al.* (1996)** compared leptin levels in 22 anorexic females and 23 female non-sufferers, finding leptin levels significantly lower in the anorexics and that leptin levels correlated positively with body weight and percentage of body fat. This supports the idea of leptin being related to AN.

- **Mayo-Smith *et al.* (1989)** found that leptin and body fat mass levels were higher in healthy low-weight females than in anorexic females, supporting the idea that leptin levels are related to the low amounts of body fat in anorexics rather than their actual body weight.

■ **Figure 5.7** Anorexics experience heightened self-control in the dorsolateral prefrontal cortex brain area when thinking about food items, but not non-food items

▨ Evaluation

- Abnormal biochemistry, like the levels of serotonin and leptin found in anorexics, may not cause the onset of the disorder, but may instead be an effect of the malnutrition associated with AN.

- Current thinking on the role of leptin is that prolonged weight loss, as seen in anorexics, leads to a continual reduction in circulating leptin levels, rather than leptin levels causing the development of anorexia. Research interest in leptin now is focused more on the possible role for leptin as a therapy to treat AN.

- Much research into AN involves female participants, thus findings cannot be generalized to males, who differ in many ways physiologically from females. For example, males have different distributions and amounts of body fat, therefore the relationship between male anorexics and neurotransmitter levels may be different to that of female sufferers.

- Research like that by **Nunn *et al.* (2012)** illustrates that the abnormal biochemistry seen in anorexics may be under genetic control, suggesting a link between genetic and neural influences.

> **LINK TO THE BIOLOGICAL APPROACH**
> The genetic, neural, biochemical and evolutionary explanations of AN all relate to the biological approach, as they see physiologically determined features, as associated with the development of the disorder.

Evolutionary explanations

Evolutionary explanation of anorexia nervosa – the perception of the disorder as being acted upon by natural selection through having an adaptive survival value.

Evolutionary explanations see AN as having an adaptive survival value that has been acted upon by natural selection. This explains why the disorder has existed throughout the ages and continues to be apparent in the population. If AN did not fulfil an adaptive purpose, then natural selection would have caused it to die out.

The reproduction suppression hypothesis: Surbey (1987)

The reproduction suppression hypothesis (RSH) sees the phenomenon of teenage girls wanting to control their weight as an evolutionary adaptation of delaying sexual maturity so that they do not get pregnant in times when food supplies are too scarce to adequately feed infants. In the Pleistocene era when most evolution occurred, food was only available periodically. Therefore, nowadays when young females are subjected to stress it causes them to react in a genetically pre-programmed way, as if food supplies were low, by excessive dieting. In this way, they attempt to gain control over their bodies and suppress getting pregnant until environmental conditions would allow them to successfully raise children.

Adaptive response to famine: Guisinger (2003)

The evolutionary explanation for the adaptive response to famine (ARF) sees AN as an adaptive response to times of food scarcity. In such times, populations would have to migrate to find foodstuffs and the hyperactivity often found in anorexics is seen as a form of 'migratory restlessness', where motivation is created to move to a more food-rich environment through loss of weight in individuals (through dieting in response to modern day pressures to be 'attractively slim') who are genetically vulnerable to the condition. In other words, AN motivated nomadic people to migrate when food supplies ran out and the behaviour is now an evolutionary remnant of those times.

Research

- **Frisch & Barbieri (2002)** reported that the majority of women require between 17 and 22 per cent of their body weight to be fat, in order for them to be able to menstruate and maintain their ovulatory cycle, thus supporting the RSH, that AN is related to a suppression of reproductive ability.

- **Ellison (2003)** investigated the relationship between disruptions to energy balance, through suppression of eating, and ovarian steroid levels, which influence a female's reproductive ability. It was found that changes in energy levels led to reductions in ovarian steroid levels, which supports the RSH, because such reductions are associated with a lesser chance of becoming pregnant.

- **Arcelus et al. (2011)** reviewed 36 studies in order to compare mortality rates of people suffering from AN with other mental disorders, finding it to have the highest death-rate, at 4 per cent, of any psychiatric disorder, with many anorexic deaths due to suicide. This weakens support for evolutionary explanations, which sees the condition as adaptive and thus useful to those with the condition; however, these findings suggest anorexia is a very maladaptive experience for many sufferers.

- **Rakison (2002)** investigated the association between eating habits and attitudes towards sexual attention. The Eating Attitudes Test-40 was given to 100 non-anorexic men, 100 non-anorexic women and 100 anorexics to assess their attitudes towards food and eating. Participants then completed a second questionnaire, which assessed attitudes towards marriage, attention from the opposite sex and active seeking of attention from the opposite sex. A negative correlation was found between high levels of disordered eating and low levels of attraction to sexual attention, which gives support to the evolutionary idea that AN is linked to a suppression of reproductive behaviour.

Evaluation

- The fact that many anorexics are male (and indeed often homosexual) goes against the RSH, which sees AN purely as an evolutionary adaptive response of females suppressing their chances of getting pregnant during times of food scarcity.

- The RSH gains support from the fact that AN does restrict physical signs of puberty, for example amenorrhea (the cessation of periods), which means that sufferers cannot get pregnant in line with the theory.

- Evolutionary theories cannot adequately explain cultural differences in levels of AN. The disorder is more prevalent in western cultures, where food scarcity is less likely than in non-western cultures. Nor can evolutionary theories explain sub-cultural differences in prevalence rates. Middle-class white girls are seen as more vulnerable than those from ethnic groupings and working-class individuals, though levels have risen in these groupings too.

- Generally, there is a lack of research support for evolutionary explanations, especially the ARF explanation, for which Guisinger herself provided no research support. The fact that other explanations have more research support implies that evolutionary explanations have less validity.

- Evolutionary explanations can be accused of being somewhat simplistic, as they tend to neglect other important factors in the causation of AN; for example, media influences upon young women to achieve skinny body shapes. Perhaps evolutionary explanations would be better included as part of a diathesis-stress explanation, where certain individuals are seen to have, through the process of evolution, a greater genetic vulnerability to developing the disorder, with environmental factors then determining whether the condition is triggered.

Strengthen your learning

1 Explain the following biological explanations of AN:
   a the genetic explanation
   b neural and biochemical explanations
   c evolutionary explanations, including the reproduction suppression hypothesis and the adaptive response to famine.

2 Summarize what research studies have suggested about biological explanations of AN.

3 Assess the biological explanations of AN in terms of their strengths and weaknesses.

4 For Oberndorfer *et al.*'s (2013) contemporary study of anorexia linked to brain region, in your own words state the:
   a aims
   b procedure
   c results
   d conclusions
   e evaluative points.

■ Psychological explanations for anorexia nervosa

FOCUS ON...

■ Psychological explanations for anorexia nervosa, including the family systems theory, social learning theory and the cognitive explanation.

Psychological explanations see AN as arising from non-physiological factors. Three possible psychological explanations are: first, the family systems theory, which sees AN as arising from dysfunctional patterns of family interaction; second, social learning theory, which sees AN as being a condition learned through the observation and imitation of role models; and third, the cognitive explanation, which sees AN as resulting from irrational thought processes.

Family systems theory – Minuchin (1979)

Family systems theory (FST) – the perception that anorexia nervosa results from dysfunctional patterns of family interaction.

The **family systems theory (FST)** sees families as intensely connected emotionally to each other, with family members seeking each other's attention and approval and continually reacting to each other's needs and moods. Thus families are interdependent units, where change in the functioning of one member affects the functioning of other members. AN is seen as developing due to dysfunctional interactions between family members, with its development often serving to prevent or reduce dissension (disagreements) within a family. For example, an adolescent fearing that arguments between parents may lead to divorce becomes anorexic to divert family attentions onto themselves, thus saving the marriage. In other words, the family is 'sick', but the anorexic becomes the 'fall guy' (takes the blame) for the family's problems, with the anorexic often fearing abandonment or worsening of the family's problems unless they accept their role.

LINK TO THE SOCIOCULTURAL APPROACH

The family systems theory explanation for AN relates to the sociocultural approach, as it focuses on social and environmental learning experiences, but also to some extent the cognitive approach, as it additionally focuses on the idea of identity and self, which involves mental processes, such as self-perception.

Enmeshment

Enmeshment – a family interactive style that inhibits each family member's sense of individuality.

Enmeshment involves dysfunctional interactions between family members inhibiting each family member's sense of individuality; for example, where families are over-protective of their children, thus preventing any sense of independence developing. This tends to occur in families that do everything together and so adolescent children striving for independence restrict their eating as a form of protest. Enmeshment therefore occurs as a type of boundary between individuals being able to distinguish themselves as separate from family units. This occurs because in the families of some anorexics there isn't enough flexibility to allow children to develop a sense of self.

Autonomy and control – the perception of anorexia nervosa as a struggle for self-management, identity and effectiveness.

Autonomy and control

Autonomy refers to the experience of choice and freedom in relation to oneself and others, and involves the development of control, identity, competence and effectiveness. The major aspect of achieving **autonomy and control** is to develop a sense of self.

An important part of the FST is that disturbances in the development of autonomy are a central feature of AN that manifest as distortions of body image, misperceptions of internal states and a paralysing sense of ineffectiveness.

Rosman et al. (1978) described five qualities of dysfunctional families that hindered the development of autonomy: 1) enmeshment, 2) over-protectiveness, 3) rigidity of style, 4) conflict avoidance and 5) involvement of the anorexic in parental conflict.

Research

- **Minuchin et al. (1978)** gave a standardized interactive task to 11 families of anorexics and 34 families of non-anorexics, finding the families of anorexics had higher levels of enmeshment, over-protectiveness, conflict avoidance and rigidity of style, supporting the idea of enmeshment and a lack of autonomy being features of AN in line with the FST.

- **Blinder et al. (1988)** reported that although anorexic families seem ideal on the surface, closer inspection reveals little expression of affection with conflict avoided at all costs, although underlying tensions are often present. Parents also put high expectations on their children to compensate for the lack of love within their marriage, with anorexics going on to use their illness to try to unite their parents. These findings support the predictions of the FST.

- **Karwautz et al. (2003)** used the Subjective Family Image Test to compare perceptions of family relationships between 31 pairs of sisters, where one sister had AN and the other did not, finding that the anorexics had lower levels of autonomy, related mainly to their relationships with their mothers (and to a lesser extent their fathers), supporting the idea of autonomy being a central feature of AN.

- **Strauss & Ryan (1987)** used questionnaires, such as the General Causality Orientations Scale, to measure the degree of autonomy in 19 anorexics and 17 non-anorexic controls, finding anorexics had less sense of autonomy, poorer self-concept and more disturbed family interactions, supporting the FST, especially the idea of autonomy disturbance.

Evaluation

- There does tend to be heightened tensions within families of anorexics. However, rather than being a precipitating trigger for the development of AN, heightened tensions could easily be the result of having an anorexic in the family.

- Dysfunctional families like those described by the FST have always existed, so it is difficult for this theory to explain the huge increase in AN throughout the population.

- **Shapiro (1981)** pointed out that deficiencies in autonomy are central to many abnormal conditions and that therefore it is not known how such deficiencies relate specifically to AN.

- **Le Grange & Eisler (2008)** report that for family therapies to be effective they have to be tailor-made to fit individual family circumstances, because uniform features of dysfunctional anorexic families do not really exist. Also treatments based around family therapies are more effective if they treat the family, not as the cause of the disorder, but as a valuable resource to help an anorexic recover from their disorder, weakening support for the FST.

Social learning theory (SLT) of anorexia nervosa – the perception of anorexia nervosa as being learned through observation and imitation.

Social learning theory

Social learning theory (SLT) sees learning occurring by social means where an observation is made of someone being rewarded for their behaviour, with this behaviour then being imitated.

The SLT of AN is based around the idea that people wish to be popular and that imitating popular people's thinness will achieve this aim. Young people are seen as especially vulnerable, as they are searching for an identity and heightened self-esteem.

SLT can explain why AN occurs more in cultures where attractiveness is associated with being skinny and why it is more of a female disorder in those cultures, as low body weight is mainly associated with attractiveness in females. Similarly, it explains the relatively high incidence of AN in homosexual men, as gay men tend to value thinness more than heterosexual men do.

LINK TO THE SOCIOCULTURAL AND COGNITIVE APPROACHES

The social learning theory explanation of AN relates to the sociocultural approach, as it focuses on social and environmental learning experiences, but also to some extent the cognitive approach, as it additionally focuses on mental processes, such as memory and attention, when observing and imitating anorexic behaviour.

Modelling

Modelling – where learning occurs vicariously by experience through observation of others.

Modelling is an important aspect of SLT, where learning involves extraction of information from observations and making decisions about the performance of the behaviour. In this way, learning occurs without noticeable changes in behaviour. There are three types of modelling stimuli:

1   A live model demonstrating the desired behaviour (such as a skinny person being complimented).

2   Verbal instruction by an individual of the desired behaviour.

3   Symbolic modelling through media presentations of the desired behaviour (such as photos of skinny fashion models in magazines).

Effective modelling depends on: a) the amount of attention given to the observed behaviour, b) retention of a mental image of the observed behaviour, c) reproduction of the mental image and d) having motivation to imitate the behaviour.

Reinforcement

Reinforcement – the consequence of a behaviour that strengthens (increases) the chances of it occurring again.

Another important part of SLT is **reinforcement**. When an observed behaviour is imitated, others respond to this; if the response is rewarding, it increases the chances of the behaviour occurring again, as the behaviour has been reinforced (strengthened). Reinforcement can be external, such as gaining approval from others for losing weight, or internal, like feeling better about oneself. Reinforcements can also be positive, such as receiving compliments for being skinny, or negative, for example not being mocked anymore for being chubby.

Vicarious reinforcement occurs when an individual imitates the behaviour of a model in an attempt to gain the reward that the model achieves through their behaviour, like the model being complimented for being skinny.

Media

Media – public forms of communication.

The **media** is a powerful force in SLT. In western cultures the media portrays extreme thinness, such as through models in women's magazines, as being desirable. These images are observed and then imitated to the point where AN develops. This can help to explain why women are likelier to be anorexic, as women are bombarded by more 'desirable' media images of thinness than men. It also explains why women who move from cultures where such media images do not occur to cultures where they do occur become more vulnerable to developing AN.

■ Research

- **Bemis (1978)** supported SLT by reviewing 20 years of Playboy centrefolds and finding the weight of models progressively decreased. Additional support came from **Garner & Garfinkel (1980)** finding that Miss America beauty queen winners have become much slimmer over time.

- **DiDomenico & Andersen (1992)** found that women's magazines had more articles and advertisements focused on losing weight than men's magazine; indeed magazines aimed at females aged 18 to 24 years had ten times more content concerning dieting than equivalent men's magazines, illustrating the power of the media as a social learning force.

- **Herzog et al. (1991)** compared 43 homosexual and 32 heterosexual men on body satisfaction and weight issues, finding homosexual men had role models who were much lighter in weight than heterosexual role models, supporting the idea that heightened levels of AN among gay men can be explained by reference to SLT.

■ **Mumford *et al.* (1991)** found heightened levels of AN among Arab and Asian women who moved to western cultures, which suggests that cultural pressures via the media were to blame, as media emphasis on dieting and female thinness is not found in their countries of origin. **Lai (2000)** supported this by finding AN increased among Chinese people in Hong Kong, as the region became more westernized.

■ **Figure 5.8** Research suggests that beauty queens have become increasingly slimmer over time, with the media encouraging girls to imitate such low-weight role models

▨ Evaluation

■ SLT cannot explain why dieting continues after the point at which compliments for losing weight stop, or indeed when negative comments commence.

■ SLT does not explain why only some women develop AN, when all women are subjected to the same media images of thinness being attractive.

■ If SLT truly can explain the development of AN through the observation and imitation of thin role models, then it suggests a practical application to counteract the disorder by the use of media images of desirable heavier women.

■ SLT is better able than biological explanations or the FST to explain why the prevalence of AN has increased and why it occurs more in females and certain cultures (due to the increased promotion of thinness in western cultures).

■ SLT does not really consider the cognitive aspects of AN; for example, the faulty perceptions of body image that often underpin the disorder.

The cognitive explanation

The **cognitive explanation** sees AN as caused by a breakdown in rational thought processes, like an individual wishing to attain an unreal level of perfection in order to be an acceptable person. This level of perception is seen as attainable by developing an extremely thin body type.

Distortions

Distorted thought processes involve errors in thinking that negatively affect perceptions of body image. These **distortions** lead an individual to adopt strict, inflexible rules about eating, with any breaking of these rules leading to a sense of guilt and failure, thus lowering self-esteem and creating self-disgust, which in turn leads to even more severe anorexic behaviour.

Cognitive explanation of anorexia nervosa – the perception of anorexia nervosa as resulting from maladaptive thought processes.

Distortions – the idea that faulty thinking negatively affects perceptions of body image.

Irrational beliefs

Irrational beliefs
– the notion that maladaptive ideas lead to the development and maintenance of anorexia nervosa.

Irrational beliefs are maladaptive ideas that lead to the development and maintenance of AN, with such irrational beliefs often resulting in anorexics misperceiving their body image and seeing themselves as fatter than they are. Anorexics will also possess flawed reasoning behind their eating habits.

Anorexics typically demonstrate 1) distortions in thinking and 2) errors in thinking. See Tables 5.4 and 5.5.

Distortions in thinking
Misperceiving the body as overweight when it is underweight
Basing self-worth only on physical appearance
Having flawed beliefs about eating and dieting

■ **Table 5.4** Anorexics' distortions in thinking

Errors in thinking
All or nothing thinking, e.g. 'I ate a chip, now I will be fat.'
Overgeneralizing, e.g. 'If I cannot restrict my eating I am a failure.'
Magnification/minimization, e.g. 'Gaining any weight is not acceptable/My weight loss is not harmful.'
Magical thinking, e.g. 'If I weighed below five stone I would be happy.'

■ **Table 5.5** Anorexics' errors in thinking

LINK TO THE COGNITIVE AND SOCIOCULTURAL APPROACHES

AN has a cognitive component, as it is characterized by distorted body perception and irrational beliefs about self-worth and body image. It also has a sociocultural component, as prevalence rates are higher in some cultural and sub-cultural groups than others, which suggests social and cultural factors exert an influence.

▓ Research

- **Garner *et al.* (1982)** compared 160 anorexic participants with 140 non-anorexic participants, finding that anorexics tended to over-estimate their weight and body size, lending support to the cognitive theory. Further support came from **Bemis-Vitouesk & Orimoto (1993)**, who found that anorexics have a consistent distorted body image and feel they must continually lose weight to be in control of their bodies, illustrating the key role that distortions play in the maintenance of AN.

- **Halmi *et al.* (2000)** got 322 anorexics to complete the Multi-Dimensional Perfectionism Scale, finding they scored much higher on a need to be perfect than a similar non-anorexic control group. The higher the needs for perfectionism, the more severe are the symptoms of anorexia. This supports the belief of the cognitive theory that anorexics wish to attain an unreal level of perfectionism to be acceptable.

- **Steinglass *et al.* (2007)** administered the Brown Assessment of Beliefs Scale (BABS) to 25 anorexics to identify the dominant belief that was inhibiting their eating. They found that 68 per cent had a main fear of gaining weight or becoming fat, with 20 per cent classed as delusional. This supports the idea of irrational thinking underpinning AN in line with cognitive theory.

- **Konstantakopoulos *et al.* (2012)** used the BABS scale with 39 anorexics and found that 28.8 per cent had delusional body image beliefs that were associated with restricted eating and body dissatisfaction, again linking irrational thinking to the onset and maintenance of AN.

■ **Figure 5.9** Anorexics often have a distorted body image in line with the cognitive theory

RESEARCH IN FOCUS

Research into the cognitive explanation of AN often uses questionnaires, such as the Brown Assessment of Beliefs Scale, generally finding that irrational thinking underpins the disorder.

1　What would the strengths and weaknesses of investigating the cognitive explanation of AN in this way be?

2　What considerations should be made when constructing such questionnaires?

3　In what ways would an experimental study be superior to a questionnaire?

Evaluation

- The cognitive theory, and research based upon it, does not clarify if maladaptive thought processes are a cause of AN or a result of being anorexic.

- Cognitive behavioural therapies have a relatively high success rate in treating AN, giving a degree of support to the cognitive theory upon which they are based.

- Most females (and many males) express dissatisfaction with their bodies and many have been/are on diets, but only a few develop AN, which the cognitive theory cannot explain.

- The multiple factors of AN converge into two key elements: low self-esteem and a high need for perfectionism, both of which are explicable by reference to the cognitive theory.

- The cognitive theory does not consider other explanations, many of which are supported by research evidence. It may well be that different explanations can be combined to give a better understanding of the causes of AN. For instance, the high drive for perfectionism exhibited by many anorexics and which is a key part of the cognitive theory may be genetically transmitted.

YOU ARE THE RESEARCHER

Explain why it would not be possible to conduct an experiment to examine whether stress leads to the development of AN.

Instead, design a study that would be ethical. Explain why this would be ethical and how you would conduct it. In what ways would this study be superior to/inferior to conducting an experiment?

Strengthen your learning

1 Explain the following psychological explanations of AN:
   a the family systems theory, including the role of enmeshment, autonomy and control
   b social learning theory, including the role of modelling, reinforcement and media
   c the cognitive approach, including the role of irrational beliefs.

2 Summarize what research studies have suggested about psychological explanations of AN.

3 Assess psychological explanations of AN in terms of their strengths and weaknesses.

SECTION SUMMARY

- Biological explanations of OCD focus on genetic, neural and evolutionary factors.
- Psychological explanations of OCD focus on behaviourist, cognitive and psychodynamic factors.
- Biological explanations of AN focus on genetic, neural and evolutionary factors.
- Psychological explanations of AN focus on the family systems theory, social learning theory and cognitive factors.

■ Assessment check

1	Discuss one or more biological explanations for one abnormal disorder.	(22 marks)
2	Evaluate one sociocultural explanation of one abnormal disorder.	(22 marks)
3	Discuss cognitive explanations of one or more abnormal disorders.	(22 marks)
4	With the use of suitable examples, discuss the prevalence rates for one abnormal disorder.	(22 marks)
5	Discuss one or more research studies of the explanation of one abnormal disorder.	(22 marks)
6	Evaluate one or more etiologies of one abnormal disorder.	(22 marks)
7	Contrast one biological and one cognitive explanation of one or more abnormal disorders.	(22 marks)

Treatments of mental disorders and their effectiveness

'Never go to a doctor whose office plants have died.'
Erma Bombeck

■ Introduction

There are a number of treatments and therapies for mental disorders, each with their strengths and weaknesses. Which treatment is used depends on a range of factors, such as which particular disorder is being addressed, cost-effectiveness and individual patients' circumstances (such as their age, mental health history and experiences with previous treatments). Eclectic (combination) treatments, where more than one simultaneous therapy is given, are often more effective than single treatments.

Therapies for mental disorders are based on different etiologies; for instance, biomedical therapies are based on the biological model's belief that mental disorders have a biological basis, while cognitive therapies are based on the cognitive viewpoint that mental disorders originate from maladaptive thinking. The success rates of specific therapies in treating mental disorders are seen as reflecting how well the psychological approaches on which they are based can explain the origins of those mental disorders. However, the concept of treatment aetiology fallacy believes it is a mistaken notion that the success of a treatment reveals the cause of a disorder.

Eclectic approaches to treatment

Eclectic treatments give greater flexibility, as they involve the combination of two or more different therapies, often to suit the particular needs of an individual or group, thus allowing more aspects of a disorder to be treated. Eclectic treatments can be:

- *Simultaneous* – where different therapies are applied at the same time.
- *Sequential* – where therapies are given consecutively to each other.
- *Stage-orientated* – where one therapy is given during the initial severe phase of a disorder and other therapies are given during the maintenance or recovery stage.

The greatest advantage of eclectic treatments is that the strengths of several therapies can be applied (such as drugs to reduce symptoms so that 'talking' therapies can be applied), though the downside is that the collective weaknesses of the therapies being applied are also apparent (such as the addictive nature of some drugs and the overall cost of applying several therapies).

The effectiveness of treatments

The effectiveness of treatments is judged by:

1 The degree to which treatments alleviate symptoms – assessed by research evidence.
2 Whether improvements in mental health are gained over the long rather than the short term – assessed in terms of relapse rates (the extent to which symptoms return over time).
3 The type, amount and severity of side effects – assessed by research evidence.
4 Cost-effectiveness, where the level of improvement in mental health is judged against the financial costs of delivering a treatment – assessed by research evidence.
5 Number of patients benefitting from a treatment: whether treatments can be applied to general populations, or are more suited to specific types, age groups, and so on – assessed by research evidence.
6 The extent to which treatments deal with the severity of disorders: whether treatments are suitable for those with severe forms of disorders or only to those with milder versions of treatments – assessed by research evidence.

7 The suitability of a therapy to be part of an eclectic treatment: the extent to which therapies are suitable to be combined with other forms of treatment in alleviating symptoms – assessed by research evidence.
8 Perception of treatments by patients: the extent to which treatments are favoured by patients – assessed by drop-out rates.

Biological treatments

FOCUS ON…

- Biological treatments of mental disorders, including drug therapy, ECT, psychosurgery and deep-brain stimulation.

Biological treatments are based on the biological/medical model, which sees mental disorders as having diagnosable physiological causes and perceives cures as emanating from rectifying the physical problems that originate from such causes. This comes through physical interventions that alter the function of neurological mechanisms, such as the brain and hormonal and neurotransmitter activity. Common treatments include, **drug therapy, electroconvulsive therapy (ECT)** and **psychosurgery**.

Psychiatric drugs modify the working of the brain, affecting mood and behaviour. Drugs enter the bloodstream to reach the brain and affect the transmission of chemicals in the nervous system known as neurotransmitters, such as dopamine, incurring a variety of effects on behaviour. Psychiatric drugs work by increasing or decreasing the availability of neurotransmitters, thus modifying their effects on behaviour. Drugs blocking the effects of neurotransmitters are called antagonists, while those mimicking or increasing the effects of neurotransmitters are called agonists.

ECT is believed to induce changes in neurotransmitter levels, including sensitivity to serotonin in the hypothalamus and an increase in the release of GABA, noradrenaline and dopamine. ECT is used against drug-resistant depression and schizophrenia, with several treatments a week given for a limited period. A general anaesthetic and a muscle relaxant are given to ensure that patients do not feel pain or convulse and incur fractures. Brain stimulation occurs through electrodes placed on the head, with a brief controlled series of electrical pulses. This causes a seizure within the brain, lasting about a minute. After 5–10 minutes, the patient regains consciousness. Unilateral ECT occurs when only the non-dominant hemisphere of the brain is stimulated, while bilateral ECT involves stimulation to both hemispheres.

Psychosurgery is generally used against depression and anxiety disorders (including OCD) when other treatments have failed, quality of life is reduced and there is enhanced risk of suicide. Psychosurgery involves the irreversible destruction of small amounts of specific pieces of brain tissue, usually in the limbic system, an area associated with emotion, for example bimedial and orbital leucotomies. There is also **deep-brain stimulation**, a less invasive and less destructive treatment involving electrodes planted in the brain.

Deep-brain stimulation – a non-invasive physical means of treating mental disorders through the application of magnetic pulses to specific brain areas.

RESEARCH IN FOCUS

1 Why might it not be possible for individuals with severe OCD to give informed consent for psychosurgery?

2 Who would give consent for them?

3 Who else cannot give informed consent?

Psychological treatments

FOCUS ON...

- Psychological treatments of mental disorders, including behavioural therapies, CBT and psychodynamic therapy.

Psychological treatments – therapies based on non-biological explanations of mental disorders, which focus on remedying psychological factors associated with disorders.

Behavioural therapies – treatment of mental disorders through modifying maladaptive behaviour by substitution of new responses.

Psychodynamic therapy – treatment of mental disorders through identifying childhood traumatic experiences and resolving them.

Cognitive behavioural therapy – treatment of mental disorders through modifying thought patterns in order to alter behavioural and emotional states.

Psychological treatments are based on non-biological explanations of mental disorders. Three such treatments are **behavioural therapies**, cognitive therapies and **psychodynamic therapies**, each of which treats mental disorders based on their viewpoint of what causes abnormal behaviours. Each has strengths and weaknesses, with each more effective in particular instances.

The behaviourist approach sees mental disorders as maladaptive (inappropriate) behaviours learned through environmental experience. Behavioural therapies replace maladaptive behaviours with adaptive (appropriate) ones, through the use of:

1 *Classical conditioning*, where learning of a desired behaviour occurs through association of a neutral stimulus with an involuntary unconditioned stimulus, such as with systematic desensitization (SD) and exposure and response prevention (ERP), both of which are treatments for OCD.

2 *Operant conditioning*, where learning occurs via reinforcement of desirable behaviour, thus increasing the chances of the behaviour occurring again, such as with behavioural activation therapy (BAT) and social skills training (SST), both of which are treatments for depression.

3 *Social learning*, where learning occurs by the observation and imitation of others modelling desirable behaviours.

The cognitive approach sees mental disorders as arising from disordered thought processes, with **cognitive behavioural therapy (CBT)**, an umbrella term for several therapies, based on the model. The idea behind CBT is that beliefs, expectations and cognitive assessments of self, the environment and the nature of personal problems affect how individuals perceive themselves and others, how problems are approached and how successful individuals are in coping with and attaining goals. CBT challenges and restructures maladaptive ways of thinking into rational, adaptive ones. Behaviour is seen as being generated from thoughts; therefore maladaptive behaviour is altered by targeting maladaptive thinking. Thoughts are perceived as affecting emotions and behaviour and so are modified to reduce symptoms. Drawings are used, illustrating links between thinking, actions and emotions, with understanding where symptoms originate from being useful in reducing symptoms.

The psychodynamic approach sees mental disorders as arising from unresolved conflicts during psychosexual stages of development in childhood. Treatments are orientated at identifying the nature of a conflict and then resolving it. As conflicts are unconscious, patients will not be aware of them and so various methods are used to extract information, allowing a therapist to gain insight into the origin of their disorder, so the patient can achieve an understanding of the repressed events occurring in their past. Various psychodynamic techniques are used by therapists to help patients gain insight into and recover from repressed conflicts. For example, dream analysis involves a therapist looking at the manifest content of a dream (what it appears to be about) to draw out the latent content (what the true meaning is), which often occurs in symbolic form (such as a sword being a symbol for a penis).

TOK link

A problem with psychodynamic explanations is the lack of objective criteria that can be measured and assessed in a scientifically valid way. The whole theory is based on non-testable, subjective viewpoints, with analysis dependent on the subjective and, some would argue, biased interpretations of psychotherapists. This is probably why there is a lot of entrenched opposition to regarding psychodynamic explanations and therapies as having any relevance to mental disorders.

Treatment can either be delivered through individual therapies, where a patient is treated on their own, or through group therapy, where a number of patients, generally with similar disorders, meet with one or more therapists and share their experiences and give mutual support to each other. Relationships with group members are seen as assisting in problem-solving and developing confidence. Patients learn about themselves, how others view them and the reactions they cause in others, all of which increase self-awareness. Therapists attempt to develop group dynamics to illustrate individual problems.

Strengthen your learning

1 Explain what is meant by eclectic treatments.

2 Explain how the effectiveness of treatments for mental health is determined.

3 Describe the following biological treatments
   a drug therapy
   b ECT
   c psychosurgery
   d deep-brain stimulation.

4 Describe the following psychological treatments:
   a behavioural therapies
   b CBT
   c psychodynamic therapies.

5 Explain the difference between individual and group therapies.

▨ Biological treatments of OCD

'Hand sanitizer is a gateway drug for OCD.'
anonymous

FOCUS ON...

- Biological treatments of OCD, including drug therapy, psychosurgery and deep-brain stimulation.
- Ringold *et al.*'s contemporary study of olanzapine augmentation of treatment-resistant OCD.

Drug therapy

Antidepressants are used to treat OCD, such as SSRIs, which elevate levels of serotonin and cause the orbital-frontal cortex to function at more normal levels. The most common SSRI used with adults is fluoxetine (Prozac). For children aged six years, sertraline is usually prescribed and fluvoxamine for children aged eight years and older. Treatment usually lasts for 12–16 weeks. Anxiolytics drugs are also used due to their anxiety-lowering properties. Antipsychotic drugs that have a dopamine-lowering effect have also proven useful in treating OCD, though are only generally given after treatment with SSRIs has not proved to be effective (or incurs serious side effects). Beta-blockers also reduce the physical symptoms of OCD. They work by countering the rise in blood pressure and heart rate often associated with anxiety, by lowering adrenaline and noradrenaline production.

KEY STUDY ## CONTEMPORARY RESEARCH

'Olanzapine augmentation for treatment-resistant obsessive-compulsive disorder'
Ringold *et al.* (2000)

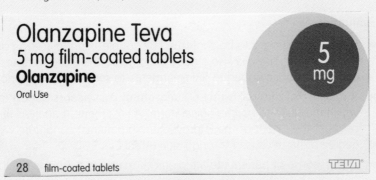

■ **Figure 5.10** Antidepressants are the most common drug used to treat OCD

Research had shown that combining the antipsychotic drug risperidone with a serotonin reuptake inhibitor (SRI) benefits patients with forms of OCD that do not respond to treatment. So the researchers here decided to assess the ability of another atypical antipsychotic, olanzapine, to do the same, as it has a similar effect on serotonin and dopamine levels.

Aims

To assess the ability of olanzapine augmented with an SRI to alleviate treatment-resistant forms of OCD.

Procedure

1 Ten adult OCD patients, whose condition had not responded to treatment of at least 60 mg a day for ten weeks of the SRI drug fluoxetine, consented to act as participants.

2 All participants had OCD for at least one year, as diagnosed by the Yale–Brown Obsessive Compulsive Scale (Y-BOCS), and had not been diagnosed with any other disorder.

3 Participants had failed a mean of 3.3 SRI trials and had a mean Y-BOCS score of 29.0.

4 Administration of fluoxetine continued, but 2.5 mg a day of olanzapine was added to the treatment for two weeks. The olanzapine was then increased to 5 mg a day and two weeks later to 10 mg a day for four more weeks.

Results

1 Nine participants completed the trial.

2 Mean Y-BOCS scores were 24.4 (-4.6, a 16 per cent reduction).

3 One patient's Y-BOCS score dropped 68 per cent, another by 30 per cent and a third by 29 per cent.

4 Only one patient was rated as 'much improved', but this improvement was maintained over the next six months, taking 5 mg daily of olanzapine.

5 Six patients experienced the side-effect of significant weight increase.

Conclusions

- Augmenting SRI treatment with olanzapine has some positive effect with treatment of resistant forms of OCD.

- The administration of simultaneous drug therapies can be more effective than single drug treatments.

Evaluation

- Results would need to be confirmed by double-blind, placebo-controlled trials to be confirmed. There is also a need to compare the effectiveness of risperidone and olanzapine when added to SRI treatments to see which is superior.

- A negative of the trial is that 60 per cent of participants put on considerable weight, which may lead to psychological harm. A cost–benefit analysis here would need to consider the extent of the improvement in patients' condition, weighed against the degree of harm caused through side effects.

- The response of patients to a biological treatment supports the idea of a biological cause to OCD, though the treatment aetiology fallacy warns that just because a disorder responds to a treatment does not necessarily mean the treatment is addressing the cause.

LINK TO THE BIOLOGICAL APPROACH

Drug therapies, psychosurgery and deep-brain stimulation all relate to the biological approach, as they exert a physiological effect in order to reduce the symptoms of OCD.

RESEARCH IN FOCUS

Ringold *et al.*'s study assessed the effectiveness of the drug olanzapine in alleviating treatment-resistant forms of OCD. Previous research had suggested the drug would be effective.

Explain why this would justify having a directional (one-tailed) hypothesis. Construct appropriate directional and null hypotheses for this study.

◾ Research

- **Flament *et al.* (1985)** tested the ability of the tricyclic antidepressant drug clomipramine to address the symptoms of childhood OCD in 19 patients, finding the drug superior over a five-week period to placebo treatment, lending support to the use of the drug. However, **Pigott & Seay (1999)**, in reviewing studies testing the effectiveness of drug therapies, found SSRIs to be consistently effective in reducing OCD symptoms, but although clomipramine proved slightly more effective, it had more serious side effects. This suggests that SSRIs should be given as a first attempt drug treatment and clomipramine should only be used when SSRIs have not proven effective.

- **Cicerone *et al.* (2000)** investigated the effect of low doses of the antipsychotic drug risperidone in treating OCD, finding treatment effective due to the drug's dopamine-lowering effect.

- **Julien *et al.* (2007)** reported that studies of SSRIs show that although symptoms do not fully disappear, between 50 to 80 per cent of OCD patients improve, allowing them to live a fairly normal lifestyle, which they would not be able to do without the treatment.

- **Soomro *et al.* (2008)** reviewed 17 studies of SSRIs versus placebo treatments involving 3097 patients and found SSRIs to be moderately effective in the short-term in treating OCD of varying duration in adults, lending a degree of support to the treatment.

- **Piccinelli *et al.* (1995)** performed a meta-analysis of 36 studies assessing the worth of antidepressants as a treatment for OCD, finding them effective in the short-term, with 61 per cent showing improved symptoms with the tricyclic antidepressant clomipramine and 28 per cent with newer SSRI medications; both treatments proved more beneficial than non-serotonergic drugs.

YOU ARE THE RESEARCHER

Design an experiment to test the effectiveness of antidepressant drugs against placebo treatment. What experimental design would be used? What would be your independent variable (IV) and dependent variable (DV)? How would you establish a double-blind procedure?

TOK link

Can biological treatments alone ever truly 'cure' mental disorders? Such treatments are based on the idea that all mental disorders have a physical cause, such as abnormally functioning biochemistry, and that treatments therefore should be solely biological in nature.

However, this neglects the important role of cognitive and sociocultural influences upon mental disorders. This probably explains why eclectic treatments that combine biological and non-biological treatments often are more effective in reducing symptoms.

◾ Evaluation

- Generally drugs do not 'cure' OCD, but reduce obsessive thoughts and compulsive behaviour to such a level that a more normal lifestyle can be achieved. Once drug taking stops, however, symptoms tend to reappear.

- A limitation of drug therapy is the side effects that patients may experience. Loss of sexual appetite/ability is common, as is irritability, sleep-pattern disturbance (insomnia/drowsiness), headaches and loss of appetite.

- Antidepressant medication may be more suitable for adults, as they are more able to tolerate and understand side effects.

- It is not certain whether drug treatments that are effective in treating OCD reduce obsessive symptoms, or instead lessen the depressive symptoms that often accompany the condition.

- Drug treatments are widely used to treat the symptoms of OCD as they are relatively cheap, do not require a therapist to administer them and are a user-friendly form of treatment, as people are used to taking medicines for illnesses.

Some would argue that because of the risk of side effects and the tendency of antidepressants to produce heightened levels of suicidal thinking, plus the effectiveness of psychological treatments, drug treatments should not be used to treat OCD.

PSYCHOLOGY IN THE REAL WORLD

Drug therapies can have a major effect in reducing the symptoms of mental disorders, but often incur serious side effects. When drug companies introduced atypical antipsychotics to treat schizophrenia, with claims of greater effectiveness and fewer side effects than older, typical types of drugs, the future looked good. But then drug companies were accused of being more motivated by money than patient welfare.

In 2011, 3.1 million Americans were prescribed antipsychotics, generating $18.2 billion (£11.6 billion) in profits. Prescriptions for atypical antipsychotics increased by 93 per cent between 2001 and 2011, though the rate of incidence of schizophrenia and depression for which they are given remained the same. Atypical antipsychotics cost about $100 (£75) per prescription, compared with only $25 (£17) for typical varieties and research has not really backed up claims that they are more effective. Although they reduce side effects associated with typical drugs, they incur serious side-effect risks of their own, which drug companies were not keen to admit to. The Johnson & Johnson pharmaceutical company was fined $2.2 billion (£1.4 billion) in the USA after allegations of 'purposely withholding findings' about antipsychotics it sold increasing the risk of strokes, diabetes and being associated with breast growth in males. Accusations have also been made about research into such drugs being largely controlled by drug companies that influence which findings are published.

Drug companies are also accused of marketing new 'improved' drugs only when their patents for older drugs run out. But are such drugs improvements? Invega was approved in 2007 as an improvement on Risperdal, the drug of which it is a metabolite, but research suggests it is no more effective, even though it is costly. When patents run out, other companies can introduce cheaper generic drugs, severely eating into drug companies' profits.

And what of other drugs? **Thomsen *et al.* (2017)** found cannabidol, an active ingredient in marijuana (which does not contain THC, an ingredient of cannabis associated with triggering schizophrenia), worked just as effectively as antipsychotics, but with far fewer side effects. However, the suspicion is that as it is much cheaper to produce it would not generate great profits, so the drug companies will not be overly keen to produce it.

Psychosurgery and deep-brain stimulation

Psychosurgery involves destroying brain tissue to disrupt the cortico-striatal circuit by the use of radio frequency waves. This has an effect on the orbital-frontal cortex, the thalamus and the caudate nucleus brain areas, and is associated with a reduction in symptoms. There has been a recent movement towards using deep-brain stimulation, which involves the use of magnetic pulses on the supplementary motor area of the brain, which is associated with blocking out irrelevant thoughts and obsessions.

Research

- **Richter *et al.* (2004)** reported that 30 per cent of OCD patients had a 35 per cent or greater reduction in symptoms, but there were occasional complications, such as urinary incontinence and seizures. As these were patients at risk of suicide who had not responded to drug therapies, the treatment can be considered relatively effective.

- **Liu *et al.* (2008)** followed up 35 OCD patients who were non-responsive to medications or psychological and behavioural treatments, and who underwent stereotactic bilateral anterior capsulotomy psychosurgery. PET scans and questionnaires were used to find that twenty patients (57 per cent) became symptom-free, ten (29 per cent) experienced significant improvements, while five (14 per cent) showed no improvements, suggesting the treatment to be safe and effective in treating OCD.

- **Kelly & Cobb (1985)** reported that 78 per cent of 49 patients suffering from OCD displayed improved symptoms 20 months after limbic leucotomies were performed, suggesting a good level of support for the treatment.

- **Hindus *et al.* (1985)** followed up gamma capsulotomy surgical cases three and seven years after treatment, finding that only a few OCD patients showed improvements in their condition, suggesting that different forms of psychosurgery have vastly different success rates.
- **Mallett *et al.* (2008)** evaluated deep-brain stimulation of the subthalamic nucleus in16 individuals with treatment-resistant OCD, comparing it with sham stimulation, and found significant symptom reduction, which suggests the treatment to be effective. This was supported by **Greenberg *et al.* (2008)** finding symptom reduction and functional improvement in 18 out of 26 OCD patients undergoing stimulation of the ventral internal capsule/ventral striatum brain area.

Evaluation

- Although psychosurgery has a relatively small success rate and can cause serious side effects, it can be seen as an acceptable treatment, as it is only used on severe forms of OCD that have not responded to other treatments, such as drug therapies, for about ten years and where there is severely diminished quality of life and/or risk of death to the patient.
- About 10 per cent of OCD patients actually get worse over time, even with drug treatments (and psychological therapies), and so psychosurgery can be deemed a valid treatment for such patients.
- Psychosurgery should only be used after patients have given fully informed consent. It is debatable whether patients with severe OCD can give fully informed consent, however, suggesting there may be ethical problems in administering the treatment.
- Whether psychosurgery should be used generally involves a cost–benefit analysis, where the possible costs, such as irreversible side effects, should be compared against the possible benefits, like the lessening of symptoms detrimental to everyday functioning.
- Psychosurgery cannot be considered to be a cure for OCD and patients who undergo neurosurgery will probably continue to need psychiatric support following the procedure, even if it is considered to be a success.

Strengthen your learning

1 Explain the following biological treatments of OCD:
   a drug therapies
   b psychosurgery
   c deep-brain stimulation.

2 Summarize what research studies have suggested about biological explanations of OCD.

3 Assess the biological explanations of OCD in terms of their strengths and weaknesses.

4 For Ringold *et al.*'s (2000) study of olanzapine augmentation for treatment-resistant obsessive-compulsive disorder, in your own words, state the:
   a aims
   b procedure
   c results
   d conclusions
   e evaluative points.

■ Psychological treatments of OCD

FOCUS ON...

■ Psychological treatments of OCD, including cognitive therapies and psychodynamic therapies.
■ Chlebowski & Gregory's contemporary study, examining the relevance of the psychodynamic perspective and the treatment of OCD.

Cognitive therapy

CBT is a common treatment for OCD, treatments occurring once every 7–14 days for about 15 sessions in total, with CBT orientated at changing obsessional thinking, such as with habituation training (HT), where sufferers relive obsessional thoughts repeatedly to reduce the anxiety created. All types of maladaptive thoughts associated with OCD can be successfully addressed with CBT; intrusive thoughts are shown to be normal and patients come to understand that thinking about a behaviour is not the same as actually doing it. Sufferers learn to focus on estimations of potential risks and realistically assess the likelihood of them occurring. Sufferers are encouraged to practise new adaptive beliefs and to disregard their former maladaptive ones. Although CBT is seen as the most effective treatment for OCD, even higher success rates are found when it is combined with drug treatments.

CBT can be given as an individual treatment, or as a group therapy, such as by group CBT (GCBT), where the basic aim, as with individual CBT, is to change obsessional thinking and develop new adaptive beliefs, but interaction with fellow OCD sufferers provides additional support and encouragement and decreases the feelings of isolation that can aggravate OCD symptoms.

GCBT for OCD often incorporates exposure and response prevention (ERP), involving exposure to a feared obsession (either imagined or for real) until the fear subsides, and response prevention, where the usual ritual response is not allowed to occur.

GCBT usually involves five to twelve participants and one or two therapists meeting once or twice a week for up to 12 sessions, with pre-, post- and follow-up measurements.

■ Research

■ **Vogel & Vogel (1992)** investigated the effectiveness of habituation training in treating OCD patients, finding declines in obsessional thinking within sessions, but not between sessions, implying that the technique is of little value in the real world.

■ **O'Connor et al. (1999)** assessed the effect of combining CBT with drug medication. Patients received one of the following: drugs and CBT together; CBT only; drugs only; or no treatment. Patients in all groups, except the no treatment group, showed improvements, but most symptom reduction was seen when drugs were combined with CBT, especially if drugs were given for a period first. This suggests that the most effective treatment is to first administer drugs to reduce symptoms, especially anxiety levels, so that CBT can then have a more beneficial effect.

■ **O'Kearney et al. (2006)** assessed the ability of CBT to treat children and adolescents with OCD, finding it effective, but more so when combined with drug treatments, demonstrating how drugs and CBT can work together to alleviate the condition.

■ **Cordioli (2008)** reviewed randomized clinical trials and meta-analyses of CBT, finding it effective in reducing OCD symptoms in 70 per cent of patients who complied with treatment, suggesting that the therapy has useful therapeutic value, though the reasons why many sufferers are non-responsive were not identifiable.

■ **Jónsson & Hougaard (2009)** found that GCBT with ERP was better than drug treatments in reducing OCD symptoms, which suggests it is a more effective treatment than drug therapy.

RESEARCH IN FOCUS

1 **Jónsson & Hougaard (2009)** had no prior knowledge of whether GCBT with ERP would be more effective than drug therapy. Would they therefore use a directional (one-tailed) or non-directional (two-tailed) experimental hypothesis? Explain your decision.

2 Compose a suitable experimental hypothesis and identify the IV and DV in the study.

■ Evaluation

- Although CBT was acknowledged to be more effective and not to have the side effects associated with OCD, is it is not suitable for patients who have difficulties talking about inner feelings, or for those who do not possess the verbal skills to do so. Maybe such patients would be more suited to drug therapies.

- Although drugs do not 'cure' OCD they may reduce anxiety and symptoms sufficiently for CBT to be successfully introduced, showing how the two treatments can be successfully combined.

- Drug treatments are lengthy in comparison to CBT; even if a patient shows improvements with drugs, they should continue taking the medication for at least 12 months to ensure their symptoms continue to improve, which suggests CBT may be more cost-effective in the long-term.

- The chances of OCD being successful are strongly correlated with the strength of the working relationship created between patient and therapist, indicating the pivotal role that the therapist plays in administering the treatment.

- Suitably trained nurses have proven as effective as psychiatrists and psychologists in treating those with OCD, demonstrating the simplicity of the treatment and its cost-effectiveness.

- The feelings of isolation that OCD often incur can be addressed by the social support that group therapies provide and the realization that others have similar problems.

LINK TO THE COGNITIVE APPROACH

CBT relates to the cognitive approach, as it focuses on replacing irrational thought processes with rational ones, as the means by which OCD symptoms can be dealt with.

Psychodynamic therapy

Psychodynamic therapies contain biological, cognitive and sociocultural elements.

Psychodynamic therapies have not been seen as an effective treatment for OCD; indeed some clinicians have perceived them as more harmful than useful in alleviating symptoms. However, there has been a recent move towards viewing certain types of psychodynamic therapies as useful with certain types of patient, especially after treatment with drugs and CBT has not reduced their symptoms. Psychodynamic therapies may especially have a useful role to play with patients who have comorbid conditions, especially those additionally suffering from borderline personality disorder (BPD) and patients whose OCD developed in adulthood due to stressors based upon interpersonal relationships, as well as those whose OCD may emanate from unresolved crises in childhood.

Dynamic deconstructive psychotherapy (DDP) is a form of psychodynamic therapy that has produced some promising results. The aims of DDP are to get patients to connect with their own emotional experiences, in order to gain a better sense of self, and to get them to connect with other people in more meaningful ways, in order to develop better interpersonal relationships. The main focus is on social interactions, with a therapist helping a patient to identify the emotions they experience in relation to their condition and getting them to explore other ways of interpreting their interactions with people. This serves the purpose of deconstructing attributions about oneself (how an individual regards themselves and their behaviour) and replacing them with more positive attributions.

DDP occurs as weekly sessions of 45 minutes for up to 12 months of treatment. Between sessions patients assess their emotional experiences by completing Daily Connection Sheets in order to build better social relationships outside of treatment. At the end of treatment, some patients will require monthly maintenance sessions or six-month blocks of 'booster' sessions.

| KEY STUDY | **CONTEMPORARY RESEARCH** |

'Is a psychodynamic perspective relevant to the clinical management of obsessive-compulsive disorder?'
Chlebowski & Gregory (2009)

Drug therapy and CBT are the accepted treatments for OCD, while psychodynamic therapies are seen as inappropriate. However, up to 60 per cent of patients do not respond adequately to drug treatment and drop-out rates during CBT are relatively high, with symptoms still persisting from a mild to moderate degree in the majority of patients treated. So in this study the researchers looked at five case studies of OCD patients treated by psychodynamic means to see if there were any circumstances in which such therapies could be of use.

Aims

1   To assess whether psychodynamic therapies are effective in treating OCD.

2   To see whether psychodynamic therapies enhance the understanding of OCD beyond biological and cognitive factors.

3   To see if there are identifiable groups of people who may benefit from psychodynamic therapies.

Procedure and findings

Five individual case studies of individuals suffering from OCD, who were treated with psychodynamic therapies, were reviewed.

1   *Case study one.* A 40-year-old mother with two young children, who was worried by obsessional thoughts of hurting her children, compulsively hid away in drawers knives, gloves, and so on that she might hurt her children with. She admitted to marital problems due to the controlling behaviour of her husband. During psychodynamic therapy, she was made aware that the lack of control she felt related to the lack of control she had as a child, while taking care of her sick mother. She was prescribed drugs and CBT, but took neither, saying that due to the realization of her lack of control, she had solved her difficulties by becoming more assertive in her marriage. Six months later her obsessional thoughts had ceased.

2   *Case study two.* A 30-year-old married female had obsessions and compulsions based on fears of the house burning down, constantly checking stoves, fires, and so on. She also had comorbid (shared) conditions of AN, bipolar disorder, borderline personality disorder (BPD) and alcohol abuse. She had previously taken SSRIs and antidepressants, but without any improvement in her condition. She was given weekly dynamic deconstructive psychotherapy (DDP), which revealed that her symptoms were a displacement of her anger and destructive wishes onto objects in her house. She was encouraged to deconstruct her distorted attributions about herself, with her condition gradually improving so that all OCD symptoms had disappeared within one year, and did not return over the next five years.

3   *Case study three.* A 22-year-old single female undergraduate, just released from psychiatric care after a suicide attempt, had obsessions of contamination and compulsions of cleaning herself, including washing and showering every 30 minutes. Previous drug treatment and CBT had not improved her symptoms. She also had AN, problems with alcohol and BPD. She began DDP, which revealed her cleaning rituals to be attempts to displace feelings of shame. After six months most of her symptoms had gone and she had finished her degree course.

4   *Case study four.* A 29-year-old married female was obsessed with the idea that bloody tampons were littering her house, though she recognized this was untrue. She had compulsions to search for them and constantly wash laundry. She had been unsuccessfully treated with CBT. Psychotherapy revealed that symptoms onset coincided with her marriage and she admitted she had a fear of sexual intercourse. The bloody tampons were interpreted as symbolizing a threatening penis, which was a displacement of her fears of sexuality. When told this, the patient became angry, stormed out and did not return.

5   *Case study five.* A 20-year-old single male student had obsessions from age 11 of losing body parts, which he constantly checked for. He also had obsessions involving staples (he avoided staplers as he feared stapling his eye to the paper) and bottles (he would open half-empty bottles as he feared part of himself was trapped in the bottle). He had a very close relationship with his mother and feared suicide when separated from her. His condition had worsened since starting university. Treatment with drugs and CBT had not worked. During 12 sessions of psychotherapy he was encouraged to concentrate on building new relationships and not on his OCD symptoms. However, he became anxious about reducing dependency on his mother, left treatment and returned to live with his mother.

Conclusions

- Some cases of OCD may arise from unresolved conflicts during the anal stage of development and psychotherapy can help such patients to identify and acknowledge their forbidden urges and ego-defences. As such, psychotherapy thus helps understanding of certain cases of OCD.

- Treatment is successful when self-esteem reaches a level that allows a patient to relinquish their obsessions and compulsions and so live without their defences.

- Psychotherapy is a useful treatment for patients who have comorbid OCD and BPD (about 25 per cent of OCD sufferers have BPD) and for patients whose OCD starts in adulthood due to interpersonal stressors and whose symptoms have symbolic significance.

Evaluation

- Psychotherapy only benefited three out of five cases, lowering support for the therapy, though where patients withdrew from therapy, continuation with treatment may have brought improvements.

- Five case studies do not really constitute a representative sample, making it difficult to generalize findings to all OCD sufferers.

- Although significant reduction of symptoms did occur, there is no scientific support for the principles of psychodynamic theory upon which psychotherapy is based. Interpretation of patients' behaviour and symptoms is subjective and may be prone to researcher bias.

- The results do suggest that blind faith in drug therapy and CBT for all OCD cases may be misplaced and that psychodynamic therapies should not be immediately dismissed, as some patients do seem to benefit.

LINK TO THE BIOLOGICAL, COGNITIVE AND SOCIOCULTURAL APPROACHES

Psychodynamic therapies for the treatment of OCD relate to the biological approach, as they refer to innate features, such as the concept of the id; but they also relate to the sociocultural approach, as they focus on social and environmental learning experiences; as well as the cognitive approach, as an important part of such therapies is patients gaining cognitive insight into and understanding of their disorder.

RESEARCH IN FOCUS

Chlebowski & Gregory used the case study method to assess the treatment of OCD by psychotherapy. Explain why this study method was chosen and what the strengths and weaknesses of the method are

▨ Research

■ **Leichsenring & Steinert (2016)** reviewed research to find that short-term psychodynamic therapy (STPP) is effective in treating OCD, which suggests that the psychodynamic explanation upon which the therapy is based is valid (see psychodynamic treatment of OCD on page 247). The treatment has 12 modules, including focusing upon the core conflictual relationship theme (CCRT) and helping to form a trusting non-judgemental relationship with the therapist (which are common to most psychodynamic treatments), as well as OCD-specific treatment elements. At the start, the CCRT associated with the symptoms of OCD are reviewed, with the CCRT having three components: (1) *the wish* (for instance, aggressive or sexual urges), (2) *response from others* (for instance, being criticized), (3) *response of self* (for instance, types of obsessions and compulsions). The therapist then relates the OCD symptoms to the sufferer's wishes and the responses of others, which permits the sufferer to have insight into their anxiety and OCD behaviour. This involves the CCRT and its OCD components being reviewed in past and present relationships, with a view to sufferers developing more rational behaviours that help them to gain control over their anxiety. OCD-specific components of the treatment include differentiating between thinking and acting (for example, understanding that having sexual urges about women does not mean the sufferer has violated them), mitigating the rigid and hyper-strict super-ego (for instance, not criticizing a sufferer for having sexual urges) and encouraging them to resist the compulsive response to such urges.

■ **Clarkin (2003)** performed a review of studies assessing the effect of psychodynamic therapies on patients with BPD, including many who had comorbid OCD. It was found that such treatments were effective and produced better improvements in condition than other forms of treatment and in many cases significantly reduced OCD symptoms. This again supports the idea of psychotherapy being useful in treating cases of comorbid OCD with BPD.

▨ Evaluation

■ **Kempke & Luyten (2007)** report that there is a previously unacknowledged overlap between psychodynamic and cognitive-behavioural explanations for OCD, especially concerning the idea of schemas that relate to perceptions of oneself and others. This suggests that therapies based upon relevant elements of both explanations may be more effective in symptom reduction than treatments based on a single explanation.

■ It may be that although psychodynamic therapy is not the most effective main treatment for OCD and has little use as a sole treatment, it may have an important role as part of an eclectic, combined treatment. Many patients respond favourably to drug therapy and CBT, but more long-term success can be gained by then adding in psychodynamic treatment to explore the deeply rooted thought patterns that develop from having OCD in order to free themselves from these patterns.

■ There is an ethical concern of harm with psychodynamic therapies, as such treatments can involve patients revisiting traumatic emotional experiences that are seen to relate to their condition. As well as being highly stressful for a patient, this can have the effect of patients abandoning treatment, as happened in two out of the five case studies reviewed by **Chlebowski & Gregory**.

■ Psychodynamic therapies are not cheap, as they require long-term treatment that is administered by a trained therapist. Therefore, such treatments are probably only justifiable for sufferers who have not responded to other more mainstream, cheaper forms of therapy, such as drugs and CBT.

■ **Shedler (2010)** argues that psychodynamic therapies are often disfavoured, not because they are ineffective, but because they are associated with discredited Freudian views of psychodynamic theories. He argues that modern forms of psychotherapy are based on more rational foundations and should be assessed on research evidence rather than unsubstantiated prejudice.

Strengthen your learning

1 Explain the following psychological treatments of OCD:
a CBT
b psychodynamic therapies.

2 Summarize what research studies have suggested about psychological explanations of OCD.

3 Assess psychological explanations of OCD in terms of their strengths and weaknesses.

4 For Chlebowski & Gregory's (2009) contemporary study of the psychodynamic perspective and its relevance to the clinical management of obsessive-compulsive disorder, in your own words, state the:
a aims
b procedure
c results
d conclusions
e evaluative points.

Biological treatments of anorexia nervosa

'How cool is it that the same God, who created mountains, oceans and galaxies, looked at you and thought the world needs one of you too.'
Anonymous

FOCUS ON...

■ Biological treatments of anorexia nervosa, including drug therapies, the mandometer and repetitive transcranial magnetic stimulation.

Drug therapy

Drugs are generally not seen as an effective treatment for AN on their own, but can have some effectiveness when combined with other psychological treatments. Antidepressant SSRIs, such as Prozac and Sarafem, are seen as useful in treating anorexics who have comorbid anxiety disorders and/or depression, with the antipsychotic drug olanzapine also sometimes used to reduce feelings of anxiety related to weight and dieting in patients who have not responded to other treatments.

SSRIs only tend to be prescribed to patients who have started to put weight on, as the risk of side effects is heightened in people who are underweight, especially that of loss of appetite and further weight loss. Also, SSRIs are generally only given to patients over the age of 18. When SSRIs are prescribed, the patient will take them for some weeks before any improvement in symptoms is seen. As well as reducing feelings of depression in anorexics, SSRIs can help patients to maintain a healthy weight once control over weight and eating has been established. SSRIs increase serotonin levels, a neurotransmitter that affects mood. Olanzapine tends to be given if SSRIs have had little beneficial effect and can help some sufferers to gain weight and reduce obsessive thinking. Drugs cannot cure anorexia but can help to control urges to binge or purge and excessive focus on food and dieting.

Research

■ **Scherag et al. (2009)** reported that the serotonergic brain system is involved in weight regulation, eating behaviour and AN. Serotonin levels were found to be increased in long-term weight-restored anorexic patients, which suggests that SSRI drugs, which affect serotonin levels, might have a role to play in the long-term treatment of AN.

■ **Biederman et al. (1985)** reported that treatment for AN in adults using only antidepressants showed no benefits in terms of weight gain, and in many cases they incurred unpleasant side effects, causing many patients to stop taking them. This was supported by **Halmi et al. (1986)** finding similar results. **Holtkamp et al. (2005)** found treatment with SSRIs alone in adolescent patients had no significant beneficial effects. Collectively, these findings suggest drug therapy alone is not effective in treating AN.

- **Kaye *et al.* (2001)** found that the SSRI Prozac, if given to anorexic patients after their weight had returned to normal, had the effect of causing them not to relapse back into weight loss and AN. Ten out of 16 (63 per cent) of anorexic patients who took Prozac after their weight returned to normal did not relapse, compared to only 3 out of 19 (16 per cent) who took a placebo. This suggests Prozac can be useful in reducing relapse rates, which can be a big problem for recovering anorexics.

- **Boachie *et al.* (2003)** found that the treatment of four anorexic patients aged between 10 and 12 years with the antipsychotic drug olanzapine led to decreases in anxiety and weight gain, which suggests such treatment alone may be useful for young patients. However, **Barbarich *et al.* (2004)** found treatment by olanzapine alone led to no weight gain in adult patients, which suggests the treatment is ineffective for older sufferers, though **McElroy *et al.* (2003)** found olanzapine useful for treating patients with severe AN, possibly due to its anxiety reducing properties lowering their fear of eating.

- **Hsu *et al.* (1991)** found that treatment with SSRIs had some effectiveness in treating AN in patients with comorbid conditions of depression and OCD, which suggests drug therapies may have a role in treating comorbid conditions.

Evaluation

- Clinicians are often reluctant to prescribe SSRIs due to their side effects, such as problems in sleeping, low sex drive, hallucinations and especially low-appetite and weight loss, which could have severe negative effects on the treatment of anorexics.

- Drug companies have been keen to promote research into the use of drugs as a treatment for AN, as if they proved effective, they would incur large profits. They would also provide a cheap and easy form of therapy compared to other forms of treatment. However, such hopes have proven to be false ones.

- Clinical trials of drug therapy for AN usually have a comparison control condition of patients who are given placebo treatment, with patients in both conditions not knowing if they have taken a drug or a placebo. This allows the true effect of the drug on reducing symptoms to be seen.

- The effectiveness that drugs do have is probably in keeping anxiety levels low in recovering patients, as elevated anxiety levels could cause fear of eating/weight increase to return, leading to spiralling back into AN.

LINK TO THE BIOLOGICAL APPROACH

Drug therapies, use of the mandometer and repetitive transcranial magnetic stimulation all relate to the biological approach, as they are seen to act upon physiologically determined features in order to reduce symptoms of AN.

Other biological therapies

Other biological therapies include:

1 *Mandometer* – a device that gives patients feedback on their rate of eating, which can be used to accelerate rate of eating in anorexics.

2 *Repetitive transcranial magnetic stimulation (rTMS)* – a treatment involving brain stimulation, usually used to treat depression and anxiety, whereby an electromagnetic coil is used to generate magnetic pulses to targeted brain areas. This induces an electrical current in specific nerve cells, which causes a stimulation that positively affects mood. Attempts are now being made to assess its effectiveness in treating AN, due to many sufferers having high levels of anxiety and comorbid conditions involving heightened levels of depression and anxiety.

Research

- **Van Elburg *et al.* (2012)** compared mandometer treatment (MT) with more usual forms of treatment (UFT) for AN, finding after treatment that 63 per cent of MT patients reached normal weight levels, compared to 85 per cent of UFT patients; this coupled with the fact that after two years more MT than UFT patients were still in treatment and that more had relapsed suggests MT is not an effective long-term treatment for AN.

■ **Van den Eynde *et al.* (2011)** gave single sessions of rTMS to anorexic patients, to find the treatment reduced sufferers' urges to restrict their eating and reduced their feelings of fullness, which restricted eating. This suggests the treatment may have a role to play in treating AN.

Evaluation

■ Worsening of mood in winter months has been seen to increase maladaptive eating behaviour in patients with BN. As this phenomenon has been successfully treated with light therapy, where patients lie under bright lights in order to elevate depressed mood, it suggests the treatment may be beneficial to anorexics who also experience worsening of mood in winter months.

■ The development of rTMS as a potential treatment for AN offers a non-invasive, biological way of treating the condition that does not involve the side effects associated with taking drugs that often lead to patients dropping out of treatment. It is probable though that rTMS would be most effective when combined with other psychological therapies, that is, as a replacement for drug therapy in combined treatments.

■ If rTMS does prove of worth, it will probably be most effective in treating anorexic patients with comorbid conditions involving low mood that negatively affect eating behaviour, such as depression and OCD, as the treatment primarily heightens mood and lowers anxiety.

■ As, despite lots of research, biological therapies do not prove to be of much benefit in treating AN, it may be that the condition is more psychological than biological in nature and so should be treated as such.

Strengthen your learning

1 Explain the following biological treatments of AN:
   a drug therapies
   b mandometer
   c repetitive transcranial magnetic stimulation.

2 Summarize what research studies have suggested about biological explanations of AN.

3 Assess the biological explanations of AN in terms of their strengths and weaknesses.

Psychological treatments of anorexia nervosa

FOCUS ON...

■ Psychological treatments of anorexia nervosa, including cognitive therapies and psychodynamic therapies.

Cognitive therapy

Cognitive behaviour therapy (CBT) is a common method of treating AN. CBT stresses the role that maladaptive cognitions (thoughts) and behaviours play in onset and maintenance of AN. Maladaptive cognitive factors include: preoccupation with weight and body shape, food and eating, negative body image, negative self-worth, negative self-evaluation and perfectionism. Maladaptive behavioural factors include: severe dieting, purging, constant weighing, self-harm.

Individuals who have negative, distorted perceptions of themselves and their bodies develop feelings of shame and disgust that trigger weight control behaviours and a repeating cycle of negative self-evaluation. CBT, delivered by a trained therapist, gets sufferers to identify the factors that help to maintain their anorexic behaviour. The main emphasis is on teaching skills to patients to help them not only understand why they are anorexic, but also to help develop new, more adaptive ways of thinking and behaving in order to maintain a stable, healthy weight.

CBT for AN occurs in three phases, which can be delivered to patients inside and outside of hospital:

1 *Behavioural phase* – therapist and patient work together to create a plan for stabilizing eating behaviour and reducing anorexic symptoms. Coping strategies are taught and practised that help the patient to deal with the intense negative emotions that can arise at this time.

2 *Cognitive phase* – cognitive restructuring skills, which help patients to identify and alter negative thinking patterns, are taught. For example, identifying that 'I can only be of worth if I lose weight' is maladaptive, and is altered to 'my happiness doesn't depend on my weight'. Also at this stage, relationship, body image and self-worth problems are addressed, as well as methods of controlling one's emotions.

3 *Maintenance and relapse prevention phase* – focus is on reducing factors that trigger anorexic thoughts and behaviour and developing strategies to prevent relapsing back into AN. After anorexic symptoms have been dealt with, the final focus is on other areas of concern and conflict that could precipitate such a relapse.

LINK TO THE COGNITIVE APPROACH

CBT relates to the cognitive approach, in that it focuses on replacing irrational thought processes with rational ones as the means by which AN symptoms can be addressed and reduced.

Research

■ **Pike (2003)** performed a study of CBT as an out-patient treatment for AN in 33 adults who had originally been hospitalized with the disorder. Participants were randomly selected to receive either CBT or nutritional advice. After one year, 22 per cent of CBT patients had either dropped out of treatment or relapsed, compared to 77 per cent of patients receiving nutritional advice. The CBT patients also had lower levels of purging and better attitudes towards and behaviours concerned with eating, which collectively suggests CBT to be an effective out-patient treatment for AN.

■ **Carter *et al.* (2009)** compared the effectiveness of CBT against group therapy (GT), as a maintenance treatment for AN patients who had regained a healthy weight. Forty-six patients received CBT and 42 patients received GT for one year each, with assessments occurring every three months. After one year, 35 per cent of CBT patients had relapsed, compared to 66 per cent of GT patients (with 12 patients dropping out of each condition), which suggests CBT is a better long-term maintenance treatment than GT for AN.

■ **Ball & Mitchell (2010)** compared CBT to behavioural family therapy (BFT) (where all family members, not just the anorexic member, are involved in therapy). Twenty-five females aged between 13 and 23 years were randomly selected for CBT or BFT, with both groups receiving 25 sessions each. Participants in both conditions generally maintained normal body weight, had regular periods, lower levels of anxiety, higher levels of self-worth and better eating habits and attitudes. However, most patients did not reach full recovery, which suggests that CBT is as effective as BFT, but that neither treatment is fully effective on its own.

■ **Bulik *et al.* (2007)** conducted a meta-analysis of 19 studies to compare the effectiveness of various type of therapy for AN. However, although the findings indicated that CBT, in combination with drug therapy, helps reduce relapse rates for patients who have regained weight, it was not possible to assess fully how CBT on its own compared to other types of therapy, including interpersonal psychotherapy and cognitive analytic therapy. This was due to small sample sizes, high drop-out rates, not taking sociodemographic factors into account (e.g. family background) and different treatments conducted at different places over differing amounts of time. This implies that further, better conducted research needs to be undertaken if CBT is to be properly assessed.

Evaluation

- It is often difficult to assess the effects of CBT, as patients have often been influenced by other previous types of treatment, and, such as in **Pike's (2003)** study, may be on medication while CBT is delivered. Therefore, it can be difficult to identify which specific treatment has had the main effect (or indeed improvement may be used to a combined effect).

- Another methodological problem with assessing the effectiveness of CBT (and other treatments) is the high drop-out rates from treatment over time. This reduces sample sizes, making generalization of findings less valid, and can obscure whether treatments are effective or not. For example, in **Ball & Mitchell's (2010)** study, 7 out of 25 patients (28 per cent) dropped out (plus there was not a 'no treatment' condition to compare recovery rates for CBT and BFT against).

- CBT is only really suitable for patients who can form a relationship with their therapist that allows them to communicate fully their thinking patterns and attitudes towards themselves and eating. As many anorexics are self-obsessed and have problems with anxiety that limit their ability to form interpersonal relationships, this may be difficult for some sufferers to achieve.

Psychodynamic therapy

Psychodynamic therapy (PDT) focuses on symptoms as being related to disturbances in relationships. For example, a sufferer may be seen as fearful of greed, which manifests itself through limiting their food intake to appear less greedy, with this perceived as being symbolic of similar patterns within a sufferer's interpersonal relationships, where there are fears of having feelings of dependency on others. Anorexics generally see dependency as a sign of weakness and so they develop anorexic behaviours as a way of showing they are not dependent on food. With the focus now on controlling food and body weight, interpersonal relationships become less important and the anorexic creates a sense of being emotionally and physically self-sufficient.

The role of a psychotherapist is to help the patient understand their unconscious thoughts, feelings and behaviour so that such insight will help them to change and repair relationships with themselves and others.

Focal psychodynamic therapy (FPT) is a form of PDT, which sees AN to be linked to unresolved conflicts that occurred in childhood, mainly during the oral stage of psychosexual development. By getting patients to assess how early childhood experiences may be linked to their anorexic behaviour, it is seen as assisting them, with help from a therapist, to find effective ways of coping with stressors and negative thoughts and feelings.

Interpersonal therapy (IT) is another form of PDT, which focuses on relationships with others and the external world as being linked to mental health. AN is seen as being related to perceptions of low self-worth and high anxiety, caused by problems with interpersonal relationships. During treatment a therapist helps a patient to assess negative factors associated with interpersonal relationships and to form and practise strategies to resolve them.

LINK TO THE BIOLOGICAL, COGNITIVE AND SOCIOCULTURAL APPROACHES

Psychodynamic therapies relate to the biological approach, as they refer to innate features, such as the concept of the id, but they also relate to the sociocultural approach, as they focus on social and environmental learning experiences, in addition to the cognitive approach, as an important part of such therapies is patients gaining cognitive insight into and understanding of their anorexia.

Research

- **Zipfel et al. (2014)** compared the effectiveness of CBT and FPT in treating AN. Eighty patients randomly assigned to each group underwent 40 treatment sessions over ten months. At the end of treatment, weight gain had occurred in both groups, with no significant differences between the two treatment groups. Further weight had been gained at a 12-month follow-up. This implies that FPT is as effective as CBT, though there was a fairly high drop-out rate (28 per cent).

- **Dare et al. (2001)** assessed the effectiveness of FPT by randomly allocating 84 patients to one of four treatment groups: one year of FPT, one year of family therapy (FT), seven months of cognitive analytic therapy (CAT) or one year of the usual out-patient low-contact treatment. At one year, all patients had improved, with one-third of FPT, CAT and FT patients showing no sign of AN. Around 80 per cent of patients in these treatment groups had increased in weight, with 38 per cent increasing by at least 10 per cent of body weight. A smaller amount of patients were assessed as 'poor' who had received FPT than any other treatment type. This suggests FPT is at least as effective as other treatment methods.

- **Egger et al. (2016)** compared the cost-effectiveness of FPT and enhanced CBT. Cost-effectiveness was calculated by assessing cost per each patient who had recovered at 22 months. It was found that FPT had lower average costs than CBT, which suggests that FPT is a relatively cost-effective treatment.

- **McIntosh et al. (2005)** assessed the effectiveness of interpersonal therapy (IT) in treating AN. Fifty-six patients either had IT, CBT or usual out-patient support. At the end of treatment, IT was the least effective treatment in reducing symptoms, which suggests the treatment is relatively ineffective. However, long-term follow-up, on average 6.7 years later, found no difference in recovery rates between all three treatments; and patients who had received IT, in particular, had improved over the long term.

- **Hartmann et al. (2010)** reported that psychodynamic therapies that focus on improving the quality of patients' interpersonal relationships lower the chances of relapse, which suggests it is this aspect of psychodynamic therapy which is effective.

> **RESEARCH IN FOCUS**
>
> **Dare et al.'s (2001)** study randomly selected participants for inclusion into four different testing conditions.
>
> 1 Explain what is meant by random selection.
>
> 2 How would random selection be achieved?
>
> 3 Give one strength and one limitation of random selection.

Evaluation

- A methodological problem in assessing forms of PDT (and other types of treatment) is that patients have different severities of AN, but this is not generally taken into account when assessing how effective treatments have been, making findings less valid.

- Individuals who are recovering from AN are seen as being difficult to work with, but this may support the basis behind PDT, as anorexics' 'difficult behaviour' may actually be an effect of the avoidant behaviours from their disorder. As they start to improve their relationships with themselves and others, such avoidant behaviours decline and symptoms begin to improve.

- Although a lot more research needs to be done into the effectiveness of PDTs, it is clear that the use of such therapies is being seen as generally more acceptable as a means of treating AN. The disorder is notoriously difficult to treat effectively in the long-term, so any new methods of treatment that have even a small degree of success will be useful to clinicians.

- One positive aspect of PDT is that it does not, unlike with drug therapies, incur any risk of side effects. One negative though is that, like CBT, a trained therapist is needed to administer the treatment, which increases the cost of the treatment.

Strengthen your learning

1 Explain the following psychological treatments of AN:
   a CBT
   b psychodynamic therapies.

2 Summarize what research studies have suggested about psychological explanations of AN.

3 Assess psychological explanations of AN in terms of their strengths and weaknesses.

Role of culture in treatment

'A mind cannot be independent of culture.'
Lev Vygotsky

FOCUS ON...

■ A consideration of how cultural factors affect the treatment of mental disorders.

Culture – the shared set of beliefs, norms, and values that groups possess.

Culture affects treatment in several ways.

First, mental health care reflects the culture it operates in. For example, in western cultures, mental health therapies are based upon western cultural viewpoints, which stress the medical model, hence the emphasis on biological treatments.

Secondly, the way patients present their symptoms, which then affects diagnosis and treatment given, differs cross-culturally. For instance, Asian patients are likelier to report physical than emotional symptoms, as there is cultural shame attached to admitting to having emotional problems.

Thirdly, how people of different cultures perceive mental disorders also affects whether individuals will seek treatment when they need it. In many cultures there is a stigma of embarrassment and shame attached to being mentally disordered that will negatively affect how other people perceive and behave towards that individual, and so they fail to seek treatment for mental problems. If they do seek help and receive treatment, then the effectiveness of the treatment might be reduced if friends and family are not supportive of that individual's treatment. In western cultures, people from minority cultural groups are also more likely to delay seeking treatment until their symptoms are severe, which can negatively affect their prospects of benefitting from treatment.

Also, in many cultures, such as in Africa, individuals with mental disorders are more likely to seek help from religious figures or traditional healers, such as herbalists and witch-doctors, which will negatively affect their chances of recovery.

Furthermore, a problem for people from ethnic minorities is that it often is not possible for them to have a therapist of the same ethnicity, as there is an under-representation of such people providing mental health care and this could affect their chances of committing to a treatment, or even seeking treatment in the first place. There are even cultural differences in which forms of treatment people prefer. For example, many black Americans prefer counselling to drug therapy, due to cultural concerns about side effects, effectiveness and addiction.

Mistrust of treatment is also a big factor, especially mistrust of mental health care that is provided mainly by people of another culture. Hospitalization and many forms of treatment are often feared, as they carry connotations of punishment, similar to being in prison; that is, being 'punished' for being mentally unsound.

Additionally, cost of treatment can also affect what type of therapies people will receive. People in many cultures and from ethnic minorities in western cultures cannot afford specialist treatments and so will often only receive low-cost treatments, such as drug therapy, even if better treatments exist. This will again negatively affect treatment outcomes (this is generally in countries where health care has to be paid for by individuals and not in countries like Great Britain where health care is provided free). Such people are also at greater risk of misdiagnosis, which could lead to incorrect and thus non-effective (or even harmful) treatments being given.

RESEARCH IN FOCUS

A problem with interpreting behaviour from different cultures is that of imposed etics. What is an imposed etic and what effect can it have?

Research

- **Lin & Cheung (1999)** found that Asian patients tend to report physical symptoms more than emotional ones, but when questioned further admit to having emotional symptoms. This supports the idea that people of different cultures selectively express (or not) symptoms in a culturally acceptable way and this can affect the type of treatment prescribed.

- **Vega et al. (1998)** reported that ethnic minorities in the USA are less likely than white people to seek mental health treatment, due partly to having negative perceptions of being mentally disordered. This accounts for such people being under-represented in mental health care and suggests that such people may incur long-term suffering and elevated risk of suicide from having such perceptions. Further support comes from **Zhang et al. (1998)**, who reported that ethnic and racial minorities in the USA are less likely than the white majority to seek mental health treatment.

- **Peifer et al. (2000)** reported that many cultural groups turn to informal sources of care, such as clergy, traditional healers and family and friends, instead of health professionals, when encountering mental health problems. This suggests that utilizing such forms of treatment would greatly lower such individuals' chances of recovery.

- **Sussman et al. (1987)** found that nearly 50 per cent of black Americans suffering from depression feared hospitalization and mental health treatments, compared to 20 per cent of their white counterparts, and these fears led to them often not seeking treatment. This suggests that black Americans are therefore likelier to have lower prospects of recovery from mental disorders.

Evaluation

- The consequences of individuals not seeking treatment due to culturally determined negative perceptions of mental disorders, or treatment not being effective due to a lack of support from family and friends, can be serious. For example, such individuals may continue to be severely affected by their condition, worsen over the long term, or even commit suicide.

- It is difficult to generalize findings from studies of mental health care to all cultures, because health care systems in different cultures vary so greatly. Findings from one culture may be due exclusively to that culture's type of mental health care system and so not be relevant to people in another culture where the health care system is very different.

- One necessary method of reducing some of the more negative effects of the role of culture in mental health treatment would be to train more clinicians of other cultures. This would mean that people, if they wished, could have a clinician of their own cultural background who understood their needs and perception of their disorder in a way that would facilitate treatment towards a more effective outcome.

- As part of their training, clinicians need to be made more aware of how cultural factors affect the treatment of mental disorders and incorporate such factors into their mental health care provision to improve patients' chances of recovery. For example, in Alaska, traditional native healers work alongside clinicians in delivering mental health care to Alaskan Indian people with effective results.

Strengthen your learning

1 In bullet-point form, describe the various ways in which culture can affect the treatment of mental disorders.

2 Summarize what research studies have suggested about ways in which culture can affect the treatment of mental disorders.

3 What other evaluative points can be made about ways in which culture can affect the treatment of mental disorders?

SECTION SUMMARY

■ Eclectic treatments combine different types of therapies together.
■ Several factors are used to assess the effectiveness of treatments.
■ Biological treatments for OCD consist of drug therapy, psychosurgery and deep-brain stimulation.
■ Psychological treatments for OCD consist of CBT and psychodynamic therapies.
■ Biological treatments of AN consist of drug therapy, the mandometer and repetitive transcranial magnetic stimulation.
■ Psychological treatments of AN consist of CBT and psychodynamic therapies.
■ Culture affects treatment in several ways.

■ Assessment check

1	Discuss one or more biological treatments for one abnormal disorder.	(22 marks)
2	Evaluate cognitive treatment of one or more abnormal disorders.	(22 marks)
3	Discuss the sociocultural approach to the treatment of one or more abnormal disorders.	(22 marks)
4	Discuss one or more research studies of the treatment of one abnormal disorder.	(22 marks)
5	Discuss ethical considerations in the treatment of one or more abnormal disorders.	(22 marks)
6	Evaluate the role of culture in diagnosis.	(22 marks)
7	Discuss research studies of the role of culture in diagnosis.	(22 marks)

Developmental psychology

'Through others we become ourselves.'
Lev S. Vygotsky

'One of the luckiest things that can happen to you in life is, I think, to have a happy childhood.'
Agatha Christie

Introduction

This chapter is concerned with how, as individuals, we develop and mature into the people we become. How we grow, think and behave as adults is the accumulation of a developmental process that, in many cases, follows a typical trajectory. However, the unique context we find ourselves in mediates that process. There are many potential factors that can shape our development throughout childhood and beyond.

This is illustrated by cases of identical twins, who are genetically 100 per cent identical, being reared apart and then reunited. For example, Jim Lewis and Jim Springer were raised apart and did not meet each other for 39 years. When reunited they found they had a lot in common such as the cigarette brand they both smoked, an aptitude for mathematics and similar occupations (security guard and police officer). However, there were also differences and teasing apart the role of heredity and environment in their development is difficult. What cases such as this one do show is that there are influences at the biological, cognitive and sociocultural levels that affect development of an individual.

Influences on cognitive and social development

FOCUS ON...

- The role of peers and play as influences on child development.
- How trauma and resilience can support or undermine development.
- The relationship between poverty/socio-economic status and development in a child.

▧ Role of peers

Development is influenced by context; there is widely accepted acknowledgement that the environment a child grows up in affects the ease and rate of their development. Urie Bronfenbrenner, in his ecological systems theory, highlighted five potential levels of influence: micro-system (e.g. home, school, immediate family); meso-system (the interaction of the factors within the micro-system, e.g. parents attending events at school); exo-system (indirect but strong effects on the child such as the parents' working environment); macro-system (cultural beliefs and customs); and chrono-system (events over the life course, such as a war). These all affect a child to a varying degree and are dependent on the individual's context.

This section will focus predominantly on the micro-system of the child and, more specifically, the peers they meet at school or close to their home. It will consider the potential influence that peers have on both cognitive and social development.

Influence of peers on cognitive development

Children can learn as much from peers as they can from their parents. This is often underplayed. An argument with a friend in childhood can teach a child many things, such as negotiation and problem-solving. Later in childhood, peer tutoring and mentoring programmes illustrate that the relationships an individual has with their peers are powerful.

Cognition is enhanced by the presence of peers. Language learning enhances and benefits from conversations between peers. If children discuss their feelings and thoughts together then the representations that a child has of emotions and feelings are improved by such dialogue. Language acquisition is also shown to be helped by learning from peers, as opposed to parents (**Pinker, 1994**). This was illustrated by a group of deaf Nicaraguan children who had no experience of a recognized language. When the children, who were all deaf, were put together as a group they developed their own sign language. This illustrates that they had collaborated to design a way of communicating with each other. Furthermore, they taught the language to new members of the group (**Senghas & Coppola, 2011**).

Piaget, a key developmental theorist (see page 294), focused upon the interaction between the child and their physical environment in his work, but he did acknowledge that peers were influential in **cognitive development**. Vygotsky also argued that peers could enhance learning of the child; when their skills or language were superior, they would act as tutor (**Stepanović, 2010**).

A key theoretical explanation for how peers affect the learning of individuals is social learning theory. This theory, developed by Bandura, explains the role of others, including peers, in learning; it is covered in more depth in Chapter 3, 'Sociocultural approach to understanding behaviour' on page 103. Throughout our lifespan we will observe the behaviour of others and, if the behaviour appears to have rewarding outcomes, then we are more likely to imitate it, especially if we see the person as a **role model**. There are mediating factors at the cognitive level such as retaining the memory of the behaviour and the ability to act that way, but Bandura argued that social learning was a powerful tool for development in an individual.

Cognitive development – the process by which thought and perception develops in an individual.

Role model – an individual looked to by others as someone to imitate.

LINK TO THE COGNITIVE EXPLANATION

Social learning is a sociocultural theory as it is social cognitive; that is, affected by others in our environment. However, it should be acknowledged that it does have cognitive elements.

◼ Research

- **Topping & Trickey (2007)** considered how peer learning in education can help the academic development of students across all ages. When reviewing the literature, he noted that the benefits to the learner are well documented, but also that the beneficial effect on the peer teaching should be noted. These are not just cognitive gains, but social gains too. This illustrates that the influence of peers is not one way in interactions and that it can be beneficial for both parties.

- **Azmitia & Hesser (1993)** examined the effectiveness of siblings and peers in helping the cognitive development of a younger child. They gave a toy-windmill-building task to older peers and older siblings with a younger child and compared the extent to which the younger child learned from the older child and the interactions between the two. The researchers found that the child was more likely to watch and follow guidance from an older sibling and also that the older siblings were more likely to help the younger child without prompting. This suggests that while peers can play a part in cognitive development, the role of siblings seems more influential in that regard. The research also highlights the role of social learning in competence for a task. The young children observed their siblings who were powerful role models and focused upon how they completed the task. This effect was not so strong with peers, but present nonetheless.

- **Ribeiro et al. (2017)** examined the language development of 539 children in Norwegian preschool child care provision. They looked at the quality of language that the individuals encountered in their peer group and how that seemed to affect development. Their results showed that the better the quality of the language in peer groups, the more advanced the development of the children. The researchers argue that the development in all children should be considered to raise the proficiency level in the whole group, rather than just concentrate on the children who were struggling, as the influence of the peer group was powerful. The effect was also more influential for children coming from a home life where the mothers were less educated. It seems as though peer influence can compensate for environments that are less helpful for cognitive development.

Influence of peers on social development

There is evidence to suggest that interactions with peers can influence the development of 'theory of mind'. This is an ability to understand someone's perspective, and that it is different from one's own perspective. Children develop this thinking skill at about three years old. By playing and interacting with other children, an individual will start the process of developing an understanding of others. This emphasis of peer interaction seems to increase with age.

▆ Research

■ Work by the researcher Judith Rich Harris emphasizes the shift to greater peer influence on individuals. In her book *The nurture assumption* she argues against the emphasis on parental influence in the environment, stating that much of the evidence of parental influence can be accounted for by genetic, rather than environmental, influences. Harris argues that it is peers that exact the greater influence, especially as the child moves into adolescence. She argues that it is the membership of a peer group, rather than a one-to-one parent–child relationship, that is responsible for the socialization of an individual (**Harris, 1995**).

■ **Brown et al. (1996)** found, when recording children's talk about mental states (i.e. feelings), that it was initially with parents then shifted to being more frequent with peers (at around four years old). This means that the role of peers in **social development** seems to increase as the child gets older.

■ Peers can help with psychological social development in later years as young adults. Using peers to teach in college settings was shown by **Hanson et al. (2016)** to enhance the well-being in students who were given peer-learning provision during their degree courses. It seems that the effect of peers in terms of social development stretches into adulthood too.

■ **Brooks et al. (2015)** researched how peer interaction could help the social development of children with poor intellectual cognitive development. They found that unstructured social activities helped all children, both those with typical cognitive development, and those with atypical cognitive development. However, the effect was greater for those with atypical intellectual abilities. This shows the power that peer interaction can have for all but that it can be particularly helpful for children struggling with other areas of development.

> **Social development** – the process by which interaction with and understanding of others develops in an individual.

▆ Evaluation

■ There is considerable overlap between cognitive and social development influence. Interaction from peers can mean enhanced language, which may in turn enhance understanding of feelings generally. This is hard to categorize as either cognitive or social. However, generally it is acknowledged that peer influence enhances both and that they are often connected.

■ Most research suggests the positive influence of peers for both social and cognitive development. However, research also suggests that it is particularly helpful for children who are disadvantaged through their home life or intellectually. This suggests that it can compensate for disadvantage and reduce the effects of other unhelpful factors.

▆ Role of play

Article 31 (Leisure, play and culture) of the Convention of the Rights of the Child (Unicef, 1989) outlines play as a right of every child.

It states that:

> *'Children have the right to relax and play, and to join in a wide range of cultural, artistic and other recreational activities.'*

This emphasis on the need to play has highlighted just how important it is to child development. This section will consider how it affects both cognitive and social development. The repercussions for policy are great. If play is considered to be a major influence in child development then there should be provision for all; and the educational system needs to take play into account, possibly by considering the optimal age for starting formal education and the type of activities needed in the classroom.

There are several types of play, which include locomotor play (physical movement), social play (interactions with others, which could include parents or other children), parallel play (when two children play alongside each other and observe what the other child is doing, or rough and tumble play), object play (playing with objects such as bricks) and language play (non-necessary talking to oneself or others). Pretend play, in children aged 15 months and over, also allows children a way in which to develop and use their imagination. All these types of play are helpful to the development of the child in different ways and facilitate cognitive and social development.

■ **Figure 6.1** An example of parallel play

PSYCHOLOGY IN THE REAL WORLD

The Batman Effect is a strategy used by teachers to help children to develop the skills to concentrate and therefore work for longer on a task. By pretending to be Batman while they are tackling a new task, children seem to be more likely to engage and persevere. **White & Carlson (2016)** examined the use of this strategy and found that four to six-year-old children were more likely to stick to a cognitive task than divert their attention to an exciting computer game if they pretended to be Batman, or a similar role model. This is a good example of how pretend play can help to foster skills.

Influence of play on cognitive development

Understanding of the world

Jean Piaget, whose ideas will be given in more detail in the cognitive development section of this chapter (see page 294), argues in his theory of child development (**Piaget, 1932**) that a child will develop cognitively through their interaction with the environment. This includes play, which allows a child to construct and test ideas about their environment through mental structures. These structures are either Functional (solid, unchanging knowledge) or Variant (ideas that could be refined through discovery and experience). Play therefore was seen as pivotal for building an idea of how the world worked and a way of testing (and revising) those ideas that had been formed. An example of this would be the idea that a tall thin container filled with 500 ml of water has more water in it than a shorter fatter container with the same quantity of water. Children aged four will believe this to be the case, and through object play with water in the primary classroom, or bath, they will start to realize that because it looks as though the water level is higher in the tall container, this is not the case. This understanding that appearance does not affect mass/volume or number is called conservation. Play facilitates the acquisition of this kind of knowledge.

Creativity

Creativity in its broadest sense is the process of producing original ideas in both art forms and in problem-solving. Play is argued to facilitate creativity in children as they are able to test ways of solving problems through object play, and, if the problem is about managing others, social play or pretend play can help resolve issues and give a potential way to deal with a problematic situation.

■ Research

- **Howard-Jones *et al.* (2010)** looked at whether unstructured play and creativity were linked. Fifty-two children aged 6–7 years old were put into two groups: structured activity and free play. The structured group were asked to copy out some text and the free play group were given some modelling dough to play with. Then both groups were given the same creativity task: producing a collage. A couple of days later the groups were reversed and had the same creativity task to complete. Creativity on the collage task was judged by ten independent judges. The results showed that when children were given the free play dough task they scored as more creative. This shows a clear relationship between creativity and free play, while controlling for individual differences in creativity.

- **Pellis & Pellis (2007)** raised two sets of rats from birth. One set of rats was allowed to play fight and the other group was prevented from doing so. Both groups had normal interactions with adult rats. The rats' brains were examined post-mortem. Researchers found that rats raised without play showed a less developed pattern of neurons in the prefrontal cortex than did rats who had been allowed to play. This suggests that there is a direct relationship between play and brain development and, in turn, this indicates that there are most likely cognitive advantages to play in non-human animals.

- **Lillard *et al.* (2013)** looked at the effectiveness of pretend play in helping development. In terms of language acquisition, executive function, conservation, intelligence and creativity the researchers found that there was a relationship between the time spent in pretend play and the level of advancement, but they argued that causation could not be established. There is a possibility that the cognitive skills facilitate pretend play, rather than the other way around.

Influence of play on social development

Emotional security is thought to be enhanced by pretend play specifically. This is because playing imaginatively, with dolls, for example, means that a child can work through any situations they may be worried about. For example, a child may be witnessing parents arguing or someone in the house being ill, and pretend play means they can think about the situation but they can do this by taking a step away from experiencing the situation themselves.

Theory of mind

Theory of mind (ToM) is the ability to understand the world or a situation from someone else's perspective. This is discussed in more detail later in the chapter, on page 292. It has been suggested, relatively recently, that play facilitates the development of this cognitive skill. Traditionally, ToM is developed around the age of three or four years old. Prior to successful development of the skill, theorists argue that social play is important as children can role play and they can think about what the other child/adult must do within the role play. As this is different from their role, it helps them to think about another person's perspective and actions.

TOK link

ToM facilitates social interaction because it helps the individual to understand other people. However, it is a thought process and, as such, bridges social and cognitive development. This means that it can be used as evidence in both cognitive and social development.

Research

- **Lillard (1993)** examined the relationship between pretend play and ToM, by reviewing research. She found that there appeared to be three reasons why the two were connected: the ability to see one object as representing another, the ability to represent one object as two things at once, and finally the ability to represent mental representations. These were key to helping develop ToM because the skill is all about looking from different perspectives.

- In work conducted by **Schwebel *et al.* (1999)** researchers found that frequency of parallel play was related to false belief (the underpinning skill behind acquiring ToM). The skill was not as well developed in children who preferred solitary play. This suggests that there is a relationship between time spent in parallel and social play and development of ToM, and it emphasizes the need for these kinds of play.

- **Pellis *et al.* (2010)** found that social development was facilitated by rough and tumble play in rats. They found that there was a relationship between the amount of time spent playing as young rats and how socially competent they are as adult rats. The researchers also went further in that they suggested that the play helped maturation of the brain, and that the facilitation of social skills was due to the brain developing at a quicker rate.

Evaluation

- The argument that social play facilitates development of ToM is not well supported by research evidence (**Smith, 2005**). The explanation itself seems to make sense, and it is entirely possible that play facilitates development, but it seems more likely to be one way of many that the skill develops. ToM can develop without lots of social play, so play is not a pivotal influence.

- A distinction needs to be made between free play and structured play (i.e. with an adult). Theorists argue that a combination of both is optimal for development. Structured play often means the environment is enriched with play-appropriate toys, and this enhances the benefits of play. However, free play is important too. Without it, the child will not have the opportunity to discover their environment and test their theories as suggested by Piaget.

- Play is not always a positive influence on development. War play, which means acting in an aggressive and/or violent way to others, and re-enactment of war-like situations is not thought to be good for all instances. In some ways it will allow children to role play, which has its advantages, but there are psychologists who argue that it is a negative influence on hard-to-manage children. It is shown to be linked to more anti-social behaviour generally and less empathic understanding (**Dunn and Hughes, 2001**). Rough and tumble play is also seen to be a negative influence in that it can become an actual fight. This is especially the case in children who lack social skills. It should be noted, however, that it develops into a fight in only about 1 per cent of cases (**Pellegrini, 2009**).

- The different types of play seem to help facilitate development in different areas. Social play will influence cognitive development in terms of language learning and understanding others, but other types of play may be more appropriate to develop other skills. This distinction is important and therefore provision for the differing types of play should be made in educational settings.

Strengthen your learning

1 Outline the influence of peers on:
   a cognitive development
   b social development.

2 Summarize what research studies have suggested about the influence of peers on cognitive and social development.

3 What other evaluative points can be made about the influence of peers on cognitive and social development?

4 Explain how play can influence:
   a cognitive development
   b social development.

5 Summarize what research studies have suggested about the influence of play on cognitive and social development.

6 What other evaluative points can be made about the influence of peers on cognitive and social development?

■ Childhood trauma and resilience

IN THE NEWS

Ψ The Psychological Enquirer

LEARNING TO LIVE WITH MULTIPLE PERSONALITIES

■ **Figure 6.2** Dissociative Identity Disorder involves the experience of multiple personalities within one body

At 40 years old, a family event gave Melanie Goodwin insight into her own problems. Until that time, she could not recall anything about the first 16 years of her life. Following the family tragedy, she became aware of multiple identities being present inside her that ranged from a 3 year old to a 16 year old, and she had more than one adult personality too. Clinicians diagnosed Melanie with Dissociative Identity Disorder (DID).

Melanie's identities switch regularly, often on a moment-by-moment basis. She describes packing to go away as difficult because the various personalities have differing tastes and needs in clothing. Inevitably, she says she has to take more than one bag of clothes to keep them all happy. Melanie does work at a local library, but the only way she can do this, she reports, is to bargain with the childlike identities to let the adult personalities be in charge during the working day on the understanding they will have time to emerge in the evening. She is married, and her husband understands her condition and helps her to deal with it. It is not easy for either of them. She has an identity that is anorexic, one that is flirty, one that is anxious and one that has attempted suicide twice, along with the childlike personalities.

Through therapy it has become apparent that the identities formed following childhood trauma, specifically child abuse. The first instance was at the age of three and that is why she and her clinicians believe the youngest identity is three years old.

DID is argued to be a way of dealing and coping with childhood trauma. The various identities have different roles: one experiences the trauma and then the other identities take over, as such, to help the individual escape the abuse and then another to act as if it has not happened. This coping method is argued to occur in cases when there is no healthy, normal attachment to a parent or other adult. DID is relatively rare. DSM-V, the 'Diagnostic and statistical manual of mental disorders', states that many of the cases report:

> 'dissociative flashbacks during which they undergo a sense of reliving of a previous event as though it were occurring in the present, often with a change of identity, a partial or complete loss of contact with or disorientation to current reality during the flashback, and a subsequent amnesia for the content of the flashback. Individuals with the disorder typically report multiple types of interpersonal maltreatment during childhood and adulthood' (p.294)

The prevalence rate is reported as 1.5 per cent.

This is an extreme version of reaction to childhood trauma, but it does illustrate the pervasive effect it can have on an individual.

Trauma

Trauma can describe a physical injury, but, in the context of this book, the focus will be on psychological trauma. Childhood abuse, a distressing incident, and being witness to violence in the home are all traumas. It can also be brought about by a one-off traumatic event. They are often called Adverse Childhood Experiences (ACEs).

The potential effects of trauma are multiple. Some individuals do not suffer ill effects, and this is one element of resilience, which will be discussed in the next section in this chapter. However, many can experience increased anxiety, addictive behaviour/substance abuse, and somatic problems, including disordered sleep and weight problems. These will be outlined below, though it should be noted that there are other effects too.

Increased anxiety

Post-traumatic stress disorder (PTSD) can occur in cases of trauma. Sufferers experience flashbacks and nightmares and find that they relive the trauma again and again. The flashbacks can be triggered by sounds, smells and other sensory input. To cope, sufferers often keep themselves busy so that they can avoid and numb the feelings they are experiencing. They often find that they are hypervigilant, which means they are in a state of tension looking for triggers, which makes relaxation difficult. There are also somatic (physical) effects such as aching muscles. PTSD is thought to occur in instances of sudden, prolonged and man-made traumas.

Addictive behaviour/substance abuse

One effect of PTSD is an increased likelihood of heavy drinking (of alcohol) and drug use. These are not always illegal drugs and addiction to painkillers can occur as a consequence of PTSD. Considering the fact that there is physical pain associated with the condition, the need for painkillers is an understandable byproduct.

Somatic problems

Children who experience childhood trauma appear to be more likely to be obese when adults. This could be connected to comfort or emotional eating, a desire to put up a barrier to sexual attention, or indeed to be more visible. There is also the possibility that the individual is disassociated from their body and therefore cannot read the cues of appetite regulation that someone who has not experienced trauma receives. Sleep disorders can also be experienced by those recovering from childhood trauma. These sleep problems do not only occur in children, but also into adulthood. This disturbance may be as a method of staying alert to avoid abuse or because of the high anxiety that traumatic incidences provoke.

KEY STUDY   ## CLASSIC RESEARCH

*'Relationship of childhood abuse and household dysfunction
to many of the leading causes of death in adults'*
Felitti *et al.* (1998)

This study looks at the effect of trauma on later life in terms of health and relationships. The focus is on long-term effects in the individual.

Aim
From 1995 to 1997 a large-scale study, nicknamed the ACEs study, was conducted which aimed to look at the relationship between trauma experienced as a child and later long-term effects.

Procedure
1   The researchers administered a questionnaire to 13,494 adults asking about seven types of Adverse Childhood Experiences (psychological, physical, or sexual abuse; violence against mother; or living with household members who were substance abusers, mentally ill or suicidal, or ever imprisoned).

2 They then also administered measures which covered health risk factors, current health and disease.

Results
The results were disturbing. They found that:

1 More than 50 per cent of participants had experienced one adverse childhood experience and around 25 per cent reported experiencing two or more events.

2 The number of ACEs and risky behaviours were closely related, with the correlation being highly significant.

3 Participants who had four or more reported ACEs were more sexually promiscuous (with more than 50 sexual partners), less likely to exercise and had increased health risks in terms of alcoholism, drug abuse, depression and suicide attempts, when compared to participants who had not experienced any trauma. The seven types of trauma were all related to risk factors. Individuals who had experienced more than one type of trauma were at greater risk of early death.

Conclusions
The researchers urged that a greater amount of research needed to be conducted. They also highlighted that the potentially difficult topic matter meant that practitioners such as doctors did not feel comfortable discussing the subject. Many treatments were reactive rather than preventative.

Evaluation
This study prompted a great deal of follow-up research and was one of the first to show the strength of the relationship between childhood trauma and adverse psychological and physical health effects.

◼ Research

- The National Child Traumatic Stress Network (USA) (**Dierkhising *et al.*, 2013**) conducted a review of adolescent trauma and substance abuse. They found that individuals who had experienced abuse or assault were three times more likely to report ongoing or previous substance abuse than those who had not experienced trauma. They also found that 70 per cent of adolescents attending substance abuse treatment programmes had experienced ACEs.

- Research conducted by **Danese & Tan (2014)** examined, using a meta-analysis, the relationship between obesity and ACEs. They found a complicated relationship and some instances where there was no connection, but they did conclude that suffering bad treatment as a child was a risk factor for obesity. They also felt that it was something that could be treated, but urged for more research into why the two were connected. This ultimately would help to design effective treatment plans.

- **Greenfield *et al.* (2011)** examined the extent to which adults were affected by ACEs. They found that childhood abuse was related to sleep pathologies, even if the abuse was only once, or infrequent. Frequent occurrences were strongly associated with poor sleep. The correlation coefficients found for all components of sleep such as quality, sleep disturbances, duration, and use of medication were all statistically significant, showing that there was a strong relationship between the frequency of ACEs and sleep problems.

- Researchers looked at the relationship between early childhood trauma and PTSD. **Powers *et al.* (2016)** used questionnaires with 328 participants to measure PTSD, psychotic disorders and level of childhood trauma and found that there was a close association between the amount of childhood trauma experienced by participants and both PTSD symptoms and psychotic episodes. This shows how early childhood trauma can lead to later mental health problems in adulthood.

Evaluation

- The strong relationships between trauma and adverse effects would suggest causation. However, as most research is correlational, causation is not clear. Given that the occurrences are in childhood, this would suggest that the behaviours did not prompt the ACEs and that a causal direction can be made in the other direction. **Whitfield *et al.* (2006)** conducted research into neurophysiological effects from trauma, which could then explain subsequent effects. He identified areas of the brain that were developmentally different in adults who had experienced trauma and suggested how those might have a behavioural effect. This goes some way to establishing causation. It also highlighted that there could be a biological underpinning to the behaviour.

- One effect highlighted by practitioners who work with sufferers of childhood trauma is an issue with cognitive processing. This manifests itself in some individuals as a problem with memory. The DSM-V documents in its diagnostic criteria for PTSD that there could be issues with remembering trauma, so it is widely acknowledged that the detail and frequency of events may be unreliable. This means the data collected for studies looking for a relationship may not be accurate. Retrospective memory recall is notoriously inaccurate. This is another reason why data accuracy may be low. This, together with the fallibility of testimony in children, means that both childhood and adulthood recall of trauma is affected.

- Trauma is difficult to discuss and measure. By researching, and asking participants to recall events, there are many potential ethical issues. These are monitored closely by the research ethics process. However, sometimes it is not possible to anticipate the effects of recall, and, depending on how someone with trauma deals with it, the process of recall could jeopardize their recovery.

YOU ARE THE RESEARCHER

You have been asked to examine the relationship between substance abuse and childhood trauma in 18- to 25-year-olds. You will do this by using questionnaires designed to ascertain the frequency of trauma and the level of substance abuse.

What are the ethical issues you must consider with any research conducted?

PSYCHOLOGY IN THE REAL WORLD

Treating trauma... the use of Eye Movement Desensitization and Re-processing (EMDR)

EMDR is currently being used to treat trauma, especially in those people diagnosed with PTSD. It involves moving your eyes from side to side, following a therapist's finger, while you record a traumatic event. Sometimes the therapist may ask you to make the side-to-side eye movements while they play a tone or tap their finger. They then try to replace the negative experience of the trauma with more positive thoughts. The therapy was conceived by an American therapist called Francine Shapiro in 1987, after taking a walk through some woods to give herself a break and to process some unpleasant thoughts. By looking backwards and forwards across the woodland scene, she found she felt a lot better. She then encouraged some of her clients to use rhythmic eye movement in therapy sessions and they too started to feel better. EMDR therapy stemmed from her work published in 1989.

It is thought to work by desensitizing the individual to the memory of the trauma and reducing its impact. It could also be that the eye movements mimic those in REM (or dream) sleep, giving the memory a less anxiety-inducing dream-like quality. Other theorists have suggested it works as it helps communication between the hemispheres, which decreases emotionality. The working memory is also thought to be implicated, as it asks the individual to complete two tasks (eye movement and recall) thus reducing the impact and emotionality of the memory.

Its advantages are that it works well across all cultures, is cost-effective, non-invasive and evidence based. Therapists are also increasingly using it with children as a method to reduce the impact of traumatic memories. Studies have shown it is effective in treating trauma (specifically those with a diagnosis of PTSD) and is especially so when compared to doing nothing or using some other methods (**Rodenburg *et al.*, 2009**) and there are now over 60,000 therapists who are trained to use it. However, the absence of any definitive explanation on how it works can make some practitioners, and clients, suspicious.

Resilience

....

Resilience – a characteristic that allows an individual to recover quickly and successfully from difficulties.

....

Resilience is defined by the Oxford dictionary as 'the capability to recover quickly from difficulties; toughness'. Other words such as 'grit' are also used to describe a similar construct. Resilience is an attribute which seems to be present in different levels in individuals. It is a measure of the extent to which an individual can cope and keep going when life has adverse events to deal with.

Measures of resilience are centred mainly on questionnaire methodology. Many measures have been developed for a variety of target populations. In a review of 19 resilience measures, **Windle et al. (2011)** established that, at that point in time, there were five questionnaires that had been tested sufficiently, as many of them were relatively new. The construct itself has only been the focus of a wealth of research in the past 15 years, although clearly it has been evident.

The types of items you would expect to see on a resilience measure are as follows:

1 I can usually look at a situation in a number of ways.

2 I am determined.

3 My life has meaning.

The resilience scale is designed to measure resilience in children aged 12 to 13 years. Those taking the measure would be expected to respond on the extent to which they agreed with the statement.

The report highlighted that cross-culturally there are issues with defining the construct, as many other cultures have words to describe a similar attribute. However, some of the measures have been translated into as many as 36 languages, so work is progressing on this aspect.

Interventions to strengthen resilience

Resilience research is very much focused upon building resilience in the population, particularly the student population. There are resources and interventions designed for such a purpose. Often they start at the level that focuses upon meeting challenge in the classroom. The idea is that this will transfer to meeting the challenges of life.

Educational interventions for resilience are becoming more widely used and these focus upon ensuring that children are prepared to persevere when meeting a challenge.

Dr Judy Willis, a neurologist and teacher, advocates a growth mindset when learning. The child should believe they can improve, which means they can feel competent and are then confident to keep learning. She also advocates failure and learning from it, together with seeing the personal relevance in learning. She states:

'By building students' resilience in this way you can help them realize that when they engage confidently with a challenge, anything is possible and failure is not something to fear. This is vitally important.'

Teachers have many resources available to them to help foster resilience. This is widespread across many countries. In 2008, 12 recommendations were published for teachers to build resilience in the classroom. These clustered under teacher–student rapport (developing strong student–teacher relationships), classroom climate (a classroom with a growth mindset, clear expectations, and a caring classroom), instructional strategies (promoting cooperation and peer teaching), and student skills (teaching life skills, extracurricular activities and effective literacy skills). This indicates that resilience can potentially be taught throughout childhood to help 'inoculate' a child against future problems and difficulties in both childhood and adulthood.

▓ Research

- ■ **Hines (2015)** conducted a meta-synthesis of 17 studies published between 1991 and 2012 on successful coping strategies used by children when they have experienced family violence. A meta-synthesis was conducted, as it was a way of pulling all the strategies together to ascertain themes. Themes identified included cultivating support and hope for the future. Resilience was identified by Hines as being key to coping with an adverse home environment, and she advocated resilience teaching being incorporated into interventions by service providers, such as social workers. This illustrates the importance of resilience in very different threatening conditions for children and how it can help them cope with being in such an environment.

- **Lin *et al.* (2014)** examined the relationship between suicidality and resilience. They found that the two factors appeared to be related throughout the lifespan, but the relationship was more complex than anticipated. In their data they found that there were other factors, such as level of social support, which increased suicidality to a greater extent and reduced the apparent relationship between resilience and suicidality once they were controlled for in the analysis. However, looking across the lifespan, the mid-life group (aged 48 to 52 years) continued to show that low resilience levels were related to thoughts about suicide. This suggests not only that the two are linked, but also that resilience varies across the lifespan.

- Resilience interventions are being widely used to try and 'inoculate' children against the negative events they may encounter in their life. One such intervention was assessed for effectiveness in children and adolescents by **Allen *et al.* (2016)**. They found that post-intervention participants reported that they felt more confident in being able to cope with problems. Parents, too, reported a behavioural effect of the intervention in children, with their stating there was a lower number of emotional and behavioural difficulties. However, this was not the case for adolescents who had received the intervention. This was explained by the researchers as being due to younger children being more 'malleable' and therefore more likely to take on the ideas the intervention taught. This means that resilience education is probably best delivered to the younger children, as they will be more likely to learn resilient behaviour. They also will benefit from it for longer and it could potentially reduce some of the factors that predispose an individual to problems in adolescence.

Evaluation

- Measures of resilience are almost always questionnaire-based. One of the key issues with this is the biased self-reporting associated with the methodology. In relation to resilience specifically, this can be altered by the situation or context that the participant is in. For example, if they are in a particularly difficult point of their life, they may feel that they do not cope as well as they generally do because they are struggling at that point. This means that the resilience level may be artificially low. However, there seems to be little other alternative in terms of methodology, as the construct is a general attribute and, as such, needs to be measured taking an overall perspective of life experience. The individual elements such as perseverance can be measured in a lab context, for example, but when combining elements, lab-based observations and tasks are not particularly helpful.

- The construct is argued to be made up of many different components. Currently there is no consensus of opinion about what the construct of resilience contains. Suggestions include hope, optimism and perseverance; however, not all measures include items for these constructs. The absence of a 'gold standard' for a definition of what resilience actually is means that research comparing studies needs to be treated with caution, as it may not be comparing like with like.

- Resilience is recognized as a construct globally. Other cultures recognize the role of resilience in well-being and coping with trauma. A concept called 'sisu' is part of Finnish culture and is part of the national character of Finland. Sisu is described as grit, bravery and hardiness. There is no direct translation into English but the closest translation is resilience. This shows that the characteristic is recognized cross-culturally and is key in combatting the effects of trauma.

Strengthen your learning

1 Explain what is meant by trauma.

2 Explain how the following can occur as a result of trauma:
   a anxiety
   b addictive behaviour/substance abuse
   c somatic problems.

3 For Fellitti *et al.*'s classic 1998 study of the effects of trauma in early life upon later health and relationships, in your own words, state the:
   a aims
   b procedure
   c results
   d conclusions
   e evaluative points.

4 Summarize what research has suggested about childhood trauma.

5 What other evaluative points can be made about childhood trauma?

6 What is resilience and how is it measured?

7 Outline interventions designed to strengthen resilience.

8 Summarize what research has suggested about interventions designed to strengthen resilience.

9 What other evaluative points can be made about interventions designed to strengthen resilience?

Poverty/socio-economic status

Figures on **poverty** suggest that one in four children in the UK live below the poverty threshold today. Psychologists have worked to establish the possible effects on child development that living in such circumstances could bring about.

The Child Poverty Action Group in the UK defines poverty as 60 per cent or less of the median income in the country. Other countries calculate their child poverty figures a different way. However, it cannot be disputed that children growing up in poverty will have a difficult childhood, with many potential consequences of their situation.

The Child Poverty Action Group focuses upon three areas in life where effects occur and influence the child's development: education, health and communities. This section will consider the potential effects in each of those domains and the evidence for the effects.

> **Poverty** – a lack of resources and means to be able to meet personal needs. People who are in poverty have low socio-economic status.

Education

Statistics consistently show that children growing up in poverty are disadvantaged in terms of educational progress. At three years old, children of low socio-economic status families lag nine months behind in developmental terms. By 14 years old they are, in terms of educational levels, five terms behind (three terms are a year, so this shows almost two years' less progress). Children on free school meals (which are provided for children from low-income households) also attain lower grades at school. In GCSEs it has been shown that they average 1.7 grades lower than their wealthier peers.

This is explained by some as due to poorer attendance, and figures do show that children from poorer backgrounds have a poorer attendance level. The absence of teaching will impinge on their ability to learn new information and they can fall behind in terms of progress quite quickly if their attendance is poor.

There is also the argument that the quality of their home life is not conducive to learning. For example, there are no books available within the home, their parents do not or cannot read and the level of stimulation is low. This is most certainly not the case for many low-income households, as parents do their best in the circumstances, but for some children the poverty of stimulus in the child's environment, which goes alongside poverty itself, is influential in poor progress.

A few parents also do not value education in the same way as many households, so the child is not encouraged to read or study. Working hard at school is not reinforced. The parents do not provide a positive role model in terms of education, and therefore the child is not encouraged to learn. This too can serve to inhibit progress.

Living in a poor neighbourhood can work against a child trying to learn for lots of different reasons. Economic instability, stress and daily risk all supersede education as a priority and, given that children in poor environments tend to have raised levels of cortisol because of stress, elevated blood pressure and adrenaline levels, the difficulty of every day for a child in such an environment is apparent. Children are often hungry if they live in a poor household and to eat is a priority above all else.

Health

Sadly, evidence suggests that living in poverty is likely to affect an individual's health adversely. This has a clear effect on development. At birth, children of low-income families weigh less than average, are more likely to be born prematurely, and more likely to die at birth. Similarly, the lifespan of someone living in poverty is less than someone who is not. There is a greater incidence of disability and chronic illness in children living in low socio-economic households.

The World Health Organization explains these health effects on its website, stating:

> '*Poverty creates ill health because it forces people to live in environments that make them sick, without decent shelter, clean water or adequate sanitation.*'

In terms of child development, poor health affects attendance in school, brain development and cognitive impairment. All these have far reaching implications for the future of the child and how they can cope with the environment they grow up in.

Healthy brain development is very influential in the ability of a child to develop along a typical development trajectory. If the home life of a child is affected by a lack of resources, such as experienced by children in poverty, then the important needs of the child for healthy brain development are not met. When this occurs children's brains may suffer from insufficient production of new brain cells, the brain may not therefore follow the healthy trajectory of maturation, and the circuitry will be affected. This will affect not only their cognitive development, but also their social development too. This will mean that their ability to function in the classroom and social environments is diminished, because they will struggle to process information and to regulate their emotions.

Communities

There are many potential effects of growing up in poverty for a child. Two key effects are safety and less opportunity to play.

Feeling safe is argued by many theorists, such as Maslow, to be an important motivator. Maslow's Hierarchy of Needs theory, developed in the 1940s, stated that there was a hierarchy of needs that formed the basis of motivation. This is illustrated in Figure 6.3.

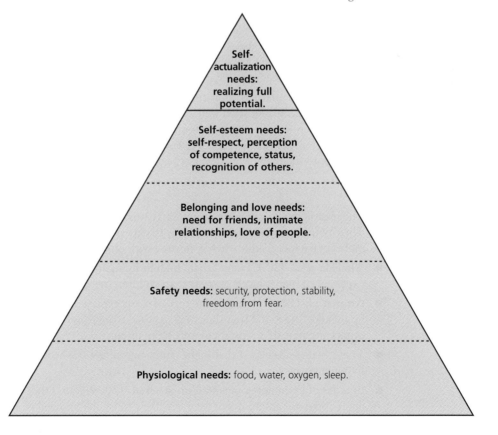

■ **Figure 6.3** Maslow's hierarchy of needs

Maslow stated that the initial needs that need to be met for an individual are physiological: food, sleep, water. If these are not met, and the person is hungry, then they will be motivated to satisfy that hunger above all else. Once the physiological needs are met then Maslow stated that the second level on the hierarchy of motivation is safety. The need to feel you are safe dominates the thought until you are in a position of safety. That stage, if achieved, is then followed by a sense of belonging and being loved, then self-esteem, and then finally you reach the pinnacle of optimal functioning, self-actualization. Self-actualization is not widespread in the population but if a child lives in a safe, warm environment that fulfils their needs, they will at least have a chance of reaching self-actualization. A child living in poverty will often struggle to fulfil the physiological needs and if the environment is then unsafe, either because of issues within the home, or the community, their chances of reaching optional functioning are thwarted in the earliest stages.

Opportunities for play are also decreased by living in an area of low socio-economic status. The Child Poverty Action Group in the UK highlights that vandalism, playground misuse and danger of injury are all potential threats to using play facilities appropriately. There are often more play facilities available in deprived areas, but there are also more potential problems with using that area. The importance of play for a child's development is outlined on page 262 in this chapter and therefore, a lack of access to safe and fully functioning play areas could affect their ability to gain the benefits of play for development.

Research

Education

- Looking at the relationship between cognitive ability, performance and low-income households, in a review of evidence, **Gottfried et al. (2003)** found a significant relationship in most studies. The researchers also found that parental involvement mediated the relationship and could reverse the effects of poverty.

- **Noble et al. (2005)** were interested in looking at the relationship between cognitive skill and socio-economic status. In their study they tested the neurocognitive performance of 60 children, 30 of whom were from low-income households and 30 were from more affluent households. They were all African–American and about 4–5 years old. They found that there were overarching and specific differences in the brains of children from the two groups. These findings were also supported by **Farah et al. (2006)**, who looked at the cognitive functioning in older children. They also found differences between the two groups, similarly divided by socio-economic status.

- The emotional effects of growing up in households with a greater level of stress and how that impinges on education were examined by **Bradley & Corwyn (2002)**. They found that children in high-stress environments display higher levels of disruptive behaviour and therefore are less able to experience a positive school life. This is due, the researchers asserted, to the inability to develop healthy academic and social skills.

Health

- The mental health of children in poverty was examined by **McCoy & Reynolds (1999)**. They found that they were more likely to experience psychiatric disturbances and poor, maladaptive social skills when compared with children from wealthier households.

- **Almeida et al. (2005)** found that children living in low socio-economic households experienced higher levels of stress than children living in more affluent homes.

- **Attar et al. (1994)** looked at the type of stress experienced by children living in poorer households and found that they were exposed to a greater number of stressors and stressful events and that those instances were more intense.

- These studies all suggest that higher stress may affect the healthy development of children living in poverty.

- In terms of brain development, **Gunnar et al. (2009)** found that children who had grown up in a stressful environment were less likely to be able to regulate their emotions due to atypical brain development.

Communities

Emery & Laumann-Billings (1998) examined the level of stress experienced in communities occupied by low-income parents and found it to be high. The researchers found that this meant that negativity and low mood were witnessed by the children, and this also meant that parents were unable to parent their children as well as they might have done without the high levels of stress. They also found that there were higher levels of disruption, separation and violence within the households. This illustrates a clear relationship between the communities affected by poverty and stress levels.

▨ Evaluation

- There are examples of children raised in low socio-economic status households who manage to reverse all the potential contraindications against their development and education. The window of opportunity to do this is often seen as being in the preschool years. **Hill-Soderlund & Braungart-Rieker (2008)** agreed with the early years being important, but they also emphasized that recovery can occur later into childhood. This means that the educational environment has the opportunity to prompt change.

- Many of the effects shown in research are correlational, which means that causation cannot be proven. There does seem to be a great deal of research to demonstrate that poverty is responsible for poor development in many spheres of life, however, but proving causation is problematic.

- There are also very many differing factors that contribute to child development and establishing the main influences is difficult. The role of poverty in preventing optimal development is known, but the extent to which it is responsible is more difficult to establish.

- It is possible that the stressors of a poor home life may occur in families that are not considered to be under the poverty line. Domestic and sexual abuses are not confined to homes with poor socio-economic status at all, and it is therefore possible that vulnerable children come from rich backgrounds too. This means, in terms of research, that the comparison between children from affluent and poor households may be inaccurate.

Strengthen your learning

1 How can poverty be defined?

2 Explain the effects that poverty can have upon:
   a education
   b health
   c community.

3 Summarize what research studies have suggested about the effects that poverty can have upon:
   a education
   b health
   c community.

4 What other evaluative points can be made about the effects that poverty can have upon:
   a education
   b health
   c community?

5 How might environment affect the biological development of a child at the genetic level? (Clue: epigenetics)

SECTION SUMMARY

- Both peers and play affect the development of a child.
- Traumatic events can inhibit both the cognitive and social development of a child.
- Resilience can act as an 'inoculating' factor against trauma experienced in childhood and adulthood.
- Poverty can affect a child's development via education, health and community influences.

Developing an identity

'Nothing of me is original. I am the combined effort of everyone I've ever known.'
Chuck Palahniuk, 'Invisible Monsters'

'They fuck you up, your mum and dad.

They may not mean to, but they do.

They fill you with the faults they had

And add some extra, just for you.'
Philip Larkin, 'This Be the Verse'

Our uniqueness as an individual is all part of forming our identity. The effect our environment has on our identity formation is discussed in this section, looking particularly at our relationships with others (the attachments we form) our gender identity and the social roles we play.

FOCUS ON...

- How attachments may influence development of an identity.
- The development of gender identity and social roles.
- How developing an identity is affected by interactions with others; specifically the development of empathy and ToM.

■ Attachment

Attachment – a close emotional bond to someone or something.

Attachments made in early life are thought to be pivotal in identity development. Attachments are defined in many ways, but they are essentially an emotional bond to a specific person that is reciprocated. Much attachment research discusses and examines relationships between a child and parent, but attachments can equally be with other relatives, friends and caregivers.

Attachments are formed by early contact such as bodily contact, mimicking, communication, smiling and eye contact. There are also developmental stages with regard to attachment formation. These were documented by **Schaffer & Emerson (1964)** and ran from the pre-attachment stage at birth, where a preference for human faces is shown through indiscriminate attachment, until 7–8 months, when more specific attachments become commonplace. From the age of nine months a child will move from one key attachment figure to multiple attachments.

■ Bowlby's theory and ideas on attachment and how it can affect development of identity

A key figure in attachment research, John Bowlby argued that the attachments a child makes are vital for healthy development. He also stated that the initial attachments formed were likely to affect all subsequent relationships. At the cognitive level, the primary attachment formed early on became the schema for subsequent attachments and relationships.

Maternal deprivation hypothesis

Maternal deprivation – separation from a mother figure.

Without a sound initial attachment figure, Bowlby argued there would be effects on behaviour that would continue across the lifespan. He also argued there would be an effect on the adult personality. Bowlby named this the **maternal deprivation** hypothesis. This idea was developed in 1965 and referred to as maternal deprivation, insinuating that it was the relationship with the mother that was important. However, it was later acknowledged that being the primary caregiver was the most important aspect and this included figures other than the mother alone. **Schaffer & Emerson (1964)** found that in 39 per cent of cases where they tested babies for strength of attachment, the mother (usually the main carer) was not the baby's main attachment figure.

In most cases, Bowlby argued that if an individual receives plenty of love and care from their primary attachment figure, then they will develop strong positive attachments throughout the lifespan. Unfortunately, however, this is not always the case. If this does not happen, an individual will struggle to form good relationships for the rest of their life.

There are instances where a primary caregiver may be separated from the child for a period of time, which Bowlby described as maternal deprivation. As relationships are so important to an individual, this deprivation can have lasting effects and give a negative representation of the world, leading to their believing it to be a hostile place. This can, in turn, affect their behaviour and increase the potential for anti-social behaviour and criminality.

KEY STUDY   CLASSIC RESEARCH

'44 thieves study of maternal deprivation'
Bowlby (1944)

Many children were evacuated from their families in the Second World War to a place perceived as safer for them. Trying to establish what the effects on a child may be if they are separated from their parents was a primary focus for psychologists in war time for this and other reasons.

Aim

Bowlby's aim was to test the maternal deprivation hypothesis by looking at a delinquent population to see whether separation had been experienced. This was to examine the potential subsequent effects of that deprivation.

Procedure

1 Bowlby interviewed 44 juvenile delinquents, who had been caught stealing from a psychiatric facility (the 'thieves'), and 44 'controls', who were also at the facility but had not stolen anything (the 'controls').

2 Bowlby, as the psychiatrist, interviewed the children and mothers separately.

3 He interviewed the juveniles first to ascertain their personalities. Bowlby diagnosed affectionless psychopathy, where there was a lack of affection for, or empathy to, others. He also established whether they felt a lack of guilt or shame at their actions and that informed the diagnosis.

4 The families were interviewed to determine whether the thieves had prolonged early separations from their primary caregiver in their first two years of life.

Results

The results were as shown in Table 6.1.

Had they been involved in offending behaviour?	Yes				No	
	44 Thieves				44 Controls	
Diagnosed as affectionless psychopaths?	Yes		No		No	
	14		30		0	
Had they been separated from primary caregiver for 6+ months before the age of two?	Yes	No	Yes	No	Yes	No
	12	2	5	25	2	42

■ **Table 6.1** Bowlby's 44 thieves study of maternal deprivation (1944)

Conclusions

The results seem to indicate that:

1 If a child has experienced early separation from the primary caregiver for more than six months then the chance that they will become delinquent is greater.

2 If a child has experienced early separation from the primary caregiver for more than six months then they are more likely to be affectionless psychopaths.

Bowlby drew conclusions that the maternal deprivation can, to some extent, explain offending behaviour.

Evaluation

This study was influential and supports the view that there are effects of separation from a primary caregiver, but has been heavily criticized for its methodology and potential bias.

Internal working model

Another key element of Bowlby's research on attachments was the idea that attachments formed early on influenced all subsequent attachments. This occurred at the cognitive level. Most babies will follow a typical stage-by-stage approach to attachment formation, but as they age the attachment will become more personalized between the two people, and this uniqueness underpins identity formation. Bowlby argued that the primary attachment was unique: it is the first to develop and the strongest of all, forming a model for relationships, which the infant will expect from others. In cognitive terms it forms a schema. Subsequent attachments are based upon this schema and this emphasizes the importance of the first attachment formed.

Critical period

Critical period – a time restricted opportunity for development of a skill or characteristic.

Bowlby also argued that the window of opportunity for forming initial attachments was limited. Much of the work to suggest this came from animal studies. Research suggested to Bowlby that there is a **critical period** for the formation of attachments, where attachment behaviours between infant and carer must occur within a certain time period if children are to form attachments. He saw attachment behaviours as useless for most children if delayed until after 12 months and useless for all children if delayed until after two and a half to three years. This has clear potential effects on the identity of an individual and it seems likely that if the critical period is missed the effects will be lifelong.

TOK link

The idea of a critical period has changed over time. **Sluckin *et al.* (1966)** questioned whether there actually was a critical period, a set time period in which imprinting must occur or it never would do so. Performing a replication of Lorenz's famous study (see next page), but using ducklings instead of goslings, he successfully imprinted them onto himself, but kept one duckling in isolation well beyond Lorenz's reported critical period (up to five days). He found it was still possible to imprint this youngster and concluded that the critical period was actually a sensitive period, a time period best for imprinting to perform, but one beyond which attachments could still be formed. This led to Bowlby changing his idea to one called a 'sensitive period'. This illustrates the changing nature of theory and how it is necessary to assimilate subsequent research findings into a theory.

Research

■ **Lorenz (1935)** found that certain animals have an innate tendency to respond immediately to parents (or who they believe to be their parent). If, for example, a gosling sees a human keeper prior to their mother, then the gosling will form an attachment with that human. This is exactly what happened with Konrad Lorenz, as a group of baby goslings imprinted onto him. This suggests that such innate 'pre-programming' provides an evolutionary advantage, as by staying close to such individuals newborn animals are safer from predators and environmental danger. This also suggests that a critical period is likely, as for attachment to have an evolutionary advantage the formation must occur early on.

■ **Schaffer & Emerson (1964)** found that multiple attachments are the norm. This suggests that the emphasis on the primary attachment may be misplaced. The research found that 39 per cent of children had their main attachment to someone other than the main carer. It is possible therefore that it is the formation of attachments that is important to the formation of identity and not specifically the primary attachment.

■ **Lamb *et al.* (1982)** studied the attachments that infants had with people like fathers, grandparents and siblings and found that infants had different attachments for different purposes, rather than attachments being a hierarchy. For example, infants go to fathers for play, but mothers for comfort. This suggests that multiple attachments are a more holistic way to develop an identity and that variety in attachments is important to this end.

■ **Hazan & Shaver (1987)** conducted some research examining Bowlby's idea that attachment type will continue on from childhood and throughout life, due to the **internal working model**. They published a 'love quiz' in a newspaper that asked about attachments from childhood and attachments now. They then classified the responses along the lines of the attachment type outlined by Ainsworth (see below). When comparing the childhood attachment style to the adult relationship style they found the two were indeed related. This supports the idea that early attachment style has a long-lasting effect on the behaviour of an individual and this could be due to schema formation.

Internal working model – an internal schema, or idea, that is formed through experience as a blue print for attachment style.

Evaluation of Bowlby's ideas

■ Care should be taken in extrapolating animal research to human behaviour. The reliance that human babies have on their mothers, owing to the fact that they are not mobile, will mean that their attachments fulfil a different need to those of animals who are more mobile at birth. Human babies are potentially much more reliant.

■ Bowlby's idea of attachment occurring as an innate process, conferring an evolutionary advantage, suggests that mere exposure to another individual is sufficient for an attachment to develop. This is supported by animal studies. However, **Schaffer & Emerson (1964)** found that attachments occurred mainly with individuals displaying sensitive responsiveness, which goes against this idea. This suggests that attachment formation is a delicate process that develops over time.

■ Research underlines the importance of attachment for a child's development and identity formation. The effects can be long term so healthy development is important, as suggested by Bowlby.

Individual differences in attachment types

Mary Ainsworth worked with John Bowlby in the 1950s and then studied mother–child relationships in the Ganda tribe of Uganda. Over nine months she observed 26 mothers, with infants ranging in age from 15 weeks to two years, for hours at a time. In addition to her observations, Ainsworth carried out interviews with the mothers. From these data she identified three types of attachments, as shown in Table 6.2.

Type of attachment	Description
Type A: Insecure–avoidant	Infants are keen to explore, have high stranger anxiety, are easy to calm and are enthusiastic at the return of their carer. Caregivers are sensitive to infants' needs.
Type B: Securely attached	Infants are willing to explore, have low stranger anxiety, are unconcerned by separation and avoid contact at the return of their caregiver. Caregivers are indifferent to infants' needs.
Type C: Insecure–resistant	Infants are unwilling to explore, have high stranger anxiety, are upset by separation and seek and reject contact at the return of their caregiver. Caregivers are ambivalent to infants' needs, demonstrating simultaneous opposite feelings and behaviours.

■ **Table 6.2** Types of attachment

In 1971 Ainsworth performed a similar study in Baltimore, USA, visiting 26 mother–child pairs every 3–4 weeks for the babies' first year of life. Each visit lasted 3–4 hours. Interviews and naturalistic observations were used, with the latter playing a greater role.

Ainsworth identified two important features of attachment, both with an adaptive survival value. First, infants seek proximity to their mothers, especially when feeling threatened. Second, secure attachments allow infants to explore (behaviour that aids cognitive and social development), using their attached figure as a safe base to explore from and return to.

In order to test the findings of these two studies, Ainsworth developed a standardized research methodology to ascertain the attachment style of children. The details of the Strange Situation procedure and results are outlined in 'Classic research' (below).

KEY STUDY **CLASSIC RESEARCH**

'*The Strange Situation*'
Ainsworth *et al.* (1978)

The Strange Situation testing procedure was created to make sense of the data Ainsworth had collected and to create a valid method of measuring attachments.

Aim

1 To assess how infants between 9 and 18 months of age behave under conditions of mild stress and novelty, in order to test stranger anxiety, separation anxiety and the secure base concept.

2 To assess individual differences between mother–infant pairs in terms of the quality of their attachments.

Procedure

1 'The Strange Situation' comprised eight episodes. Each of these lasted for about three minutes, except episode one, which lasted for 30 seconds.

2 Every aspect of the participants' behaviour was observed and videotaped, with most attention given to reunion behaviours, the infants' responses to their mothers' return. Data were combined from several studies. In total 106 infants were observed.

3 The testing room was an unfamiliar environment (hence the name 'Strange Situation'), comprising an 81 square foot area divided into 16 squares to help record movements.

4 Five categories were recorded:
   a proximity- and contact-seeking behaviours
   b contact-maintaining behaviours
   c proximity- and interaction-avoiding behaviours
   d contact- and interaction-resisting behaviours
   e search behaviours.

5 Every 15 seconds, the category of behaviour displayed was recorded and scored on an intensity scale of 1 to 7.

Episode	Persons present	Brief description
1	Mother, infant, observer	Observer introduces mother and infant to experimental room, then leaves.
2	Mother, infant	Mother is passive while the infant explores.
3	Stranger, mother, infant	Stranger enters. First minute: stranger silent. Second minute: stranger converses with mother. Third minute: stranger approaches infant. After three minutes, mother quietly leaves.
4	Stranger, infant	First separation episode. Stranger's behaviour is geared towards that of the infant.
5	Mother, infant	First reunion episode. Stranger leaves. Mother greets and/or comforts infant, then tries to engage infant again in play. Mother then leaves, saying 'bye-bye'.
6	Infant	Second separation episode. Infant is alone.
7	Stranger, infant	Continuation of second separation. Stranger enters and gears her behaviour to that of the infant.
8	Mother, infant	Second reunion episode. Mother enters, greets and then picks up infant. Meanwhile, stranger quietly leaves.

■ **Table 6.3** The Strange Situation

Results

1 Generally infants explored the playroom and toys more enthusiastically when only the mother was present than either a) after the stranger entered or b) when the mother was absent.

2 Reunion behaviours reflected three types of attachment:

Type A: insecure–avoidant – 15 per cent of infants ignored their mother and were indifferent to her presence. Level of play was not affected either by the mother's presence or absence. Infants displayed little stress when she left and ignored or avoided her when she returned. Infants reacted to the mother and stranger in similar ways, showing most distress when left on their own.

Type B: securely attached – 70 per cent of infants played contentedly when their mother was present, whether or not a stranger was present, but were distressed when she left. On her return they sought comfort from her, calmed down and restarted to play. Mother and stranger were treated very differently.

Type C: insecure–resistant – 15 per cent of infants were fussy and wary, even with their mother present. They were distressed by her leaving and sought contact with her on her return, but simultaneously showed anger and resisted contact (for example, putting out their arms to be picked up, then fighting to get away once they had been picked up).

Conclusions

● Sensitive responsiveness is the major factor determining the quality of attachments, as sensitive mothers correctly interpret infants' signals and respond appropriately to their needs. Sensitive mothers tend to have securely attached babies, whereas insensitive mothers tend to have insecurely attached babies.

● The individual differences in attachment show the underpinning of identity formation, as research supports the idea that attachment style is a blue print for subsequent attachment style and hence personality.

Evaluation

- The Strange Situation methodology developed by Ainsworth has been used widely to examine the attachment types that underpin individual development, as it is one influence that leads to development of identity.

- Ainsworth's work focused upon attachment being unchangeable. If a child was securely attached, for example, they would use that attachment style throughout their development. However, this is unlikely. A child will react to its parent and the context it is in, so if the mother, for example, is stressed or unwell one day, then the behavioural pattern of the child could be very different.

- The artificial nature of the Strange Situation is such that it could elicit unnatural behaviours from a child. Therefore, researchers have questioned its validity, in that it is not measuring what it is designed to measure. It can be said that it measures attachment style in an unfamiliar situation. Running it at home would, they argue, improve its validity.

- The fact that the mother is being observed with her child may also mean that she does not act in a natural way. She may feel pressure to be more attentive to her child than she would be ordinarily, to be seen as a good mother by the researchers. This is social desirability bias and could affect the reliability of the measure, meaning the child acts in an atypical way to how it would do normally.

- The methodology has been criticized for ethics because the child can feel and display real stress when separated from its mother, or left with a stranger. There were provisions in place to deal with this, in that they would bring the stage to an early finish, but psychologists argue it could still have an effect on the child, causing psychological harm.

There is a problem with having merely three attachment styles. **Main & Solomon (1986)** found an additional attachment type, insecure–disorganized (Type D), displayed by a small number of children, whose behaviour is a confusing mixture of approach and avoidance behaviours. This additional attachment style was integrated into the theory by Ainsworth later. The four category model was tested in young adults by **Bartholomew & Horowitz (1991)**, looking at the robustness of the styles within the model. Their work supported the later four-category model which followed the work of Main and Solomon.

LINK TO THE SOCIOCULTURAL LEVEL OF ANALYSIS

There appear to be some cultural differences in the way that the attachment styles are distributed in comparison to Ainsworth's research. Work by **Van IJzendoorn & Kroonenberg (1988)** found variations, such as the highest proportion of insecure–avoidant attachment was found in German participants and the highest proportion of insecure–resistant children was found in Japanese participants. This suggests that culture has a modifying effect on the type of attachment style elicited by the parenting practices. It should be noted, however, that in all countries the highest proportion of attachment style was secure attachment, suggesting that there are cultural similarities too and other influences on attachment style other than culture. Cross-cultural studies like these can suffer from an imposed etic, where researchers analyse findings in a biased manner, in terms of their own cultural beliefs, wrongly imposing cultural-specific beliefs onto other cultures. For instance, Ainsworth, an American, assumed that separation anxiety was an indication of secure attachment, but it may represent something else in other countries.

YOU ARE THE RESEARCHER

Design a research study to compare the strength of attachment a grandparent has with their child. How might you do this? Think about the methodology you could use. What methodological and ethical problems might there be with your design?

Strengthen your learning

1 What is an 'attachment'?

2 How are attachments formed?

3 Why did John Bowlby believe attachments to be so important?

4 Explain Bowlby's maternal deprivation hypothesis.

5 For Bowlby's classic 1944 study of 44 juvenile thieves, in your own words, state the:
   a aims
   b procedure
   c results
   d conclusions
   e evaluative points.

6 Explain Bowlby's concepts of the:
   a internal working model
   b critical period.

7 Summarize what research has suggested about Bowlby's ideas about attachment.

8 What other evaluative points can be made about Bowlby's ideas about attachment?

9 Outline Ainsworth's types of attachment. Make sure you describe them in terms of both an infant and their caregiver's characteristics.

10 For Ainsworth *et al.*'s classic 1978 study of 'The Strange Situation', in your own words, state the:
    a aims
    b procedure
    c results
    d conclusions
    e evaluative points.

Gender identity and social roles

▣ Development of gender identity

Gender identity – our experience of our own gender. This can be the same as the one assigned at birth, or in some cases, may not be.

For many people, their **gender identity** is assigned at birth. One of the first things the midwife or doctor will tell parents is the gender of their newborn. A host of behaviours are associated with that gender label. How do children develop their gender identity? What social roles are connected to the genders?

There are biological, cognitive and sociocultural explanations of how gender identity is formed. One of each of these theories is outlined in the section below.

Biological explanations for the development of gender identity

The biological explanation for gender identity development that is discussed in this section is biochemical and more specifically hormonal.

The DNA of most individuals has either an XX chromosomal combination (female) or an XY combination, which is male. These chromosomes dictate hormonal response in the foetus, with all embryos being female initially but then, by eight weeks into the pregnancy, XY chromosomes will have triggered the gonads to become testes. These produce high levels of testosterone and this leads to the foetus becoming male. This higher level of testosterone in the foetus continues until 24 weeks into development, but then the levels drop again until full gestation. There is a surge of male hormones again in male babies after birth and, once again, the hormonal levels differ within the sexes until six months. The levels then drop again, and spike in puberty.

This biological explanation, however, merely describes the physical differences between the sexes. Biopsychologists argue that it is these differences which underpin the behavioural differences witnessed between the genders. Some of the support for this idea of hormones influencing gender-typical behaviour comes from individuals who have atypical hormonal development. Girls who have congenital adrenal hyperplasia (CAH), an inherited condition, have an enlarged adrenal gland. This triggers higher levels of testosterone (among other hormonal effects) and can cause genitalia that appear male, no periods at puberty, a deep voice and facial hair. In terms of behaviour, such girls show preference for 'male' toys such as cars and guns and they are as likely to choose boys as playmates as girls. The differences in behavioural preferences persist despite girls with CAH being raised as girls and being given the gender identity of 'girl'. Researchers argue that this supports the biological explanation of gender identity, as the non-stereotypical behaviour overrides the societal and parental input to have typically female behaviour.

There is also information to suggest that maternal testosterone levels in pregnancy and a girl's testosterone levels in adolescence dictate how stereotypically feminine their behaviour is.

▣ Research

- **Hines and Kaufmann (1994)** observed that girls with CAH chose boys and girls in equal numbers as playmates, whereas girls without CAH, from the same family, preferred to play with girls for 90 per cent of the time. This supports the view that there is a difference in gender preferences in playmate choice and, more specifically, it can be argued that there is a biological reason for that behaviour.

- Testosterone levels experienced by the mother in pregnancy seem to influence play preferences in three-year-old girls. **Hines _et al._ (2002)** found that women who had higher testosterone levels during pregnancy had daughters who displayed male-typical preferences in play choice and toy preference.

KEY STUDY **CONTEMPORARY RESEARCH**

'_Sex role identity related to the ratio of second to fourth digit length in women_'
Csathó et al. (2003)

The influence of hormones is documented as affecting gender identity, but this is a difficult area for experimentation.

Aim
The aim of the study was to examine the extent to which prenatal hormones (i.e. androgens such as testosterone) influence sex role identity in women.

Procedure
1 This study was conducted on female adults aged between 19 and 26 years old.
2 There was no way to measure the pre-birth hormones in the mothers of these women, but there is a well-documented physical effect of high testosterone levels in pregnancy. This can be done by examining the ratio between the second and fourth fingers on the daughter's hand. This is called the 2D:4D ratio.
3 In cases where the index finger is longer than the ring finger, this is termed a high 2D:4D ratio. When the ring finger is longer than the index finger, this is a low 2D:4D ratio. Some scientists believe that a low ratio could be an indicator for higher prenatal testosterone levels, as often men have a low ratio in the general population. Csathó used this indicator to surmise that women with a low ratio were exposed to higher levels of testosterone in the womb.
4 The researchers gave the participants a questionnaire called the Bem Sex Role Inventory (BSRI) to ascertain how stereotypically feminine or masculine they were. Details on this questionnaire are given in the next section on page 288.

Results
They found that both men and women with low 2D:4D ratios on the right hand were more likely to demonstrate a masculinized bias on the Sex Role Inventory. However, it should be noted that the effect was not significant on the left hand.

Conclusions

This study does support the biological underpinning of gender identity.

Evaluation

- It could be argued that using an indirect measure of prenatal hormones is problematic. So too is the use of the Bem Sex Role Inventory, which has come under criticism for being a measure of personality rather than sex role identity.

- There is also a strong potential for self-report bias with such a measure. The fact that the two hands do not both show effects is questionable, although the researchers did argue that the right hand was more sensitive to prenatal hormones than the left. Why this should be the case is not yet understood.

- There is evidence to support the biological underpinning of gender identity, but there are issues with some of the methods used. Many experiments and research show that there are associations between hormone levels and reported gender identity development, but causation is difficult to establish.

■ Evaluation

- Intersex individuals and people with atypical hormonal levels are used to argue that the gender identity of an individual is biological. This can be seen as problematic, in that it is also possible that the idea of gender being binary (i.e. an individual is a boy or a girl) is a misnomer. The evidence base for gender being non-binary is growing and it seems that biological sex is also along a continuum. As the gender assigned by looking at the external genitalia is the one assigned at birth for most people, then it is possible that hormonal, chromosomal and internal physical indicators of biological sex and thus gender are non-binary. Gender assignment at birth may require more testing than is currently available.

- Teasing apart the influences of biology from the cognitive and sociocultural influences is very difficult. It seems likely that it could be a combination of factors that explain gender identity development. The following explanations describe other proposed explanations for such development.

Cognitive explanation of gender development: Kohlberg's theory of gender constancy (1966)

Gender development – the process by which gender identity can be formed.

Cognitive explanations of **gender development** focus on how children's thinking about gender develops, with thinking occurring in qualitatively different stages. Gender identity is seen to result from children actively structuring their own experiences, rather than being a passive (non-interactive) outcome of social learning. Kohlberg's theory of gender constancy sees thinking and understanding as the basis behind gender identity and gender role behaviour. Kohlberg perceives children as developing an understanding of gender in three distinct stages, with gender role behaviour apparent only after an understanding emerges that gender is fixed and constant. Gender schema theory shares the same cognitive view of gender understanding, but perceives children as having schemas for gender at an earlier stage than Kohlberg.

An important difference between the two theories is that schema theory believes that children only need gender identity to develop gender-consistent behaviours, while Kohlberg sees the acquisition of gender constancy as necessary first.

Kohlberg's theory of gender development is a stage theory that explains how a child formulates an understanding of their gender and others' gender too. The label they are assigned at birth means they know which gender they need to identify with. They then go through three stages which give them a progressively greater understanding of their gender. Around the age of seven years old the understanding of gender is complete. Kohlberg's stages are outlined in Table 6.4.

Stage 1: Gender labelling (basic gender identity)
Occurs between 18 months and three years, and refers to children's recognition of being male or female. Kohlberg sees an individual understanding their gender as a realization that allows them to understand and categorize their world. This knowledge is fragile, with 'man', 'woman', 'boy' and 'girl' little more than labels, equivalent to personal names. Children sometimes choose incorrect labels and do not realize that boys become men and girls become women.

Stage 2: Gender stability
By the age of 3–5 years, most children recognize that people retain gender for life, but rely on superficial, physical signs to determine gender. If someone is superficially transformed – for example, a woman having long hair cut short – children infer that the person has changed gender.

Stage 3: Gender constancy (consistency)
By about age 6–7 years, children realize that gender is permanent, e.g. if a woman has her head shaved, her gender remains female. Gender constancy represents a kind of conservation, an understanding that things remain the same despite changing appearance. Gender understanding is complete only when children appreciate that gender is constant over time and situations.

■ **Table 6.4** Kohlberg's stages of gender development

Once gender constancy has been reached a child will observe and follow the behaviours of people who have also been assigned that gender.

Research

- **Slaby & Frey (1975)** conducted research with findings that supported Kohlberg's theory. The researchers interviewed two- to five-year-old children to assess their level of gender constancy and then several weeks later showed them a film of a man and woman performing gender-stereotypical activities. They found that the children with high levels of gender constancy focused more on same-sex models than children who had low levels. The attentional focus of children with high levels of gender constancy suggests that they observe and notice the behaviours of people of the same gender as them, so they can form a full understanding of the gender role they have been assigned.

- When **Rabban (1950)** asked children of varying ages about gender, he found that there were key age differences. For example, children up to the age of three could say what their gender was but not why they had been assigned that gender, or that it would remain the same. That understanding increased with age. His findings supported Kohlberg's theory of gender identity development being a stage process.

- **Thompson (1975)** found similar results to Rabban (above) in that gender identity development appears to be a process in stages. He found, that at two years, children given pictures of boys and girls could successfully select same-sex ones, which showed they could identify genders in themselves and others. The findings with older children also illustrated that greater understanding of gender identity developed with age.

Evaluation

- Kohlberg's theory is well supported by research evidence, which suggests that the gender identity of a child develops as a stage process and that the ages for each stage are robust. This suggests there may be a biological underpinning to the cognitive processes as the child matures.

- Looking at the theory and ages suggested by Kohlberg, gender-specific behaviour should not occur until the child is in the gender-constancy stage. This, however, is not what is observed in the children who are younger. They do adopt gender-specific behaviour earlier than Kohlberg's theory says they should, so this calls both the ages and stages into question.

- The theory concentrates on cognitive factors and overlooks important cultural and social factors, such as the influence of parents and friends. Their influence is discussed in the section below. Social learning is a powerful theory of gender identity development (see below) and is actually in some ways incorporated into Kohlberg's theory, as it explains how gender-appropriate behaviour is acquired by children once they reach gender constancy. However, it can be argued that its role is underplayed because of the focus on cognition.

Sociocultural explanations of the development of gender identity: social learning theory

Social learning theory explains gender-identity development by the child observing those around them of the same gender and imitating gender-specific behaviours. There are no age-related stages involved. The theory when applied to gender explains it as an ongoing process. Influences on gender-identity development include all people within a child's environment whom they regard as role models, for reasons centring on status, skill, age and gender. The same-sex parent provides one such role model but so too do other family members, such as older siblings and peers.

Peers can influence a child as role models of behaviour. If the child sees them as influential owing to skill, strength of personality or achievement, they will observe and follow their behaviour. Clearly, they will adopt gender-specific behaviours when they are the same gender. Children tend to select other children of the same gender as themselves to act as role models. As gender-appropriate behaviour is more exaggerated in social situations, the role that peers play in the development of gender identity is very important. Indeed, it could possibly be more influential than the role of parents. During social interactions peers will reinforce gender-typical behaviour, criticize non-gender-appropriate behaviour and, as a consequence, a child will be more likely to act in a gender-appropriate way.

■ Research

- Research indicates that there are gender differences between the reinforcement of behaviours. **Block (1983)** found that boys are positively reinforced more for imitating behaviours reflecting independence, self-reliance and emotional control, while girls are reinforced for dependence, nurturance, empathy and emotional expression. This suggests that SLT can explain why males and females acquire different gender roles, as the roles encouraged fit with the gender roles prevalent in society.

- 'Traditional' families, in which the parents have roles of men working outside the home and women staying at home, seem to elicit more gender-appropriate behaviours. **Fagot & Leinbach (1995)** found that there is greater use of gender labels and gender-role stereotyping in such households by young children. This reinforces the idea that parents act as role models for gender-specific behaviour.

- **Pauletti *et al.* (2014)** looked at the extent to which peers punished non-gender stereotypical behaviour and whether that changed over time. They observed and interviewed 195 boys and girls, aged around ten years. Through the findings they established that boys and girls differ in terms of how tolerant they are of non-typical behaviour, but this is moderated by how strong their gender identity is. This means that the reinforcement of gender-stereotypical behaviour varies from peer to peer and it is dependent on how strong a child feels about their gender identity. The area is more complex than social learning theory may suggest.

- **Renold (2001)** found that final-year primary school girls who sought academic success were bullied and ostracized by both boys and girls and such girls had problems establishing a feminine role that did not revolve around boys and presenting their body in certain ways. This illustrates how peers play a strong role in policing stereotypical gender roles, strongly supporting social learning theory.

■ Evaluation

- As social learning theory does not stipulate age-related stages in its theory, it struggles to explain the differences in understanding shown by children. The stage models such as Kohlberg's theory do have research support for age-related understanding, and social learning fails to explain these findings.

- Social learning theory can successfully describe how children acquire gender-stereotypical behaviour and it also explains how stereotypical behaviour is perpetuated throughout society. However, as there is no biological underpinning in the theory, it cannot explain how the stereotypes arose in the first place. It also struggles to explain how gender roles that are atypical arise, as within society the emphasis is on the traditional or typical. So, while the theory is comprehensive, it cannot explain all aspects of gender roles.

■ In some families, there are gender behaviours that vary between same-sex siblings. This is harder to understand, as the parents are presumably acting in the same way with both siblings. It can be argued that peers could explain this difference, but a complete reversal within a family is difficult to explain using social learning.

Social roles

Social role – a pattern of behaviours, beliefs and norms that an individual will adopt if given a role in society.

A social role is a pattern of behaviours, beliefs and norms that an individual will adopt if given a role in society. Social roles are what is expected within that society, and therefore can alter from culture to culture. Examples of social roles are sometimes found within a family, for example mother, father or grandparent. Equally, social roles can be related to professions such as policeman or teacher. At a cognitive level, social roles are a type of schema or script, which allows people to understand first how they should act, or how someone else should act.

Gender behaviour is said to be a social role where there is an expectation of how a boy/man and a girl/woman are expected to act. In 1971, Bem examined gender roles and developed a measure of personality characteristics and whether that typified the gender roles in society (**Bem & Bem, 1971**). The inventory has a list of 60 items, 20 deemed 'masculine' (e.g. independent, competitive, ambitious), 20 deemed feminine (e.g. yielding, sensitive to others' needs, loves children, etc.) and 20 deemed neutral (e.g. helpful, happy and jealous). Individuals completing the measure state how much those characteristics are like them. This gives a score along the masculinity and femininity scales. So, a high masculine score together with a low feminine score is, Bem argued, characteristic of someone with a masculine gender role. The opposite is true for a feminine gender role. If someone scores high on both masculine and feminine characteristics they are deemed to be androgynous, someone who has both masculine and feminine characteristics. If they score low on both the masculine and feminine scale, they are labelled 'undifferentiated', where neither gender role is adopted.

The Stanford prison study, conceived and run by Zimbardo in 1973 (**Haney et al., 1973**), was not designed to test social roles. The key aim was to find out the effects of taking on the roles of prisoner and guard within a simulated environment. However, the results illustrated just how easily we can slip into and fulfil social roles. The study is outlined in the 'Classic study' box below.

KEY STUDY | **CLASSIC RESEARCH**

'*The Stanford Prison study*'
Haney *et al.* (1973)

Social roles clearly play a part in identity formation and also on behaviour. This study is designed to consider the extent to which enforced social roles can affect an individual.

Aim

The researchers were interested in finding out the effects of taking on the roles of prisoner and guard within a simulated environment.

Procedure

1 Participants for the Stanford Prison study were recruited from the student population of Stanford University and were all tested for good physical and mental health. They were then randomly assigned the roles of prisoner or guard.

2 At the outset they were all escorted to the basement at Stanford University, which had been converted into a prison set by police officers. Guards were given uniforms, handcuffs and whistles. Prisoners, on the other hand, were dressed in smocks, rubber sandals and a nylon cap. Then prisoners were stamped with an ID number and had an ankle lock chain fitted. From then on the participants, having been assigned their respective roles, coexisted in the prison environment.

Results

1 Roles were adopted surprisingly quickly with some of the guards being particularly zealous in the role, being quick to withdraw privileges for punishments, together with using solitary confinement and making prisoners wash the toilets with bare hands.

2 Prisoners too adopted the role they had been given, and were often obedient and apathetic, as though accepting the situation they were in. There were, however, some very negative effects for some of the prisoners, who suffered health issues, such as a rash, and one being released from the experiment early because he had a severe 'emotional disturbance'.

3 It seemed that both the social roles of guard and prisoner had been adopted rapidly and they continued to develop and become more entrenched with time. The experiment was finished early for ethical reasons, lasting only a week.

Conclusions

The speed and extent to which roles were adopted shows that first humans like to take on social roles, even negative ones. It also shows how powerful social roles are in affecting behaviour.

Evaluation

There has been some argument that the artificial environment and experimental conditions elicited atypical behaviour and that the behaviour observed would not occur 'in real life'. However, the extent to which the prisoners were affected shows they were not play acting; they actually did adopt the role of prisoner. There was a cumulative effect in terms of the guards' aggression levels towards the prisoners, suggesting that as time went on they took on more of the role. This again means that play acting was unlikely.

Strengthen your learning

1 Outline biological explanations for the development of gender identity.

2 Summarize what research studies have suggested about biological explanations for the development of gender identity.

3 What other evaluative points can be made about biological explanations for the development of gender identity?

4 For Csathó *et al.*'s 2003 contemporary study of 'Sex role identity related to the ratio of second to fourth digit length in women', in your own words, state the:
   a aims   **c** results   **e** evaluative points.
   b procedure   **d** conclusions

5 Outline Kohlberg's cognitive theory of gender constancy.

6 Summarize what research studies have suggested about Kohlberg's cognitive explanation for the development of gender constancy.

7 What other evaluative points can be made about Kohlberg's cognitive explanation for the development of gender constancy?

8 Outline the following sociocultural explanations of gender identity:
   a social learning theory
   b social roles.

9 Summarize what research studies have suggested about sociocultural explanations for the development of gender identity.

10 What other evaluative points can be made about sociocultural explanations for the development of gender identity?

11 For Zimbardo's classic prison simulation study (Haney *et al.*, 1973), in your own words, state the:
   a aims   **c** results   **e** evaluative points.
   b procedure   **d** conclusions

Development of empathy and theory of mind

Development of empathy

Empathy can be described as the ability to understand and experience or share the feelings of others. One key aspect of empathy is understanding that other people have different feelings and experiences from yourself, and this is termed theory of mind. This will be discussed in greater depth in the next section, but this section considers what some psychologists argue is the biological underpinning of empathy: mirror neurons.

The Shared Manifold Hypothesis (**Gallese, 2001**) outlined how this could occur. Mirror neurons are specific neurons which are activated in the brain of someone observing someone else and they fire in a way that mimics the actions of the person being observed. So, if someone is pulling up their socks and another individual is watching, the mirror neurons of the observer will fire in a way that indicates they are also completing the action, but in a weaker form. This explains the acting out of movement, but how does this help us understand what the person may be feeling, which is an essential part of development of empathy? It is argued by Gallese that understanding thought and emotion can be done by recognizing emotion and states using non-verbal communication. If you see someone smile at you, your mirror neurons will re-enact that smile within you, in a milder form, and you will take on the emotion associated with that smile. At the other end of the emotional spectrum, if you see someone crying, that too will make you feel sadness, via your mirror neurons. Mirror neurons take the observation beyond mere understanding of another's thoughts or feelings to where the observer experiences those emotions, in a diluted form. In the case of empathy, merely understanding the emotions of another and feeling sorry for them is sympathy. The mirror neurons take it a step further to where feeling or sharing in their pain/sadness/happiness means they have empathy.

Empathy occurs globally and cross-culturally. It is not necessary to understand the language of someone who is happy. It is observed in their non-verbal communication. Emotion is expressed in facial expressions in the same way across the world. So empathy can occur cross-culturally, too, as no language is needed to understand emotion.

Research

- **Corradini & Antonietti (2013)** conducted a review of the research literature looking at the psychological and neurobiological mechanisms underlying development of empathy. They found that there was good empirical support for the role of mirror neurons in empathy and that it was an essential part of the development of the cognitive skill.

- **Kaplan & Iacoboni (2006)** conducted research using an fMRI scanner on participants asked to watch video clips of people cleaning up cups, or drinking from cups using different types of grip on the cups. The grips were designed to be appropriate for the action, so when drinking a hot drink you would expect someone to use a precision grip (using the handle) rather than a full grip (wrapping fingers round the cup) because the cup would be hot. Participants were only asked to watch the clips and pay full attention while they were in the scanner. They also subsequently completed an empathy questionnaire, which included items such as 'When I watch a good movie, I can very easily put myself in the place of a leading character.' The researchers found that there was a correlation between the score on the empathy questionnaire and the activity level of the mirror neurons, particularly when the video showed someone picking up a hot drink, with their hands around the seemingly 'hot' cup. This demonstrates that there was a connection between mirror neuron activation and potentially emotional/painful occurrences, supporting the role of mirror neurons in empathy development.

- Using fMRI, **Schulte-Rüther et al. (2007)** found that mirror neurons were implicated in both motor cognition and interpersonal cognition. This supports the idea that face-to-face interpersonal interactions are supported by the mirror neuron system and that this is important for experiencing empathy.

IN THE NEWS

Ψ The Psychological Enquirer

ARE MIRROR NEURONS THE REASON WHY WE ENJOY SCARY MOVIES?

How often have you sat watching a romantic movie mopping up the tears with a firmly clutched handkerchief? Probably more times than you care to admit. And how many times have you sat peeping through gaps in your fingers, petrified at some scary scene in a horror movie? And yet why do we love such experiences so? Perhaps mirror neurons are the answer.

■ **Figure 6.5** Are mirror neurons the reason we enjoy the experience of watching a scary movie?

Mirror neurons are nerves in the brain that are active not only when we perform certain behaviours ourselves, but also when we observe them being performed by others, which allows individuals to share the feelings of others without having to think about it. This could be the reason, then, why we become so emotionally involved in films, because we 'mirror' the feelings apparently being experienced by the actors and actresses in front of us.

But is this true? It reads as though it could be true, but where is the evidence? Mirror neurons were discovered by Italian scientists studying monkeys in the 1990s and the popular press has promoted the view that their discovery was a 'great scientific breakthrough', with all kinds of claims being promoted as 'truths'. Neuroscientist V.S. Ramachandran, for instance, stated that mirror neurons underpin what it is to be human and that they are responsible not just for empathy, but also for language and the evolution of culture, including the use of tools and fire. He even goes as far as to say that when mirror neurons do not work, the result is autism.

However, researchers have found it difficult to identify and interpret mirror neuron activity in humans and there are many types of mirror neurons with apparently different functions. Also, humans can understand the intentions of others even when they have never performed such actions themselves. Mirror neurons are an exciting discovery, but only through patient scientific research will the true significance of any observed phenomena be revealed and any true student of psychology should remember this.

■ Evaluation

- Much of the research on mirror neurons has been gathered from animal studies. This is problematic if talking about a higher order cognitive skill such as empathy. Some would argue that, while activation of mirror neurons can be observed successfully in non-human animals, extending that work to development of empathy is too far. There has been research conducted on human mirror neurons but there is a need, some argue, for a greater body of evidence.

- It is argued that stating that the mirror neuron system underlies all experiences of empathy may be misplaced. It cannot easily explain how empathy can be felt when you cannot see the person, for example in a letter, where there are no non-verbal cues such as voice or facial expression.

■ Moebius syndrome is a type of paralysis that means an individual cannot express emotion on their face and the mirror neurons will be affected accordingly. However, **Rives Bogart & Matsumoto (2010)** found that this did not hinder individuals with the syndrome being able to recognize emotion, which means that the Shared Manifold Hypothesis may be flawed in the emphasis it puts on mirror neurons being necessary for development of empathy.

Development of theory of mind

A key component to development of empathy is the cognitive development of theory of mind (ToM). Anytime you hear someone say, 'I think he is angry about us being late' or 'She was unsure of her answer to my question', you know that the person speaking has ToM. It can be defined as the ability to attribute mental states, knowledge, wishes, feelings and beliefs to oneself and others. In everyday language that means the ability to put oneself in another's shoes.

At a young age (from birth) children have egocentric thinking; the idea that their experience is the world and their experience is the same as everyone else's experience. From around the age of four years such thinking changes and this is the point at which ToM develops. Children start to realize that other people have a mind too, and that it is feeling and thinking differently to their mind.

ToM is investigated by presenting children with false belief tasks. This involves witnessing a scene and being asked to interpret it from the viewpoint of one of the characters in the scene. If they can do this, they are seen as having developed a ToM. If children instead interpret the scene from their own egocentric viewpoint, they are seen as not having a ToM. Such research generally indicates that children around the age of four give egocentric answers (have a false belief) and thus have not developed a ToM, while by six years of age most children can perform the task and thus do have a ToM.

With the development of ToM comes the ability to manipulate and deceive others by hiding one's emotions and intentions. This occurs from three years of age. It is possible there is a more primitive earlier version of ToM, called shared attention mechanism (SAM), developing at 9–18 months of age, which allows two people to realize that they are witnessing the same thing.

Research

■ **Wimmer & Perner (1983)** used models to act out a story to four-, six- and eight-year-olds about a boy called Maxi who put some chocolate in a blue cupboard. While Maxi was absent, the children saw his mother transfer the chocolate to a green cupboard. The children were asked where Maxi would look for the chocolate. Most six- and eight-year-olds gave the blue cupboard as the correct answer, while most four-year-olds said they would look in the green cupboard. They thought Maxi would act on the basis of his false belief, implying that they had not developed a ToM.

■ It seems that development of mind can be encouraged by certain activities in preschool children. **Sigirtmac (2016)** found that learning and practising chess could facilitate development of ToM. The researchers administered ToM tests to two groups of participants, who were between four and six years old. They found that the scores of children who had chess training were higher (significantly so) than the scores of other children on ToM tests. This suggests that although ToM development may be innate, the environment can have an effect that encourages its development.

■ **Bartsch & Wellman (1995)** found that ToM acquisition follows a common developmental pattern in both US and Chinese children, suggesting that as it is cross-cultural, the ability is biologically controlled. This is further supported by **Avis & Harris (1991)**, who found that children in both developed and non-developed countries realize that at four years of age people can have false beliefs, supporting the idea of biological maturation.

Evaluation

- The age at which ToM develops is not without debate. There is disagreement as to whether this occurs at the age of four or more gradually from two years of age and upwards.

- Younger children may fail to understand false belief tasks such as that used by **Wimmer & Perner (1983)**, not because they do not have a ToM, but because the language of the questions is too complex. For instance, 'Where will he look for the chocolate?' could be taken by a child to mean 'Where is the chocolate?' This means that the validity of the false belief tests is questionable.

- **Bloom & German (2000)** argue that passing a false belief task involves having more than a ToM. Even if young children do understand that beliefs can be false, the task given in many studies is very complex, such as following the actions of two characters in a scenario, remembering what events have occurred and understanding the specific meaning of the question asked of them. Such requirements may be beyond young children, even if they do have a ToM. They also argue that there is more to having a ToM than passing false belief tasks. Children below the age of two, who tend to fail false belief tests, can initiate pretend play and understand the pretending of others, which would suggest an ability to understand the mental states of others. Again, this means that the testing method may lack validity.

- The evidence to suggest that ToM can be taught (see **Sigirtmac 2016** above) would indicate that the environment can have an effect on development. This means that the idea of an innate mechanism that develops at a certain age is potentially erroneous. It seems more likely that there is an innate mechanism but that the appropriate environment can trigger activation. The role of play in developing ToM is discussed earlier in the chapter on page 264. This means that the age by which ToM develops could be earlier in some cases and there is likely to be a wide range of ages at which it develops in individuals.

YOU ARE THE RESEARCHER

You have been given the task of designing some research that looks at the relationship between gender and the age at which empathy develops. How might you do this in an age-appropriate way? What ethical and methodological considerations must you make given that the participants will be a young age?

Strengthen your learning

1 What is meant by:
   a empathy
   b theory of mind?

2 Outline the Shared Manifold Hypothesis in terms of how mirror neurons may explain empathy.

3 Summarize what research studies have suggested about the relationship between mirror neurons and empathy.

4 What other evaluative points can be made about the relationship between mirror neurons and empathy?

5 Outline the development of ToM.

6 Explain how false belief tasks are used to assess the development of ToM.

7 Summarize what research studies have suggested about the development of ToM.

8 What other evaluative points can be made about the development of ToM?

SECTION SUMMARY

- The quality of attachments and the attachment style of a child are part of their identity formation.
- The development of gender identity can be explained at the biological, cognitive and sociocultural levels.
- Social roles are an important part of human behaviour as they contribute to the identity of the individual.
- Development of empathy, a cognitive construct, can be explained biologically using mirror neurons.
- Development of theory of mind underpins empathy and this occurs around the age of four.

Developing as a learner

Learning is an essential part of development for a child and continues to be so throughout the lifespan. This section considers how cognitive development and brain development facilitate that learning.

'Live as if you were to die tomorrow. Learn as if you were to live forever.'
Mahatma Gandhi

> ### FOCUS ON...
>
> ■ Cognitive development with a focus on the theories of Piaget and Vygotsky.
> ■ Brain development and how that biological development can be influenced by other factors.

■ Cognitive development

Two theorists of cognitive development are discussed within this section: Piaget and Vygotsky. They both attempt to explain how children's mental abilities develop and how their thinking matures. Piaget's theory is focused on the stages of development of thought processes, acknowledging their biological underpinning. You could therefore argue that Piaget's theory is an explanation that incorporates predominantly cognitive explanations with some biological consideration too. Vygotsky, on the other hand, sees cognitive development as a product of learning, so, as a consequence, his theory is more influenced by sociocultural aspects.

Piaget's theory of cognitive development

Piaget was intrigued by how intelligence changes in the individual throughout their development. He devised and conducted experiments to test what a child could achieve at stages in their childhood.

Piaget considered carefully how the child learned from their environment and how the process of acquiring understanding came about. He was also interested in how children adapted to change within their environment.

Piaget suggested that learning occurs through interaction and adaptation to their environment. Key aspects are:

1 The process of adaption – which involves accommodation and assimilation; fitting knowledge into new schemas and altering schemas to fit in new knowledge respectively.

2 The process of equilibration – which involves feeling in a state of understanding (equilibrium) and not understanding (disequilibrium).

3 Schemas – these are the ideas we form to understand and predict the world around us (see the cognitive explanations for human behaviour on page 63).

4 Operations – a combination of schemas drawn together.

Newborn babies have reflexes, such as the sucking reflex; this means the child has a way of discovering and learning from the environment around them. Cognitive development can be seen through the example of the innate schema of sucking. At first babies suck everything they come into contact with in the same inborn manner; this is called assimilation (part of the process of adaption) and involves fitting new environmental experiences into existing schemas. If this is possible, infants are in a state of equilibrium (part of the process of equilibration), a pleasant state of balance.

When infants find something new which they cannot suck in the usual way, such as drinking from a cup, they experience disequilibrium (the other part of the process of equilibration), an unpleasant state of imbalance. Children are naturally motivated to return to the balanced state of equilibrium, which is achieved by accommodating the new experience (the other part of the process of adaption). This involves altering existing schemas to accommodate (fit in) new experiences, such as using new lip shapes to drink/suck out of different things.

Therefore, cognitive development involves constantly swinging between equilibrium and disequilibrium, through a continuous series of assimilation (fitting knowledge into new schemas) and accommodation. When new schemas are formed, assimilation allows for practice of the new experiences until they are automatic. This process continues through life, but is most apparent in the first 15 years.

Stages of cognitive development

Piaget 's theory suggests a series of stages of development. He also asserted that these stages were innate, global and invariant. As children move from stage to stage they have a mixture of abilities from both stages until they move to the next stage.

The stages are outlined in Table 6.5.

Sensorimotor stage (birth to 2 years)	New schemas arise from matching sensory to motor experiences as the child explores the environment to a greater degree. Object permanence occurs at age two as children develop what is known as GSF (general symbolic function), which is the ability to form mental images of an object and retain them when an object disappears.
Pre-operational stage (2–7 years)	Internal images, symbols and language develop; this enables interaction with the environment. The child is influenced by how things seem, not logic. This is called centration. Thinking is still very simple. Between four and seven years children become intuitive, but still struggle with logic. They are also egocentric, which means they see the world as their world and do not think of it as separate from them.
Concrete operational stage (7–11 years)	Development of conservation (use of logical rules), but only if situations are concrete, not abstract. A child at this stage struggles to think in an abstract way. Decline of egocentrism. Children are able to see the perspective of others.
Formal operational stage (11+ years)	Abstract manipulation of ideas (concepts without physical presence). Some individuals never achieve this stage. It is the most advanced and sophisticated.

■ **Table 6.5** Piaget's stages of cognitive development

LINK TO BOTH COGNITIVE AND BIOLOGICAL EXPLANATIONS

Piaget's work focuses upon the cognitive development of children but he acknowledged that there was a biological underpinning to his theory.

KEY STUDY CLASSIC RESEARCH

'*The Swiss Mountain Scene study*'
Piaget & Inhelder (1956)

Piaget observed that pre-operational children, aged between two and seven, show errors in logic, as they are egocentric (they can see the world from their own point of view only). This was demonstrated in this study by children only being able to select pictures of a view they could see themselves (see Figure 6.6). The study, though, is not without its criticisms.

■ **Figure 6.6** A child looking at a mountain scene

Aim

To see whether children who are less than seven years of age are able to see the model of a mountain scene from their own viewpoint only.

Procedure

1 Children aged between four and eight years were presented with three papier-mâché mountains of various colours, each with something different on the top: a red cross, a covering of snow or a chalet.

2 Children walked round the model, exploring it, then sat on one side while a doll was placed on one of the other sides.

3 Children were then shown ten pictures of different views of the model, including the doll's and their own. They were asked to select the picture representing the doll's view.

Results

Four-year-olds chose the picture matching their own view. Six-year-olds showed some understanding of other viewpoints, but often selected the wrong picture. Seven- and eight-year-olds consistently chose the picture representing the doll's view.

Conclusions

Four-year-olds are unaware that there are viewpoints other than their own. Children under seven years are subject to the egocentric illusion, failing to understand that what they see is specific to their position. Instead, they believe that their own view represents 'the world as it really is'.

Evaluation

● Swiss mountains are outside of most children's experience; therefore, what Piaget witnessed, due to his poor methodology, was not egocentrism but a lack of understanding.

● The study is not actually an experiment, as it has no independent variable, but instead is a 'controlled observation'.

● **Hughes & Donaldson (1979)** found that 90 per cent of children aged between three and a half and five years could hide a doll in a 3D model of intersecting walls where a police doll could not see it, but they could see it, as they used their experience of playing hide-and-seek to do so, suggesting that young children are not egocentric. Similarly, **Gelman (1979)** found that four-year-olds adjust their explanations of things to a blindfolded listener to make them clearer and use simpler forms of speech when talking to two-year-olds. This would not be expected if they were egocentric.

● These studies support the idea that Piaget may have underestimated the age at which children stop being egocentric.

▨ Research

■ **Piaget & Cook (1952)** got seven-year-olds to agree that two identically shaped beakers, A and B, contained equal amounts of liquid. Having witnessed liquid from beaker A being poured into beaker C, a taller, thinner beaker that contained the same amount, the children stated that C contained more, which suggests they cannot conserve. However, **Donaldson (1978)** argues that as the same question is asked twice, the children think a different answer is required, suggesting that Piaget's methodology was not suitable for such young children.

■ In another conservation task of number, **Piaget (1960)** laid out two equally spaced rows of counters and pre-operational children agreed that there was the same number in both rows. One of the rows, in sight of the child, was compressed (the counters were moved closer to each other) and children stated that the longer line had more. **McGarrigle & Donaldson (1975)** repeated the study and children again initially agreed that the two rows contained the same number. Then 'naughty teddy', a glove puppet, 'secretly' pushed one of the rows together and children stated they still contained the same number. The researchers argue that children believe, from experience, that adults are always changing things, so a different answer is needed when adults meddle with the counters. Similarly, **Berko & Brown (1960)** argues that children misinterpret the words 'more' and 'less' as meaning 'taller' and 'shorter', again suggesting Piaget's findings were due to poor methodology.

■ **Inhelder & Piaget (1958)** asked participants to consider which of three factors (the length of some string, the heaviness of some weights or the strength of push) was the most important in assessing the speed of the swing of a pendulum. The solution is to change one variable at a time, for example try different lengths of string with the same weight, and children in the formal operational stage were able to do this, but younger children could not, as they tended to try several variables at once. This suggests that children in the formal operational stage can think logically in an abstract manner in order to see the relationships between things.

Evaluation

■ **Marwaha et al. (2017)** tested children aged four to seven for their level of intuitive thinking, in line with Piaget's theory. The researchers also looked at the relationship with IQ. Three hundred children were tested overall and it was found that their abilities supported Piaget's theory in that age group and that there was a gradual progression to more mature thinking throughout the ages from four to seven years old. The more advanced children in terms of their maturity of thinking also measured higher in IQ tests.

■ Piaget stimulated interest in cognitive development, with his theory becoming the starting point for many later theories and research. **Schaffer (2004)** believes it to be the most comprehensive account of how children come to understand the world, even though it has declined in importance in more recent years.

■ As cross-cultural evidence implies that the stages of development (except formal operations) occur as a universal, invariant sequence, it suggests cognitive development is a biological process of maturation. However, **Dasen (1977)** believes that as formal operational thinking is not found in all cultures, this stage is not genetically determined. Also, the fact that not all individuals seem to acquire formal operational thinking, and of those that do, it is at different ages, suggests this stage is not as uniform and invariant as others, which additionally suggests it is not biologically determined. Another major criticism of the theory is that Piaget neglected the important role of emotional and social factors in intellectual development and, in doing so, overemphasized cognitive aspects of development.

■ Piaget saw language ability as reflecting an individual's level of cognitive development, while theorists like Bruner argued it was the other way round, with language development preceding cognitive development.

■ Piaget's often poor methodology, such as using research situations that were unfamiliar to children, led him to underestimate what children of different ages could achieve. This means that the stages may be accurate, but that the ages in which they occur may be underestimated.

■ **Meadows (2006)** argues that Piaget saw children as being independent from others as they constructed their knowledge and understanding of the physical world and thus excluded the contribution of others to cognitive development. This important omission of the social nature of learning (how it is influenced by others) is a major feature of Vygotsky's theory (see below).

Vygotsky's theory of cognitive development

Due to his untimely death at the age of 38, Vygotsky's theory was not fully formed. However, it is often given equal weight in developmental text books and focuses upon the sociocultural aspect of cognitive development, which is an area in which Piaget's theory is criticized.

Vygotsky saw cognitive development as a cultural construct, influenced by the learning of norms and attitudes of whichever culture a child is raised within. He also emphasized the role of others as tutors, facilitating cognitive development in children. These tutors are not necessarily professional. Learning happens outside of an educational context.

One way this occurs is learning from older influences which happen through interactions with caregivers, thus passing cultural attitudes and beliefs from one generation to another, developing them further, then handing them on to the next generation. The interaction also helps progress in terms of cognitive development.

Cognitive development occurs first on a social level, through interaction between people (interpsychological), and second on an individual level within a child (intrapsychological). Even higher-level cognitive functions and concepts were seen by Vygotsky as originating through interactions between individuals.

> **LINK TO BOTH COGNITIVE AND SOCIOCULTURAL EXPLANATIONS**
> Vygotsky's work, like Piaget's, focuses upon the cognitive development of children, but he emphasized the role of culture so can be said to incorporate that level of explanation into his theory too.

Internalization and the social nature of thinking

The ability to think and reason by and for oneself is called inner speech or verbal thought. Infants are born as social beings, capable of interacting with others, but able to do little practically or intellectually by themselves. Gradually, children become more self-sufficient and independent, and by participating in social activities their abilities develop.

For Vygotsky, cognitive development involves active internalization of problem-solving processes, taking place as a result of mutual interaction between children and people they have social contact with. This therefore replaces Piaget's 'child as a scientist' idea (that children construct and test out their own theories about the world) with the 'child as an apprentice' idea, where cultural skills and knowledge are gained through collaboration with those who possess them.

The zone of proximal development

The zone of proximal development (ZPD) is the distance between current and potential ability. Cultural influences and knowledgeable others push children through the ZPD and on to tasks beyond their current ability.

Mentors (trusted advisors) with understanding of an area encourage and assist children in their learning. The mentor's role in regulating performance gradually reduces, as a child becomes more able, with the child being given increased opportunity to perform the task independently.

Scaffolding

Scaffolding is a concept that sees cognitive development as being assisted by sensitive guidance, with children being given clues as to how to solve a problem, rather than being given the actual solution – for example, being advised to create the border of a jigsaw first and then fill in the interior. At first a child will need such guidance, but as they increasingly master a task, the scaffolding is removed so that they can stand alone to complete the task.

With scaffolding, learning first involves shared social activities until individuals can self-scaffold, with learning eventually becoming an individual, self-regulated activity.

Semiotics

Semiotics involves the use of signs and symbols to create meaning. Vygotsky saw semiotics as assisting cognitive development through the use of language and other cultural symbols, which act as a medium for knowledge to be transmitted, turning elementary mental functions into higher ones.

At first, children use pre-intellectual language for social and emotional purposes, where words are not symbols for the objects they represent but instead reflect properties of the objects, with pre-linguistic thinking occurring without the use of language. From around two years of age, language and thinking combine so that speech and thought become interdependent (dependent on each other), with thinking thus becoming an internal conversation. Such development occurs in several phases:

- Social speech (birth to three years) – involving pre-intellectual language.
- Egocentric speech (3–7 years) – involving self-talk/thinking aloud.
- Inner speech (7+ years) – where self-talk becomes silent and internal, and language is used for social communications.

Concept formation

Vygotsky (1934) gave children blocks with nonsense symbols on them and they had to work out what the symbols meant. Four different approaches were observed, from which Vygotsky proposed four stages of concept formation (see Table 6.6).

Vague syncretic	Trial-and-error formation of concepts without comprehension of them. Similar to Piaget's pre-operational stage.
Complex	Use of some strategies to comprehend concepts, but not very systematic.
Potential concept	More systematic use of strategies, with one attribute being focused on at a time – for example, weight.
Mature concept	Several attributes can be dealt with systematically – for example, weight and colour. Similar to Piaget's formal operations.

■ **Table 6.6** Vygotsky's four stages of concept formation

■ Research

- **Wood & Middleton (1975)** observed mothers using various strategies to support four-year-olds in building a model that was too difficult for the children to do themselves. Mothers who were most effective in offering assistance were ones who varied their strategy according to how well a child was doing, so that when a child was progressing well they gave less specific help, but when a child struggled they gave more specific guidance until the child made progress again. This highlights the concept of the ZPD and shows that scaffolding is most effective when matched to the needs of a learner, so that they are assisted to achieve success in a task that previously they could not have completed alone.
- **McNaughton & Leyland (1990)** observed mothers giving increasingly explicit help to children assembling progressively harder jigsaws, which illustrates how scaffolding and sensitivity to a child's ZPD aid learning.
- **Gredler & Gilbert (1992)** reported that in New Guinea the symbolic use of fingers and arms when counting among natives limited learning, supporting the idea of cultural influence on cognitive development.

> **YOU ARE THE RESEARCHER**
>
> Design an experiment that compares the ability of five-year-old children to build a Lego model of a farm, either on their own or with scaffolding in the form of guidance from a mentor (as suggested by Vygotsky's theory).
>
> Consider what type of experimental design to use, what the IV and DVs would be and where you would be best situating the experiment. Justify your choices.

■ Evaluation

- There are strong central similarities between Piaget's and Vygotsky's theories, and it has been suggested that combining the two may be feasible and desirable in order to gain a fuller understanding of children's cognitive development. They would also, if combined, cover both cognitive and sociocultural levels of explanation equally.
- As Vygotsky focused upon the role of the tutor in the child's environment, his theory has applicability in the field of education. For example, psychologists have taken the concepts of scaffolding and peer tutoring and applied them to an educational setting. Teachers use scaffolding to teach concepts and it is used widely in mathematics education. The idea of peer tutoring is also used successfully across the world in formal educational settings. The work of Garetsky (above) supports the effectiveness of this application.

■ Vygotsky's theory was developed within a collectivist culture and is more suited to such cultures, with their stronger element of social learning than individualistic western cultures. However, it should be noted that different cultures emphasize different skills and learning goals and yet Vygotsky's concepts of sensitive guidance, scaffolding and ZPD are applicable in all cultures, suggesting his concepts to be 'culture-fair'. There are further criticisms though as the theory can also be accused of overemphasizing the role of social factors at the expense of biological and individual ones. Learning would be faster if development depended on social factors only, so there are clearly other factors involved. An example of this was suggested by **Schaffer (2004)** in his criticism of Vygotsky's theory. He argued that it failed to include important emotional factors, such as the frustrations of failure and the joys of success, as well as failing to identify the motivational factors children use to achieve particular goals.

Strengthen your learning

1 Explain Piaget's theory of cognitive development in terms of the:
a process of adaption
b process of equilibration.

2 Describe an example of your own to show your understanding of the processes of adaption and equilibration.

3 Outline Piaget's stages of cognitive development, ensuring that you include the ages at which they occur.

4 Summarize what research has suggested about Piaget's theory of cognitive development.

5 Assess Piaget's theory in terms of its strengths and weaknesses.

6 For Piaget & Inhelder's classic 1956 Swiss mountain study, in your own words, state the:
a aims
b procedure
c results
d conclusions
e evaluative points.

7 Explain Vygotsky's theory of cognitive development. Include reference to:
a internalization and the social nature of thinking
b the zone of proximal development
c scaffolding
d semiotics
e concept formation.

8 Summarize what research has suggested about Vygotsky's theory of cognitive development.

9 Assess Vygotsky's theory in terms of its strengths and weaknesses.

▒ Brain development

As with other areas of the body, the brain is a developing organ that has a lifelong developmental process. The biological section on neuroplasticity (page 13) illustrates how the physiology can change in response to learning and trauma. That change is lifelong, as you can learn until the day you die.

The physical developmental trajectory of the brain

There is a typical developmental trajectory for the brain, which is expected by medical professionals. Overall the volume of the brain increases as the child grows in size, but this halts at around 11 years old for girls and 15 years old for boys. The grey matter volume, which is the brain tissue that contains synapses, increases and then decreases in volume a few years earlier than the total volume. However, the white matter, that is, brain tissue containing all the connections between the grey matter, continues to increase in volume throughout childhood and adolescence.

Grey matter, which is where the synapses are found, seems to vary in terms of maturation, depending on the function of that area of the brain. The first areas to mature are the motor and sensory areas, which then are ready to map onto higher order function as the child makes sense of the world. The latest area to develop is called the prefrontal cortex, which seems to enable higher order thinking such as judgement, decision-making and impulse control. This helps to moderate emotional decision-making and happens during adolescence.

The increase in white matter throughout childhood and adolescence means that the child's brain can increase connectivity as they need to be able to accommodate their learning. The more a connection is used, the thicker the volume of that connection which facilitates function. In adolescence, there is a process of pruning where connections are jettisoned and strong connections made stronger, so the brain is refining its activity in response to learning. A useful analogy which explains this process was suggested by **Power *et al.* (2010)**. They likened this stage to language, where pre-adolescence the brain learns the alphabet and during adolescence it learns how to use the alphabet to form many different words. This symbolizes the idea of an increased number of connections.

Influences on the developmental trajectory of the brain

Genes and environment

Although these developmental changes appear to be universal, there is evidence that the development of the brain is not only affected by genes but also by the individual's environment. The genes seem to determine the changes in grey and white matter, but these too are influenced by age, with the heritable element increasing with age for white matter volume and decreasing for grey matter volume. So, therefore, if there is a family history of high levels of white matter in the brain, then this deviation from the normal levels becomes more apparent as the individual gets older and the differences increase. Any atypical development in grey matter becomes less obvious with age. It is also thought that individuals may have genes that trigger disorders at certain ages.

Male/female differences

There are gender differences in the likelihood of developing neuropsychiatric disorders; and the development of these disorders, if affecting both genders, can vary between genders. Therefore, looking at the developmental differences between brains of the genders is informative.

The respective volume of white, grey and total volume of the brain varies, on average, between genders. Indeed, the cortical structure of the brain is shown to be robustly different between genders.

Of course, this refers to average differences between genders and there will always be differences within the genders so there is an overlap between some male and female brains. They are not anatomically different; it is the thickness of the tissue that varies so differentiating male and female brains is not a straightforward task. The developmental differences can be compared to height differences in men and women. Overall, the average height of men is greater than that of women, but there are women who are taller than men. This means that a person's gender cannot be determined by looking at their height. It is the same for developing brains. Capacity for learning may be skewed to particular skills, but both genders have a similar capacity for learning.

Toxins

Toxins – poisonous substances that are in the environment or in substances that may be ingested.

Toxins in the environment are thought to affect brain development. In a widespread study in 2006 in the USA, scientists identified toxins implicated in causing abnormal development and the possible effects. Some of the toxins included heavy metals (such as lead and mercury), organophosphates (which are found in insecticides), nicotine, alcohol and even excessive exposure, via supplements, of vitamin A. The brain development effects can occur *in utero* so an individual's brain is vulnerable to toxins prior to birth. This means learning potential is affected. An example of this is Foetal Alcohol Syndrome (FAS) – see 'In The News' (below).

IN THE NEWS

Ψ The Psychological Enquirer

FOETAL ALCOHOL SYNDROME

■ **Figure 6.7** Foetal Alcohol Syndrome is caused by excessive alcohol consumption during pregnancy

Every year it is estimated that up to 7500 babies are born in the UK showing some of the symptoms associated with Foetal Alcohol Syndrome (FAS). Matthew Verity was the first child in the country to be diagnosed with the syndrome in 1977. He was aged 30 at the time of the article's publication.

Matthew has major problems with his memory and needs to stick lists around his flat to remind himself of what he needs to do that day. This includes basic acts of taking care of himself, such as how to get dressed and to eat breakfast. He needs a list for shopping which, in itself, is not unusual, but if there are any changes in the layout of his local supermarket he is lost and unable to adapt to the changes without facing a great number of issues.

Matthew's mother was a binge drinker and this continued while she was pregnant with him. She was a teacher and she kept her drinking secret from all, including her husband. He found out, and urged her to seek help when she was four months pregnant. It is thought that the damage to the brain happened before then. The alcohol passes through the mother's bloodstream to the child's blood. As the foetus is immature it cannot metabolize the alcohol and, as a consequence, the foetal brain and body are damaged. Development from then on is atypical. In Matthew's case, this has left him with severe intellectual and cognitive impairment and he also has physical effects, such as an abnormally small head. FAS can also cause facial abnormalities and often the ears are set lower down on the head.

Matthew is affected in terms of social development and cognitive development. He has trouble maintaining and making friendships and his memory is very unreliable. His foster family worked hard with him throughout his childhood and he thrived within their care, but the effects that his mother's drinking has caused are unlikely to go away.

This case shows the wide-ranging physical, cognitive and social effects that toxins have on brain development and the enduring, indeed lifelong, effects that this can have on an individual's learning.

■ Research

Atypical development of the brain has been linked to disorders. One such example is Autistic Spectrum Disorder (ASD). ASD is defined as having symptoms as follows:

■ ongoing social problems that include difficulty communicating and interacting with others

■ repetitive behaviours, as well as limited interests or activities

■ symptoms that typically are recognized in the first two years of life

■ symptoms that hurt the individual's ability to function socially, at school or work, or other areas of life.

Research has identified that there could be a brain development issue in the development of the disorder. Through brain imaging research, **Esquivel-Alvarez & Shahdiani (2015)** identified that the brain development of those diagnosed with ASD differed from the norm in terms of grey and white matter development, cortical thickness and the myelination (the production of myelin sheath which helps in conducting messages along the axon of the neuron). Shahdiani also observed widespread differences throughout the brain, indicating that the behaviour could be a manifestation of abnormal brain development.

Albert *et al.* (2013) reviewed literature examining decision-making in adolescence. Research suggests that brain development at that time may affect decision-making and risk-taking behaviour. However, along with brain development, the researchers also looked at other potential effects on the decision-making in that life stage. They found that studies also emphasized the social aspects, as adolescents are heavily influenced by peers. Albert *et al.* asserted that as the brain develops it was not just the neuronal connections in the frontal lobe that moderated the risky decision-making, but also that the maturing brain facilitates self-regulation and allows the individual to be able to resist peer influence.

Lopez-Larson *et al.* (2011) found significant gender differences in male and female brain development from the age of 11 to 35 years. The area of key difference was that there was a greater amount of neuronal connections in the amygdala (an area linked to emotion) and hippocampus (implicated in memory).

KEY STUDY CONTEMPORARY RESEARCH

'A window of opportunity for cognitive training in adolescence'
Knoll *et al.* (2016)

Much brain development research focuses on the brains of children; however, lifelong learning indicates that the brain continues to develop beyond that life stage.

Aim
The researchers were interested in examining opportunities for learning beyond childhood and the extent to which brain development facilitates this.

Procedure
1   The sample consisted of 633 11- to 33-year-olds, divided into four age groups, and they were each assigned to one of three possible training groups.
2   All the groups were asked to complete 20 days of training on either perception of magnitude, reasoning or facial recognition.

Results
1   The training worked in different ways for each cognitive skill.
2   For perception of quantity the training only worked on late adolescents and adults. Interestingly, the training for reasoning was successful across all ages. However, training did not improve for the facial recognition task at any age.

Conclusion
This suggests that for certain cognitive skills, learning appears to be superior later in adolescence and adulthood. The early adolescent brain is not as receptive to development and change. The implications of this for brain development are that research should consider the 'developing brain' beyond adolescence and also that there could be age stages in the education system where learning may be slower, or not happen at all for certain cognitive skills.

Evaluation

- This study is important in that it illustrates that brain development continues past childhood and adolescence.
- The large sample size also makes the findings more robust.

Evaluation

■ The influence of the environment on the developing brain is widely acknowledged in the literature. However, the degree to which brain development and the environment are responsible for the behaviour of an individual is not easy to ascertain. These factors almost certainly combine, but deciding the most influential cannot be done.

■ The various ways of gathering data on brain development could all be seen as problematic. One of the key issues is the number of cases included in research. Brain imaging research traditionally uses small samples, owing to participant availability, cost and equipment availability. This means that generalizing to the whole population is difficult, especially considering that brains are unique. That said, there are general observed trends in brain development.

■ The trajectory of brain development is focused mainly on childhood. However, the idea that this should be the main focus has been questioned following research findings that the brain learns effectively and develops further across the lifespan. The research by Knoll and colleagues (see 'Contemporary research' above) is an example of where brain development needs to be considered beyond the traditional era of childhood.

Strengthen your learning

1 Explain the physical development trajectory of the brain.

2 Outline the following influences upon the development trajectory of the brain:
   a genes and environment
   b gender differences
   c toxins.

3 Summarize what research studies have suggested about the physical development trajectory of the brain.

4 What other evaluative points can be made about the physical development trajectory of the brain?

5 For Knoll *et al.*'s contemporary 2016 study of cognitive training in adolescence, in your own words, state the:
   a aims
   b procedure
   c results
   d conclusions
   e evaluative points.

SECTION SUMMARY

■ Piaget suggested a theory of cognitive development with biological underpinnings.
■ Vygotsky's theory of cognitive development focused upon explaining the thinking of a child as an interaction between the child and the culture they grow up in.
■ Brain development varies across childhood and into adulthood in terms of the proportion of grey and white brain matter.
■ Brain development is affected by such factors as genes, gender and toxins in the environment.

'*Healthy citizens are the greatest asset any country can have.*'
Winston S. Churchill

Introduction

Health psychology considers both physical and psychological health and well-being. By understanding the thought processes, external factors and biology involved in engaging in health behaviours, both good and bad, health psychology can work in both a reactive and proactive way to try and raise the general health of the population.

It considers how health can be affected at the biological, cognitive and sociocultural levels. If you consider an individual and their health, it is clear that their biology can affect how they feel (for example, via a virus or tumour) but the way that they think and the beliefs they hold, such as how likely they are to recover, can also have an effect. These beliefs will also affect how likely they are to take part in healthy/unhealthy behaviours. Sociocultural factors such as their ethnicity and level of wealth will also be an influence on how healthy they are.

Health psychologists are widely involved in providing insights into 'good' and 'bad' health behaviours and their input in health promotion can be invaluable. This section considers the areas of health determinants, health problems and health promotion.

Determinants of health

> **FOCUS ON...**
>
> - Understanding and evaluating the biopsychosocial model of health and well-being.
> - The influence of dispositional factors in determining health.
> - How health beliefs can affect the health of the individual.
> - The influence of both risk and protective factors on health.

■ Biopsychosocial model of health and well-being

Biomedical – relates to both biology and medicine.

Psychosomatic – when a health condition may be caused, or made worse, by a mental factor such as internal conflict or stress.

Holistic – consideration of the whole person, including psychological and social factors as well as biological symptoms.

For many years the **biomedical** model of health and well-being was the dominant explanation for health. This means that healthcare within society was viewed and organized around this perspective. There were key assumptions made by the model.

The core assumption was that ill health and sickness came from the environment in a biological form such as a bacteria or virus. All illness was caused by a biological reason. As such, the individual who was ill was in no way responsible for becoming sick. This also meant that illness was seen as a change in the physical state of the individual and that a return to health meant that the physical change should be treated biologically or physically by a health professional. This model also was dichotomous in that it sees individuals as either healthy or ill.

In the twentieth century, this model was moderated by the introduction of **psychosomatic** and behavioural medicine. Psychosomatic as a word is a combination of psych (mind) and soma (body). This was introduced following the publication of Sigmund Freud's ideas.

So there was an acknowledgement of the role of mind in health, and the introduction of behavioural medicine introduced the idea of preventative medicine; changing how an individual behaves to maintain health.

Health psychology as a discipline sees illness differently from the biomedical model. It does not regard poor health as having a purely biological cause and has replaced this idea with the health of an individual being due to a complex system of interacting forces. This is a **holistic** viewpoint. The shift means that they see an individual as responsible for their own health. Treatment is advocated using a series of professionals who can help with all aspects; treatment is no longer seen as the domain of doctors only. The dichotomous viewpoint of healthy/ill is also argued to be outdated and most health professionals would advocate seeing health/illness along a continuum, with full health at one end and very ill at the other. Health is ultimately seen as an interaction between body and mind. One model which acknowledges this interaction is the biopsychosocial model.

The biopsychosocial model

This model acknowledges both the influence of biology and psychology in illness but also highlights the influence of environmental factors such as poverty and working conditions. It was developed by **Engel (1978)** and is an integrative model.

Engel stated that there were three key elements to health and illness – biology, psychology and social – all with relatively equal influence on health.

The biological element referred to all the causes focused upon by the biomedical model. These included viruses, bacteria and damage to physiology (such as a stroke causing a brain lesion). The second element, psychology, focused upon the behaviour of the individual in terms of lifestyle choice (smoking, drinking alcohol, etc.) and their thought processes (their beliefs). Their resilience in terms of coping is also part of this element, together with perceived stress and pain levels. The third element, which incorporates research in such fields as sociology, is social factors. These refer to such influences as class, ethnicity, employment and wealth. With the factors come 'norms' of behaviour, such as whether you should smoke or not, and pressures from family and peers. For the social element of the model, it is acknowledged that there is massive variability in terms of the extent to which someone may become ill. For example, two people may have a cough that has been present for three weeks. One of these people may realize that this could be an indication that something serious is wrong so they seek advice from a GP. However, the other person with the same condition may be part of a family unit who do not advocate seeing a doctor, and therefore a more serious illness, such as lung cancer, could be missed.

Culture too plays a part in the model at this level. A culture can determine whether an individual is likely to seek help for their medical problem, or not. It can equally affect the adoption of protective behaviours to maintain good health. An example of this is screening for illness or inoculation against illness. Sub-cultures too can have an effect. For example, **Zola (1966)** noticed that Italian Americans report a larger number of symptoms than Irish Americans. However, the Irish Americans reported many more issues with respiratory problems, particularly the ear, nose and throat. There is no clear reason for this difference other than cultural norms.

TOK link

Reductionism can be defined as the attempt to explain any act by reducing it to a simpler level. Holism, however, is when the interaction of different factors affecting a behaviour is taken into account in an explanation – it does not focus on one specific part of an explanation. Reductionism is often a criticism levelled at explanations for behaviour in psychology. The biopsychosocial model of health behaviour considers many levels of behaviour. It is therefore a holistic model.

▨ Research

■ The impact of the biopsychosocial model was measured by **Miró et al. (2009)** in patients with muscular dystrophy (a muscle wasting disease that is genetic). They looked specifically at the chronic pain the patients were experiencing from their condition. They asked 182 patients to complete a series of questionnaires about their pain levels, psychological and demographic factors, together with any injuries they had. Psychological functioning measures were also included to assess the cognitive aspects of their pain. It was found that all the elements, biological, social and psychological, played a part in the patients' pain experience, which strongly supported the model and helped the researchers to identify key factors in pain management for people suffering from muscular dystrophy.

- **Habtewold et al. (2016)** applied the biopsychosocial model to patients who had been affected physically by Type 2 diabetes and psychologically by depression. They examined the extent to which social variables should be taken into account to reduce levels of depression. They found that marital status, negative life events and poor social support all played a part in the levels of the depression experienced. This supports the idea that social factors are influential and that all three elements of the model need consideration for treatment of the patients.

- Further support for the biopsychosocial model was found by **McNamara & McCabe (2012)**, who looked at explaining the exercise levels taken by elite Australian athletes. The researchers were interested to see what exercise dependence was related to within the athlete's world. A holistic approach was taken in the research, when they compared athletes who indicated exercise dependency (using a measure) and those who did not. They found there were differences at the physical level (in terms of higher body mass in 'dependent' athletes) and also at the cognitive level in terms of their beliefs relating to exercise. They also had lower levels of social support and higher levels of pressure from coaches. McNamara & McCabe suggested that the explanation needed to take all the levels of explanation into account to satisfactorily explain exercise dependence and that no one factor alone was responsible for the behaviour.

Evaluation

- The biopsychosocial model of health has been embraced within the profession. For example, in terms of psychological illness, addiction is acknowledged as having all three elements and influences in the DSM-V, the manual used for diagnosis of mental disorder. There is mention of biological mechanisms such as brain reward circuitry, cognitive influences such as memory and genetic and environmental influences. These are discussed in detail in this chapter.

- Engel has been criticized for merely acknowledging the factors that affect illness and not the impact of illness on those factors. His critics argue that he does not make a full holistic argument. They say there is a two-way exchange of biological, psychological and social factors. So, for example, the world of a patient includes all three types of influence of their health but, in turn, their health has an effect on the three areas of biology, psychology and social factors too, like feeling pain, which then affects the patient's mental health and consequently the close family are affected too.

- Critics also argue that there is more emphasis on certain factors than others within the medical profession. For example, some practitioners focus on the physical or biological elements because they may be easier to treat. It is argued that it is difficult for practitioners to consider all three levels of influences. With a limited amount of time and resources it is difficult for those treating illness to find out about all the elements of the illness and the patient's life. Therefore, the treatment of the biology is very often the focus of their work.

- By shifting the focus from the biological model to the biopsychosocial model the focus on blame can be argued to shift from the biology of an individual, which some see as out of their control, to elements such as how they think and interact being a factor in their illness. This can appear as if the blame lies with the patient and this is, for some, victimizing them again.

Strengthen your learning

1 Outline the biopsychosocial model of health and well-being, including focus on:
   a biological
   b psychological
   c social
   d cultural and sub-cultural factors.

2 Summarize what research has suggested about the biopsychosocial model of health and well-being.

3 Assess the biopsychosocial model in terms of strengths and weaknesses.

■ Dispositional factors and health beliefs

IN THE NEWS

Ψ The Psychological Enquirer

ANT MCPARTLIN IN REHAB FOR DRUG ADDICTION

Ant McPartlin, one-half of the celebrity duo Ant and Dec, was admitted into a rehabilitation clinic for drug addiction. He stayed in the clinic for two months while he was treated for painkiller addiction and alcohol dependency.

The addiction is believed to have started following a knee operation two years ago, when Ant was prescribed painkillers to help him cope with the pain. Ant also explained how he had started drinking heavily, so alcohol abuse was also an issue. He was urged to seek help from his friend Declan Donnelly and his wife and family. The presenter stated how doctors told him he had come close to killing himself with the behaviour.

Following two months of rehab Ant left the clinic and reported that he felt well and positive. The general public reacted to this news with surprise and sympathy. There were many well-wishers as Ant McPartlin is a popular celebrity. The story illustrates how addiction can affect someone who has a seemingly good and successful life.

It is recognized that there are dispositional, risk and protective factors that can increase or decrease chances of health behaviours in everyone. Addiction is one of those health behaviours and will be examined in this chapter.

There are direct and indirect influences on health. For example, beliefs can lead to a direct effect, such as feeling that you are very stressed at any point in time having an immediate physical effect on your biology. However, it could equally prompt you to adopt a behaviour such as smoking a lot of cigarettes or drinking heavily, which will have a detrimental effect in the long term.

Dispositional factors

Dispositional factors are internal factors that affect health and are characteristics of an individual. They can include anything from genetics to personality and are mostly indirect and out of the individual's control (to some extent), but this does not make them any less important. Genetic vulnerability and personality are considered with regard to health behaviour below. This section looks specifically at addiction. Probably the best way to describe addiction is to refer to the diagnostic manual to see what is now defined as dependence. This varies depending on whether it is dependence on substance (like nicotine) or behavioural (like gambling). Alcohol is given separate diagnostic criteria, which are similar to substance-related addiction. There is a list of 11 symptoms, of which two need to be evident for diagnosis to be made. They also need to be present together in the same 12-month period. Examples of the indicators are:

- taking the substance in larger amounts, or for longer than intended
- wanting to cut down or stop using the substance, but not being able to
- spending a lot of time getting, using, or recovering from use of the substance
- cravings and urges to use the substance
- not managing to do what you should at work, home or school because of substance use.

It is evident that the symptoms of a problem do not vary significantly from each other. Broadly speaking, there are key behaviours such as over-use, taking the substance even when you know it is bad for you, problems maintaining everyday activities and ineffective efforts to stop.

Genetic vulnerability

There is thought to be a genetic influence on development of addiction, much like many other behaviours. **Nielsen *et al.* (2009)** compared DNA from former heroin addicts and non-addicts, and they found a connection between the genetics of the individual and their genetic make-up.

However, it is absolutely necessary for there to be a gene–environment interaction for this to occur. The individual will plainly not become addicted if they are not exposed to the substance or the opportunity within their environment. Therefore, genetic vulnerability should be seen as an interaction.

Twin studies have been useful for picking up on a heritability component to addiction. So too have linkage studies of addiction to substances and genetic make-up. These have shown an association between genes and: 1) alcohol (**Foroud *et al.*, 2000**); 2) nicotine (**Li *et al.*, 2004**); and 3) cocaine (**Gelernter, 2005**). Twin studies are useful for picking up on genetic vulnerability because the incidence rates in identical twins (who are 100 per cent genetically similar) and non-identical twins (who are only 50 per cent genetically similar) can be compared. Other linkage studies have found a similar relationship.

The way genetics can increase our likelihood of becoming addicted when looking at substance addiction is the way our body responds to a drug. We can be more susceptible to its positive or negative effects. In the case of alcohol, the way the genetic code affects the likelihood of addiction is the way in which alcohol is metabolized by the body. The first reaction of our body to alcohol is to metabolize it to acetaldehyde then to acetic acid. The acid is released into our urine very quickly, otherwise we can feel nauseous. In about 50 per cent of people from Asia, their genetic code does not facilitate the release of the acetic acid into the urine so they feel nauseous when drinking alcohol. Clearly this means their chance of addiction is slim to none.

LINK TO BIOLOGICAL EXPLANATION

Genetic vulnerability is a biological dispositional factor in its purest form. The vulnerability cannot be controlled in any way and is determined at conception.

▮ Research

- **Tsuang *et al.* (1996)** used data from the Vietnam Era Twin Registry to evaluate the genetic influence on addiction. They looked at the records of 3000 male twins. To define addiction, they deemed it to be the use of an illegal drug at least once a week. The data showed that there was a significant difference in the concordance rates of MZ (identical) and DZ (non-identical) twins. This suggests that there is a genetic component to the addiction.

- **Kendler *et al.* (1997)** found that the concordance rates for alcohol abuse in MZ twins were significantly higher than for DZ twins. The data was gathered from the Swedish Twin Registry and the sample size was large, at almost 9000 twin pairs. The data had been collected over a 40-year period and the researchers found that the heritability figure stayed constant over time. This too suggests that there is a genetic component to addiction.

- **Kendler & Prescott (1998)** compared concordance levels of drug abuse among MZ and DZ twins. The classification of drug abuse was the criteria set out by DSM-IV and data from nearly 2000 twins was used. They found concordance rates for using, abusing or being dependent on drugs were higher for MZ than for DZ twins. For cannabis use, concordance was 54 per cent for MZ twins against 42 per cent for DZ twins. For lifetime cannabis abuse, concordance was 47 per cent in MZ twins against 8 per cent for DZ twins. For cannabis dependence, concordance was 35 per cent in MZ twins against 0 per cent in DZ twins. These figures indicate there is a genetic link to use of drugs.

- **DiFranza (2008)** found that 10 per cent of teenage smokers who went on to be nicotine addicts had strong cravings for smoking two days after first inhaling and 35 per cent within one month, suggesting that nicotine is strongly addictive, with long-term use not necessary for addiction. The fact that those who had cravings early on were 200 times more likely to become daily smokers suggests a genetic vulnerability. It seems that they are genetically more susceptible to feeling the effects of the drug.

▓ Evaluation

- There seems to be a wealth of research indicating that there is a genetic vulnerability to addiction, although no concordance rates in twin studies have ever shown 100 per cent concordance, so it is clearly a genetic predisposition rather than a certainty.

- It appears that the genetic link to addiction varies across substances, which means that the vulnerability is not general but specific to certain substances. This, in turn, means that if an individual is never exposed to the substance they will never realize that they have that genetic vulnerability, as they may not react in the same way to other substances.

- The role of the environment is also vital in considering genetics. This is particularly so with addiction, as many factors affect the predisposition to addiction, such as exposure to the drug, availability, stress, family influence and peers.

- There may be a fundamental issue in drawing conclusions from twin studies, as MZ twins are more likely to be treated similarly by parents than DZ twins. This means that concordance rate differences may be accounted for by upbringing rather than genetic similarity. This weakens the argument for a genetic vulnerability to addiction.

Personality

It is argued that people who have pathological personalities are more likely to become addicts because the drug or behaviour they are addicted to initially offers them a relief. Pathological personalities are types that have a predominantly negative persona. Their personality means they may be more stressed and find life difficult. The temporary high gained from playing a fruit machine or drinking a vodka and tonic, for example, would make them more likely to keep doing it. This means ultimately that the personality triggers the addiction rather than the other way round.

Addictive personality

> **Neuroticism** – a personality characteristic that is characterized by high levels of worry, anxiety and depressed mood.
>
> **Psychoticism** – a personality characteristic that is characterized by high levels of aggressiveness and hostility to others.

Various theorists have proposed the existence of an addictive personality. **Eysenck (1997)** outlined a model that suggested addictions occur because of personality type and the needs of the personality. He argued that those with high **neuroticism** levels were predisposed to addictions. Neuroticism is characterized by high levels of anxiety and irritability. He also added that high levels of **psychoticism** were linked to addiction because this meant that the individual was aggressive and emotionally detached, so the high associated with drugs or certain behaviours helped this.

Eysenck also argued that there was a biological basis to personality and therefore the personality was inherited. Following this argument through, it would seem to suggest that someone is born with a predisposition to their personality.

Cloninger's (1987) tri-dimensional theory of addictive behaviour suggests that there are three key traits – novelty seeking, harm avoidance and reward dependence – that make an individual liable to substance abuse.

Novelty seeking is the need for change and stimulation. Individuals will actively seek new environments and experience, almost as if they have a low boredom threshold. This element makes them more likely to seek out sensations from drugs.

Harm avoidance is the amount that a person worries and sees the negative elements of a situation. This can affect their likelihood of taking a drug and therefore becoming addicted to it. Cloninger's theory suggests that addiction occurs in individuals with a low level of harm avoidance.

Reward dependence in an individual is when someone reacts and learns from a rewarding situation quickly. This also predisposes them to addiction, as the rewarding effects are experienced quickly and easily.

LINK TO THE COGNITIVE EXPLANATION

Personality is defined as a cognitive dispositional factor, as it is a pattern of thought processes that leads to behaviour.

KEY STUDY | # CONTEMPORARY RESEARCH

'The relationship between stress, personality, family functioning and internet addiction in college students'
Yan *et al.* (2014)

This section considers the dispositional factors in health behaviours, specifically addiction. The research conducted by Wansen Yan et al. examined the different potential influences underpinning internet addiction. This addiction could also inform researchers on other addictive behaviours such as gambling.

Aim

The researchers' aim was to examine whether there is a relationship between stress levels, personality traits, and family functioning in relation to internet addiction.

Procedure

1 892 participants (407 males and 485 females) had complete data sets out of an original sample of 1065 college students. They were selected from across China.

2 Each participant completed five measures using a questionnaire format.

 a Demographic variables. A questionnaire was used to collect data on gender, age, education grade, university and province.

 b Family functioning. To measure how well the family of each participant functions, the researchers used the Family Adaptability and Cohesion Scale, a 30-item measure that looks at the adaptability and cohesiveness of the family, examining such things as the strength of the emotional bond between members and the level of connection between members.

 c Addiction level. The Chen Internet Addiction Scale was used for this purpose. It is a 26-item scale, which considers compulsive use, withdrawal effects, tolerance, time management, interpersonal problems and health problems.

 d Personality. The Eysenck personality questionnaire was given to participants. This had 48 items with yes/no response options that measured the level of extraversion, neuroticism and psychoticism for each participant.

 e Stress. To measure stress levels the researchers administered the Adolescent Self-rating Life Events checklist, which looks at the amount of life change the individual has been through in the last 12 months. There is a positive correlation between the number and degree of life changes experienced and stress.

Results

1 It was found that almost 10 per cent of the sample had severe internet addiction and just over 11 per cent (100 students) had mild internet addiction.

2 No link was found between the demographic variables and level of addiction.

3 The group with severe addiction had low family functioning levels, implying that poor family relationships were influential. However, this could have occurred after the addiction.

4 The severely addicted group also had higher levels of neuroticism and psychoticism and lower levels of extraversion, as indicated by the personality questionnaire.

5 The severely addicted group had higher scores on the life changes measure than the non-addicted participants, which suggests they had experienced higher levels of stress over the previous 12 months. The mildly addicted students answered no differently to the non-addicted participants on the measures of personality.

Conclusion

To conclude, it appears therefore that personality, stress and family functioning all play a part in addictive behaviour.

Evaluation

- The psychological processes underlying these factors were not in any way tested by this research. It is merely correlational, so only a relationship can be ascertained. This means that the factors could be vulnerability factors, or they could equally be by-products of being addicted. Looking, for example, at the family functioning measure, it is possible that a consequence of the severe internet addiction experienced by about 100 of the participants could have placed considerable strain on relationships due to their lack of interaction at home and at social occasions.

- The fact that there was missing data from so many students may mean that the sample is biased, as it is essentially self-selecting. It could be that some students who were severely addicted did not wish to contribute their data. Exactly how this would affect the outcome is not known, but caution should be used in drawing conclusions from the figures showing the number who were severely/mildly addicted. It is possible this is higher in the college student population because internet-addicted individuals may be less likely to fill out the questionnaires as they have other priorities, such as being on the computer. This means the exact relationship cannot be established. The number of measures used would have meant there were a lot of questions to answer, so it is possible that participants dropped out because they found the procedure too time-consuming.

▧ Research

- **Howard *et al.* (1997)** in a meta-analysis of the studies investigating Cloninger's tri-dimensional theory found that novelty seeking does predict alcohol abuse in teenagers and young adults. It also predicts anti-social behaviour in those alcoholics. However, harm avoidance and reward dependence do not seem as clearly linked to addictive behaviours and the relationship is less consistent. This suggests all three dimensions do not contribute to addictive behaviour equally and that personality may not play a key part in addiction.

- Work by **Zuckerman (1983)** on sensation seeking shows a link between the need for novelty and addictive behaviours. Cloninger's novelty seeking and Zuckerman's sensation seeking are very closely linked, so this supports Cloninger's ideas too.

- **Yan *et al.* (2014)** (see 'Contemporary research' above) show that there is a relationship between personality characteristics and addiction. The research looked specifically at Eysenck's theory and found evidence to suggest that high levels of neuroticism, high levels of psychoticism and low levels of extraversion were linked to internet addiction. These findings support Eysenck's ideas, although the low levels of extraversion found in the study contradict Cloninger's theory that novelty seeking is a characteristic predisposing an individual to addiction. Extraversion is a personality characteristic that seeks out stimulation, so this would suggest that extraversion would be at a high level in addicts, if Cloninger's theory is correct.

Evaluation

- There is evidence to suggest that personality traits are implicated in an individual's likelihood of becoming an addict. However, to argue that there is an addictive personality that is inherited seems less plausible.

- The possession of certain traits does not automatically mean that addiction will occur; it is merely a predisposition. There are lots of other factors involved that influence the behaviour.

- Evidence suggests that certain traits are high in predictive validity with regards to addictive behaviour. However, the research indicates only likelihood and cannot fully explain the mechanism or cause underlying the behaviour. This makes it incomplete.

- The role of personality in addiction is complex as cause and effect is difficult to establish. This means that it is not always clear whether the addiction has altered the personality or vice versa, that is, has the individual's personality predisposed them to addiction?

> ### YOU ARE THE RESEARCHER
> Personality is often measured using questionnaires. If you were to design a questionnaire to test Cloninger's theory, what kind of items would you include? Remember that your questionnaire would have to test all three dimensions of the personality.
>
> What ethical considerations would you have to take into account with your questionnaire?
>
> How could you test the validity of the questionnaire you developed?

Health beliefs

There are several key theories for beliefs about health and this section outlines three: the health belief model, the theory of planned behaviour and Prochaska's six-stage model of behaviour change.

Health belief model

This model was generated in the 1970s to understand why preventative behaviours were not employed by individuals to protect their health. The take-up rate of screening, for example, was lower than expected. It provides a way to ascertain the likelihood of someone using the facilities and services available to them, adding insight into the actions of the population.

Likelihood of engagement is established by looking at how at risk individuals feel they are and whether they evaluate the service/facility positively.

There are key elements in the model centred on individual perceptions, modifying factors and likelihood of acting. In terms of individual perceptions, the perceived susceptibility to the consequences of not acting and the perceived severity of not acting (i.e. Will it kill me, or am I at risk with the intervention?) influence the behaviour. Modifying factors also include the benefits of acting (Will I feel fitter?), demographic variables such as age (I am too old to try), the threat level (This will definitely kill me if I do not do it) and cues to action (such as the health promotion campaign or the death of a loved one). Finally, the likelihood of action relates to the costs, barriers and benefits of acting, for example the accessibility of a service or the likelihood of making friends.

This model is illustrated in Figure 7.1.

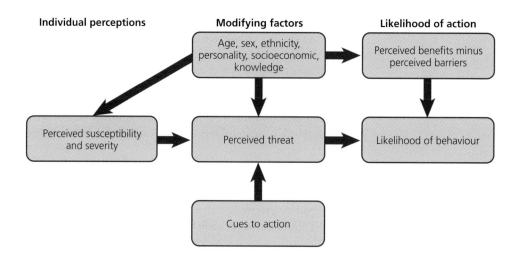

Individual perceptions   Modifying factors   Likelihood of action

Age, sex, ethnicity, personality, socioeconomic, knowledge

Perceived benefits minus perceived barriers

Perceived susceptibility and severity

Perceived threat

Likelihood of behaviour

Cues to action

■ **Figure 7.1** Health belief model

▨ Research

■ **De Wit & Stroebe (2004)** make the point, when reviewing the health belief model, that a questionnaire has not yet been developed that tests the model in its entirety. There are ways of measuring each component, but not the model. This means that the model's predictive validity (i.e. how much it can actually predict the likelihood of acting upon a behaviour) is difficult to ascertain. It also means that each of the elements may be viewed differently by different researchers. In effect, there is no clear definition for each element in terms of experimentation, yet.

■ **Gorin & Heck (2005)** found that the model was able to predict the uptake for a cervical cancer screening programme reasonably accurately. In the study they found that demographic variables such as age and marital status played a large influence in uptake. This supports the health belief model.

■ **Wringe *et al.* (2009)** conducted research in rural Tasmania into uptake for an HIV treatment programme. They found that the biggest determinant of uptake was the accessibility, which acted as a large barrier for some individuals. This demonstrates that the most influential factors in the model can vary from country to country.

▨ Evaluation

■ There is no account of the emotions involved in the decision-making process. The model acts as if an individual is rational, but decisions are often emotive and there is no evidence of this as a modifying factor. Some researchers argue this is accounted for within the model in the cost/barriers and cues to action section because phobia of hospitals would act as a barrier and the death of a loved one would act as a cue to action, but there is no acknowledgement of emotion as a mediating influence per se.

■ The model is argued to be good for explaining individual behaviours such as attending a screening test or having inoculations. It is, however, not able to explain general attitudes to health. Looking at the development of the model, however, it was designed to examine likelihood of uptake of a behaviour, so it can be argued that the model is fit for purpose.

■ The lack of a questionnaire to measure the model as a whole means that the model has never been tested as a whole entity and this has implications for its validity. However, as the model does not claim to calculate the likelihood quantitatively, it is perhaps sufficient that it brings all the various elements involved in decision-making together.

■ The research from **Wringe *et al.* (2009)** above suggests that although the model is cognitive, there is cultural influence on beliefs. Therefore, the model should take this into account and identify where this may occur.

The theory of planned behaviour

The theory of planned behaviour is a refinement of the model of reasoned action, which stated that a change in addictive behaviour was underpinned by decision-making processes. **Ajzen (1991)** developed the model to explain how beliefs affect behaviour change and it is a general model that can be related to many health behaviours, including addiction. In terms of addiction, the model may explain why someone might be successful in quitting addictive behaviours and why someone else might not.

The core idea of the model is that if we are to predict the outcome of a treatment programme, we need to consider the beliefs, influences and motivation of an addict to the proposed change. There are four parts to the model:

1 *Attitude and behavioural beliefs.* Behavioural beliefs are the attitudes towards the behaviour. In the context of addiction, this would be a recognition that the behaviour is having a negative effect on the addict and that giving up is a good idea. This is key to the process of recovery.

2 *Subjective norms and normative beliefs.* Normative beliefs are the beliefs of the group to which the addict feels they belong. If, for example, a drug addict was surrounded by friends who were also addicts and did not wish to give up, then the likelihood of the addict joining a treatment programme and staying on it would be diminished.

3 *Perceived behavioural control.* Control beliefs focus on the factors an addict believes are present and that may affect the treatment. It is very much their perceived idea of the situation and not the reality. So, for example, if they think that they cannot ensure they will attend sessions or stay away from situations that challenge their resolve, the likelihood of the treatment working for them is decreased. This is not particularly what will happen, more what they believe will happen. It should be noted that Ajzen proposed that perceived control was linked directly to behaviour and could therefore be a predictor of behaviour on its own.

4 *Behavioural intentions.* The behavioural intentions are a combination of the other three factors. These all contribute to the level of intention, which is essentially the motivation to engage with the programme. This process is illustrated in Figure 7.2.

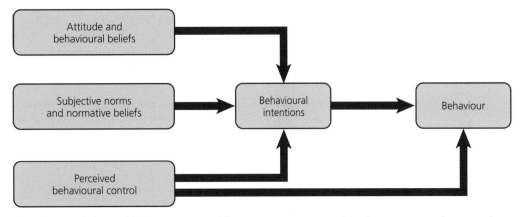

■ **Figure 7.2** Theory of planned behaviour (Ajzen, 1991)

The theory of planned behaviour is used by practitioners to predict the outcomes of potential treatment programmes. They can establish why someone wants to quit and the amount of resolve they have to do so. The first section of the model, which focuses on behavioural beliefs, is important to ensure they access the treatment initially. The second stage of normative beliefs ensures the social support is present and that negative peer and family influence can be dealt with. The final section of perceived control is a good indicator for the success of the programme. If an addict does not believe that they can stop their addictive behaviour, for example by stopping gambling or giving up smoking, it is unlikely that they will do so.

▦ Research

- **Webb & Sheeran (2006)** conducted a meta-analysis of 47 studies using the model. They found that the level of intention is linked to behavioural change, but that the link is small, so scoring high for intention with the model actually only prompts a small behaviour change. This suggests that the theory can explain behavioural change, but to a lesser degree than originally thought.

- **Godin & Kok (1996)** reviewed how successful the theory was for predicting health-related behaviours generally. Their findings were positive, showing a significant correlation between the behaviours and the intention level predicted by the model. They also found that the level of perceived behavioural control made a significant contribution towards predicting the behaviours in half of the studies.

- **Oh & Hsu (2001)** used a questionnaire to assess gamblers' previous gambling behaviour, their social norms, attitudes, perceived behavioural control (such as perceived gambling skills and levels of self-control), along with behavioural intentions. A positive correlation was found between attitudes and behavioural intentions and actual behaviour, supporting the model.

- **Walker *et al.* (2006)** used interviews to assess whether theory of planned behaviour could explain gambling behaviour. They found that behavioural beliefs and normative beliefs were important, but that perceived behavioural control was not. Intention was, however, found to be a good predictor of behavioural change. This seems to support some elements of the model but not others.

▦ Evaluation

- The theory is used widely in health psychology and health economics (which looks at cost-effectiveness of treatments). This suggests that practitioners acknowledge its validity and deem its predictive power as useful.

- There is no consideration of emotion within the model, which can influence the likelihood of behavioural change. This is especially the case with addiction, which is a vulnerable state and influenced by mood.

- A strength of the model is its acknowledgement of the role of peers in influencing behaviour. This influence does not stop once the behaviour is developed and therefore should be considered in predicting outcomes of behaviour change programmes.

- The model relies on self-report measures to gauge its effectiveness. This is a potential problem as the participants could be irrational and liable to downplay the level of their addiction. This means that the effectiveness measures may be unreliable.

- The practical application of this model is one of its strengths. Practitioners can use it to decide whether an intervention will be effective, and as such, time and money are not spent if it is not going to be effective for the individual.

Prochaska's six-stage model of behaviour change to addictive behaviour

Prochaska's (1977) model offers an explanation for the process of changing from unhealthy to healthy behaviours. He and his colleagues felt that change of behaviour was often portrayed as an immediate jump from unhealthy to healthy and that in reality this was simply not the case. He argued that there are stages, a series of transitions in thinking and action that lead to someone actually changing. He also argued that once their behaviour had changed, it was not a constant state and relapse could occur. Indeed, it could occur at any stage in the process.

The six stages are outlined in Table 7.1. There is also a quote of what someone in that stage might be expected to say.

Stage	Outline of stage	Potential quote
1 Pre-contemplation	This is when the individual will be aware that what they are doing is unhealthy, but they do not feel they need to do anything about it at this point.	'I am OK right now'
2 Contemplation	In this stage individuals show an awareness that they need to take action, but they do not do it. It is often described as a stage of inertia, when people know the right thing to do but they do not act on it.	'I will change, tomorrow'
3 Preparation	This stage is the first point at which action is taken. It is also important in that if the behaviour change is planned, it has a greater chance of succeeding. Behaviours at this stage are dependent on the aspect being changed, but they include things such as ensuring that there are no social events that might tempt a relapse in the early days, planning distractors to keep the individual busy, and deciding on rewards to keep motivation strong.	'I'm changing next month so I need to plan how I will do it'
4 Action	This is when the plan is put into action. Smoking is stopped, alcohol is no longer drunk and this is the first time the person actually makes the change of behaviour. This stage lasts six months until it is deemed to be the next stage of maintenance. Relapse can happen at this stage.	' I have stopped'
5 Maintenance	This stage can be lengthy, and starts to ensure that the initial enthusiasm and motivation do not wane. Maintenance strategies are employed, such as realizing the benefits of adopting the healthier behaviour, rewarding oneself for stopping, and keeping focused on the long-term goal of termination. Relapse can still occur at this stage.	'I have still stopped!'
6 Termination	Termination was added to a revision of the model in 1992. This is a stable state and is the point at which there is no longer any temptation and there is maximum confidence in the ability to resist the behaviour. Some people never achieve this stage, instead staying in the stage of maintenance for many years. However, this stage means the change is complete – relapse cannot occur.	'I will never do it again'

■ **Table 7.1** Prochaska's six stages

The model is used to explain the change of all unhealthy behaviours to healthy ones, including addiction.

The model also outlines what may make the person move on and progress from stage to stage. Variables suggested include self-efficacy (their confidence in their ability), helping relationships at home and in their social support network and reinforcement management (making sure the rewards from healthy behaviours are greater than those from unhealthy behaviours).

Research

■ Smoking cessation programmes based on this theory can be successful. A meta-analysis of five studies by **Velicer *et al.* (2007)** showed that there was a robust 22–26 per cent success rate, which compares favourably with other interventions. The researchers also found no demographic differences in success (gender, age, etc.); therefore, it would suggest that it suits all groups. They did find, however, that success was dependent on the smoking habits (e.g. frequency) of the individual.

■ **Parker & Parikh (2001)** looked at how successful Prochaska's theory was in aiding planning programmes of health care interventions. They found the model performed well and helped facilitate the organizing and planning of successful programmes.

■ A randomized control trial conducted by **Aveyard *et al.* (2009)** found that there was no increase in effectiveness if an intervention was tailored to the stages of change of the individual trying to stop smoking. This clearly contradicts the evidence found by **Velicer *et al.* (2007)**.

Evaluation

■ Evidence on the effectiveness of the model is mixed. This can be seen from the Research section above.

■ **Noel (1999)** developed a modified version of the model, which proposed that behavioural change is not linear and that the stages are more like 'influences'. So anyone going through a process of behaviour change has more or less influence from the stages at any one time. For example, someone may take action for most of the time but also have periods where they are judged to be in the contemplation stage. It seems that the division between the stages may not be as clear cut as suggested by Prochaska. This idea is further supported in a 2002 review of the model **(Littell & Girvin, 2002)** where the discussion stated that the stages are not exclusive and therefore should not be seen as stages at all.

■ Looking at change as a series of stages means that interventions can be designed to match the stage that the individual is currently in. This is argued to mean that interventions incorporating the model should work better than those that see it in a less dynamic way.

■ The model has led to measures being developed to allow individuals to be classified on which stage they are currently in. Perhaps the one which is the most widely used is URICA (University of Rhode Island Change Assessment scale), which measures the pre-contemplation, contemplation, action and maintenance stages. Adaptations have been made to make the scales more behaviour-specific, depending on which unhealthy behaviour is being changed. This means that there has been a practical application to the theory, and that appropriate interventions can be administered depending on the stage.

Strengthen your learning

1   What is meant by dispositional factors?

2   Explain how the following can affect addiction:
    a genetic vulnerability
    b personality.

3   Summarize what research studies have suggested about how the following can affect addiction:
    a genetic vulnerability
    b personality.

4   What other evaluative points can be made about how the following can affect addiction:
    a genetic vulnerability
    b personality?

5   For Yan *et al.*'s contemporary 2014 study of the relationship between stress, personality, family functioning and internet addiction in college students, in your own words, state the:
    a aims
    b procedure
    c results
    d conclusions
    e evaluative points.

6   Outline:
    a the health belief model
    b the theory of planned behaviour
    c Prochaska's six-stage model of behaviour change.

7   Summarize what research studies have suggested about:
    a the health belief model
    b the theory of planned behaviour
    c Prochaska's six-stage model of behaviour change,

8   Assess the following in terms of their strengths and weaknesses:
    a the health belief model
    b the theory of planned behaviour
    c Prochaska's six-stage model of behaviour change.

▨ Risk and protective factors

Risk and protective factors are rather like two sides of the same coin. A risk factor will increase the likelihood of developing a bad health or bad health behaviour, whereas protective factors reduce that risk. Both differ from determining factors in that they can, to some extent, be controlled. Each individual has a combination of both risk and protective factors and the resultant combination can be positive (in that an aspect of bad health is avoided) or negative (in that they become more likely to develop bad health if the risks outweigh the protective factors).

The 'In the News' feature opposite illustrates ways that an individual can be at greater risk of suicide owing to family influences and stress, both of which are discussed as risk factors below. They also act as protective factors in other contexts. Some family influence is positive and there is reduced pressure to do well, so stress levels are low.

IN THE NEWS

Ψ The Psychological Enquirer

THE SILICON VALLEY SUICIDES

Palo Alto in California is the location of multi-national companies such as Facebook and Google. The families living there are often affluent and it is not unusual for Chinese families to settle in the area temporarily so that the children can access the education provided at the local high schools. These high schools have a phenomenally successful academic track record, and a higher than average percentage of its senior students getting into top universities after graduation. However, the schools in the area also unfortunately have experienced a higher than average number of its students committing suicide: five times higher than the national average.

Many questions have been raised about why this occurs. The area is affluent (double the median in California) and the students too have much of what they need in terms of cars, phones, and so on. However, they do report that the levels of stress that the culture of achievement places them under means they do not feel the benefits of wealth. There is an expectation of high achievement within much of the community and students often have a phenomenal amount of time at extracurricular activities. All of which contribute to a pressured environment.

■ **Figure 7.3** It has been suggested that stress may have played a part in the high level of student suicides in Silicon Valley

After the suicide of a student called Cameron Lee who, to parents and peers, appeared happy and well, a fellow student called Martha Cabot uploaded a YouTube video, which urged a change in attitude. She focused upon the parents and the stress they exert. The following are quotes from the video. She says:

'We love our Moms and we love our Dads but calm down.'

'The amount of stress on a student is ridiculous. Students feel the constant need at our school of having to keep up with all the achievements.'

'We'll do just fine, even though we got a B minus on that chem test. And no, I won't join the debate team for you.'

She does acknowledge in the information under the video that 'stress' is not definitively the cause of the suicides. However, there does appear to be a relationship in terms of poor health with students in this position. There is also an increase in unhealthy behaviours such as alcohol and drug abuse. **Luthar & Latendresse (2005)** talk about a u-shaped curve, in terms of poor health and unhealthy behaviours, where it is the most-rich and the most-poor students who display a link to poor health (drug abuse, anxiety and depression).

This illustrates that influences from the environment can act as risk factors for an individual, increasing unhealthy behaviour and poor mental health.

Risk and protective factors for health can occur at the biological, psychological and social levels and they are defined as being risk/protective factors because of exposure to them in the environment. For this section, we will consider factors influencing the development of an addiction at all three levels. Biological factors are strictly dispositional factors as they are internal factors that affect health, but there are biological reactions to psychological or cognitive risk factors such as stress. For risk and protective factors, there are both cognitive and social factors. At the cognitive level, we will look at the influence of stress. Finally, at the social level we will consider family influences, specifically social learning and peer influence.

Stress

It is easy to see why high levels of stress would make you more vulnerable to addiction. Turning to behaviours and drugs that give a temporary relief from stress is a type of coping mechanism. Stress can be short term or long term and it is the long-term exposure to stress that could increase the likelihood of someone becoming addicted. High stress in this instance is a risk factor, low stress a protective factor.

There would be mediating factors, however, so someone might experience high stress, but have a lot of social support and other ways of coping with it. It is possible that it is not the level of stress, but the ability to cope with it that predisposes   someone to addiction.

There are higher levels of stress in cities or areas with a high population, and this is also related to addictive behaviour as the number of addicts is greater in overcrowded urban environments. However, cause and effect cannot be established as this is a correlation. The relationship is complex and it could be that addicts live in those areas because of the availability of drugs or cheaper living costs.

There is also the possibility that the two are related because addiction prompts high levels of stress owing to the problems it causes with money.

> **LINK TO THE BIOLOGICAL EXPLANATION**
>
> Stress is a cognitive state as the individual has to perceive a situation as stressful. However, there is a biological effect from the reaction of the body in terms of raised heart rate and sweating. This indicates that there are multiple biological effects occurring in response to a stressor.

Research

- **Yan et al. (2014)** (see 'Contemporary research' on page 311) show that there is a link between stress and addiction. The measure used was life changes which are linked to stress. However, it could be argued that the measure may lack validity.

- **Tavolacci et al. (2013)** examined the risk factors in developing addiction at university. Their argument was that it was a stressful time and that this predisposed students to addictive disorders. They compared highly stressed students (using a perceived stress scale) with students who were feeling less stressed and found that high perception of stress was related to smoking regularly, alcohol abuse problems and risk of cyber addiction (addiction to the internet). This suggests that stress and vulnerability to addiction are linked, although a cause-and-effect relationship cannot be established through this research as it is correlational.

■ **Figure 7.4** Studies have found that addiction to the internet can be related to high perception of stress

- **Sinha (2001)** found in a review of research that stress plays an important role in perpetuating drug abuse and relapse. The mechanism was not made clear from the research, and ideas about how this happened could merely be suggested. This demonstrates a link between stress and addiction, but also that more research into the possible mechanism is necessary.
- **Piazza *et al.* (1989)** tested rats for vulnerability to addiction through stress. They achieved a state of stress in the rats by pinching their tails and found that rats were more likely to seek out and ingest amphetamines the more stressed they became. This research too indicates a relationship between stress and addiction, but as the research is conducted on animals there are issues with generalizing the findings to human behaviour. There is also no insight on why there is a relationship in terms of thought processes or biological mechanisms.

PSYCHOLOGY IN THE REAL WORLD

Screening the older generation for addiction: November 2014

A nursing home in the Bronx, New York has decided that its residents need to be screened for addiction as they have noted that they are vulnerable at key times. One such potential time seems to occur when they are administered strong pain killers to reduce discomfort following surgery. The nursing home targets recent patients who have had surgery for joint replacements or heart conditions. Other occasions when the nursing home believes residents are vulnerable is when they have had a recent bereavement, or life change such as retirement.

The residents are screened as part of their care programme, and if issues with addiction are picked up, they are offered help for their addiction.

Risk factors were clearly identified in this example and appropriate preventative measures were put in place to try and ensure that the vulnerability to addiction did not manifest into actual addiction.

Evaluation

- There is an issue with establishing cause and effect through research. High stress levels may indeed be linked to the likelihood of becoming addicted, but they could equally be a by-product of being addicted.
- Stress research is often conducted on animals because of the ethical issues of using humans. This means that there are issues with applying the research to human behaviour. There is no way of knowing, for example, how stressed the animal feels or indeed if they are definitely stressed, so it can be argued that there are issues with validity.
- Research in this field is useful in terms of developing a practical application. It is feasible that a vulnerability measure could be developed to help predict the likelihood of becoming addicted due to stress levels. A stress level could also be used to help predict the likelihood that someone might relapse, as relapses and stress levels are closely linked.

Family influences

There are two key ways that families can influence addictive behaviour: social learning and expectancies. They can either put an individual at risk of addiction, or protect them to some extent from developing addictive behaviour.

Social learning is the learning of behaviour by observation of role models in the environment. If the individual sees that model rewarded for their behaviour then the vicarious reinforcement is going to increase the likelihood of the observer imitating the behaviour. It is clear how that could occur with addictive substances within a family. However, it should be noted that the addiction is not the imitated behaviour; it is the desire to try the substance that is the influence.

LINK TO SOCIOCULTURAL LEVEL OF ANALYSIS

Social learning is a sociocultural explanation for why someone is more or less likely to develop an addiction. There are elements of cognitive processing, such as the level of motivation, but on the whole it is social cognitive and therefore fits within the category of sociocultural explanations.

▨ Research

- **Akers & Lee (1996)** found that the social learning process was important in explaining smoking behaviours in adolescents. They looked over five years at the smoking levels of 454 young adults aged 12 to 17 and found that social influences affected the smoking behaviours of these participants, to try smoking, continue smoking or quit smoking. One of the sources of social learning tested was family influences.
- **Yan et al. (2014)** (see 'Contemporary research' on page 311) show that there is a relationship between the cohesiveness of the family and the likelihood of internet addiction.

▨ Evaluation

- The relative influence of the family will vary dependent on the age and the strength of relationship for an individual. It may be that at a younger age the influence of the family to try, or abstain from, a substance or behaviour could be much greater than in an older individual. Therefore, family influence is not constant throughout the lifespan.
- There is not a certainty that if a child observes a behaviour they will definitely imitate that behaviour. There are mediating cognitive processes that influence whether a behaviour is imitated or not. This means that motivations to behave in a certain way, such as start smoking, are influenced by other sources which may counteract the family influence. For example, seeing a parent smoke is in no way a guarantee that the children will smoke too.
- It is very difficult to gauge the relative influence of the family against all the other potential influences. All that can be said is that the family can influence behaviour and the likelihood to use a substance. However, how that influence compares with peer influence, for example, is difficult to ascertain

Peers

Given that social influence is often seen as the psychological explanation for initiation to addictive behaviours, the influence of peers is potentially great. However, as with many of the vulnerability factors, proving causation is problematic. It is just as possible that choice of peer groups is influenced by addiction. So an addict might choose a peer group that allows them easy access to the focus of the addiction (e.g. drug) and they may choose a non-judgemental peer group.

Peers are influential at the intervention stage, too, as they can provide access to drugs and may encourage a relapse. It is argued that these social influences should be taken into account when designing and delivering an intervention programme to try to ensure maximum success levels.

▨ Research

- In a longitudinal study by **Bullers et al. (2001)** it was found that selection of the peer group followed addiction in many cases and that it was the greatest influential direction. Social influence had less of an effect. This indicates that the peer group you are part of may not be a strong risk factor.
- **Leshner (1998)** believes treatment strategies must include social context elements, such as peer groups, as well as biological and behavioural ones if they are to be successful, as recovered addicts may relapse when leaving a clinic due to the original social context still being in place. Peer groups can therefore be helpful or unhelpful in helping some recover from addiction.
- **Bauman & Ennett (1996)** argued that much research states that peer influence is a reason behind substance abuse. However, upon reviewing the literature they found that often it was not tested as a construct and that it is possible that the influence level is overestimated.
- Work by **Kobus (2003)** suggested, through reviewing the literature, that the effect of peer influence on smoking behaviour was more subtle than often thought and that the media, family and neighbourhood were also involved. They agreed with the idea of peer influence

for both encouraging and deterring smoking, but argued that the psychological processes behind the behaviour needed more research as they may be more influential risk factors than peer influence per se.

Evaluation

- Peer group influences are just one of many social context effects. Others include such factors as economic and social deprivation, and all should be considered when assessing levels of vulnerability to dependency, as dependency is rarely related to just one factor.

- It is difficult to ascertain the level of influence from peers. Distinguishing the influence of friends from that of family is impossible and therefore it is difficult to establish exactly the extent to which someone is influenced by their peers.

- The influence of peers is likely to be greater at different ages. The work of **Harris (1998)** states that peer influence increases during adolescence, so substance abuse in young adults is likely to be influenced by peers to a greater extent than parents.

Strengthen your learning

1 What is meant by:
   a risk
   b protective factors?

2 Explain how stress can affect vulnerability to addiction.

3 Summarize what research studies have suggested about how stress can affect vulnerability to addiction.

4 What other evaluative points can be made about how stress can affect vulnerability to addiction?

5 Explain how family influences can affect vulnerability to addiction.

6 Summarize what research studies have suggested about how family influences can affect vulnerability to addiction.

7 What other evaluative points can be made about how family influences can affect vulnerability to addiction?

8 Explain how peers can affect vulnerability to addiction.

9 Summarize what research studies have suggested about how peers can affect vulnerability to addiction.

10 What other evaluative points can be made about how peers can affect vulnerability to addiction?

SECTION SUMMARY

- The biopsychosocial model of health behaviour is an integrative model which considers biological, psychological and sociocultural elements of health.
- Dispositional factors such as genetic vulnerability and personality are implicated in health behaviour.
- Health beliefs described by the health belief model, the theory of planned behaviour and Prochaska's six-stage model demonstrate how thought processes can affect health.
- Risk and protective factors such as stress, expectancies, family and peer influences all play a part in affecting the likelihood of suffering ill health.

■ Assessment check

1	Evaluate the biopsychosocial model of health and well-being.	(22 marks)
2	Discuss research studies related to the biopsychosocial model of health.	(22 marks)
3	Discuss the influence of dispositional factors on health-related behaviour.	(22 marks)
4	Evaluate health beliefs as determinants of health.	(22 marks)
5	Discuss one or more research studies of determinants of health.	(22 marks)
6	Discuss risk and protective factors as determinants of health.	(22 marks)

Health problems

'Health is the greatest possession. Contentment is the greatest treasure. Confidence is the greatest friend.'
Lao Tzu

'Addiction isn't about substance – you aren't addicted to the substance, you are addicted to the alteration of mood that the substance brings.'
Susan Cheever

■ Explanations of health problems

The first three chapters of this book considered three levels of explanation in psychology: biological, cognitive and sociocultural. These three overarching ways can be used to explain a specific behaviour such as addiction. The following section looks at the three ways these perspectives explain addiction behaviour, specifically smoking addiction.

FOCUS ON...

■ How health problems can be explained. Ensure you pay equal attention to all three levels of explanation.
■ The prevalence of health problems in the population and the issues with calculating incidence problems.

Brain neurochemistry: the role of dopamine

Dopamine is implicated in addiction as the addictive substance or behaviour prompts a high through boosting the activity of the brain's reward system. This system is found in the centre of the brain and is a complex circuit of neurons that produces a high, like euphoria, which means the individual is tempted to take the drug again or repeat the behaviour.

The brain mechanism is basically a pathway of neurons that is activated by the neurotransmitter dopamine. The source of the activation is the ventral tegmental area (VTA), which has many dopamine neurons. This then triggers activation in the limbic system (specifically the nucleus accumbens) and this subsequently boosts activity in the prefrontal cortex.

This activity is called the 'common reward pathway', as it is associated with the feeling of euphoria. As the level of emotion experienced by this pathway is so high, it explains how an addiction can be formed through repetitive behaviour. As time goes on, and through repeated usage, the level of drug needed to elicit the reaction becomes greater. This occurs due to a change in the neuronal structure in the pathway, which accounts for tolerance levels increasing in an individual and also why the individual craves the drug or wishes to carry out the behaviour. Addiction is the result.

LINK TO BIOLOGICAL EXPLANATION

The dopamine hypothesis is a biological explanation for addiction because it focuses on brain physiology and biochemicals.

■ Research

■ **Dani & Biasi (2001)** found that part of the reason nicotine is so addictive is because it acts upon the dopaminergic systems, which helps to reinforce rewarding behaviour. This shows a direct relationship between the neural mechanisms in the brain and the rewarding effects felt while smoking.

■ **Watkins et al. (2000)** reviewed the research into the neurobiology of nicotine addiction. They found that dopamine release was reduced following chronic exposure to nicotine. This means that tolerance of the drug occurs owing to the level of reward felt decreasing.

- **Di Chiara (2000)** argues that dopamine is one of the main causes for the addictive nature of nicotine. The rewarding aspect of the drug such as the feeling of pleasure is released through dopaminergic activity so is responsible for the addictive nature of the drug. If pleasure was not felt then the smoker would not continue to smoke over time.

■ Evaluation

- The researchers argue that this is only part of the neural action and that dopamine is not the whole story. It is likely that the reason why nicotine is so addictive is due to several complex explanations.
- The role of dopamine could explain how there appears to be a genetic link to addiction. It is possible that the dopaminergic mechanism in some individuals leads them to feel the rewarding aspects of drugs to a greater level.
- The evidence base for research in this area is often using animals as a sample. This means the findings may not be generalizable to humans. They also potentially lack validity because the feelings associated with addiction and drug use cannot be measured successfully because of a lack of communication.
- The dopamine explanation for addiction is purely biological and, as a consequence, the psychological aspects of addiction are largely ignored. It is likely that dopamine, although implicated, is not the whole picture, and many levels of explanation should be considered. It can therefore be said to be reductionist.

Cognitive explanation of smoking addiction

Expectancies

Expectancies are the associations we make from observing the environment around us. In other words, we may learn from our environment that if we drink a lot of alcohol then we will get ill (because we witnessed our older brother doing this). Another application is that if we smoke cigarettes then we will appear cool (because we saw a rock star doing this).

These expectancies are formed from our learning and experience, which in turn is often our home environment. They are a form of schema. This then can explain to some extent how our family and others in our environment can influence our likelihood of addiction. It can increase or decrease the likelihood of trying substances or behaviours and, as a consequence, can influence our chance of becoming addicted.

> **LINK TO COGNITIVE EXPLANATION**
>
> As expectancies are formed through schemas they are a cognitive construct. They are formed through experience but can influence the likelihood of getting addicted, maybe through faulty schemas giving an inaccurate expectancy of becoming addicted to any given substance.

■ Research

- **Christiansen *et al.* (1989)** have shown that the expectancies of adolescents can be used to predict drinking problems in later life. When sampling a group of 11- to 14-year-olds they found that the amount and how often they drank a year later was linked to their expectancies and beliefs. This research shows the importance of environmental influence on later behaviour, so the influence of the family is potentially significant.
- **Dunn & Goldman (1998)** found that when they measured the expectancies of 7- to 18-year-olds they mirrored those of adults. This suggests that the adults in a child's environment can heavily influence their attitude towards substance use and therefore potentially addiction.
- **Brown *et al.* (1998)** examined the way that expectancies can affect treatment for addiction. They found that addicts who had underestimated the effects of withdrawal (low expectancy) were less likely to recover from addiction. This suggests that expectancies are important in recovering from addiction, but lower expectancies may also mean that the addiction is more likely to occur in the first place.

▨ Evaluation

■ Schemas are powerful influences on behaviour and are formed through experience. However, the extent to which they are influential in behaviour is difficult to gauge precisely. It seems likely that they are a key influence but are only part of the picture.

■ Peer influence also helps to form expectancies, as they can alter the schema for social situations where the initial contact with a drug occurs. For this reason, it is likely that peers are more likely than families to help the formation of schemas and their assimilation by an individual.

Sociocultural explanation of smoking addiction

Sociocultural explanations for addiction look to the environment to explain why someone becomes addicted to a substance or behaviour. This chapter has previously looked at how addiction could be more likely to occur in terms of the environment; namely through family and peer influence. However, it can also explain how the behaviour occurs in the first place and then becomes addictive behaviour. The most widely acknowledged environmental influence to developing addiction is explained using learning theories, specifically social learning, and operant and classical conditioning. This will be examined in the following section, referring specifically to smoking behaviour.

Learning theory as applied to smoking behaviour

> **Operant conditioning (OC)** – learning due to the positive or negative consequences of the behaviour.

Smoking behaviour is well explained by learning theory as a two-stage process involving social learning theory and **operant conditioning (OC)**.

Social learning theory

The basic assumptions of social learning explanations for behaviour are that behaviour is learned from the environment and this occurs when an individual observes others and takes note of the reinforcement or punishment they receive. More detail on social learning theory (SLT) can be seen in the section headed 'Social cognitive theory' in Chapter 3 on page 109.

Social learning provides a sound explanation for how someone starts smoking. An individual observes role models smoking and experiences the vicarious reinforcement of social learning. Vicarious reinforcement is seeing someone else receiving a reward. This process is especially powerful in young people and this is also when most first experience smoking. Initiation of smoking is therefore well explained by peer pressure and social influences.

Operant conditioning (behaviourist explanation)

Operant conditioning is another learning principle of the behaviourist approach. It works on the principle of learning by consequence. There are three key ways this can occur: positive reinforcement, negative reinforcement and punishment.

In general terms these three principles can make behaviour more or less likely. If you apply this to a school-based example of whether to complete a piece of homework or not, you would find that the:

1 Positive reinforcement would be potential better grades, teacher approval and praise.

2 Negative reinforcement would be avoiding disapproval from teachers and parents, avoiding a detention, teacher's anger.

   Both of these would be more likely to make you do the work.

3 However, punishment for not completing homework would be the disapproval from teachers and parents, detention and the teacher's anger.

   This makes NOT doing the homework less likely.

If you apply these principles to smoking, that is, whether to have a cigarette or not, you would find examples of positive reinforcement such as potentially feeling calmer and the negative reinforcement of smoking would be avoiding the bad feelings of withdrawal to nicotine. Both of these would be more likely to make you smoke.

OC explains why smoking continues and is due to the positive reinforcement that nicotine induces. It can give a pleasant feeling that is rewarding for the individual. The Law of Effect makes it more likely to keep reoccurring as positive reinforcement is involved.

Cue reactivity (behaviourist explanation using classical conditioning)

Cue reactivity with regard to smoking behaviour involves associations made through **classical conditioning (CC)**. The key idea is that learning occurs through classical conditioning when an association is made between a previously neutral stimulus and reflex response. This reflex response can be positive or negative. If the association of the stimulus is with a positive feeling, then that positive feeling will arise whenever the person comes into contact with that specific stimulus. The same is true for negative associations.

Cues in the environment, such as someone sitting outside the pub on a summer's evening with a pint of beer in one hand and a cigarette in the other, for example, might cause an association to form between the pint of beer and the need for a cigarette. This means that the two go together and it is strange for the person not to smoke while drinking alcohol. In classical conditioning terms, the pint glass serves as a conditioned stimulus to cue the craving for a cigarette. This association makes giving up hard in certain environments and makes someone more likely to smoke, perpetuating the addiction.

> **Classical conditioning (CC) –** an association between a previously neutral object/ situation (stimulus) and a strong emotional response.

Research

- **Brynner (1969)** found that media images of smoking create perceptions of it being attractive and tough. This increases the motivation for wanting to smoke, and if role models are smoking in the media, they could provide models for social learning in the audience. This lends support to SLT being implicated in smoking.

- The US National Institute on Drug Abuse (NIDA) found that 90 per cent of US smokers started smoking as adolescents, which was attributed mainly to observing and imitating peers **(Weitzman & Ying-Yeh Chen, 2005)**. This suggests that the decision to start smoking is due in part to social learning factors.

- In research with monkeys, **Goldberg et al. (1981)** used a system where the monkeys had to press a lever to receive nicotine. The researchers found that the monkeys pressed the lever at a rate that was similar to the level that would be expected with cocaine. This suggests addictive behaviour and the idea that it is accessed for its reinforcing effect. Operant conditioning as an explanation for addiction therefore has research support.

- **Calvert et al. (2010)** reports that smokers shown cigarette packets experienced strong activation in the ventral striatum and nucleus accumbens brain areas, suggesting a biological explanation of craving behaviour. However, this also supports the idea of cue reactivity and the brain activation may show the neural basis for classical conditioning.

Evaluation

- There is sound research support for learning theory as an explanation for addiction. However, it seems that only looking to operant conditioning, for example, is reductionist and more specifically an example of stimulus-response reductionism. Reductionism in this sense means lacking detail or oversimplified. There are many other factors involved in the behaviour.

- Learning theory cannot explain why one person may smoke for a short amount of time and not become addicted to the nicotine, whereas another may be addicted. If learning theory is to be believed then any behaviour that is rewarded will be repeated. This is clearly not the case, so the theory is flawed when considering individual differences.

- Operant conditioning cannot easily explain why someone would initially start smoking but can explain why they might get addicted to it. Social learning is able to explain the initial behaviour, so perhaps a more convincing explanation would be to combine the two learning explanations.

Strengthen your learning

1 Explain the role of dopamine in addiction.

2 Summarize what research studies have suggested about the role of dopamine in addiction.

3 What other evaluative points can be made about the role of dopamine in addiction?

4 Outline the cognitive explanation of addiction to smoking, including reference to expectancies.

5 Summarize what research studies have suggested about the cognitive explanation of addiction to smoking.

6 Assess the cognitive explanation of addiction to smoking in terms of its strengths and weaknesses.

7 Outline the sociocultural explanation of addiction to smoking.

8 Summarize what research studies have suggested about the sociocultural explanation of addiction to smoking.

9 Assess the sociocultural explanation of addiction to smoking in terms of its strengths and weaknesses.

10 Outline the learning theory explanation of addiction to smoking, including reference to social learning theory, operant conditioning and cue reactivity (classical conditioning).

11 Summarize what research studies have suggested about the learning theory explanation of addiction to smoking.

12 Assess the learning theory explanation of addiction to smoking in terms of strengths and weaknesses.

▨ Prevalence rates of health problems

A key consideration when examining health problems is the prevalence of the problem within the population. Prevalence is the word used to describe the rate of occurrence of a health problem. Knowledge of how widespread a problem is helps to inform priorities in terms of resources but, arguably more importantly, it can raise awareness about a health problem. Prevalence statistics are often a powerful tool in health promotion campaigns.

An example of reported prevalence rates is the figures reported in DSM-V, the diagnostic and statistical manual. For example, for addictive behaviour, these are divided up into the specific substances or behaviours that the addiction is linked to.

Alcohol addiction (or alcohol use disorder) is described as a common disorder in the diagnostic manual. Figures from the United States are reported stating the following information:

■ Rates of the disorder indicate that more adult men (12.4 per cent) than adult women (4.9 per cent) are diagnosed.

■ There is a reduction in long-term (i.e. more than a year) incidence in middle age, with the highest incidence rate occurring in the 18 to 29 years old age group.

The reported prevalence statistics for *gambling disorder* are lower:

■ The rates reported in the DSM-V (2013) show an incidence rate of 0.2 to 0.3 per cent in the general population.

■ The lifetime prevalence rate is 0.4 to 1 per cent.

■ For women (0.2 per cent) there is a lower lifetime prevalence rate compared to men (0.6 per cent).

These are reported from diagnosis rates and this is problematic for many reasons. The evaluation section below outlines why the figures could be inaccurate for prevalence figures in all disorders.

▨ Research

■ The relation between awareness of the symptoms of high blood pressure and prevalence rates was highlighted in work conducted by **Wu *et al.* (2008)**. They looked at the prevalence within the population in China and the awareness levels, finding that the two were closely linked. This illustrates that there is a relationship between both prevalence and awareness.

- **Keyes *et al.* (2010)** examined the effect of stigma on treatment being sought by those suffering from alcohol disorders. They found that the level of stigma perceived by the individuals mediated their willingness to access treatment centres. This could mean that prevalence rates reported will be lower than the actual number in the population.
- **Hoffman & Kopak (2015)** compared the criteria for diagnosis of alcohol use disorders (AUDs) between DSM-V and ICD-10. Severe cases would be diagnosed by practitioners using either manual; however, this was not the case with less severe cases. They found the criteria differ in the two manuals in terms of both the mild and moderate cases. This clearly will affect global prevalence figures reported.

Evaluation of the accuracy of prevalence rates

There is a key relationship between prevalence and awareness. The more widespread a problem is, the more likely people are to be aware of it. However, this relationship can work the other way. Prevalence rates can increase due to awareness both within the general and practitioner population. It is for this reason that prevalence rates cannot be entirely accurate for some health problems.

There is also a key relationship between diagnosis and prevalence, as ultimately, a case will not be counted within prevalence figures if not diagnosed formally. There is an issue with individuals seeking help in some cases owing to stigma. There can be a worry that some health problems, if diagnosed, are not viewed sympathetically by society. This was the case for mental health problems within many cultures and is still the case in some areas of the world today. In the example of addiction prevalence statistics, the individual with the addiction knows that acknowledging the problem and seeking help would mean a period of withdrawal from the substance or behaviour. This is unthinkable for some individuals who are addicted and they will therefore refuse to seek diagnosis and help.

Issues with diagnosis also mean that global prevalence figures are problematic. Diagnosis varies from country to country and the priorities within a country's health system will affect the likelihood of diagnosis. The criteria for diagnosis vary from country to country and therefore when comparing prevalence rates globally, the statistics are not always as directly comparable as they might seem to be. For example, the two key diagnostic manuals for mental health disorders (DSM-V and ICD-10) used currently are referred to across the world, with some countries favouring one manual over the other. Their criteria for diagnosis vary, meaning that diagnosis for the same disorder could differ depending on the manual used.

For prevalence rates to be accurate it is important that diagnosis is correct and standardized. If this is not the case then the statistics compiled will not compare like with like. Diagnostic manuals are designed to help standardize the diagnosis of physical and mental problems. For mental disorder, even though a symptomatology is described from diagnosis there is room for individual difference. This makes diagnosis subjective. For example, in DSM-V the first diagnostic criterion for major depressive disorder is stated as: 'Depressed mood most of the day, nearly every day, as indicated by either subjective report (e.g. feels sad, empty, hopeless) or observation made by others (e.g. appears tearful).' Looking at this wording it seems that diagnosis is made on judgement of either the individual being diagnosed, or those around them. Both judgements are opinion-based and therefore potentially unreliable.

Prevalence rates are also weakened by the samples that provide the statistics. These can be self-selecting. If medical diagnosis is the source of the information then, even with its associated problems of reliability, all the statistics can be derived from official records. This is not always where prevalence records come from. If taken from survey samples the respondents are self-selecting. This means potentially that very busy people will not respond, or those who struggle with literacy will not want to complete a survey. Given the notoriously slow response rate for questionnaires and surveys generally, the prevalence rates derived from such means are likely to be inaccurate.

CONTEMPORARY RESEARCH

'A case study of mental health prevalence statistics'
McManus *et al.* (2016)

The following research is a report compiled for the UK government on the prevalence of mental health issues.

Aim

The report was designed to give information on how common mental health problems are in England and also gathered data on the services treating mental health problems.

Procedure

The data was gathered in 2014 using the Adult Psychiatric Morbidity Survey, which gives information on both treated and untreated psychiatric disorder. As this is the third of such surveys, the research methods have become standardized so that prevalence rates can be compared.

Results

Statistics documented by the report showed that:

1 One in six people experienced a common mental disorder (e.g. depression or anxiety) in the last week.

2 Common mental disorders (such as depression or anxiety) are more common among women than among men. This gender difference is most pronounced among those aged 16 to 24.

3 The percentage of people reporting a common mental disorder has risen since 1993. The figure was 15.5 per cent in 1993 but had risen to 18.9 per cent in 2014.

4 Unemployed and economically inactive people are more likely to report common mental disorders.

Conclusions

Mental health problems are on the increase in the general population and there are groups with higher numbers reported.

Evaluation

The strengths of the research as given by the researchers were as follows:

1 The sample came from the general population rather than patient lists, which gives a fuller picture of the prevalence, as it includes people who have not yet accessed treatment.

2 The survey used validated screeners and assessments for collecting the data, which provided information on people who might not yet be diagnosed.

3 The survey collects more data, including demographic data, on each individual so the data has depth.

4 There was permission sought for collecting more data later so there is an opportunity for longitudinal data on individuals.

However, the researchers did acknowledge limitations in the data:

1 The sample is limited to private households only. This means that it is a biased sample, which will not collect data from all demographic groups in the general population. Indeed, some of those not included, such as the homeless, are known to suffer a higher percentage of mental health problems. However, the percentage of people omitted was argued to be very small and therefore the statistics would not be significantly different anyway.

2 The response rate was 57 per cent. This means that some of the people contacted did not take part, either because the communication did not reach them, or they refused to take part. This means that the sample is self-selected and could be biased. The researchers introduced a weighting system that addressed this issue to some extent.

3 Questionnaires and measures were used online, but it is possible that clinical interviews would have been more reliable had they been carried out by a mental health professional.

4 The sensitive nature of the topics may mean that the accuracy of the data could be compromised. Although the sensitive data is collected online, there still could be an issue with honesty with questions being so personal. Prevalence rates could therefore be underreported.

5 It should be recognized that the prevalence figures can only ever be estimates of the general population. They could be higher, or lower, than the actual figure.

YOU ARE THE RESEARCHER

Reports state that the number of mental health problems in secondary age students is increasing. You have been commissioned by the National Health Service to examine this worrying increase.

How could you design a study to investigate the potential reason behind this increase? Justify your choice of methodology.

Strengthen your learning

1 What is meant by prevalence rates of health problems?

2 What are the prevalence rates for:
a alcohol
b gambling addiction?

3 Summarize what research studies have suggested about prevalence rates for addiction.

4 From McManus *et al.*'s contemporary 2016 study of mental health prevalence statistics, in your own words, state the:
a aims
b procedure
c results
d conclusions
e evaluative points.

SECTION SUMMARY

- Explanations of health problems can include differing levels of explanations, such as biological, cognitive and sociocultural explanations.
- The biological explanation for addiction is the role of dopamine, a neurotransmitter.
- The cognitive explanation for addiction is expectancies based on schemas gathered through experience.
- The sociocultural explanation for addiction is learning theory, specifically operant and classical conditioning (cue reactivity).
- Prevalence rates of health problems are indications of the incidence rate in the population.
- There are problems with compiling accurate prevalence rates, as issues with diagnosis and sample bias skew statistics.

■ Assessment check

1 Contrast explanations of health problems. (22 marks)
2 Discuss research studies related to one or more explanations of health problems. (22 marks)
3 Discuss one explanation of health problems. (22 marks)
4 Discuss prevalence rates of health problems. (22 marks)
5 Evaluate research studies related to prevalence rates of health problems. (22 marks)
6 With the use of suitable examples discuss ethical considerations of research into health problems. (22 marks)

Promoting health

'Smoking is a custom, loathsome to the eye, hateful to the nose, harmful to the brain, dangerous to the lungs ...'
King James 1, in what is argued to be the first health promotion statement (transcribed by Jones, 1985: 1763)

Health promotion is communication with targeted groups or the general public to encourage good health behaviours. They use all communication mediums and we will all have been the recipient of health promotions communication at one time or another.

FOCUS ON...

- Health promotion approaches and how effective they are.
- Health promotion tools and their effectiveness.
- How effective health promotion programmes are and how they are evaluated.

As the models of health have changed through time so too has health promotion. The medical model concentrated on specific interventions with a heavy use of trained medical staff, but as health came to be seen holistically, the emphasis moved to informing the individual. There has also been a move to encompass consideration of complementary and alternative therapies as the influence of the medical model has diminished.

Alongside the medical model, health promotion has embraced the idea of environmental and social influences on health, such as peer influence and poverty.

In an attempt to encourage good health globally, the World Health Organization has defined five key principles to outline the areas that health promotion should consider:

1 The general population as a whole should be considered for health promotion, not just specific target groups who could contract specific diseases.
2 The promotion should be focused on the cause of the health problem, including the individual's environment.
3 Health promotion should be a combination of complementary methods and a variety of communication mediums should be used.
4 Promotion should try to include public participation and encourage the formation of self-help groups.
5 Health professionals should be consulted and involved in health promotions.

These principles clearly acknowledge the role of the health professional, the individual and the social and environmental factors in the good health of the global population.

■ The approaches of health promotion

Marks & Allegrante (2005) classified the ways of tackling health promotion into three categories: the self-empowerment approach, the behaviour change approach, and lastly the community development approach.

Self-empowerment approach

This approach focuses on the control of the individual over their body and environment. It is likely that adherence to the programme and thus its success will be increased if the individual affected feels they have some control over the outcome, which means they will also be more likely to do something about their health. This means taking a less prescriptive approach and encouraging individuals to take lifestyle choices that will impact on their general health.

A good example of such an approach is the 'This Girl Can' campaign, which aims to address the issue of low sports participation numbers in women. Fear of judgement was identified as a barrier to women taking part in sport, owing to being concerned about their appearance, thinking they are not good at sport and prioritizing others over themselves. The campaign was designed to address those fears in women directly and it used a film of real women exercising, together with slogans such as 'sweating like a pig', 'feeling like a fox', 'I jiggle therefore I am' and 'I kick balls, deal with it'.

■ **Figure 7.5** This Girl Can campaign

The campaign, which resulted in 1.6 million women starting to exercise, is ongoing.

Community development approach

The community development approach is just that: health promotion within the community so that the environment of the individual changes and social support is available. Self-help groups are an example of this kind of health promotion.

In Beijing, China there is a landmark known as the Temple of Heaven. Every morning large numbers of retired people gather in the grounds to do some form of activity together in groups. Tai chi, choirs and line dancing, among other activities, are on offer. It is apparent to visitors that there is a strong sense of community and support. It promotes activity and companionship, which supports good health.

■ **Figure 7.6** The Temple of Heaven gardens in China, where retired people gather in the morning to do activities together

LINK TO THE SOCIOCULTURAL EXPLANATION

The community development approach to health depends on changing the environment so that it is encouraging of good health behaviours. It is therefore a sociocultural approach to health promotion.

Behaviour change approach

This approach to health promotion focuses on the cognitive level. People hold beliefs that are not realistic. These are particularly damaging from a health perspective, where faulty thinking causes an individual to feel they are not at risk of poor health or a specific disease. A public health campaign can address that misperception by presenting facts and highlighting who might be at risk. There are ways of doing this.

For example, message content has been shown to be more effective if both sides of the argument are given. The individual receiving the message retains an element of control, which makes it more attractive.

Another way is to present information including statistics that can be perceived in several ways by an individual; so if, for example, you say the risk of a disease is a 10 per cent, this can be seen either as risky or minimal depending on the context.

Health promotion campaigns using this approach are designed to change the individual's way of thinking about their health. This can be done in a variety of different ways, for example by giving facts and the reality of the situation so that they do not hold misperceptions that they are not affected.

An example of this approach was the one taken to challenge the idea that heart disease only affected men. It was designed by the British Heart Foundation and involved erecting temporary cardboard gravestones in five UK cities. The gravestones had words such as 'Mum' and 'Grandma' written on them to raise awareness of potential female fatalities from heart-disease-related problems. This campaign also aimed to raise money, which it did, over £1 million.

The AIDS campaign of the 1980s also used shock images to raise awareness of the condition. At that point there was no known treatment, so the diagnosis was a death sentence. Prior to the campaign the disease was seen as affecting homosexuals, so the government wanted to address that misperception. The campaign image was striking in that it emphasized the terminal prognosis for that time, with gravestones, flowers and black and white images.

LINK TO THE COGNITIVE EXPLANATION

The self-empowerment and behaviour change approaches are cognitive as they are designed to change the thinking of the target population. By affecting how individuals feel about themselves and how they think about the health risk or behaviour, the campaign approach should encourage them to make behavioural changes.

KEY STUDY ## CONTEMPORARY RESEARCH

'When scary messages backfire: Influence of dispositional cognitive avoidance on the effectiveness of threat communications'
Nestler & Egloff (2010)

Sometimes a health promotion campaign does not get the desired results. This can be due to unpredicted reactions by the general public.

Aim

This research was conducted to identify when a health promotion message does not work in the way that is expected, and why.

Procedure

1 Nestler & Egloff looked at the reactions of participants to two health messages, one a very 'high threat' communication, the other low threat. It was thought that the high-threat communication would prompt healthier choices, as people would be scared about the consequences of unhealthy behaviours. Researchers also looked at the type of thinking style the participants had in threatening situations, specifically their level of cognitive avoidance (measured by a questionnaire). This is a disposition for avoiding unwelcome or threatening information. The argument was that high cognitive avoiders would read the threat as lower than it actually was, as they would be avoiding the reality of the message.

2 Two health messages were given to participants, both hypothetical. They talked about how levels of caffeine consumption could affect the likelihood of developing a fictional condition called Xyelinenteritis, which was described as a digestive disease. In the high-threat condition, participants were told that caffeine could cause Xyelinenteritis, which would then lead to stomach cancer. In the low-threat condition this link to cancer was not mentioned. Both groups were informed that they should reduce their caffeine consumption.

Results

Nestler & Egloff found that cognitive avoidance levels did affect the reaction of participants and the level of threat they perceived. In high-cognitive avoiders researchers found that they underplayed the threat level in the high-threat condition to below that of the low-threat communication and were consequently less likely to reduce caffeine intake. This shows that not everyone reacts similarly to health promotion literature and campaigns and assumptions cannot be made about reactions of individuals. This is because of differing cognitive styles.

Conclusions

This research examines the behaviour change approach and shows that assumptions cannot be made about how someone will react to information they are given.

Evaluation

This is important work looking at the thought processes involved behind health promotion and, as such, has a useful application for ensuring that campaigns are appropriate for all. This will improve their effectiveness.

Research

- In a review of health promotion literature, **Wallerstein (1992)** found that a lack of power, or lack of control, is a risk factor for disease. Self-empowerment can therefore be shown to be an important factor in health promotion, although measuring self-empowerment is difficult to do in a valid and reliable way, so the exact effect is difficult to ascertain.

- **Armstrong (2000)** examined the use of garden programs in New York State to facilitate health promotion. She found that gardens in low-income areas were four times more likely to help the communities they served in terms of issues of social support, and so on. Health benefits were evident too. This illustrates that community health and well-being can be enhanced by a better social and physical environment.

Evaluation

- The self-empowerment strategy to improve health is seen by some as placing the blame of poor health onto the individual. Dispositional factors, as outlined in the first section of this chapter, illustrate that this is out of the control of the individual in some cases.

- Conversely, self-empowerment techniques in health promotion are designed to give the individual control over their health. Lack of control is linked to poor health due to the level of stress it induces. Therefore, by making an individual feel in control, not only are they more likely to do something and act, but also their levels of stress are reduced. This means that the health benefits will be two-fold.

- Self-empowerment has been shown to help adherence to good health practices. For example, **Funnell & Anderson (2004)** looked at adherence to medication regimes in diabetics and they found when the patient retained an element of control they were more likely to stick to the medication administration needed. This meant their illness was well managed. Self-empowerment health promotion campaigns therefore not only help to initiate healthy behaviour, they also increase the likelihood of the behaviour continuing.

- Research by **Nestler & Egloff (2010)**, above, illustrates that assuming a message will be perceived a certain way is problematic. There are no guarantees that the target population will react how they 'should'. This means that campaigns are very difficult to design and execute effectively.

Strengthen your learning

1 In your own words, state the World Health Organization's five key principles to encourage good health.

2 Explain the:
   a self-empowerment approach to health promotion, with focus on the 'This Girl Can' campaign
   b community development approach, including reference to the Temple of Heaven
   c behaviour change approach, including reference to the British Heart Foundation campaign and the 1980s AIDS awareness campaign.

3 Summarize what research studies have suggested about approaches to health promotion.

4 Assess approaches to health promotion in terms of their strengths and weaknesses.

5 For Nestler & Egloff's 2010 contemporary study of 'when scary messages backfire', in your own words, state the:
   a aims
   b procedure
   c results
   d conclusions
   e evaluative points.

6 Explain the role of the following as tools of health promotion:
   a mass media
   b legislation
   c source characteristics.

7 Summarize what research studies have suggested about the role of the following as tools of health promotion:
   a mass media
   b legislation
   c source characteristics.

8 What other evaluative points can be made about the role of the following as tools of health promotion:
   a mass media
   b legislation
   c source characteristics?

Tools of health promotion

Role of mass media

Corcoran (2007) defined the mass media as including television, radio, print-based media and electronic/social media. This is a key tool for health promotion owing to the reach of its various mediums.

Within health promotion a campaign usually uses several elements, but the emphasis is now moving to social media, although this depends on the audience it is trying to reach.

One of the key advantages of using the mass media is that a campaign can be targeted and portray simple messages; these have impact and, owing to their simplicity, can be emotive and easy to remember. The problem arising in recent times is the amount of false information that can be circulated, especially on social media. An example of this was the incorrect publication of information on the contraceptive pill and blood clots, which led to a decrease in numbers of women taking the pill and consequently an increase in abortion rates. Something similar happened with research that suggested autism could be developed following the MMR vaccine, although the research was later shown to be falsified. This led to a decrease in parents having their children vaccinated, which led to dire consequences in terms of children developing measles, mumps and rubella.

Legislation

Legislation can be used to promote health behaviours by restricting the availability of products, such as alcohol, that can lead to poor health. It can also be helpful in terms of making products too expensive via taxation and finally advertising can be restricted. All these measures have been used to try and decrease the number of smokers. For example, in the UK there are age restrictions on buying cigarettes, the packets are taxed heavily and cigarette advertising is also banned from the mass media. There are even restrictions now on the packaging of cigarettes in an effort to make them less attractive.

Source characteristics

The choice of person giving the message in a health promotion affects the likelihood of it being effective. There must be a similarity between the messenger and the recipient of the message. For example, in the Everyman Campaign launched by the Institute of Cancer Research in 1999, pop star Robbie Williams was selected to get the message about testicular cancer across to the target audience (men). He was chosen as a role model to men aged 20 to 35. In the advert Robbie wears a pair of false breasts and says 'Hey you know, if you men paid more attention to these (*grabbing his crotch*) instead of these (*pointing to the false breasts*) then maybe fewer of us would be dying of testicular cancer. So go and check 'em out.'

Research

■ **Figure 7.7** Everyman, the campaign to raise awareness of testicular and prostate cancer, used celebrities such as Robbie Williams to promote their message

■ **Sharf (1997)** conducted an analysis of the use of online discussion forums for breast cancer awareness. She found that the forums helped foster awareness and self-empowerment in women and also that there was much social support expressed for each other. This illustrates the important role that mass media can play in promoting positive health behaviours.

■ **Meyers *et al.* (2009)** reported a 17 per cent decrease in hospital admissions for acute myocardial infarctions (heart attacks) following a smoking ban in public places, enforced using legislation. This shows a direct use of legislation in promoting good health and reducing illness.

- **Chapman & Leask (2001)** argued that sometimes use of a celebrity/role model can be counterproductive in promoting healthy behaviour. In Australia, in 1998, Shane Warne, a famous cricketer, was a key figure in a smoking cessation attempt, paid for by a pharmaceutical company. Unfortunately, he failed to stop smoking and the resultant effects were very negative for the company. Part of the issue was the large payment he received. This illustrates that paying large amounts of money to celebrities can be counterproductive. The fact that he did not actually stop smoking also caused a very negative reaction and a lot of press coverage.

Evaluation

- The use of mass media in a health promotion campaign is now a necessity. Organizing an effective campaign without harnessing the help of mass media is difficult. However, it also has the potential to backfire and work against those promoting good health, as in the example of Shane Warner (see **Chapman & Leask, 2001** above).

- The process of legislating health is a long one, so using the law as a method of health promotion is often too drawn out, especially when quick action is needed. Often legislation is the end result of campaigns that have failed to change behaviour in a sufficient number of the population.

- Selection of an appropriate role model to figurehead a campaign is a difficult choice. It relies upon the ability of the celebrity to act in a healthy way too and to ensure there is no negative press during the campaign. However, although potentially a risky strategy, there is little doubt that the correct figurehead for a campaign can be very powerful.

Evaluating the effectiveness of health promotion campaigns

The effectiveness of health promotion is not just important to measure because of the costs of the campaign, but also to ensure the message has been conveyed sufficiently. If not, then more campaigning may be necessary.

Evaluation is a process involving setting aims and choosing the most appropriate evaluation method(s). The choice is dependent on resources available to you, such as the research team size, facilities, services and material resources. It is necessary to have a baseline measure which may come, for example, in the form of statistics. This allows the researcher to start to build a 'before campaign' and 'after campaign' picture.

Each campaign has its own aims and objectives and evaluation of the effectiveness must focus specifically on those aims and objectives. For example, if the campaign is focused upon drug use in 18- to 25-year-olds, they must be the target population for the measure of effectiveness.

One of the most important aspects of designing an evaluation is to find a good way of taking a baseline measure. This means you can establish a 'before' picture. This can be done by using statistics. Often the baseline measure forms the case for the campaign, as it illustrates a need for the intervention.

Research

- **Van Hasselt et al. (2015)** conducted a review of health promotion effectiveness evaluation in severe mental illness. They found that there were key areas that were not being considered in making the decision of the effectiveness. One example was measuring akathisia, which is restlessness or fidgeting. This is characteristic in many patients with severe mental illness and is a behavioural characteristic observed by others. Any intervention should be effective in reducing this physical effect. In the literature this was never used as a measure of effectiveness. They also found that some measures were inappropriate, such as self-report for smoking. If someone is mentally ill this judgement is problematic. Indeed it could be argued that this method is not accurate in those not severely mentally ill. This suggests that context must be considered when designing a campaign, especially with a clinical population.

- **Pommier *et al.* (2010)** reviewed evaluating health promotion in schools. They developed a research protocol to be used by researchers based on good practice. Key aspects were ensuring that both qualitative and quantitative methods were used and ensuring that the design was realistic as this would ensure it was completed properly and there would be sufficient uptake in schools.

Evaluation

- One of the hardest things to do once you have designed a baseline measure and run the intervention is to show that any changes in statistics can be attributed to the intervention itself. Causation often cannot be proven, but if your pre-intervention statistics and measures are comprehensive then your case can be stronger.
- **Allen & Flack (2015)** in their paper on the ethics of health promotion evaluation talk about issues in the evaluation of campaigns in terms of accuracy and honesty. They talk about how the need to show a positive effect can affect researcher integrity, with figures being skewed when the researcher has a conflict of interest. This means that the reliability of research into effectiveness needs to be considered carefully.
- Determining the level of effectiveness is difficult in health promotion. If the sample is large, a significant effect or significant relationship can be reported. The actual figures of people affected can be surprisingly low. Whether this is a sufficient number is in some ways affected by the motivations and costs involved.
- Evaluation must be specific to the context. The requirements of mental health interventions and schools both require due consideration considering their vulnerable populations. A 'one size fits all approach' is not appropriate for all campaigns.
- The case study below of Stoptober ('Psychology in the real world') illustrates how a campaign can be assessed.

PSYCHOLOGY IN THE REAL WORLD

Case study of a health promotion

Aim

Stoptober is an annual campaign to encourage cigarette smokers in the UK to stop smoking for the month of October.

The campaign

In 2012, Stoptober was the first national smoking cessation campaign that was aimed at all smokers in the country, urging them to quit for one month. It is now an annual campaign that is designed to focus upon stopping for four weeks, with the idea that this will mean that smokers stop for good. The first year it ran was 2012 and it used the mass media, including social media, to send a sustained message to smokers to be smoke-free for the duration of October. The smokers who pledge to give up are supported by health professionals such as GPs and pharmacies and all smokers who intend trying to quit. They also receive an online pack and digital tools such as apps to help and support them. In addition they are offered the chance to be sponsored by family and friends to encourage them to stay smoke-free for the whole month. In 2017, Public Health England also encouraged use of e-cigarettes to help the process for the first time.

This is an example of the use of mass media to promote good health. The message is simple: Quit smoking for October and you will find it easier to stop smoking totally.

Theory behind the campaign

Principle 1: Social cognitive theory argues that if there is a group of people focused upon a common goal, then the message of that goal, such as 'Quit smoking for a month', will be stronger. In other words, the influence of being part of a group will amplify the effect.

Principle 2: SMART goals are more likely to be effective. The goals set by Stoptober are Specific (stop smoking), Measurable (you either smoke or you do not), Achievable (it is possible to stop), Realistic (it is only for one month, initially) and Time based (one month). This means that the message is clear and positive.

Principle 3: PRIME theory argues that for behaviour change to work it has to consider the whole motivation system. Stoptober did so by positive messaging throughout to try and combat those moments of weakness. The fact that many others were also quitting meant that there was an overall effect on levels of motivation. The level of support available online and in the environment also helped those trying to stay smoke-free by making them feel supported.

Effectiveness

Brown *et al.* (2014) examined the effectiveness of the first 2012 Stoptober campaign. They did this by comparing the numbers of smokers trying to quit before and during the campaign. Brown had the details of 31,366 smokers who had reported smoking in the period 2007 to 2012 (when the campaign was released). They were both cigarette and other forms of tobacco smokers. The researchers asked the participants to report any attempts to quit smoking they had made in the period leading up to the Stoptober campaign. They also asked them to report when the attempts were and how often they had made a serious attempt to stop. They also gave demographic information such as their age, gender and social-grade. In addition, they were asked to give details on how many cigarettes they smoked per day (or pipes or cigars).

Researchers then examined the number of attempts to stop in October, compared with the average number over the preceding months. They examined if there was an interaction in the month of October. Patterns were observed year on year as there are expected peaks in the number of quit attempts at certain points in the year, as part of the annual cycle. For example, there is always a peak in attempts to stop smoking at the beginning of January in line with the idea of new year's resolutions.

In terms of effectiveness, one measure used was the number of live years gained. This is the expected extension to lifespan that would occur if someone stopped smoking permanently. The statistics for this assessment also took age into account, as it was recognized that the age at which the person stopped smoking would mean that they would benefit to a varying degree (older people would gain less).

The researchers were also aware of potential relapse so, when calculating the projected figures on live years added onto life, set the potential number of 'permanent quitters' at 2.5 per cent. They argued this to be a realistic and conservative figure based on previous research of quit attempts.

Results

The results found were as follows:

- Quit attempts were higher in October 2012 than in previous months and years.

- October was traditionally a month with lower-than-average attempts to stop smoking. However, in 2012 this pattern was reversed, with an increase in attempts to stop of 4.15 per cent.

- There was no evidence that Stoptober was effective in certain demographic groups. The effect seemed to be equivalent over the whole social spectrum.

- Cost-effectiveness of the campaign was calculated to be greatest for people in the 35 to 44-year-old age group and least cost-effective for those under 35 years old.

- The research also looked at effectiveness in terms of public health impact. The number of participants to have given up as a result of the campaign was described as being 8817, which was from a total number of quit attempts of 352,662.

Evaluation

- A causal association cannot be made, as this research measured effectiveness by comparing average figures and the difference in October of the campaign year. It is possible that there were other factors that affected the success or otherwise of the campaign.

- The campaign compared well with other attempts to encourage cessation of smoking. However, its main aim was to elicit a mass-cessation and this was not achieved, given that the number of smokers in England at that time far exceeded the number who actually tried to stop.

- This campaign did not use the usual tactic employed by mass media campaigns of a negative message which arouses fear. It was an encouraging and positive message of cessation being a possibility. This was an important message for planning future campaigns. It could be argued that this campaign used a self-empowerment approach.

- The fact that there was no apparent demographic effect would suggest that it is possible to design a campaign which promotes good health for all. This then has the potential to be wider reaching.

YOU ARE THE RESEARCHER

Choose a health promotion campaign and design a method to evaluate its effectiveness. What would you use as measures? What ethical and methodological considerations would you have to make?

Strengthen your learning

1 Explain how the effectiveness of health promotion campaigns is evaluated.

2 Summarize what research studies have suggested about evaluating the effectiveness of health promotion campaigns.

3 What other evaluative points can be made about evaluating the effectiveness of health promotion campaigns?

4 Explain how the effectiveness of the 'Stoptober' campaign was assessed. How effective was the campaign concluded to be?

5 What evaluative points can be made about the assessment of the effectiveness of the 'Stoptober' campaign?

SECTION SUMMARY

- Health promotion uses various approaches to encourage good health choices, including the self-empowerment approach, the behaviour change approach and the community development approach.
- To do this, different tools are used such as the mass media, legislation and source characteristics (appropriate delivery of the message).
- Health promotion programmes have been shown to be successful in several ways, but measuring the effectiveness of a campaign is difficult.

■ Assessment check

1	Discuss the ethical considerations of research into health promotion.	(22 marks)
2	Discuss health promotion.	(22 marks)
3	Discuss one or more studies related to the effectiveness of health promotion programmes.	(22 marks)
4	Evaluate the effectiveness of health promotion programmes.	(22 marks)
5	Discuss the effectiveness of two health promotion programmes.	(22 marks)

Psychology of human relationships

'Together we cast a single shadow on the wall.'
Doug Fetherling (1979)

Introduction

Personal relationships – close connections formed between people through emotional bonds and interactions.

Romantic, family and friendship partnerships are our main types of **personal relationships**, though any situation involving interaction between individuals can be considered a form of personal relationship, such as those with people at work or team mates in sports situations. Psychologists have especially been interested in the reasons why personal relationships form, the role of communication within relations, especially in their maintenance, and explanations for why personal relationships break down.

IN THE NEWS

Ψ The Psychological Enquirer

TWO HEARTS BEATING AS ONE

■ **Figure 8.1** Two hearts beating as one

Gordon Yeager's girlfriend Norma, aged 18, graduated from high school in State Center Iowa, USA, at 10 a.m. on 26 May 1939. At 10 p.m. that night the couple got married. Always together, they went on to have a full life, working as partners in several businesses, socializing and travelling. At home they sat side by side in two adjoining chairs, Gordon, the outgoing 'hyper' one, who could be seen in his nineties working on the roof of his house, Norma, the supporting, quieter one.

They were married for 72 years until a car accident left them in intensive care, though all the time their concerns were only for each other's injuries. When it was realized that they would not recover, their beds were moved together so they could hold hands. Gordon stopped breathing and died at 3:38 p.m. on 19 October 2011. But the surprise came when his relatives realized his heart monitor was still functioning. The nurse explained that Gordon was picking up Norma's heartbeat through her hand. Their son Dennis exclaimed, 'Oh my gosh, Mom's heart is beating through him.' Norma died exactly one hour later, at 4.38 p.m. The couple were put in a coffin together holding hands, cremated and their ashes were buried together.

Most people would agree that Gordon and Norma married for love, but there are many factors in why people are attracted and form relationships with each other, whether it be for evolutionary, social exchange, equity or financial purposes. Not everyone is as fortunate as Gordon and Norma – 42 per cent of marriages in Britain end in divorce, though 16 per cent of married couples will celebrate their 60th wedding anniversary.

Interestingly, stories like that of Gordon and Norma's deaths are not that unusual. Bereaved widows and widowers are 30 per cent more likely to die within six months of their partner's death than people of the same age who have not lost a partner. There is even emerging evidence, like that of **Ferrer *et al.* (2013)**, that romantic partners' heartbeats become synchronized (beat in time with each other) and that is possibly a reason why the number one cause of death for bereaved spouses is sudden cardiac death.

Formation of personal relationships

- The evolutionary explanation for partner preferences.
- The relationship between sexual selection and human reproductive behaviour.
- Attractiveness, body symmetry and waist-to-hip ratio as indicators of genetic fitness.
- Male and female strategies in reproductive behaviour.
- What research studies inform about the evolutionary explanation for partner preferences.
- An assessment of the evolutionary explanation for partner preferences.

Successful romantic relationships are seen as a prime route to happiness. As well as being a means of raising children, successful romantic relationships are an important source of self-esteem and personal fulfilment. Psychologists have considered a range of explanations for the formation of relationships, which take on board a range of biological as well as psychological factors.

Evolutionary explanation for partner preferences

'Maternity is a matter of fact, paternity a matter of opinion.'
American proverb

Evolution – the process of adaptation through natural selection.

Human reproductive behaviour – the different mating strategies used by males and females.

Sexual selection – the selection of characteristics that increase reproductive success.

Charles Darwin (1809–1882) explained that within each animal species, including humans, there is variation, making people non-identical. Part of the variation comes from differences in individuals' genes, 50 per cent inherited from each parent, but genes (strands of DNA) can also undergo mutation, a random change affecting an individual's physiology and behaviour, which sometimes give individuals an advantage when competing for resources such as food, territories and mates. Such individuals stand more chance of surviving into adulthood and reproducing offspring who will also have the mutated gene, with the characteristic determined by the mutation becoming more widespread over time. This evolutionary process of gradual changes to our genetic make-up is known as natural selection. One important way in which **evolution** works to shape **human reproductive behaviour** is that of **sexual selection**.

LINK TO THE BIOLOGICAL APPROACH

The evolutionary explanation for partner preferences links to the biological approach, as it sees evolution as genetically transmitted between generations. Reproductive strategies that have a survival value are passed on to the next generation through genetic material and over time become more widespread in a population.

The relationship between sexual selection and human reproductive behaviour

The evolutionary approach (also known as the sociobiological explanation) is a biological explanation that sees males and females being subjected to different selective pressures, which therefore leads them to use different strategies to maximize their reproductive potentials.

Sexual dimorphism concerns the different characteristics that male and female humans possess – for example, males are generally larger and more muscular than females. Evolution explains sexual dimorphism as developing through the process of natural selection, because the evolution of different features gave an adaptive advantage – that is, it increased the chances of survival into adulthood and sexual maturity, where genes are passed to the next generation.

Sexual selection involves the natural selection of characteristics increasing reproductive success. For example, if muscularity increases a male's chances of being chosen as a mate, the characteristic becomes enhanced as a sexually selected one and over generations males will become progressively more muscular.

Reproductive success involves the production of healthy offspring, surviving to sexual maturity, and the offspring reproducing themselves, and differences between male and female sexual behaviour will arise, as they are subject to different selective pressures. These differences occur due to anisogamy, the difference between the nature and amount of gametes (sperm and eggs) produced.

Males produce lots of small, highly mobile sperm, about 110 million sperm per ejaculation, enough to populate Britain twice over, and males can fertilize many females at little cost to reproductive potential. Before the advent of DNA testing, males could not be sure of paternity (that the child is theirs), so natural selection favours male behaviours maximizing the number of potential pregnancies, resulting in intrasexual competition between males (where males compete for mating opportunities with females), and polygamy, where one male mates with more than one female. Therefore, a male's best strategy to heighten his chances of reproducing genes into the next generation is to have as much sex as possible with as many females as possible. Various male strategies have arisen, for instance seeking females displaying signs of fertility, such as health, youth and childbearing hips, as mating with fertile females enhances the chances of successful reproduction (see 'Male strategies', on page 345).

Females produce a few, relatively large eggs, each one representing a sizeable reproductive investment, though she can always be sure of maternity. Females are fertile for about 25 years – ovulating one egg a month, they therefore have only 300 opportunities to reproduce. Males can, in theory, reproduce as much as three times a day and remain fertile for longer – the oldest documented father was Nanu Ram Jogi, an Indian farmer who fathered a child at the age of 90. The oldest documented mother conceiving without hormone treatment was Dawn Brooke of Guernsey, who gave birth in 1997 aged 59 – her pregnancy was so unexpected it was believed to be cancer. Therefore, females must be more selective about who they mate with, as each mating involves a sizeable part of reproduction potential compared with that of males.

Natural selection therefore favours female behaviours, maximizing the chances of successful reproduction through various strategies, including careful mate selection, monogamy (having only one sexual partner) and high parental investment. Females seek males displaying genetic fitness, such as strength, status and resources. Females indulge in inter-sexual competition, where females choose males from those available. Females also utilize practices like courtship, which help to select the best male from those available and also serve to make males invest time, effort and resources in them and in any resulting offspring, thus increasing the chances that the male will not desert them and will offer more protection and resources to the female and her children (see 'Female strategies', on page 346).

TOK link

Evolutionary explanations, such as that for partner preferences, see behaviour as being biologically determinist, where behaviour is coded into genes and is thus unconscious. This may be true for many animal species, but human behaviour is also motivated by higher-level cognitive processes, which means that humans have a degree of free will and are thus able to consciously control their behaviour. Maybe this explains why some humans choose partners for reasons other than increasing reproductive potential

'Boys think girls are like books – if the cover doesn't catch their eye they won't bother to read what's inside.'
Marilyn Monroe

Attractiveness

Physical attractiveness – the degree to which an individual's external characteristics are considered pleasing or beautiful.

Physical attractiveness in females is valued by males as an indicator of health and fertility, two of the qualities needed to produce and raise children. Younger women are seen as more attractive, as they tend to be more fertile. Females are more attracted to men, often older, who have access to resources, as this indicates an ability to provide for a female and her children. Although physical attractiveness is less important, females are choosier in selecting mates, as their investment is greater. Females are also attracted to kindness in males, as it indicates a willingness to share resources.

Body symmetry and waist-to-hip ratio

Body symmetry and waist-to-hip ratio are forms of physical attractiveness that indicate genetic fitness, with males and females who possess near-perfect body symmetry having 2 to 3 times as many sexual partners as those with asymmetrical bodies. Facial symmetry is especially seen as attractive, as it is regarded as the best predictor of body symmetry. Symmetry is particularly attractive in males, as symmetry requires genetic precision, and only males with good genetic quality can produce it. Generally symmetry itself is not directly attractive, but other characteristics related to body symmetry, such as being more dominant or having higher self-esteem, are.

Waist-to-hip ratio is an important aspect of female attractiveness, as females with a larger waist-to-hip ratio are associated with greater reproductive ability – they have 'childbearing hips' see Figure 8.2). A small waist also suggests a woman is not carrying another man's child.

■ **Figure 8.2** Which of these three images is the most attractive? Evolutionary theory predicts the one in the middle with a waist-to-hip ratio of 0.7, compared with 0.6 on the left and 0.8 on the right

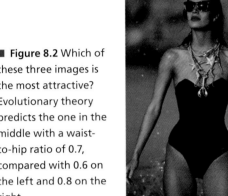

YOU ARE THE RESEARCHER

A female's hip-to-waist ratio is seen as an indicator of her reproductive ability. Therefore, evolutionary theory would predict that males will prefer the middle of the three pictures in Figure 8.2. Test this out by designing a suitable experiment that uses an opportunity sample. What will your IV and DV be?

Previous research suggests the middle picture will be preferred – this should help you decide when composing your experimental hypothesis if you will need a one-tailed (directional) or two-tailed (non-directional) hypothesis.

What type of graph will be appropriate to display your data? Remember to title and label it.

'Courtship – a man pursuing a woman until she catches him.'
Anonymous

Male strategies

Several male strategies have evolved seeking to maximize opportunities for mating success, including the following:

■ *Courtship rituals* – allow males to display genetic potential, through characteristics and resource abilities.

■ *Size* – males evolved to be bigger, demonstrating strength for success in competition against other males. Weaponry evolved in some species, for example antlers in deer.

■ *Sperm competition* – natural selection acted on males, making them more competitive by producing larger testicles, bigger ejaculations and faster-swimming sperm.

■ *Mate guarding* – males fear being cuckolded (where another male gets their partner pregnant) and spending resources raising another male's child. Males therefore indulge in mate guarding, where they keep an eye on and remain in close contact with female partners to prevent them mating with other males. **Buss & Schmidt (1993)** believes while men are fearful of partners being sexually unfaithful, females worry about emotional unfaithfulness, due to a fear of their partner spending resources on other females.

■ *Sneak copulation* – males mate with females other than their partners if given the opportunity, as it increases their chances of reproductive success. Women gain from this, too, as having different fathers brings a wider genetic diversity to their children, increasing survival chances. Females can also gain an adaptive advantage by being in a relationship with a resource-rich male, while getting pregnant through a sneaky copulation with a genetically fit 'stud', though if found out she risks abandonment and being left to raise the child without male resources. Research is somewhat contradictory, with indications of varying levels of children born through sneak copulations.

'To catch a husband is an art; to hold him is a job.'
Simone de Beauvoir (1949)

Female strategies

Several female strategies have evolved that maximize opportunities for mating success, including:

■ *Sexy sons' hypothesis* – females select attractive males as they will produce sons with the same attractive features, increasing their sons' and thus their own reproductive fitness.

■ *Handicap hypothesis* – **Zahavi (1975)** believes females select males with handicaps because it advertises ability to thrive despite handicaps, demonstrating superior genetic quality. This may explain females finding males attractive who drink or take drugs in large amounts, as they are demonstrating an ability to handle toxins, a sign of genetic fitness.

■ *Courtship* – females use courtship to select males on the basis of reproductive fitness, through males demonstrating strength, health and ability to provide resources. Prolonged courtship rituals also benefit females, as they make males invest time, effort and resources, increasing the chances of males not deserting after successful matings, so investing more resources in females and their offspring. Thus the human practice of dating, with males investing resources to females.

PSYCHOLOGY IN THE REAL WORLD

One practical application of evolutionary theory of relationships concerns heterosexual men learning skills to seduce women based upon evolutionary theory. The first stage involves creating opportunities to exploit evolved cues of what women find attractive in men, such as demonstrating charm and humour, as these are seen as 'honest' signals of high mate value. Conversation and acts that stress generosity and wealth will also create a good impression. Another male strategy is to befriend an attractive woman and use her as 'bait' to attract other attractive females. Subsequent strategies establish comfort and trust, such as through touch and eye contact to create bonding. Then finally seduction can occur where passion towards sexual activity is created by building intimacy through shared experiences and self-disclosure.

Although such practices may seem ethically questionable, their effectiveness is supported by the comfortable living being earned by a growing number of 'pick-up coaches' who teach such skills. The success of Neil Strauss's best-selling book 'The Game: Penetrating the secret society of pick-up artists' (2006) is one such example.

KEY STUDY ## CONTEMPORARY RESEARCH

'Sex differences in jealousy: the recall of cues to sexual and emotional infidelity in personally more and less threatening context conditions'
Schutzwohl & Koch (2004)

Previous research had indicated men to be more jealous of sexual infidelity than women and women to be more jealous of emotional infidelity than men. This study tested the assertion by examining male and female decision times in deciding jealousy choice.

Aim

To test **Buss & Schmidt's (1993)** belief that males fear sexual infidelity more, while females fear emotional infidelity more.

Procedure

1   An opportunity sample of 100 male and 100 female German university students formed the sample. Experimental procedures, scenarios and response alternatives were presented on a computer screen.

2   Participants were presented with four scenarios involving social situations, each with a choice of two alternative responses. Only the responses to scenario four were of interest to the study.

3   Participants were asked to vividly imagine the scenarios before responding. They were told that the scenarios referred to romantic relationships they had been in, were currently in or would like to be in.

4   Scenario four read as follows:

> *'Imagine that you discover your partner formed both a deep emotional and a passionate sexual relationship with another person. Which aspect of your partner's involvement would make you more jealous?*
>
> *The deep emotional relationship.*
>
> *The passionate sexual relationship.'*

5   The description of sexual and emotional infidelities was counterbalanced across participants. Choices were recorded, along with the times taken to make a decision after scenario presentation.

Findings

1   Both sexes reported more jealousy concerning the partner's emotional involvement, but more males (37 per cent) than females (20 per cent) selected their partner's sexual involvement as making them more jealous.

2   Women who selected emotional infidelity reached their decision faster than women selecting sexual infidelity.

3   Men who selected sexual infidelity reached their decision faster than men selecting emotional infidelity.

Conclusions

●   Men who are more jealous of sexual infidelity employ less elaborate decision strategies than men who are more jealous of emotional infidelity, while women who are more jealous of emotional infidelity employ less elaborate decision strategies than women who are more jealous of sexual infidelity.

●   Men and women who choose their adaptively primary infidelity type – that is, sexual for men, emotional for women – rely on their initial response tendency suggested by their respective jealousy mechanism, whereas men and women selecting their adaptively secondary infidelity type engage in additional considerations that lead them to override their initial response tendency.

Evaluation

●   Previous results from similar research, suggesting that women who select the emotional infidelity option engage in a more elaborate decision-making process than women selecting sexual infidelity, are refuted by this study.

●   The study does not identify the exact nature of the decision processes undertaken, especially by men, when selecting their adaptively secondary infidelity type.

RESEARCH IN FOCUS

Schutzwohl & Koch (2004) found a significant difference between male and female jealousy and would thus have been able to accept their experimental hypothesis. However, in doing so there would be a chance of making a Type I error.

1 What is a Type I error and under what circumstances would it occur?

2 Explain how a Type II error differs from a Type I error and under what circumstances it would occur.

Research

■ **Buss (1989)** tested participants from 37 cultures, finding that males prefer young, physically attractive females, while females prefer resource-rich, ambitious, industrious males, supporting the idea that gender-based ideas of attractiveness are biological in nature.

■ **Davis (1990)** performed a content analysis of personal advertisements, finding that men look for health and attractiveness, while offering wealth and resources. Females look for resources and status, while offering beauty and youth, supporting the idea of evolutionary based gender differences in relationship formation. Additional support came from **Dunbar & Waynforth (1995)**, who analysed 900 personal advertisements from four US newspapers, to find that 42 per cent of males sought youthfulness, while only 25 per cent of females did. Of males, 44 per cent sought attractiveness, while only 22 per cent of females did, supporting the sociobiological idea that males and females have different reasons for forming relationships.

■ **Pawlowski & Dunbar (1999)** examined the idea that older women do not disclose their true age in personal advertisements because men tend to judge prospective female partners on age, as it correlates with fertility. This was found to be true, especially for women aged 35–50, implying that women disguise their age in order to find high-quality partners before reproductive opportunities are ended by the menopause.

■ **Toma et al. (2008)**, who used personal advertisements to research males, found that men thought it more acceptable to lie about their education and income than females, while **Kurzban & Wedden (2005)** found females more likely to declare their weight as less than it was. This illustrates how resource richness is seen as attractive in males, while physical attractiveness as a sign of fertility is seen as attractive in females.

■ **Cartwright (2000)** found that women with symmetrical breasts were more fertile than more asymmetrically breasted women, supporting the idea that body symmetry indicates reproductive fitness. Additional support comes from **Penton-Voak et al. (2001)**, who found that females prefer males with greater facial symmetry, an indication of developmental stability that would be passed on to their sons, increasing reproductive potential.

■ **Langlois & Roggman (1990)** used computer-composite images to produce faces of varying symmetrical quality, finding a preference for symmetrical faces, faces identical in shape and form on both sides. This applied to both male and female faces. **Cartwright (2000)** supported this, finding that men prefer photographs of women with symmetrical faces and vice versa.

■ It seems that symmetry, which tends to be inherited, equates with fitness. Only individuals with good genes and food supplies develop perfectly symmetrical faces.

■ **Singh (1993)** used data from 50 years of beauty contest winners and Playboy centrefolds to assess waist-to-hip ratios of attractive women. He found that a small waist set against full hips was a consistent feature of female attractiveness, while breast size, overall body weight and physique varied over the years, suggesting that waist-to-hip ratio is an indicator of reproductive ability.

■ **Swami & Furnham (2006)** found that the optimum waist-to-hip ratio of 0.7:1 corresponds closely to supermodels, such as Anna Nicole Smith (0.69), Kate Moss (0.66) and Cindy Crawford (0.69), supporting Singh's findings.

■ Different studies into children born as a result of human sneak copulations have found differing figures. **Peritz & Rust (1972)** found a figure of only 0.03 per cent, while **Ridley (1993)** found a much higher 20 per cent. **Simmons et al. (2003)** gave a questionnaire on lifetime sexual behaviour to 416 Australian women and men, finding 27.9 per cent of males and 22.2 per cent of females admitted to cheating on partners, which suggests a sizeable minority of both sexes use the strategy, supporting evolutionary theory.

YOU ARE THE RESEARCHER

Design a study using a content analysis of personal advertisements (adverts in a newspaper where people seek relationships) to see if the evolutionary predictions that men will offer wealth and resources while seeking health and fertility are true. After locating a newspaper with personal advertisements, you will need to create coding units to categorize the qualities you are assessing. Use a random sample of the adverts available. Once you've quantified your data (by counting the number of times each quality appears within your sampled adverts) you will need to create a suitable graph and table to display your data in.

Evaluation

- Much early evidence for children born from sneak copulations is based on questionnaires and blood samples, so may not be reliable. Estimates of children born from sneak copulations also vary widely, which may be due to cultural differences, or to the types of samples used – for instance, using DNA data where males had suspicions of non-paternity is more likely to find such evidence. Evidence from supposedly monogamous species in the animal kingdom is supportive though, with **Birkhead (1990, cited in Birkhead & Moller, 1998)** using DNA sampling to find that 8 per cent of zebra finch offspring result from females' sneaky copulations with non-partner males.

- **Miller & Fishkin (1997)** sees evolution as shaping human culture – that is, language, art, humour and music, which act as courtship displays, attracting sexual partners.

- The evolutionary explanation presumes heterosexuality and that all relationships are sexual; it is therefore oversimplified and cannot explain long-distance romantic relationships, like those conducted over the internet. It also cannot explain couples choosing not to have children, as it assumes all relationships are motivated by a desire to reproduce.

- **Diamond (1992)** believes males, especially in early adulthood, use drugs and indulge in risky behaviours, like bungee jumping, to advertise their reproductive fitness in the face of adversity, providing support for the handicap hypothesis.

- The practice of checking partners' mobile phone records, email accounts, and so on, can be regarded as a modern form of mate guarding, where checks are made on partners to see whether they have been sexually/emotionally unfaithful.

- Younger males sometimes desire substantially older women – this goes against evolutionary theory, but may occur due to males wanting to mate with females proven to be fertile.

- Females often alter their appearance through the use of make-up and cosmetic surgery and lie about their age in order to appear younger and more fertile. Males use deceit to exaggerate their resource capabilities and feign love in order to persuade females to mate with them. This supports the idea of males and females using different strategies to maximize reproductive potential.

- Women do not need men in the way they once did and as predicted by evolutionary theory. Females in western cultures have greater financial security and employment opportunities, and this has occurred simultaneously with a rise in single women having children – according to the **Office for National Statistics (2014)**, 82,000 single women over the age of 30 had babies in Britain in 2006, and 25 per cent of British families are single-parent families (90 per cent are female-led). These statistics are not consistent with women needing male partners to provide for them and their offspring.

- Evolutionary theory explains female choosiness and male competitiveness in terms of maximizing reproductive potential. However, this can also be explained by gender role socialization.

TOK link

Evolutionary explanations, such as those for partner preferences, often gather evidence from animal studies. However, this poses problems of generalization to humans, as human behaviour is influenced more by higher cognitive processes than with animal species.

YOU ARE THE RESEARCHER

Test out Pawlowski & Dunbar's claim (see page 348) that women disguise their age by using personal advertisements from newspapers to see whether there is a difference in the number of women and men not stating their age (or giving an age range rather than a precise age). If the researchers are correct, more women should not state their age. You will need an equal number of male and female advertisements.

'What you seek is seeking you.'
Jalal ad-Din Muhammad Rumi (1250)

'You don't always get to choose who you fall in love with.'
Stephani Hecht (2010)

Strengthen your learning

1   Explain, from an evolutionary viewpoint, why males and females have different strategies to maximize reproductive success.

2   What is sexual dimorphism?

3   Explain why attractiveness in females is valued by males.

4   Explain how symmetry and hip-to-waist ratios are forms of attractiveness.

5   Outline male strategies for maximizing mating success.

6   Outline female strategies for maximizing mating success.

7   For Schutzwohl & Koch's (2004) study of sexual differences in jealousy, in your own words, state the:
    a aims   c results   e evaluative points.
    b procedure   d conclusions

8   Summarize what other research studies have suggested about evolutionary explanations for partner preferences.

9   Provide an assessment of evolutionary explanations for partner preferences in terms of strengths and weaknesses.

The matching hypothesis

FOCUS ON...

■ The matching hypothesis as an explanation for relationship formation.
■ What research has informed about the matching hypothesis as an explanation for relationship formation.
■ An assessment of the matching hypothesis as an explanation for relationship formation.

Matching hypothesis – the idea that individuals are unconsciously motivated to form romantic relationships with those of perceived similar attractiveness.

Walster et al.'s (1966a) matching hypothesis argues that when initiating romantic relationships, individuals seek partners who are most like themselves in terms of physical attractiveness. This involves individuals assessing their own level of physical attractiveness and then focusing attention upon potential partners of perceived similar physical attractiveness, as there is seen to be less chance of being rejected. It has also been hypothesized that individuals will feel more secure in a relationship with someone of equal physical attractiveness, owing to fears that a more attractive partner might be tempted to end the relationship if a more physically attractive partner became available.

Research

- **Brigham (1971)** found that physically attractive people are seen as having desirable personality characteristics, including being sociable, interesting, exciting and sexually warm, supporting the idea of the Halo effect, where people's whole personality is judged on the basis that they are physically attractive.

- **Gunnell & Ceci (2010)** found that physically less attractive people are 22 per cent more likely to be convicted in courts of law and receive prison sentences of on average 22 months longer than physically attractive people. This supports the Halo effect that physically attractive people are generally seen as more trustworthy than less physically attractive people.

- **Walster & Walster (1969)** told students they had been assigned an ideal partner for a forthcoming dance event, though selections had actually been made at random. The students met up before the dance and those who had been paired up with partners of similar physical attractiveness to themselves expressed greater liking of their partners than those who had been paired up with partners of dissimilar levels of physical attractiveness. This supports the matching hypothesis.

- **Murstein (1972)** asked participants to assess from photographs the physical attractiveness levels of genuine couples and non-genuine couples (who had been put together for the purpose of the study). It was found that the real couples were more likely to be judged as of similar levels of attractiveness to each other than the non-genuine couples, thus supporting the matching hypothesis.

- **Taylor et al. (2011)** used profiles and photographs from an online dating site to assess the matching hypothesis, finding that initial attraction (assessed by whether communication was requested) was based on levels of physical attractiveness, which did not support the matching hypothesis. However, replies were more likely to be sent to individuals who were judged to be of similar levels of physical attractiveness and agreements to 'communicate' were also more likely to occur among couples of similar physical attractiveness. This suggests the matching hypothesis applies more to later stages of the dating process rather than explaining initial attraction.

YOU ARE THE RESEARCHER

Test out the matching hypothesis by conducting a correlational analysis where you find about ten wedding photographs from a newspaper or the internet (not of famous people). Cut them up so that you can paste all the male photos onto one sheet and the female photos onto another sheet. Get male participants to rate the females on physical attractiveness from 1 to 10 (where 1 is very unattractive and 10 is very attractive), while similarly getting female participants to do the same with male images. Compose suitable correlational hypotheses and plot your data onto a scattergram.

Evaluation

- Walster et al.'s original matching hypothesis stated that individuals would desire to partner someone as socially desirable as themselves. However, over time the hypothesis has come to be regarded as one focused solely on levels of physical attractiveness, something it was not orientated towards.

- In an earlier study **Walster et al. (1966b)** actually found that participants liked people who were more physically attractive and that physical attractiveness was the best indicator by both males and females of wanting to see someone again. This goes against the matching hypothesis, though when asked months later, it was found that participants who actually did date their partner again were of similar levels of physical attractiveness, which supports the hypothesis.

- Although physical beauty is an important form of attractiveness, those without it can compensate through complex matching, where they may pair up with a more physically attractive partner by being attractive in other ways, such as through wealth or domestic skills.

- Evolutionary theory suggests that men value physical attractiveness more in women than women do in men, which means it is easier for men to compensate through other means for not being physically attractive.

- In many cultures, such as those practising arranged marriages, senior family members are regarded as better judges of who is compatible as a partner for their children and therefore attractiveness will be judged on factors other than physical attractiveness.

Social exchange theory

'I told her I'd wait forever for her, but that was before I found somebody else who'd give me a lift home.'
Jared Kintz (2010)

FOCUS ON...

- Social exchange theory, equity theory and Rusbult's investment theory as explanations for relationship maintenance.
- Thibaut & Kelley's four-stage model of social exchange.
- Walster's four principles of equity.
- What research has informed about social equity theory and Rusbult's investment theory as explanations for relationship maintenance.
- An assessment of social exchange theory, equity theory and Rusbult's investment theory as explanations for relationship maintenance.

Social exchange theory – an economic explanation of relationships based on maximizing profits and minimizing costs.

There are different versions of **social exchange theory** (SET), but underlying all of them is the idea that in any relationship both partners are continually giving and receiving items of value to and from each other and, as people are fundamentally selfish, relationships continue only if both partners feel they are getting more out of the relationship than they are putting in.

The theory sees people as perceiving their feelings for others in terms of profit (the rewards obtained from relationships minus the costs). The greater the rewards and the lower the costs, the greater the profit and therefore the greater the desire to maintain the relationship.

Interactions between partners can be 'expensive', as they take time, energy and commitment, and may involve unpleasant emotions and experiences. Therefore, for a relationship to be maintained, individuals must feel they are receiving more than they put in. The theory also sees social interactions as involving an exchange of rewards, such as affection, intimate information and status. The degree of attraction or liking between partners reflects how people evaluate the rewards they receive relative to those given.

Thus SET is a sociocultural explanation of personal relationships that focuses on economics and explains relationships in terms of maximizing benefits and minimizing costs. The 'social exchange' is the mutual exchange of rewards between partners, like friendship and sex, and the costs of being in the relationship, such as freedoms given up. A person assesses their rewards by making two comparisons:

1   *The comparison level (CL)* – where rewards are compared against costs to judge profits.

2   *The comparison level for alternative relationships (CLalt)* – where rewards and costs are compared against perceived rewards and costs for possible alternative relationships.

A relationship is maintained if rewards exceed costs and the profit level is not exceeded by possible alternative relationships.

Thibaut & Kelley (1959) proposed a four-stage model of SET, setting out how relationships could be maintained (see Table 8.1). It perceives that over time people develop a predictable and mutually beneficial pattern of exchanges, assisting the maintenance of relationships.

Stage	Description
Sampling	Rewards and costs are assessed in a number of relationships
Bargaining	A relationship is 'costed out' and sources of profit and loss are identified
Commitment	Relationship is established and maintained by a predictable exchange of rewards
Institutionalization	Interactions are established and the couple 'settle down'

■ Table 8.1 Thibaut & Kelley's four-stage model

Research

- **Hatfield (1979)** looked at people who felt over- or under-benefited in their relationships. The under-benefited felt angry and deprived, while the over-benefited felt guilty and uncomfortable, supporting the theory by suggesting that regardless of whether individuals are benefited, they do not desire to maintain a relationship if it is unequal.

- **Mills & Clark (1980)** identified two kinds of intimate relationship: the communal couple, where each partner gives out of concern for the other, and the exchange couple, where each keeps mental records of who is 'ahead' and who is 'behind'. This indicates that there are different types of relationships and that SET can be applied to some of them, but not universally to all.

- **Rusbult (1983)** asked participants to complete questionnaires over a seven-month period concerning rewards and costs associated with relationships, finding that social exchange theory did not explain the early 'honeymoon' phase of a relationship when balance of exchanges was ignored. However, later on, relationship costs were compared against the degree of personal satisfaction, suggesting that the theory is best applied to the maintenance of relationships.

- **Rusbult (1983)** found that the costs and rewards of relationships were compared against the costs and rewards of potential alternative relationships in order to decide whether the relationship should be maintained, supporting the social exchange model's idea that people assess rewards by making comparisons.

- **Rusbult & Martz (1995)** found that women who had been physically assaulted by their partners and were living in a women's refuge were likely to return to their abusive partners, as they did not have better alternatives, often because of low levels of education, no job prospects and little access to money. This supports SET, as even though the women were in abusive relationships, the profits were seen to exceed the costs.

Evaluation

- **Rubin (1983)** believes that although people are not fundamentally selfish, attitudes towards others are determined to a large extent by how rewarding we think they are for us, supporting the theory.

- **Sedikides (2005)** claims that people are capable of being unselfish – doing things for others without expecting anything in return. This is most evident in relationships with those emotionally closest to us. Sedikides believes that individuals can bolster their partner's self-esteem when they are faced with failure and other stressful life events. Therefore, the view of humans as being out for what they can get is simplistic and inaccurate.

- **Fromm (1962)** argues against the theory, defining true love as giving, as opposed to the false love of the 'marketing character', where people expect to have favours returned.

- The social exchange theory was modified into the **equity theory**, which concerns balance and stability in relationships and is a logical progression.

- **Argyle (1988)** criticized methodologies that evaluate social exchange theory, declaring them contrived and artificial, with little relevance to real life.

- Research has concentrated on the short-term consequences of relationships rather than the more important, long-term maintenance of relationships.

- The theory applies to people who 'keep score'. **Murstein et al. (1977)** devised the exchange orientation tool, identifying such scorekeepers, who are suspicious and insecure, suggesting that the theory only suits relationships lacking confidence and mutual trust.

Equity theory – an economic explanation of relationships based on motivation to achieve fairness and balance.

Rusbult's investment model – an explanation that sees relationship satisfaction as dependent upon a consideration of perceived benefits, costs and the quality of possible alternative relationships..

RESEARCH IN FOCUS

Participants used in studies of **Rusbult's investment model** tended to know they were taking part in a study, so there may have been a risk of demand characteristics.

Explain what demand characteristics are and what psychologists can do to minimize their effects.

YOU ARE THE RESEARCHER

Assess social exchange theory by combining the experimental method with a questionnaire to compare two groups of people in romantic relationships, such as people from different age ranges or different genders, by asking them to state what they give and receive in their relationships.

What type of experimental method would this be? What experimental design would you use? What would the IV and DV be? For the questionnaire would you use open or closed questions? How would you compile your data?

Construct a suitable table and graph to display your data.

PSYCHOLOGY IN THE REAL WORLD

■ **Figure 8.3** Carol Santa Fe and partner

Human romantic relationships can take many forms other than just between heterosexual and homosexual partners. In 2017, 45-year-old Carol Sante Fe married Sante Fe railway station in California, USA (taking the railway's surname). She claims they have been in love for 36 years, that she has had sex with the building, and visits every day to spend time with her partner. During the pet rocks craze of the 1970s (where people bought rocks as pets), several women went through marriage ceremonies to their rocks. These are examples of objectum sexuality, where people develop sexual feelings for inanimate objects. Marrying convicted murderers on 'Death Row' whom women have never actually physically met is another quite common phenomenon, as is the more recent trend for virtual weddings, where people create avatars and get married in cyberspace; indeed there are many websites where people can indulge in virtual fantasy relationships. Any psychological theory that is fully valid should be able to explain all relationships like these and not just the more 'traditional' ones.

Equity theory

'Fairness does not mean everyone gets the same.

Fairness means everyone gets what they need.'
Rick Riordan (2005)

Equity in relationships does not mean equality; instead it is a belief that individuals are motivated to achieve fairness in relationships and to feel dissatisfied with inequity (unfairness). Definitions of equity within a relationship can differ between individuals.

The formation and maintenance of relationships occurs through balance and stability. Relationships where individuals put in more than they receive, or receive more than they put in, are inequitable, leading to dissatisfaction and possible dissolution (ending of the relationship). The recognition of inequity within a relationship presents a chance for a relationship to be saved – that is, maintained further by making adjustments so that there is a return to equity.

Relationships may alternate between periods of perceived balance and imbalance, with individuals being motivated to return to a state of equity. The greater the perceived imbalance, the greater the efforts to realign the relationship, provided that a chance of doing so is perceived to be viable.

Walster *et al.* (1978) saw equity as based on four principles, as set out in Table 8.2.

Principle	Description
Profit	Rewards are maximized and costs minimized
Distribution	Trade-offs and compensations are negotiated to achieve fairness in a relationship
Dissatisfaction	The greater the degree of perceived unfairness, the greater the sense of dissatisfaction
Realignment	If restoring equity is possible, maintenance will continue, with attempts made to realign equity

■ **Table 8.2** The four principles of equity

Research

- **Argyle (1977)** found that people in close relationships do not think in terms of rewards and costs unless they feel dissatisfied, implying that equity, at least in a conscious fashion, is not a valid explanation of relationship maintenance.

- **Murstein & MacDonald (1983)** supported Argyle, finding that a conscious concern with 'getting a fair deal', especially in the short term, makes compatibility hard to achieve, especially between married couples.

- **Canary & Stafford (1992)** devised the Relationship Maintenance Strategies Measure (RMSM), using it to assess degree of equity in romantic relationships. A link was found between degree of perceived equity and the prevalence of maintenance strategies, implying that equitable relationships are maintained.

- **Dainton (2003)** studied 219 individuals in romantic relationships, finding that those in relationships of perceived inequity had low relationship satisfaction, but were motivated to return to an equitable state to maintain the relationship, suggesting that equity is a main factor in relationship satisfaction and maintenance.

- **Yum *et al.* (2009, cited in Lawton, 2012a)** looked at different types of heterosexual romantic relationships in six different cultures. As predicted by equity theory, maintenance strategies differed, with individuals in perceived equitable relationships engaging in most maintenance strategies, followed by those in perceived over-benefited and under-benefited relationships. Cultural factors had little effect, suggesting that equity theory can be applied to relationships across cultures.

TOK link

Cross-cultural studies, such as **Yum *et al.*'s (2009)** study of heterosexual relationships in different cultures, compare people from different cultures on an important variable. If behaviour is found to be similar in different cultures then this suggests the behaviour is innate, while if the behaviour differs across cultures, then it suggests the behaviour is more environmental in nature.

Evaluation

- Equity theory still portrays people as selfish. Many researchers, like **Duck (1988)**, prefer to see people as concerned with an equitable distribution of rewards and costs for themselves and their partners.

- **Kelley & Thibaut (1978)** proposed *interdependence theory*, which suggests that not all social interactions reflect a shared desire for equity and fair exchange. Intimate relationships are varied and complex, and partners' motives and desires can clash as well as coincide, producing many outcomes, including aggression, altruism, competition, capitulation (giving in), cooperation and intransigence ('digging your heels in'). Interdependence theory goes beyond individual partners, considering the harmony and/or conflict between attitudes, motives, values or goals of people in social relationships.

- **Sprecher (1986)** believes that close relationships are too complex to allow for precise assessment of various rewards and costs involved in establishing equity.

- **Mills & Clark (1982)** believe that it is not possible to assess equity in loving relationships, as much input is emotional and therefore unquantifiable, and to do so diminishes the quality of love.

- Equity seems more important to females, suggesting that the theory is not applicable to both genders. **Hochschild & Machung (1990)** found that women do most of the work to make relationships equitable.

- Some research suggests that equity theory does not apply to all cultures. **Moghaddam et al. (1993)** found that US students prefer equity (fairness), but European students prefer equality, suggesting that the theory reflects the values of US society.

Rusbult's investment model of commitment

'He's Mr Right, but I'm always right.'
Mara Lawton (2014)

As another sociocultural explanation, Rusbult's theory attempts to identify the determinants of relationship commitment and is comprised of three factors positively linked with commitment: satisfaction level, the comparison with alternatives and size of investment.

1 *Satisfaction level* refers to the positive v. negative effect experienced in a relationship. Satisfaction is influenced by the degree to which a partner meets an individual's needs, for example the extent to which a partner meets one's emotional and sexual needs.

2 *Comparison with alternatives* refers to the perceived desirability of the best alternative to the current relationship and is based upon the extent to which an individual's needs could be met within that alternative relationship, for example the extent to which a potential alternative partner could meet one's emotional and sexual needs. If such needs could be better met elsewhere then the quality of alternatives is high. If such needs are best met within the current relationship then commitment is stronger.

3 *Investment size* refers to the amount and importance of the resources associated with a relationship and such resources would decline in value or be lost if the relationship was to end. Partners invest directly into relationships, such as the time and effort put into the relationship, as well as indirect investments, such as shared friends, children and co-owned material possessions. After investments have occurred, commitment is heightened as ending a relationship would then become more costly.

There are also two variables linked to commitment:

1 *Equity* is the degree of 'fairness' within a relationship. Inequity (perceived unfairness) leads to distress and lack of satisfaction with a relationship and thus less commitment to it. Such distress can be relieved by ending the relationship.

2 *Social support* is the degree of care and assistance available from others, such as from family and friends. If such others approve of a relationship it produces a positive influence that increases commitment to the relationship.

Research

- **Lin & Rusbult (1995)** found that although findings were inconsistent, females generally reported higher satisfaction levels, poorer scores for quality of alternatives, greater investments and stronger overall commitment. This suggests gender differences may exist, with females demonstrating greater dependence and stronger commitment than males.

- **Rusbult *et al.* (1998)** gave the investment model scale (IMS) questionnaire to student participants in relationships, to find that commitment in relationships was positively correlated with satisfaction level, negatively correlated with the quality of alternatives and positively correlated with investment size, supporting all three factors of Rusbult's model.

- **Rusbult *et al.* (1998)** administered the IMS questionnaire to participants in homosexual relationships, finding support for all factors of the model, as did **Duffy & Rusbult (1986)** when administering the same questionnaire to individuals in marital relationships, which suggests that the model explains commitment in a variety of relationships.

- **Van Lange *et al.* (1997)** found support for all factors of the model in Taiwanese participants and this was coupled with similar results found by **Lin & Rusbult (1995)** with Dutch participants, which suggests the model has cross-cultural validity.

Evaluation

- Research indicates that Rusbult's model with its focus on commitment and what individuals have invested is a better predictor of long-term maintenance in relationships than equity theory.

- Rusbult's model can explain why partners remain in abusive relationships, as the cost of losing what they have invested and committed to in the relationship may be too great, with no possible alternative relationships to turn to.

- The investment model is able to explain infidelity, as such behaviour occurs when there is low satisfaction with a current relationship and high satisfaction with an alternative relationship, with both these factors serving to erode commitment.

- Research that supports the investment model is highly reliant on self-report measures, which may be subject to socially desirable and idealized answers, as well as researcher bias, casting some doubts on the validity of the results.

Strengthen your learning

1 Explain the matching hypothesis as an explanation of relationship formation.

2 Summarize what research studies have suggested about the matching hypothesis.

3 What other evaluative points can be made about the matching hypothesis?

4 Outline each of the following as explanations of relationship maintenance:
   a social exchange theory (including Thibaut & Kelley's four-stage model of SET)
   b equity theory (including Walster *et al.*'s. four principles of equity)
   c Rusbult's investment model of commitment.

5 Summarize what research studies have suggested about
   a social exchange theory
   b equity theory
   c Rusbult's investment model of commitment.

6 Provide an assessment of each of the following in terms of their strengths and weaknesses:
   a social exchange theory
   b equity theory
   c Rusbult's investment model of commitment.

- The formation of personal relationships can be explained by reference to evolution, with males and females having developed different strategies to maximize reproductive success.
- The matching hypothesis sees individuals as forming relationships with those of similar levels of perceived attractiveness.
- Social exchange theory, equity theory and Rusbult's investment model are economic explanations of relationships based on considerations of costs and rewards.

Role of communication in personal relationships

'The most important thing in communication is hearing what isn't said.'
Peter Drucker

Communication –
methods of sending and receiving information.

Attribution – the process by which individuals explain the causes of behaviour and events.

Self-disclosure – the revealing of personal information about oneself to another.

Communication between individuals is an important factor in the formation and maintenance of relationships, with the quality of communication being a vital part in the building and developing of interpersonal relationships. Relationships often end when individuals stop communicating. Effective communication is especially important to individuals who lack trust and self-esteem, as it often serves to clear up misunderstandings and anxieties and to build-up confidence within a relationship.

Factors that affect the quality of communication within a relationship include:

- **Attribution**
- **Self-disclosure**

FOCUS ON...

- Attribution as a factor affecting the quality of communication within relationships.
- The effects of internal and external attributions, emotional and motivational states, egocentric bias and the theory of minding the close relationship upon communication within relationships.
- What research has informed about attribution as a factor affecting the quality of communication within relationships.
- An assessment of attribution as a factor affecting the quality of communication within relationships.
- Self-disclosure as a factor affecting the quality of communication within relationships, including face-to-face and virtual relationships.
- What research has informed about self-disclosure as a factor affecting the quality of communication within relationships.
- An assessment of self-disclosure as a factor affecting the quality of communication within relationships.

Attribution theory

Heider (1958) saw humans as 'amateur scientists', trying to understand each other's behaviour by collecting information until they found a reasonable explanation. For example, is someone in an angry mood, because they're a naturally angry person, or has something in the environment made them angry? Two basic attributions (reasons) for behaviour were identified:

1 *Internal attribution* – a person behaves in a certain way because of something personal about them, like their attitude or character.

2 *External attribution* – a person behaves a certain way due to characteristics of the situation they are in.

Attributions are highly affected by emotional and motivational states, with individuals often using attributions to portray themselves positively and others negatively, such as by deflecting blame onto others. **Jones & Davis (1965)** argued that we pay particular attention to intentional behaviour (rather than accidental or unthinking behaviour).

So, for example, in a relationship, if a person burst into tears during a conversation, then their partner may analyse this behaviour by reference to whether they normally behave in this way, whether they have been insensitive and provoked this reaction, whether there is an identifiable reason for the behaviour (such as they've had a bad day at work), or whether there is some intention behind the behaviour (e.g. attention seeking) that reflects the partner's personality.

So in relationships, when negative outcomes occur, there is a tendency to see these as due to egocentric bias, where individuals seek to protect their levels of self-esteem by attributing their behaviour to factors in the external situation and their partner's behaviour due to defects in their personality. The motivation for doing this can often relate to wanting to control or punish one's partner, with **Newman (1981)** believing that attribution is a form of persuasion and ongoing communication in interpersonal relationships that influences their development and maintenance over time.

There are gender differences in the way men and women process attributions. Females tend to process and analyse reasons for issues and events in relationships more than men, with males only indulging in extensive attribution when there are relationship problems.

Harvey & Omarzu (1999) proposed the theory of **minding the close relationship**, which argues that in healthy relationships individuals mutually take care to make positive, but accurate attributions about their partners. This sees communication in relationships as being a mutual, constant process of self-disclosing to partners and seeking self-disclosure from them. Flexibility in making attributions in response to new information is also important, as is sometimes making negative attributions in order to promote discussion and solve relationship problems. This results in a build-up of trust and admiration for one's partner.

Minding the close relationship – the idea that in healthy relationships individuals mutually take care to make positive, but accurate attributions about their partners.

Research

- **Orvis et al. (1976)** got couples to list examples of behaviour for which partners had different explanations. It was found that for behaviours which resulted in negative outcomes participants tended to see themselves as blameless, while placing guilt onto their partner, and this was more apparent in problematic relationships. In more harmonious relationships, participants attributed negative outcomes to the situation rather than their partner's personality. This supports the idea of egocentric bias in attribution and illustrates how motivational factors are important in making attributions in personal relationships.

- **Harvey et al. (1978)** found that in problematic relationships, partners made different attributions about their problems, in line with Orvis et al.'s findings, but that they also were not able to predict their partner's attributions. This suggests a breakdown in, or lack of, communication between partners may be central to the experience of relationship problems.

- **Holtzworth-Monroe (1988)** used self-reports to study violent relationships, finding that abused women, although not blaming themselves for their partners' violence, did attribute the violence to external factors, with violent partners also offering external attributions for their actions. This supports the idea that attribution theory can be used to explain the quality of interpersonal relationships.

Evaluation

- The egocentric bias seen when assigning attributions to relationship behaviour may be negatively affecting relationships by itself, or may just be an indicator that the relationship already has problems.

- The fact that there are gender differences in how and when males and females partake in attribution processes backs up the idea that there also gender differences in how men and women experience relationship breakdown.

- Studies of attribution in relationships tend to use self-reports, such as interviews and questionnaires. Such methods are prone to several influences that can affect the validity of findings. For example, idealized answers where participants answer as they'd like to be rather than how they actually are, and socially desirable answers, where participants give answers that conform to social expectations rather than their true feelings.

- Studies of attribution in relationships can involve probing sensitive areas, such as physical abuse in relationships, infidelity, and so on. Therefore, care should be taken that research methods, such as the framing of questions, do not have the potential to cause unacceptable levels of distress, that the right to withdraw is clearly explained and that a thorough debriefing takes place after the research is conducted.

- Communication plays an even bigger role in **virtual relationships (VRs)**, where people interact purely via social media.

....
Virtual relationships (VRs) – non-physical interactions between people communicating via social media.
....

TOK link

Many research studies of attribution in relationships use interviews and questionnaires. Although such studies cannot establish causality, as they are not conducted under controlled conditions, they do have the advantage of producing quantitative (numerical) data, which can be subjected to statistical analysis to draw conclusions, as well as qualitative (non-numerical) data, which is another dimension to the results, by including people's beliefs and feelings about a research area. This allows greater depth and detail to be added to findings and may even identify possible new areas for research.

Self-disclosure

'It takes a lot of courage to show your dreams to someone else.'
Erma Bombeck

Self-disclosure (SD) involves communicating personal information about oneself to another. The revealing of such personal information leads to a build-up of intimacy, essential to the development and maintenance of relationships. SD is seen as especially important in the modern phenomenon of virtual relationships (VRs), where people interact and form strong interpersonal relationships through social media.

SD occurs more easily in VRs as people can self-disclose with less fear of social embarrassment. This is similar to **Rubin's (1975)** 'strangers on a train' phenomenon, where individuals reveal more to a stranger as they do not have knowledge of, or access to, the stranger's social circle. However, strangers tend to only meet once; VRs allow for continued interactions, meaning trusting relationships can often be built more quickly and with more intimacy than face-to-face (FTF) relationships.

SD in VRs tend to be based on more meaningful factors, for example shared attitudes and interests, rather than the more superficial factors found with FTF relationships, such as physical attractiveness. Also, due to the anonymity of VRs, SD tends to be about one's 'true' self rather than a publicly presented 'false' self and such real intimacies help build a stronger, more meaningful relationship. This means, due to the level of communication, that VRs have greater potential to be more long-lasting than FTF relationships.

SD can create high levels of affection that are sustained if people in VRs go on to physically meet. This occurs due to the initial lack of physical information (such as a person's level of physical attractiveness), which can help form initial impressions of individuals that become resistant to change. As deep VRs form without physical information, such information will not be that influential when people meet in person.

Intimate communication occurs more with VRs, because of a lack of gating, the limiting factors that can affect the formation and maintenance of FTF relationships. Visible features, such as a lack of physical attractiveness, a tendency to stutter or be shy, for example, are not apparent in VRs, so less physically beautiful, less confident and less socially gifted individuals have a better chance of developing a meaningful relationship. This means that, owing to the high levels of intimacy reached, progressing on to physically meeting each other will not be damaged by revealing a lack of physical attractiveness, and so on, due to the degree of intimacy established.

There are dangers though of communication in VRs. People can misrepresent themselves online more easily and because of the anonymous nature of the internet individuals are more at risk of being harassed than in FTF relationships. A recent phenomenon of communicating via VR is sexting, the sending of sexually explicit photos/videos. This occurs as probably people feel less inhibited in their behaviour on social media than in real life, but there are dangers, such as being blackmailed or coerced into such behaviour against one's will. There is also the possibility that people may become over-dependent on VRs so spend less time learning FTF relationship skills.

Research

■ **Peter *et al.* (2005)** found introverts were motivated to communicate online to compensate for their lack of social skills, which increased their motivation to make friends online, leading, in turn, to more self-disclosure and thus more intimate VRs. This suggests that quieter, shy people are more attracted to self-disclose in VR. However, it was also found that extroverts self-disclosed more in VR, which helped to develop their relationships further too, illustrating again how personality mediates VR. This was supported by **Schouten *et al.* (2007)** finding that people high in social anxiety revealed greater self-disclosure in VR owing to the lack of non-verbal cues in online communications, supporting the idea that people who have problems socializing in the physical world are able to self-disclose more in VR.

■ **McKenna & Bargh (2000)** surveyed 568 internet users to find that 54 per cent had gone on to physically meet virtual friends and 63 per cent had talked on the phone. In a two-year follow-up study, 57 per cent revealed their VR had continued and increased in intimacy. Romantic relationships fared even better, with 70 per cent of relationships formed online enduring beyond two years compared with more than 50 per cent of physical relationships that fail within two years. The results illustrate how communication in VR can help such relationships develop into physical enduring ones.

■ Data from the **Pew Research Internet Project (2014)** shows that 9 per cent of American mobile phone owners have sent a sext; with individuals in relationships just as likely to do so as single people. This suggests that this form of uninhibited self-disclosure is a quite common occurrence.

■ **McKenna *et al.* (2002)** got participants to either interact with a partner in person for 20 minutes on two 'real' occasions, or via an internet chat room first before meeting face to face. In the final condition, participants interacted with one partner in person and another via an internet chat room, but unbeknown to both partners they were actually the same participants (the order in which people met in this final condition was counterbalanced). Each participant was paired with an opposite-sex partner on ten occasions. It was found that partners were liked more when they met via the internet than face to face in all situations because communications were seen as more intimate. This supports the idea that when in face-to-face interactions, superficial gating features, such as degree of physical attractiveness, dominate and overwhelm other factors that lead to more intimate disclosure and greater attraction.

RESEARCH IN FOCUS

A lot of the research into VR is conducted with interviews and questionnaires. Explain why the findings of such research can be invalid owing to participants giving idealized answers and socially desirable answers.

Evaluation

■ One of the dangers of self-disclosure in VR is that individuals may present their ideal self to their virtual partner, rather than their real self, faults and all. Therefore, the intimacy created can lead to idealization of a virtual partner, which the person cannot live up to in reality.

■ Research has not really discriminated between different types of intimacy and the effects these have on the degree of attraction an individual feels towards a partner. For example, the intimate physical nature of sexting is very different to the intimate revelations of one's inner thoughts and feelings.

■ The internet and other forms of social media may be creating social pressure upon individuals to conform to certain levels of intimate disclosures that they are not truly happy with. This is especially true of sexting where many individuals, often female, report pressure on them to send sexts.

■ The **absence of gating** features in VR means that there is a much wider potential group of people to form relationships with online, as VR will, from the start, communicate more upon common interests, attitudes, and so on, rather than being limited by more superficial but dominant gating features, such as level of physical attractiveness.

> ## PSYCHOLOGY IN THE REAL WORLD
>
> The fact that people who lack social skills are especially attracted to virtual relationships suggests a practical application in using VR as a therapy for the socially inept to learn social skills that are useful for shaping social relationships in the real world. Such a therapy could also be used to help those with social phobias (fear of social situations) overcome their fears.

Strengthen your learning

1 Outline attribution theory as a factor affecting communication within relationships – ensure you include in your answer:
  a the difference between internal and external attributions
  b why attributions are especially affected by motivational and emotional states
  c the role of egocentric bias.

2 Explain the theory of 'minding the close relationship'.

3 Outline self-disclosure as a factor affecting communication within relationships – ensure you include in your answer why self-disclosure is especially important in virtual relationships.

4 Summarize what research studies have suggested about the following as factors affecting communication within relationships:
  a attributions   b self-disclosure.

5 What other evaluative points can be made about the following as factors affecting communication within relationships:
  a attributions   b self-disclosure?

Explanations for why relationships change or end

> '*Stop going to a dry well for water.*'
> Arabic proverb

Dissolution – the process by which romantic relationships break down.

If psychologists can understand better the reasons why relationships break down, then it may lead to more effective strategies for saving relationships that are in trouble. Two well regarded models of **dissolution** (relationship breakdown) are those of Duck and Lee.

FOCUS ON...

■ Duck and Lee's models as explanations for relationship breakdown.
■ The phases and stages of relationship breakdown.
■ What research has informed about Duck and Lee's models as explanations for relationship breakdown.
■ An assessment of Duck and Lee's models as explanations for relationship breakdown.

▓ Duck's phase model of relationship breakdown

Duck (2001) proposed three general reasons for why relationships break up.

1 *Pre-existing doom* – incompatibility and failure are fairly much guaranteed from the start of the relationship.

2 *Mechanical failure* – two compatible, well-meaning people grow apart and find that they cannot live together any longer (this is the most common cause).

3 *Sudden death* – the discovery of infidelity (cheating) or the occurrence of a traumatic incident (such as a huge argument) leads to immediate ending of a relationship.

Duck proposed several other factors as contributing to relationship dissolution:

- *Predisposing personal factors* – e.g. individuals' bad habits or emotional instabilities.
- *Precipitating factors* – e.g. exterior influences, such as love rivals, process features, such as incompatible working hours, emergent properties, for instance lack of relationship direction, and attributions of blame, such as perceiving that someone else is to blame.
- *Lack of skills* – e.g. being sexually inexperienced.
- *Lack of motivation* – e.g. perceiving inequity.
- *Lack of maintenance* – e.g. spending too much time apart.

Duck believed that the 'official' reasons given to others, including partners, to justify breaking up are more interesting psychologically than the real reasons. The psychology of break-up involves many individual psychological processes, group processes, cultural rules and self-presentation to others.

As **Duck (2001)** said:

'Truly committed romantic relationships involve the foregoing of other romantic relationships and commitment to only one partner ... So, the ending of a romantic relationship indicates two people are now legitimately available as partners for other relationships. This requires them to create a story for the end of the relationship that leaves them in a favourable light as potential partners. Romantic relationships are, therefore, typically ended publicly in a way that announces the ex-partners' freedom from the expectations of exclusive commitment.'

Duck (1982) sees dissolution as a personal process, but one where partners regard how things will look to friends and social networks. Duck therefore suggested an account of dissolution involving four sequential phases. This explanation begins where one partner is sufficiently dissatisfied with the relationship over a long enough period of time to consider ending it.

The four phases (see Table 8.3) in **Duck's phase model** are:

1 *Intrapsychic* – one partner privately perceives dissatisfaction with the relationship.

2 *Dyadic* – the dissatisfaction is discussed. If it is not resolved, there is a move to the next stage.

3 *Social* – the breakdown is made public. There is negotiation about children, finances and so on, with wider families and friends becoming involved.

4 *Grave dressing* – a post-relationship view of the break-up is established, protecting self-esteem and rebuilding life towards new relationships.

> **Duck's phase model**
> – an explanation that sees dissolution occurring through a series of four sequential stages.

■ **Figure 8.4**
Duck's theory sees relationship breakdown as occurring in four phases

Threshold	Phase	Characteristic behaviours
'I can't stand this any more'	Intrapsychic phase	Personal focus on partner's behaviour Assess adequacy of partner's role performance Depict and evaluate negative aspects of being in the relationship Consider costs of withdrawal Assess positive aspects of alternative relationships Face 'express/repress dilemma' – whether you should express your dissatisfaction or keep it to yourself
'I'd be justified in withdrawing'	Dyadic phase	Face up to 'confrontation/avoidance dilemma' Confront partner Negotiation through 'our relationship' talks Attempt repair and reconciliation? Assess joint costs of withdrawal or reduced intimacy
'I mean it'	Social phase	Negotiate post-dissolution state with partner Initiate gossip/discussion in social network Create publicly negotiable face-saving/blame-placing stories and accounts Consider and face up to implied social network effect
'It's now inevitable'	Grave-dressing phase	Perform 'getting over it' activities Retrospective, reformative post-mortem attribution Publicly distribute own version of break-up

■ **Table 8.3** The main thresholds and phases of dissolving personal relationships (based on Duck, 1982; from Duck, 1998)

▨ Research

- **Kassin (1996, cited in Lawton, 2012b)** found that women are more likely to stress unhappiness and incompatibility as reasons for dissolution, while men blame lack of sex. Women wish to remain friends, while males want a clean break, suggesting gender differences that Duck's model does not consider.

- **Argyle (1988, cited in Argyle, 1992)** found that women identified lack of emotional support as a reason for dissolution, while men cited absence of fun, again suggesting gender differences that the model does not explain.

- **Hatfield *et al.* (1984)** reported that when an individual experiences initial dissatisfaction with a relationship they are burdened by resentment and feelings of being 'under-benefited', which leads to social withdrawal so that the individual can consider their position, thus supporting the notion of an intrapsychic phase.

- **Akert (1992, cited in Lawton, 2012b)** found that the person who instigated the break-up suffers fewer negative consequences than the non-instigator, suggesting individual differences in the effects of dissolution that the model does not explain.

- **Tashiro & Frazier (2003)** performed a survey of 92 students about their experiences after relationship breakdowns, finding a number of personal growth factors that helped with future relationships, such as feeling stronger, more independent and better off emotionally. Participants also felt they had gained wisdom that would help them with future relationships and that their relationships with friends had strengthened. This supports Duck's idea that through grave-dressing processes people are able to recover and move on after relationship dissolution.

YOU ARE THE RESEARCHER

Design an interview that investigates the reasons why romantic relationships fail and the stages through which breakdowns occur. Will you use a structured, semi-structured or unstructured interview technique and open or closed questions or a mixture of the two? Once you have decided, compose your questions. How will you deal with possible interviewer effects when interviewing both males and females? Finally you will need to decide how to assess and present your data.

▨ Evaluation

- The theory has face validity as it is an account of relationship breakdown that most people can relate to through their own and/or others' experiences.

- The view of dissolution as a process, rather than an event, is widely accepted. This view applies to the breakdown of friendships as well as sexual relationships, including marriages. However, the theory applies mainly to romantic relationships because these are exclusive in a way that friendships generally are not.

- The theory does not focus exclusively on individual partners, but takes their social context into account. As **Duck (2001)** says:

  'Break-up involves not only the individual creating the break-up, but the psychological sense of integrity of the person to whom it all happens ... But a lot that happens is done with an eye on the group that surrounds the person.'

- The theory does not take into account why dissatisfaction occurred in the first place; its starting point is where dissatisfaction has already set in. Therefore, it fails to provide a complete picture of dissolution.

- Duck's four phases are not universal – they do not apply in every case of relationship breakdown – nor do they always occur in the order described.

- The model does not usually apply to homosexual relationships, which may not involve some of the decisions over children that heterosexuals have to consider. Additionally, it does not apply to heterosexual couples who decide not to have children.

- The model is simplistic, as it does not account for relationships such as casual affairs and friendships.

- **Rollie & Duck (2006)**, responding to criticisms, modified the theory to add a fifth phase of resurrection after that of grave dressing, which represented a period of reconfiguration of self and preparation for new relationships. They also added a new element, whereby communication patterns within each phase could result in a reversion to an earlier, more positive state of the relationship rather than progressing on to the next phase of the break-up.

Lee's model of relationship dissolution

'I like my relationships like I like my eggs. Over easy.'
Jared Kintz (2010)

> **Lee's stage model** – an explanation that sees dissolution occurring through a series of five sequential stages.

Lee's stage model (1984) proposed a five-stage model of relation breakdown, similar to Duck's explanation in being a stage theory and perceiving dissolution as a process occurring over time, rather than just a single event. The theory was reached by analysing data from relationship break-ups. See Table 8.4.

Stage of dissolution	Description
Dissatisfaction	An individual becomes dissatisfied with the relationship
Exposure	Dissatisfaction is revealed to one's partner
Negotiation	Discussion occurs about the nature of the dissatisfaction
Resolution	Attempts made to resolve the dissatisfaction
Termination	If the dissatisfaction is not resolved, the relationship ends

■ **Table 8.4** Lee's five-stage model of relationship dissolution

Research

- **Lee (1984)** created his theory after conducting a survey of 112 break-ups of non-marital romantic relationships, finding that the negotiation and exposure stages were most distressing and emotionally exhausting. Individuals who missed out stages, going straight to termination, were those with less intimate relationships. Those going through the stages in a lengthy and exhaustive fashion felt attracted to their former partner after termination and experienced greater feelings of loss and loneliness.

- **Argyle & Henderson (1984)** asked participants to consider whether rule violations were to blame for personal relationship breakdown. Rule violations were found to be important factors, with jealousy, lack of tolerance for third-party relationships, disclosing confidences, not volunteering help and public criticism being most critical, suggesting that Lee's explanation is not complete, as it does not account for these factors.

■ (*Research studies relating to Duck's model can also be applied to Lee's theory, so are a valid means of answering exam questions on relationship change or end.*)

Evaluation

■ The theory is simplistic, as it cannot explain the whole range of relationships and reasons for dissolution.

■ The strengths of Lee's research were that a lot of information was gathered and the sample was large. However, it only contained students in premarital relationships, so may not relate to other types of romantic relationships, especially long-term relationships involving children and shared resources.

■ Lee's theory is more positive than Duck's, as it sees more opportunities for problematic relationships to be saved.

■ Lee's theory (like Duck's) cannot explain abusive relationships, where the abused partner may not initiate the stages of dissolution, being reluctant to reveal their dissatisfaction. Instead, the abused partner may simply walk away from the relationship.

■ Stage theories describe the process of dissolution, but do not provide explanations of why the process occurs.

■ Lee's theory (like Duck's) is culturally specific, as there are cultural differences in relationship dissolution that these models do not explain. Many non-individualistic cultures have arranged marriages, which tend to be more permanent and involve whole families in crises.

■ Both theories can be seen as reductionist, in focusing only on romantic heterosexual relationships, which suggests they are not applicable to friendships, homosexual relationships, and so on.

Strengthen your learning

1   Outline, in your own words, Duck's three general reasons for relationship breakdown.

2   What other factors does Duck see to be related to relationship breakdown?

3   Outline Duck's four phases of relationship breakdown.

4   Outline, in your own words, Lee's theory of relationship breakdown; include in your answer Lee's five stages of relationship dissolution.

5   Summarize what research has suggested about:
    a Duck's theory   b Lee's theory.

6   What other evaluative points can be made about:
    a Duck's theory   b Lee's theory?

SECTION SUMMARY

■ An individual's attributional style influences the quality of communication within relationships and affects the development and maintenance of relationships over time.

■ Individuals who make positive, accurate attributions about their partners tend to have healthy relationships.

■ Self-disclosure of personal information helps build-up intimacy in relationships, especially in virtual relationships.

■ Self-disclosure is easier with virtual relationships due to the lack of limiting gating features.

■ The breakdown of relationships is seen as occurring in sequential stages, such as in Duck and Lee's theories.

■ **Assessment check**

1	Discuss two explanations for the formation of personal relationships.	(22 marks)
2	Evaluate one explanation for the formation of personal relationships.	(22 marks)
3	Discuss the role of communication in personal relationships.	(22 marks)
4	Discuss what research studies have suggested about the role of communication in personal relationships.	(22 marks)
5	Outline and evaluate two explanations for why relationships change or end.	(22 marks)
6	Discuss what research studies have suggested about explanations for why relationships change or end.	(22 marks)

Social responsibility

Every day individuals will find themselves in situations where others need help. This could range from risking your life to save somebody else, to holding a door open for someone. There are various factors which influence whether help will be given and to what degree.

FOCUS ON...

- Bystanderism as an explanation for helping behaviour.
- The case of Kitty Genovese as an example of bystander intervention.
- The number of witnesses, the type of emergency, emotional arousal, cognitive appraisals and social identity as factors in bystander behaviour.
- Darley & Latane's five-stage model of bystander behaviour.
- Darley & Latane's classic study of bystander intervention.
- What research has informed about bystanderism.
- An assessment of bystanderism.

▨ Bystanderism

'What hurts the victim most is not the cruelty of the oppressor, but the silence of the bystander.'
Elie Wiesel

Bystanders – people who witness events without intervening or offering assistance.

Bystanders are people who witness events, but do not intervene or offer assistance. The true story of Kitty Genovese (see below), where a woman was brutally murdered and no one tried to help her, generated a lot of interest from psychologists in trying to explain such behaviour.

The rape and murder of Kitty Genovese

■ **Figure 8.5** Kitty Genovese

In 1964, 28-year-old bar manager Kitty Genovese was brutally raped and murdered outside her apartment in New York. Winston Moseley was convicted of her murder and sentenced to life imprisonment (he died in prison in 2016). Two weeks after the incident the *New York Times* ran a story that claimed up to 38 people witnessed the event, but none had gone to her assistance or phoned the police. This phenomenon became known as the 'bystander effect' and the 'Genovese syndrome'. Public reaction was one of anger and disgust; how could people be so indifferent to the plight of another? It was this incident that proved to be the inspiration for psychologists to conduct research and try and explain such behaviour. (Incidentally, many details of the newspaper story were actually untrue; there were far fewer witnesses to the crime than claimed, phone calls to the police were made and a woman did go to Kitty's assistance, so perhaps the reasons why people were so eager to believe the story is the most striking feature of this whole incident.)

IN THE NEWS

Ψ The Psychological Enquirer

THREE PEOPLE ON TRIAL IN THE GERMAN CITY OF ESSEN FOR FAILING TO ASSIST A PENSIONER WHO HAD COLLAPSED AFTER ENTERING A BANK CASHPOINT

■ **Figure 8.6** Making not helping others a criminal act

In 2017 an 83-year-old pensioner collapsed in a bank, hitting his head on the tiled floor. Three people ignored the pensioner, even stepping over his unconscious body. A fourth customer reported the incident, but it took 20 minutes for medical care to arrive. The pensioner died a week later. Two of the accused, identified from CCTV, claimed they thought the pensioner was a homeless man, even though he was well dressed. All three people are to stand trial, as in Germany it is a crime, punishable by up to a year in jail, not to respond to a medical emergency; people must at least inform medical authorities of an incident if they lack medical skills themselves. The incident has sparked angry debate in Germany, with some suggesting it symbolizes a coarsening of society, with many people indifferent to their fellow citizens' welfare.

This incident closely resembles that of the famous 1964 rape and murder of Kitty Genovese in New York, though in this case people really did ignore the welfare of a person in need. Psychologists have used the concept of bystanderism, the behaviour of witnesses to incidents where others come to harm, to explain such behaviour. This particular incident resembles that of a study done by Piliavin, where differences in helping behaviour by witnesses were noted between a frail old man with a stick and a drunk who had apparently collapsed on a train. It may well be that society is not actually becoming more unhelpful and uncaring about the plight of others, but just that when certain social factors are in place, helping behaviour does not readily occur.

Reasons for bystanderism

Number of witnesses

The greater the number of witnesses, then the less likely it is that others will intervene. Three reasons for this have been put forward.

1 *Diffusion of responsibility* – the belief that the more witnesses there are, then the more likely it is that someone else will help. Therefore, each bystander feels less obligated to intervene.

2 *Pluralistic ignorance* – the belief that if others are not helping, then the situation cannot be an emergency and therefore help is not required.

3 *Evaluation apprehension* – the belief that if an individual intervenes, then their actions will be rated by others. This is seen as creating a reluctance to help.

Type of emergency

Whether bystanders intervene is heavily dependent on whether an emergency is perceived as being one for which help is required. Bystanders are much more likely to intervene, even if there is risk to personal safety, when a situation is seen as an emergency.

Emotional arousal

The Arousal: Cost–Reward Model sees the chances of bystander intervention occurring as being dependent on whether such intervention would reduce the emotional arousal caused by an incident. This requires a cost-reward analysis, where the costs of helping, such as physical effort, risk of harm, and so on, are compared against the costs of not helping, such as criticism from others and self-blame.

Cognitive appraisals

Darley & Latane (1970) proposed a five-stage model of bystander behaviour, the main principle of which was that individuals make a number of swift assessments in deciding whether or not to help. Each appraisal (assessment) that is met by a positive response moves the individual onto the next appraisal. If all appraisals are positive, then help is offered. If any appraisal is negative, then help is not offered. See Table 8.5.

Stage	Description
Stage one	Attention is directed to the situation
Stage two	Assess whether the situation is an emergency or not
Stage three	Personal responsibility is assumed for dealing with the situation
Stage four	Assess whether you have the necessary skills to help, e.g. medical skills
Stage five	Action to help is given

■ Table 8.5 Darley & Latane's (1970) five-stage model of bystander behaviour

The model assumes that individuals think about situations and make logical decisions about them, rather than acting from instinct or their emotions.

Social identity

The likelihood of bystander intervention is affected by an individual's social identity. If a person who is identified as in need of help is seen as a member of one's one social group (in-group) they are more likely to be given help than if the individual is seen as a member of another social group (out-group).

> ### LINK TO THE COGNITIVE APPROACH
> Studies of bystander behaviour focus to a great extent on cognitive factors; for instance, cognitive appraisals and how bystanders decide what type of emergency is in play. Therefore, bystanderism can be placed to some extent within the cognitive approach.

CLASSIC RESEARCH

'Bystander intervention in emergencies: Diffusion of responsibility'
Darley & Latane (1968)

The researchers, inspired by the Kitty Genovese incident, were interested in what effect the number of witnesses had upon whether individual witnesses would intervene in a situation.

Aim

To assess the effect of the number of witnesses to an event on whether an individual witness would intervene in the event.

Procedure

1   A laboratory experiment was conducted on university students. Participants were placed in booths on their own and asked to take part in an intercom discussion about university life. Participants were asked to speak for two minutes each. There were three conditions:

   a   *Condition one*: Participants believed they were taking part in an intercom discussion with one other person.

   b   *Condition two*: Participants believed they were taking part in an intercom discussion with two other people.

   c   *Condition three*: Participants believed they were taking part in an intercom discussion with five other people.

2   An emergency was created by a pseudo-participant (who has explained that they suffer from epilepsy) appearing to have an epileptic fit and asking for assistance over the intercom.

3   The researchers recorded:

   a   the percentage of participants in each condition who intervened within four minutes

   b   how long it took participants to intervene.

Results

1   *Condition one*: 100 per cent of participants intervened, with the average time taken to intervene being 52 seconds.

2   *Condition two*: 85 per cent of participants intervened, with the average time taken to intervene being two minutes.

3   *Condition three*: 62 per cent of participants intervened, with the average time taken being nearly three minutes.

Conclusions

● As the number of people in a group increases, the chances of an individual in that group intervening in an emergency decreases, as individuals feel less personal responsibility for taking action, a phenomenon known as diffusion of responsibility.

Evaluation

● Evaluation apprehension could also explain the findings, where individuals do not intervene as they fear the embarrassment of being judged by others for their actions. The bigger the group, then the greater the evaluation apprehension and the less chance of intervening.

- As a laboratory experiment the study lacks ecological validity. In real-world situations an incident might not so easily be perceived as an emergency, as in this study, and participants' attention may be distracted elsewhere, decreasing the chances of intervention.
- The use of pseudo-participants (such as the apparent student with epilepsy) would be regarded as unethical now, as it involves deceit, which means that informed consent could not be gained. Unacceptable levels of distress may have been caused to participants too.

Research

- **Darley & Latane (1969)** got participants to fill in questionnaires in a room that gradually filled with smoke. When a participant was alone in the room, 75 per cent left to report the incident, but when a participant was placed with two pseudo-participants who ignored the smoke, only 10 per cent reported the incident. This supports the idea of pluralistic ignorance, where if others are not seen to react then an incident is not seen as an emergency and so bystander intervention does not take place.
- **Piliavin *et al.* (1969)** conducted a field experiment on the New York subway system. A researcher acted being either a partially sighted passenger with a white cane, or a drunken passenger with a bottle of alcohol, who collapsed onto the train floor. In variations of the study, the person collapsing was either black or white. If no passengers helped within 70 seconds, a pseudo-participant went to help to see what effect that would have on helping behaviour. It was found that the number of passengers in the train made no difference if the collapsing passenger was partially sighted; help was given rapidly, whether they were black or white. The drunken passenger was helped 50 per cent of the time, without the pseudo-participant going to help, though the time taken was longer. The results do not support diffusion of responsibility, as the size of the group of witnesses had no effect on the likelihood of helping, but support instead the idea of cost-reward analysis where the drunk was helped less, because the cost of helping is relatively high (e.g. he could be violent) and the cost of not helping is low (e.g. few people would look negatively on someone not helping a drunk). However, the cost of helping the partially sighted person is quite low (e.g. less chance of them being violent) while the cost of not helping would be high (negative opinions of others).
- **Levine *et al.* (2005)** got a pseudo-participant to fall over in front of 35 Manchester United fans, dressed in either a Manchester United or a Liverpool football shirt. (There was also a control condition where the injured person wore a neutral shirt.) When the injured person was dressed in a Manchester United shirt, 12 fans helped him and one did not; when dressed in a neutral shirt, four fans helped and eight did not; and when dressed in a Liverpool shirt, three fans helped and seven did not. This supports the idea of social identity affecting the likelihood of bystander intervention, where individuals are likelier to assist those they identify with.
- **Fischer *et al.* (2011)** performed a meta-analysis of 105 bystander intervention studies involving 7,700 participants, to find that people were more likely to intervene when situations were seen as dangerous emergencies and when the costs of intervention were physical. This supports the Arousal: Cost–Reward Model that dangerous situations produce high levels of arousal, which are reduced by helping behaviour.

Evaluation

- The likelihood of bystander intervention is dependent on many factors, which need to be considered collectively rather than individually, as that is how such factors occur in real-life situations.
- Another important consideration is that of personality. Some people may intervene in situations as they have less fear of injury or embarrassment than others, or because they are more socially responsible and helpful.

- Some criticize the idea of the five-stage model as being unrealistic, as people do not 'mechanically' scan through a series of judgements, but rather act immediately without any thought.

- Many of the studies into the bystander effect are now considered unethical, as they often involved deceit through the use of pseudo-participants and caused harm by creating elevated levels of stress.

YOU ARE THE RESEARCHER

Design a field experiment where a person lays on the floor, possibly ill or injured. Have a group of pseudo-participants either walk by the person or stop to enquire if they are okay. Then record whether real bystanders walk by or stop to assist. What will your IV and DV be? What type of sample are you using? Compose suitable hypotheses and create a table and graph to display your data.

What ethical considerations are there with this study? Do you think it is ethically okay to conduct this study? Explain your answer.

Strengthen your learning

1 What are bystanders?

2 Explain how the following factors affect bystander behaviour:
   a the number of witnesses
   b type of emergency
   c emotional arousal.

3 Outline Darley & Latane's five-stage model of bystander behaviour.

4 For Darley & Latane's (1968) classic study, in your own words, state the:
   a aims
   b procedure
   c results
   d conclusions
   e evaluative points.

5 Explain how social identity can affect bystander behaviour.

6 Use your knowledge of bystander behaviour to explain the case of Kitty Genovese.

7 Summarize what research studies have suggested about bystander behaviour.

8 What other evaluative points can be made about bystander behaviour?

Prosocial behaviour

'No one has ever become poor by giving.'
Anne Frank

Prosocial behaviour
– behaviour that is intended to benefit others.

Prosocial behaviour is characterized as voluntary behaviour intended to help others. Such behaviour is generally motivated by concerns for the rights and welfare of others, due to feelings of empathy and concern for others. Prosocial behaviour is, therefore, the opposite of anti-social behaviour.

Psychologists have been interested in identifying the factors that motivate and affect prosocial behaviour. Biological theories see prosocial behaviour as having an evolutionary survival value, such as described in the kin selection theory, while other more psychological theories see learning experiences as vital in cultivating such behaviour, such as in the empathy–altruism theory.

Altruism is the idea of unselfish prosocial behaviour where an individual does something at a cost to themselves in order to benefit another. Arguments are still ongoing about whether altruism actually exists. Some argue that no one ever performs an action without there being some reward for that individual, while others contend that humans do exist who are truly unselfish in their actions. Altruism among related individuals is explained by kin selection theory, where sacrifices are made by an individual to benefit genetically related others, while reciprocal altruism explains actions that benefit non-related individuals, as being where individuals perform acts that benefit others in the expectation that for doing so they will similarly be helped by others at a later date.

FOCUS ON...

- Hamilton's kin selection theory and Batson's empathy–altruism theory as explanations of prosocial behaviour.
- Batson *et al.*'s. classic study of empathy–altruism.
- What research has informed about Hamilton's kin selection theory and Batson's empathy–altruism theory as explanations of prosocial behaviour.
- An assessment of Hamilton's kin selection theory and Batson's empathy–altruism theory as explanations of prosocial behaviour.
- Green beard genes as an alternative biological explanation of kin selection.

Hamilton's kin selection theory (1964)

'An ounce of blood is worth more than a pound of friendship.'
Spanish Proverb

Hamilton's kin selection theory – an explanation that sees helping behaviour as directed at increasing the reproductive chances of genetically related individuals.

Evolution sees behaviours that increase an individual's survival chances as being acted upon by natural selection so that such behaviours are passed on to children through genes, thus becoming more widespread in a population. The idea of altruism seems therefore to oppose evolutionary theory, as altruistic behaviour involves a cost to an individual to benefit others, such a cost might even be the loss of that individual's life in order to save those of others. But **Hamilton's kin selection theory** is based on the idea of inclusive fitness, which not only considers the effect of a behaviour on an individual's survival and reproduction level (direct fitness), but also upon the survival and reproduction of relatives (indirect fitness), because we share genetic material with our relatives. Thus, when an individual performs an action at a cost to themselves, but which benefits their relatives, the reward of the action is to increase the survival and reproduction chances of their own genes contained with others. This is the idea of kin selection. The theory also argues that the closer the genetic relationship between an individual and others, such as a father and his children, and the more relatives that will benefit from an individual's altruistic behaviour, then the greater the risks and efforts an individual will make to benefit those others.

Many examples of kin selection are seen in the animal world, especially in animals that live in social groups where many members will be related to each other and thus share genetic material. For example, an adult zebra risking or losing its life to prevent a lion from killing its young. Similar examples can be argued for among humans, such as reducing your own survival and reproduction chances by donating a kidney to a family member, thus increasing their survival and reproduction chances.

Kin selection theory, like many evolutionary explanations, allows predictions to be made, based on evolutionary theory, as to how individuals will act in the real world. These predictions can then be checked to assess their validity, with such research generally tending to support the theory.

LINK TO BIOLOGICAL APPROACH

Hamilton's kin selection theory sees altruistic behaviour as having been passed on to us through our genes by our ancestors, as it had a survival value to help related people, even if it had a cost to us individually, and has therefore been acted upon by natural selection to become more widespread in the population. Therefore, it is part of the biological approach, as it sees altruistic behaviour as part of the gene pool.

■ Research

- **Milius (1998)** studied alarm-calling behaviour in ground squirrels, to find that alarm calls to alert others to the presence of a predator occurred more often by an individual when it had relatives nearby. This supports kin selection theory, as making alarm calls lowers the survival chances of the individual making them, in revealing the individual to the predator, but heightens the survival chances of relatives by alerting them to the danger so they can escape.

■ **Smith (2007, cited in Smith & Read, 2008)** even found evidence of kin selection in plants. It was found that when sea rocket plants had to share a pot to grow in, genetically unrelated plants competed for soil nutrients by promoting aggressive root growth, but they did not do this in the presence of genetically related plants. As kin selection seems to occur in so many divergent life forms, it supports the idea of the behaviour having a biological evolutionary based origin.

■ **Essock-Vitale (1985)** interviewed hundreds of women in Los Angeles, USA, finding that although non-related friends were willing to help each other, this tended to concern acts of reciprocal helping, where such helping would be rewarded by that person doing something for the other in return. In contrast high levels of non-reciprocal helping (where nothing was gained in return) were found to occur for related individuals. This suggests that reciprocal altruism is a better explanation for prosocial behaviour among non-related persons and kin selection for prosocial behaviour among related persons.

■ **Madsen *et al.* (2007)** got British and South African Zulu participants to endure as long as possible a painful bodily position, with participants' relatives receiving increasing rewards of money or food for the longer the body position was endured. It was found that the greater the level of genetic relatedness between an individual enduring the body position and the recipient of the food or money, then the longer the body position would be held for. This strongly supports the idea behind kin selection theory that prosocial behaviour is based upon genetic relatedness.

■ **Whiting & Whiting (1975)** assessed prosocial behaviour in children from six different cultures, finding wide differences in levels of helping behaviour, from 100 per cent in Kenyan children, down to just 8 per cent in American children. The fact that differences exist cross-culturally in levels of prosocial behaviour suggests the behaviour is more learned than innate, which goes against kin selection theory.

LINK TO THE SOCIOCULTURAL APPROACH

There is a link to the sociocultural approach, as studies like that of **Whiting & Whiting (1975)** have found wide differences in levels of prosocial behaviour in different cultures, which suggests that cultural factors influence levels of helping behaviour.

Evaluation

■ The theory does not really explain the mechanisms by which kin selection calculations and decisions are made. For example, three siblings contain 150 per cent of an individual's genes (one and half times what that individual actually has), so it would make sense for the individual to sacrifice themselves for three siblings, but not for one sibling and two cousins (who would collectively possess 75 per cent of the individual's genes). In dangerous situations, such as attack by predators, it is difficult to see how individuals would have the time to make such calculations.

■ The theory has face validity from observing the everyday behaviour of individuals; for example, an individual leaving sums of money to different relatives in their will that reflect how closely related they are to each other.

■ Kin selection theory's explanatory power is limited, as it only explains prosocial behaviour between related individuals. The theory also has problems explaining individual differences in levels of helping behaviour, as evolutionary theory predicts that levels of helping behaviour would be universal.

■ Kin selection theory argues that altruism (non-selfish behaviour) does not exist, but is explicable as 'selfishness in disguise' (performing acts to benefit your own genes).

- **Alonso & Shuck-Paim (2002)** argue that the behaviours that kin selection theory seeks to explain are not really altruistic behaviours, as they tend to be group behaviours, similar behaviours carried out over long periods of time by many members of a social group. Therefore, such behaviours may be better explained through reciprocal altruism and may be learned rather than being innate evolutionary ones.
- Many close human relationships are based upon shared experiences, not genes, such as that between adoptive parents and adopted children. Kin selection theory cannot explain acts of sacrifice between such attached persons.

Batson's empathy–altruism theory (1987)

'Practice kindness all day to everybody and you will realize you're already in heaven.'
Jack Kerouac

Batson's empathy–altruism theory – an explanation that sees helping behaviour as motivated by unselfish concern for the needs of others.

Batson's empathy–altruism theory believes that altruism as truly unselfish behaviour actually exists, as individuals will help others, at a price to themselves, purely out of concern for the well-being of others. His central idea is that if we can feel empathy (experience the feelings of others) by perspective taking (accessing the viewpoint of others) then we are motivated to help those people, regardless of the cost to ourselves. When empathy is not felt, individuals will only help others if, by doing so, the benefits of the action outweigh the costs.

Identifying a person who is in need of help is seen as producing one of two types of emotional reaction:

1 *Personal distress* – feelings of concern or anxiety are generated that cause discomfort.

2 *Empathetic concern* – feelings of sympathy are generated for the person in need of help.

Motivation for helping another caused by feelings of personal distress is based on reducing one's own levels of discomfort. This is egoist (selfish) helping, as it is based on one's own feelings rather than the feelings of others.

Motivation for helping another caused by feelings of sympathy for another is based on reducing the discomfort of others. This is altruistic (unselfish) helping, as it is based on the feelings of others rather than one's own feelings.

There is some research support for empathy–altruism, though Batson himself admits that such behaviour is relatively rare.

KEY STUDY   CLASSIC RESEARCH

'Is empathic emotion a source of altruistic motivation?'
Batson *et al.* (1981)

Batson and his co-workers devised a clever method of creating and manipulating empathy levels so that they could assess the effect on prosocial behaviour. The technique involved assessing the degree to which participants would swap positions with a girl, Elaine, so that they and not Elaine received painful electric shocks.

Aim
To test whether empathy would lead to altruistic rather than egoistic motivation to help another in distress.

Procedure

1 Forty-four female student participants drew lots to see if they would be an observer or the recipient of electric shocks in a study concerning working in harsh conditions. It was rigged so they were always the observer (but believing they could have been the recipient).

2 Participants filled out a questionnaire that measured their attitudes, values and interests.

3 They then witnessed a fellow student, Elaine, apparently receiving painful electric shocks. Participants were then given an unexpected opportunity to receive the remaining shocks instead of Elaine.

4   Participants were told if they did not take her place, they would either have to watch her receive the rest of the shocks (difficult escape condition) or they could leave and not see Elaine get the rest of the shocks (easy escape condition).

5   Participants were given what they believed to be Elaine's answers to the questionnaire. They either received answers similar to their own (similar victim condition) or dissimilar (dissimilar victim condition).

6   There were 11 participants in each of the four conditions (though four participants' data was removed, as they didn't believe the shocks to be real).

7   Elaine's 'performance' in receiving the shocks was actually viewed via a videotape, where she explains how she has experienced shocks before, has a fear of them and reacts badly to them.

8   Whether a participant would swap places was recorded, as well as the number of shocks (up to a maximum of eight) they would take.

Results

1   All participants agreed that the shocks seemed painful to a fairly equal degree.

2   When Elaine was seen as having similar attitudes, values and interests, 91 per cent in the easy escape condition consented to take her place and 82 per cent in the difficult escape condition.

3   When Elaine was seen as having dissimilar attitudes, values and interests, 18 per cent in the easy escape condition consented to take her place and 64 per cent in the difficult escape condition.

	Dissimilar victim	Similar victim
Easy escape	18 per cent	91 per cent
Difficult escape	64 per cent	82 per cent

■ **Table 8.6** Results of research to test whether participants in a study would help others in distress

Conclusions

● The findings supported the empathy–altruism hypothesis.

● In the dissimilar victim condition, where empathy was low, and helping behaviour egoistic (selfish), the manipulation of difficulty to escape had a big effect. When escape was easy, participants were less likely to take the shocks, as a less costly way of lowering their discomfort was to leave, but when escape was difficult, participants were more likely to swap with Elaine, as receiving the remaining shocks was less costly than the discomfort of watching Elaine receive them.

● In the similar victim condition, where empathy was high and helping behaviour altruistic (unselfish), whether escape was easy or difficult had little effect on participants' willingness to swap with Elaine. As their motivation was to reduce Elaine's discomfort they were likely to help even when escape from helping was fairly easy.

Evaluation

● A laboratory experiment was used, so the findings lack ecological validity, as they do not necessarily reflect behaviour in real-life situations.

● The procedure used is now seen as being highly unethical. Deceit was used in getting participants to believe Elaine was receiving electric shocks, that she was a fellow participant and that they had randomly been selected to be observers. This means that informed consent could not be gained. High levels of harm were caused too, through getting participants to believe Elaine was being hurt, by the stress of believing they might receive the shocks too and the guilt of not swapping with Elaine. Although the right to consent was stressed and a full debriefing took place, many would argue this would not alleviate or justify the deceit and harm involved.

Research

- **Batson *et al.* (1981)** conducted a second experiment, where instead of a similarity condition, empathy was manipulated by getting participants to swallow a tablet after being told it would either make them temporarily feel warm and sensitive to others (personal distress condition) or temporarily experience feelings of unease and discomfort (empathic concern condition). (The tablet was actually a harmless placebo.) There were, as before, conditions of 'easy to escape' and 'difficult to escape'. As expected, participants in the personal distress condition reported experiencing empathic concern feelings due to the apparent effect of the tablet, while those in the empathic concern condition reported feelings of personal distress due to the apparent effect of the tablet. It was found that 33 per cent of participants in the personal distress condition, when it was easy to escape offered to swap with Elaine and 75 per cent when it was difficult to escape. However, 83 per cent of participants in the empathic concern condition, when it was easy to escape offered to swap with Elaine, compared to 58 per cent when it was difficult to escape. The findings support the empathy–altruism theory, as they suggest that when empathic concern is high people will help others, regardless of whether it is easy or difficult to escape, while when empathic concern is low, people will only help when it is difficult to escape without helping.

- **Singer *et al.* (2013)** used brain scanning technology to identify the right supramarginal brain area (part of the cerebral cortex) as highly involved in the experience of empathy, with highly empathetic people having high activity in this brain area. This suggests that empathy has an innate biological component so that only those with naturally high levels of empathy would be capable of exhibiting unselfish altruistic behaviour.

Evaluation

- Although research like **Singer et al.'s** suggests empathy–altruism is largely an innate behaviour, other research has identified activities whereby participation can raise the ability to feel empathy. For example, taking part in painful physical exercise makes individuals more empathetic to suffering in others, while regular participation in volunteering activities also seems to have an effect in raising concern for others. This suggests that such activities may affect the activation levels of the right supramarginal brain area, making individuals more able to display empathy–altruism, thus fortifying empathy and altruism at a neurobiological level for each individual.

- The idea of empathy–altruism is well supported by research evidence and also allows predictions to be made about what circumstances are necessary for acts of empathy–altruism to occur.

- Empathy does not always precede (come before) altruistic behaviour; research suggests there are other valid explanations of such behaviour. Therefore empathy–altruism cannot be seen as an 'explain-all' theory, but rather as just one of the factors that influence altruistic behaviour.

- Although research supports the idea of empathy–altruism, it has not been possible to see whether altruistic behaviour is motivated mainly by empathy for others or by the desire to escape from one's own negative emotions.

PSYCHOLOGY IN THE REAL WORLD

Green beard genes: an alternative biological explanation to kin selection

A '**Green beard' gene** was first suggested by Richard Dawkins in his book '*The Selfish Gene*' (1976) and is seen as being one that allows its bearer to recognize their difference from others (like having a naturally green beard would do) and to recognize the trait in others (fellow individuals with green beards) and to behave positively towards such individuals (and negatively towards those without it), even if they are not seen as genetically related individuals. This is a somewhat different explanation than kin selection, which sees altruism as occurring only between related individuals in a non-specific way. Although dismissed by many as purely a hypothetical idea, **Keller & Ross (1998)** reported evidence of a 'Green beard gene' in red fire-ants, who live in colonies containing several unrelated egg-laying queens. Worker ants in the colony were seen to kill queens that did not bear a particular gene that they did, which the researchers believe is detected by an odour (smell) cue.

■ **Figure 8.7** Recognizing someone with a green beard

Strengthen your learning

1   What is prosocial behaviour?

2   What is altruism? Why might it not exist?

3   Outline Hamilton's kin selection theory.

4   Outline Batson's empathy–altruism theory.

5   For Batson *et al.*'s (1981) classic study, outline in your own words the:
    a aims
    b procedure
    c results
    d conclusions
    e evaluative points.

6   Summarize what research studies suggest about:
    a Hamilton's kin selection theory
    b Batson's empathy–altruism theory.

7   Provide an assessment of the following in terms of their strengths and weaknesses:
    a Hamilton's kin selection theory
    b Batson's empathy–altruism theory.

8   What are green beard genes? Is there any research support for their existence?

Promoting prosocial behaviour

'No one is useless in this world who lightens the burdens of another.'
Charles Dickens

FOCUS ON...

■ Perspective taking, prosocial moral reasoning, high self-esteem, emotional well-being and attributional style as factors associated with the development of prosocial behaviour.
■ The influence of schools and parenting styles on prosocial behaviour.
■ The PATHS programme as an example of prosocial behaviour.
■ What research has informed about schools and parenting style on prosocial behaviour.
■ An assessment of schools and parenting style on prosocial behaviour.

Perspective taking
– individuals who can perceive the viewpoints of others are more able to develop prosocial behaviours.

Prosocial moral behaviour – individuals whose actions are based on belief systems centred on the welfare of others are more able to develop prosocial behaviours.

High self-esteem – those with elevated levels of self-worth are more able to develop prosocial behaviours.

Emotional well-being – individuals with positive mental health are more able to develop prosocial behaviours.

Attributional style – individuals who believe they influence events through personal effort are more able to develop prosocial behaviours.

Prosocial behaviour concerns the voluntary actions of an individual which are intended to benefit another person or society as a whole. Promoting prosocial behaviour is advantageous, as such behaviour is associated with many desirable outcomes. Individuals who exhibit sharing, helping and cooperating behaviours generally have high levels of social competence (are able to interact positively with others), are liked by others and do well academically. Developing prosocial behaviour is also directly related to the reduction of anti-social behaviour and thus the costs such behaviour incur upon society.

Psychological research has identified several factors that are associated with the development of prosocial behaviour:

1 **Perspective taking** – individuals who are able to empathize (see from another person's viewpoint) are more easily able to develop prosocial behaviours, as the motivation for such behaviour involves having concern for the welfare of others.

2 **Prosocial moral reasoning** – individuals who base their behaviour on belief systems centred on the welfare of others can also more easily develop prosocial behaviours, again because such behaviour is focused on concern for others.

3 **High self-esteem** – individuals who have elevated levels of self-worth, as well as a sense of competence in what they do, are more able to interact effectively with others and thus develop prosocial behaviour.

4 **Emotional well-being** – individuals who have good mental health are able to function effectively at work and in their interpersonal relationships, so have more scope to be able to develop prosocial behaviours.

5 **Attributional style** – individuals who can take responsibility for themselves and their actions, as they see themselves able to influence events through their own efforts (internal attribution), tend to view themselves and their environment more positively than people who believe they cannot influence events (external attribution), and so are more able to develop prosocial behaviours.

These factors can generally be influenced through parenting and teaching styles, as well as interactions with peers.

Schools

Schools can provide learning experiences that develop the skills necessary for prosocial behaviour. This can occur directly through the actual content of educational programmes, as well as indirectly through providing opportunities for meaningful interactions between peers that allow them to develop and practise the social and cognitive skills necessary for prosocial behaviour.

Prosocial behaviour can be promoted through lessons that provide cooperative and collaborative learning activities; for example, activities where students have to work together to achieve goals. Such activities allow students to develop their ability to interact with others in positive ways through the development of perspective taking, empathy and prosocial moral reasoning. Partnering less and more able students with each other to work towards collective goals is also a useful way of promoting prosocial behaviour, as it provides opportunities for them to work together in cooperative and collaborative ways and thus learn the positive value of participating in prosocial behaviours.

Some schools provide students with specific prosocial learning programmes, such as the PATHS Programme for Schools, which is used in primary schools to promote the development of self-control, emotional awareness and interpersonal problem-solving skills. This is delivered in specific lessons, using specially designed materials and delivered by trained personnel. Research suggests such programmes have a positive impact upon students in the short and long-term, though their costs and finding space for them within the curriculum can sometimes be problematic.

PSYCHOLOGY IN THE REAL WORLD

PATHS Programme for Schools

The PATHS Programme for Schools is an example of a prosocial behaviour programme, which is used in several countries, including Canada, Great Britain and New Zealand. The aim is to aid the development of self-control, emotional awareness and interpersonal problem-solving skills in children by improving levels of self-esteem, self-control, emotional intelligence, conflict control and academic performance, while lowering levels of aggression, emotional distress and problem behaviours. Initial sessions focus on developing children's understanding of their own and others' emotions, before moving on to learning self-control, which is seen as essential in helping reduce problem behaviours focused around anger and frustration. Subsequent sessions then focus on social problem-solving, where skills for making decisions that involve the needs and concerns of others are taught, and developing positive, caring relationships with peers.

A mixture of formal teaching, video demonstrations and opportunities for role-playing are used, with all sessions delivered by trained members of staff.

Parenting styles

Research has shown that certain 'positive' parenting styles are associated with the development of prosocial behaviours (just as some 'negative' parenting styles are associated with high incidence of anti-social behaviour). This includes the parenting of young children, but 'positive parenting' has maximum effect on the development of prosocial behaviours in adolescents.

The two most important factors for 'positive parenting' are having secure attachment patterns with parents, which are developed in early childhood (but can be developed at any stage of development), and the use of balanced positive discipline, where using disciplinary practices that are loving, empathetic and respectful is seen as strengthening relationships with parents and leading eventually to individuals developing a conscience that is guided by compassion for the needs of others.

Traditional 'authoritarian' parenting is seen as incurring negative outcomes, as it instils fear and shame in children, which is associated with increased risks of future anti-social behaviour, for example crime and drug abuse. Authoritarian parenting can also weaken the trust between a parent and child, which harms the attachment bond. Alternatively, balanced positive discipline is a parenting tool based on helping a child to develop a conscience that will be guided by self-discipline (where a child monitors their own behaviour from a moral viewpoint) and concern for others. Techniques include offering a child choices, making positive changes, sensitivity to strong emotions and making decisions together.

LINK TO THE SOCIOCULTURAL AND COGNITIVE APPROACHES

As schooling and parenting styles provide opportunities for individuals to learn the social skills necessary for the development of prosocial behaviours, they can be considered part of the sociocultural approach. Similarly, as schooling and parenting also allow opportunities for individuals to develop the cognitive abilities associated with prosocial behaviour, they can also be considered part of the cognitive approach.

Research

- **The SEAK Project Trust (2015)** found that in schools where the PATHS Programme for Schools was used, there was an increase in academic achievement of 11 per cent, as well as decreases in aggressive behaviour and increases in the ability to tolerate frustration. Children were seen to possess high levels of empathy and emotional understanding and were better able to understand problems and independently develop strategies to solve them. Increased health was also associated with the programme, by being associated with lower levels of childhood obesity. This suggests that prosocial behaviour interventions in schools are highly effective in developing a wide range of desirable outcomes.

- **Spivak & Dulak (2015, cited in Durwin & Reese-Weber, 2018)** reviewed recent studies to find that schools that used active learning programmes, such as cooperative learning, and emphasized caring relationships with teachers and peers developed higher levels of prosocial behaviour among students. Such schools also tended to provide opportunities for students to develop prosocially and provided role models who demonstrated prosocial behaviours. Targeted programmes, such as those specifically orientated to children who were seen as being anti-social, were also successful, but only when delivered by highly trained staff. This supports the idea that prosocial behaviour can be developed as part of children's education.

■ **Flook *et al.* (2015)** assessed the effects of a 12-week mindfulness-based Kindness Curriculum programme delivered to 68 preschool children. A control group of children who did not receive the programme was also used. It was found that children who attended the programme had greater improvements in social competence, got better marks and showed better emotional development. The control group showed more selfish behaviour. Children who were seen as being initially low in levels of social competence benefited most from the programme. This illustrates that prosocial teaching programmes can be delivered effectively from an early age, but are possibly most effective when targeted at those who will benefit from them most.

■ **Farrant *et al.* (2011)** studied the parenting styles used with 72 children aged between four and six years of age, finding a positive correlation between parenting styles that encouraged children to develop empathy for and appreciation of the perspective of others and the development of prosocial behaviour. This suggests parents have a key role to play in developing prosocial behaviour, to go alongside initiatives within schools.

■ **Carlo *et al.* (2007)** used questionnaires to assess the relationship between parental styles and prosocial behaviour in 233 American adolescents. A positive correlation was found between the use of 'positive parenting' and the incidence of prosocial behaviour. The most important factor seemed to be the development of empathy with others that developed from the use of positive parenting, with this then leading to the development of prosocial behaviour. The findings illustrate the important role parenting style can play in affecting levels of prosocial behaviour.

■ **Knafo-Noam *et al.* (2015)** reviewed studies to report that higher levels of prosocial behaviour were found among adolescents whose parents demonstrated prosocial behaviour themselves and gave their children opportunities to develop prosocial behaviour. Warm, responsive and sensitive parenting styles that generated empathy were also seen to be important, as did the use of balanced positive discipline, which emphasized the emotional states of others in need. This demonstrates the important influence of parenting upon prosocial behaviour.

RESEARCH IN FOCUS

A lot of research into promoting prosocial behaviour uses correlational analysis. Explain why such a research method cannot establish causality (cause-and-effect relationships).

Evaluation

■ Although the desirability of prosocial behaviour, and thus programmes that promote it, are recognized within education, such programmes are rare, as they are costly and difficult to include within often already crowded student timetables. Traditional academic subjects, for example mathematics, are often more favoured in terms of directed resources, such as funding and teacher availability.

■ Promoting prosocial behaviour within educational institutions, such as schools and colleges, is desirable, as the positive psychological functioning that comes from having such programmes reduces the time and cost of dealing with maladaptive and anti-social behaviours, as such behaviours are greatly reduced.

■ Although schooling and parenting can be used to develop prosocial behaviour, research, for example twin studies, suggests that the ability to be prosocial also has a genetic component, which suggests there may be a limit to the influence that parenting and schooling can have on prosocial behaviour levels. It may well be that certain individuals have an innate temperament (personality) which makes it difficult for them to empathize and develop prosocial behaviours.

- Many schools give their students a short programme of several weeks of lessons designed to increase mindfulness (empathy) and prosocial behaviour. Although better than no programme at all, more long-term changes towards prosocial behaviour are seen if such lessons feature as a regular part of students' timetables throughout their time at school.

- One way for schools to boost the effect of prosocial behaviour programmes is to identify within individual subjects opportunities for students to practise and develop prosocial learning. For example, physical education and games lessons provide many opportunities for cooperating, collaborating and basing behaviour upon emotional maturity focused on the perspectives of others.

Strengthen your learning

1   Explain why prosocial behaviour is advantageous.

2   Outline, in your own words, factors associated with the development of prosocial behaviour.

3   Explain how prosocial behaviour can be promoted by:
    a schools   b parenting styles.

4   Outline the PATHS programme as a means of promoting prosocial behaviour.

5   Summarize what research has suggested about the following as methods of promoting prosocial behaviour:
    a schools   b parenting styles.

6   What other evaluative points can be made about the following as methods of promoting prosocial behaviour:
    a schools   b parenting styles?

SECTION SUMMARY

- Bystanderism is affected by the number of witnesses to an event, the type of emergency, emotional arousal and cognitive appraisals.
- Prosocial behaviour can be explained by individuals helping related persons and by individuals acting altruistically through concern for the welfare of others.
- Prosocial behaviour can be affected through parenting and teaching styles and interactions with peers, by factors of perspective taking, prosocial moral reasoning, high self-esteem, emotional well-being, and attributional style.

■ Assessment check

1 Discuss one or more explanations of bystanderism.	(22 marks)
2 Outline and evaluate research studies of bystanderism.	(22 marks)
3 Discuss research studies of bystanderism.	(22 marks)
4 Evaluate theories of prosocial behaviour.	(22 marks)
5 Outline and evaluate one biological and one non-biological theory of prosocial behaviour.	(22 marks)
6 Discuss what research studies have suggested about promoting prosocial behaviour.	(22 marks)
7 Evaluate methods of promoting prosocial behaviour.	(22 marks)

Group dynamics

'Alone we can do so little, together we can do so much.'
Helen Keller

Group dynamics – the positive and negative forces operating within groups of people.

Social psychologists have been interested for a long time in understanding **group dynamics**, the ways in which members of social groups interact with each other, within and between groups, in order to understand the positive and negative outcomes that are produced.

Cooperation and competition are separate and opposite social situations, where individuals either unite and work together, or oppose and work against each other towards a goal. Research has shown that they are complementary phenomena, each exerting an influence over the other.

Prejudice and discrimination are seen as negative outcomes of group dynamics that can have extremely harmful consequences for society. The reasons why such prejudice and discrimination arise and are maintained are studied by psychologists in order to gain a fuller understanding of the group dynamics behind them, so that effective long-term strategies to reduce their impact can be constructed.

Similarly psychologists study the origins of conflict between groups in order to understand the dynamics underpinning such conflict, so that again effective strategies to reduce such harmful consequences can be devised.

When studying group dynamics, psychologists have used laboratory-based experiments and observations conducted within naturalistic environments, as well as sociograms and diagrams, constructed from answers to questionnaires that show levels of liking and disliking between group members.

FOCUS ON...

- The effects of cooperation and competition on behaviour.
- Deutsch's theory of cooperation and competition, including the Crude Law of Social Relations.
- The jigsaw classroom as an example of cooperative learning.
- The evolutionary adaptive value of cooperation.
- Game theory as an explanation of cooperative and competitive behaviour.
- What research has informed about Deutsch's theory, evolution and cooperation and game theory.
- An assessment of Deutsch's theory, evolution and cooperation and game theory.

Cooperation and competition

'Competition is the law of the jungle, but cooperation is the law of civilization.'
Peter Kropotkin

Cooperation – when two or more people work together towards the same end.

Competition – when two or more individuals struggle against each other for a goal that cannot be shared.

Although **cooperation** and **competition** are generally seen as being separate and, indeed, factors opposite to each other, it is actually very rare to find either occurring without the other, as they tend to perform a contributory influence upon each other in producing behaviour. For example, members of a football team cooperate with each other in order to win a game, but compete against each other to see who will be seen as the best player in the team.

Competition often requires initial cooperation in setting up rules without which meaningful competition would not be possible. Also, cooperation would not often be the powerful force that it is without the pressure of competition that motivates individuals to cooperate.

The theory of cooperation and competition: Deutsch (1949b)

Deutsch proposed that the degree to which members of a group see their goals as being shared ones affects the way in which those goals are pursued and their chances of success. Cooperation, he argued, led to group processes that produced better outcomes than if individuals competed against each other on their own. Cooperation has positive effects, including effective communication, helpfulness, coordination of effort, respect, agreement and empathy. Competition has negative effects, including poor communication, obstructiveness, disagreement and conflict. Deutsch therefore saw cooperation as superior, not just in terms of producing better outcomes, but also in producing a more caring and harmonious society.

Deutsch saw cooperative and competitive goals as interdependent and the actions taken towards goals as either being effective (ones that increase the chances of an individual achieving their goal) or bungling (ones that decrease an individual's chances of achieving their goal), with these actions affected by:

- *Substitutability* – the degree to which a person's actions are able to meet the intentions of another.
- *Cathexis* – how able an individual is to evaluate themselves and their environment.
- *Inducibility* – how ready an individual is to accept the influence of another.

With his **Crude Law of Social Relations**, Deutsch argued that being cooperative tends to lead individuals to being cooperative again in the future and that being competitive leads to more competition. In other words, the effects of cooperating, such as creating more helpfulness and trust between individuals, and the effects of competition, such as poorer communication and increased suspicion of others, are actually the factors that lead to people being cooperative and competitive in the first place. This is an example of a self-reinforcing feedback loop, where the effects of something heighten the chances of it happening again repetitively.

Research

■ **Johnson & Johnson (1989)** reviewed studies to find that cooperation, compared to competition, produced greater group productivity, more favourable interpersonal relations, better psychological health and higher self-esteem. Cooperation also led to more constructive resolution of conflicts, illustrating the superiority of cooperation over competition in producing a better functioning, more harmonious society.

■ **Aronson *et al.* (1978)** assessed why strong emphasis on competition within school classrooms was not delivering positive results. Students using competitive techniques were compared against those made to use cooperative techniques, with the results showing increases in self-esteem, motivation, interpersonal attraction and empathy in those using cooperative techniques, as well as improvements in academic performance, especially among students from ethnic minorities. The findings thus support Deutsch's theory that cooperation produces better outcomes than competition.

YOU ARE THE RESEARCHER

Design a study to compare whether working cooperatively or competitively in a class produces better test results. You will need to decide what the cooperative and competitive behaviours will be and what the learning task will be. Divide your sample randomly into two groups, one to work cooperatively and one to work competitively (this will be an IMD). You'll also need to compose some test questions to assess which group has learned best. What will your IV and DV be? Compose suitable hypotheses and decide how you will assess and present your data.

Evaluation

■ Deutsch's theory could be said to lack ecological validity, as much early research was laboratory based and thus not applicable to real-world situations. However, subsequent research was performed in real-life institutional settings, such as in schools and business settings, and produced similar results, which suggests the theory has external validity. The theory has also underpinned a lot of successful conflict resolution through the use of cooperative rather than competitive techniques.

■ Deutsch's theory was the first of its kind and led to interest and research into the relative effects of cooperation and competition and thus a greater understanding of how they affect and interact with each other. Other subsequent theories, such as **game theory**, can be seen to have their origins in Deutsch's theory.

■ An important measure of the validity of an explanation of a theory is the theory's ability to produce effective practical applications. As Deutsch's theory has led to many such applications in a wide range of real-life settings, it can be considered a highly effective theory.

RESEARCH IN FOCUS

When designing experimental studies, such as those into the effects of cooperation and competition on group performance, researchers need to manipulate an independent variable (IV) and set up a dependent variable (DV). Explain the purpose of an IV and a DV in an experiment.

What were the IV and DV in **Aronson *et al.*'s (1978)** study?

PSYCHOLOGY IN THE REAL WORLD

The jigsaw classroom is a cooperative learning technique developed by Elliot Aronson (1971), which is used in schools to reduce racial tensions, promote better learning, heighten motivation and increase the enjoyment of learning. It is the element of 'interdependence', where children learn from each other and do not try to outdo each other, which is most important, as children enhance each other's learning, rather than inhibiting it, as happens in traditional competitive learning environments. The technique has proven very effective and is now common in schools in many countries.

Evolution and cooperation

At first inspection cooperation does not seem to make sense from an evolutionary viewpoint. Individuals should engage in behaviours that maximize their individual survival and reproduction chances. Cooperation therefore would seem to be a costly behaviour that benefits others, so should not be favoured by evolution. However, cooperating with others can benefit the individual, as when we help others it increases the chances that others will help us (a phenomenon known as reciprocal altruism). Also, cooperative behaviour often involves working with others whom we are genetically related to, so helping them actually increases the survival and reproduction chances of our own genes, which we share with them (a phenomenon known as kin selection).

Cooperating with others in a group therefore benefits an individual, as group members are better able to work together in competing against other groups for limited resources and this can be seen in warfare, where a cooperative body of warriors (an army) competes against another cooperative body of warriors to gain territory, resources, and so on. The resources cannot be won by one individual, so working together to share them is the best method of securing at least some resources. Cooperation between group members also often involves those who are related to each other, which has an additional evolutionary advantage in line with kin selection theory. Humans have even evolved ways to detect shirkers and cheaters, those members of groups who do not contribute fully, or try to maximize their gaining of resources at the expense of other group members. This has led to forms of social punishment, such as group members being ostracized (excluded from the benefits of group membership).

LINK TO BIOLOGICAL APPROACH

As cooperative behaviours can be argued to have evolved, owing to gaining valuable resources through cooperative efforts with others increasing survival and reproductive chances, cooperation can be regarded as part of the biological approach.

Research

- **Boyd & Richerson (2009)** reported that cultural differences between groups led to competition between such groups and thus to natural selection favouring behaviours that increase competitive ability. Meanwhile within cultural groups, natural selection favoured genes that increased cooperative behaviours, as such behaviour increased reproductive success. This suggests that competitive and cooperative behaviour co-evolved, with both having a complementary influence upon each other.

- **Binmore (2007)** demonstrated a problem with cooperative behaviour known as *by-product benefit*, where 'free-riders' take advantage of the fact that cooperation, such as when hunting, produces greater rewards than competitively hunting on your own. The free-rider does not contribute much (or at all) to the cooperative behaviour, but shares in the rewards. **Gardner et al. (2009)** showed how this problem is dealt with by a technique called *enforcement*, where free-riders are punished for their non-involvement in cooperative behaviours, by not having resources shared with them or being ostracized from group interactions. Also relevant here is *reciprocal cooperation*, where individuals cooperate with those who have cooperated fully with them in the past and will not cooperate with those known to be free-riders.

▨ Evaluation

- ■ Evolutionary explanations of cooperation and competition can successfully explain how such behaviours have a complementary effect on each other to heighten reproductive success and can explain how such behaviours arose in the first place. Evolutionary theory can also explain the wide range of cooperative and competitive behaviours that animals and humans show in differing situations.

- ■ As cooperative and competitive skills can be successfully taught, for example in classroom settings, it suggests that they are not as biologically determined as evolutionary theory would suggest.

- ■ Much of the research into evolutionary explanations of cooperation and competition are animal based, presenting problems of generalization of findings to humans. Human behaviour tends to involve higher order cognitive processing more than with animal behaviour. However, research using humans has tended to produce similar results to animal studies, supporting the explanation's validity.

▨ Game theory

Game theory is an explanation of social behaviour that focuses on how individuals interact cooperatively and competitively in the pursuit of goals. There are two aspects to game theory:

1 *Cooperative game theory* – focuses on how individuals cooperate in groups in competition against other groups to achieve goals.

2 *Non-cooperative game theory* – focuses on how individuals interact to achieve their own goals.

Researchers devised a series of games for individuals to play so that they could study human cooperative and competitive behaviour and identify the important factors that influence whether behaviour is cooperative or competitive. Such games, like the prisoner's dilemma, involve allowing players to behave cooperatively or competitively, with different rewards for differing types of behaviour. Research identified that in some situations cooperation is favoured, while in others competition is favoured, with factors such as the personalities of individuals, the level of communication between individuals, size of groups and the level of reciprocal behaviour seen as important. Personality also plays a part, with some people always competing, some always cooperating, and some being very conformist by mirroring other people's behaviour, for instance they begin by cooperating, but then compete if other people do.

The most important finding is that game theory shows that individuals do not always behave in ways that maximize their gaining of rewards. Therefore, human social behaviour is not always logical.

▨ Research

- ■ **Deutsch & Krauss (1960)** got two participants to play a game. Each participant is told they own a trucking company and have to deliver some goods as quickly as possible. There is a longer route and a shorter route along a one-lane road. To drive on the shorter route, players have to cooperate and take turns to use it. Each player can also shut a gate that stops the other player using the shorter route. The most profitable strategy is to cooperate, but players instead spend most time competing by shutting the gate. This illustrates how in some situations, even when it is an inferior tactic, people will compete rather than cooperate.

- ■ **Davis (1997)** gave two participants the 'prisoner's dilemma', where each is accused of a crime and if neither of them confesses, each will get a one-year sentence, while if both confess each will get a 40-year sentence. Additionally, if one confesses, that player gets a three-month sentence, while the other gets a 20-year sentence. There is a relatively good payoff if they cooperate and both do not confess (each get only one-year sentence), but generally players compete by confessing and hoping the other one does not, in the hope of only getting three months. This again shows that people will compete in some situations where cooperating would have been more profitable.

- ■ **Guth et al. (1982)** devised the 'ultimatum game' for two players, where one player receives a sum of money and proposes to the other player how it should be split between them. The second player can either accept the offer or reject it, a choice which means both players receive nothing. It would be expected that the first player would offer the second player a low sum that they would choose, as a low sum would be worse than nothing. But receivers tend to reject offers they see as too low (below 30 per cent of the money), while proposers tend not to make very low offers to the receiver, but ones of 40 to 50 per cent of the money. This suggests that people will be fair to others and that those who do not behave fairly will be punished, even when doing so incurs a cost to the punisher. An altruistic punishment is one where receivers reject unfair offers to teach the other player a lesson, so reducing the chances of them making a similarly unfair offer in the future, thus benefitting receivers in the future. A self-control punishment is where receivers reject unfair offers purely to punish the other player for making such an offer.

- **Wichman (1970)** found that if players in the prisoner's dilemma were not allowed to communicate with each other, about 40 per cent of responses were cooperative, but this increased to 70 per cent when they were allowed to communicate, illustrating the important role communication plays in cooperative and competitive behaviour.

- **Komorita & Lapworth (1982)** found that when the prisoner's dilemma was modified so that groups of people could play, cooperative behaviour increased as the size of the group increased, demonstrating the importance of group size in determining cooperative and competitive behaviour.

YOU ARE THE RESEARCHER

Females are generally seen as being more cooperative than males, who tend to be more competitive. Use the 'prisoner's dilemma' (see **Davis, 1997**) to assess whether there are gender differences in cooperative and competitive behaviour. This will be an IMD. Compose a suitable one-tailed (directional) hypothesis and create a table and graph to display your data. What conclusions do your data allow you to make?

Evaluation

- Cultural factors seem to play a role in determining if behaviour is cooperative or competitive. **Werner (1979)** reported that Americans will generally choose to be competitive and that this tendency is learned during childhood.

- Game theory produces results that lack ecological validity, as research findings come from playing artificial games that may not reflect how humans behave in real-life situations.

- Whether or not individuals will behave cooperatively or competitively depends not on any single factor, but rather on a complex interaction of external factors, such as the size of a group, and internal factors, for example personality.

RESEARCH IN FOCUS

Game theory tends to use games such as the 'prisoner's dilemma' and the 'ultimatum game' as a basis for research. Explain why such studies can be accused of lacking ecological validity.

Strengthen your learning

1 Outline Deutsch's theory of cooperation and competition – ensure you include his Crude Law of Social Relations.

2 Explain how cooperation has an evolutionary adaptive (survival) value.

3 Outline game theory.

4 Summarize what research has suggested about the following as explanations of cooperation and competition:
   a Deutsch's theory   b the evolution of cooperation   c game theory.

5 What other evaluative points can be made about the following as explanations of cooperation and competition:
   a Deutsch's theory   b the evolution of cooperation   c game theory?

Cohesion

'The way a team plays as a whole determines its success.'
Babe Ruth

■ The effects of cohesion on cooperation between group members.
■ The effects of task and social cohesion on group performance.
■ The effects of cohesion on co-active and interactive groups.
■ The effects of social loafing on group performance.
■ What research has informed about the effects of cohesion and social loafing on group performance.
■ An assessment of the effects of cohesion and social loafing on groups.

> **Cohesion** – the degree of unity between members of a social group.

Effective groups are ones that have cohesion (work together well). **Cohesion** can be affected by group dynamics of leadership, intergroup relationships (how well group members get on with and work with each other) and role-definition. For example, groups in which members have clearly defined roles will be more effective; this is why sports teams often have clearly defined positions, such as defender, attacker, midfielder, and so on.

Group cohesion can be an effect or cause of cooperation between group members and works in two ways:

1 The total sum of forces binding a group together.
2 Resistance by the group to disruptive forces.

Early research examined the role of individuals within a group; more recent research has concentrated on studying groups as a whole. Five measures are usually taken of group cohesiveness by the use of questionnaires, such as the Group Evaluation Questionnaire:

1 Measure the degree of interpersonal attraction between group members.
2 Measure each individual's desire to remain within the group.
3 Measure the level of closeness and identification felt by group members.
4 Measure the attractiveness of the group to individuals.
5 A combination of 1 to 4 above.

Cohesion does not guarantee a cooperative group success and it is often the effective performance of a group that creates more cohesion.

Carron (1982) pointed out the difference between:

■ *Task cohesion* – how well a cooperative group works as a unit.

■ *Social cohesion* – how well group members like each other and identify with the group.

Successful performances rely more on task cohesion, though the relation between cohesion and performance is also dependent on the type of group structure (kind of team) involved. Group structure can either be:

■ *Co-active* – relates to situations where members perform the same task at different times and do not require others to be successful for them to be successful, e.g. batting at cricket.

■ *Interactive* –r elates to situations involving a high degree of work effort, not just the sum of individual efforts, e.g. hockey.

Interactive groups are more successful when high cohesion is perceived by group members. For such groups, high cohesion is more important than individuals' skill levels.

Co-active groups can be successful when low cohesion is perceived by group members, as rivalries and the competitive behaviour they motivate between team members become a spur to success, driving individuals to greater performances. The West German men's rowing eight at the 1968 Olympics loathed each other so much they didn't talk to one another. They won gold.

Generally, the more that group members are interdependent and the more group performance depends on cooperative action, the greater the role for cohesion.

Cohesion can adversely affect performance, as in small groups high cohesion hinders individuals from expressing their individuality. High group cohesion may also lead to individuals performing to the same standard, minimizing healthy competition within the group, especially in training. In this, conflict within the team should be created to heighten motivation.

Research

- **Mullen & Copper (1994)** performed a meta-analysis of 66 cohesion–performance relationships from 49 studies of sports, business and military groups, finding that the relationship between cohesion and performance was due to task commitment rather than interpersonal attraction or group pride, suggesting task (not social) cohesion is important for performance.

- **Carron *et al.* (2002)** performed a meta-analysis of 46 studies, finding no difference in the relationship between task cohesion and performance between co-active and interactive sports teams. In both types of sports, high task cohesion was related to good performances, suggesting that high task cohesion is beneficial to all teams and going against the idea that low task cohesion is necessary for co-active teams to perform well. It may be low social cohesion driving co-active teams to greater performances, not task cohesion.

- **Rovio *et al.* (2009)** found that high cohesion in an ice-hockey team led to impaired performances, due to pressures for individual players to perform similarly and conform to group norms, illustrating how high cohesion can have adverse effects on performance.

Evaluation

- **Escovar & Sim (1974)** argued that interpersonal attraction is not part of group cohesion, as it does not explain cohesion in response to adversity, for example in response to the threat of group defeat, and it does not explain improvements in interactions between group members.

- The effects of cohesion on performance are difficult to assess, as situations differ from one another widely in terms of the different levels of team cohesion needed for success.

Aids and barriers to team cohesion

Cooperative groups with cohesion are more successful, possessing greater group identity and staying together longer, allowing development of successful skills and strategies, as well as pulling together more persistently in the face of adversity. Therefore, establishing and maintaining cohesion is desirable, with several aids and barriers to this process. Removal of such barriers is an aid to increased cohesion by itself.

Social loafing

Ringelmann (1913) found the greater the size of a group, the less effort was put in by individual members. If one person is pulling on a rope they will put in 100 per cent effort, if two people are pulling they will put in 93 per cent average individual effort, while eight people will put in just 49 per cent individual effort.

> **Social loafing** – the phenomenon of people exerting less individual effort in a group than when on their own.

Some reasons for **social loafing** concern cohesion; for example, diffusion of responsibility, where decreased effort occurs owing to the lack of identifiability of individual efforts. This barrier to cohesive performance can be addressed by setting group members identifiable individual roles, like monitoring individual performances and giving individual feedback to reinforce good practice. **Latane (1980)** argued that if individual members are more identifiable, the group situation provides a social incentive, through group cohesion, to perform better. The establishment of set individual roles also addresses the problem of group cohesion hindering performance owing to a loss of individuality within the group and the loss of healthy competition between group members.

Research

- **Ingham *et al.* (1974)** asked blindfolded participants to pull on a rope in the belief that other people were also pulling. As the perceived size of the group increased, individual effort decreased, in line with Ringelman's idea of social loafing. Ingham backed up his findings using Olympic rowing times to show that coxed fours were only 13 per cent faster than coxed pairs and coxed eights only 23 per cent faster than coxed pairs.

■ **Gross (1982)** found that sports players who received feedback about individual performances outperformed those that didn't, illustrating how the negative effects of social loafing can be reduced in cooperative groups.

Evaluation

■ Cohesiveness is not a static state. Adjustments are constantly needed to address fluctuations in cohesion, like those through changes in group members and changes to group goals.

■ Other factors contribute to social loafing, as well as cohesion, like loss of control and distraction of the group, for example. Therefore, the effect is not just due to a lack of cohesion.

■ Cohesion is measured through sociograms: diagrams that show interpersonal relationships between group members. These highlight less preferred group members and cliques, thus providing an opportunity for such harmful cliques to be broken up and to formulate strategies to include 'outsiders' more effectively into a group.

PSYCHOLOGY IN THE REAL WORLD

Evolutionary theory explains how social exclusion strategies are used to punish group members who do not contribute fully to group behaviour, or who are seen to work against the group.

One real-world example is the treatment of women who had relationships with invading German soldiers during the Second World War. In the Channel Islands, a British territory between England and France, such women were derogatively called 'Jerry bags' and ostracized (excluded) from society. After the defeat of the Germans, many of these women had their heads shaved and were paraded through the streets to be mocked and abused.

■ **Figure 8.8** 'Jerry bags' often had their heads shaved as a form of public humiliation

---

Strengthen your learning

1   What is cohesion?

2   Explain how cohesion can affect cooperation within groups. Be sure to include references to task and social cohesion, as well as co-active and interactive groups.

3   Explain how and why social loafing affects group performance.

4   Summarize what research has suggested about the effects of the following on cooperative group performance:
    a   cohesion
    b   social loafing.

5   What other evaluative points can be made about the following on cooperative group performance:
    a   cohesion
    b   social loafing?

Prejudice

'Prejudices are what fools use for reason.'
Voltaire

FOCUS ON...

- Prejudice as an attitude.
- Social identity theory, stereotyping, conformity, realistic conflict theory and the authoritarian personality, as explanations for prejudice.
- Tajfel's classic minimal groups study, as an exploration of social identity theory.
- Sherif *et al.*'s. Robbers Cave classic study, as an exploration of realistic conflict theory.
- What research has informed about social identity theory, stereotyping, conformity, realistic conflict theory and the authoritarian personality, as explanations for prejudice.
- An assessment of social identity theory, stereotyping, conformity, realistic conflict theory and the authoritarian personality, as explanations for prejudice.

Prejudice – an unfair or unreasonable idea or feeling that is not based on fact.

Discrimination – treating someone in an unfair manner based on their sex, race, age, etc.

Social identity theory (SIT) – the idea that individuals discriminate positively towards 'in-group' members and against 'out-group' members.

Stereotyping – a type of cognitive bias that concerns grouping types of individuals together on the incorrect basis that they all possess the same quality.

Conformity – yielding to group norms that discriminate in favour of 'in-group' members and against 'out-group' members.

Realistic conflict theory (RCT) – the idea that prejudice arises through competition between 'in' and 'out' groups over valuable resources.

The **authoritarian personality** – the idea that prejudice arises from the possession of certain characteristics nurtured in childhood.

Prejudice is an attitude that is not based on fact, which is held about someone or something. Any attitude has three components: *cognitive* (beliefs about an attitude object, whether false or true), *affective* (emotions concerned with an attitude object) and *behavioural* (actions towards an attitude object). For example:

- *Cognitive*: 'All blondes are stupid.'
- *Affective*: 'Blondes really annoy me.'
- *Behavioural*: 'I own a company, but I wouldn't employ any blondes.'

Although prejudices can sometimes be positive ones, they are generally negative in terms of the harmful **discrimination** they motivate against people we hold prejudiced attitudes about: for example, racial discrimination, where people from ethnic minorities are distrusted and abused. Psychologists are therefore interested in studying prejudice so that effective strategies can be devised to reduce its negative discriminatory effects upon society.

'Prejudice is a great time saver, you can form opinions without having to get to the facts.'
E.B. White

Explanations for prejudice

There are five basic explanations given for prejudice: **social identity theory, stereotyping, conformity, realistic conflict theory** and the **authoritarian personality**. However, conformity and stereotyping can be largely considered as part of social identity theory.

Social identity theory: Tajfel & Turner (1979)

Social identity theory (SIT) is based on the idea that self-esteem (self-value) is central to an individual's identity and that in order to feel good about ourselves, we need to feel good about the social groups we feel we belong to ('in-groups'). The theory has three components:

1 *Social categorization* – a person perceives themselves as having similar characteristics to members of a social group.

2 *Social identification* – a person moves on to classifying themselves as a member of that social group (an 'in-group') by adopting the group's norms (ways of thinking and behaving) and attitudes.

3 *Social comparison* – a person compares themselves, as a member of their 'in-group', as being superior to 'out-group' members (people who belong to other social groups), which leads to treating 'out-group' persons in a prejudiced and discriminatory way.

SIT also includes the 'out-group' homogeneity (similarity) effect, where members of 'out-groups' are not only seen as different from 'in-group' members, but as being more similar to each other than 'in-group' members.

■ **Figure 8.9** Henri Tajfel

KEY STUDY   CLASSIC RESEARCH

'Experiments in intergroup discrimination: the minimal group paradigm'
Tajfel (1970)

Tajfel was a British psychologist whose parents were Polish Jews murdered by the Nazis. Thus Tajfel had a lifelong interest in understanding the reasons why intergroup prejudice arose. In this particular study he wanted to see whether prejudice and discrimination between groups could be created by randomly assigning people to groups. Would such individuals categorize and identify themselves as belonging to these groups and then behave negatively towards each other, even though none of these individuals had any prejudices towards each other before the study began?

Aim

To see whether prejudice would arise between people with no previous prejudice towards each other, simply by placing them into different groups.

Procedure

1   The participants were 64 schoolboys from Bristol, England aged between 14 and 15 years.

2   Boys believed they were divided into groups on the basis of minimal tasks they had to perform (tasks that they would not feel very passionately about); this formed the basis of two experiments.

3   Experiment one – boys were told they were taking part in a study of visual judgement. They were shown 40 clusters of dots on a screen and asked to say how many there were. They were then told they were being put into groups of being either an 'over-estimator or 'under-estimator' (all groupings were actually done randomly). Boys were then asked to give small rewards of money to a pair of boys who were either 'in-group' or 'out-group' members, by using a book of matrices. Each matrix had a pair of numbers that converted into money (1 point = 1 pence).

4   Experiment two – boys believed they had been divided into two groups on the basis of their preferences for 12 paintings by Paul Klee and Wassily Kandinsky (this was in fact done randomly). As per experiment one, boys chose from matrices of pairs of numbers, but this time the researchers gave the boys three choices:

   a   *maximum joint profit* – giving the largest amount to members of both groups

   b   *maximum in-group profit* – giving the largest amount to an in-group member, regardless of the amount to an out-group member

   c   *maximum difference* – giving the largest possible difference in amounts between an in-group and out-group member.

A

Matrix 1

219	216	213	210	27	24	21	0	1	2	3	4	5	6
6	5	4	3	2	1	0	21	24	27	210	213	216	219

Matrix 2

12	10	8	6	4	2	0	21	25	29	213	217	221	225
225	221	217	213	29	25	21	0	2	4	6	8	10	12

B

Matrix 3

1	2	3	4	5	6	7	8	9	10	11	12	13	14
14	13	12	11	10	9	8	7	6	5	4	3	2	1

Matrix 4

18	17	16	15	14	13	12	11	10	9	8	7	6	5
5	6	7	8	9	10	11	12	13	14	15	16	17	18

C

Matrix 5

214	212	210	28	26	24	22	21	3	7	11	15	19	23
23	19	15	11	7	3	21	22	24	26	28	210	212	214

■ **Figure 8.10** Examples of Tajfel's matrices

Results

1 *Experiment one* – the amounts allocated were fairly similar if pairs consisted of two in-group or two out-group members, but when allocating money to an in-group and an out-group member, most boys gave more to the in-group member.

2 *Experiment two* – again the amounts allocated were fairly similar if pairs consisted of two in-group or two out-group members, but when allocating money to an in-group and an out-group member, they would choose the maximum difference, even if it meant giving the in-group member less money than choosing the 'maximum in-group profit' option.

Conclusions

- Prejudice can be created simply by getting individuals to identify with an 'in-group' and see others as 'out-group' members.

- Discrimination against 'out-group' members is more important than rewarding 'in-group' members.

Evaluation

- Tajfel's 'minimal groups' studies lack ecological validity, as the tasks performed were not everyday life ones. However, very little of importance was at stake in these tasks, so in real-life situations where consequences were greater, perhaps even stronger prejudice and discrimination should be expected.

- Another methodological consideration in the 'minimal groups' studies is demand characteristics. The matrices could have been perceived as a competitive game (especially as boys and not girls were involved) that they were expected to try and 'win', and it was this expectation that shaped their behaviour.

Stereotyping

'I live bigger than your labels.'
Rachel Fershleiser

Stereotyping is a type of cognitive bias that concerns grouping types of individuals together on the incorrect basis that they all possess the same quality, for example that all red-haired people are aggressive. It involves cognitively (mentally) classifying groups of people on the similarities they have and how they differ from other groups of people. This has an evolutionary adaptive survival value in simplifying the world and the people within it, making it easier to make decisions about how to deal with people. However, such mental 'short-cuts' of 'out-groups' often tend to be negative, leading to suspicion, fear and discrimination against members of such groups. Conversely, in line with SIT, stereotypes of 'in-group' members tend to be positive, leading to preferential discriminatory behaviour towards their members. The way in which stereotypes develop can also be explained by reference to SIT, as part of the social-categorization, social-identification and social-comparison processes.

Prejudiced attitudes and discriminatory behaviour towards minority groups, including ethnic minorities, homosexuals and transsexuals, religious groups, and so on, can be seen to be based on incorrect stereotyped beliefs that are generalized to all members of the minority group. Any actual example of stereotypical behaviour that is experienced, such as a blonde-haired person behaving stupidly, is portrayed in an exaggerated way as being an example of 'typical blonde behaviour, it's what they're all like, and this is why they can't be trusted', while any non-stereotypical behaviour experienced, such as a blonde person behaving intelligently, is ignored. In this way, stereotyping helps to maintain prejudiced views against 'out-group' members and the discriminatory behaviour that comes with holding such views.

Conformity

'We are half ruined by conformity, but we would be wholly ruined without it.'
Charles Dudley Warner (1896)

Normative social influence – a motivational force to be liked and accepted by a group.

Compliance – publicly but not privately going along with majority influence to gain approval.

Identification – public and private acceptance of majority influence in order to gain group acceptance.

Internalization – public and private acceptance of majority influence due to adoption of the majority's belief system.

Conformity involves adhering to the norms (expected ways of thinking and behaving) of 'in-groups' (and conversely not adhering to the norms of 'out-groups'). Therefore, individuals will adopt, in line with SIT, prejudiced, stereotypical beliefs about members of 'out-groups' and conform to behaving in a discriminatory way against such people. This is known as **normative social influence** and involves **compliance**, where individuals adopt the norms of a social group in order to be accepted and not rejected by that group. However, this is a weak form of conformity, as it only involves public, but not private agreement with the group's norms. A stronger form of conformity is **identification**, where, due to membership of an 'in-group' having desirable outcomes, individuals take on the norms of a social group both publicly and privately, as in the social identification component of SIT. The strongest form of conformity is **internalization** (also known as true conformity), where an individual fully adopts the belief system of an 'in-group' (including their beliefs about and behaviours towards members of 'out-groups') with such beliefs and behaviours maintained even when an individual isn't in the company of other 'in-group' members. It may be that individuals with low self-esteem have a greater need for social acceptance into 'in-groups' so will display more conformity to social norms of prejudice to 'out-groups'.

Research

- **Crandall & Stangor (2005)** found that when participants were told that the members of their 'in-group' held a certain belief, they were more likely to report holding this belief themselves than those who had not been told this. This supports the idea that, in line with SIT, people conform to 'in-group' norms of beliefs and behaviours.

- **Jones *et al.* (1981)** asked student participants in four different 'dining' clubs to rate members of their own and other clubs on personality dimensions. It was found that participants rated members of other groups ('out-groups') as more similar to each other (the 'out-group homogeneity effect') than in their own 'in-group'. This is in line with SIT and also demonstrates a stereotyping effect, where people are grouped together by similarities, whether they are true or not.

- **Nelson *et al.* (1990)** asked participants to judge the height of men and women from a booklet of photographs, each photograph showing one person. Participants were told, 'In this booklet, the men and women are actually of equal height. We have taken care to match the heights of the men and women pictured. That is, for every woman of a particular height, somewhere in the booklet there is also a man of that same height. Therefore, in order to make as accurate a height judgement as possible, try to judge each photograph as an individual case; do not rely on the person's sex.' However, despite being told this and the offer of a $50 prize for the person making the most accurate judgements, males were perceived to be on average several inches taller than women. This suggests that people are unable to break free of gender stereotypes, even when knowing they are not true, which illustrates the strength of stereotyping in maintaining prejudices.

- **Minard (1952)** observed the behaviour of black and white coal miners in the USA, finding that below ground where the social norm was being friendly with workmates, 80 per cent of white miners were friendly to black colleagues, but above ground where the social norm was to act in racially prejudiced ways only 20 per cent of white miners were friendly to black colleagues. This supports the idea of prejudice due to conformity, where people adopt the norms of a given situation in order to fit in.

- **Pettigrew (1959)** studied the relationship between conformity and prejudice, finding highly conformist white South African students tended to be more prejudiced against black people than white students with low levels of conformity. This suggests that highly conformist people have a greater need for social approval (acceptance into an 'in-group') and so are prepared to show more prejudice to achieve it. This adds a personality dimension to the conformist explanation of prejudice.

- **Rogers & Frantz (1962)** found that white immigrants to Rhodesia (now Zimbabwe) became more prejudiced to black people the longer they lived in the country, which suggests they learned and conformed to social norms of prejudice in order to be accepted into an 'in-group' and avoid their rejection by not displaying prejudice.

Evaluation

- SIT explains why prejudice occurs even when an out-group poses no threat to an in-group and there is no competition over resources, owing to a need to discriminate against others in order to boost self-esteem.

- Some individuals seem to have a greater need than others for self-esteem and so develop stronger social identities. Adorno's authoritarian personality (page 398) may better explain such people's prejudiced views.

- Although stereotypes are automatically triggered when we meet people (and the way we behave towards them), **Devine (1989)** argues that there is an important personality difference, as she sees low-stereotype people as able to actively inhibit (block out) such stereotypes, while high-prejudice people do not. This important difference is explicable by reference to Adorno's concept of the authoritarian personality.

- Although conformity offers a plausible explanation for prejudice, social norms change over time, which therefore does not explain why such prejudiced views are maintained.

- There are different types of conformity – compliance, identification and internalization – which have different strengths in terms of their degree of private acceptance and how much they affect a person's belief system; and this can explain why different individuals have different degrees of prejudice towards 'out-group' members.

- Conformity to 'in-group' norms of prejudice can be seen to have an evolutionary adaptive value, as being accepted as a member of a social group increases survival and reproductive chances, especially when competing against 'out-groups' for valuable resources.

LINK TO BIOLOGICAL APPROACH

Stereotyping can be seen to have an evolutionary survival value, through simplifying the world and the people within it, making it easier to make decisions as to how to deal with people. Conformity also has an evolutionary basis, as membership of 'in-groups' and discriminating against 'out-groups' increases individual survival and reproduction chances. Therefore, prejudice can be argued to be part of the biological approach.

Realistic conflict theory

Realistic conflict theory (RCT) explains how intergroup rivalry over conflicting goals and competition for valuable resources can lead to prejudice.

Groups may have different goals or beliefs, such as the differing views of political parties and religious groups; and groups may also have to compete against each other for access to resources, such as finances, territory, food and reproductive opportunities (sexual mates). Competition can also be for social status, with increased levels giving easier access to power and resources.

Prejudice develops due to feelings of distrust, fear and resentment towards other competing groups, especially when only the 'winning' group can achieve their goal or gain the desired resources. Such feelings can also arise over worries that resources, status, and so on, already possessed by a group may be 'stolen' by an 'invading' group. The intergroup conflicts that occur over competition for goals and resources lead to discriminatory behaviour and the level of prejudice and discrimination is determined by the level of importance placed upon achieving group goals and securing valuable resources, as well as the degree of intergroup conflicts to secure such goals and resources.

LINK TO THE SOCIOCULTURAL APPROACH

As RCT and SIT both focus on the human need to feel a sense of belonging with and connectedness to others, they can be considered to be part of the sociocultural approach.

KEY STUDY   ## CLASSIC RESEARCH

'Inter-group conflict and cooperation: The Robbers Cave experiment'
Sherif *et al.* (1961)

Turkish–American Muzafer Sherif is considered one of the founders of social psychology and conducted much ground-breaking research. In this particular study, he and his team were interested in identifying and assessing the factors associated with intergroup conflict and cooperation. They were especially interested in doing this under real-life conditions and came upon the idea of using a boy's summer camp to build separate friendship groups and then artificially create conflict and competition between the groups of boys to see if negative attitudes and behaviours would develop between the groups. The final part of his study was designed to see if it was then possible to reduce prejudice between the groups through the use of cooperative tasks.

Aims

1   To see whether friendship groups could be created among boys who had no previous relationships with each other, by getting them to interact in group activities with common goals.

2   To see whether intergroup conflict and hostility could be created through conditions of competition and group frustration.

Procedure

1   The participants were 22 boys, aged 11 to 12 years, attending an isolated 300-acre summer camp at Robbers Cave State Park, Oklahoma, USA.

2   Stage one: the boys were split into two groups of 12 who lived, worked and played separately from each other. Activities with a common goal were introduced that needed cooperation to accomplish, such as pitching tents, making meals and going on a treasure hunt. The two groups of boys performed these activities separately and out of sight of the other group.

3   Stage two: the two groups of boys were then brought together to engage in a competitive tournament, comprising ten sporting events. Points were also awarded for other things, like the tidiness of their cabins. A trophy, medals and knives for all group members would be awarded to the winning group.

4   Stage three: seven equal-status contact situations were introduced where boys from both groups had to interact, such as filling in questionnaires, viewing films and eating together. After this, the water supply was cut off, with the only means of restoring it being with the two groups working together. Other cooperative tasks then introduced included pooling money together to go and watch a film, pulling on a rope together to get a truck started, making meals and putting up tents together.

Results

1   By the end of stage one, two friendship groups had been created with unmistakeable group structures and each with a discernible leader and a status hierarchy. Each group had developed its own norms and punishments for deviant behaviour (behaviour that broke group norms). One group had taken to calling itself the 'Rattlers' and the other group called itself the 'Eagles'.

2   Before the competition began the 'Eagles' burned the 'Rattlers' flag and the camp counsellors (the researchers) had to break up a fight between the two groups. The researchers engineered the results of the competition so that the 'Eagles' won, at which point the 'Rattlers' stole their medals and knives.

3   All boys expressed preferences for in-group members. Members of the 'Rattlers' stereotyped themselves as 'brave', 'tough' and 'friendly' and the majority of the 'Eagles' as 'sneaky', 'stinkers' and 'smart Alecks', with the 'Eagles' having similar self-stereotypes and views of the 'Rattlers'.

4   At stage three, the introduction of the seven equal-status contact situations had no effect on reducing prejudice between the two groups. However, the later cooperative tasks had a gradual effect in making group divisions disappear. Sixty-five per cent of friendship choices were now made from the other group, with stereotypes of other group members also becoming more positive.

Conclusions

● Prejudice towards an 'out-group' can occur through competition for resources that only one group can achieve.

● Contact with an 'out-group' is insufficient by itself for prejudice to be reduced.

● Prejudice can be reduced and positive relationships established between previously hostile groups, by working towards goals that require cooperative action.

Evaluation

● The researchers had pre-conceived ideas about what they thought the results would be. This may have led to researchers interpreting the behaviour of the boys in subjective ways that 'proved' their hypotheses.

- The contrived nature of the study, involving manipulation of various parts of the research setting, such as ensuring the 'Eagles' won, sabotaging the water supply, and encouraging the boys to cooperate with each other, may have created demand characteristics where the boys formed impressions of how the researchers wanted them to act and then behaved accordingly.

- In order to elicit natural behaviour, the researchers did not inform the boys they were taking part in a study of prejudice and this could be regarded as unethical, as deceit was used; this means informed consent was not gained, nor was a right to withdraw given to the boys. Harm may also have been caused by subjecting individuals to hostility and prejudice from other boys. There is no indication given that the boys were debriefed after the study had concluded.

Research

Michigan National Election Studies (1972) assessed data on reactions to a government plan to racially integrate schools by bussing white and black children to the same schools. It was found that white people generally opposed the idea, as they felt the advantages they held of better wealth, education and career prospects for their children would be at threat if black children were given access to these resources. This supports the idea of RCT that prejudice can arise between groups competing for the same limited resources.

Evaluation

- RCT can explain why competition for valuable resources in communities comprising different social groups can present potentially harmful consequences.

- RCT only explains prejudice as arising between groups of fairly equal status. **Duckitt (1994)** argues that when competing social groups are of unequal status, the higher status group dominates, leading to the lower status group either accepting the dominant group's attitudes and behaviours in order to avoid harmful conflict, or rejecting the lower status placed upon them and responding with conflict and hostility, as in gaining rights for black people through the civil rights movement in the USA.

- RCT can be seen to have face validity in terms of real-world situations. For example, **Brain (2012, cited in Boyd-Barrett, 2017)** argues that prejudice and hostility between Ukraine and Russia arose over competition between who controls the flow of gas (a valuable resource) to Europe, as Russian gas pipelines have to pass through Ukraine.

TOK link

Theories and models are explanations of phenomena. One way of assessing the validity (accuracy) of theories and models is to examine the degree of research support they have. However, to be considered valid, theories and models should also produce effective practical applications. Therefore, to be seen as valid, theories of prejudice should lead to effective means of reducing discrimination against prejudiced groups. For example, Sherif successfully used realistic conflict theory to create methods of reducing intergroup hostility by encouraging cooperative behaviours towards shared goals.

Authoritarian personality

'Intolerance of ambiguity is the mark of an authoritarian personality.'
Theodor Adorno

The authoritarian personality (AP) sees certain personality characteristics to be associated with a tendency to being prejudiced. Such people are also seen as being highly conformist and obedient.

First proposed by **Fromm (1941)**, the AP sees individuals who hold right wing, conservative views as having a personality type characterized by a belief in absolute obedience, submission to authority and domination of minorities. It is probably best summed up by the phrase 'Might is right'. **Adorno *et al.* (1950)** saw people of this type as having insecurities that led them to be hostile to people from minority social groups, and having a belief in a need for power and toughness, which leads them to be highly obedient to authority. Adorno additionally saw the personality type as being shaped in early childhood by hierarchical, authoritarian parenting. To measure an individual's degree of authoritarian personality, Adorno constructed the F-scale questionnaire, which has 30 questions assessing 9 personality dimensions (the 'F' stands for 'fascist').

More recently, **Jost *et al.* (2003)** has claimed that the authoritarian personality is motivated by thought processes which underpin a desire to reduce the fear and anxiety that other social groups will introduce harmful social change.

Research

- **Adorno *et al.* (1950)** gave the F-scale questionnaire to hundreds of American participants. Forty high scorers and 40 low scorers were then interviewed and it was found that high scorers had more prejudiced beliefs about people from minority social groups, such as Jewish people. This supports the idea that prejudice can arise from having an authoritarian personality.

- **Harding *et al.* (1969)** reviewed several studies to report that individuals who were prejudiced towards Jewish people also tended to be prejudiced towards black people and indeed towards people of all minority groups, which supports the idea that those with an AP are generally disposed to be prejudiced towards minority groups.

- **Akrami (2005)** got 183 Finnish students to each complete five questionnaires measuring levels of different forms of prejudice, including homophobia, sexism and prejudice against intellectually disabled people, as well as levels of general prejudice. It was found that all measures of prejudice were highly positively correlated, which supports the central idea of the AP that prejudice is formed from personality characteristics disposing individuals to be hostile to minority groups.

YOU ARE THE RESEARCHER

Design and conduct a correlational study to assess the claim that people with an authoritarian personality are more prejudiced. To measure the AP, you can download a copy of the F-scale from the internet, or a more up-to-date measure is the Right Wing Authoritarianism scale. You will then need to design a questionnaire that measures prejudice. You'll need about 10 to 15 questions. Remember to consider the ethical issue of harm when composing your questions. It will also be important to conduct a debriefing that explains there are no right or wrong answers to these questions. Compose suitable correlational hypotheses and a scattergram to plot your data. What conclusions can you draw from your data?

Evaluation

- The AP can explain prejudice towards minority social groups, but has difficulty in explaining other forms of prejudice, such as ageism and sexism.

- Research in to the AP tends to use questionnaires, which can be subject to socially desirable answers, where people answer untruthfully by giving answers that society expects of them, rather than their true personal beliefs. Whether this means that levels of prejudice associated with the AP would be over or under-emphasized is not certain.

- Although the F-scale has some research support, supposedly authoritarian individuals do not always score as highly on all the dimensions as the theory would predict.

- The F-scale suffers from response bias, as the scale is worded in a confirming direction. Therefore, if individuals agree with items they are rated as authoritarian. **Altemeyer (1981)** produced the less biased Right Wing Authoritarianism scale (RWA), which has an equal number of pro- and anti-statements.

RESEARCH IN FOCUS

Adorno *et al.*'s (1950) study into prejudice and the authoritarian personality used a correlational design.

1 Give one strength and one weakness of such a design.

2 How does a positive correlation differ from a negative one?

3 What type of graph is used to plot correlational data?

Strengthen your learning

1 Define prejudice.

2 Give an example of your own of prejudice as an attitude. Be sure to include a cognitive, affective and behavioural component.

3 Outline, in your own words, the following explanations of prejudice:
   a social identity theory
   b stereotyping
   c conformity
   d realistic conflict theory
   e the authoritarian personality.

4 Explain why stereotyping and conformity can be seen as part of social identity theory.

5 For Tajfel's (1970) classic minimal groups study, in your own words state the:
   a aims
   b procedure
   c results
   d conclusions
   e evaluative points.

6 For Sherif *et al.*'s. (1961) Robbers Cave classic study, in your own words state the:
   a aims
   b procedure
   c results
   d conclusions
   e evaluative points.

7 Summarize what research has suggested about the following as explanations of prejudice:
   a social identity theory
   b stereotyping
   c conformity
   d realistic conflict theory
   e the authoritarian personality.

8 Provide an assessment of the following as explanations of prejudice, in terms of their strengths and weaknesses:
   a social identity theory
   b stereotyping
   c conformity
   d realistic conflict theory
   e the authoritarian personality.

SECTION SUMMARY

- Cooperation and competition are complementary forces that exert an influence upon each other in social situations.
- Cooperation can be seen to have evolved, as it has an adaptive survival value.
- Game theory explains how individuals interact cooperatively and competitively in the pursuit of goals.
- Cooperative group performance is affected by levels of cohesion and through social loafing.
- Prejudice and discrimination can be explained by reference to social identity theory, stereotyping, conformity, realistic conflict theory and the authoritarian personality.

Origins of conflict and conflict resolution

'No matter how thin you slice it, there will always be two sides.'
Baruch Spinoza

FOCUS ON...

- Destructive and constructive conflict resolution.
- The characteristics of conflict.
- How conflicts arise.
- Types of behaviour arising from conflicts.
- Social identity theory and realistic conflict theory as explanations for conflict.
- Deutsch's Crude Law of Social Relations, three-step collaborative conflict resolution and interactive conflict resolution, as methods of conflict resolution.
- What research has informed about methods of conflict resolution.
- An assessment of explanations of conflict and methods of their resolution.

Origins

Conflict – a dispute that arises over individuals holding incompatible viewpoints.

A **conflict** is a dispute that arises owing to two incompatible viewpoints. Conflicts are a natural product of human interactions and indeed can be positive as well as negative in nature. **Deutsch (1949a)** distinguishes between destructive conflict, which is to be avoided, and constructive conflict, which he sees as an essential and valuable part of human creativity. When conflict leads to violence, then it can be seen as destructive, though it has been argued that the threat of violence can be a route to reducing conflicts.

Mack & Snyder (1957) believe that conflict can be characterized by four conditions: (1) the presence of two or more separate parties, (2) a scarce or valuable resource, (3) mutually opposed goals, (4) the possibility of behaviour designed to injure others. Conflicts can occur between individuals, social groups or indeed nations and can therefore be interpersonal, intergroup and international.

Conflicts can be seen as cognitive rather than behavioural in nature, as conflicts arise from a perception of incompatibility between groups and are resolved by removing that perception and replacing it with one of compatibility. Conflict behaviours, such as violence against specific groups of people, are an effect of perceiving there to be a conflict rather than being a cause of such conflict.

Conflicts arise in two ways: first, over issues of interest, where conflicting groups agree on their goals, but disagree about how to achieve them, generally over the distribution of resources between groups (like allocation of funding to different groups); and second, over issues of value, where conflict arises over fundamental beliefs (like those between different religious groups). These conflicts are harder to resolve. In terms of rewards, zero sum conflicts, where one group wins all of a resource, so that the other group gets none, are the hardest to resolve.

Conflict resolution – the means by which a peaceful solution is found to settle a dispute.

The social environment in which conflicts occur is also important. Conflicts that are managed in a structured environment, where behaviour takes place as specified by agreed norms (such as in collective bargaining between trade unions and management), are carried out in a cooperative manner that seeks to find shared goals. If during the **conflict resolution** disagreements occur, agreed procedures are put in place to find a compromise. However, conflicts that occur in an unstructured environment, such as during a revolution, do not have shared goals, as they tend to concern zero sum conflicts and are conducted in a hostile, distrustful, competitive manner that can lead to destructive violence.

Kriesberg (1982) argues that three basic types of behaviour arise from conflicts: persuasion, coercion and reward.

1 *Persuasion* – attempts are made to influence other groups by reasonable arguments, references to common interests and shared values and norms of fairness. Such behaviour tends to occur through verbal discussion and has a low cost to all concerned parties.

2 *Coercion* – attempts are made to influence other groups through imposing unacceptable costs and/or threats of injury and actual violence. Such behaviour can be verbal or physical and can incur high costs to all concerned parties.

3 *Reward* – attempts are made to influence other groups through promises of benefits and, as with coercion, are dependent on the responses of other concerned parties. Such behaviour can be verbal or physical and incurs some costs in having to pay out rewards.

Generally, conflicts are resolved by replacing positions of disagreement and incompatibility between groups with cooperation and interdependent goals.

> **LINK TO THE COGNITIVE APPROACH**
>
> As conflicts arise from a perception of incompatibility between groups and because such conflicts are resolved by replacing that perception with one of compatibility, conflict behaviours and conflict resolution behaviours can be viewed as part of the cognitive approach.

Conflicts can be seen as cognitive rather than behavioural in nature, as conflicts arise from a perception of incompatibility between groups and are resolved by removing that perception and replacing it with one of compatibility. Conflict behaviours, such as violence against specific groups of people, are an effect of perceiving.

Social identity theory

Social identity theory (SIT) (see page 391) sees prejudice as explaining the origins of conflict. SIT argues that conflict against 'out-groups' arises purely out of individuals identifying themselves as being members of 'in-groups'. SIT sees individuals as gaining identity and self-esteem from membership of 'in-groups', with self-esteem linked to the status of one's 'in-group'. If the status of an 'in-group' is low or gaining access to valuable resources is difficult, self-esteem will be low but can be increased by moving to a higher status 'in-group' or improving the social status of one's existing 'in-group'. These options often are not available, especially to minority groups, so conflict between groups arises. (**Tajfel's 1970** minimal groups experiment would be a useful source of research evidence here.)

Realistic conflict theory

Similarly to SIT, *realistic conflict theory (RCT)* (see page 396) sees prejudice as explaining the origins of conflict. RCT argues that conflict arises from social groups competing for resources that only one group can achieve, with 'out-group' members viewed through negative stereotypes and treated with hostility during the conflict. RCT also argues that conflict can be reduced by the formation of shared, interdependent goals (goals that have to be worked through together by all groups involved in a conflict). The action of cooperatively working towards a goal reduces negative stereotypes and hostility, and thus can resolve the conflict. (**Sherif's 1961** Robbers Cave study would be a useful source of research evidence here.)

▓ Methods of conflict resolution

> *'Peace is not the absence of conflict, but the ability to handle conflict by peaceful means.'*
> Mahatma Ghandi

Deutsch (1949a)

Morton Deutsch argues that constructive processes of resolving conflicts are similar in nature to the cooperative processes used in problem-solving. Deutsch's Crude Law of Social Relations (see page 383) can be used here to explain how to foster such cooperative processes; friendly, helpful, empathetic behaviours lead to cooperative responses by others, while hostile, suspicious and domineering behaviours provoke destructive competitive responses in others.

Deutsch sees cooperative behaviours as leading to constructive resolution of conflicts, with social support essential to creating and maintaining cooperative behaviours. He also sees constructive resolution as likelier when the individuals involved in a conflict can reframe their goals so that they become shared, interdependent ones. This means that the conflict then becomes a joint problem of groups involved in a conflict, so that the success of one group in reaching their goal becomes associated with other groups reaching their goals too. This can only occur if all groups engage in cooperative norms, such as honesty, respect for others, forgiveness, positivity and seeking common ground. These norms are based on shared values of equality, reciprocity (mutual benefits) and non-violence, which Deutsch believes can create common ground, even between very opposed groups.

Deutsch also argues that successful conflict management requires skills and knowledge. First are the skills necessary to create and maintain effective working relationships between groups involved in a conflict. Second are the skills required to sustain cooperative behaviours throughout a conflict, while third are the skills necessary for group problem-solving and decision-making.

Such skills for effective conflict management can be learned and must be expressed within an environment that is supportive of all involved groups, if cooperative attitudes and behaviours are to be maintained.

Three-step collaborative conflict resolution

- Step 1: *Recognition that there is a problem* – involves all concerned parties outlining what they think the problem consists of and suggesting what they want, with other parties listening. Should occur in a calm and respectful way.

  Suggestions should not be stated as criticisms of other parties and should be stated in a positive way. Listening should involve attempts to understand and empathize with other parties' perspectives without criticism.

- Step 2: *Exploration of underlying concerns* – involves all concerned parties outlining their fears, desires and other factors of importance to them. Again other parties listen and a calm respectful environment is required.

  A commitment is required by all parties to try and find a means of resolution by identifying factors that will achieve a resolution that is agreeable to all parties. This is achieved by attempting to understand other parties' concerns. Conflicts will need to be explored in depth rather than by trying to find a quick solution.

- Step 3: *Creation of mutually agreeable solution* – an agreed plan of action that meets the concerns of all parties is negotiated. In order to meet all parties' concerns, the eventual solution may not match what any party originally wanted, but will be seen as a win–win solution, not because one party got what it wanted (and the other didn't), but because it has addressed the concerns of all in a cooperative and respectful manner.

  All parties need to be receptive to new ideas and thinking should be positive so that solutions which address all parties' concerns can be created. This may require modification to suggestions that were outlined in step one. There also needs to be a belief that mutually agreeable resolutions can be found. Other parties should not be told what they need to do.

Interactive conflict resolution: Kelman (2008)

The interactive conflict resolution (ICR) approach uses trained conflict managers to resolve disputes between conflicting parties and is especially designed to resolve complex and lengthy disputes.

1 Talks initially take place with involved parties separately from each other, in order mainly to prepare the parties to be constructive in discussions with the other parties. This occurs in workshops where parties are shown cooperative means of interaction, such as being empathetic, respectful and seeking mutually agreeable goals, and are encouraged to resist negative forms of interaction, such as criticism, hostility, competitiveness and threatening behaviours.

2 Parties then progress on to discussions with each other, again in workshops supervised by trained conflict managers and conducted in a structured environment, with agreed norms of behaviour. Reasons for the conflict occurring are explored, particularly those concerning threatened needs for recognition, security, autonomy (independence) and justice.

3 Solutions are sought that meet the needs of all parties through taking part in joint problem-solving. Agreements are reached between the parties themselves, rather than having compromises imposed upon them by conflict managers. This increases the chances of long-term commitment to the resolution by all parties.

Research

- **Fisher (1997)** reviewed the use of workshops in ICR and found that they improved attitudes held by groups towards other groups involved in conflict disputes, as well as improving the complexity of thinking about conflicts and possible ways of resolving them. Workshops were also seen to improve levels of communication between disputing groups, which suggests that ICR is a valid means of resolving conflicts.

- **Freeman & Fisher (2012)** assessed the effectiveness of ICR in resolving a political uprising in India and in trying to establish peace between warring Turkish and Greek groups in Cyprus. In both disputes, workshops lasting several days were held, first with separate parties and then with both conflicting parties together. Progress was made in both disputes in establishing more cooperative behaviours and empathetic views between conflicting groups. This had the effect of preventing the disputes from escalating into destructive violent behaviour, though complete resolution of political differences and goals was not possible in either case. This suggests that ICR does have positive effects, especially in stabilizing conflicts, but that disputes which involve parties with very different values and beliefs are difficult to resolve.

- **Deutsch (1973)** reviewed several studies assessing the impact of cooperation and competition on conflict resolution, to find that while competition was associated with tactics of coercion, threats, deception, suspicion, hostility and attempts to highlight differences between groups, which did not lead to successful conflict resolution, cooperation was associated with stressing similarities in beliefs, helpfulness, trustworthiness, sensitivity, friendliness and de-emphasizing differences, which did lead to successful conflict resolution. This supports the Crude Law of Social Relations that cooperation and not competition provides the most effective route to solving disputes between groups.

- **Kriesberg (2003)** reviewed attempts to resolve several international conflicts, such as the struggle of the African National Council to overthrow apartheid in South Africa, the Zapatista uprising against the government in Mexico and the civil rights movement in Northern Ireland. It was found that persuasion, through the use of reasonable viewpoints and, to a lesser extent, rewards, through the promise of benefits to other groups, produced more effective resolutions than the use of coercion, where attempts were made to bully other groups into submission. This supports the idea that different behaviours arising from conflicts have different levels of success in resolving them.

- **Overton & Lowry (2013)** assessed the use of conflict management in health care, where conflicts often arise due to the high-pressure nature of the job. It was found that conflict management resulted in improved teamwork, productivity and patient and employee satisfaction. Improving communication skills between workers led to a 30 per cent improvement in the quality of work produced, a 40 per cent increase in productivity and a 50 per cent decrease in costs. Conflict management training did not reduce the number of conflicts, but impacted on how conflicts were perceived and handled, leading to fewer negative outcomes. The critical factors were seen to be encouraging compromise and collaboration, so that all concerned parties felt their needs were being addressed, and providing a structured 'safe' environment (one of mutual respect) for conflicts to be resolved within. This illustrates how when conflicts are successfully addressed, multiple benefits result to an organization and the individuals within it.

RESEARCH IN FOCUS

Explain the ethical considerations that would arise in conducting experimental studies into conflict resolution. What alternative research methods are more likely to be conducted in this area? What would be the strengths and weaknesses of conducting such studies?

▨ Evaluation

- ▨ **Gelfand & Brett (2004)** state that people in individualistic cultures tend to adopt a more confrontational, competitive viewpoint in conflicts than people from collectivist cultures, who are more concerned with establishing positive, cooperative relationships. This suggests there are important cultural differences to consider in understanding conflicts and their resolution.

- ▨ One of the unanswered questions in this area is whether it is possible to develop a general model of conflict resolution that can be applied across different types and levels of conflict; for instance, between romantic-relationship conflicts involving two individuals and political disputes involving groups of people with different political views and values. Kriesberg, one of the leading exponents in the field, cautions that there is no single formula for resolving conflict.

- ▨ When disputes involve parties with very different belief and value systems, it is extremely difficult to find common ground upon which to establish cooperative behaviours of trust, empathy and concern for the needs of others. The best that can often be hoped for in such situations is to stop the conflict from escalating any further into destructive levels of violence.

- ▨ It would be difficult to set up experimental studies of conflict resolution, as this would involve setting up artificial conflicts, which could create ethical issues of harm and deceit. Sherif's 'Robber's Cave' and Tajfel's 'Minimal Costs' studies did this to some extent and ethical issues resulted in both studies.

- ▨ One problem in assessing the effectiveness of conflict resolution methods is that success in resolving conflicts should be considered over the long-term. It may appear, in the immediate sense, that conflicts have been resolved, but then the conflict may arise again several years later, which would suggest that the underlying reasons for the conflict had not originally been successfully addressed. In Northern Ireland, 'The Good Friday Agreement' of 1998 seemed to have established peace between warring parties and the establishment of a power-sharing government at Stormont. Yet by 2017 this had broken down, resulting in the closing down of the Northern Ireland Parliament and the threat of a return to direct rule from England.

TOK link

To assess whether methods of conflict resolution work in the long-term would require longitudinal studies to be done. This involves conducting a study at regular intervals over a long period of time. In this way, trends can be seen (changes over time). However, participants are often reluctant to commit for such lengthy periods. Another problem is that of atypical sample attrition, where participants of one type drop out over time, making the results increasingly unrepresentative.

PSYCHOLOGY IN THE REAL WORLD

Research into conflict resolution has led to the establishment of many organizations who specialize in conflict resolution. For example, 'Relate' is a relationship counselling service that offers therapy, workshops and mediation services for couples experiencing romantic-relationship conflicts. They help 150,000 people a year in Britain, with 80 per cent of respondents reporting that the organization strengthened their relationships.

ACAS is an organization that successfully provides mediation for conflicts between employers and employees, such as those between management and trade unions. It also runs training courses for managers and human relations staff, with their work having been seen to boost productivity and profitability and improve harmony and motivation in the workplace, which has resulted in fewer future conflicts arising.

Strengthen your learning

1   What is a conflict?

2   Name and describe the four conditions that characterize conflicts.

3   Explain the two ways in which conflicts arise.

4   How does the environment they occur in affect conflicts?

5   Outline, in your own words, the basic types of behaviour that can arise from conflicts.

6   Explain how the following can explain the origins of conflict:
    a   social identity theory
    b   realistic conflict theory.

7   Outline the following methods of conflict resolution:
    a   Deutsch's Crude Law of Social Relations
    b   three-step collaborative conflict resolution
    c   interactive conflict resolution.

8   Summarize what research has suggested about the following as methods of conflict resolution:
    a   Deutsch's Crude Law of Social Relations
    b   three-step collaborative conflict resolution
    c   interactive conflict resolution.

9   What other evaluative points can be made about conflict resolution?

SECTION SUMMARY

- Conflicts are a natural product of human interactions and can be constructive or destructive.
- Social identity theory and realistic conflict theory can be used to explain the origin of conflicts.
- Conflicts are resolved through the use of cooperative processes, such as seen in the three-step collaborative conflict resolution and the interactive conflict resolution techniques.

■ Assessment check

1	Discuss cooperation and competition in human relationships.	(22 marks)
2	Discuss what research studies have suggested about cooperation and competition in human relationships.	(22 marks)
3	Evaluate explanations for prejudice and discrimination.	(22 marks)
4	Outline and evaluate research studies of prejudice and discrimination.	(22 marks)
5	Discuss origins of conflict and conflict resolution.	(22 marks)
6	Outline and evaluate methods of conflict resolution.	(22 marks)
7	Discuss what research studies have suggested about the origins of conflict and conflict resolution.	(22 marks)

IN THE NEWS

Ψ The Psychological Enquirer

THE INTERESTING CASE OF KLUGER HANS

Kluger Hans (Clever Hans in English) was a horse who had apparently been taught mathematics by his owner, Wilhelm Von Osten, and could perform simple arithmetic tasks, such as adding, subtracting, dividing and multiplying, by tapping out the correct answer with his hooves. There was no deliberate deception involved; Von Osten truly believed his horse had the ability to perform these sums. A panel of 13 experts headed by psychologist Carl Stumpf investigated Von Osten's claims and concluded in 1904 that the horse was genuine and no trickery was involved. Kluger Hans became front page news around the world, but further evaluation by Oskar Pfungst in 1907 found that Kluger Hans only answered correctly if his questioner knew the answer to the question being asked and if he could see Von Osten, his questioner. Eventually Pfungst realized the horse would stop tapping his hoof as, when he reached the right answer, Von Osten's eyebrows would go up.

■ **Figure 9.1** Many experts were convinced that Kluger Hans was a horse who truly had a knowledge of mathematics

The curious case of 'Kluger Hans' is a good example of the design-making decisions psychologists must make in order to devise research that produces valid results and allows greater understanding of the mind and behaviour, in this case the mind and behaviour of a horse.

The study demonstrates some of the problems psychologists may face and have to overcome in order to have results that truly show the effect of an IV upon a DV and not that of confounding variables. For example, with the study of 'Kluger Hans' there initially was observer bias (see Chapter 4, page 154), where an investigator's cognitive bias allows them to unconsciously influence participants' behaviour, often resulting in gaining the findings the researcher expects or desires to occur. Only by using a double-blind technique (see Chapter 4, page 150) can this problem be counteracted. If Kluger Hans's questioner did not know the answer to the written question he was holding up for the horse to read, or if the horse could not see his questioner, he could not demonstrate his seemingly intelligent behaviour.

Experimental study

FOCUS ON...

- The purpose of the internal assessment.
- Requirements for SL and HL students.
- Points to consider.
- Choosing an experiment.
- Dos and don'ts for the internal assessment.
- Where to locate information on the experimental method, types of experiment, experimental designs, ethical consideration and data analysis.
- An example study: Sheldrake's 'Experiments on the sense of being stared at' (1998).
- Writing up the report, including presentation, the title page, the introduction component, the exploration component, the analysis component, the evaluation component, references and appendices.
- The assessment criteria.

Introduction to the internal assessment

The purpose of the internal assessment is for students to get some hands-on experience of what it is to be a 'proper' psychologist by conducting some actual research for themselves. Not only should this activity be enjoyable and motivating in itself, but also it will demonstrate to students how psychology works, especially in helping to understand the essential role that research plays in the subject, and allow them to demonstrate skills and knowledge learned during the course. Students should also gain a familiarity with how research is used to evaluate psychological theories and explanations, allowing such explanations and theories to be either validated (accepted) or falsified (rejected).

SL/HL requirements

The requirements for SL and HL students are the same: to investigate a published study, theory or model relevant to their learning in psychology, by carrying out an experimental study and reporting the findings.

SL students

The report is worth 25 per cent of overall marks.

HL students

The report is worth 20 per cent of overall marks.

Points to consider

1 Students should seek advice from their teachers on what experiment to choose, what practical and ethical issues need to be considered and how their work will be assessed.

2 Students are required to work in groups of two to four students.

3 SL and HL students can work together.

4 Students can include in the group virtual (online) members of other schools who are studying IB psychology.

5 Members of the group can be students studying related courses, either IB or non-IB.

6 The research method, materials, participants and operationalization of the independent and dependent variables will be the same and result from the group working together.

7 Once data has been collected, each student should work independently of each other in writing up the research report, including the analysis of data and the conclusions drawn.

8 Students should discuss their internal assessment work with their teacher and should not be penalized (in terms of marks awarded) for doing so.

9   Teachers are allowed to give oral and written advice on how to improve the work for one draft of the study. The next version submitted is the final version and cannot be changed once it has been submitted.

10 The same piece of work cannot be submitted to meet the requirements of the internal assessment and the extended essay.

11 The research study cannot be of any other method than that of an experiment.

12 Students' work must be completely their own with no plagiarism occurring (presenting the work of another as your own). Referencing others' work (such as by describing previous relevant research) is allowable, as long as sources are credited.

13 Ethical considerations must be adhered to in planning, carrying out and writing up the report.

Choosing an experiment

1   The topic chosen can be from any area of psychology (not just those on the specification).

2   The theory or model on which the study is based must have appeared in a peer-reviewed journal.

3   The study or model used must be linked to the student's aims and objectives and the reason for conducting the experiment should be explained.

TOK link

Although psychology uses the experimental method, common to the natural sciences, there always remains the problem that the investigation of psychological phenomena is not merely confined to physically observable and measurable factors. For example, Sheldrake's belief that some people may have a psychic ability to detect unseen stares does not completely lend itself to a form of investigation that focuses solely on objective criteria.

Dos and don'ts for the internal assessment

1   In the internal assessment, students are only allowed to have one IV.

2   The study on which the experiment is based may have several conditions for the IV. Students can either replicate all the conditions, or simplify the experiment so that there are only two conditions.

3   The way in which the IV is operationalized may differ from the original study, in order to suit the specific circumstances of the study.

4   Variables that are based on pre-existing characteristics of participants are not acceptable for the internal assessment. These include:
    a   *Gender* (comparing the performance of males and females)
    b   *Age* (comparing participants of different age groups)
    c   *Native language* (comparing speakers of two different languages)
    d   *Culture* (comparing participants from different cultural groups)
    e   *Education* (comparing participants from different classes/schools)
    f   *Socio-economic status* (comparing participants of different wealth or class groupings)
    g   *Handedness* (comparing left- and right-handed participants)

5   Also not acceptable are experiments that include:
    a   *Placebos*
    b   *Ingestion and exhalation* (studies involving eating, drinking, smoking, taking drugs)
    c   *Deprivation* (studies involving denial of essential requirements, such as sleep or food)

Knowledge of experiments

Referral should be made to Chapter 4 in this book when designing and carrying out the study, and analysing the data produced, especially the sections covering the experimental method, types of experiments, types of experimental design, scientific processes (including ethical considerations) and data analysis.

EXAMPLE STUDY # SHELDRAKE (1998)

For the purposes of explaining what will be necessary for the internal assessment to be carried out, reference will be made to **Sheldrake's (1998)** laboratory experiment into whether or not people have the seemingly psychic ability to detect unseen stares.

Sheldrake (1994), from earlier work by **Titchener (1898)**, who reported the phenomenon whereby people feel a tingling sensation on their neck when being stared at, proposed the *'Alice Through the Looking-Glass'* theory of perception, where perception is seen as a two-way process involving a movement of light into the body and an outward projection from the body of mental images. He therefore saw the mind as being able to reach out and 'touch' the things we look at, so that people should be able to detect being stared at by an unseen person, due to the physical strains and pressures of the tendons, skin, muscles and joints being exerted by the person doing the staring. This led him to design and conduct a study whereby participants underwent 20 trials each, using more or less equal amounts of control (not being stared at) and experimental (being stared at) trials. Each trial lasted about 10 seconds and the order of control and experimental trials was presented as random sequences, with the experimenter who was present during the study unaware of the content of these sequences. The findings were subjected to statistical analysis and a significant difference was found beyond chance factors that led Sheldrake to conclude that the ability to detect unseen stares is a real phenomenon that gives support to his theory of perception.

Sheldrake's claims are, however, very controversial and have led to claims and counter-claims about the validity of his findings, mostly centring on his methodology (how he conducted his studies).

For more information on Sheldrake's work visit:

http://sheldrake.org
http://www.sheldrake.org/files/pdfs/papers/JCSpaper1.pdf
http://citeseerx.ist.psu.edu/viewdoc/download?doi=10.1.1.692.8890&rep=rep1&type=pdf

TOK link

Sheldrake's research into unseen stares is classed as a part of parapsychology, the study of extraordinary phenomena, and this branch of psychology highlights the important point that science must always study phenomena with an open mind and be ready to accept results that are contradictory to one's own beliefs. Pre-judgements about the impossibility of phenomena are as inappropriate in science as being biased in favour of such abilities existing.

Writing up the report

Once a practical has been designed, approved, carried out and made sense of through analysis, there comes the task of writing up the practical report. There is a set convention on how such reports are written, with the overriding principle that they are written up in such a way to permit replication by others wanting to check the reliability of results.

It is usual to write up research in continuous prose, in the past tense, avoiding slang terms/colloquialisms and with a clear, unambiguous writing style.

Presentation

1 The report should be between 1800 and 2200 words, not including the appendices.
2 The report should be divided into the following components:
   a *Title page* (not assessed, but essential for identification/verification purposes)
   b *Introduction*
   c *Exploration*
   d *Analysis*
   e *Evaluation*

f *References* (not assessed, but must be included for verification purposes)

g *Appendices* – should include: raw data tables, calculations/statistical test results, consent forms (unfilled), copy of standardization and debriefing notes and list of materials used

Title page

The title page should contain the following:

1 *Title of the investigation*
2 *IB candidate code*
3 *IB candidate codes for all group members*
4 *Day, month and year of submission*

The introduction component

The introduction component should contain the following:

The aims of the study

(See Chapter 4, page 161.)

An aim is a precise statement of why a study is taking place. It should include what is being studied and what the study is trying to achieve. **For example, the aim in Sheldrake's (1998) study was 'to investigate whether people have the ability to detect an unseen person staring at them'.**

The study on which the report is based

The study on which the experiment is based (or is a replication of) should be identified, explained and referenced. **For instance, Sheldrake's (1998) study was based upon Titchener's (1898) 'Alice Through the Looking-Glass' theory of perception.**

Literature review

Research studies and theories relevant to the experiment should be presented and explained, including their relevance to the experiment being undertaken. **For example, in Sheldrake's study, not only was Titchener's 'Alice Through the Looking-Glass' theory of perception explained, but also previous, relevant research studies and their findings, such as that of Poortman (1959) and Williams (1983), who both found that participants could detect if they were being stated at to an extent that was beyond the boundaries of chance.**

Hypotheses

The null and experimental (research) hypotheses should be clearly stated and should contain the independent variable and dependent variable in operationalized form.

The experimental hypothesis must be either directional (one-tailed) or non-directional (two-tailed). Directional hypotheses are used when previous research evidence suggests results will go in one particular direction, or when replicating a previous study that also used a directional hypothesis.

For example, in Sheldrake's study the directional (one-tailed) experimental hypothesis was:

'Participants will be significantly more able to detect whether an unseen person is staring at them.'

While the null hypothesis was:

'There will be no significant difference between the number of times participants can and cannot detect an unseen person staring at them.'

A directional (one-tailed) hypothesis was justified as most previous research suggested that participants would be able to detect being stared at to an extent that was beyond chance factors.

At the end of the study either the experimental or the null hypothesis will be accepted and the other one rejected.

◼ The exploration component

The exploration component should contain the following.

Experimental design

(See Chapter 4, page 166.)

TOK link

There is no 'best' type of experimental design and each should be considered in terms of its strengths and weaknesses. Repeated measures is often most favoured, as its strengths generally outweigh its weaknesses, especially as it is usually possible to counterbalance order effects, which is its main weakness. There are, however, situations where independent groups or matched pairs designs are best to use, but as with repeated measures there will always be drawbacks to consider.

The type of experimental design used should be included and justified. This will be one of the following: the repeated measures design, the independent groups design, or the matched pairs design. **For example, Sheldrake's unseen stares study used a repeated measures design as participants performed under both conditions of the IV.**

Sampling method and participants

(See Chapter 4, page 162.)

1   The type of sampling method should be identified and explained in terms of how it relates to the experiment being undertaken. This will probably be one of the following: random sampling, opportunity sampling, self-selected (volunteer) sampling, purposive sampling or snowball sampling; although other acceptable sampling methods could be utilized.

2   Relevant details of the sample should be included, such as overall number of participants, number of males and females, age range of participants, background of participants and what the target population was (the population that the sample represents/is drawn from). How participants were allocated to testing conditions should also be recorded.

   For example, Sheldrake (1998) used an opportunity sample of 160 children (80 male and 80 female), aged 8–16 years, made available to him from eight different schools in America and Germany and who were randomly allocated to experimental conditions.

TOK link

It is important when conducting research to create representative samples, ones that occur without bias in selection. The best way to accomplish this is to use random sampling. This is not as easy as it sounds, however, as humans are very poor at making random choices. If you ask ten people to randomly select a number between 1 and 10, each of the ten numbers should, theoretically, be chosen once, but certain numbers will be favoured more than others. The use of non-representative samples can seriously confound results, which is why unbiased methods of selection, such as names drawn from a hat, should always be used wherever possible.

Procedure

1   The procedure used in the study should be described in sufficient detail to allow full replication.

2   The use of standardized instructions, informed consent form, debriefing statement, and so on, should be referenced here, but the actual documents placed in the appendices.

3   Choice of materials used in conducting the study should be referenced and explained here. A list of all materials used should be placed in the appendices.

4   Ethical considerations, including how they were dealt with should be explained here. (See Chapter 4, page 168.)

5   The independent variable and dependent variable should be identified here in fully operationalized form. (See Chapter 4, page 149) **For example, in Sheldrake's (1998) study the IV was clearly operationalized as being whether an unseen person is staring at someone or not, while the DV was clearly operationalized as the number of times participants can or cannot detect unseen stares.**

6   The way in which extraneous variables were controlled to try and prevent them confounding the results should be detailed here. This should only include extraneous variables that were relevant to the experiment being undertaken. (See Chapter 4, page 149.)

In Sheldrake's study, for instance, if participants had received feedback (by being told whether each individual decision on whether they were being stared at, or not, was correct or wrong), then the feedback could have formed an extraneous variable of their being able to learn the supposedly random sequence of whether they were being stared at or not. This would have meant that the researchers could not be certain whether a participant's performance was due to the extraneous variable or to the effect of the manipulated IV on the DV. Results would have been confounded and worthless. This was easily controlled though, by participants not being given such feedback.

There potentially were demand characteristics (see Chapter 4, page 150) in Sheldrake's study, because in his study participants may answer 'yes' or 'no' in response to being asked whether an unseen person is staring at them, not because they believe their answers are true, but because they are nervous about being tested or because they wish to give the answer they think is required. Clearly stated standardized instructions were given to participants to explain to them the purpose of the study and how they should respond.

Observer bias (see Chapter 4, page 154) could have occurred in Sheldrake's study, because the researcher could unconsciously have suggested to a participant whether they should be saying 'yes' or 'no' in response to being asked if an unseen person was staring at them (see 'The interesting case of Kluger Hans', page 407). This was dealt with by use of a double-blind procedure (see Chapter 4, page 150) where the researcher, as well as the participants, was unaware of the randomized sequences of whether an unseen person was staring at them or not. Another researcher, who was not present during testing, produced the random sequences.

Also in Sheldrake's study, investigator effects (see Chapter 4, page 150) could possibly have occurred that biased the researchers' interpretation of data. For example, the researcher could interpret non-committal answers such as 'maybe he's staring' as a correct answer, thus increasing the chances of 'proving' their hypothesis. This was dealt with by standardized instructions clearly stating that participants' answers could only be 'yes' or 'no'.

TOK link

Researchers generally have expectations (and even preferences) about how research will turn out, but this can create a serious bias that acts to confound results. Sheldrake reports that when believers in the ability to detect unseen stares replicate his study, they tend to find the ability is real, while when sceptics perform the research they generally do not find evidence to support its existence. They cannot both be right. Only by conducting completely bias-free research can truly effective research ever be performed.

7   Details of any pilot study conducted (see Chapter 4, page 166) should be described here, including identification of extraneous variables and any procedural/methodological changes that were made as a result of conducting the pilot study.

In Sheldrake's study, pilot studies identified the extraneous variables described above and allowed changes to be made to the methodology to try and eliminate any confounding effect upon the measurement of the DV.

▨ The analysis component

1 The analysis component of the report details the use of descriptive and inferential statistics to analyse the results (see Chapter 4, pages 176 and 182).

2 An appropriate results table, which addresses the hypothesis, should be placed here, clearly titled and labelled. **For example, Sheldrake produced tables that showed the total number of correct and incorrect responses to questions asking participants whether they were being stared at.**

3 Appropriate graphs should be placed here, which address the hypothesis, clearly titled and labelled. **For example, Sheldrake used a bar chart to display findings, as the data were non-continuous.**

4 A statement of the measure(s) of central tendency should be placed here (calculations relevant to this should be referenced here and placed in the appendices). **For example, Sheldrake calculated mean scores for incorrect and correct responses.**

5 A statement of the measure of dispersion should be placed here (calculations relevant to this should be referenced here and placed in the appendices). **For example, Sheldrake used standard deviation in his calculations.**

6 Reporting of inferential statistics used, including justification for their use, should be located here. **For example, Sheldrake subjected his data to statistical analysis by use of a chi-squared inferential test, as he a) was looking for a difference between two conditions, b) used an independent groups design, and c) had a nominal level of data.**

7 The interpretation of statistical findings should be placed here, including critical value and significance level used, and be clearly linked to the hypotheses. **For example, Sheldrake reported his finding of participants being able to detect being stared at, or not, with 56.9 per cent accuracy and gave details of his chi-squared statistical analysis to show that this was beyond chance factors, which allowed him to reject his null hypothesis.**

TOK link

Experiments generate numerical data that is made sense of by statistical analysis, such as descriptive statistics (e.g. measures of central tendency and dispersion), as well as inferential statistical tests. Through this scientifically approved process, hypotheses are accepted or rejected, but is it ever really possible to take the emotional phenomenon of human experience and reduce it down to mere numbers? Does human experience always go beyond such simplistic analysis?

▨ The evaluation component

In the evaluation component, the findings from the study are discussed in comparison to the research/theory/model that the study is based upon. **For example, in Sheldrake's study the similarity in findings to those of Poortman (1959) were discussed, as well as other relevant research studies featured in the introduction.**

The discussion should also contain:

1 Interpretation of descriptive statistics. **For example, Sheldrake discussed how an accuracy level of 56.9 per cent in assessing whether a person was being stared at or not suggested that people do possess the ability to detect unseen stares. Additionally, Sheldrake discussed the fact that more participants (97) gave correct answers than those (42) giving wrong answers (with 21 giving an equal number of right and wrong answers) and that most people were better at detecting they were being stared at than not being stared at, and that these findings too supported the experimental hypothesis.**

2 Interpretation of inferential statistics. **For example, Sheldrake reported details of how his chi-squared analysis allowed him to reject his null hypothesis.**

3 Identification of limitations of the student's research in relation to the design, sample and procedure. **For example, Sheldrake discussed the possibility of how subtle cues, such as the use of peripheral vision (seeing out of the side of their eyes), may have allowed participants to see if they were being stared at or not.**

4   Suggestions for modification to address limitations of the student's research. **For example, Sheldrake suggested performing the research with blindfolded participants to remove the possibility of them using peripheral vision to detect whether they were being stared at or not.**

5   Ideas for future, related research. **For instance, Sheldrake suggested future research that investigated if the effect would still occur to the same significant degree if blindfolded participants were stared at through a closed window.**

6   Conclusions drawn from the findings. **For example, Sheldrake concluded that the results of his statistical analysis, and the fact that similar patterns of results were found in the eight different locations in which the study was carried out, suggest the ability to detect unseen stares is a real one and may have an evolutionary survival value in allowing animals to detect the presence of an unseen predator.**

References

The references are not assessed, but must be included for the report to be regarded as having been completed in the conventional manner and to avoid any suspicion of academic misconduct (not acknowledging the work and ideas of others).

Work cited within the report listed should be written in the standard expected format.
For example, as in Sheldrake's study:

Poortman, J.J. (1959) 'The feeling of being stared at', *Journal of the Society for Psychical Research* 40, 4–12.

Titchener, E.B. (1898) 'The feeling of being stared at', *Science New Series* 8, 895–7.

Appendices

The appendices are not considered in the total word count. Their inclusion is necessary so that all sources, calculations, materials, and so on, referenced in the study can be checked.

The appendices should include:

- *Raw data and calculations* (these can be in print-out or written form)
- *A list of materials used*
- *A copy of standardized instructions and debriefing statement*
- *A copy of a blank informed consent form*

Assessment criteria

The IB has assessment criteria against which practical reports will be judged, done internally by a teacher and later on externally by a moderator appointed by the exam board. Therefore, each section of the report should be written in a way that attempts to maximize attainment of the marks available for each assessment criterion. There are no differences in criteria between SL and HL students.

Listed below are the assessment criteria descriptors needed to secure all the available marks.

Introduction component (6 marks)

- The aim of the study is clearly stated and its relevance to the study explained.
- The theory/model upon which the study is based is described and a clear explanation of how it links to the study is provided.
- The independent variable and the dependent variable are appropriately stated and operationalized within the experimental or null hypotheses.

Exploration component (4 marks)

- The research design is explained.
- The sampling technique is explained.
- The choice of participants is explained.
- Controlled variables are explained.
- Choice of materials is explained.

Analysis (6 marks)

- Descriptive and inferential statistics have been appropriately and accurately applied.
- A graph has been appropriately presented that relates to the hypothesis.
- The statistical findings have been interpreted in relation to the data produced and linked to the hypothesis.

Evaluation (6 marks)

- The findings from the study have been discussed in relation to the theory/model upon which the study was based.
- Strengths and limitations of the design, sample and procedure, which are relevant to the study, are given and explained.
- Modifications are given, justified and explained that address the limitations of the study that have been identified.

Glossary

Abnormality – a psychological or behavioural state leading to impairment of interpersonal functioning and/or distress to others.

Absence of gating – the lack of limiting factors upon the formation of virtual relationships that form barriers to the creation of physical relationships.

Acculturation – the process by which an individual learns culturally appropriate behaviour and cultural norms for a new culture.

Action potentials – electrical activity which travels down the neuron. At the synapse, they may be transmitted to the next neuron, or they may be stopped.

Affordances – the quality of objects that permits actions to be carried out on them.

Aim – a precise statement of why a study is taking place.

Amygdala – brain area associated with the influence of emotion on cognitive processes.

Anorexia nervosa (AN) – an eating disorder characterized by an obsessive desire to lose weight by refusing to eat.

Articulatory process (AP) – part of the phonological acoustic store, allows sub-vocal repetition of information within the store.

Attachment – a close emotional bond to someone or something.

Attribution – the process by which individuals explain the causes of behaviour and events.

Attributional style – individuals who believe they influence events through personal effort are more able to develop prosocial behaviours.

Authoritarian personality – the idea that prejudice arises from the possession of certain characteristics nurtured in childhood.

Autonomy and control – the perception of anorexia nervosa as struggle for self-management, identity and effectiveness.

Batson's empathy–altruism theory – an explanation that sees helping behaviour as motivated by unselfish concern for the needs of others.

Behavioural categories – dividing target behaviours into subsets of behaviours through use of coding systems.

Behavioural therapies – treatment of mental disorders through modifying maladaptive behaviour by substitution of new responses.

Behaviourist explanation of OCD – the perception of the disorder as being learned from environmental interactions.

Biological approach – model of abnormality that perceives mental disorders as illnesses with physical causes.

Biological explanation of OCD – the perception of the disorder as determined by physiological means with treatments based upon chemical means.

Biological treatments – therapies based on the biological/medical model, which perceive cures as emanating from rectifying the physical problems that caused a disorder.

Biomedical – relates to both biology and medicine.

Bottom-up (direct) processing – perception that arises directly from sensory input without further cognitive processing.

Bystanders – people who witness events without intervening or offering assistance.

Capacity – the amount of information that can be stored at a given time.

Case studies – individual (or small group) cases that are unique in some way and therefore studied by researchers for that uniqueness.

Cell membrane – the outer covering of neurons. The cell membrane for neurons is composed of layers that allow it to transmit electrical impulses.

Central executive (CE) – oversees and coordinates the components of working memory.

Chunking – method of increasing STM capacity by grouping information into larger units.

Classical conditioning (CC) – an association between a previously neutral object/situation (stimulus) and a strong emotional response.

Clinical bias – systematic deviation from validity of diagnosis.

Cognitive approach – model of abnormality that perceives mental disorders as due to negative thoughts and illogical beliefs.

Cognitive behavioural therapy – treatment of mental disorders through modifying thought patterns in order to alter behavioural and emotional states.

Cognitive biases – illogical, systematic errors in thinking that negatively affect decision-making.

Cognitive development – the process by which thought and perception develops in an individual.

Cognitive explanation of anorexia nervosa/OCD – the perception of the disorder as resulting from maladaptive thought processes.

Cohesion – the degree of unity between members of a social group.

Collectivism – a perspective that emphasizes the well-being and needs of the group or nationality.

Communication – methods of sending and receiving information.

Competition – when two or more individuals struggle against each other for a goal that cannot be shared.

Compliance – publicly but not privately going along with majority influence to gain approval.

Compulsions – uncontrollable urges to repetitively perform tasks and behaviours.

Computerized axial tomography (CAT) – a brain imaging technique which gives a still picture of the brain, using X-rays.

Confabulation – the spontaneous production of false memories, which are believed to be true.

Confirmation bias – favouring information that supports an established belief.

Conflict – a dispute that arises over individuals holding incompatible viewpoints.

Conflict resolution – the means by which a peaceful solution is found to settle a dispute.

Conformity – yielding to group norms that discriminate in favour of 'in-group' members and against 'out-group' members.

Confounding variables – uncontrolled extraneous variables that negatively affect results.

Content analysis – a method of quantifying qualitative data through the use of coding units.

Cooperation – when two or more people work together towards the same end.

Correlational data – data produced from correlational studies.

Correlational studies – a research method that measures the strength of relationship between co-variables.

Co-variables – the variables measured in a correlation.

Critical period – a time restricted opportunity for development of a skill or characteristic.

Crude Law of Social Relations – the idea that cooperation leads individuals to being cooperative again in the future, while being competitive leads to more competitive behaviour in the future.

Cue-utilization theory – an explanation that sees high levels of emotion focusing attention on the emotionally arousing elements of an environment, so that these elements become encoded in memory and not the non-emotionally arousing elements.

Cultural bias – the tendency to over-diagnose members of other cultures as suffering from mental disorders.

Cultural relativism – the idea that definitions of what is normal functioning vary from culture to culture and have equal validity.

Culture – the shared set of beliefs, norms, and values that groups possess.

Day care – care provided for children while their parents are occupied, usually at work. Day care can include nurseries, nannies and childminders.

Decision-making – a cognitive process involving making a choice from available options.

Deep-brain stimulation – a non-invasive physical means of treating mental disorders through the application of magnetic pulses to specific brain areas.

Demand characteristics – a research effect where participants form impressions of the research purpose and unconsciously alter their behaviour accordingly.

Dependent variable (DV) – the factor measured by researchers in an investigation.

Deviation from ideal mental health – failure to meet the criteria for perfect psychological well-being.

Deviation from social norms – behaviour that violates a society's accepted rules.

Diagnosis – identification of the nature and cause of a mental disorder.

Diathesis-stress explanation of OCD – the perception that the disorder results from a combination of factors that include both nature and nurture elements.

Digital amnesia – the tendency for individuals to forget information that has been stored on digital devices.

Digital technology (DT) – electronic devices and systems that generate, process and store data.

Discrimination – treating someone in an unfair manner based on their sex, race, age, etc.

Dissolution – the process by which romantic relationships breakdown.

Distortions – the idea that faulty thinking negatively affects perceptions of body image.

Drug therapy – treatment of mental disorders by chemical means.

DSM-V – diagnostic classification system produced and used in the USA.

Duck's phase model – an explanation that sees dissolution occurring through a series of four sequential stages.

Duration – the length of time information remains within storage.

Eclectic treatments – the use of multiple therapies in the treatment of mental disorders.

Electroconvulsive therapy (ECT) – treatment of mental disorders by application of electrical voltages across the brain.

Electroencephalography (EEG) – a method of measuring brain activity using electrodes attached to the scalp.

Emic – when the researcher conducts research within their own culture and has a relativist viewpoint (an insider's viewpoint). They therefore do not generalize the findings to other cultures.

Emotion – a state of mind determined by one's mood.

Emotional well-being – individuals with positive mental health are more able to develop prosocial behaviours.

Empathy – the ability to understand and experience or share the feelings of others.

Encoding – the means by which information is represented in memory.

Enculturation – the process by which an individual learns culturally appropriate behaviour and cultural norms of their own culture.

Enmeshment – a family interactive style that inhibits each family member's sense of individuality.

Episodic buffer (EB) – temporary store of integrated information from the central executive, phonological loop, visuospatial sketchpad and LTM.

Episodic memory (EM) – a form of LTM for events occurring in an individual's life.

Equity theory – an economic explanation of relationships based on motivation to achieve fairness and balance.

Ethical issues – the rules governing the conduct of researchers in investigations.

Etic – when a researcher conducts research outside of their culture and holds a universalist perspective. This then becomes an imposed etic (an outsider's viewpoint).

Evolution – the process of adaptation through natural selection.

Evolutionary explanation of anorexia nervosa/OCD – the perception of the disorder as being acted upon by natural selection through having an adaptive survival value.

Experimental method – a research method using random allocation of participants and the manipulation of variables to determine cause and effect.

Extraneous variables – variables other than the IV that might affect the DV.

Extrapolation – the term used when findings of animal research are used to help explain human behaviour.

Eyewitness testimony – the recall of observers of events previously experienced.

Failure to function adequately – an inability to cope with day-to-day living.

Family systems theory (FST) – the perception that anorexia nervosa results from dysfunctional patterns of family interaction.

Field experiment – experiment conducted in a naturalistic environment where the researchers manipulate the independent variable.

Flashbulb memory – a strong, vivid memory of an event with a high emotional impact.

Functional magnetic resonance imaging (fMRI) – a brain imaging technique involving detection of differences in magnetization between poor or rich oxygenated blood flow.

Fundamental attribution bias – the tendency to see favourable outcomes as being a result of actions under our control and unfavourable outcomes as being due to factors not under our control.

Game theory – an explanation of social behaviour that focuses on how individuals interact cooperatively and competitively in the pursuit of goals.

Gender development – the process by which gender identity can be formed.

Gender identity – our experience of our own gender. This can be the same as the one assigned at birth, or in some cases, may not be.

Genetic explanation of anorexia nervosa/OCD – the perception of the disorder as resulting from an inherited predisposition.

Globalization – global trade, cooperation and geographical mobility across cultures.

Glocalization – the adaptation of globalization to the local environment.

Graphs – easily understandable, pictorial representations of data.

Green beard genes – genes that allow a bearer to recognize a difference in themselves from others and to behave positively towards other individuals with that difference.

Group dynamics – the positive and negative forces operating within groups of people.

Hamilton's kin selection theory – an explanation that sees helping behaviour as directed at increasing the reproductive chances of genetically related individuals.

Heuristics – making decisions by the use of mental short-cuts that focus on one aspect of a problem while ignoring others.

High self-esteem – those with elevated levels of self-worth are more able to develop prosocial behaviours.

Hindsight bias – the tendency to see an event as having been predictable, even though there was no information for predicting this occurrence at all.

Holistic – consideration of the whole person, including psychological and social factors as well as biological symptoms.

Horizon ratios – invariant sensory information concerning the position of objects in relation to the horizon.

Hormones – chemical messengers released from glands throughout the body.

Human reproductive behaviour – the different mating strategies used by males and females.

Hypothesis – precise, testable research prediction.

ICD-10 – diagnostic classification system produced by the World Health Organization and used in Great Britain.

Identification – public and private acceptance of majority influence in order to gain group acceptance.

Illusion of control – the idea that people's understanding of a situation is illogical in order for them to believe they can influence external events.

Independent groups design (IGD) – experimental design in which each participant performs one condition of an experiment.

Independent variable (IV) – the factor manipulated by researchers in an investigation.

Individualism – a perspective that emphasizes the well-being and needs of the individual.

Inductive content (thematic) analysis – a method of qualitative research linked to content analysis, which involves analysing text in a variety of media to identify the patterns within it. A coding system may be needed to sort the data and to help to identify patterns.

Inferential testing – statistical procedures that make predictions about populations from mathematical analysis of data taken from samples.

In-group – the group an individual belongs to.

Inner scribe (IS) – part of the VSS, stores information about the physical relationships of items.

Insufficient anchoring judgement – the tendency to not update decisions as new information becomes available.

Internal working model – an internal schema, or idea, that is formed through experience as a blue print for attachment style.

Inter-observer reliability – where observers consistently code behaviour in the same way.

Internalization – public and private acceptance of majority influence due to adoption of the majority's belief system.

Interviews – self-report method where participants answer questions in face-to-face situations.

Investigator effects – a research effect where researcher features influence participants' responses.

Irrational beliefs – the notion that maladaptive ideas lead to the development and maintenance of anorexia nervosa.

Laboratory experiment – experiment conducted in a controlled environment allowing the establishment of causality.

Lee's stage model – an explanation that sees dissolution occurring through a series of five sequential stages.

Leptin – a hormone produced by fat cells associated with the regulation of energy intake and expenditure.

Long-term memory (LTM) – a permanent store holding limitless amounts of information for long periods.

Magnetic resonance imaging (MRI) – a still picture of the brain which can inform on the structure. The pictures are compiled using the measurement of radio frequency.

Matched pairs design (MPD) – experimental design where participants are in similar pairs, with one of each pair performing each condition.

Matching hypothesis – the idea that individuals are unconsciously motivated to form romantic relationships with those of perceived similar attractiveness.

Maternal deprivation – separation from a mother figure.

Measures of central tendency – methods of estimating mid-point scores in sets of data.

Measures of dispersion – measurements of the spread of scores within a set of data.

Media – public forms of communication.

Meta-analysis – a statistical technique of combining the findings of several similar studies to give a more typical overview.

Minding the close relationship – the idea that in healthy relationships individuals mutually take care to make positive, but accurate attributions about their partners.

Misleading information/questions – information or questions that suggest a desired answer.

Modelling – where learning occurs vicariously by experience through observation of others.

Mood-congruence effect – the ability of individuals to retrieve information more easily when it has the same emotional content as their current emotional state.

Mood-state dependent retrieval – the ability of individuals to retrieve information more easily when their emotional state at the time of recall is similar to their emotional state at the time of encoding.

Multi-store model (MSM) – an explanation of memory that sees information flowing through a series of storage systems.

Mundane realism – the extent to which findings of studies can be generalized to real-life settings.

Myth of multitasking – the false belief that humans can simultaneously perform cognitive tasks.

Natural experiment – experiment where the independent variable varies naturally.

Naturalistic observations – surveillance and recording of naturally occurring events.

Neural explanation of anorexia nervosa/OCD – the perception of the disorder as arising from abnormally functioning brain mechanisms.

Neural transmission – the way the signal is transmitted down the neuron to the next synapse.

Neuron – the way the brain can transmit activation. There are billions of neurons in the human brain.

Neuroplasticity – the ability of the nervous system, especially the brain, to adapt to the environment and to replace function following damage.

Neuroticism – a personality characteristic that is characterized by high levels of worry, anxiety and depressed mood.

Neurotransmitters – biochemicals found within the brain that play an important part in transmitting messages from neuron to neuron.

Nomothetic – the idea that people can be regarded as groups and theories/explanations are therefore generalizable.

Normal distribution – data with an even distribution of scores either side of the mean.

Normative social influence – a motivational force to be liked and accepted by a group.

Obsessions – forbidden or inappropriate ideas and visual images leading to feelings of extreme anxiety.

Obsessive-compulsive disorder (OCD) – anxiety disorder characterized by persistent, recurring, unpleasant thoughts and repetitive, ritualistic behaviours.

Operant conditioning (OC) – learning due to the positive or negative consequences of the behaviour.

Operationalization of variables – the process of defining variables into measureable factors.

Optical array – the structure of patterned light received by the eyes.

Optic flow patterns – unambiguous sources of information that directly inform perception.

Out-group – the groups that an individual is not a member of.

Oxytocin – a hormone which is implicated in maternal behaviours and attachment formation.

Perception – the interpretation of sensory data.

Perceptual defence – the process by which stimuli are not perceived or are distorted due to their threatening or offensive nature.

Personal relationships – close connections formed between people through emotional bonds and interactions.

Perspective taking – individuals who can perceive the viewpoints of others are more able to develop prosocial behaviours.

Phonological loop (PL) – component of the WMM that deals with auditory information.

Physical attractiveness – the degree to which an individual's external characteristics are considered pleasing or beautiful.

Pilot studies – small-scale practice investigations.

Placebo effect – where improvement in a patient's condition is due to expectation of improvement rather than any actual therapeutic effect.

Positron emission tomography (PET) – a brain imaging method that gives a moving picture of brain activity. This is achieved by tracking radiation levels in the brain.

Post-event information – misleading information added to an event after it has occurred.

Poverty – a lack of resources and means to be able to meet personal needs. People who are in poverty have low socio-economic status.

Prejudice – an unfair or unreasonable idea or feeling that is not based on fact.

Primary acoustic store (PAS) – part of the phonological loop, stores words heard.

Probability – the likelihood of events being determined by chance.

Procedural memory (PM) – type of LTM for the performance of particular types of action.

Prosocial behaviour – behaviour that is intended to benefit others.

Prosocial moral behaviour – individuals whose actions are based on belief systems centred on the welfare of others are more able to develop prosocial behaviours.

Psychodynamic explanation of OCD – the perception of the disorder as resulting from unresolved traumatic experiences occurring during psychosexual stages of development in childhood.

Psychodynamic therapy – treatment of mental disorders through identifying childhood traumatic experiences and resolving them.

Psychological treatments – therapies based on non-biological explanations of mental disorders, which focus on remedying psychological factors associated with disorders.

Psychosomatic – when a health condition may be caused, or made worse, by a mental factor such as internal conflict or stress.

Psychosurgery – treatment of mental disorders by irreversible destruction of brain tissue.

Psychoticism – a personality characteristic that is characterized by high levels of aggressiveness and hostility to others.

Qualitative data – non-numerical data expressing meanings, feelings and descriptions.

Quantitative data – data occurring in numerical form.

Quasi-experiment – experiment where the independent variable occurs naturally without manipulation from the researcher.

Questionnaires – self-report method where participants record their own answers to a preset list of questions.

Realistic conflict theory (RCT) – the idea that prejudice arises through competition between 'in' and 'out' groups over valuable resources.

Reciprocal determinism – a term defined by Bandura as the way an individual affects their environment and vice versa.

Reconstructive memory – the phenomenon by which memories are not accurate versions of events experienced, but instead are built from schemas active at the time of recall.

Reinforcement – the consequence of a behaviour that strengthens (increases) the chances of it occurring again.

Relativism – the viewpoint that behaviour is culture-dependent and therefore not generalizable across cultures.

Reliability – the extent to which a test or measurement produces consistent results.

Reliability of diagnosis – the consistency of diagnosis.

Reliability of memory – the extent to which memory produces consistent results.

Repeated measures design (RMD) – experimental design where each participant performs all conditions of an experiment.

Replicability – being able to repeat a study to check the validity of the results.

Repression – a form of motivated forgetting where emotionally threatening memories are hidden in the unconscious mind to prevent feelings of anxiety.

Research methods – the means by which explanations are tested.

Resilience – a characteristic that allows an individual to recover quickly and successfully from difficulties.

Role model – an individual looked to by others as someone to imitate.

Rusbult's investment model – an explanation that sees relationship satisfaction as dependent upon a consideration of perceived benefits, costs and the quality of possible alternative relationships.

Sampling – the selection of participants to represent a wider population.

Schema – a readiness to interpret sensory information in a preset manner.

Self-disclosure (SD) – the revealing of personal information about oneself to another.

Self-report techniques – participants giving information about themselves without researcher interference.

Self-serving bias – favouring information that displays oneself in a favourable way.

Semantic memory (SM) – type of LTM for meanings, understandings, and other concept-based knowledge.

Sensory memory (SM) – a short-duration store holding impressions of information received by the senses.

Sexual selection – the selection of characteristics that increase reproductive success.

Short-term memory (STM) – a temporary store holding small amounts of information for brief periods.

Significance levels – statistical criteria determining if observed differences/relationships are beyond the boundaries of chance.

Social development – the process by which interaction with and understanding of others develops in an individual.

Social exchange theory – an economic explanation of relationships based on maximizing profits and minimizing costs.

Social identity theory (SIT) – the idea that individuals discriminate positively towards 'in-group'

members and against 'out-group' members.

Social learning theory (SLT) of anorexia nervosa – the perception of the disorder as being learned through observation and imitation.

Social loafing – the phenomenon of people exerting less individual effort in a group than when on their own.

Social role – a pattern of behaviours, beliefs and norms that an individual will adopt if given a role in society.

Sociocultural approach – model of abnormality that perceives mental disorders as determined by social and cultural environments.

Statistical infrequency – exhibiting behaviours that numerically are rare.

Stereotypes – a collection of beliefs or attitudes held towards someone due to their membership of a group.

Stereotyping – a type of cognitive bias that concerns grouping types of individuals together on the incorrect basis that they all possess the same quality.

Synapse – the small fluid-filled gap between neurons which is essential for transmission of the nerve signals.

Synaptic transmission – the process of signal from neuron to neuron.

Testosterone – a hormone that is an androgen (a male hormone). It is generally found in lower levels in the female population than it is in men.

Texture gradient – surface patterns that provide sensory information about objects.

Thinking – the actions of the conscious mind to interpret, plan and make predictions about the world around us.

Top-down (indirect) processing – perception that involves cognitive processing that goes beyond mere sensory input.

Toxins – poisonous substances that are in the environment or in substances that may be ingested.

Type I errors – when a difference/relationship in a data set is accepted as a real one and is not.

Type II errors – when a difference/relationship in a data set is rejected, but actually does exist.

Universalism – the viewpoint that all humans are the same and behaviour is generalizable globally.

Validity – the extent to which results accurately measure what they are supposed to measure.

Validity of diagnosis – the accuracy of diagnosis.

Virtual relationships (VRs) – non-physical interactions between people communicating via social media.

Visual cache (VC) – part of the VSS, stores information about form and colour.

Visuospatial sketchpad (VSS) – component of the WMM that deals with visual information and the physical relationship of items to each other.

Working memory model (WMM) – an explanation that sees short-term memory as an active store holding several pieces of information simultaneously.

Xenophobic – a dislike of people from other countries.

References

Chapter 1

Andics, A., Gácsi, M., Faragó, T., Kis, A. and Miklósi, Á. (2014) Voice-sensitive regions in the dog and human brain are revealed by comparative fMRI. *Current Biology*, 24(5), 574–578.

Andrews-McClymont, J.G., Lilienfeld, S.O. and Duke, M.P. (2013) Evaluating an animal model of compulsive hoarding in humans. *Review of General Psychology*, 17(4), 399–419.

Aspinall, P., Mavros, P., Coyne, R. and Roe, J. (2015) The urban brain: analysing outdoor physical activity with mobile EEG. *British Journal of Sports Medicine*, 49(4), 272–276.

Azari, N.P., Nickel, J., Wunderlich, G., Niedeggen, M., Hefter, H., Tellmann, L., *et al.* (2001) Neural correlates of religious experience. *European Journal of Neuroscience*, 13(8), 1649–1652.

Bateson, P., Biggs, P., Cuthbert, A., Cuthill, I., Festing, M., Keverne, E.B., *et al.* (2004) *The Use of Nonhuman Animals in Research: A Guide for Scientists*. London: The Royal Society.

Beltz, A.M., Swanson, J.L. and Berenbaum, S.A. (2011) Gendered occupational interests: prenatal androgen effects on psychological orientation to Things versus People. *Hormonal Behaviour*, 60(4), 313–317.

Bennett, A.J. (2012) Animal research: the bigger picture and why we need psychologists to speak out. *Psychological Science Agenda*, April, 162–174.

Bombari, D., Preuss, N. and Mast, F.W. (2014) Lateralized processing of faces. *Swiss Journal of Psychology*, 73, 215–224.

Bouton, C.E., Shaikhouni, A., Annetta, N.V., Bockbrader, M.A., Friedenberg, D.A., Nielson, D.M., *et al.* (2016) Restoring cortical control of functional movement in a human with quadriplegia. *Nature*, 533(7602), 247–250.

Brunner, H.G., Nelen, M., Breakefield, X.O., Ropers, H.H. and Van Oost, B.A. (1993) Abnormal behavior associated with a point mutation in the structural gene for monoamine oxidase A. *Science*, 262, 578–578.

Buss, D.M. (1989) Sex differences in human mate preferences: evolutionary hypotheses tested in 37 cultures. *Behavioral and Brain Sciences*, 12(1), 1–14.

Campbell, A. (2008) Attachment, aggression and affiliation: the role of oxytocin in female social behavior. *Biological Psychology*, 77(1), 1–10.

Cases, O., Seif, I., Grimsby, J., Gaspar, P., Chen, K., Pournin, S., *et al.* (1995) Aggressive behavior and altered amounts of brain serotonin and norepinephrine in mice lacking MAOA. *Science*, 268(5218), 1763–1766.

Clancy, B., Finlay, B.L., Darlington, R.B. and Anand, K.J.S. (2007) Extrapolating brain development from experimental species to humans. *Neurotoxicology*, 28(5), 931–937.

Clapcote, S.J., Lipina, T.V., Millar, J.K., Mackie, S., Christie, S., Ogawa, F., *et al.* (2007) Behavioral phenotypes of Disc1 missense mutations in mice. *Neuron*, 54(3), 387–402.

Clarke, S., Assal, G. and de Tribolet, N. (1993) Left hemisphere strategies in visual recognition, topographical orientation and time planning. *Neuropsychologia*, 31(2), 99–113.

Collins, K. and Mohr, C. (2013) Performance of younger and older adults in lateralised right and left hemisphere asymmetry tasks supports the HAROLD model. *Laterality: Asymmetries of Body, Brain and Cognition*, 18(4), 491–512.

Conner, R.L. and Levine, S. (1969) The effects of adrenal hormones on the acquisition of signaled avoidance behavior. *Hormones and Behavior*, 1(1), 73–83.

Conroy-Beam, D., Buss, D.M., Pham, M.N. and Shackelford, T.K. (2015) How sexually dimorphic are human mate preferences? *Personality and Social Psychology Bulletin*, 41(8), 1082–1093.

Crisp, A.H., Hall, A. and Holland, A.J. (1985) Nature and nurture in anorexia nervosa: a study of 34 pairs of twins, one pair of triplets, and an adoptive family. *International Journal of Eating Disorders*, 4(1), 5–27.

Czaczkes, T.J., Grüter, C., Ellis, L., Wood, E. and Ratnieks, F.L. (2013) Ant foraging on complex trails: route learning and the role of trail pheromones in Lasius niger. *Journal of Experimental Biology*, 216(2), 188–197.

Danelli, L., Cossu, G., Berlingeri, M., Bottini, G., Sberna, M. and Paulesu, E. (2013) Is a lone right hemisphere enough? Neurolinguistic architecture in a case with a very early left hemispherectomy. *Neurocase*, 19(3), 209–231.

Davis, K.L., Kahn, R.S. and Davidson, M. (1991) Dopamine in schizophrenia: a review and reconceptualization. *The American Journal of Psychiatry*, 148(11), 1474–1486.

Daw, N. (2012) *How Vision Works: The Physiological Mechanisms Behind What We See*. Oxford: Oxford University Press.

Dawkins, M.S. (1990) From an animal's point of view: motivation, fitness, and animal welfare. *Behavioral and Brain Sciences*, 13(1), 1–9.

De la Plata, C.D.M., Hart, T., Hammond, F.M., Frol, A.B., Hudak, A., Harper, C.R., *et al.* (2008) Impact of age on long-term recovery from traumatic brain injury. *Archives of Physical Medicine and Rehabilitation*, 89(5), 896–903.

Domanski, C.W. (2013) Mysterious 'Monsieur Leborgne': the mystery of the famous patient in the history of neuropsychology is explained. *Journal of the History of the Neurosciences*, 22(1), 47–52.

Dundas, E.M., Plaut, D.C. and Behrmann, M. (2015) Variable left-hemisphere language and orthographic lateralization reduces right-hemisphere face lateralization. *Journal of Cognitive Neuroscience*, 27(5), 913–925.

Fuhrmann, D., Knoll, L.J. and Blakemore, S.J. (2015) Adolescence as a sensitive period of brain development. *Trends in Cognitive Sciences*, 19(10), 558–566.

Gerra, G., Avanzini, P., Zaimovic, A., Sartori, R., Bocchi, C., Timpano, M., *et al.* (1999) Neurotransmitters, neuroendocrine correlates of sensation-seeking temperament in normal humans. *Neuropsychobiology*, 39(4), 207–213.

Gottesman, I.I., McGuffin, P. and Farmer, A.E. (1987) Clinical genetics as clues to the 'real' genetics of schizophrenia (a decade of modest gains while playing for time). *Schizophrenia Bulletin*, 13(1), 23–48.

Hare, R.M., Schlatter, S., Rhodes, G. and Simmons, L.W. (2017) Putative sex-specific human pheromones do not affect gender perception, attractiveness ratings or unfaithfulness judgements of opposite sex faces. *Royal Society Open Science*, 4(3), 160831.

Harlow, H.F. (1959) The development of learning in the rhesus monkey. *American Scientist*, 47, 459–479.

Harlow, H.F. and Harlow, M.K. (1969) Effects of various mother-infant relationships on rhesus monkey behaviors. *Determinants of Infant Behavior*, 4, 15–36.

Healy, D. (2015) Serotonin and depression. *BMJ*, 350, h1771.

Hettema, J.M., Neale, M.C. and Kendler, K.S. (2001) A review and meta-analysis of the genetic epidemiology of anxiety disorders. *American Journal of Psychiatry*, 158(10), 1568–1578.

Hodgkin, A.L. and Huxley, A.F. (1952) A quantitative description of membrane current and its application to conduction and excitation in nerve. *Journal of Physiology*, 117(4), 500–544.

Hooijmans, C.R., Leenaars, M. and Ritskes-Hoitinga, M. (2010) A gold standard publication checklist to improve the quality of animal studies, to fully integrate the Three Rs, and to make systematic reviews more feasible. *Alternatives to Lab Animals*, 38(2), 167–182.

Hu, L. (2016) Functional reorganization of the primary somatosensory cortex of a phantom limb pain patient. *Pain Physician*, 19, E781–E786.

Hugdahl, K. and Westerhausen, R. (eds) (2010) *The Two Halves Of The Brain: Information Processing in the Cerebral Hemispheres.* Cambridge, MA: MIT Press.

Hummer, T.A. and McClintock, M.K. (2009) Putative human pheromone androstadienone attunes the mind specifically to emotional information. *Hormones and Behavior*, 55(4), 548–559.

Hyde, K.L., Lerch, J., Norton, A., Forgeard, M., Winner, E., Evans, A.C., *et al.* (2009) The effects of musical training on structural brain development. *Annals of the New York Academy of Sciences*, 1169(1), 182–186.

Kandel, E.R. and Squire, L.R. (2000) Neuroscience: breaking down scientific barriers to the study of brain and mind. *Science*, 290(5494), 1113–1120.

Kawai, R., Markman, T., Poddar, R., Ko, R., Fantana, A.L., Dhawale, A.K., *et al.* (2015) Motor cortex is required for learning but not for executing a motor skill. *Neuron*, 86(3), 800–812.

Kellogg, W.N. and Kellogg, L.A. (1933) *The Ape and the Child: A Study of Environmental Influence on Early Behaviour.* New York and London: McGraw-Hill.

Kennedy, J.S. (1992) *The New Anthropomorphism.* Cambridge, UK: Cambridge University Press.

Kirkpatrick, M.G., Lee, R., Wardle, M.C., Jacob, S. and De Wit, H. (2014) Effects of MDMA and intranasal oxytocin on social and emotional processing. *Neuropsychopharmacology*, 39(7), 1654–1663.

Klinteberg, B.A. and Magnusson, D. (1989) Aggressiveness and hyperactive behaviour as related to adrenaline excretion. *European Journal of Personality*, 3(2), 81–93.

Komori, M., Kawamura, S. and Ishihara, S. (2009) Averageness or symmetry: which is more important for facial attractiveness? *Acta Psychologica*, 131(2), 136–142.

Lorenz, K. (1935) Der kumpan in der umwelt des vogels. *Journal für Ornithologie*, 83(3), 289–413.

Low, P., Panksepp, J., Reiss, D., Edelman, D., Van Swinderen, B. and Koch, C. (2012, July) The Cambridge declaration on consciousness. *Francis Crick Memorial Conference,* Cambridge, UK, 7 July.

Lycett, J.E. and Dunbar, R.I. (2000) Mobile phones as lekking devices among human males. *Human Nature*, 11(1), 93–104.

Mason, G.J. (1991) Stereotypies: a critical review. *Animal Behaviour*, 41(6), 1015–1037.

Mazur, A. (1983) Hormones, aggression, and dominance in humans. In B.B. Svare (ed.) *Hormones and Aggressive Behavior* (pp. 563–576). New York: Plenum Press.

McMahon, C.R., Harcourt, R., Bateson, P. and Hindell, M.A. (2012) Animal welfare and decision making in wildlife research. *Biological Conservation*, 153, 254–256.

Mehta, P.H. and Beer, J. (2010) Neural mechanisms of the testosterone–aggression relation: the role of orbitofrontal cortex. *Journal of Cognitive Neuroscience*, 22(10), 2357–2368.

Moeller, F., Dougherty, D.M., Swann, A.C., Collins, D., Davis, C.M. and Cherek, D.R. (1996) Tryptophan depletion and aggressive responding in healthy males. *Psychopharmacology*, 126(2), 97–103.

Mostafa, T., El Khouly, G. and Hassan, A. (2012) Pheromones in sex and reproduction: do they have a role in humans? *Journal of Advanced Research*, 3(1), 1–9.

Nesse, R.M. and Williams, G.C. (1995) *Why We Get Sick.* New York: Times Books.

Ohlson, K. (2002) It takes two: studying twins is still a vital tool for 21st-century geneticists, even with the human genome map at their fingertips. Kristin Ohlson gets stuck into the nature-nurture debate. *New Scientist*, 176(2363), 42–45.

Overgaard, M. (2011) Visual experience and blindsight: a methodological review. *Experimental Brain Research*, 209(4), 473–479.

Passamonti, L., Crockett, M.J., Apergis-Schoute, A.M., Clark, L., Rowe, J.B., Calder, A.J., *et al.* (2012) Effects of acute tryptophan depletion on prefrontal-amygdala connectivity while viewing facial signals of aggression. *Biological Psychiatry*, 71(1), 36–43.

Peck, J.A. and Ranaldi, R. (2014) Drug abstinence: exploring animal models and behavioral treatment strategies. *Psychopharmacology*, 231(10), 2045–2058.

Pinto, Y., Neville, D.A., Otten, M., Corballis, P.M., Lamme, V.A., de Haan, E.H., *et al.* (2017) Split brain: divided perception but undivided consciousness. *Brain*, 140(5), 1231–1237.

Pitman, R.K. (1989) Animal models of compulsive behavior. *Biological Psychiatry*, 26(2), 189–198.

Ratcliff, J.J., Greenspan, A.I., Goldstein, F.C., Stringer, A.Y., Bushnik, T., Hammond, F.M., *et al.* (2007) Gender and traumatic brain injury: do the sexes fare differently? *Brain Injury*, 21(10), 1023–1030.

Russell, M.J., Switz, G.M. and Thompson, K. (1980) Olfactory influences on the human menstrual cycle. *Pharmacology Biochemistry and Behavior*, 13(5), 737–738.

Santana, E.J. (2016) The brain of the psychopath: a systematic review of structural neuroimaging studies. *Psychology and Neuroscience*, 9(4), 420–443.

Schwarz, S. and Hassebrauck, M. (2012) Sex and age differences in mate-selection preferences. *Human Nature*, 23(4), 447–466.

Sperry, R.W. (1968) Hemisphere deconnection and unity in conscious awareness. *American Psychologist*, 23(10), 723–733.

Stelzer, J., Lohmann, G., Mueller, K., Buschmann, T. and Turner, R. (2014) Deficient approaches to human neuroimaging. *Frontiers in Human Neuroscience*, 8, 462.

Stern, K. and McClintock, M.K. (1998) Regulation of ovulation by human pheromones. *Nature*, 392, 177–179.

Szycik, G.R., Mohammadi, B., Hake, M., Kneer, J., Samii, A., Münte, T.F., *et al.* (2017) Excessive users of violent video games do not show emotional desensitization: an fMRI study. *Brain Imaging and Behavior*, 11(3), 736–743.

Takatsuru, Y., Fukumoto, D., Yoshitomo, M., Nemoto, T., Tsukada, H. and Nabekura, J. (2009) Neuronal circuit remodeling in the contralateral cortical hemisphere during functional recovery from cerebral infarction. *Journal of Neuroscience*, 29(32), 10081–10086.

Thiebaut de Schotten, M., Dell'Acqua, F., Ratiu, P., Leslie, A., Howells, H., Cabanis, E., *et al.* (2015) From Phineas Gage and Monsieur Leborgne to HM: revisiting disconnection syndromes. *Cerebral Cortex*, 25(12), 4812–4827.

Tops, M., Buisman-Pijlman, F.T. and Carter, C.S. (2013) Oxytocin and attachment facilitate a shift from seeking novelty to recognizing and preferring familiarity. In M. Kent, M.C. Davis and J.W. Reich (eds) *The Resilience Handbook: Approaches to Stress and Trauma* (pp. 115–130). London: Routledge.

Torgersen, S. (1983) Genetic factors in anxiety disorders. *Archives of General Psychiatry*, 40(10), 1085–1089.

Verhaeghe, J., Gheysen, R. and Enzlin, P. (2013) Pheromones and their effect on women's mood and sexuality. *Facts, Views and Vision: Issues in Obstetrics, Gynaecology and Reproductive Health*, 5(3), 189–195.

Voigt, J.P. and Fink, H. (2015) Serotonin controlling feeding and satiety. *Behavioural Brain Research*, 277, 14–31.

Wei, N., Yong, W., Li, X., Zhou, Y., Deng, M., Zhu, H., *et al.* (2015) Post-stroke depression and lesion location: a systematic review. *Journal of Neurology*, 262(1), 81–90.

Zuckerman, M. (ed.) (1983) *Biological Bases of Sensation Seeking, Impulsivity, and Anxiety*. Hillsdale, NJ: Lawrence Erlbaum.

Chapter 2

Alkhalifa, E. (2009) Exhibiting the effects of the episodic buffer on learning with serial and parallel presentations of materials. *Informing Science Journal*, 12, 57–71.

Alloway, T. (2006) How does working memory work in the classroom? *Educational Research and Reviews*, 1, 134–139.

Allport, G. and Postman, L. (1947) *The Psychology of Rumor*. New York: Holt, Rinehart and Winston.

Anderson, R. and Pichert, J. (1978) Recall of previously unrecallable information following a shift in perspective. *Journal of Verbal Learning and Verbal Behavior*, 17, 1–12.

Anokhin, P. (1973) *Biology and Neurophysiology of the Conditioned Reflex and Its Role in Adaptive Behavior*. Oxford: Pergamon Press.

Ares, G., Giménez, A., Bruzzone, F., Vidal, L., Antúnez, L. and Maiche, A. (2013) Consumers' visual processing of food labels: results from an eye-tracking study. *Journal of Sensory Studies*, 28, 138–153.

Azar, B. (2007) Making sense of semantic memory. *Monitor on Psychology*, 38(5), 16.

Baddeley, A. (1966) Influence of acoustic and semantic similarities on long-term memory for word sequences. *Quarterly Journal of Experimental Psychology*, 18(4), 302–309.

Baddeley, A. (1996) Exploring the central executive. *Quarterly Journal of Experimental Psychology A*, 49(1), 5–28.

Baddeley, A. (2000) Binding in visual working memory: the role of the episodic buffer. *Neuropsychologia*, 49(6), 1393–1400.

Baddeley, A. and Hitch, G. (1974) Working memory. In G.H. Bower (ed.) *The Psychology of Learning and Motivation: Advances in Research and Theory* (Vol. 8, pp. 47–89). New York: Academic Press.

Baddeley, A., Buchanan, M. and Thomson, N. (1975) Word length and the structure of short-term memory. *Journal of Verbal Learning and Verbal Behavior*, 14(6), 575–589.

Bahrick, H.P., Bahrick, P.O. and Wittinger, R.P. (1975) Fifty years of memory for names and faces: a cross-sectional approach. *Journal of Experimental Psychology: General*, 104, 54–75.

Bartlett, F. (1932) *Remembering: A Study in Experimental and Social Psychology*. Cambridge, UK: Cambridge University Press.

Bettman, J.R. Luce, M.F. and Payne, J.W. (1998) Constructive consumer choice processes. *Journal of Consumer Research*, 25(3), 187–217.

Bitterman, M. and Kniffin, C. (1953) Manifest anxiety and 'perceptual defense'. *Journal of Abnormal and Social Psychology*, 48(2), 248–252.

Bower, G.H. (1981) Mood and memory. *American Psychologist*, 36, 129–148.

Brandt, C., Mathers, C., Oliva, M., Brown-Sims, M. and Hess, J. (1975) Examining district guidance to schools on teacher evaluation policies in the Midwest region. *Issues and Answers Report*. Washington, DC: US Department of Education, Institute of Education Sciences, National Center for Education Evaluation and Regional Assistance, Regional Educational Laboratory Midwest.

Brasel, S., Zimbardo, P. and Slavich, G.A. (2006) A blind mind's eye: perceptual defense mechanisms and aschematic visual information. In C. Pechmann and L. Price (eds) *NA – Advances in Consumer Research* (Vol. 33, p. 305), Duluth, MN: Association for Consumer Research.

Brochet, F., Morot, G. and Dubourdieu, D. (2001) The colour of odors. *Brain and Language*, 79(2), 309–320.

Brown, R. and Kulik, J. (1977) Flashbulb memories. *Cognition*, 5(1), 73–99.

Bruner, J.S. and Minturn, A.L. (1955) Perceptual identification and perceptual organisation, *Journal of General Psychology*, 53, 21–28.

Carr, N. (2010) The juggler's brain. In N. Carr (ed.) *The Shallows: What the Internet Is Doing to Our Brains* (pp. 115–143). New York; London: W.W. Norton Publishing Company.

Christianson, S.A. and Hubinette, B. (1993) Hands up! A study of witnesses' emotional reactions and memories associated with bank robberies. *Applied Cognitive Psychology*, 7(5), 365–379.

Cohen, W. and Levinthal, D. (1990) Absorptive capacity: a new perspective on learning and innovation. *Administrative Science Quarterly*, 35(1), 128–152.

Creem-Regehr, S., Willemsen, A., Gooch, A. and Thompson, W. (2003) The effects of restricted viewing conditions on egocentric distance judgments. *Journal of Vision*, 3, 16.

Crowder, R. (1993) Short-term memory: where do we stand? *Memory and Cognition*, 21(2), 142–145.

Daneman, M. and Carpenter, P. (1980) Individual differences in working memory and reading. *Journal of Verbal Learning and Verbal Behavior*, 19(4), 450–466.

Deffenbacher, K. (1983) The influence of arousal on reliability of testimony. In S.M.A. Lloyd-Bostock and B.R. Clifford (eds) *Evaluating Witness Evidence* (pp. 235–251). Chichester: Wiley.

D'Esposito, M., Detre, J.A., Alsop, D.C., Shin, R.K., Atlas, S. and Grossman, M. (1995) The neural basis of the central executive system of working memory. *Nature*, 378(6554), 279–281.

Devlin Committee Report (1976) *Report of the Committee on Evidence of Identification in Criminal Cases*. London: HM Stationery Office.

Dijksterhuis, J. (2004) Think different: the merits of unconscious thought in preference development and decision. *Journal of Personality and Social Psychology*, 87(5), 586–598.

Drace, S. (2013) Evidence for the role of affect in mood congruent recall of autobiographic memories. *Motivation and Emotion*, 37(3), 623–628.

Eysenck, M. and Keane, T. (1990) *Cognitive Psychology: A Student's Handbook*. New York: Psychology Press.

Fagot, J. and Cook, R.G. (1996) Evidence for large long-term memory capacities in baboons and pigeons, and its implications for learning and the evolution of cognition. *Proceedings of the National Academy of Sciences*, 46, 17564–17567.

Finke, C., Esfahani, N. and Ploner, C. (2012) Preservation of musical memory in an amnesic professional cellist. *Current Biology*, 22, 591–592.

Fluke, S.F., Webster, R.J. and Saucier, D.A. (2010) *Re-examining the Form and Function of Superstition*. Poster presented at the annual conference of the Society for Personality and Social Psychology, San Antonio, TX.

Folkman, S. and Lazarus, R. (1988) Coping as a mediator of emotion. *Journal of Personality and Social Psychology*, 54, 466–475.

Foster, R., Libkuman, T., Schooler, J. and Loftus, E. (1994) Consequentiality and eyewitness person identification. *Applied Cognitive Psychology*, 8, 107–121.

Frichtel, M. and Lecuyer, R. (2007) The use of perspective as a depth cue with a 2D display in 4 and 5-month-old infants. *Infant Behavior and Development*, 30, 409–421.

Frost, N. (1972) Encoding and retrieval in visual memory tasks. *Journal of Experimental Psychology*, 95(2), 317–326.

Gathercole, S. and Baddeley, A. (1993) Phonological working memory: a critical building block for reading development and vocabulary acquisition? *European Journal of Psychology of Education*, 8(3), 259–272.

Gibson, J-J. (1966) *The Senses Considered as Perceptual Systems*. Boston, MA: Houghton Mifflin.

Goldman, W.P. and Seamon, J.G. (1992) Very long-term memory for odors: retention of odor-name associations. *American Journal of Psychology*, 105(4), 549–563.

Gregory, R. (1970) *The Intelligent Eye*. London: Weidenfeld and Nicolson.

Hancock, P. and Warm, J. (1989) A dynamic model of stress and sustained attention. *Human Factors*, 5, 519–537.

Hardy, G. and Legge, D. (1968) Cross-modal induction of changes in sensory thresholds. *Quarterly Journal of Experimental Psychology*, 20(1), 20–29.

Hastie, R. and Dawes, R.M. (2001) *Rational Choice in an Uncertain World: The Psychology of Judgment and Decision Making*. Thousand Oaks, CA: Sage Publications.

Herlitz, A., Nilsson, L.-G. and Bäckman, L. (1997) Gender differences in episodic memory. *Memory and Cognition*, 25(6), 801–811.

Hirst, W., Phelps, E., Buckner, R., Budson, A., Cuc, A. and Gabrieli, J. (2011) Long-term memory for the terrorist attack of September 11: flashbulb memories, event memories, and the factors that influence their retention. *Journal of Experimental Psychology: General*, 138(2), 161–176.

Holmes, D. (1990) The evidence for repression: an examination of sixty years of research. In J.L. Singer (ed.) *Repression and Dissociation* (pp. 85–102). Chicago: University of Chicago Press.

Jacobs, J. (1887) Experiments in prehension. *Mind*, *12*, 75–79.

Kaplan, R. and Manicavasagar, V. (2001) Is there a false memory syndrome? A review of three cases. *Comparative Psychiatry*, 42(4), 342–348.

Karon, B. and Widener, A. (1997) Repressed memories and World War II: Lest we forget! *Professional Psychology: Research and Practice*, 28(4), 338–340.

Kaspersky laboratory international survey (2015) Available at: www.kaspersky.com/about/press-releases/2017_users-most-sensitive-data.

Klauer, K. and Zhao, Z. (2004) Double dissociations in visual and spatial short-term memory. *Journal of Experimental Psychology: General*, 133(3), 355–381.

Klingberg, T., Fernell, E., Olesen, P.J., Johnson, M., Gustafsson, P., Dahlström, K., *et al.* (2002) Computerized training of working memory in children. *Journal of American Academic Child Adolescent Psychiatry*, 44(2), 177–186.

Kohlberg, L. (1969) Continuities and discontinuities in childhood and adult moral development. *Human Development*, 12, 93–120.

LaBar, K. and Phelps, E. (1998) Arousal-mediated memory consolidation: role of the medial temporal lobe in humans. *Psychological Science*, 9(6), 490–493.

Lawson, E. and McKinnon, D. (1999) Research on self-serving biases of teachers and students: the impact of deception. Paper presented at the AARE annual conference, Melbourne, Australia.

Lawton, J-M. (2015) Cognitive psychology: memory. In J-M. Lawton and E. Willard (eds) *AQA Psychology for A Level, Year One* (pp. 51–99). London: Hodder Education.

Lawton, J-M., Gross, R. and Rolls, G. (2011) *Psychology A2 for AQA(A)*. London: Hodder Education.

Lazarus, R. (1982) Thoughts on the relation between emotion and cognition. *American Psychologist*, 37(9), 1019–1024.

Lazarus, R.S. and McCleary, R.A. (1951) Autonomic discrimination without awareness: a study of subception. *Psychological Review*, 58(2), 113–122.

Le Doux, J.E. and Brown, R. (2017) A higher-order theory of emotional consciousness. *PNAS*, 114(10), E2016–E2025.

Liao, Y.C. (2007) Effects of computer-assisted instruction on students' achievement in Taiwan: a meta-analysis. *Computers and Education*, 48(2), 216–233.

Loftus, E.F. (1975) Leading questions and the eyewitness report. *Cognitive Psychology*, 7, 560–572.

Loftus, E.F. and Palmer, J.C. (1974) Reconstruction of automobile destruction: an example of the interaction between language and memory. *Journal of Verbal Learning and Verbal Behavior*, 13(5), 585–589.

Loftus, E.F. and Pickrell, J.E. (1995) The formulation of false memories. *Psychiatric Annals*, 25, 720–725.

Loftus, E.F. and Pickrell, J.E. (2003) Make my memory: how advertising can change our memories of the past. *Psychology and Marketing*, 19(1), 1–23.

Loftus, E., Loftus, G. and Messo, J. (1987) Some facts about weapon focus. *Law and Human Behavior*, 11, 55–62.

Logie, R. (1995) *Visuo-spatial Working Memory.* Hillsdale, NJ: Erlbaum.

Logothetis, N. and Pauls, J. (1995) Shape representation in the inferior temporal of monkeys. *Current Biology*, 1(5), 552–563.

Lou, Y. (2001) Small group and individual learning with technology: a meta-analysis. *Review of Educational Research*, 71(3), 449–52.

Marsh, D.M. and Hanlon, T.J. (2007) What we want to see: confirmation bias in animal behavior. *Ethology*, 113(11), 1089–1098.

Marsh, R.L., Sebrechts, M.M., Hicks, J.L. and Landau, J.D. (1997) Processing strategies and secondary memory in very rapid forgetting. *Memory and Cognition*, 25, 173–181.

Mayer, R.E. and Moreno, R. (1998) A split-attention effect in multimedia learning: evidence for dual processing systems in working memory. *Journal of Educational Psychology*, 90, 312–320.

McGinnies, E. (1949) Emotionality and perceptual defense. *Psychological Review*, 56(5), 244–251.

Miller, G. (1956) The magical number seven, plus or minus two: some limits on our capacity for processing information. *Psychological Review*, 63, 81–97.

Moran, J., Ferdig, R., Pearson, D., Wardrop, J. and Blomeyer, R. (2008) Technology and reading performance in the middle-school grades: a meta-analysis with recommendations for policy and practice. *Journal of Literacy Research*, 40, 6–58.

Mueller, P. and Oppenheimer, D. (2014) The pen is mightier than the keyboard. *Psychological Science*, 25(6), 1159–1168.

Murdock, B.B. (1962) The serial position effect of free recall. *Journal of Experimental Psychology*, 64(5), 482–488.

Neisser, U. (1967) *Cognitive Psychology.* Englewood Cliffs, NJ: Prentice-Hall.

Nelson, T.O. and Rothbart, R. (1972) Acoustic savings for items forgotten from long-term memory. *Journal of Experimental Psychology*, 93(2), 357–360.

Ochsner, K.N. (2000) Are affective events richly remembered or simply familiar? The experience and process of recognizing feelings past. *Journal of Experimental Psychology: General*, 129, 242–261.

Payne, J. (1976) Heuristic search processes in decision making. *Advances in Consumer Research*, 3, 321–327.

Payne, J., Bettman, J. and Johnson, E. (1988) Adaptive strategy selection in decision-making. *Journal of Experimental Psychology: Learning Memory and Cognition*, 14(3), 534–552.

Peterson, L.R. and Peterson, M.J. (1959) Short-term retention of individual verbal items. *Journal of Experimental Psychology*, 58, 193–198.

Phelps, E., Ling, S. and Carrasco, M. (2006) Emotion facilitates perception and potentiates the perceptual benefits of attention. *Psychological Science*, 17(4), 292–299.

Prabhakaran, V., Narayanan, K., Zhao, Z. and Gabrieli, J. (2000) Integration of diverse information in working memory within the frontal lobe. *Natural Neuroscience*, 3, 85–90.

Rahman, A. and Crouch, G. (2015) Risky choice framing effects on travellers' time-of-booking decisions. *Tourism Travel and Research Association: Advancing Tourism Research Globally*, 25.

Reitman, J.S. (1974) Without surreptitious rehearsal, information in short-term memory decays. *Journal of Verbal Learning and Verbal Behavior*, 13, 365–377.

Rizzolati, G. and Sinigaglia, C. (2008) The functional role of the parieto-frontal mirror circuit: interpretations and misinterpretations. *Nature Reviews Neuroscience*, 11, 264–274.

Roediger, H. and Karpicke, J. (2006) Test-enhanced learning: taking memory tests improves long-term retention. *Psychological Science*, 17(3), 249–255.

Sacks, O. (2007) *Musicophilia: Tales of Music and the Brain.* New York: Knopf.

Schank, R. and Abelson, R. (1977) *Scripts, Plans, Goals, and Understanding.* Hillsdale, NJ: Erlbaum Associates.

Schmidt, H., Peeck, V., Paas, F. and Van Breukelen, V. (2000) Remembering the street names of one's childhood neighbourhood: a study of very long-term retention. *Memory*, 8(1), 37–49.

Schwartz, B., Ward, A., Monterosso, J., Lyubomirsky, S., White, K. and Lehman, D.R. (2002) Maximizing versus satisficing: happiness is a matter of choice. *Journal of Personality and Social Psychology*, 83(5), 1178–1197.

Scoville, W.B. and Milner, B. (1957) Loss of recent memory after bilateral hippocampal lesions. *Journal of Neurology, Neurosurgery and Psychiatry*, 20, 11–21.

Simon, H, (1974) How big is a chunk? *Science*, 183, 482–488.

Slatcher, R. and Trentacosta, C.J. (2011) A naturalistic observation study of the links between parental depressive symptoms and preschoolers' behaviors in everyday life. *Journal of Family Psychology*, 25(3), 444–448.

Snyder, M. and Uranowitz, S.W. (1978) Reconstructing the past: some cognitive consequences of person perception. *Journal of Personality and Social Psychology*, 36, 941–950.

Solley, C. and Haigh, G. (1948) How children perceive Santa Claus. *Psychology*, 27, 203–208.

Sparrow, B., Liu, J. and Wegner, D. (2011) Google effects on memory: cognitive consequences of having information at our fingertips. *Science*, 333(6043), 776–778.

Speisman, J.C., Lazarus, R.S., Mordkoff, A. and Davison, L. (1964) Experimental reduction of stress based on ego-defense theory. *Journal of Abnormal and Social Psychology*, 68, 367–380.

Sperling, G. (1960) The information available in brief visual presentations. *Psychological Monographs*, 74(11), 1–29.

Stewart, V. (1973) Test of the carpentered world: hypothesis by race and environment in America and Zambia. *International Journal of Psychology*, 8, 83–94.

Sundstrom, M. (2011) Modeling recall memory for emotional objects in Alzheimer's disease. *Neuropsychology, Development and Cognition. Section B: Aging Neuropsychology and Cognition*, 18(4), 396–413.

Treisman, A. (1964) Selective attention in man. *British Medical Bulletin*, 20, 12–16.

Trojani, L. and Grossi, D. (1995) Phonological and lexical coding in verbal short-term memory and learning. *Brain Language*, 51(2), 336–354.

Tulving, E. (1972) *Episodic and Semantic Memory*. London: Academic Press.

Turnbull, C. (1961) *The Forest People*. New York: Simon & Schuster.

Ucross, C. (1987) Mood state-dependent memory: a meta-analysis. *Cognition and Emotion*, 3(2), 139–169.

Van Gorp, W., Wilkins, J.N., Hinkin, C.H., Moore, L.H., Hull, J., Horner, M.D., *et al.* (1999) Declarative and procedural memory functioning in abstinent cocaine users. *Archives of General Psychiatry*, 56(1), 85–89.

Vicari, S., Menghini, D., Di Paola, M., Serra, L., Donfrancesco, A., Fidani, P., *et al.* (2007) Acquired amnesia in childhood: a single case study. *Neuropsychologia*, 45, 704–715.

Wagenaar, W. (1986) My memory: a study of autobiographical memory over six years. *Cognitive Psychology*, 18, 225–252.

Walsh, D. and Thompson, L. (1978) Age differences in visual sensory memory. *Journal of Gerontology*, 33(3), 383–387.

Warren, W. (1984) Perceiving affordances: visual guidance of stair climbing. *Journal of Experimental Psychology: Human Perception and Performance*, 10(5), 683–703.

Wood, W., Zivcakova, L., Gentile, P., Archer, K., De Pasquale, D., and Nosko, A. (2012) Examining the impact of off-task multi-tasking with technology on real-time classroom learning. *Computers and Education*, 58, 365–374.

Zajonc, R.B. (1984) On the primacy of affect. *American Psychologist*, 39(2), 117–123.

Zeelenberg, R. and Bocanegra, B. (2010) Auditory emotional cues enhance visual perception. *Cognition*, 115(1), 202–206.

Chapter 3

Abrams, D.E. and Hogg, M.A. (1990) *Social Identity Theory: Constructive and Critical Advances*. New York: Springer-Verlag.

Adams, G., and Plaut, V.C. (2003) The cultural grounding of personal relationship: friendship in North American and West African worlds. *Personal Relationships*, 10(3), 333–347.

Asch, S.E. (1955) Opinions and social pressure. *Readings About the Social Animal*, 193, 17–26.

Asendorpf, J.B. and Motti-Stefanidi, F. (2017) A longitudinal study of immigrants' peer acceptance and rejection: immigrant status, immigrant composition of the classroom, and acculturation. *Cultural Diversity and Ethnic Minority Psychology*, 23(4), 486–498.

Bandura, A. (1977) *Social Learning Theory*. Englewood Cliffs, NJ: Prentice Hall.

Bandura, A. and Huston, A.C. (1961) Identification as a process of incidental learning. *Journal of Abnormal and Social Psychology*, 63(2), 311–318.

Bandura, A., Ross, D. and Ross, S.A. (1961) Transmission of aggression through imitation of aggressive models. *Journal of Abnormal and Social Psychology*, 63(3), 575–582.

Becker, A.E., Burwell, R.A., Herzog, D.B., Hamburg, P. and Gilman, S.E. (2002) Eating behaviours and attitudes following prolonged exposure to television among ethnic Fijian adolescent girls. *British Journal of Psychiatry*, 180(6), 509–514.

Bogdonoff, M.D., Klein, R.F., Estes, E.H., Shaw, D.M. and Back, K.W. (1961) Modifying effect of conforming behavior upon lipid responses accompanying CNS arousal. *Clinical Research*, 9, 135.

Bond, R. and Smith, P.B. (1996) Culture and conformity: a meta-analysis of studies using Asch's (1952b, 1956) line judgment task. *Psychological Bulletin*, 119(1), 111–137.

Booth, N.S. (1975) Time and change in African traditional thought. *Journal of Religion in Africa*, 7(2), 81–91.

Church, A.T., Katigbak, M.S. and del Prado, A.M. (2010) Cultural similarities and differences in perceived affordances of situations for Big Five behaviors. *Journal of Research in Personality*, 44(1), 78–90.

Cleland, J. and Cashmore, E. (2016) Football fans' views of racism in British football. *International Review for the Sociology of Sport*, 51(1), 27–43.

Crutchfield, R.S. (1955) Conformity and character. *American Psychologist*, 10(5), 191–198.

de Mamani, A.W., Weintraub, M.J., Maura, J., Martinez de Andino, A., Brown, C.A. and Gurak, K. (2017) Acculturation styles and their associations with psychiatric symptoms and quality of life in ethnic minorities with schizophrenia. *Psychiatry Research*, 255, 418–423.

Deutsch, M. and Gerard, H.B. (1955) A study of normative and informational social influences upon individual judgment. *Journal of Abnormal and Social Psychology*, 51(3), 629–636.

Efremkin, E. (2016) At the intersection of modernities: migrants as agents of economic and cultural change. *Journal of Contemporary History*, 51(3), 531–554.

Eisenberg, J., Lee, H-J., Brück, F., Brenner, B., Claes, M-T., Mironski, J, *et al.* (2013) Can business schools make students culturally competent? Effects of cross-cultural management courses on cultural intelligence. *Academy of Management Learning and Education*, 12(4), 603–621.

Elliott, J. (1968–2011) The University of Iowa libraries. UI Collection Guides – Jane Elliott papers, 1968-2011, http://collguides.lib.uiowa.edu/?IWA0832#contentDescription.Date (accessed 23 February 2018).

Errington, F. and Gewertz, D. (1989) *Cultural Alternatives and a Feminist Anthropology: An Analysis of Culturally Constructed Gender Interests in Papua New Guinea*. Cambridge, UK: Cambridge University Press.

Fitneva, S.A., Lam, N.H.L. and Dunfield, K.A. (2013) The development of children's information gathering: to look or to ask? *Developmental Psychology*, 49(3), 533–542.

Fuller, B., Holloway, S.D. and Liang, X. (1996) Family selection of child-care centers: the influence of household support, ethnicity, and parental practices. *Child Development*, 67(6), 3320–3337.

Gineikiene, J. and Diamantopoulos, A. (2017) I hate where it comes from but I still buy it: countervailing influences of animosity and nostalgia. *Journal of International Business Studies*, 48(8), 992–1008.

Gong, T. (2010) Exploring the roles of horizontal, vertical, and oblique transmissions in language evolution. *Adaptive Behavior*, 18(3–4), 356–376.

Hall, R.E. (2013) The idealization of light skin as vehicle of social pathogen vis-à-vis bleaching syndrome: implications of globalization for human behavior. *Journal of Human Behavior in the Social Environment*, 2(4) 552–560.

Henrich, J., Heine, S.J. and Norenzayan, A. (2010) Beyond WEIRD: towards a broad-based behavioral science. *Behavioral and Brain Sciences*, 33(2–3), 111–135.

Hildebrand, D., DeMotta, Y. Sen, S. and Kongsompong, K. (2013) In-group and out-group influences on the consumption behavior of minority groups: the case of gay men. *Journal of Public Policy and Marketing*, 32, 70–78.

Hofstede, G (1983) National cultures in four dimensions: a research-based theory of cultural differences among nations. *International Studies of Management and Organization*, 13(1–2), 46–74.

HŘebÍČková, M. and Graf, S. (2014) Accuracy of national stereotypes in central Europe: out-groups are not better than in-group in considering personality traits of real people. *European Journal of Personality*, 28(1), 60–72.

Jenness, A. (1932) The role of discussion in changing opinion regarding a matter of fact. *Journal of Abnormal and Social Psychology*, 27(3), 279–296.

Kaya, M and Oran, G. (2015) The transmission of socio-cultural codes in teaching Turkish as a foreign language. *Procedia: Social and Behavioral Sciences*, 186, 1208–1213.

Kim, R, and Coleman, P.T. (2015) The combined effect of individualism–collectivism on conflict styles and satisfaction: an analysis at the individual level. *Peace and Conflict Studies*, 22(2), 137–159.

Kim, S.H and Kim, S. (2016) National culture and social desirability bias in measuring public service motivation. *Administration and Society*, 48(4), 444–476.

Koopmans, L., Bernaards, C.M., Hildebrandt, V.H., Lerner, D., de Vet, H.C. and van der Beek, A.J. (2016) Cross-cultural adaptation of the Individual Work Performance Questionnaire. *Work*, 53(3), 609–619.

Lakey, P.N. (2003) Acculturation: a review of the literature. *Intercultural Communication Studies*, 12(2), 103–118.

Lamm, B., Keller, H., Teiser, J., Gudi, H., Yovsi, R.D., Freitag, C., *et al.* (2017) Waiting for the second treat: developing culture-specific modes of self-regulation. *Child Development*, 6 June.

Lavine, R.A. (2009) Personality traits across cultures and research on obedience. *American Psychologist*, 64(7): 620a.

Lim, H. and Park, J-S. (2013) The effects of national culture and cosmopolitanism on consumers' adoption of innovation: a cross-cultural comparison. *Journal of International Consumer Marketing*, 25(1), 16–28.

Maes, H., Neale, M.C., Kendler, K.S., Martin, N.G., Heath, A.C. and Eaves, L.J. (2006) Genetic and cultural transmission of smoking initiation: an extended twin kinship model. *Behavior Genetics*, 36(6), 795–808.

McSweeney, B., Brown, D. and Iliopoulou, S. (2016) Claiming too much, delivering too little: testing some of Hofstede's generalisations. *Irish Journal of Management*, 35(1), 34–57.

Mead, M. (1963) *Sex and Temperament in Three Primitive Societies* (Vol. 370). New York: Morrow.

Mesoudi, A. (2016) Cultural evolution: a review of theory, findings and controversies. *Evolutionary Biology*, 43(4), 481–497.

Milgram, S. (1963) Behavioral study of obedience. *Journal of Abnormal and Social Psychology*, 67(4), 371–378.

Mischel, W. (1958) Preference for delayed reinforcement: an experimental study of a cultural observation. *Journal of Abnormal and Social Psychology*, 56(1), 57–61.

Mori, K, and Arai, M. (2010) No need to fake it: reproduction of the Asch experiment without confederates. *International Journal of Psychology*, 45(5), 390–397.

Neto, F. (2002) Acculturation strategies among adolescents from immigrant families in Portugal. *International Journal of Intercultural Relations*, 26(1), 17–38.

Oishi, S. (2010) The psychology of residential mobility: implications for the self, social relationships, and well-being. *Perspectives on Psychological Science*, 5(1), 5–21.

Pennington, C.R., Heim, D., Levy, A.R. and Larkin, D.T. (2016) Twenty years of stereotype threat research: a review of psychological mediators. *PLOS One*, 11(1), e0146487.

Pourrazavi, S., Allahverdipour, H., Jafarabadi, M.A. and Matlabi, H. (2014) A socio-cognitive inquiry of excessive mobile phone use. *Asian Journal of Psychiatry*, 10, 84–89.

Rabellino, D., Morese, R., Ciaramidaro, A., Bara, B.G. and Bosco, F.M. (2016) Third-party punishment: altruistic and anti-social behaviours in in-group and out-group settings. *Journal of Cognitive Psychology*, 28(4), 486–495.

Rhee, J., Zhao, X., Jun, I. and Kim, C. (2017) Effects of collectivism on Chinese organizational citizenship behavior: guanxi as moderator. *Social Behavior and Personality: An International Journal*, 45(7), 1127–1142.

Ritzer, G. (1993) *The McDonaldization of Society*. Newbury Park, CA: Pine Forge Press.

Roca, J, and Urmeneta. A. (2013) Bi-national weddings in Spain: a recent and increasingly frequent phenomenon in the context of the globalization of the marriage market. *Procedia: Social and Behavioral Sciences*, 82, 567–573.

Roldán-Chicano, M.T., Fernández-Rufete, J., Hueso-Montoro, C., García-López, M., Rodríguez-Tello, J. and Flores-Bienert, M.D. (2017) Culture-bound syndromes in migratory contexts: the case of Bolivian immigrants. *Revista Latino-Americana de Enfermagem*, 25, e2915.

Schaffer, B.S. and Riordan. C.M. (2003) A review of cross-cultural methodologies for organizational research: a best-practices approach." *Organizational Research Methods*, 6(2), 169–215.

Schmitz, L. and Weber, W. (2014) Are Hofstede's dimensions valid? A test for measurement invariance of uncertainty avoidance. *Interculture Journal: Online-Zeitschrift für Interkulturelle Studien*, 13(22), 11–26.

Schuetz, A., Farmer, K. and Krueger, K. (2017) Social learning across species: horses (equus caballus) learn from humans by observation. *Animal Cognition*, 20(3), 567–573.

Serafini, K., Wendt, D.C., Omelas, I.J., Doyle, S.R. and Donovan, D.M. (2017) Substance use and treatment outcomes among Spanish-speaking Latino/as from four acculturation types. *Psychology of Addictive Behaviors*, 31(2), 180–188.

Shih, M., Pittinsky, T.L. and Ambady, N. (1999) Stereotype susceptibility: identity salience and shifts in quantitative performance. *Psychological Science*, 10(1), 80–83.

Sobol, K., Cleveland, M. and Laroche, M. (2018) Globalization, national identity, biculturalism and consumer behavior: a longitudinal study of Dutch consumers. *Journal of Business Research*, 82, 340–353.

Steele, C.M., and Aronson, J. (1995) Stereotype threat and the intellectual test performance of African Americans. *Journal of Personality and Social Psychology*, 6(5), 797–811.

Tadmor, C.T., Galinksy, A.D. and Maddux, W.W. (2012) Getting the most out of living abroad: biculturalism and integrative complexity as key drivers of creative and professional success. *Journal of Personality and Social Psychology*, 103(3), 520–542.

Tajfel, H., Billig, M.G., Bundy, R.P. and Flament, C. (1971) Social categorization and intergroup behaviour. *European Journal of Social Psychology*, 1(2), 149–178.

Tobin, K. (1987) Forces which shape the implemented curriculum in high school science and mathematics. *Teaching and Teacher Education*, 3(4), 287–298.

Tönnies, F. and Loomis, C.P. (1957) *Community and Society*. Mineola, NY: Courier Corporation.

Ventriglio, A., Ayonrinde, O. and Bhugra, D. (2016) Relevance of culture-bound syndromes in the 21st century. *Psychiatry and Clinical Neurosciences*, 70(1), 3–6.

Wang, W. and Vallotton, C. (2016) Cultural transmission through infant signs: objects and actions in US and Taiwan. *Infant Behavior and Development*, 44, 98–109.

Wardell, J.D., Read, J.P., Colder, C.R. and Merrill, J.E. (2012) Positive alcohol expectancies mediate the influence of the behavioral activation system on alcohol use: a prospective path analysis. *Addictive Behaviors*, 37(4), 435–443.

Williams, T. and Williams, K. (2010) Self-efficacy and performance in mathematics: reciprocal determinism in 33 nations. *Journal of Educational Psychology*, 102(2), 453–466.

Zhou, L., Wang, J.J., Chen, X., Lei, C., Zhang, J.J. and Meng, X. (2017) The development of NBA in China: a glocalization perspective. *International Journal of Sports Marketing and Sponsorship*, 18(1), 81–94.

Chapter 4

Adorno, T.W., Frenkel-Brunswik, E., Levinson, D.J. and Sanford, R.N. (1950) *The Authoritarian Personality*. New York: Harper and Row.

Ainsworth, M., Bell, S. and Stayton, D. (1971) Individual differences in strange-situation behavior of one-year-olds. In H.R. Schaffer (ed.) *The Origins of Human Social Relations* (pp. 17–58). London, New York: Academic Press.

Baddeley, A. (1966) Influence of acoustic and semantic similarities on long-term memory for word sequences. *Quarterly Journal of Experimental Psychology*, 18(4), 302–309.

Becker, A., Burwell, L.A., Herzog, D., Hamburg, P. and Gilman, S. (2002) Eating behaviours and attitudes following prolonged exposure to television among ethnic Fijian adolescent girls. *British Journal of Psychiatry*, 180(6), 509–514.

Bulik, C., Berkman, N., Brownley, K., Sedway, J. and Lohr, K. (2007) Anorexia nervosa treatment: a systematic review of randomized controlled trials. *International Journal of Eating Disorders*, 40, 310–320.

Canary, D. and Stafford, L. (1992) Relational maintenance strategies and equity in marriage. *Communication Monographs*, 59, 243–267.

Carlo, G., McGinley, M., Hayes, R., Batenhorst, C. and Wilkinson J. (2007) Parenting styles or practices? Parenting, sympathy, and prosocial behaviors among adolescents. *Journal of Genetic Psychology*, 168, 147–176.

Chlebowski, S. and Gregory, R. (2009) Is a psychodynamic perspective relevant to the clinical management of obsessive-compulsive disorder? *American Journal of Psychotherapy*, 63(3), 245–256.

Costello, E., Compton, S., Keeler, G. and Angold, A. (2003) Relationships between poverty and psychopathology: a natural experiment. *JAMA*, 290(15), 2023–2029.

Dainton, M. (2003) Equity and uncertainty in relational maintenance. *Western Journal of Communication*, 67(2), 164–186.

Darley J. and Latane, B. (1968) Bystander intervention in emergencies: diffusion of responsibility. *Journal of Personality and Social Psychology*, 8(4), 377–383.

Davis, E. (1990) Men as success objects and women as sex objects: a study of personal advertisements. *Sex Roles*, 23, 43–50.

D'Esposito, M., Detre, J.A., Alsop, D.C., Shin, R.K., Atlas, S. and Grossman, M. (1995) The neural basis of the central executive system of working memory. *Nature*, 378(6554), 279–281.

Einstein, D.A. and Menzies, R.G. (2003) The presence of magical thinking in obsessive compulsive disorder. *Behaviour Research and Therapy*, 42, 539–549.

Festinger, L. (1957) *A Theory of Cognitive Dissonance*. Stanford, CA: Stanford University Press.

Fleischmann, M. and Pons, S. (1989) Electrochemically induced nuclear fusion of deuterium. *Journal of Electroanalytical Chemistry*, 261(2), 301–308.

Freud, A. and Dann, S. (1951) An experiment in group upbringing. *The Psychoanalytic Study of the Child*, 6(1), 127–168.

Grootheest, D., Cath, D., Beekman, A. and Boomsma, D. (2005) Twin studies on obsessive-compulsive disorder: a review. *Twin Research and Human Genetics*, 8(5), 450–458.

Haney, C., Banks, W.C. and Zimbardo, P.G. (1973) A study of prisoners and guards in a simulated prison. *Naval Research Review*, 30, 4–17.

Herlitz, A., Nilsson, L-G. and Bäckman, L. (1997) Gender differences in episodic memory. *Memory and Cognition*, 25(6), 801–811.

Klauer, K. and Zhao, Z. (2004) Double dissociations in visual and spatial short-term memory. *Journal of Experimental Psychology: General*, 133(3), 355–381.

Koluchova, A. (1972) Severe deprivation in twins: a case study. *Journal of Child Psychology and Psychiatry*, 13, 107–114.

Koluchova, A. (1991) Severely deprived twins after 22 years' observation. *Studia Psychologia*, 33, 23–28.

Lawton, J-M. (2012) *My Revision Notes: AQA(A) A2 Psychology*. London: Hodder Education.

Lin, Y-H.W and Rusbult, C.E. (1995) Commitment to dating relationships and cross-sex friendships in China and America. *Journal of Social and Personal Relations*, 12, 7–26.

Loftus, E.F. and Pickrell, J.E. (2003) Make my memory: how advertising can change our memories of the past. *Psychology and Marketing*, 19(1), 1–23.

Marsh, D.M. and Hanlon, T.J. (2007) What we want to see: confirmation bias in animal behavior. *Ethology*, 113(11), 1089–1098.

Murstein, B. (1972) Physical attractiveness and marital choice. *Journal of Personality and Social Psychology*, 22(1), 8–12.

Piliavin, I., Rodin, J. and Piliavin, J. (1969) Good Samaritanism: an underground phenomenon? *Journal of Personality and Social Psychology*, 13, 289–299.

Schmidt, H., Peeck, V., Paas, F. and Van Breukelen, V. (2000) Remembering the street names of one's childhood neighbourhood: a study of very long-term retention. *Memory*, 8(1), 37–49.

Sears, D. (1986) College sophomores in the laboratory: influences of a narrow data base on social psychology's view of human nature. *Journal of Personality and Social Psychology*, 51(3), 515–530.

Simmons, L., Firman, R., Rhodes, G. and Peters, M. (2003) Human sperm competition: testis size, sperm production and rates of extra pair copulations. *Animal Behaviour*, 68(2), 297–302.

Slatcher, R. and Trentacosta, C.J. (2011) A naturalistic observation study of the links between parental depressive symptoms and preschoolers' behaviors in everyday life. *Journal of Family Psychology*, 25(3), 444–448.

Stice, E., Fisher, M. and Martinez, E. (2004) Eating disorder diagnostic scale: additional evidence of reliability and validity. *Psychological Assessment*, 16(1), 60–71.

Williams, L. (1984) The classic rape: when do victims report? *Social Problems*, 31(4), 459–467.

Word, C., Zanna, M. and Cooper, J. (1974) The nonverbal mediation of self-fulfilling prophecies in interracial interaction. *Journal of Experimental Social Psychology*, 10, 109–120.

Chapter 5

Abed, R. and Pauw, K. (1998) An evolutionary basis for obsessive-compulsive behaviour. *Behavioural Neurology*, 11, 245–250.

Abelson, R. and Langer, E. (1974) A patient by any other name... clinician group: difference in labeling bias. *Journal of Consulting and Clinical Psychology*, 42, 4–9.

Abramowitz, J. (2006) The psychological treatment of obsessive-compulsive disorder. *Canadian Journal of Psychiatry*, 51, 407–416.

Adler, A. (1930) *The Pattern of Life*. Eastford, CT: Martino Fine Books.

Allen, K.L. (2013) DSM–IV-TR and DSM-V eating disorders in adolescents: prevalence, stability and psychosocial correlates in population based sample of male and female adolescents. *Journal of Abnormal Psychology*, 122, 720–732.

Anand, B. and Brobeck, J. (1952) Hypothalamic control of food intake in rats and cats. *Yale Journal of Biology and Medicine*, 24, 123–140.

Arcelus, J., Mitchell, A., Wzales, J. and Neilsen, S. (2011) Mortality rates in patients with anorexia nervosa and other eating disorders: a meta-analysis of 36 studies. *Archives of General Psychiatry*, 68(7), 724–731.

Bachner-Melman, R., Lerer, E., Zohar, A.H., Kremer, I., Elizur, Y., Nemanov, L., *et al.* (2007) Anorexia nervosa, perfectionism, and dopamine D4 receptor (DRD4). *American Journal of Medical Genetics B: Neuropsychiatric Genetics*, 144B(6), 748–756.

Bailer, U.F., Frank, G.K., Henry, S.E., Price, J.C., Meltzer, C.C., Weissfeld, L., *et al.* (2005) Altered brain serotonin 5-HT1A receptor binding after recovery from anorexia nervosa measured by positron emission tomography and [carbonyl11C]WAY-100635. *Archives of General Psychiatry*, 62, 1032–1041.

Ball, J. and Mitchell, P. (2010) A randomized control study of cognitive behavior therapy and behavioral family therapy for anorexia nervosa patients. *Eating Disorders: The Journal of Treatment and Prevention*, 12(4), 303–314.

Barbarich, N.C., McConaha, C.W., Gaskill, J., La Via, M., Frank, G.K., Achenbach, S., *et al.* (2004) An open trial of olanzapine in anorexia nervosa. *Journal of Clinical Psychiatry*, 65(11), 1480–1482.

Barrett, P. and Healey, L. (2002) Do parent and child behaviours differentiate families whose children have obsessive-compulsive disorder from other clinic and non-clinic families? *Journal of Child Psychology and Psychiatry*, 43(5), 597–607.

Baxter, L.R. (1992) Neuroimaging studies of obsessive-compulsive disorders. *The Psychiatric Clinics of North America*, 15, 871–884.

Beck, A.T. (1963) Thinking and depression, idiosyncratic content and cognitive distortions. *Archives of General Psychiatry*, 9, 324–333.

Becker, A., Burwell, L.A., Herzog, D., Hamburg, P. and Gilman, S. (2002) Eating behaviours and attitudes following prolonged exposure to television among ethnic Fijian adolescent girls. *The British Journal of Psychiatry*, 180(6), 509–514.

Bemis, K.M. (1978) Current approaches to the etiology and treatment of anorexia nervosa. *Psychological Bulletin*, 85, 593–617.

Bemis-Vitousek, K. and Orimoto, L. (1993) Cognitive-behavioral models of anorexia nervosa, bulimia nervosa, and obesity. In P. Kendall and K. Dobson (eds) *Psychopathology and Cognition* (pp. 191–243). New York: Academic Press.

Biederman, J., Herzog, D.B., Rivinus, T.M., Harper, G.P., Ferber, R.A. and Rosenbaum, J.F. (1985) Amitriptyline in the treatment of anorexia nervosa: a double-blind, placebo-controlled study. *Journal of Clinical Psychopharmacology*, 5(1), 10–16.

Blinder, B., Chaitin, B. and Goldstein, R. (1988) *The Eating Disorders*. Dana Point, CA: PMA Publishing Corporation.

Boachie, A., Goldfield, G.S. and Spettigue, W. (2003) Olanzapine use as an adjunctive treatment for hospitalized children with anorexia nervosa: case reports. *International Journal of Eating Disorders*, 33(1), 98–103.

Brooks, S., Owen, G., Uher, R., Friederich, H., Giampietro, V., Brammer, M., *et al.* (2011) Differential neural responses to food images in women with bulimia versus anorexia nervosa. *PLoS One*, 6, e22259.

Bulik, C., Berkman, N., Brownley, K., Sedway, J. and Lohr, K. (2007) Anorexia nervosa treatment: a systematic review of randomized controlled trials. *International Journal of Eating Disorders*, 40, 310–320.

Bulik, C., Sullivan, P., Tozzi, F., Furberg, H., Lichtenstein, P. and Pedersen, N. (2006) Prevalence, heritability and prospective risk factors for anorexia nervosa. *Archives of General Psychiatry*, 63, 305–312.

Buttolph, M.L. and Holland, A.D. (1990) Obsessive-compulsive disorders in pregnancy and childbirth. In M. Jenike, L. Baer and W. Minichiello (eds) *Obsessive-Compulsive Disorders: Theory And Management* (pp. 89–97). Chicago, IL: Year Book Medical.

Carr, A.T. (1974) Compulsive neurosis: a review of the literature. *Psychological Bulletin*, 81, 311–318.

Carter, J., McFarlane, T., Bewell, C., Olmsted, M., Woodside, D. and Kaplan, A. (2009) Maintenance treatment for anorexia nervosa: a comparison of cognitive behavior therapy and treatment as usual. *International Journal of Eating Disorders*, 42, 202–207.

Chepko-Sade, D., Reitz, K. and Sade, D. (1989) Sociometrics of Macaca Mulatta IV: network analysis of social structure of a pre-fission group. *Social Networks*, 11(3), 293–314.

Chlebowski, S. and Gregory, R. (2009) Is a psychodynamic perspective relevant to the clinical management of obsessive-compulsive disorder? *American Journal of Psychotherapy*, 63(3), 245–256.

Cicerone, K., Dahlberg, C., Kalmar, K., Langenbahn, D., Malec, J., Bergquist, T., *et al.* (2000) Evidence-based cognitive rehabilitation: recommendations for clinical practice. *Archives of Physical Medicine and Rehabilitation*, 81(12), 1596–1615.

Clark, D.A. (1992) Depressive, anxious and intrusive thoughts in psychiatric inpatients and outpatients. *Behaviour Research and Therapy*, 30, 93–102.

Clarkin, J.F. (2003) The development of a psychodynamic treatment for patients with borderline personality disorder: a preliminary study of behavioural change. *Journal of Personality Disorders*, 15(6), 487–495.

Cochrane, R. (1977) Mental illness in immigrants to England and Wales: an analysis of mental hospital admissions. *Social Psychiatry*, 12(1), 25–35.

Cordioli, V. (2008) Cognitive-behavioral therapy in obsessive-compulsive disorder. *Revista Brasilia de Psiquiatria*, 30(2), s65–72.

Darcy, A. and Lin, I.H. (2012) Are we asking the right questions? A review of assessment of males with eating disorders. *Eating Disorders: The Journal of Treatment and Prevention*, 20(5), 416–426.

Dare, C., Eisler, I., Russell, G., Treasure, J. and Dodge, L. (2001) Psychological therapies for adults with anorexia nervosa: randomised controlled trial of out-patient treatments. *British Journal of* Psychiatry, 178(3), 216–221.

Davis, L., Yu, L., Keenan, C., Gamazon, E., Konkasbaev, A., Derks, E., *et al.* (2013) Partitioning the heritability of Tourette syndrome and obsessive compulsive disorder reveals differences in genetic architecture. *PLOS Genetics*, 9, e1003864.

Deacon, B. and Abramowitz, J. (2004) Cognitive and behavioral treatments for anxiety disorders: a review of meta-analytic findings. *Journal of Clinical Psychology*, 60(4), 429–441.

de Rosnay, M., Cooper, P.J., Tsigaras, N. and Murray, L. (2006) Transmission of social anxiety from mother to infant: an experimental study using a social referencing paradigm. *Behaviour Research and Therapy*, 44(8), 1165–1175.

DiDomenico, L. and Andersen, A. (1992) Diet vs. shape content of popular male and female magazines: a dose-response relationship to the incidence of eating disorders? *International Journal of Eating Disorders*, 11(3), 283–287.

Di Nardo, P.A. and Barlow, D.H. (1988) *Anxiety Disorders Interview Schedule-Revised (ADIS-R)*. Albany, NY: Graywind.

Eddy, K., Dorer, D., Franko, D., Tahilani, K., Thompson-Brenner, H. and Herzog, D. (2008) Diagnostic crossover in anorexia nervosa and bulimia nervosa: implications for DSM-V. *American Journal of Psychiatry*, 165(2), 245–250.

Egger, N., Wild, B., Zipfel, S., Junne, F., Konnopka, A., Schmidt, U., *et al.* (2016) Cost-effectiveness of focal psychodynamic therapy and enhanced cognitive-behavioural therapy in out-patients with anorexia nervosa. *Psychological Medicine*, 46(16), 3291–3301.

Einstein, D.A. and Menzies, R.G. (2003) The presence of magical thinking in obsessive compulsive disorder. *Behaviour Research and Therapy*, 42, 539–549.

Ellison, P. (2003) Energetics and reproductive effort. *American Journal of Human Biology*, 15(3), 342–351.

Fallon, B. and Nields, J. (1994) Lyme disease: a neuropsychiatric illness. *American Journal of Psychiatry*, 151(11), 1571–1583.

Feldman, M. (2007) Eating disorders in diverse lesbian, gay, and bisexual populations. *International Journal of Eating Disorders*, 40(3), 218–226.

Fisher, S. and Greenberg, R. (1996) *Freud Scientifically Reappraised: Testing the Theories and Therapy.* Chichester, UK: John Wiley & Sons.

Flament, M., Rapoport, J. and Berg, J. (1985) Clomipramine treatment of childhood obsessive-compulsive disorder. *Archives of General Psychiatry*, 42(10), 977–983.

Foa, E., Freund, B. and Steketee, G. (1987) Compulsive activity checklist: psychometric analysis with obsessive compulsive disorder. *Behavioural Assessment*, 9(1), 67–79.

Fontenelle, L., Mendlowicz, M., Marques, C. and Versiani, M. (2004) Trans-cultural aspects of obsessive-compulsive disorder: a description of a Brazilian sample and a systematic review of international clinical study. *Journal of Psychiatric Research*, 38(4), 403–411.

Frisch, R. and Barbieri, R. (2002) *Female Fertility and the Body Fat Connection.* Chicago, IL: University of Chicago Press.

Garcia, J. and Koelling, R. (1966) Relation of cue in consequence to avoidance learning. *Psychonomic Science*, 4, 123–124.

Garner, D. and Garfinkel, P. (1980) Cultural expectations of thinness in women. *Psychological Reports*, 47, 484–491.

Garner, D., Olmsted, M., Bohr, Y. and Garfinkel, P. (1982) The eating attitudes test: psychometric features and clinical correlates. Psychological Medicine, 12(4), 871–878.

Gehring, W., Himle, J. and Nisenson, L.G. (2000) Action-monitoring dysfunction in obsessive-compulsive disorder. *Psychological Science*, 11(1), 1–6.

Geller, D.A., Doyle, R., Shaw, D., Mullin, B., Coffey, B., Petty, C., *et al.* (2006) A quick and reliable screening measure for OCD in youth: reliability and validity of the obsessive compulsive scale of the Child Behavior Checklist. *Comprehensive Psychiatry*, 47(3), 234–240.

Goldberg, D. and Huxley, P. (1992) *Common Mental Disorders: A Bio-Social Model*. London; New York: Tavistock/Routledge.

Gothelf, D., Presburger, G., Zohar, A.H., Burg, M., Nahmani, A., Frydman, M., *et al.* (2004) Obsessive-compulsive disorder in patients with velocardiofacial (22q11 deletion) syndrome. *American Journal of Medical Genetics B: Neuropsychiatric Genetics*, 126B(1), 99–105.

Greenberg, D. and Witztum, E. (1994) The influence of cultural factors on obsessive compulsive disorder: religious symptoms in a religious society. *Israel Journal of Psychiatry and Related Sciences*, 31(3), 211–220.

Greenberg, B., Gabriels, L., Malone, D., Rezai, A., Friehs, G. and Okun, M. (2008) Deep brain stimulation of the ventral internal capsule/ventral striatum for obsessive-compulsive disorder: worldwide experience. *Molecular Psychiatry*, 15(1), 64–79.

Grinspoon, S., Gulick, T., Askari, H., Landt, M., Lee, K., Anderson, E., *et al.* (1996) Serum leptin levels in women with anorexia nervosa. Journal of Clinical Endocrinology and Metabolism, 81(11), 3861–3863.

Grootheest, D., Cath, D., Beekman, A. and Boomsma, D. (2005) Twin studies on obsessive-compulsive disorder: a review. *Twin Research and Human Genetics*, 8(5), 450–458.

Gross, R. (1996) http://aqabpsychology.co.uk/2010/07/obsessive-compulsive-disorder-introduction-explanations-and-treatments (accessed 25 January 2018).

Guisinger, S. (2003) Adapted to flee famine: adding an evolutionary perspective on anorexia nervosa. *Psychological Review*, 110(4), 745–761.

Gunewardene, A., Huon, G.F. and Zheng, R. (2001) Exposure to westernization and dieting: a cross-cultural Study. *International Journal of Eating Disorders*, 29, 289–293.

Hakonarson, H., Wang, K., Zhang, H., Bloss, C., Duvvur, V., Kaye, W., *et al.* (2010) A genome-wide association study on common SNPs and rare CNVs in anorexia nervosa. *Molecular Psychiatry*, 16, 949–959.

Halmi, K., Eckert, E., La Du, T. and Cohen, J. (1986) Anorexia nervosa: treatment efficacy of cyproheptadine and amitriptyline. *Archives of General Psychiatry*, 43, 177–181.

Halmi, K., Sunday, S., Strober, M., Kaplan, A., Woodside, D., Fichter, M., *et al.* (2000) Perfectionism in anorexia nervosa: variation by clinical subtype, obsessionality, and pathological eating behaviour. *American Journal of Psychiatry*, 157(11), 1799–1805.

Hartmann, A., Zeeck, A. and Barrett, M. (2010) Interpersonal problems in eating disorders. *International Journal of Eating Disorders*, 43(7), 619–627.

Herzog, D., Newman, K. and Warshaw, M. (1991) Body image dissatisfaction in homosexual and heterosexual males. *Journal of Nervous and Mental Disease*, 179(6), 356–359.

Hindus, P., Bergström, K. and Levander, S. (1985) Gamma capsulotomy in anxiety and OCD. *Abstracts of the World Congress of Biological Psychiatry*, Abstract 311.7.

Holmes, D. (1990) The evidence for repression: an examination of sixty years of research. In J. Singer (ed.) *Repression and Dissociation: Implications for Personality, Theory, Psychopathology, and Health* (pp. 85–102). Chicago, IL: University of Chicago Press.

Holtkamp, K., Konrad, K., Kaiser, N., Ploenes, Y., Heussen, N., Grzella, I., *et al.* (2005) A retrospective study of SSRI treatment in adolescent anorexia nervosa: insufficient evidence for efficacy. *Journal of Psychiatric Research*, 39(3): 303–310.

Horwath, E. and Weissman, M. (2000) The epidemiology and cross-national presentation of obsessive-compulsive disorder. *The Psychiatric Clinics of North America*, 23(3), 493–507.

Hsu, L., Clement, L., Santhouse, R. and Ju, R. (1991) Treatment of bulimia nervosa with lithium carbonate: a controlled study. *Journal of Nervous and Mental Diseases*, 179, 351–356.

Hu, X., Lipsky, R., Zhu, G., Akhtar, L., Taubman, J., Greenberg, D., *et al.* (2006) Serotonin transporter promoter gain-of-function genotypes are linked to obsessive-compulsive disorder. *American Journal of Human Genetics*, 78(5), 815–826.

Jahoda, M. (1958) *Current Concepts of Positive Mental Health*. New York: Basic Books.

Jónsson, H. and Hougaard, E. (2009) Group cognitive behavioural therapy for obsessive-compulsive disorder: a systematic review and meta-analysis *Acta Psychiatrica Scandinavica*, 119(2), 98–106.

Julien, D., O'Connor, K.P. and Aardema, F. (2007) Intrusions related to obsessive-compulsive disorder: a question of content or context. *Journal of Clinical Psychology*, 65, 709–722.

Karwautz, A., Nobis, G., Haidvogl, M., Wagner, G., Hafferl-Gattermayer, A., Wöber-Bingöl, C., *et al.* (2003) Perceptions of family relationships in adolescents with anorexia nervosa and their unaffected sisters. *European Child and Adolescent Psychiatry*, 12(3), 128–135.

Kaye, W.H., Nagata, T., Weltzin, T.E., Hsu, L.K., Sokol, M.S. and McConaha, C. (2001) Double-blind placebo-controlled administration of fluoxetine in restricting- and restricting-purging-type anorexia nervosa. *Biological Psychiatry*, 49(7), 644–652.

Kelly, D. and Cobb, J. (1985) Limbic leucotomy in the treatment of severe intractable obsessive-compulsive neurosis. Paper presented at the Fifth World Congress of Biological Psychiatry, Philadelphia.

Kempke, S. and Luyten, P. (2007) Psychodynamic and cognitive-behavioral approaches of obsessive-compulsive disorder: is it time to work through our ambivalence? *Bulletin of the Menninger Clinic*, 71(4), 291–311.

Khandelwal, S., Sharan, P. and Saxena, S. (1995) Eating disorders: an Indian perspective. *International Journal of Social Psychiatry*, 41(2), 132–146.

Kirsch, I., Moore, T., Scoboria, A. and Nicholls, S. (2002) The emperor's new drugs: an analysis of antidepressant medication data submitted to the U.S. Food and Drug Administration. *Prevention and Treatment*, 5(1), Article ID 23.

Konstantakopoulos, G., Varsou, E., Dikeos, D., Ioannidi, N., Gonidakis, F., Papadimitriou, G., *et al.* (2012) Delusionality of body image beliefs in eating disorders. *Psychiatry Research*. 200(2–3), 482–488.

Kortegaard, L., Hoerder, K., Joergensen, J., Gilberg, C. and Kyvik, K. (2001) A preliminary population-based twin study of self-reported eating disorder. *Psychological Medicine*, 31, 361–365.

Lai, K. (2000) Anorexia nervosa in Chinese adolescents – does culture make a difference? *Journal of Adolescence*, 23(5), 561–568.

Lawton, J-M. (2012) *AQA(A) A2 Psychology Student Unit Guide (New Edition): Unit 4*. London: Hodder Education.

Leckman, J.F. and Chittenden, E.H. (1990) Gilles de La Tourette's syndrome and some forms of obsessive-compulsive disorder may share a common genetic diathesis. *L'Encephale*, 16, 321–323.

Le Grange, D. and Eisler, I. (2008) Family interventions in adolescent anorexia nervosa. *Child and Adolescent Psychiatric Clinics of North America*, 18, 159–173.

Leichsenring, F. and Steinert, C. (2016) Psychodynamic therapy of obsessive-compulsive disorder: principles of a manual guided approach. *World Psychiatry*, 15(3), 293–294.

Lenane, N., Swedo, S., Leonard, H., Pauls, D., Sceery, D. and Rapaport, J. (1990) Psychiatric disorders in first degree relatives of children and adolescents with obsessive compulsive disorder. *Journal of the American Academy of Child and Adolescent Psychiatry*, 29(3), 407–412.

Lin, K. and Cheung, F. (1999) Mental health issues for Asian Americans. *Psychiatric Services*, 50(6), 774–780.

Liu, K., Zhang, H., Liu, C., Guan, Y., Lang, L., Cheng, Y., *et al.* (2008) Stereotactic treatment of refractory obsessive compulsive disorder by bilateral capsulotomy with 3 years follow-up. *Journal of Clinical Neuroscience*, 15(6), 622–629.

Lomax, C., Oldfield, V. and Salkovskis, P. (2009) Clinical and treatment comparisons between adults with early- and late-onset obsessive-compulsive disorder. *Behaviour Research and Therapy*, 47(2), 99–104.

Makino, M., Tsuboi, K. and Dennerstein, L. (2004) Prevalence of eating disorders: a comparison of western and non-western countries. *Medscape General Medicine*, 6(3), 49.

Mallet, L., Polosan, M., Jaafari, N., Baup, N., Welter, M.L., Fontaine, D., *et al.* (2008) Subthalamic nucleus stimulation in severe obsessive-compulsive disorder. *New England Journal of Medicine*, 359, 2121–2134.

Mathis, M., Alvarenga, P., Funaro, G., Torresan, R., Moraes, I., Torres, A., *et al.* (2011) Gender differences in obsessive-compulsive disorder: a literature review. *Revista Brasileira de Psiquiatria*, 33(4), 390–399.

Mayo-Smith, W., Hayes, C., Biller, B., Klibanski, A., Rosenthal, H. and Rosenthal, D. (1989) Body fat distribution measured with CT: correlations with healthy subjects, patients with anorexia nervosa and patients with Cushing syndrome. *Radiology*, 170, 515–518.

McElroy, S., Hudson, J., Malhotra, S. and Welge, J. (2003) Citalopram in the treatment of binge-eating disorder: a placebo-controlled trial. *Journal of Clinical Psychiatry*, 64, 807–813.

McIntosh, W., Jordan, J., Carter, F., Luty, S., McKenzie, J.M., Bulik, C., *et al.* (2005) Three psychotherapies for anorexia nervosa: a randomized, controlled trial. *American Journal of Psychiatry*, 162(4), 741–747.

Meyer, V. and Cheeser, S. (1970) *Behaviour Therapy in Clinical Psychology*. New York: Science House.

Minuchin, S. (1979) Constructing a therapeutic reality. In E. Kaufman and P.N. Kaufman (eds) *Family Therapy of Drug and Alcohol Abuse* (pp. 5–18). London: Tavistock.

Minuchin, S., Rosman, B.L. and Baker, L. (1978) *Psychosomatic Families: Anorexia Nervosa in Context*. Cambridge, MA: Harvard University Press.

Mumford, D., Whitehouse, A. and Platts, M. (1991) Sociocultural correlates of eating disorders among Asian schoolgirls in Bradford. *British Journal of Psychiatry*, 158, 222–228.

Nasser, M. (1986) Comparative study of the prevalence of abnormal eating attitudes among Arab female students of both London and Cairo universities. *Psychological Medicine*, 16(3), 621–625.

Nicholls, D., Chater, R. and Lask, B. (2000) Children into DSM don't go: a comparison of classification systems for eating disorders in childhood and early adolescence. *International Journal of Eating Disorders*, 28(3), 317–324.

Noonan, J.R. (1971) An obsessive-compulsive reaction treated by induced anxiety. *American Journal of Psychotherapy*, 25(2), 293–295.

Nunn, K., Frampton, I. and Lask, B. (2012) Anorexia nervosa – a noradrenergic dysregulation hypothesis. *Medical Hypotheses*, 78(5), 580–584.

Oberndorfer, T., Simmons, A., McCurdy, D., Strigo, I., Matthews, S., Yang, T., *et al.* (2013) Greater anterior insula activation during anticipation of food images in women recovered from anorexia nervosa. *Psychiatry Research*, 214, 132–141.

O'Connor, K., Todorov, C., Robillard, S., Borgeat, F. and Brault, M. (1999) Cognitive-behaviour therapy and medication in the treatment of obsessive-compulsive disorder: a controlled study. *Canadian Journal of Psychiatry*, 44, 64–71.

O'Kearney, R., Anstey, K. and von Sanden, C. (2006) Behavioural and cognitive behavioural therapy for obsessive compulsive disorder in children and adolescents. *Evidence-Based Child Health: A Cochrane Review Journal*, 2, 1283–1313.

Pato, M., Schindler, K. and Pato, C. (2001) The genetics of obsessive-compulsive disorder. *Current Psychiatry Report*, 3, 163–168.

Pavlov, I. (1903) The experimental psychology and psychopathology of animals. The 14th International Medical Congress, Madrid, Spain, 23–30 April.

Peifer, K., Hu, T. and Vega, W. (2000) Help seeking by persons of Mexican origin with functional impairments. *Psychiatric Services*, 51(10), 1293–1298.

Peterson, B., Leckman, J. and Scahill, I. (1992) Steroid hormones and CNS sexual dimorphisms modulate symptom expression in Tourette's syndrome. *Psychoneuroendocrinology*, 17, 553–563.

Piccinelli, M., Pini, S. and Bellantuono, C. (1995) Efficacy of drug treatment in obsessive-compulsive disorder: a meta-analytic review. *British Journal of Psychiatry*, 166, 424–443.

Pichichero, M. (2009) OCD and streptococcal infection clinical. *Psychiatry News*, www.questia.com/read/1G1-90794698/ocd-and-streptococcal-infection-guest-editorial (accessed 22 January 2018).

Pigott, T. and Seay, S. (1999) A review of the efficacy of selective serotonin reuptake inhibitors in obsessive-compulsive disorder. *Journal of Clinical Psychiatry*, 60, 101–106.

Pike, K. (2003) Cognitive behavior therapy in the posthospitalization treatment of anorexia nervosa. *American Journal of Psychiatry*, 160(11), 2046–2049.

Polimeni, J. (2005) Could obsessive-compulsive disorder have originated as a group-selected adaptive trait in traditional societies? *Medical Hypotheses*, 65(4), 655–664.

Rachman, S. and Hodgson, R. (1980) *Obsessions and Compulsions*. Englewood Cliffs, NJ: Prentice Hall.

Raevuori, A., Keski-Rahkonen, A. and Hoek, H. (2014) A review of eating disorders in males *Current Opinion in Psychiatry*, 27(6), 426–430.

Rakison, D.H. (2002) www.psy.cmu.edu/~rakison/sampleresearch.pdf (accessed 24 January 2018).

Richter, E.O., Davis, K.D. and Hamani, C. (2004) Cingulotomy for psychiatric disease: microelectrode guidance, a callosal reference system for documenting lesion location, and clinical results. *Neurosurgery*, 54, 622–628.

Ringold, A.L., Elliott, M. and Koran, L. (2000) Olanzapine augmentation for treatment-resistant obsessive-compulsive disorder. *Journal of Clinical Psychiatry*, 61(7), 514–517.

Rosenhan, D, (1973) On being sane in insane places. *Science*, 179(4070), 250–258.

Rosenhan, D.L. and Seligman, M.E.P. (1989) *Abnormal Psychology, 2nd Edition*. New York: W.W. Norton.

Rosman, B., Baker, L. and Minuchin, S. (1978) *Psychosomatic Families: Anorexia Nervosa in Context*. Cambridge, MA: Harvard University Press.

Salzman, L. (1980) Psychotherapy with the obsessive personality. In T.B. Karasu and L. Bellak (eds) *Specialized Techniques in Individual Psychotherapy*. New York: Brunner-Mazel.

Samuels, J., Shugart, Y.Y., Grados, M.A., Willour, V.L., Bienvenu, O.J., Greenberg, B.D., *et al.* (2007) Significant linkage to compulsive hoarding on chromosome 14 in families with obsessive–compulsive disorder: results from the OCD Collaborative Genetics Study. *American Journal of Psychiatry*, 164(3), 493–499.

Saxena, S. and Rauch, S.L. (2000) Functional neuroimaging and the neuroanatomy of obsessive–compulsive disorder. *Psychiatric Clinics of North America*, 23, 563–586.

Scherag, S., Hebebrand, J. and Hinney, A. (2009) Eating disorders: the current status of molecular genetic research. *European Child and Adolescent Psychiatry*, 19, 211–226.

Schwartz, J.M., Stoessel, P.W., Baxter, L.R., Jr, Martin, K.M. and Phelps, M.E. (1996) Systematic changes in cerebral glucose metabolic rate after successful behavior modification treatment of obsessive–compulsive disorder. *Archives of General Psychiatry*, 53, 109–113.

Scott-Van Zeeland, A., Bloss, C., Tewhey, R., Bansal, V., Torkamani, A., Libiger, O., *et al.* (2014) Evidence for the role of EPHX2 gene variants in anorexia nervosa. *Molecular Psychiatry*, 19(6), 724–732.

Seligman, M. (1971) Phobias and preparedness. *Behaviour Therapy*, 2(3), 307–320.

Shapiro, D. (1981) Reliability of four quadrant model of self-control: ratings by experts in Type A behavior/health psychology, East-West psychology, and sex role psychology. *Psychologia: An International Journal of Psychology in the Orient*, 25, 149–154.

Shedler, J. (2010) The efficacy of psychodynamic psychotherapy. *American Psychologist*, 65(2), 98–109.

Soomro, G., Altman, D., Rajagopal, S. and Oakley-Browne, M. (2008) Selective serotonin re-uptake inhibitors (SSRIs) versus placebo for obsessive compulsive disorder *Cochrane Database of Systematic Reviews*, 1, CD001765.

Steinglass, J., Eisen, J., Attia, E., Mayer, L. and Walsh, T. (2007) Is anorexia nervosa a delusional disorder? An assessment of eating beliefs in anorexia nervosa. *Journal of Psychiatric Practice*, 13(2), 65–71.

Stewart, M., Brown, J., Weston, W., McWhinney, I., McWilliam, C. and Freeman, T. (2003) *Patient Centred Medicine: Transforming The Clinical Method, 2nd Edition*. Oxford: Radcliffe Medical Press.

Stewart, S., Rosario, M., Brown, T., Carter, A.S., Leckman, J.F., Sukhodolsky, D., *et al.* (2007) Principal components analysis of obsessive-compulsive disorder symptoms in children and adolescents. *Biological Psychiatry*, 61, 285–291.

Stice, E., Fisher, M. and Martinez, E. (2004) Eating disorder diagnostic scale: additional evidence of reliability and validity. *Psychological Assessment*, 16(1), 60–71.

Strauss, J. and Ryan, R.M. (1987) Autonomy disturbances in subtypes of anorexia nervosa. *Journal of Abnormal Psychology*, 96, 254–258.

Surbey, M. (1987) Anorexia nervosa, amenorrhea and adaptation. *Ethology and Sociobiology*, 8(3), 47–62.

Sussman, L., Robins, L. and Earls, F. (1987) Treatment-seeking for depression by black and white Americans. *Social Science and Medicine*, 24(3), 187–196.

Sysko, R. and Walsh, B. (2011) Does the broad categories for the diagnosis of eating disorders (BCD-ED) scheme reduce the frequency of eating disorder not otherwise specified? *International Journal of Eating Disorders*, 44, 625–629.

Szasz, T. (1960) *Myth of Mental Illness*. New York: Harper & Row.

Tallis, F. (1995) The characteristics of obsessional thinking: difficulty demonstrating the obvious? *Clinical Psychology and Psychotherapy*, 2(1), 24–39.

Tang, R., Ji Noh, H., Wang, D. and Sigurdsson, F. (2014) Candidate genes and functional noncoding variants identified in a canine model of obsessive-compulsive disorder. *Genome Biology*, 15(3), R25.

Thomsen, K.R., Thylstrup, B., Pedersen, M.M., Pedersen, M.U., Simonsen, E. and Hesse, M. (2017) Drug-related predictors of readmission for schizophrenia among patients admitted to treatment for drug use disorders. *Schizophrenia Research*, epub ahead of print, doi: 10.1016/j.schres.2017.09.026.

Van den Eynde, F., Suda, M., Broadbent, H., Guillaume, S., Van den Eynde, M., Steiger, H., *et al.* (2011) Structural magnetic resonance imaging in eating disorders: a systematic review of voxel-based morphometry studies. *European Eating Disorders Review*, 20(2), 94–105.

Van Elburg, A., Hillebrand, J., Huyser, C., Snoek, M., Kas, M., Hoek, H., *et al.* (2012) Mandometer treatment not superior to treatment as usual for anorexia nervosa. *International Journal of Eating Disorders*, 45(2), 193–201.

Vega, W., Kolody, B., Aguilar-Goxiola, S., Alderete, E., Catalano, R. and Caraveo-Anduaga, J. (1998) Lifetime prevalence of DSM-III-R psychiatric disorders among urban and rural Mexican Americans in California. *Archives of General Psychiatry*, 55, 771–778.

Vogel, P. and Vogel, E. (1992) Therapist manual for exposure treatment of obsessive-compulsives. *Psychotherapy: Theory, Research, Practice and* Training, 29, 368–375.

Weltzin, T., Cornella-Carlson, T., Fitzpatrick, M.E., Kennington, B., Bean, P. and Jefferies, C. (2012) Treatment issues and outcomes for males with eating disorders. *Eating Disorders*, 20(5), 444–459.

Wilfley, D., Bishop, M., Wilson, D. and Agras, W. (2007) Classification of eating disorders: toward DSM-V. *Journal of Eating Disorders*, 40, 123–129.

Winter, D.A. (1999) Psychological problems: alternative perspectives on their explanation and treatment. In D. Messer and F. Jones (eds) *Psychology and Social Care*. London: Jessica Kingsley.

Xia, L. (2012) Chinese citizens sent to mental hospitals to quiet dissent. *USA* Today, 29 December 2011.

Zhang, A.Y., Snowden, L.R. and Sue, S. (1998) Differences between Asian- and White-Americans' help-seeking and utilization patterns in the Los Angeles area. *Journal of Community Psychology*, 26, 317–326.

Zipfel, S., Wild, B., Groß, G., Friederich, H.C., Teufel, M., Schellberg, D., *et al.*, on behalf of the ANTOP study group (2014) Focal psychodynamic therapy, cognitive behaviour therapy, and optimised treatment as usual in outpatients with anorexia nervosa (ANTOP study): randomised controlled trial. *Lancet*, 383, 127–137.

Zohar, J., Insel, T., Zohar-Kadouch, R., Hill, J. and Murphy, D. (1987) Serotonergic responsivity in obsessive-compulsive disorder: effects of chronic chloipramine treatment. *Archives of General Psychiatry*, 45, 167–172.

Chapter 6

Ainsworth, M., Blehar, M. Waters, E. and Wall, S. (1978) Patterns of attachment: a psychological study of the strange situation. *Child Development*, 41, 49–67.

Albert, D., Chein, J. and Steinberg, L. (2013) The teenage brain: peer influences on adolescent decision making. *Current Directions in Psychological Science*, 22(2), 114–120.

Allen, S.F., Pfefferbaum, B., Nitiema, P., Pfefferbaum, R.L., Houston, J.B., McCarter III, G.S., *et al.* (2016) Resilience and coping intervention with children and adolescents in at-risk neighborhoods. *Journal of Loss and Trauma*, 21(2), 85–98.

Almeida, D.M., Neupert, S.D., Banks, S.R. and Serido, J. (2005) Do daily stress processes account for socioeconomic health disparities? *The Journals of Gerontology Series B: Psychological Sciences and Social Sciences*, 60(2), S34–S39.

Attar, B.K., Guerra, N.G. and Tolan, P.H. (1994) Neighborhood disadvantage, stressful life events and adjustments in urban elementary-school children. *Journal of Clinical Child Psychology*, 23(4), 391–400.

Avis, J. and Harris, P.L. (1991) Belief-desire reasoning among Baka children: evidence for a universal conception of mind. *Child Development*, 62(3), 460–467.

Azmitia, M. and Hesser, J. (1993) Why siblings are important agents of cognitive development: a comparison of siblings and peers. *Child Development*, 64(2), 430–444.

Bartholomew, K. and Horowitz, L.M. (1991) Attachment styles among young adults: a test of a four-category model. *Journal of Personality and Social Psychology*, 61(2), 226–244.

Bartsch, K. and Wellman, H.M. (1995) *Children Talk About the Mind*. Oxford: Oxford University Press.

Bem, S.L. and Bem, D.J. (1971) *Training the Woman to Know Her Place: The Power of a Nonconscious Ideology*. Pittsburgh, PA: Know Incorporated.

Berko, J. and Brown, R. (1960) Psycholinguistic research methods. In P.H. Mussen and A.L. Baldwin (eds) *Handbook of Research Methods in Child Development* (pp. 517–557). New York: Wiley.

Block, J.H. (1983) Differential premises arising from differential socialization of the sexes: some conjectures. *Child Development*, 54(6), 1335–1354.

Bloom, P. and German, T.P. (2000) Two reasons to abandon the false belief task as a test of theory of mind. *Cognition*, 77(1), B25–B31.

Bowlby, J. (1944) *Juvenile Thieves*. London: Bailliere, Tindall and Cox.

Bradley, R.H. and Corwyn, R.F. (2002) Socioeconomic status and child development. *Annual Review of Psychology*, 53(1), 371–399.

Brooks, B.A., Floyd, F., Robins, D.L. and Chan, W.Y. (2015) Extracurricular activities and the development of social skills in children with intellectual and specific learning disabilities. *Journal of Intellectual Disability Research*, 59(7), 678–687.

Brown, J.R., Donelan-McCall, N. and Dunn, J. (1996) Why talk about mental states? The significance of children's conversations with friends, siblings, and mothers. *Child Development*, 67(3), 836–849.

Corradini, A. and Antonietti, A. (2013) Mirror neurons and their function in cognitively understood empathy. *Consciousness and Cognition*, 22(3), 1152–1161.

Csathó, A., Osváth, A., Bicsák, E., Karádi, K., Manning, J. and Kállai. J. (2003) Sex role identity related to the ratio of second to fourth digit length in women. *Biological Psychology*, 62(2), 147–156.

Danese, A. and Tan, M. (2014) Childhood maltreatment and obesity: systematic review and meta-analysis. *Molecular Psychiatry*, 19(5), 544–554.

Dasen, P.R. (1977) *Piagetian Psychology: Cross-cultural Contributions*. Oxford: Gardner.

Dierkhising, C.B., Ko, S.J., Woods-Jaeger, B., Briggs, E.C., Lee, R. and Pynoos, R.S. (2013) Trauma histories among justice-involved youth: findings from the National Child Traumatic Stress Network. *European Journal of Psychotraumatology*, 4(1), 20274.

Donaldson, M. (1978) *Children's Minds*. Glasgow: Fontana/Collins.

Dunn, J. and Hughes, C. (2001) 'I got some swords and you're dead!': violent fantasy, antisocial behavior, friendship, and moral sensibility in young children. *Child Development*, 72(2), 491–505.

Emery, R.E. and Laumann-Billings, L. (1998) An overview of the nature, causes, and consequences of abusive family relationships: toward differentiating maltreatment and violence. *American Psychologist*, 53(2), 121–135.

Esquivel-Alvarez, Y. and Shahani, L. (2015) Cognitive impairment in Asperger syndrome. In A. Costa and E. Villalba (eds) *Horizons in Neuroscience Research* (pp. 117–122). New York: Nova Science Publishers.

Fagot, B.I. and Leinbach, M.D. (1995) Gender knowledge in egalitarian and traditional families. *Sex Roles*, 32(7–8), 513–526.

Farah, M.J., Shera, D.M., Savage, J.H., Betancourt, L., Giannetta, J.M., Brodsky, N.L., *et al.* (2006) Childhood poverty: specific associations with neurocognitive development. *Brain Research*, 1110(1), 166–174.

Felitti, V.J., Anda, R.F., Nordenberg, D., Williamson, D.F., Spitz, A.M., Edwards, *et al.* (1998) Relationship of childhood abuse and household dysfunction to many of the leading causes of death in adults. The Adverse Childhood Experiences (ACE) Study. *American Journal of Preventive Medicine*, 14(4), 245–258.

Gallese, V. (2001) The Shared Manifold hypothesis. From mirror neurons to empathy. *Journal of Consciousness Studies*, 8(5–6), 33–50.

Gelman, R. (1979) Preschool thought. *American Psychologist*, 34(10) 900–905.

Gottfried, A.W., Gottfried, A.E., Bathurst, K., Guerin, D.W. and Parramore, M.M. (2003) Socioeconomic status in children's development and family environment: infancy through adolescence. In M.H. Bornstein and R.H. Bradley (eds) *Socioeconomic Status, Parenting, and Child Development* (pp. 189–207). Mahwah, NJ: Lawrence Erlbaum.

Gredler, G.R. (1992) *School Readiness: Assessment and Educational Issues*. Brandon, VT: Clinical Psychology Publishing Company, Inc.

Greenfield, E.A., Lee, C., Friedman, E.L. and Springer, K.W. (2011) Childhood abuse as a risk factor for sleep problems in adulthood: evidence from a US national study. *Annals of Behavioral Medicine*, 42(2), 245–256.

Gunnar, M.R., Frenn, K., Wewerka, S.S. and Van Ryzin, M.J. (2009) Moderate versus severe early life stress: associations with stress reactivity and regulation in 10–12-year-old children. *Psychoneuroendocrinology*, 34(1), 62–75.

Haney, C., Banks, W.C. and Zimbardo, P.G. (1973) A study of prisoners and guards in a simulated prison. *Naval Research Reviews*, 9, 1–17.

Hanson, J.M., Trolian, T.L., Paulsen, M.B. and Pascarella, E.T. (2016) Evaluating the influence of peer learning on psychological well-being. *Teaching in Higher Education*, 21(2), 191–206.

Harris, J.R. (1995) Where is the child's environment? A group socialization theory of development. *Psychological Review*, 102(3), 458–489.

Hazan, C. and Shaver, P. (1987) Romantic love conceptualized as an attachment process. *Journal of Personality and Social Psychology*, 52(3), 511–524.

Hill-Soderlund, A.L. and Braungart-Rieker, J.M. (2008) Early individual differences in temperamental reactivity and regulation: implications for effortful control in early childhood. *Infant Behavior and Development*, 31(3), 386–397.

Hines, L. (2015) Children's coping with family violence: policy and service recommendations. *Child and Adolescent Social Work Journal*, 32(2), 109–119.

Hines, M. and Kaufman, F.R. (1994) Androgen and the development of human sex-typical behavior: rough-and-tumble play and sex of preferred playmates in children with congenital adrenal hyperplasia (CAH). *Child Development*, 65(4), 1042–1053.

Hines, M., Golombok, S., Rust, J., Johnston, K.J., Golding, J. and the Avon Longitudinal Study of Parents and Children Study Team (2002) Testosterone during pregnancy and gender role behavior of preschool children: a longitudinal, population study. *Child Development*, 73(6), 1678–1687.

Howard-Jones, P.A., Bogacz, R., Yoo, J.H., Leonards, U. and Demetriou, S. (2010) The neural mechanisms of learning from competitors. *Neuroimage*, 53(2), 790–799.

Hughes, M. and Donaldson, M. (1979) The use of hiding games for studying the coordination of viewpoints. *Educational Review*, 31(2), 133–140.

Inhelder, B. and Piaget, J. (1958) *The Growth of Logical Thinking From Childhood to Adolescence: An Essay on the Construction of Formal Operational Structures (Developmental Psychology)*. New York: Basic Books.

Kaplan, J.T. and Iacoboni, M. (2006) Getting a grip on other minds: mirror neurons, intention understanding, and cognitive empathy. *Social Neuroscience*, 1(3–4), 175–183.

Knoll, L.J., Fuhrmann, D., Sakhardande, A.L., Stamp, F., Speekenbrink, M. and Blakemore, S-J. (2016) A window of opportunity for cognitive training in adolescence. *Psychological Science*, 27(12), 1620–1631.

Lamb, M.E., Hwang, C-P., Frodi, A.M. and Frodi, M. (1982) Security of mother-and father-infant attachment and its relation to sociability with strangers in traditional and nontraditional Swedish families. *Infant Behavior and Development*, 5(2–4), 355–367.

Lillard, A.S. (1993) Young children's conceptualization of pretense: action or mental representational state? *Child Development*, 64(2), 372–386.

Lillard, A.S., Lerner, M.D., Hopkins, E.J., Dore, R.A., Smith, E.D. and Palmquist, C.M. (2013) The impact of pretend play on children's development: a review of the evidence. *Psychological Bulletin*, 139(1), 1–34.

Lin, I-H., Ko, C.H., Chang, Y.P, Liu, T.L, Wang, P.W., Lin, H.C., *et al.* (2014) The association between suicidality and Internet addiction and activities in Taiwanese adolescents. *Comprehensive Psychiatry*, 55(3), 504–510.

Lopez-Larson, M.P., Andersen, J.S, Ferguson, M.A. and Yurgelun-Todd, D. (2011) Local brain connectivity and associations with gender and age. *Developmental Cognitive Neuroscience*, 1(2), 187–197.

Lorenz, K. (1935) Der kumpan in der umwelt des vogels. *Journal für Ornithologie*, 83(3), 289–413.

Main, M. and Solomon, J. (1986) Discovery of an insecure-disorganized/disoriented attachment pattern. In M. Yogman and T.B. Brazelton (eds) *Affective Development in Infancy* (pp. 95–124). Norwood, NJ: Ablex.

Marwaha, S., Goswami, M. and Vashist, B. (2017) Prevalence of principles of Piaget's theory among 4–7-year-old children and their correlation with IQ. *Journal of Clinical and Diagnostic Research: JCDR*, 11(8), ZC111–ZC115.

Maslow, A.H. (1943) A theory of human motivation. *Psychological Review*, 50(4), 370–396.

McCoy, A.R. and Reynolds, A.J. (1999) Grade retention and school performance: an extended investigation. *Journal of School Psychology*, 37(3), 273–298.

McGarrigle, J. and Donaldson, M. (1975) Conservation accidents. *Cognition*, 3(4), 341–350.

McNaughton, S. and Leyland, J. (1990) The shifting focus of maternal tutoring across different difficulty levels on a problem-solving task. *British Journal of Developmental Psychology*, 8(2), 147–155.

Meadows, S. (2006) *The Child as Thinker: The Development and Acquisition of Cognition in Childhood*. London: Routledge.

Noble, K.G., Norman, M.F. and Farah, M.J. (2005) Neurocognitive correlates of socioeconomic status in kindergarten children. *Developmental Science*, 8(1), 74–87.

Pauletti, R.E., Cooper, P.J. and Perry, D.G. (2014) Influences of gender identity on children's maltreatment of gender-nonconforming peers: a person × target analysis of aggression. *Journal of Personality and Social Psychology*, 106(5), 843–866.

Pellegrini, A.D. (2009) *The Role of Play in Human Development*. New York: Oxford University Press.

Pellis, S.M. and Pellis, V.C. (2007) Rough-and-tumble play and the development of the social brain. *Current Directions in Psychological Science*, 16(2), 95–98.

Pellis, S.M., Pellis, V.C. and Bell, H.C. (2010) The function of play in the development of the social brain. *American Journal of Play*, 2(3), 278–296.

Piaget, J. (1932) *The Moral Development of the Child*. London: Kegan Paul.

Piaget, J. (1960) The general problems of the psychobiological development of the child. In J. Tanner and B. Inhelder (eds) *Discussions on Child Development* (Vol. 4, pp. 3–27). London: Tavistock.

Piaget, J. and Cook. M. (1952) *The Origins of Intelligence in Children* (Vol. 8, No. 5). New York: International Universities Press.

Piaget, J. and Inhelder, B. (1956) *The Child's Concept of Space*. New York: Routledge and Kegan Paul.

Pinker, S. (1994) *The Language Instinct*. New York: William Morrow and Company.

Power, J.D., Fair, D.A., Schlaggar, B.L and Petersen, S.E. (2010) The development of human functional brain networks. *Neuron*, 67(5), 735–748.

Powers, A., Fani, N., Cross, D., Ressler, K.J. and Bradley, B. (2016) Childhood trauma, PTSD, and psychosis: findings from a highly traumatized, minority sample. *Child Abuse and Neglect*, 58, 111–118.

Rabban, M. (1950) Sex-role identification in young children in two diverse social groups. *Genetic Psychology Monographs*, 42, 81–158.

Renold, E. (2001) 'Square-girls', femininity and the negotiation of academic success in the primary school. *British Educational Research Journal*, 27(5), 577–588.

Ribeiro, L.A., Zachrisson, H.D. and Dearing, E. (2017) Peer effects on the development of language skills in Norwegian childcare centers. *Early Childhood Research Quarterly*, 41, 1–12.

Rives Bogart, K. and Matsumoto, D. (2010) Facial mimicry is not necessary to recognize emotion: facial expression recognition by people with Moebius syndrome. *Social Neuroscience*, 5(2), 241–251.

Rodenburg, R., Benjamin, A., de Roos, C., Meijer, A.M. and Stams, G.J. (2009) Efficacy of EMDR in children: a meta-analysis. *Clinical Psychology Review*, 29(7), 599–606.

Schaffer, H.R. (2004) *Introducing Child Psychology*. Oxford: Blackwell Publishing.

Schaffer, H.R. and Emerson, R.E. (1964) The development of social attachments in infancy. *Monographs of the Society for Research in Child Development*, 29(3), 1–77.

Schulte-Rüther, M., Markowitsch, H.J., Fink, G.R. and Piefke, M. (2007) Mirror neuron and theory of mind mechanisms involved in face-to-face interactions: a functional magnetic resonance imaging approach to empathy. *Journal of Cognitive Neuroscience*, 19(8), 1354–1372.

Schwebel, D.C., Rosen, C.S. and Singer, J.L. (1999) Preschoolers' pretend play and theory of mind: the role of jointly constructed pretence. *British Journal of Developmental Psychology*, 17(3), 333–348.

Senghas, A. and Coppola, M. (2011) Getting to the point: how a simple gesture became a linguistic element in Nicaraguan signing. In G. Mathur and D.J. Napoli (eds) *Deaf Around the World: The Impact of Language* (pp. 127–143). Oxford: Oxford University Press.

Sigirtmac, A.D. (2016) An investigation on the effectiveness of chess training on creativity and theory of mind development at early childhood. *Educational Research and Reviews*, 11(11), 1056–1063.

Slaby, R.G. and Frey, K.S. (1975) Development of gender constancy and selective attention to same-sex models. *Child Development*, 46(4), 849–856.

Sluckin, W., Taylor, K.F. and Taylor, A. (1966) Approach of domestic chicks to stationary objects of different texture. *Perceptual and Motor Skills*, 22(3), 699–702.

Smith, P.K. (2005) Social and pretend play in children. In A.D. Pellegrini and P.K. Smith (eds) *The Nature of Play: Great Apes and Humans* (pp. 173–209). New York: Guilford Press.

Stepanović, I. (2010) The role of peer interaction in cognitive development: Piagetian and Vygotskyan perspective. *Psihološka istraživanja*, 13(2), 219–240.

Thompson, S.K. (1975) Gender labels and early sex role development. *Child Development*, 46(2), 339–347.

Topping, K.J. and Trickey, S. (2007) Collaborative philosophical enquiry for school children: cognitive effects at 10–12 years. *British Journal of Educational Psychology*, 77(2), 271–288.

Van IJzendoorn, M.H. and Kroonenberg, P.M. (1988) Cross-cultural patterns of attachment: a meta-analysis of the strange situation. *Child Development*, 59(1), 147–156.

Vygotsky, L. (1934) *Thought and Language*, trans. E. Hanfmann and G. Vakar. Cambridge, MA: MIT Press, 1962.

White, R.E. and Carlson, S.M. (2016) What would Batman do? Self-distancing improves executive function in young children. *Developmental Science*, 19(3), 419–426.

Whitfield, C., Anda, R.F., Felitti, V.J., Bremner, J.D., Walker, J.D., Perry, B.D., *et al.* (2006) The enduring effects of abuse and related adverse experiences in childhood. *European Archives of Psychiatry and Clinical Neuroscience*, 256(3), 174–186.

Willis, J. (2016) The science of resilience: how to teach students to persevere. *The Guardian*, 12 January.

Wimmer, H. and Perner, J. (1983) Beliefs about beliefs: representation and constraining function of wrong beliefs in young children's understanding of deception. *Cognition*, 13(1), 103–128.

Windle, G., Bennett, K.M. and Noyes. J. (2011) A methodological review of resilience measurement scales. *Health and Quality of Life Outcomes*, 9(1), 8.

Wood, D. and Middleton, D. (1975) A study of assisted problem-solving. *British Journal of Psychology*, 66(2), 181–191.

Chapter 7

Ajzen, I. (1991) The theory of planned behavior. *Organizational Behavior and Human Decision Processes*, 50(2), 179–211.

Akers, R.L. and Lee, G. (1996) A longitudinal test of social learning theory: adolescent smoking. *Journal of Drug Issues*, 26(2), 317–343.

Allen, J. and Flack, F. (2015) Evaluation in health promotion: thoughts from inside a human research ethics committee. *Health Promotion Journal of Australia*, 26(3), 182–185.

Armstrong, D. (2000) A survey of community gardens in upstate New York: implications for health promotion and community development. *Health and Place*, 6(4), 319–327.

Aveyard, P., Massey, L., Parsons, A., Manaseki, S. and Griffin, C. (2009) The effect of transtheoretical model based interventions on smoking cessation. *Social Science and Medicine*, 68(3), 397–403.

Bauman, K.E. and Ennett, S.T. (1996) On the importance of peer influence for adolescent drug use: commonly neglected considerations. *Addiction*, 91(2), 185–198.

Brown, J., Kotz, D., Miche, S., Stapleton, J., Walmsley, M. and West, R. (2014) How effective and cost-effective was the national mass media smoking cessation campaign 'Stoptober'?. *Drug and Alcohol Dependence*, 135, 52–58.

Brown, S.A., Myers, M.G., Lippke, L., Tapert, S.F., Stewart, D.G. and Vik, P.W. (1998) Psychometric evaluation of the Customary Drinking and Drug Use Record (CDDR): a measure of adolescent alcohol and drug involvement. *Journal of Studies on Alcohol*, 59(4), 427–438.

Brynner, J. (1969) *The Young Smoker: Smoking Among Schoolboys*. London: HM Stationery Office.

Bullers, S., Cooper, M.L. and Russell, M. (2001) Social network drinking and adult alcohol involvement: a longitudinal exploration of the direction of influence. *Addictive Behaviors*, 26(2), 181–199.

Calvert, C., Allen-Brunner, W. and Locke, C.M. (2010) Playing politics or protecting children. *Journal of Legislation*, 36, 201–248.

Chapman, S. and Leask, J-A. (2001) Paid celebrity endorsement in health promotion: a case study from Australia. *Health Promotion International*, 16(4), 333–338.

Christiansen, B.A., Smith, G.T., Roehling, P.V. and Goldman, M.S. (1989) Using alcohol expectancies to predict adolescent drinking behavior after one year. *Journal of Consulting and Clinical Psychology*, 57(1), 93–99.

Cloninger, C.R. (1987) A systematic method for clinical description and classification of personality variants: a proposal. *Archives of General Psychiatry*, 44(6), 573–588.

Corcoran, N. (2007) Mass media in health communication. In N. Corcoran (ed.) *Communicating Health: Strategies for Health Promotion* (pp. 73–95). London: Sage Publications.

Dani, J.A. and Biasi, M. (2001) Cellular mechanisms of nicotine addiction. *Pharmacology Biochemistry and Behavior*, 70(4), 439–446.

De Wit, J. and Stroebe, W. (2004) Social cognition models of health behaviour. In A. Kaptein and J. Weinman (eds) *Health Psychology* (pp. 52–83). Oxford, UK: Blackwell.

Di Chiara, G. (2000) Role of dopamine in the behavioural actions of nicotine related to addiction. *European Journal of Pharmacology*, 393(1), 295–314.

DiFranza, J.R. (2008) Hooked from the first cigarette. *Scientific American*, 298(5), 82–87.

Dunn, M.E. and Goldman, M.S. (1998) Age and drinking-related differences in the memory organization of alcohol expectances in 3rd-, 6th-, 9th-, and 12th-grade children. *Journal of Consulting and Clinical Psychology*, 66(3), 579–585.

Engel, G.L. (1978) The biopsychosocial model and the education of health professionals. *Annals of the New York Academy of Sciences*, 310(1), 169–181.

Eysenck, H.J. (1997) Addiction, personality and motivation. *Human Psychopharmacology-Clinical and Experimental*, 12(2), S79–S87.

Foroud, T., Bice, P., Castelluccio, P., Bo, R., Miller, L., Ritchotte, A., *et al.* (2000) Identification of quantitative trait loci influencing alcohol consumption in the high alcohol drinking and low alcohol drinking rat lines. *Behavior Genetics*, 30(2), 131–140.

Funnell, M.M. and Anderson, R.M. (2004) Empowerment and self-management of diabetes. *Clinical Diabetes*, 22(3), 123–127.

Gelernter, J., Panhuysen, C., Weiss, R., Brady, K., Hesselbrock, V., Rounsaville, B., *et al.* (2005) Genomewide linkage scan for cocaine dependence and related traits: significant linkages for a cocaine-related trait and cocaine-induced paranoia. *American Journal of Medical Genetics Part B: Neuropsychiatric Genetics*, 136(1), 45–52.

Godin, G. and Kok, G. (1996) The theory of planned behavior: a review of its applications to health-related behaviors. *American Journal of Health Promotion*, 11(2), 87–98.

Goldberg, S.R., Morse, W.H. and Goldberg, D.M. (1981) Acute and chronic effects of naltrexone and naloxone on schedule-controlled behavior of squirrel monkeys and pigeons. *Journal of Pharmacology and Experimental Therapeutics*, 216(3), 500–509.

Gorin, S.S. and Heck, J.E. (2005) Cancer screening among Latino subgroups in the United States. *Preventive Medicine*, 40(5), 515–526.

Habtewold, T.D., Alemu, S.M. and Haile, Y.G. (2016) Sociodemographic, clinical, and psychosocial factors associated with depression among type 2 diabetic outpatients in Black Lion General Specialized Hospital, Addis Ababa, Ethiopia: a cross-sectional study. *BMC Psychiatry*, 16(1), 103.

Harris, J.R. (1998) *The Nurture Assumption: Why Children Turn Out the Way They Do*. New York: The Free Press.

Hoffmann, N.G. and Kopak, A.M. (2015) How well do the DSM-5 alcohol use disorder designations map to the ICD-10 disorders? *Alcoholism: Clinical and Experimental Research*, 39(4), 697–701.

Howard, M.O, Kivlahan, D. and Walker, R.D. (1997) Cloninger's tridimensional theory of personality and psychopathology: applications to substance use disorders. *Journal of Studies on Alcohol*, 58(1), 48–66.

Kendler, K.S. and Prescott, C.A. (1998) Cannabis use, abuse, and dependence in a population-based sample of female twins. *American Journal of Psychiatry*, 155(8), 1016–1022.

Kendler, K.S., Prescott, C.A., Neale, M.C. and Pedersen, N.L. (1997) Temperance board registration for alcohol abuse in a national sample of Swedish male twins, born 1902 to 1949. *Archives of General Psychiatry*, 54(2), 178–184.

Keyes, K.M., Hatzenbuehler, M.L., McLaughlin, K.A., Link, B., Olfson, M., Grant, B.F., *et al.* (2010) Stigma and treatment for alcohol disorders in the United States. *American Journal of Epidemiology*, 172(12), 1364–1372.

Kobus, K. (2003) Peers and adolescent smoking. *Addiction*, 98(S1), 37–55.

Leshner, A.I. (1998) Drug addiction research: moving toward the 21st century. *Drug and Alcohol Dependence*, 51(1), 5–7.

Li, M.D., Kane, J.K., Wang, J. and Ma, J.Z. (2004) Time-dependent changes in transcriptional profiles within five rat brain regions in response to nicotine treatment. *Molecular Brain Research*, 132(2), 168–180.

Littell, J.H. and Girvin, H. (2002) Stages of change: a critique. *Behavior Modification*, 26(2), 223–273.

Luthar, S.S. and Latendresse, S.J. (2005) Children of the affluent: challenges to well-being. *Current Directions in Psychological Science*, 14(1), 49–53.

Marks, R. and Allegrante, J.P. (2005) A review and synthesis of research evidence for self-efficacy-enhancing interventions for reducing chronic disability: implications for health education practice (part II). *Health Promotion Practice*, 6(2), 148–156.

McManus, S., Bebbington, P., Jenkins, R. and Brugha, T. (eds) (2016) *Mental Health and Wellbeing in England: Adult Psychiatric Morbidity Survey 2014*. Leeds: NHS Digital.

McNamara, J. and McCabe, M.P. (2012) Striving for success or addiction? Exercise dependence among elite Australian athletes. *Journal of Sports Sciences*, 30(8), 755–766.

Meyers, D.G., Neuberger, J.S. and He, J. (2009) Cardiovascular effect of bans on smoking in public places: a systematic review and meta-analysis. *Journal of the American College of Cardiology*, 54(14), 1249–1255.

Miró, J., Raiche, K.A., Carter, G.T, O'Brien, S.A., Abresch, R.T., McDonald, C.M., *et al.* (2009) Impact of biopsychosocial factors on chronic pain in persons with myotonic and facioscapulohumeral muscular dystrophy. *American Journal of Hospice and Palliative Medicine*, 26(4), 308–319.

Nestler, S. and Egloff, B. (2010) When scary messages backfire: influence of dispositional cognitive avoidance on the effectiveness of threat communications. *Journal of Research in Personality*, 44(1), 137–141.

Nielsen, D.A., Yuferov, V., Hamon, S., Jackson, C., Ho, A., Ott, J., *et al.* (2009) Increased OPRM1 DNA methylation in lymphocytes of methadone-maintained former heroin addicts. *Neuropsychopharmacology*, 34(4), 867–873.

Noël, Y. (1999) Recovering unimodal latent patterns of change by unfolding analysis: application to smoking cessation. *Psychological Methods*, 4(2), 173–191.

Oh, H. and Hsu, C.H.C (2001) Volitional degrees of gambling behaviors. *Annals of Tourism Research*, 28(3), 618–637.

Parker, K. and Parikh, S.V. (2001) Applying Prochaska's model of change to needs assessment, programme planning and outcome measurement. *Journal of Evaluation in Clinical Practice*, 7(4), 365–371.

Piazza, P.V., Deminière, J.M., Le Moal, M. and Simon, H. (1989) Factors that predict individual vulnerability to amphetamine self-administration. *Science*, 245(4925), 1511–1514.

Pommier, J., Guével, M-R. and Jourdan, D. (2010) Evaluation of health promotion in schools: a realistic evaluation approach using mixed methods. *BMC Public Health*, 10(1), 43.

Prochaska, J.O. and Velicer, W.F. (1997) The transtheoretical model of health behavior change. *American Journal of Health Promotion*, 12(1), 38–48.

Sharf, B.F. (1997) Communicating breast cancer on-line: support and empowerment on the Internet. *Women and Health*, 26(1), 65–84.

Sinha, R. (2001) How does stress increase risk of drug abuse and relapse? *Psychopharmacology*, 158(4), 343–359.

Tavolacci, M.P., Ladner, J., Grigoni, S., Richard, L., Viller, H. and Decehlotte, P. (2013) Prevalence and association of perceived stress, substance use and behavioral addictions: a cross-sectional study among university students in France, 2009–2011. *BMC Public Health*, 13(1), 724.

Tsuang, M.T., Lyons, M.J., Eisen, S.A., Goldberg, J., True, W., Lin, N., *et al.* (1996) Genetic influences on DSM-III-R drug abuse and dependence: a study of 3,372 twin pairs. *American Journal of Medical Genetics Part A*, 67(5), 473–477.

Van Hasselt, F.M., Oud, M.J.T. and Loonen, A.J.M. (2015) Practical recommendations for improvement of the physical health care of patients with severe mental illness. *Acta Psychiatrica Scandinavica*, 131(5), 387–396.

Velicer, W.F., Redding, C.A., Sun, X. and Prochaska, J.O. (2007) Demographic variables, smoking variables, and outcome across five studies. *Health Psychology*, 26(3), 278–287.

Walker, M., Toneatto, T., Potenza, M.N., Petry, N., Ladouceur, R., Hodgkins, D.C., *et al.* (2006) A framework for reporting outcomes in problem gambling treatment research: the Banff, Alberta Consensus. *Addiction*, 101(4), 504–511.

Wallerstein, N. (1992) Powerlessness, empowerment, and health: implications for health promotion programs. *American Journal of Health Promotion*, 6(3), 197–205.

Watkins, S.S., Koob, G.F. and Markou, A. (2000) Neural mechanisms underlying nicotine addiction: acute positive reinforcement and withdrawal. *Nicotine and Tobacco Research*, 2(1), 19–37.

Webb, T.L. and Sheeran, P. (2006) Does changing behavioral intentions engender behavior change? A meta-analysis of the experimental evidence. *Psychological Bulletin*, 132(2), 249–268.

Weitzman, E.R. and Chen, Y-Y. (2005) The co-occurrence of smoking and drinking among young adults in college: national survey results from the United States. *Drug and Alcohol Dependence*, 80(3), 377–386.

Wringe, A., Roura, M., Urassa, M., Busza, J., Athanas, V. and Zaba, B. (2009) Doubts, denial and divine intervention: understanding delayed attendance and poor retention rates at a HIV treatment programme in rural Tanzania. *AIDS Care*, 21(5), 632–637.

Wu, Y., Huxley, R., Li, L., Anna, V., Xie, G., Yao, C., *et al.* (2008) Prevalence, awareness, treatment, and control of hypertension in China. *Circulation*, 118(25), 2679–2686.

Yan, W., Li, Y. and Sui, N. (2014) The relationship between recent stressful life events, personality traits, perceived family functioning and internet addiction among college students. *Stress and Health*, 30(1), 3–11.

Zola, I.K. (1966) Culture and symptoms – an analysis of patients' presenting complaints. *American Sociological Review*, 31(5), 615–630.

Zuckerman, M. (ed.) (1983) *Biological Bases of Sensation Seeking, Impulsivity, and Anxiety*. Hillsdale, NJ: Lawrence Erlbaum Associates.

Chapter 8

Adorno, T.W., Frenkel-Brunswik, E., Levinson, D.J. and Sanford, R.N. (1950) *The Authoritarian Personality*. New York: Harper and Row.

Akrami, N. (2005) *Prejudice: The Interplay of Personality, Cognition, and Social Psychology*. Doctoral thesis, Uppsala University.

Alonso, W. and Shuck-Paim, C. (2002) Sex-ratio conflicts kin selection, and the evolution of altruism. *Proceedings of the National Academy of Sciences USA*, 99, 6843–6847.

Altemeyer, B. (1981) *Right-Wing Authoritarianism*. Winnipeg: University of Manitoba Press.

Argyle, M. (1977) Predictive and generative rules models of P x S interaction. In D. Magnusson and N.S. Endler (eds) *Personality at the Crossroads: Current Issues in Interactional Psychology* (pp. 53–370). Hillsdale, NJ: Lawrence Erlbaum Associates.

Argyle, M. (1988) *Bodily Communication, 2nd ed*. New York: Methuen.

Argyle, M. (1992) *The Social Psychology of Everyday Life*. London: Routledge.

Argyle, M. and Henderson, M. (1984) The rules of friendship. *Journal of Social and Personal Relationships*, 1(2), 211–237.

Aronson, E., Blaney, N., Stephin, C., Sikes, J. and Snapp, M. (1978) *The Jigsaw Classroom*. Beverly Hills, CA: Sage Publishing Company.

Batson, C. (1987) Prosocial motivation: is it ever truly altruistic? *Advances in Experimental Social Psychology*, 20, 65–122.

Batson, D., Duncan, B., Ackerman, P., Buckley, T. and Birch, K. (1981) Is empathic emotion a source of altruistic motivation? *Journal of Personality and Social Psychology*, 40(2), 290–302.

Binmore, K. (2007) *Game Theory: A Very Short Introduction*. Oxford: Oxford University Press.

Birkhead, T. and Moller, A. (1998) *Sperm Competition and Sexual Selection*. San Diego, CA: Academic Press.

Boyd, R. and Richerson, P. (2009) Culture and the evolution of human cooperation. *Philosophical Transactions of the Royal Society of London B: Biological Sciences*, 364(1533), 3281–3288.

Boyd-Barrett, O. (2017) *Western Mainstream Media and the Ukraine Crisis: A Study in Conflict Propaganda*, London: Routledge.

Brigham, J.C. (1971) Ethnic stereotypes. *Psychological Bulletin*, 76, 15–33.

Buss, D. (1989) Sex differences in human mate preferences: evolutionary hypotheses tested in 37 cultures. *Behavioral and Brain Sciences*, 12(1), 1–14.

Buss, D. and Schmitt, D. (1993) Sexual strategies theory: an evolutionary perspective on human mating. *Psychological Review*, 100, 204–232.

Canary, D. and Stafford, L. (1992) Relational maintenance strategies and equity in marriage. *Communication Monographs*, 59, 243–267.

Carlo, G., McGinley, M., Hayes, R., Batenhorst, C. and Wilkinson, J. (2007) Parenting styles or practices? Parenting, sympathy, and prosocial behaviors among adolescents. Journal of. Genetic Psychology, 168, 147–176.

Carron, A.V. (1982) Cohesiveness in sports groups. *Journal of Sport Psychology*, 4, 323–138.

Carron, A.V., Coleman, M. and Wheeler, J. (2002) Cohesion and performance in sport: a meta-analysis. *Journal of Sport and Exercise Psychology*, 24, 168–188.

Cartwright, J. (2000) *Evolution and Human Behavior: Darwinian Perspectives on Human Nature*. Cambridge, MA: MIT Press.

Crandall, C. and Stangor, C. (2005) Conformity and prejudice. In J.F. Dovidio, P. Glick and L.A. Rudman (eds) *On the Nature of Prejudice: Fifty Years After Allport* (pp. 295–309). Malden, MA: Blackwell.

Dainton, M. (2003) Equity and uncertainty in relational maintenance. *Western Journal of Communication*, 67(2), 164–186.

Darley, J. and Latane, B. (1968) Bystander intervention in emergencies: diffusion of responsibility. *Journal of Personality and Social Psychology*, 8(4), 377–383.

Darley, J. and Latane, B. (1969) Bystander apathy. *American Scientist*, 57, 244–268.

Darley, J. and Latane, B. (1970) *The Unresponsive Bystander: Why Doesn't He Help?* New York: Appleton-Century Crofts.

Davis, E. (1990) Men as success objects and women as sex objects: a study of personal advertisements. *Sex Roles*, 23, 43–50.

Davis, M. (1997) *Game Theory: A Nontechnical Introduction*. New York: Dover Publications, Inc.

Deutsch, M. (1949a) An experimental study of the effects of cooperation and competition upon group processes. *Human Relations*, 2, 199–231.

Deutsch, M. (1949b) A theory of cooperation and competition. *Human Relations*, 2, 129–151.

Deutsch, M. (1973) *The Resolution of Conflict: Constructive and Destructive Processes*. New Haven, CT: Yale University Press.

Deutsch, M. and Krauss, R. (1960) The effect of threat upon interpersonal bargaining. *Journal of Abnormal and Social Psychology*, 1(2), 181–189.

Devine, P. (1989) Stereotypes and prejudice: their automatic and controlled components. *Journal of Personality and Social Psychology*, 56(1), 5–18.

Diamond, J.M. (1992) *The Third Chimpanzee: The Evolution and Future of the Human Animal*. New York: Harper Perennial.

Duck, S. (ed.) (1982) *Personal Relations 4: Dissolving Personal Relationships*. New York: Academic Press.

Duck, S. (1988) *Relating to Others*. Chicago, IL: Dorsey.

Duck S, (1998) *Handbook of Personal Relationships: Theory, Research and Interventions*. Chichester, UK: John Wiley & Sons.

Duck, S. (2001) Breaking up: the dissolution of relationships. *Psychology Review*, 7(3), 2–3.

Duckitt, J. (1994) *The Social Psychology of Prejudice*. New York: Praeger.

Duffy, S. and Rusbult, C. (1986) Satisfaction and commitment in homosexual and heterosexual relationships. *Journal of Homosexuality*, 12(2), 1–23.

Dunbar, R. and Waynforth, D. (1995) Conditional mate choice strategies in humans: evidence from 'Lonely Hearts' advertisements. *Behaviour*, 132(9), 755–779.

Durwin, C. and Reese-Weber, M. (2018) *EdPsych Modules, Third Edition*. Thousand Oaks, CA: SAGE.

Escovar, L. and Sim, F. (1974) The cohesion of groups: alternative conceptions. Paper presented at the meeting of the Canadian Sociology and Anthropology Association, Toronto.

Essock-Vitale, S. (1985) Women's lives viewed from an evolutionary perspective. I. Sexual histories, reproductive success, and demographic characteristics of a random sample of American women. *Ethology and Sociobiology*, 6, 137–154.

Farrant, B., Devine, T., Mayberry, M. and Fletcher, J. (2011) Empathy, perspective taking and prosocial behaviour: the importance of parenting practices. *Infant and Child Development*, 21(2), 175–188.

Ferrer, E., Helm, J. and Sabarra, D. (2013) Assessing cross-partner associations in physiological responses via coupled oscillator models. *Emotion*, 12(4), 748–762.

Fischer, P., Krueger, J., Greitemeyer, T., Vogrincic, C., Kastenmüller, A., Frey, D., *et al.* (2011) The bystander-effect: a meta-analytic review on bystander intervention in dangerous and non-dangerous emergencies *Psychological Bulletin*, 137(4), 517–537.

Fisher, R. (1997) *Interactive Conflict Resolution*. Syracuse, NY: Syracuse University Press.

Flook, L., Goldberg, S., Pinger, L. and Davidson, R. (2015) Promoting prosocial behaviour and self-regulatory skills in preschool children through a mindfulness-based Kindness Curriculum. *Developmental Psychology*, 51(1), 44–51.

Freeman, L. and Fisher, R. (2012) Comparing a problem-solving workshop to a conflict assessment framework: conflict analysis versus conflict assessment in practice. *Journal of Peacebuilding and Development*, 7(1), 66–80.

Fromm, E. (1941) *Escape from Freedom*. New York: Farrar & Rinehart.

Fromm, E. (1962) *Beyond the Chains of Illusion: my Encounter with Marx and Freud*. New York: Continuum.

Gardner, A., Griffin, A. and West, S. (2009) Theory of co-operation. In *Encyclopaedia of Life Sciences (ELS)*. Chichester, UK: John Wiley & Sons.

Gelfand, J. and Brett, J (2004) *The Handbook of Negotiation and Culture*. Stanford, CA: Stanford University Press.

Gross, A. (1982) Twenty years of deception in social psychology. *Personality and Social Psychology Bulletin*, 8, 402–408.

Gunnell, J. and Ceci, S. (2010) When emotionality trumps reason: a study of individual processing style and juror bias. *Behavioural Sciences and the Law*, 28, 850–877.

Guth, W., Schmittberger, R. and Schwarze, B. (1982) An experimental analysis of ultimatum bargaining. *Journal of Economic Behavior and Organization*, 3(4), 367–388.

Hamilton, W. (1964) The genetical evolution of social behaviour. II. *Journal of Theoretical Biology*, 7(1), 17–52.

Harding, J., Proshansky, H., Kutner, B. and Chein, I. (1969) Prejudice and ethnic relations. In G. Lindzey and E. Aronson (eds) *The Handbook of Social Psychology* (Vol. 5) (pp. 1–76). Reading, MA: Addison-Wesley.

Harvey, J. and Omarzu, J. (1999) *Minding the Close Relationship*. Cambridge, UK: Cambridge University Press.

Harvey, J.H., Ickes, W.J. and Kidd, R.F. (eds) (1978) *New Directions in Attribution Research* (Vol. 2). Hillsdale, NJ: Erlbaum.

Hatfield, E. (1979) Equity and extramarital sex. In M. Cook and G. Wilson (eds) *Love and Attraction: An International Conference* (pp. 323–334). Oxford: Pergamon Press.

Hatfield, E., Utne, M., Traupmann, J. and Greenberger, D. (1984) Equity, marital satisfaction, and stability. *Journal of Social and Personal Relationships*, 1, 323–332.

Heider, F. (1958) *The Psychology of Interpersonal Relations*. Eastford, CT: Martino Fine Books.

Hochschild, A. and Machung, A. (1990) *The Second Shift*. New York: Avon Books.

Holtzworth-Munroe, A. (1988) Causal attributions in marital violence: theoretical and methodological issues. *Clinical Psychology Review*, 8, 331–344.

Ingham, A., Levinger, G., Graves, J. and Peckham, V. (1974) The Ringelmann effect: studies of group size and group performance. *Journal of Experimental Social Psychology*, 10, 371–384.

Johnson, D. and Johnson, R. (1989) *Cooperation and Competition: Theory and Research*. Edina, MN: Interaction Book Company.

Jones, E. and Davis, K. (1965) From acts to dispositions: the attribution process in social psychology. In L. Berkowitz (ed.) *Advances in Experimental Social Psychology* (Vol. 2, pp. 219–266). New York: Academic Press.

Jones, E., Wood, G. and Quattrone, G. (1981) Perceived variability of personal characteristics in in-groups and out-groups: the role of knowledge and evaluation. *Personality and Social Psychology Bulletin*, 7, 523–528.

Jost, J., Glaser, J., Kruglanski, A. and Sulloway, F. (2003) Political conservatism as motivated social cognition. *Psychological Bulletin*, 129(3), 339–375.

Keller, L. and Ross, K. (1998) Selfish genes: a green beard in the red fire ant. *Nature*, 394, 573–575.

Kelley, H. and Thibaut, J. (1978) *Interpersonal Relations: A Theory of Interdependence*. New York: Wiley-Interscience.

Kelman, H.C. (2008) Conflict resolution and reconciliation: a social-psychological perspective on ending violent conflict between identity groups. *Landscapes of Violence*, 1(1), Article 5.

Knafo-Noam, D., Serbin, A. and Moss, E. (2015) The influential child: how children affect their environment and influence their own risk and resilience. *Development and Psychopathology*, 27, 947–951.

Komorita, S. and Lapworth, W. (1982) Alternative choices in social dilemmas. *Journal of Conflict Resolution*, 26(4), 692–708.

Kriesberg, L. (1982) Social conflict theories and conflict resolution. *Peace and Change*, 8(2–3), 3–17.

Kriesberg, L. (2003) *Constructive Conflicts: From Escalation to Resolution*. Lanham, MD: Rowman and Littlefield.

Kurzban, R. and Wedden, J. (2005) Higher values connote higher sociosexuality. *Evolution and Human Behaviour*, 26, 227–244.

Langlois, J. and Roggman, L. (1990) Attractive faces are only average. *Psychological Science*, 1, 115–122.

Latane, B. (1980) Many hands make light work: the causes and consequences of social loafing. *Journal of Personality and Social Psychology*, 37(6), 822–832.

Lawton, J-M. (2012a) *AQA(A) A2 Psychology Student Unit Guide (New Edition): Unit 3*. London: Hodder Education.

Lawton, J-M. (2012b) *My Revision Notes: AQA(A) A2 Psychology*. London: Hodder Education.

Lee, L. (1984) Sequences in separation: a framework for investigating endings of the personal (romantic) relationship. *Journal of Personal and Social Relationships*, 1(1), 49–73.

Levine, M., Prosser, A., Evans, D. and Reicher, S. (2005) Identity and emergency intervention: how social group membership and inclusiveness of group boundaries shape helping behaviour. *Personality and Social Psychology Bulletin*, 31, 443–453.

Lin, Y-H. and Rusbult, C.E. (1995) Commitment to dating relationships and cross-sex friendships in China and America. *Journal of Social and Personal Relations*, 12, 7–26.

Mack, R. and Snyder, R. (1957) The analysis of social conflict – toward an overview and synthesis. *Journal of Conflict Resolution*, 1(2), 105–110.

Madsen, E., Tunney, R., Fieldman, G., Plotkin, H., Dunbar, R., Richardson, J., *et al.* (2007) Kinship and altruism: a cross-cultural experimental study. *British Journal of Psychology*, 98(2), 339–359.

McKenna, K. and Bargh, J. (2000) Plan 9 from cyberspace: the implications of the Internet for personality and social psychology. *Personality and Social Psychology Bulletin*, 4, 57–75.

McKenna, K., Green, A. and Gleason, M. (2002) Relationship formation on the internet: what's the big attraction? *Journal of Social Issues*, 58(1), 9–31.

Michigan National Election Studies (1972) *Michigan Election Returns, 1972: Precinct-Level (ICPSR 62)*, www.icpsr.umich.edu/icpsrweb/ICPSR/studies/62 (accessed 28 January 2018).

Milius, S. (1998) The science of eeek. What a squeak can tell researchers about life, society and all that. *Science News*, 154, 174–175, https://blumsteinlab.eeb.ucla.edu/wp-content/uploads/sites/104/2017/05/SciNews12Sept98.pdf (accessed 27 February 2018).

Miller, L.C. and Fishkin, S.A. (1997) On the dynamics of human bonding and reproductive success. In J.A. Simpson and D.T. Kendrick (eds) *Evolutionary Social Psychology* (pp. 197–236). Mahwah, NJ: Lawrence Erlbaum Associates.

Mills, J. and Clark, M.S. (1980) Communal and exchange relationships. Paper presented at a meeting of the Society of Experimental Social Psychologists, Palo Alto, California.

Mills, J. and Clark, M.S. (1982) Communal and exchange relationships. *Review of Personality and Social Psychology*, 3, 121–144.

Minard, R. (1952) Race relationships in the Pocahontas coal field. *Journal of Social Issues*, 8(1), 29–44.

Moghaddam, F.M., Taylor, D.M. and Wright, S.C. (1993) *Social Psychology in Cross-Cultural Perspective*. New York: W.H. Freeman & Co.

Mullen, B. and Copper, C. (1994) The relation between group cohesiveness and performance: an integration. *Psychological Bulletin*, 115, 210–227.

Murstein, B. (1972) Physical attractiveness and marital choice. *Journal of Personality and Social Psychology*, 22(1), 8–12.

Murstein, B. and MacDonald, M. (1983) The relationship of 'exchange-orientation' and 'commitment' scales to marriage adjustment. *International Journal of Psychology*, 18(3–4), 297–311.

Murstein, B., Cerreto, M. and MacDonald, M. (1977) A theory of the effect of exchange-orientation on marriage and friendship. *Journal of Marriage and the Family*, 39, 543–548.

Nelson, T., Biernat, M. and Manis, M. (1990) Everyday base rates (sex stereotypes): potent and resilient. *Journal of Personality and Social Psychology*, 59, 664–675.

Newman, H. (1981) Communication within ongoing intimate relationships: an attributional perspective. *Personality and Social Psychology Bulletin*, 7, 59–70.

Office for National Statistics (2014) *Families and Households: 2014*, www.ons.gov.uk/peoplepopulationandcommunity/birthsdeathsandmarriages/families/bulletins/familiesandhouseholds/2015-01-28 (accessed 27 February 2018).

Orvis, B.R., Kelley, H.H. and Butler, D. (1976) Attributional conflict in young couples. In J.H. Harvey, W. Ickes and R. Kidd (eds) *New Directions in Attribution Research* (Vol. 1, pp. 353–386). Hillsdale, NJ: Erlbaum.

Overton, A. and Lowry, A. (2013) Conflict management: difficult conversations with difficult people. *Clinics in Colon and Rectal Surgery*, 26(4), 259–264.

Pawlowski, B. and Dunbar, R. (1999) Impact of market value on human mate choice decisions. *Proceedings of the Royal Society of London B: Biological Sciences*, 266(1416), 281–285.

Penton-Voak, I., Jones, B., Little, A., Baker, S., Tiddeman, B., Burt, D., *et al.* (2001) Symmetry, sexual dimorphism in facial proportions and male facial attractiveness. *Proceedings of the Royal Society of London B: Biological Sciences*, 268(1476), 1617–1623.

Peritz, E. and Rust, P. (1972) On the estimation of the nonpaternity rate using more than one blood-group system. *American Journal of Human Genetics*, 24(1), 46–53.

Peter, J., Valkenburg, P. and Schouten, A. (2005) Developing a model of adolescent friendship formation on the internet. *Cyberpsychology and Behavior*, 8(5), 423–430.

Pettigrew, T. (1959) Regional differences in anti-Negro prejudice. *Journal of Abnormal Psychology*, 59(1), 28–36.

Pew Research Internet Project (2014) *Social Media Update 2014*, www.pewinternet.org/2015/01/09/social-media-update-2014/ (accessed 28 January 2018).

Piliavin, I., Rodin, J. and Piliavin, J (1969) Good Samaritanism: an underground phenomenon? *Journal of Personality and Social Psychology*, 13, 289–99.

Ridley, M. (1993) *The Red Queen: Sex and the Evolution of Human Nature*. New York: Viking.

Ringelmann, M. (1913) Research on animate sources of power: the work of man. *Annales de l'Institut National Agronomique*, 2nd series, 12, 1–40.

Rogers, A. and Frantz, C. (1962) *Racial Themes in Southern Rhodesia: The Attitudes and Behavior of the White Population*. New Haven, CT: Yale University Press.

Rollie, S.S. and Duck, S.W. (2006) Divorce and dissolution of romantic relationships: stage models and their limitations. In J.H. Harvey and M.A. Fine (eds) *Handbook of Divorce and Relationship Dissolution* (pp. 223–240). New York: Routledge.

Rovio, E., Eskola, J., Kozub, S.A., Duda, J.L. and Lintunen, T. (2009) Can high group cohesion be harmful? *Small Group Research*, 40(4), 421–435.

Rubin, L.B. (1983) *Intimate Strangers: Men and Women Together*. New York: Harper and Row.

Rubin, Z. (1975) Disclosing oneself to a stranger: reciprocity and its limits. *Journal of Experimental Social Psychology*, 11, 233–260.

Rusbult, C. (1983) A longitudinal test of the investment model: the development (and deterioration) of satisfaction and commitment in heterosexual involvements. *Journal of Personality and Social Psychology*, 45, 101–117.

Rusbult, C. and Martz, J. (1995) Remaining in an abusive relationship: an investment model analysis of nonvoluntary dependence. *Personality and Social Psychological Bulletin*, 21(6), 558–571.

Rusbult, C.E., Bissonnette, V.I., Arriaga, X.B. and Cox. C.L. (1998) Accommodation processes during the early years of marriage. In T.N. Bradbury (ed.) *The Developmental Course of Marital Dysfunction* (pp. 74–113). New York: Cambridge University Press.

Rusbult, C.E., Martz, J.M. and Agnew, C.R. (1998) The investment model scale: measuring commitment level, satisfaction level, quality of alternatives, and investment size. *Personal Relationships*, 5, 357–391.

Schouten, A., Valkenberg, J. and Peter, J. (2007) SD precursors and underlying processes of adolescents' online self-disclosure: developing and testing an 'internet-attribute-perception' model. *Journal of Media Psychology*, 10(2), 292–315.

Schutzwohl, A. and Koch, S. (2004) Sex differences in jealousy: the recall of cues to sexual and emotional infidelity in personally more and less threatening context conditions. *Evolutionary Psychology*, 25(4), 249–257.

Sedikides, C. (2005) Close relationships – what's in it for us? *The Psychologist*, 18, 490–493.

Sherif, M., Harvey, O., White, J., Hood, W. and Sherif, C. (1961) *Inter-Group Conflict and Cooperation: The Robbers Cave Experiment*, Norman, OK: University of Oklahoma Book Exchange.

Simmons, L., Firman, R., Rhodes, G. and Peters, M. (2003) Human sperm competition: testis size, sperm production and rates of extra pair copulations. *Animal Behaviour*, 68, 297–302.

Singer, A.C., Carr, M.F., Karlsson, M.P. and Frank, L.M. (2013) Hippocampal SWR activity predicts correct decisions during the initial learning of an alternation task. *Neuron*, 77(6), 1163–1173.

Singh, D. (1993) Adaptive significance of female physical attractiveness: role of waist-to-hip ratio. *Journal of Personality and Social Psychology*, 65(2), 293–307.

Smith, S. and Read, D. (2008) *Mycorrhizal Symbiosis, Third Edition*. New York: Academic Press.

Sprecher, S. (1986) The relation between inequity and emotions in close relationships. *Social Psychology Quarterly*, 49(4), 309–321.

Swami, V. and Furnham, A. (2006) The science of attraction. *The Psychologist*, 19, 362–365.

Tajfel, H. (1970) Experiments in intergroup discrimination. *Scientific American*, 223, 96–102. In P. Banyard and A. Grayson (eds) *Introducing Psychological Research* (pp. 69–74). London: MacMillan Press LTD, 1996.

Tajfel, H. and Turner, J. (1979) An integrative theory of intergroup conflict. In W.G. Austin and S. Worchel (eds) *The Social Psychology of Intergroup Relations* (pp. 33–47). Monterey, CA: Brooks/Cole.

Tashiro, T. and Frazier, P. (2003) 'I'll never be in a relationship like that again': personal growth following romantic relationship breakups. *Journal of Personal Relationships*, 10(1), 113–128.

Taylor, L., Fiore, A., Mendelsohn, G. and Cheshire, C. (2011) 'Out of my league': a real-world test of the matching hypothesis. *Personality and Social Psychological Bulletin*, 37(7), 942–954.

The SEAK Project Trust (2015) *Promoting Alternative Thinking Strategies (PATHS): Evaluation Report and Executive Summary*, https://educationendowmentfoundation.org.uk/public/files/Support/Campaigns/Evaluation_Reports/EEF_Project_Report_PromotingAlternativeThinkingStrategies.pdf (accessed 28 January 2018).

Thibaut, N. and Kelley, H. (1959) *The Social Psychology of Groups*. New York: Wiley.

Toma, C., Hancock, J. and Ellison, N. (2008) Separating fact from fiction: an examination of deceptive self-presentation in online dating profiles. *Personality and Social Psychology Bulletin*, 34(8), 1023–1036.

Van Lange, P., Otten, W., De Bruin, E. and Joireman, J. (1997) Development of prosocial, individualistic, and competitive orientations: theory and preliminary evidence. *Journal of Personality and Social Psychology*, 73(4), 733–746.

Walster, E. and Walster, G. (1969) The matching hypothesis. *Journal of Personality and Social Psychology*, 4, 508–510.

Walster, E., Aronson, V., Abrahams, D. and Rottman, L. (1966a) Matching hypothesis. In H. Reis and S. Sprecher (eds), *Encyclopedia of Human Relationships* (pp. 1065–1067). Thousand Oaks, CA: Sage, 2009.

Walster, E., Aronson, V., Abrahams, D. and Rottman, L. (1966b) Importance of physical attractiveness in dating behavior. *Journal of Personality and Social Psychology*, 4(5), 508–516.

Walster, E., Walster, W. and Berscheid, E. (1978) *Equity: Theory and Research*. Boston, MA: Allyn and Bacon.

Werner, E. (1979) *Cross-Cultural Child Development. A View from the Planet Earth*. Monterey, CA: Brooks-Cole.

Whiting, B. and Whiting, J. (1975) *Children of Six Cultures: A Psycho-Cultural Analysis*. Cambridge, MA: Harvard University Press.

Wichman, H. (1970) Effects of isolation and communication on cooperation in a two-person game. *Journal of Personality and Social Psychology*, 16, 114–120.

Zahavi, A. (1975) Mate selection – a selection for a handicap. *Journal of Theoretical Biology*, 53(1), 205–214.

Chapter 9

Poortman, J.J. (1959) The feeling of being stared at. *Journal of the Society for Psychical Research*, 40, 4–12.

Sheldrake, R. (1994) *Seven Experiments that Could Change the World*. London: Fourth Estate.

Sheldrake, R. (1998) The sense of being stared at: experiments in schools. *Journal of the Society for Psychical Research*, 62, 311–323.

Titchener, E.B. (1898) The feeling of being stared at. *Science New Series*, 8, 895–897.

Williams, L. (1983) Minimal cue perception of the regard of others: the feeling of being stared at. Paper presented at the 10th Annual Conference of the Southeastern Regional Parapsychological Association, Carrollton, GA, 11–12 February.

Index